IN MIXED COMPANY

COMPANY

Small Group Communication

Communication

THIRD EDITION

IN MIXED COMPANY

Small Group
Communication

THIRD EDITION

J. DAN ROTHWELL

Cabrillo College

Harcourt Brace College Publishers

Fort Worth Philadelphia San Diego New York Orlando Austin San Antonio
Toronto Montreal London Sydney Tokyo

Publisher	Christopher P. Klein
Acquisitions Editor	Carol Wada
Project Editors	Cheryl Hauser
	Kylie E. Johnston
Production Manager	Kathleen Ferguson
Art Director	Pat Bracken

© R. Llewellyn/SuperStock

ISBN: 0-15-5039857
Library of Congress Catalog Card Number: 97-71151

Address for Orders:
Harcourt Brace College Publishers
6277 Sea Harbor Drive
Orlando, FL 32887-6777
1-800-782-4479

Address for Editorial Correspondence:
Harcourt Brace College Publishers
301 Commerce Street, Suite 3700
Fort Worth, TX 76102

Website address:
http://www.hbcollege.com

Harcourt Brace & Company will provide complimentary supplements or supplement packages to those adopters qualified under our adoption policy. Please contact your sales representative to learn how you qualify. If as an adopter or potential user you receive supplements you do not need, please return them to your sales representative or send them to: Attn: Returns Department, Troy Warehouse, 465 South Lincoln Drive, Troy, MO 63379.

Printed in the United States of America

7   8   9   0   1   2   3   4   5   6   039   10   9   8   7   6   5   4   3   2

Revising a highly successful, critically acclaimed textbook is always a challenging prospect. One doesn't want to mess with success. Accordingly, I have preserved the essence of this text. The central unifying theme, that cooperation in small groups is usually superior to competition, remains. *In Mixed Company*, however, doesn't just advocate cooperation and teamwork in small groups. You can find such advocacy in numerous group textbooks. *In Mixed Company* thoroughly develops cooperation in small groups as a unifying theme—explaining in detail why cooperation is superior to competition—and describes specifically how to structure cooperation into small group decision making and problem solving. You will find no more thorough treatment of this essential theme in any textbook available. Not only have I maintained cooperation as a central theme for the third edition of *In Mixed Company*, but I have expanded its development.

Specific revisions I have chosen to make for this edition consist mostly of expansion of topics and themes covered in previous editions. Let me emphasize, however, that this revision is far more than cosmetic. I have made many substantive changes. More specifically, the key revisions made in this edition consist of the following:

1. All chapters have been thoroughly *updated*. One hundred and thirty-two references, all dated in the 1990s, have been added and numerous examples have been replaced with more current illustrations.
2. *"Closer Looks"* were critically acclaimed features of the previous two editions and have been updated where necessary. I have also added a half-dozen Closer Looks.
3. *Gender*, a subject that received considerable attention in the second edition, is discussed in significantly greater detail and depth. I have organized extensive discussions of gender-specific issues relevant to small group communication into "Focuses on Gender," which are Closer Looks with a specific theme. The Focuses on Gender are in addition to the shorter, less detailed references to gender already integrated throughout the text.
4. *Culture*, a subject that also received considerable focus in the second edition, is given significantly greater attention. I have organized extensive discussions of culture and ethnicity issues relevant to communication into "Focuses on Culture," which are also Closer Looks with a specific theme. Focuses on Culture are in addition to the shorter, less-detailed references to these topics integrated throughout the text.
5. Always a central theme, *teamwork* and *team building* receive even greater emphasis. Chapter Four in particular has been expanded to include the five elements that build teamwork. These five essential elements are then applied in ensuing chapters.

6. *Ethics*, a subject of only minor concern in previous editions, has become a more important topic in this edition.
7. *Electronic technology* (e.g., Internet, electronic brainstorming, electronic meetings) and its impact on small group decision making and problem solving receives added emphasis. Integrating this material throughout the text seemed preferable to treating electronic technology almost as an afterthought in a final chapter.
8. The treatment of *critical thinking*, previously covered extensively in Chapters Six and Seven and Appendix B, is expanded; especially the structure of an argument.

More generally, I have excised redundant material and replaced commonplace examples with sharper illustrations.

Reviewers of the second edition have raised two issues that I would like to address. First, the suggestion has been made that I write a separate chapter on the influence of gender and culture/ethnicity on small groups. I agree, however, with Broome and Fulbright's (1995) viewpoint that a separate chapter does not fully integrate these subjects into discussions of small group process. Since gender and culture are relevant to issues discussed in *every* chapter of this text, integrating discussion of gender and culture into each chapter seems preferable to setting aside such discussion and reserving it for a later chapter. Such integration also reduces redundant references to material previously covered in earlier chapters.

Second, a couple of reviews have commented on the number of "unsuccessful and negative groups" included in the Closer Looks. I respectfully disagree with the observation. The examples cited—the Juan Corona murder trial, the Blandina Chiapponi case study, the Night Stalker, and the McMartin Preschool case—although involving instances of violence, actually illustrate highly successful group decision making. In each case, the small groups avoided common pitfalls of group decision making. Effective action was taken. These few Closer Looks cited are vivid cases, so they tend to overshadow the far greater number of illustrations used that are positive in nature and do not deal with dramatic instances of violence in our society. I have not ignored the observation, however. I have included additional positive and successful small groups in the Closer Looks.

OBJECTIVES FOR STUDENTS

I have three paramount objectives for students: that the material presented be clear and comprehensible, that the text be pragmatic, and that the text be highly readable. Regarding the first objective—*clarity and comprehension*—I have included an outline prior to each chapter. "Focus Questions" precede most major sections of each chapter to direct your attention to key points. I have integrated hundreds of examples—most of them actual occurrences rather than contrived instances—to illustrate concepts. A number of extended examples, called "Closer Look," will aid your comprehension of the significant concepts discussed in each chapter. I also have included tables, each one called a "Second Look," that act as succinct summaries of complicated and/or detailed material. I am told by my students that these are very useful when studying for exams. Finally, a glossary of key terms for quick reference appears at the end of the text. Terms that are in **boldfaced** type throughout the text are included in the glossary.

I have attempted to realize my second objective—*pragmatism*—in a couple of ways. Recognizing that theory helps us understand how groups work but is limited unless it is applied practically to our everyday lives, I have chosen a wide range of examples and illustrations that show how the theory makes sense in real life. I have not simply described what competent communication is, but have also indicated, step-by-step, how you can become a competent communicator in groups.

My third paramount objective—*readability*—has been no small challenge. Sportswriter Red Smith once remarked, "There is nothing to writing. All you do is sit down at the typewriter and just open a vein." Although long ago I consigned my typewriter to a trash heap and replaced it with a more efficient, but sometimes maddening, computer, I also did my share of bleeding while writing this text. I've spilled many a corpuscle attempting to write a different kind of textbook—one that might stir interest, not act as a sedative. The risk I run in telling you this, obviously, is that you may respond, "And that's the best you could do?" Alas, yes. Whatever the shortcomings of this work, I was ever mindful of my audience. Having myself experienced studenthood for some twenty years, I am intimately acquainted with tedious textbooks. I have a fair number of them on my bookshelves. They remind me how not to write one. I am as impatient with authors who produce a theoretically competent work, but seem clueless when it comes to stimulating reader interest in the material, as I imagine you are.

Textbooks are not meant to read like spy thrillers, but they certainly shouldn't read like instructions for filling out your income tax forms, either. I strongly believe that textbooks should not induce a coma-like state in the reader. Unlike calculus, which I have no idea how to make interesting, human communication should be a fascinating subject for most people. I have made a genuine attempt to excite interest in a subject—competent communication in groups—that plays such an integral part in our lives.

Toward this end, I have searched in obvious and not-so-obvious places for the precise example, the amusing illustration, the poignant instance, and the dramatic case to enhance reader enjoyment. I also have attempted to enliven the writing style by incorporating colorful language and lively metaphors that bring interesting images to mind. Finally, where applicable, I have related stories that I hope will invite the reader to turn the pages and become interested in the subject of competent communication in groups. Easily half of the energy I expended on this project was spent on readability.

OBJECTIVES FOR INSTRUCTORS

My objectives for this text are somewhat different for instructors than they are for students. For instructors, my *principal objectives* are that the text be theoretically and conceptually sound, current, innovative yet user-friendly, and involving for the reader.

The first objective—*soundness of theory and concept*—has been achieved according to reviewers of all three editions. I appreciate their affirmation and guidance. I was spared a few embarrassments thanks to their conscientious critiques.

The second objective—*currency*—can be demonstrated less subjectively than the first. Close to a third of the more than 700 references are citations from the 1990s, and two-thirds are since 1985. I have incorporated many of the latest findings and conclusions from recent research in my discussion of group communication concepts and processes. In all subject areas I have searched energetically for the very latest research and insights. I have also referred to numerous recent events to illustrate key points.

The third objective—*innovative yet user-friendly*—proved to be the biggest challenge of the three. What I have attempted to do is cover all the familiar and essential topic areas, yet complement these with subject matter either covered in far less depth or ignored in other texts. I have covered, often in great detail, all of the top twenty-five topic areas identified in the Warnemunde (1986) study of actual instructional emphases in group communication classes nationwide.

Subjects included in this text that are either unique or covered in greater depth than in other texts on small group communication are as follows:

1. A communication competence perspective provides a clear communication focus for the text. The communication competence model is thoroughly integrated into every chapter, not just mentioned in the first chapter, then dropped entirely from later discussions.
2. Cooperation and teambuilding in small groups is a unifying theme of the text. A thorough critique of competition in groups is presented in Chapter Four and the five essential elements for structuring cooperation into small group is developed, then applied in ensuing chapters.
3. Consistent with the title of this book, *In Mixed Company,* gender and culture issues and research are thoroughly integrated into *every* chapter.
4. Power, a topic virtually ignored by other small group texts, is developed in two comprehensive chapters.
5. Conflict is discussed throughout the text, with a final focus chapter at the end.
6. Critical thinking in small groups is discussed extensively (see Chapters Six and Seven and Appendix B).
7. Special sections on dealing with social loafers and difficult group members, subjects of great concern to students, are discussed in detail.
8. Creative problem solving receives substantial treatment with emphasis on framing/reframing and integration techniques.
9. Public speaking in group situations is discussed in Appendix A. Managing

speech anxiety, gaining and maintaining audience attention, organizing and outlining a speech, and using visual aids effectively are emphasized.

I have attempted to realize the fourth objective—*reader involvement*—in several ways. Initial "Focus Questions" require the reader to be looking for answers to these questions as they read the material. "Questions for Critical Thinkers" at the end of each chapter require reader application, analysis, and evaluation of ideas and concepts covered. Thought questions at the end of every Closer Look invite readers to contemplate significant issues, sometimes of an ethical nature, and such reflection will likely stimulate interesting class discussion. Many examples, riddles, case studies, and questions sprinkled throughout the text challenge readers to work with the material as it is presented.

In addition to these four objectives, there are several *special features* that warrant brief mention. First, the "perpendicular pronoun" *I* is used throughout the text. I recognize that this is not standard academic practice, yet I feel that first person singular speaks more directly and personally to students than the more bloodless and oblique style of writing common in most textbooks.

Second, I have adopted a more *narrative or storytelling style* than is usual in textbook writing. Research (Fernald, 1987) confirms that students prefer the narrative style and benefit greatly from it in both comprehension and recall of information. The Closer Looks, plentiful examples, and the personal experiences sewn into the fabric of the text are narrative in nature.

Third, since I emphasize in my discussion of communication competence in Chapter One that "knowing how is not showing how," my colleagues and I have put together an Instructor's Manual composed of original classroom exercises that employ the learning-by-doing approach common in group communication classes. Having tired long ago of using excellent but shopworn group exercises such as "Lost on the Moon" and "Winter Survival," we have replaced the classic case studies, simulations, and structured experiences with original, and we think better, alternatives. Some students have already been "Lost on the Moon" several times in business, sociology, psychology, or counseling classes and workshops, and they have survived several plane crashes in the frozen North. Having alternatives available can be helpful in avoiding redundancy and keeping our group communication courses fresh. We call your attention especially to the "Group Polarization and Pressure," "Group Synergy," "Group Size," "Abandon Ship," and "Power Carnival" exercises as examples of enormously successful classroom-tested original group communication exercises that accompany this text.

Fourth, the Instructor's Manual includes a sample course syllabus relevant for both the quarter and semester system. One notable testing feature is the Cooperative Exam in both objective and essay form. My colleagues and I have had great success incorporating cooperative learning strategies into the group communication course. A Cooperative Group Examination is one way simultaneously to test students and to apply the text material on building cooperation.

I have also produced a videotape entitled *Working Together*, shot in documentary style, which illustrates several key classroom activities (e.g., "Power

Carnival," "Group Synergy"). This video can serve either as a substitute for doing the activities in class or as a visual guide showing how to conduct these very successful exercises in your class. The videotape is available as a textbook ancillary.

Although there is no ideal organizational pattern, my schema for the chapter sequence is quite simple. I begin with a theoretical foundation (Chapters One and Two), progress to how groups form and develop (Chapter Three), then proceed to a discussion of how to establish the proper climate for the group to work effectively (Chapter Four). I then explain what roles group members are likely to play (Chapter Five) and discuss decision making/problem solving—the primary work to be performed by most groups, with special focus on critical thinking (Chapters Six and Seven). Finally, I explore in substantial detail the close connection between power and conflict (Chapters Eight, Nine, and Ten). I can see other ways of organizing this same material, but the order I have chosen works well for me, and students seem satisfied with the sequence of topics.

ACKNOWLEDGMENTS

My sincere thanks are extended to all those who reviewed this text. A few reviewed it several times, proving that some of my colleagues haven't learned how to exercise their assertiveness and say no.

Those who deserve my gratitude for reviewing the second edition are Joseph Hemmer, Carroll College; James Keaten, University of Northern Colorado; Andrea Mitnick, Pennsylvania State University—Delaware City; and Edwina Stoll, De Anza College. Those who receive my heartfelt thanks for reviewing the first edition are Debbie Analauren, Cabrillo College; Carole Barry, Cabrillo College; Sheryl Bowen, Villanova University; Judith Bunyi, Iowa State University; Barbara Eakins, Wright State University; Betty Ensminger, Mission College; Barbara Gordon, Iowa State University; Michael Holmes, Purdue University; Larry Hugenberg, Youngstown State University; Sharon Kirk, La Salle University; Dan Millar, Indiana State University; Charlotte Morrison, Cabrillo College; Mark Murphy, Everett Community College; Michael Nicolai, University of Wisconsin—Stout; Gregg Phifer, Florida State University; Rod Stanton, Cabrillo College; Edwina Stoll, De Anza College; Vic Wall, Cleveland State University; Marcy Wieland, Cabrillo College; and Mary Wiemann, Santa Barbara City College. Many of the best features of this text resulted from suggestions of the reviewers.

Special thanks go to Topsy Smalley, reference librarian at Cabrillo College, who located references and material for this edition that would have remained forever hidden from me if I hadn't the benefit of her Herculean effort. I continue to be amazed by her skills and unflagging energy, and I never cease appreciating her cheerful attitude when she assists faculty.

My gratitude is also extended to Carol Wada who guided the second and third editions. It is a pleasure to work with such a capable and pleasant editor.

Finally, I express my heartfelt gratitude to my colleagues in the Speech department at Cabrillo College. You are a continuing source of inspiration for me, and you demonstrate daily that cooperation and teamwork can be practical realities, not merely wishful thinking.

ABOUT THE AUTHOR

J. Dan Rothwell is chair of the Speech Communication Department at Cabrillo College. He has a B.A. in American History from the University of Portland (Oregon), an M.A. in Rhetoric and Public Address, and a Ph.D. in Communication Theory. His M.A. and Ph.D. are both from the University of Oregon. He is the author of *Telling It Like It Isn't: Language Misuse and Malpractice* and co-author (with James Costigan) of *Interpersonal Communication: Influences and Alternatives*.

Professor Rothwell encourages feedback and correspondence from both students and instructors regarding *In Mixed Company*. Anyone so inclined may communicate with him by e-mail at darothwe@cabrillo.cc.ca.us or by snail-mail care of the Speech Communication Department, Cabrillo College, Aptos, CA 95003. Dr. Rothwell may also be reached by phone at 1-408-479-6511.

CONTENTS

CHAPTER FOUR: Developing the Group Climate 94

CHAPTER FIVE: Roles and Leadership in Groups 137

CHAPTER SEVEN: Group Discussion: Effective Decision Making and Problem Solving 210

Communication Competence

If you want to find out what people think about groups, ask them. I did. I passed out a questionnaire in a couple of my group communication classes. The results were quite revealing. The great majority of students had negative things to say about their experiences in groups. Comments included: "If God had ordered a committee to create the world, they'd still be discussing proposals." "For every group I've enjoyed, there have been a dozen groups looking to make my life miserable—and succeeding." "I hate groups. I hate group assignments. I hate teachers who require group assignments. Take the hint."

Surveys in the business world duplicate the reactions of my students. A survey (in Alexander, 1989) by Robert Half International, a consulting firm, found that executives spend approximately twenty-one weeks a year in group meetings and six of those weeks' worth of meetings were considered a total waste of time. That's equivalent to a year of fruitless effort in less than a decade. Consultant Steven Kaye (in Norman, 1996) estimates that this waste equals 20 percent of the total payroll of U.S. companies, or $420 billion a year. Stephen Winston, a time-management consultant and author, observes, "Most people I've talked to in the ranks see meetings as a species of event that's a drag" (in Alexander, 1989, p. 1PC).

Sorensen (1981) coined the term **grouphate** to describe how loathsome the group experience is for many people. Sorensen's research supports the view expressed by my students and business executives. She claims that most individuals do not like or enjoy working in groups.

Her most interesting result, however, shows a <u>direct relationship between the grouphate phenomenon and communication competence</u>. Those individuals least hostile to working in groups have the most instruction in effective group communication. Unfortunately, most people do not receive the requisite training in group communication, so grouphate flourishes. When we lack the training and thus the necessary knowledge and skills to function competently, we are inclined to avoid group membership (Leary, 1983), making any improvement in this regard unlikely.

I've entitled this book *In Mixed Company*. Often when groups form, you get potluck. You don't always get to choose your officemates, roommates, or housemates. The particular mix of individuals composing your group may not be ideal from your perspective. One response to other than "ideal" groups is grouphate. Another possibility, however, is to view this situation as a challenge. Some individuals experience grouphate when faced with a less-than-preferred mix of group members because they lack communication knowledge and skills to handle effectively a diversity of personalities. I recognize the reality of grouphate, but I also embrace the view that most group experiences can be highly positive.

As Sorensen's research suggests, competent communication makes a difference in our evaluation of groups. Similar to so many other experiences in life, if we obtain the knowledge and skills necessary to perform at an optimum level, we tend to enjoy the experience much more than if we flounder in confusion, ignorance, and ineptitude or merely muddle through more by chance than by choice.

Groups are inescapable. Most of you spend a substantial portion of your daily lives in groups of one sort or another. College students list as many as twenty-four groups that they belong to with eight as about average (Brilhart and Galanes, 1995). Even if you cared to try, you cannot escape groups. Your family is a group. So are athletic and debate teams; church and study groups; fraternities and sororities; bridge, poker, and chess clubs; boards, councils, and task forces; policy, executive, and ad hoc committees; discussion groups; quality-control circles and circles of friends; and personal growth, self-help, and therapy groups of almost infinite variety. This list could easily be expanded two- or threefold.

Groups are unavoidable unless you plan to live your life alone in a cave, but groups also are essential to our society. As Frey (1994) observes, "The small group is clearly the tie that binds, the nucleus that holds society together" (p. ix). Tropman (1988) claims, "Most of the important decisions that affect your work life are made by groups" (p. 7). McCann and Margerison (in Cathcart and Samovar, 1992) echo this view when they point out, "Today's business environment is so complex and in such a continual state of change that success often depends on the outputs of teams or work groups rather than the efforts of a single person" (p. 55). In a national survey of the 750 top U.S. companies, 71.4 percent of respondents considered "ability to work in teams" to be an essential employment qualification for graduates with a Masters of Business Administration (in DuBois, 1992).

Reliance on groups will not diminish in the future; quite the opposite. In the early 1980s, only 5 percent of U.S. employees were involved in self-managed work teams. By 1992, approximately 20 percent worked in such teams. By the year 2000, nearly 50 percent of U.S. employees will participate in self-managed work teams (Freeman, 1996). The American Association for the Advancement of Science, in a 1989 report, recommended that "the collaborative nature of science and technological work should be strongly reinforced by frequent group activity in the classroom" (in Wooley, 1990, p. 32). The National Council of Teachers of English and the National Council of Teachers of Mathematics have concurred.

Advances in computers and electronic technology will not slow the trend toward groups—quite the contrary. As Berge (1994) explains, "Electronic discussion groups will play an ever increasing role within the information culture. Netgroups often serve as powerful tools in the retrieval and exchanging [*sic*] of information, bringing together persons with similar interests regardless of geographic distance or the time constraints dictated by face-to-face meetings" (p. 111).

Groups are here to stay. Grouphate may not be transformed by competent communication into grouplove, where you hold hands with group members and sing "We Are the World." Nevertheless, does it not make eminently good sense, since so much of your life revolves around groups, that you should learn to communicate competently in this arena and thereby maximize the benefits of group participation for yourself and others? The <u>central purpose of this textbook</u>, then, is to teach you how to be a competent, skillful communicator in groups.

In this chapter, I will lay the theoretical groundwork for a communication competence approach to groups. My <u>objectives</u> are:

1. to correct some common misconceptions regarding the human communication process,
2. to explain what communication is, and
3. to identify broadly what constitutes competent communication.

MYTHS ABOUT COMMUNICATION

Before I tackle the question, "What is communication?" and then more specifically, "What is *competent* communication?" let me sweep out some of the musty misconceptions you may have stored in your intellectual attics regarding the communication process. As American humorist Josh Billings once remarked, foolishness springs not so much from what a person doesn't know, but from what a person "does know that ain't so." Consider just three myths widely promulgated in recent years that merit the trash heap.

Myth #1: Communication Is a Panacea

Communication has been packaged as a panacea, a cure-all for almost anything that ails us. Communication has been sold as the magic elixir, hawked by con artists, gurus with gimmicks, pop psychologists practicing without licenses, and all sorts of profiteers looking to make a fast buck with fast talk.

<u>Communication improvement is not the magical answer to all our woes.</u> When a woman is regularly abused by her male partner, ending the relationship is usually the best course of action. Trying to listen more empathically to his excuses for treating her abominably may simply nurture an illusion that this relationship is worth maintaining. Sometimes more communication aggravates differences between people and exposes qualities in others we may find unappealing.

Communication is a tool that, in the possession of someone skillful, can be used to help solve many problems. Communication, however, is not an end in itself but merely a means to an end. You will not solve all your problems by learning to communicate more effectively, because not all problems are communication based.

Myth #2: Communication Can Break Down

Communication does not "break down" (Ruben, 1978). Machines break down; they quit, and if they belong to me they do so with amazing regularity. Human beings continue to communicate even when they may wish not to do so. The view that communication breakdowns occur comes from a recognition that we do not always achieve our goals through communication. But failure to achieve our goals may occur even when communication between the parties in conflict is exemplary. So where's the breakdown?

In the movie *Cool Hand Luke,* the Paul Newman character, Luke, an inmate in a repressive U.S. prison run by a sadistic warden, is beaten and tossed into a ditch for his rebelliousness. The warden, played by Strother Martin, utters that memorable line, "What we have here is a failure to communicate." What we actually have is the defiance of oppressive authority. The warden has not achieved his goal: namely, to force Luke to conform to the prison rules. Luke's act of defiance is a test of wills and a rejection of the warden's power, not a communication breakdown.

We sometimes draw the mistaken conclusion that disagreement constitutes a communication breakdown. I may understand your message perfectly, however, but simply dislike what I'm hearing. In this case there is a difference of opinion, not a communication breakdown.

Myth #3: Communication Encompasses a Set of Specific Skills

The skills orientation to communication assumes that "if I learn a few magical communication skills, I will become a much better communicator." This skills-without-relevant-knowledge approach to communication, so prevalent in "how-to" guides filling the self-help section of local bookstores, calls to mind the story of the gorilla who amazed everyone with his ability to drive a golf ball consistently more than 400 yards. When his trainer proposed that the gorilla be allowed to compete against professionals in a golf tournament, a chorus of objections arose, until one of the golfers happened to observe the gorilla play a practice round. Not only did the gorilla drive the ball more than 400 yards on his opening drive, landing on the edge of the first green about fifteen feet from the hole, but his next shot also traveled more than 400 yards. The gorilla was clueless when it came to knowing when to use his driving skill and when to give it a rest. He had been taught a skill separated from knowledge of the game.

Communication does not exist in a vacuum. Learning how to "express your feelings honestly," for example, is a useful communication skill in many circumstances. Expressing any feelings uncritically, however, no matter how hurtful, shocking, or self-indulgent, is the act of a petulant child, not a mature adult.

Communication involves much more than learning a few isolated skills. Without understanding the complexities of the communication process, no amount of skills training will prove to be very meaningful, and may prove to be harmful.

Teaching communication skills without knowledge, without a well-researched theoretical map guiding our behavior, is like constructing a house without a carefully developed set of blueprints. All the skills necessary to build a house won't be very useful without a thoughtful plan to guide the construction and prevent collapse of the structure. The blueprint I offer you as a guide to learning how to communicate and function effectively in small groups is the communication competence model presented later in this chapter.

COMMUNICATION DEFINED

At this point I have indicated what communication is not. What it is can be seen most clearly by first considering several fundamental principles.

Focus Questions
1. How are content and relationship dimensions of messages different from each other?
2. "Meaning is within each of us, not in the symbols." What does this mean?

Communication Is Transactional

Wendall Johnson once defined human communication as "a process with four legs." Merely sending a message does not constitute communication. There has to be a receiver, but communication is more than a mere transmission of information from sender to receiver and back again like ping-pong balls batted to and fro. Communication is a **transaction.** This means that each person communicating is both a sender and receiver simultaneously, not merely a sender *or* a receiver. As you speak you receive mostly nonverbal feedback from listeners and this, in turn, influences the messages that you continue to send. Skillful communicators read feedback accurately and adjust their ensuing message appropriately.

Communication as transaction also means that all parties communicating have an impact on each other. We are mutually defined in relation to each other as we send and receive messages simultaneously (Stewart, 1986). A leader of a group must have followers or she cannot claim such a role. The messages we send and the feedback we receive from others influence our perceptions of who we are in relation to other group members and who they are in relation to us. This can be seen clearly by examining messages more closely.

Every message has two dimensions—content and relationship (Watzlawick et al., 1967). The content dimension refers to what is actually said. The relationship dimension of a message refers to how that message defines or redefines the relationship between group members.

I knew a couple whose teenagers addressed them both by their first names. The kids made statements such as, "Bob! Give me your car keys" and "Beth! Do my laundry." Compare these statements to "Dad, may I please have the keys to the car?" or "Mom, will you do me a big favor and wash my clothes for me?" Both messages have the same essential content, but the relationship dimension is clearly different.

The first two messages exhibit disrespect and define the relationship as one where the teenager orders the parents, not the other way around as we're more accustomed to experiencing. The second two messages, however, are requests, not orders. There is an outward display of respect for the parents and deference to their authority. The power relationship is a more traditional one of parents in control and teenager asking for favors. Of course, nonverbal aspects of these messages must also be considered. The first set of messages could be said facetiously and the second set could be delivered in a condescending tone of voice. In such cases, the relationship dimension of each message is changed.

While the content of two messages may be the same but the relationship dimension may be different, the reverse may also be true. "May I stay the weekend with my friend Sally?" and "May I borrow $100 from you?" are messages that display different content but essentially the same relationship. What is requested differs, but in each case respect is shown to the party with the power to grant the request.

These examples illustrate the difference between content and relationship dimensions of messages, but they represent one-way communication devoid of feedback. They are not transactional. The following tongue-in-cheek example offered by humorist Dave Barry (1986) illustrates communication as transaction:

YOU: How is this wine that costs $12 a bottle?
WINE STEWARD: We use that primarily as a disinfectant.
YOU: I see. Then we'll have something much more expensive.
WINE STEWARD: Excellent choice. (p. 63)

The wine steward, whose job requires a certain deference to the customer's wishes, in this transaction actually is shown deference by the customer who is influenced by the wine steward's initial sarcastic disapproval.

When we are in a group, every utterance, choice, and action continually defines and redefines who we are in relation to other group members and who they are in relation to us. This "definition-and-response-to-definition process," as Stewart (1986) puts it, is ongoing and unavoidable. Individuals affect the group and the group affects the individual. Communication in groups is a continuous series of transactions.

Communication Is a Process

Communication between people is a process, not a static entity. We constantly adapt to the changes that affect any relationship. Events can and do alter how we view others and what kind of interaction will take place between us.

Identifying communication as a process recognizes "events and relationships as dynamic, on-going, ever-changing, continuous" (Berlo, 1960, p. 24). Communication reveals the dynamic nature of relationships and events. Nothing stands still.

Communication is a process because changes in events and relationships are part of a continuous flow. As Trenholm and Jensen (1988) aptly explain:

If we try to understand a river by analyzing a bucket of water drawn from it, we are not studying the river as a whole. The same is true of communication. Individual sentences, words, or gestures make sense only when we see them as part of an ongoing stream of events. To understand communication, we have to look at how what we do and say is connected to what others do and say. We have to view communication as an ongoing process. (p. 5)

Students, for instance, affect the quality of instruction by their attitudes and degree of interest for the subject matter. What students do and say markedly influences the quality of their educational experience as much as what teachers do and say. Great lectures may fall flat with students who don't care or have an antagonistic relationship with the instructor. Conversely, mediocre presentations by instructors can be made more dynamic by the enthusiastic participation of students who may want their teacher to succeed because they like him or her personally. Students may be bored one minute and attentive the next. Relationships between teacher and students may change in the short time of a single class period, especially when controversial material is presented.

We cannot freeze relationships in time. Every conversation is a point of departure for an ensuing conversation. Every communication experience is the result of an accumulation of experiences preceding the present one. Each new experience affects future transactions. Human communication is a process.

Communication Is Sharing Meaning

The world we live in is not instantly intelligible to us from the moment of birth. We inhabit a world devoid of meaning. Human sense experiences do not come to us neatly packaged in ordered bundles. Life becomes intelligible to us when we assign form, shape, and structure to our experience with external "reality." In the absence of assigned order and structure, our world is chaotic, incomprehensible. Human needs cannot be satisfied adequately in such a disorganized environment.

Our world, our external "reality" becomes meaningful through communication with others. You do not establish meaning in social isolation. Sharing your ideas, feelings, ruminations, experiences, even intuitions with others, and they in turn doing likewise is all part of the process of constructing meaning, of determining connections and patterns in our minds, of making sense of our world.

Sharing meaning, however, is not necessarily a neutral event. Our constructions of reality can affect others, sometimes powerfully. In fact, one way leadership in groups has been conceptualized is in terms of meaning construction. Those who can "make sense" out of the shared experience of the group typically emerge as leaders (Smircich and Morgan, 1982). "We're poor because we're a minority" and "Government is the problem not the solution" are constructions of reality that, when shared with others, can profoundly affect those who find that such meaning constructions make sense. Sharing meaning can produce action and sometimes reactions.

We share meaning via verbal and nonverbal messages. Although we commonly separate verbal and nonverbal communication, they are inextricably interconnected. The problem of mixed messages shows the inseparable connection between verbal and nonverbal communication. Messages can become mixed when there is positive verbal and negative nonverbal feedback, or vice versa. When there is incongruity between the verbal and the nonverbal feedback, this indicates to the group that what you say and what you honestly believe are not identical. The words say one thing but gestures, facial expressions, eye contact, posture, tone of voice, and physical proximity to the group may leak contradictory information. Attempting to wipe that contemptuous opinion off your face while offering praise can be a real challenge.

The consequences of mixed messages can be serious. Leathers (1979), in his study of twenty problem-solving groups, found that mixed messages had a highly disruptive impact on the groups. Those who have to deal with the mixed messages of others find such inconsistent messages and contradictory meanings anxiety-producing and difficult to respond to in socially acceptable ways (Leathers, 1986).

So we share meaning with others via inseparably interconnected verbal and nonverbal symbols. The meaning we share, however, is not derived from the symbols themselves because a symbol represents something other than itself but bears no actual relationship to that which it represents. Meaning is derived from the associations or connections people make when using symbols. <u>Meaning is within each of us, not in the symbols</u>. The story about a psychiatrist giving a Rorschach inkblot test to a client demonstrates this point. When asked to identify the meaning for each inkblot, the client responds to the first, "a couple making love," to the second, "a nude woman silhouetted behind a shower door," and to the third, "a couple walking naked hand-in-hand." The psychiatrist pauses, then remarks, "Mr. Smith, you seem obsessed with sex." Mr. Smith indignantly retorts, "What do you mean? You're the one showing me the dirty pictures." Meaning is in the eye of the beholder. There is no inherent meaning in any symbol anymore than there is essential meaning in any inkblot.

Consider the cross-cultural difficulties the British and Americans have understanding the English language. Our *private* school is Britain's *public* school; our *first* floor is their *second* floor. *Boot* to us is a type of shoe, but to the British it is also the *trunk* of a car. Likewise, remarking at the dinner table in England, "I couldn't eat anything more; *I'm stuffed*" will invite an awkward silence (the voice of experience). *To be stuffed* is considered an offensive remark. It is little wonder that George Bernard Shaw reputedly remarked, "Great Britain and America are two countries separated by the same language." The referents (the object, concept, or event referred to by a word) for more than 4,000 English words are different when used in one country or the other (Bryson, 1990). Same words but different referents shows that no word has meaning apart from people using the verbal symbol.

Nonverbal symbols likewise have no natural connection with their referents. Rock musician Frank Zappa made this abundantly clear when he appeared on a TV talk show hosted by an acerbic individual named Joe Pine. This incident occurred in the 1960s when a person's appearance was a subject of no small controversy. The most distinctive aspect of the show was Pine's abrasiveness and shabby treatment of his guests, whom he tried to make look foolish. Pine had an amputated leg, but this was unremarkable until Zappa appeared on his show. When Zappa, sporting shoulder-length hair, was introduced to the audience, the following exchange took place:

PINE: I guess your long hair makes you a girl.
ZAPPA: I guess your wooden leg makes you a table. (in Cialdini, 1993, p. 224)

The lightening-quick ad lib by Zappa exposed the absurdity of attaching any natural and unalterable meaning to a nonverbal symbol.

<u>Symbols, both verbal and nonverbal, derive a particular meaning from the totality of the context in which they appear.</u> We derive meaning for the symbols from who uses them and where, when, why, and how they are used. For instance, what does the nonverbal act of hanging pears on barren trees in winter communicate to you? Without knowing the context, it probably means very little. Do you realize that historians, however, may record this act as the precipitating event that led to the revolution against Nicolae Ceausescu, murderous dictator of Romania? In one of his final speeches, Ceausescu boasted that Soviet-style reform would infiltrate Romania "when apple trees grow pears" (in "New rulers," 1989, p. 1A). A group of college students in Bucharest, in a taunting act of defiance, set about hanging any pears they could find on the trees, which were denuded by the bitter winter weather and were lining the capital's main street. This symbolic gesture of defiance so infuriated Ceausescu that he directed his secret police to identify the parties responsible, then had them attack the students in their dormitory, killing many. Angry students took to the university square to protest, where more than 100 were slaughtered. The country seized upon this massacre as a rallying point for outright rebellion. The government collapsed and Ceausescu was hastily tried and executed in December 1989.

I have thus far discussed what communication is not and conversely what communication is. To summarize by way of definition, **communication** *is a transactional process of sharing meaning with others*. The intricacies of sharing meaning with others in group situations will become more apparent when I discuss what constitutes *competent* communication, the next topic for consideration.

COMMUNICATION COMPETENCE

Knowing what constitutes human communication does not tell you *how* to engage in the process in a competent manner. In order to accomplish this goal you must first understand what it means to communicate competently—the objective of this next section.

Focus Questions
1. How do you determine communication competence?
2. Does appropriateness of communication require unswerving conformity to group rules and standards?
3. Does being a competent communicator mean never engaging in poor communication practices?

Competence Defined

There are several definitions of communication competence offered. Littlejohn and Jabusch (1982) define it as "the ability and willingness of an individual to participate responsibly in a transaction in such a way as to maximize the outcomes of shared meanings" (p. 30). Trenholm (1988) defines **communication competence** as "the ability to communicate in a personally effective and socially appropriate manner" (p. 11). Adler and Towne (1996) define it as "the ability to get what you are seeking from others in a manner that maintains the relationship on terms that are acceptable to all parties" (p. 42). Although there is not one definition of communication competence that satisfies everyone, there are several points of agreement among most communication experts regarding this concept.

Matter of Degree Communication competence is a relative concept—a matter of degree (Spitzberg and Cupach, 1989). We speak of communicators along a continuum from "highly competent" or *proficient* all the way to "incompetent" or *deficient* with designations such as "minimally functional" and "average" as gradations along the continuum. All of us have varying levels of success in social interactions. All of us have our communication pluses and minuses given certain situations and circumstances. Therefore, the label "competent communicator" is a judgment of an individual's proficiency in a particular set of circumstances, not a designation of that person's identity as a human being. In another context, this same person might be judged "minimally functional" or "moderately skillful."

We-not-Me Oriented Since communication is transactional, competence can only be ascertained in terms of our relationships with others. You can't be declared competent unless you're tested on the proving ground of human relations. In groups, our primary attention is on the group (we) not the individual (me), unless the individual has direct bearing on the success or failure of the group. This, of course, is not the same as saying that groups should always supersede individual interests. Nevertheless, trying to achieve your individual goals at the expense of the group usually produces unsatisfactory outcomes for both you and the group. Zander (1982) even goes so far as to claim, "A body of people is not a group if the members are primarily interested in individual accomplishment" (p. 2).

There are potential dividends when group members assume a We-orientation. Usually, helping others satisfy their goals creates an environment conducive to the satisfaction of your own goals. Ridgeway (1982) found that one way for women and ethnic minorities to overcome bias that prevents them from achieving high status in a group is to act in a group-oriented, not a self-oriented, manner.

 FOCUS ON CULTURE

The Imperial "I" versus the Authoritarian "We"

The American emphasis on personal independence and individual uniqueness is characterized by the familiar maxim "It's the squeaky wheel that gets the grease.'' Asian cultures such as Japan and Singapore, which emphasize conformity and interdependence, espouse the maxim ''The nail that sticks up gets hammered down.'' A recent poll (in Simons and Zielenziger, 1996, p. 22A) of 131 businesspeople, scholars, government officials, and professionals in eight East Asian countries and the United States showed glaring differences in the value placed on order and personal rights and freedoms. When asked the question *''Which of the following are critically important to your people?''* the results were as follows:

	Asians	**Americans**
1. An orderly society	70%	11%
2. Personal freedom	32%	82%
3. Individual rights	29%	73%

All cultures vary in the degree of emphasis they place on people exploring their uniqueness and independence versus their conformity and interdependence. This **individualism-collectivism** continuum is thought by some scholars to be the most important dimension that distinguishes one culture from another (Hui and Triandis, 1986). It is a values debate at the center of the communication competence model's We-orientation perspective.

The autonomy of the individual is of paramount importance in individualist cultures, hence, the emphasis placed on ''self-actualization'' and ''personal growth.'' Words such as *independence, self, privacy,* and *rights* imbue cultural conversations. Individualist cultures have an ''I'' consciousness where competition, not cooperation, is encouraged; decision making is predicated on what is best for the individual even if this sacrifices the group welfare; private property, thoughts, and opinions are valued; and individual achievement and initiative are stressed (Samovar and Porter, 1995).

In collectivist cultures, by contrast, commitment to the group is paramount. Words such as *loyalty, responsibility* (to the group welfare), and *community* imbue collectivist cultural conversations. Collectivist cultures have a ''We'' consciousness where cooperation, not competition, is emphasized; individuals often downplay personal goals in favor of advancing goals of a valued group (family, organization, etc.); and privacy is sacrificed for the good of the group (Samovar and Porter, 1995).

In an individualist country, a person faced with the difficult choice between accepting a career promotion that requires a move across the country and staying put in order to avoid a difficult, even unhappy, transition for other family members would likely choose the promotion. In a collectivist culture, the choice would likely be to forego the promotion for the sake of the family, unless the larger group, such as the corporation, supersedes the family in importance (Brislin, 1993).

All cultures have both individualist and collectivist tendencies, but one tends to predominate over the other (Gudykunst, 1991). In a worldwide study of work-related values in forty countries, the United States ranks number one in individualism. Venezuela is the most collectivist with other countries such as Mexico, Thailand, Singapore, and Japan ranking on the collectivist side of the continuum (Hofstede, 1980). Approximately 70 percent of the world's population lives in collectivist cultures (Triandis, 1990).

In the United States, the preoccupation with individualism has drawn fire. Psychologist Carol Tavris (1982) argues that individualism in the United States has become excessive, producing what she terms the "Imperial I." The individual is king, regal in importance. Groups often are thought to exist to satisfy the needs of individual members, not to advance the greater social welfare. Sociologist Charles Derber (1996) claims, "As individualism intensifies, the balance of commitment can tilt so far toward the self that the family and other building blocks of society decompose. . . . Americans converted to the reigning ideology of 'looking out for number one' are proving ready to sacrifice not only outsiders but their kin on the altar of their own needs and pleasures" (p. 111).

Controversial author Charles Sykes (1992) argues that Americans have become so self-absorbed that we have turned ourselves into a whimpering "nation of victims" whose chief concern is "not with others, but with the *self*" (p. 22). The war cry of the Imperial Self is "I Deserve," as in "I deserve happiness, fulfillment, health, and wealth." Failing to get our just "deserves," disappointment inevitably ensues, followed by a tendency to blame others for personal failures or shortcomings.

Pollster Andrew Kohut, concluding from his own 1990 national survey (in Derber, 1996), describes young people in the United States as a "generation of self-centered know-nothings." Only about 25 percent consider "helping make the community a better place" a priority, and many are "so self-absorbed" that they would not assist others even in the most critical emergencies. Kohut claims that the United States is embarking on a new "Age of Indifference." This is harsh criticism indeed, but criticism widely shared by young people about their own generation (Kanter and Mirvis, 1989). A more recent national survey, however, provides cause for optimism. An impressive 78 percent of 18-to-24-year-olds expressed concern over the "disappearance of community," and 95 percent agreed that "when people get involved, they can really make a difference" (in McLeod and Cooper, 1996).

Excessive individualism doesn't require excessive collectivism as a solution. The Authoritarian "We" need not replace the Imperial "I." You don't need to bow down in homage to the group when individualism is de-emphasized. The dangers of group pressure, blind conformity to groups, and deindividuation, issues that will be discussed at length later in this book, remind us of the risks involved from excessive loyalty to any group.

Collectivist cultures require a level of conformity and sometimes authoritarian rule that would send shudders down the spines of most Americans. Singapore, for example, levies heavy fines on anyone littering, smoking in public places, or failing to flush public toilets, which are monitored by government employees (Bordewich, 1995). An ABC "20/20" episode aired on December 17, 1993, revealed that chewing gum is outlawed in Singapore, traffic laws are monitored by video cameras set up at busy intersections; censorship of printed material, CDs, and motion pictures is widespread; only the police can own guns; and political opposition to the government is a risky undertaking, often resulting in fines and imprisonment for dissidents. Solving community problems requires community-wide effort and a We-not-Me focus, but individual aspirations and freedoms do not have to be extinguished.

Individualist and collectivist values do not always conflict (Schwartz, 1990). When an individual learns conflict management skills or improves interpersonal communication skills, the group likely benefits as well as the group member. Nevertheless, <u>if groups are to succeed, individual goals and agendas should be of secondary, not primary importance</u>.

Larson and LaFasto (1989), in a comprehensive study of seventy-five diverse teams, found that the "what's in it for me" orientation of team members was a primary impediment to effective teamwork and group success. Mountain climber George McLeod notes that the least effective mountaineering and exploration teams are those impeded by "skiving," whereby team members conserve energy and resources in order to achieve individual rather than team objectives. Sir Edmund Hillary, who, along with his climbing partner was the first to conquer Mount Everest, made this assessment of the May 1996 mountain climbing disaster, the worst ever on Everest: "There has been an erosion of mountaineering values. It used to be a team effort. Nowadays, it's much too everybody-for-himself. That can get you killed. Tenzing and I got to the top *together,* it wasn't first one then the other" (in "Hillary," 1996, p. 41).

Equally unsettling is the conclusion of the Federal Aviation Administration's 1987 investigative report into safety-related incidents involving the operation of Delta Airlines. The report states, "There is no evidence that Delta's crews are (on the whole) either unprofessional or purposefully negligent. Rather, it was observed that crew members are frequently acting as individuals rather than as members of a smoothly functioning team" (Witkin, 1987, p. 1). Lack of teamwork and excessive individualism were among the causes of the collision of a KLM 747 and a Pan Am 747 at the Tenerife airport in the Canary Islands on March 27, 1977 (Weick, 1990). This air disaster, the worst ever in commercial aviation history, killed 583 passengers.

The We-orientation is a difficult lesson to learn in a Me-oriented culture, but the lesson can be absorbed. Contrast the individualism of track sensation Carl Lewis with the collectivism of the U.S. women's basketball team at the 1996 Olympic Games in Atlanta.

When Lewis won the long jump for the fourth straight Olympics, he had tied for the most Olympic gold medals ever won by a single individual—nine total. Immediately he began lobbying for a place on the men's 4×100-meter relay team in order to get one last chance to earn another gold medal and go down in history as the most decorated Olympian ever. Interviewed on CNN, Lewis implored viewers to "call the Olympic people" and "make your voice heard" (in Purdy, 1996, p. 1D). Lewis had not qualified for the relay team at the Olympic Trials because he finished last in the 100-meter final. The fact that placing Lewis on the relay team meant pulling off one of the U.S. sprinters who had qualified for the team, thus squashing that runner's Olympic dream, seemed less important to Lewis than personal glory. Lewis had been invited to work out with the relay team as an alternate in case he was needed in the event of injury to a team member. Lewis declined. The U.S. relay team had the fastest

The Tenerife air disaster, the worst in commercial aviation history, was caused partly by a lack of teamwork and excessive individualism.

qualifying time but lost to the Canadian team in the finals. The distraction of the Lewis controversy may or may not have contributed to the second-place finish; there is no way to determine this. Nevertheless, Carl Lewis clearly showed the individualist philosophy at work in a not-so-noble finish to his phenomenal Olympic career.

The U.S. women's basketball team, in contrast, worked together for a year developing teamwork and cohesiveness. All team members made significant sacrifices in order to take a year out of their lives, traveling more than 100,000 miles to put a winning team together. The women's team won all sixty games it played (fifty-two preparation games and eight Olympic contests). They defeated a very capable team from Brazil in the Olympic final, 111–87. A similar Brazilian team had defeated the United States by 37 points in the 1994 Pan Am Games. The 111 points scored by the Americans was an Olympic record. Tara VanDerveer, the gifted U.S. coach, noted after her team had won the gold medal, "There's a stereotype that women can't work together. What makes this special is that people had a team agenda. They weren't individuals. This team put the gold medal as their mission" (in Killion, 1996, p. 3D).

Carl Lewis demonstrated how difficult it is to put aside individualism even when collectivism is clearly required, and the women's basketball team demonstrated that even in a highly individualist culture, collectivist behavior is possible. Embracing the We-orientation and de-emphasizing the Me-orientation in the United States will not come quickly nor easily. The United States does not have

The 1996 U.S. Women's Olympic basketball team was a model of teamwork that produced success.

to become a collectivist culture where the group is supreme, but the Imperial "I" is the antithesis of teamwork and community. As Larson and LaFasto (1989) pointedly state:

> The potential for collective problem-solving is so often unrealized and the promise of collective achievement so often unfulfilled, that we exhibit what seems to be a developmental disability in the area of social competence. . . . Clearly, if we are to solve the enormous problems facing our society, we need to learn how to collaborate more effectively. We need to set aside individual agendas. (pp. 13–14)

Working together cooperatively in common purpose is no easy task, as any of my group discussion students will readily attest. Nevertheless, <u>dethroning the Imperial "I" and emphasizing team building and collaborative effort can prove beneficial to both individuals and society</u>.

Questions for Thought

1. Do you agree that the United States has become excessively Me-oriented? Are young people especially self-centered or do critics overstate this claim? How would you defend your answer?
2. Has the United States become "a nation of victims" as Sykes claims? Provide examples to support your position.
3. Singapore has low crime, safe cities, low unemployment, and few homeless. The United States has the opposite. Should we strive to become collectivist and emulate the Singaporeans?
4. Could the United States ever become a collectivist nation given our individualist history?

Effectiveness Communication competence is predicated on results. Effectiveness, or how well we have progressed toward the achievement of goals, is a litmus test of competence (Spitzberb and Cupach, 1989). Someone who knows what changes in communication behavior need to be made, wants to make these changes, but never does can hardly be deemed a competent communicator.

Individual effectiveness, however, may be deemed incompetent "if such effectiveness precludes the possibility of others accomplishing their own goals" (Spitzberg and Cupach, 1989, p. 20). A We-orientation requires concern for others as well as self. Consequently, <u>communication competence in groups necessitates behavior that is both effective *and* appropriate</u>.

Appropriateness Spitzberg and Cupach (1989) stipulate that appropriateness involves "the avoidance of violating social or interpersonal norms, rules, or expectations" (p. 7). The difficulty determining appropriateness in a particular context can be readily seen from the following intercultural example:

> An American college student, while having a dinner party with a group of foreigners, learns that her favorite cousin has just died. She bites her lip, pulls herself up, and politely excuses herself from the group. The interpretation given to this behavior will vary with the culture of the observer. The Italian student thinks, "How insincere; she doesn't even cry." The Russian student thinks, "How unfriendly; she didn't care enough to share her grief with her friends." The fellow American student thinks, "How brave; she wanted to bear her burden by herself." (DeVito, 1990, p. 218)

Appropriateness of your communication cannot be determined by merely examining a message isolated from the rich complexity of context. <u>We determine appropriateness by analyzing what (message) is communicated, who (sender) communicates the message to whom (receiver), why (purpose) the communicator does it, where (setting), when (time), and how (way) it is done.</u>

For instance, we may self-disclose intimate information about ourselves to members of some groups but not others. If we attend a therapy group on marriage, self-disclosing will be expected and encouraged because it is compatible with the group's purpose for being. If, however, we are talking to a group of fellow Rotarians at the monthly noon meeting, very personal self-disclosure may induce members to suck their lunch down their windpipes. The purpose of Rotary is not therapeutic, so the expecations regarding what constitutes appropriate communication in this context are different than you will find at the local meeting of Alcoholics Anonymous.

If a group meets in a tavern, the setting communicates informality. There will be less concern for propriety in language usage and behavior. If a group meets in the plush surroundings of an upscale law firm, however, norms and expectations relevant to the setting dictate communication of a more formal, less relaxed nature. Great attention to proper communication etiquette will be encouraged by this setting.

Additionally, the time we choose to criticize, congratulate, or ignore group members can easily become an issue of appropriateness. If a group member criticizes you for poor performance on a project after others have similarly rebuked you, it may seem like piling on. Is the criticism in front of others or in private? Is the tone of voice used sarcastic, contemptuous, or soothing? Is there a power difference between you and the person criticizing your performance? All of these factors and more constitute the context for analyzing the appropriateness of our communication.

Although appropriateness of communication is determined on the basis of group rules and norms within a specific context, rules and norms are not inviolate. Some group rules should be changed. Most of the time, however, we merely need to adapt to the rules of the group, not tramp all over them. As Getter and Nowinski (1981) explain, communication becomes inappropriate if it violates rules and expectations of the group when such violations "could have been averted, without sacrifice of the goal, by more appropriate actions" (p. 303).

When we need to change the rules in order to be appropriate, the change should be mutually agreed to by group members. Professors who want to interact socially with their seminar students must work out a modification of the rules and expectations students have for professor-student relationships. As long as the students agree to the modification, appropriateness is maintained. If the professor persists in pushing the socializing, however, when students clearly demur, then such persistence becomes inappropriate. When such persistence takes place interpersonally, it is labeled harassment.

Elements of Competence

Four elements can be extracted from the above definition of communication competence, which provides a framework for analysis of small group communication. These four elements are knowledge, skills, sensitivity, and commitment (Shockley-Zalabak, 1988). I will briefly discuss each one of these elements.

Knowledge   I have already noted the centrality of appropriateness and effectiveness to the definition of communication competence. <u>Communication, however, may be appropriate but not effective, and vice versa</u>. Knowledge of the context is essential in order to comprehend when the two are likely to diverge and when they will likely converge. To make this point clear, consider this example:

> Brian Holtz is a U.S. businessperson assigned by his company to manage its office in Thailand. Mr. Thani, a valued assistant manager in the Bangkok office, has recently been arriving late for work. Holtz has to decide what to do about this problem. After carefully thinking about his options, he decides there are four possible strategies:
>
> 1. Go privately to Mr. Thani, ask him why he has been arriving late, and tell him that he needs to come to work on time.
> 2. Ignore the problem.
> 3. Publicly reprimand Mr. Thani the next time he is late.
> 4. In a private discussion, suggest that he is seeking Mr. Thani's assistance in dealing with employees in the company who regularly arrive late for work, and solicit his suggestions about what should be done. (Lustig and Koester, 1993, pp. 68–69)

What choice would you make? The first option is a typical American way of handling this type of situation. It is direct and probably would be effective in getting Mr. Thani to arrive at work on time. Nevertheless, considering the Thai culture (context) where one person does not directly criticize another person, this choice would be very inappropriate, even embarrassing. Conversely, the second choice would be appropriate but hardly effective since Mr. Thani would likely persist in his tardiness. The third choice would be neither appropriate nor effective. Public humiliation would likely induce Mr. Thani, a valuable employee, to resign in shame. Thus, the fourth choice is best because it is both appropriate and effective (Lustig and Koester, 1993). Mr. Thani would receive the message indirectly that he must arrive at work on time, yet he can "save face." He can respond affirmatively to the indirect request that he change his behavior from tardiness to punctuality without suffering public humiliation.

Knowledge in any communication situation is critical, whether the context is another culture or our own. We cannot determine what is appropriate and effective without knowledge of the expectations, rules, and norms operating in a given situation.

We don't always make the wisest communication choices, but we are likely to make a fair number of foolish ones if our limited knowledge shields us from appropriate alternatives. You can exercise considerably more control over your life when your knowledge of what is required in a given communication situation to be appropriate and effective is more than just superficial. In matters communicative, a little knowledge is like a dim bulb in a dark alley. There's just enough illumination to show you how lost you are but not enough light to provide proper direction. If you are uncertain what is expected or required in a given situation you should seek knowledge from those who are likely to know and can enhance your understanding.

Skills   Communication competence encompasses the ability to apply your knowledge in actual situations. <u>Knowing how is not showing how</u>. One study of undergraduate women (Christensen et al., 1980) found that even though all subjects at the same time recognized body language cues that signaled discomfort of the person interviewed, and even though all subjects were instructed to change topics immediately if the interviewee exhibited signs of discomfort, nevertheless, half the subjects continued asking questions on the topic much beyond what was appropriate. All subjects who failed to adjust their communication in an appropriate way had scored poorly on an earlier questionnaire measuring "social competence" (communication appropriateness). Even when subjects were told in advance what the appropriate behavior was, they still showed lack of skill in responding to the situation.

A **communication skill** is "the successful performance of a communication behavior . . . (and) the ability to repeat such a behavior" (Spitzberg and Hecht, 1984, p. 577). There is abundant evidence that links communication skills with success or failure in the workplace. Benson (1983), in a survey of personnel managers at 175 large companies, found "oral communication skills" listed as the number one factor in obtaining employment for graduating business students. Communication skills were rated as *more* important than work experience, technical competence, resume, degree, grade point average, letters of recommendation, and a host of lesser factors. Endicott (1979) surveyed 170 well-known business and industrial firms and asked them to list the most common reasons why they did *not* offer jobs to applicants. At the top of the list were "inability to communicate" and "poor communication skills." The Secretary's Commission on Achieving Necessary Skills of the U.S. Labor Department (1991) reports that speaking, listening, decision-making, and problem-solving skills are necessary for high job performance. Another study found that the essential skills needed to be a competent employee are interviewing, listening, planning and conducting meetings, resolving conflicts, and public speaking (Engleberg and Wynn, 1995), all communication-based skills.

Learning communication skills requires practice. You can read a book on negotiating conflict, but unless you have actually negotiated in real situations, you have nothing more than book knowledge without the requisite skills.

Of course, competence in communication is not simply a matter of learning a single skill or even a set of skills. As I indicated earlier, skills without knowledge of when and how to use them are mostly useless, even harmful. The key is learning many skills and using them flexibly given the proper knowledge of what's appropriate for a given context.

Wiemann and Backland (1980), reviewing a vast quantity of research on communication competence, conclude that <u>individuals with flexible communication skills are more competent than those who are locked into a narrow range of possible responses</u>. Interestingly, individuals in same-sex groups exhibit a greater degree of flexibility in their communication than do individuals in mixed-sex groups (Bate, 1988). Presence of the opposite sex in a group situation tends to produce more dominance from men and more hesitance to offer opinions from women. Mixed company can present its own challenges for those striving to communicate competently.

Sensitivity The We-orientation requires a sensitivity to what is best for the group to achieve its goals. Sensitivity for the competent communicator means having your antenna extended to pick up any signals from the group that indicate disharmony, conflict, disenchantment, frustration, anger, and the like. Problems that lie just below the surface of consciousness go unattended by groups and magnify difficulties unless members are sensitive to the nuances and subtleties of communication transactions between members.

Sensitivity for the competent communicator also means showing concern for others, not just yourself. This means treating members with respect, dignity, and caring. The Golden Rule captures the essence of sensitivity. Treat others as you would have them treat you.

CLOSER LOOK

Is EST a Sterling Model of Communication Sensitivity?

Sensitivity is not the lesson taught by many "encounter groups" popular with the American public for over two decades. The most visible, popular, and controversial encounter group was EST (Erhard Seminars Training), created by Werner Erhard (real name Jack Rosenberg), a former used car and encyclopedia salesman. EST purported to teach individuals how to gain personal freedom and seize control over their lives, worthy goals to be sure. Many participants to this day defend EST as responsible for transforming their lives.

From the standpoint of communication sensitivity, EST fell short in several ways. First, EST promulgated a Me-oriented philosophy "of full-blown narcissism" (Galanter, 1989). The individual, according to the EST viewpoint, owes allegiance to no one other than self. EST participants "often feel released from the commitments born out of fidelity to their fellow humans, allowing them to indulge themselves without guilt" (p. 82). From this viewpoint, individuals have no need to pick up signals from the group and adjust their communication accordingly. If there is disharmony, anger, or frustration within the group, that's someone else's problem. What matters is the self, not others. The welfare of the individual, not the well-being of the group, is of paramount importance.

Second, closely associated with this Me-not-We viewpoint is the assertion by EST trainers that "if it happened, you chose it." Kaminer (1993) calls this "the myth of total control" (p. 159). Hassan (1988) cites an example of a woman named Carol who described her experience with an EST trainer:

I remember asking a question of the seminar leader, and his response was something like "How would you know? You are sitting in the victim's row!" When he asked why I was sitting there, I explained it was because I had diabetes. In a matter of moments he accused me of creating my own diabetes in order to get my father's attention when I was a little girl. . . . He more or less stated that if I just wanted to "uncreate" my medical condition, I could do so because I had the power to create reality. It was a good thing I never stopped taking my insulin. I could have died. (p. 85)

This "no excuses" philosophy, on the surface, has appeal. It is empowering. You are totally responsible for your successes and failures. You completely control your life and what happens to you. Don't whine and complain about your misfortunes. Act!

As appealing as this philosophy may appear to be as an antidote to the "nation of victims" mentality previously discussed (and there is truth in the assertion that we do create our own realities in *some* instances), deeper reflection reveals an insensitive blame-the-victim viewpoint. If *everything* that happens to you is because you chose it to happen, then what conclusion should you draw regarding victims of rape, incest, sexual harassment, genetic diseases, the Holocaust? Don't evil intentions of others, environment, heredity, and ignorance ever act as causes of personal tragedies? Is compassion merely "a waste of psychic energy" as Kaminer (1993, p. 67) claims EST taught?

Third, methods used by trainers during EST sessions also invite serious questions regarding communication sensitivity. What lesson is taught by trainers when they verbally abuse participants, shout obscenities at them, and encourage other group participants to follow their lead by verbally beating up on other trainees (Galanter, 1989; Kaminer, 1993)? As Singer (1995) notes, "Anyone who challenges the trainer will be humiliated and verbally mashed" (p. 193). What are we to make of training methods that push some participants until they experience psychotic episodes, paranoid delusions, hallucinations, and severe depression (Galanter, 1989; Singer, 1995)?

In 1985, Erhard changed the name of EST to The Forum, giving it a more benign packaging. Erhard also franchised Transformational Technologies, described in brochures as "a network of independent professional management consulting firms" (in Singer, 1995, p. 202). Erhard sold his interest in The Forum in 1991 amidst business disputes, an IRS inquiry, an ugly divorce, and charges by his daughters of physical, emotional, and sexual abuse, but his influence is felt even today (Conway and Siegelman, 1995). As Singer (1995) explains:

> Werner Erhard's thinking, as put forth in EST, the Forum, and Transformational Technologies, was, in fact, the inspiration for many of the training programs that became popular. . . . In a sense, these programs were successful at injecting into the corporate world a fascination with New Age thinking that remains present to this day. Lifespring, Actualizations, MSIA/Insight, PSI World, and the many affiliates of Transformational Technologies, among others, all incorporate techniques modeled after those introduced by Erhard. (Singer, 1995, p. 205)

One current popular offspring of EST is the Sterling Institute. The parallels to EST manifested by the Sterling Institute's group training are striking. The founder of the Sterling Institute, A. Justin Sterling (real name Arthur Kasarjian), took EST training in the 1970s. Soon after, he began offering one-day workshops for women that espoused the philosophy that women's career aspirations conflict with their need to yield to men (Lubman, 1996). The Sterling Institute was established soon after, offering separate group seminars for men and women.

The Institute's stated purpose is to "transform the quality of people's relationships by defining differences between men and women" (in Lubman, 1996, p. 16A). These differences center on the assertion that men are aggressive by nature and women need to indulge men. Sterling asserts that women are totally responsible for making relationships work. He writes in his 1992 book for women entitled *What Really Works With Men,* "In a serious, long-term relationship with a man, there is absolutely no room for your ego. Get it stroked elsewhere" (in Lubman, 1996, p. 16A). Several male participants claim that Sterling warned groups never to confide honest feelings to women because they'll "use it against you" (in Lubman, 1996, p. 16A).

Sterling Institute trainers, similar to EST trainers, are abusive to participants in group workshops (Lubman, 1996). Encouraged to disclose sexual escapades and traumatic experiences and vent anger at the opposite sex, trainees who show reticence to do so or who question the trainer's methods during the group workshops are verbally accosted. Women have formally complained to the FBI about the abuse, and the Better Business Bureau in 1996 rated the Sterling Institute as "unsatisfactory" due to the complaints of verbal abuse and physical threats. Trainers, and Sterling himself, were charged by some trainees with making profane and obscene descriptions of women. The men's weekend group trainings are also controversial. They end in naked "rites of passage." Males are warned that participants "may threaten or engage in acts of physical violence" during these weekends (in Lubman, 1966, p. 16A).

EST, and copycat groups such as the Sterling Institute, remind us that communication sensitivity is a matter of both philosophy and practice. EST purported to transform people's lives, and it undoubtedly did for some, but it did so by preaching a Me-oriented philosophy of self-absorption seemingly devoid of compassion for the less fortunate and by communicating an insensitivity to those clearly troubled by the abrasive methods used by trainers. Likewise, the Sterling Institute purports to transform people's lives but it serves up a misogynist philosophy, and anyone who resists choking down the offensive women-are-the-problem point of view are verbally assaulted by trainers.

Questions for Thought

1. In your mind, does the fact that a majority of participants in EST and its close cousins (the Sterling Institute, Lifespring, etc.) proclaim benefits from participation in such encounter groups and justify their philosophies and training techniques?
2. Can you justify the harsh methods used by trainers?

Commitment   There is no substitute for your commitment to self-improvement. The predominant value of the competent communicator is the desire to avoid previous mistakes and find better ways of communicating with group members. Someone who makes the same mistakes repeatedly and shows little interest in altering his or her behavior is a nuisance. In an organization, they're either fired or promoted to their maximum level of incompetence.

Commitment to improving your communication effectiveness requires self-monitoring. When you interact in groups you have to be a *participant-observer.* You assume a detached view of yourself. You analyze your communication behavior looking for areas where you can improve, noting areas where you have been successful. Ultimately, the competent communicator considers it a personal responsibility to interact with group members as effectively and productively as possible. You do this because you want the group to succeed, not because someone holds a gun to your head.

SECOND LOOK

Communication Competence

Definition	Elements
• Matter of degree	• Knowledge
• We-not-Me oriented	• Skills (flexibility)
• Effectiveness	• Sensitivity
• Appropriateness (who, what, where, when, why, how)	• Commitment

FOCUS ON GENDER

Gender and Communication Competence

Elbert Hubbard defined talk as "To open and close the mouth rapidly while the bellows in the throat pumps out the gas in the brain." This view of talk corresponds well with the stereotypic assessment of female conversation—all gas and no substance, yet voluminous in quantity. So do women talk endlessly about trivialities and are men "jerks" for thinking they do?

It may appear to men that women chatter about trivialities and it may appear to women that men are jerks for thinking so, but these perceptions are grounded in a misunderstanding of how differently men and women view the purpose of conversation. Deborah Tannen (1990), in her provocative book, *You Just Don't Understand: Women and Men in Conversation,* explains that for most women talk is primarily a means to "establish connections and negotiate relationships," but for most men "talk is primarily a means to preserve independence and negotiate and maintain status in a hierarchical social order" (p. 77).

All conversations include both dimensions of status and connection, but status is usually given far more relative weight by men and connection is usu-

<u>ally given far more relative weight by women</u>. The status dimension is very different from the connection dimension as indicated below, and therefore they produce very different communication expectations and patterns.

STATUS ←——————————→ **CONNECTION**

Independence (separateness)   Interdependence (intimacy)
Competition (contest)   Cooperation (consensus)
Power (control)   Empowerment (choices)

In mixed-sex groups, men's speech consists mostly of task-oriented, instrumental communication such as giving information, opinions, and suggestions (James and Drakich, 1993). Men usually see talk as a contest, an opportunity to establish or increase status in the eyes of group members. Thus, men report their knowledge to the group. They tell more jokes than women typically do, impart more information and advice, and offer more solutions to problems. Why? Because this spotlights them as experts (status enhancing). Giving advice, stating points of view, and displaying one's expertise can raise one's status in a group.

Conversely, women's speech consists more of supportive and facilitative communication such as agreeing, giving indications of interest in what others are saying, and encouraging others to participate in group discussions (James and Drakich, 1993). Women in mixed-sex groups make references to personal experiences, sometimes as proof for a point. They try to connect with other speakers, share feelings, and listen intently to establish rapport (Tannen, 1990). Displaying interest in other group members and offering encouragement to them establishes an interpersonal connection.

The prevailing cultural belief that women are verbose and men are taciturn doesn't fit this explanation of gender differences in communication. This is not a problem since the belief is largely a myth. <u>In mixed-sex group discussions, men usually outtalk women, not the other way around</u>. In fifty-six studies dealing with the question of talkativeness, the majority found men outtalk women (James and Drakich, 1993). Only two studies showed that women outtalk men. Report talk (providing information, displaying expertise, solving problems, etc.) usually takes up more total talking time than rapport talk (encouraging others, agreeing, asking for more information, etc.). Speaking for longer periods of time is also a sign of power. Thus, men, focusing on status in group discussions, must talk a great deal, while women, focusing on connection, talk but also listen intently.

So why is there a stereotype that women chatter and men talk little when the research indicates otherwise? Even when females speak significantly less often than males, both sexes tend to perceive women as more talkative (Sadker and Sadker, 1985). Tannen (1990) argues that <u>men talk more in public situations and women talk more in private situations</u>. She contends that men talk more in groups because they feel the need to establish or maintain their status in the eyes of group members. In private situations, at home with his partner, a man feels less stress to impress. Private time is down time. When a woman wants to discuss the events of the day, this may be perceived by a man to be trivial chatter interfering with relaxation because it has no apparent instrumental value. It is talking when no talk is perceived to be necessary (James and Drakich, 1993). (Male silence during conflicts can also be a controlling strategy, forcing women to work harder and talk more in order to keep a discussion going.) Women, however, see talk as essential to establishing and maintaining close relationships, so they talk more in private with their partners yet often complain that they are living with silent partners who are also poor listeners.

The very act of listening, however, has different meaning for men and women (Tannen, 1990). For men, listening, especially for a lengthy period of time without interruption, labels them as subordinate to the speaker. This places men in a seemingly one-down, low-status position that is uncomfortable. For women, the act of listening is an opportunity to connect on a personal level with the speaker, to show interest, to confirm what is said, and to appreciate the information imparted. Listening inattentively or interrupting to seize conversational control would be insensitive to the feelings of the speaker.

One of the most widely reported claims about male-female communication patterns is that men interrupt more than women, especially in mixed-sex group discussions. I made such a claim in the previous two editions of this textbook. An extensive review of the literature on this subject by James and Clarke (1993), however, shows no significant differences between the sexes in number of interruptions. This is especially true the more recent the study (reinforcing the necessity to update constantly our conclusions about male-female communication patterns). In fact, there are typically more interruptions in all-female groups than in all-male groups. Women, however, seem to interrupt to express interest, enthusiasm, or to establish rapport more than men do in same-sex groups.

So are men jerks for seeing conversation as a contest, an opportunity to enhance status, and are women meek and passive for seeing conversation as an opportunity to bond with others? Such interpretations are extremely limiting and simplistic. Consider the tendency of women to encourage members to participate in group discussions while men rarely show such a tendency. How should this be interpreted? One interpretation could be that men are insensitive jerks. Tannen (1990), however, offers this possible interpretation: ''Men who approach conversation as a contest in which everyone competes for the floor might be treating women as equals, expecting them to compete for the floor like everyone else'' (p. 211). I would add further that, for men, to be invited into a conversation is a loss of status. It spotlights their nonparticipation and puts them on the spot to display their knowledge when they may have nothing to share. In every instance where I have polled the men in my classes on this issue, only a very few, sometimes none, of the males have said that they feel pleased to be invited into a conversation, especially when they have no special expertise on the topic being discussed. Having to reveal one's ignorance in front of the group is embarrassing. From this perspective, to invite another group member into a group discussion without any clear understanding as to why a person has been quiet could be perceived as insensitive and clumsy.

In a similar vein, men and women in organizational settings see the same behavior but perceive it differently. For example, in one study, women managers expressed a need to be involved with subordinates but male managers expressed a preference for autonomy (independence)—leaving subordinates alone to do their jobs (Statham, 1987). The author of this study concludes the following:

> Men managers leave women subordinates to struggle on their own because they believe this is the "best way to manage." Men subordinates resent women managers who "stand over their shoulders" because this signals to them a lack of confidence, while the woman believes she is demonstrating her "concern for the employee." And women resent men who "dump the work" onto others or who in other ways are perceived as not contributing as much as women. (Statham, 1987, p. 425)

Not all men and women will follow the pattern outlined by Tannen. Tannen allows for exceptions. Some men will more closely resemble the "female" pattern of communication described by Tannen and some women will more closely resemble the "male" pattern. Mostly, however, men and women exhibit recognizable, documented patterns of communication that manifest differences between the sexes when they engage in group discussion. As Tannen (1990) argues: "Pretending that women and men are the same hurts women, because the ways they are treated are based on the norms for men. It also hurts men who, with good intentions, speak to women as they would to men, and are nonplussed when their words don't work as they expected, or even spark resentment and anger" (p. 16).

Given their differences, how do men and women communicate competently with each other? First, knowledge of the different assumptions made by men and women regarding conversations has to be broadened. Men and women need to "take each other on their own terms rather than applying the standards of one group to the behavior of the other" (Tannen, 1990, p. 120). Women will continue to misjudge men if they apply the single standard of connection to all conversations, and men will continue to misjudge women if they continue to apply the single standard of status to all conversations. <u>Both status and connection are legitimate standards for assessing conversations.</u>

Second, adaptation to each other's style of conversation must take place. <u>Men and women should exhibit skill flexibility when conversing with each other, and this means seeing both status and connection as appropriate.</u> Men could make fewer interruptions to seize conversational control, be more attentive listeners, ask more questions to clarify points or seek information, and encourage women to join the conversation when appropriate. This all shows flexibility and a concern for connection without the appearance of subservience. Women who learn assertiveness skills expand their opportunities to be heard without losing their sensitivity to the importance of connection.

There is one final point that is noteworthy. Individuals, even if they don't fit the usual male-female pattern identified by Tannen, will tend to emphasize one dimension (status or connection) more than the other as a habitual pattern. Knowing this will allow you to adjust your communication appropriately as described above.

Questions for Thought

1. Can you think of additional ways men and women can adjust their conversational styles in order to reduce misunderstandings and increase effectiveness?
2. Do the typical male-female patterns of conversation identified by Tannen correspond with your experience of communicating in mixed-sex groups?

In summary, human communication is a transactional process of sharing meaning with others. Communication competence, a recurring theme throughout this book, is composed of knowledge, skills, sensitivity, and commitment. Learning to communicate competently in groups is of vital importance to all of us. With this as a backdrop, let's explore how groups function as systems.

QUESTIONS FOR CRITICAL THINKERS

1. Are some statements always racist and sexist? Explain your answer in terms of "Meaning is within each of us, not in the symbols."
2. Does competent communication ever necessitate dishonesty? Explain.
3. When you are a member of a group should you always exhibit commitment to the group?

Groups as Systems

On December 31, 1974, William O. Douglas, Supreme Court justice and energetic defender of liberal causes, suffered a serious stroke. The severity of the
situation was increased by the fact that Justice Douglas was a determined man.
He insisted on resuming his judicial duties even when he was clearly unable
to function effectively due to his stroke. Bob Woodward and Scott Armstrong
(1979) describe the effect on the entire group of one of its members struck down
by illness:

> The other Justices had been waiting in the conference room for some time. . . . White
> seethed with impatience. He had expected Douglas to retire. Burger was polite and
> helpful. Brennan sat beside Douglas, assisting him with the files and papers. The
> conference ended at 3:45, earlier than usual.
>
> The rest of the week was torture for the other Justices. Douglas was in constant
> pain and barely had the energy to make his voice audible. He was wheeled in and
> out of conference, never staying the entire session, leaving his votes with Brennan
> to cast. Powell counted the number of times Douglas fell asleep. Brennan woke him
> gently when it came time to vote. . . . The tension grew. "Get him out of here,"
> White once told Datcher [Douglas's messenger], who had been summoned to wheel
> the sleeping Douglas from the conference room. (pp. 389–92)

Douglas, a once-towering legal figure, had become a nuisance to the Court,
keeping the highest judicial body in the country from efficiently performing its
vital duties.

One way to analyze a group such as the Supreme Court is to view it as a
system. A **system** is a set of interconnected parts working together to form a
whole in the context of a changing environment (Infante et al., 1993; Littlejohn,
1989). The Supreme Court is a system. Individual justices interrelate with one
another to form the Supreme Court. What happens to one justice affects the
entire Court. What happened to Douglas seriously affected the Court as a
whole, and all of the justices had to adapt to the changes in the health of one
of their colleagues.

The operations, behaviors, and functions that occur within a group can be
explained perceptively in terms of systems theory. Understanding in what ways
a group is a system can assist you in comprehending how a group carries on
its business both effectively and ineffectively.

Understanding what a system is and how it relates to groups will be seen
more clearly when I discuss the three principal elements that characterize all
systems. They are **interconnectedness of parts, adaptability to change,** and the
influence of size.

I have three overall <u>objectives</u> in this chapter. They are:

1. to explain the primary elements of a system and apply them to groups,
2. to define groups within a systems context, and
3. to set the boundaries of this book, specifying what size and types of groups
   will receive special emphasis.

INTERCONNECTEDNESS OF PARTS

Focus Questions
1. The ripple effect in a system means what?
2. What is synergy? How does it affect a group?

Every system is a collection of integrated parts that comprise a whole. All parts interconnect and work together. Thus, analyzing a single part without looking at its interconnectedness to the whole is relatively meaningless, just as determining the communication competence of a single act separated from a specific context is pointless. A daughter staying out late at night is an event that cannot be evaluated or analyzed appropriately without looking at the group affected. In some families and circumstances, such an occurrence might be cause for alarm, involving every family member in a frantic effort to locate her whereabouts. In other families and circumstances, this same event might be viewed more casually. This next section will discuss specific ways interconnected parts impact a group.

A group is a system composed of interconnected parts.

Ripple Effect

In a system, one part can have a significant impact on the whole (Galvin and Brommel, 1986), creating a **ripple effect** or a chain reaction of one system part on the whole system. This ripple effect spreads across the entire system much like a pebble tossed into a pond disturbs the water and forces adjustments.

The massive 1989 Gulf of Alaska oil spill by the tanker Exxon *Valdez* produced devastating environmental damage and a ripple effect throughout much of the food chain. Comedian Jay Leno highlighted this fact with the quip, "Fish sticks now come in two styles: leaded and unleaded."

The influenza pandemic of 1918-19 sickened over one *billion* people, half the world's total population at the time, and left 21 million people dead worldwide (half a million in the United States)—equivalent to our twentieth-century world wars. So virulent was the virus that there was an instance reported of women boarding a New York subway in Coney Island feeling mild fatigue and being found dead when the subway train pulled into Columbus Circle some forty-five minutes later. This lethal disease that began in Europe quickly spread to every nation on the planet. Even remote parts of the world fell victim to the pandemic. Nearly 20 percent of Western Samoa died from the disease, and entire Inuit villages in isolated parts of Alaska were decimated (Garrett, 1994).

In the 1960s, Marshall McLuhan coined the term "global village" to describe the interconnectedness of the world community. The mobility of the human population has vastly increased since the great pandemic of 1918, making the spread of diseases such as Ebola virus and AIDS a cause for greater concern. If you want to scare yourself silly, don't take in a horror movie, read Laurie Garrett's nightmarish nonfiction book, *The Coming Plague*. Famed president of the U.S. National Institutes of Health and Nobel laureate Joshua Lederberg told a 1994 Manhattan gathering of investment bankers, "The world really is just a village. Our tolerance of disease in any place in the world is at our own peril" (in Garrett, 1994, p. 619). What happens in remote parts of Africa, Asia, or anywhere else in the world can have cataclysmic chain reactions on the world's population. Every part of society is affected by an epidemic. Stresses are put on health care systems overwhelmed by the number of deathly ill patients. The economic system is impacted because a major portion of the workforce is sick at home, productivity drops, consumers stay away from stores, and construction of homes and businesses decline creating chain reactions of layoffs, unemployment and welfare claims, increases in poverty, and so forth.

Even a seemingly insignificant part of a system can generate an enormous negative ripple effect. Honeybees, for instance, viewed by many to be a nuisance at picnics or branded as "killer bees" in overwrought made-for-TV movies, pollinate more than 100 crops in the United States. Entomologist Richard Hellmich notes, "Every third mouthful of food or drink you take is there because of honeybees" (in "Beekeepers get set," 1990, p. 16A). Pesticides sprayed in agriculture, among other causes, threaten to deplete the honeybee population. There are about half as many bees in the United States today as there were fifty years ago. Stephen Buchmann, coauthor of *The Forgotten Pollinators*, notes, "If bees continue to decline, there will be a $5 billion to $8 billion increase in food costs" (in "To bee," 1996, p. 60). Even minor alterations in one part of the ecosystem generate alterations in the entire ecosystem.

On a less global scope, the family as a group demonstrates nicely the interconnectedness of parts in a system and the resulting ripple effect of a single part on the whole. The family is the principal group in our society. The family is also a system. If a parent dies, the family as a unit may have to deal with a severe loss of income. Tumultuous disruption may be the consequence. Selling the family house, moving to a new town or state, entering strange schools, feeling the pinch of tight finances, and watching the remaining parent scramble for employment are just some of the potentially unsettling effects of a death in the family. What happens to one member influences all members.

The ripple effect an individual has on an entire group, of course, does not always have to be a negative experience for a group. When a parent gets a job promotion or a significant raise in pay, all members stand to gain from the good fortune. If a child wins a scholarship to a major university, the entire family potentially benefits from the news. Accomplishments of individual family members may motivate others in the group to seek similar goals.

One part of a system affects the entire system. This principle underscores the importance you should place on your own communication in groups. Your competent communication can raise the level of effectiveness of the entire group. Anything less than competent communication can markedly diminish the group's performance.

Synergy

The whole is not necessarily equal to the sum of its parts. The whole may be, and often is, greater than the sum of its individual parts. This effect is called synergy. **Synergy** (syn=together + ergon=work) is the result of different system components working together and yielding a greater total effect than the sum of the individual components could have produced. When the joint action of group members produces performance that exceeds expectations based on perceived abilities and skills of individual members, synergy has occurred (Salazar, 1995).

The synergistic quality of group decision making is analogous to mixing drugs or chemicals. Some combinations of drugs, such as certain types of chemotherapy, can produce more effective results than single drugs working alternately but not together. The potency of some pesticides, when mixed together, increase dramatically. One study at Tulane University found that mixing two common pesticide chemicals, endosulfan and dieldrin, didn't double their potency but instead increased their potency by as much as 1,600 times. As endocrinologist John A. McLachlan, who led the Tulane University team that did the study, explains, "Instead of one plus one equaling two, we found that one plus one equals a thousandfold" (in "Playing havoc," 1996, p. 14A).

A creative synergy is often produced when talented people work together effectively. If the task calls for creativity, groups often outperform even a creative individual. That is why comedy writers for television shows frequently work as teams.

Synergy occurs in a group because a system's parts do not work independently of one another. They are interconnected. One study of military tank crews illustrates synergy in a human system (Tziner and Eden, 1985). In those crews composed of soldiers with uniformly high ability, performance far exceeded what was predicted based on individual abilities. As Chairman of the Joint Chiefs of Staff, Colin Powell touted the benefits of synergy as a military strategy in time of war ("New Pentagon," 1991).

In the 1980 Winter Olympics, the U.S. hockey team was given virtually no chance of defeating the powerful Soviet Union. Two weeks before the Olympics the Soviets had demolished the same team from the United States by the humiliating score of 10-3. This was the same Soviet team that had defeated a National Hockey League All-Star team a year earlier and would do it again a few weeks after the Olympics. Nevertheless, in one of the most stunning upsets in sports history, the United States won the hockey game 4-3 and went on to win the gold medal. On the basis of individual talent the Soviets should have won with ease. The inspired U.S. team, however, playing before a home crowd in Lake Placid, New York, produced synergy from collective effort melded into virtually flawless teamwork. Synergy is one reason why sports championships are decided by actually playing the game and not relying on "experts" to decide how the game should turn out. Sometimes the underdog pulls off a synergistic miracle.

Synergy is produced only when group members work in an interconnected way. If group members work independently by completing individual assignments on their own and the group merely compiles the results without the benefit of group discussion, no synergy will occur (Fandt, 1991). For instance, if your group took an essay test and each member was assigned one question to answer, no synergistic benefit would occur if group members did not discuss rough draft answers with the whole group prior to a final draft.

Systems don't always produce synergy. Sometimes they produce negative synergy. **Negative synergy** is the result of different system components working together and yielding a worse total effect than the sum of the individual components could have produced. The whole is worse than the sum of its parts. Negative synergy is like mixing alcohol and tranquilizers, causing suicidal effects. When the joint action of group members produces a worse result than expected based on perceived individual abilities and skills of members, negative synergy has occurred (Salazar, 1995). When group members are ignorant on a subject, resistant to change, or share a collective bias or mindset, the result of mixing together their individual contributions can produce decisions beyond bad.

One such instance occurred in the early 1980s. As part of an effort to sell Congress and the American public on the survivability of nuclear war and the necessity of spending four billion dollars to implement a civil defense plan, the Federal Emergency Management Agency (FEMA) downplayed the horror of nuclear holocaust. A December 1980 FEMA publication stated, "With reasonable protective measures, the United States could survive nuclear attack and go on to recovery within a relatively few years" (in Scheer, 1982, p. 111). FEMA compounded this widely recognized absurdity with plans to evacuate whole cities (as if an aggressor would provide a week's warning in advance of an attack). Incredibly, FEMA also instructed survivors to fill out change-of-address cards with their post offices following the nuclear attack (apparently so the IRS could still collect taxes from traumatized survivors). FEMA presumed that life would return to something approaching normality soon after nuclear bombs had decimated a substantial portion of the human species (not to mention most post offices).

FEMA's Alice-in-Wonderland civil defense plan makes as much sense as satirical advice given in the "Meet Mr. Bomb" spoof edited by Tony Hendra (1982), in which citizens are instructed to prepare for the 4,000-degree centigrade temperature at ground zero by spending ten to fifteen minutes a day in a clothes dryer. I have to assume that members of FEMA were ignorant of or blind to the true cataclysmic effects of total nuclear war when issuing their advice. To assume otherwise would necessitate an even less charitable conclusion about FEMA members.

On a less global scale, negative synergy can be seen in a group dialogue recorded by Hirokawa (1987). The group is deliberating a "winter survival" task whereby items must be ranked according to their utility in improving the group's survival in a wilderness area. Here the actual process of negative synergy becomes apparent.

B: This may sound crazy, but I say we go for the radio.
A: Why the radio? It's broken.
B: I know, I know . . . but that doesn't mean we can't use it.
C: I don't understand.
A: I think I do . . . but go ahead.
B: OK, like here's what I'm thinking. I remember, like I'm a fan of "Star Trek," right . . . anyway, like on one show, Spock and Kirk are being held prisoners and they make this makeshift radio to call for help. So, like here's what I was thinking we could do . . . we could use the parts to build our own transmitter.
A: Right . . . like we could take the antenna and place it on a high tree . . . run wires down, and start building a transmitter, maybe then send Morse codes. We wouldn't have to talk.
B: What about power, though?
A: We could use the battery from the plane.
B: But that's not on the list here and we were told not to assume other things aside from the list.
C: We could use solar power.
B: Yeah, the sun . . . or electrical power . . . build our own generator . . . like on "Gilligan's Island," remember where he was on a stationary bicycle?
A: Do we know codes?
C: I know S-O-S . . . three dots, three dashes, three dots . . .
B: Anyway, no matter. Just keep sending signals—any signals. . . .
C: So we go with the radio?
B: Yeah, I bet no one else thought of it. (p. 22)

In this illustration there is no indication that any of the group members knows anything about building a transmitter or generator. In point of fact, such an endeavor actually succeeding would be quite improbable even if MacGyver (to continue the group's reference to television shows) were available. Bad ideas in this group are simply compounded one upon the other—negative synergy at work.

ADAPTABILITY TO CHANGE

In a human system, adaptability is the modification of the structure and/or function of the system in response to changing conditions. Every system reacts to change in its own way. Two groups, for instance, that begin at the same point and experience similar environmental conditions may turn out very differently. Conversely, two groups that begin at very different points and experience dissimilar environmental conditions may turn out very similarly. In other words, groups with a similar or identical final goal (e.g., financial security) may reach that end in highly diverse ways (called **equifinality** in the somewhat ponderous systems lingo).

Focus Questions
1. Why do groups establish boundaries? How do they establish boundaries?
2. Can groups ever become too open? Too closed?
3. Is it better to be more open than closed?

Openness and Change

Groups are never in a static state. Groups are in a constant state of becoming. In human systems, change cannot cease. You do not have a choice between change and no change. The relevant choice is, "Can the group adapt to the inevitable changes that are certain to occur?"

Openness in a system refers to continuous interaction with the outside environment. Systems require matter, energy, and information (input) from outside in order to function. All living systems are open to some degree. No group, for instance, can be completely isolated from its outside environment and survive. Even cloistered monasteries require some input from outside of the group. Outsiders must be transformed into new members or the group will eventually cease to exist. Some information is bound to leak into even the most sheltered groups.

Openness and change go hand in hand in a system. As systems open to the outside, new input inevitably disturbs the system by producing change. Admit women into a previously all-male club, boardroom, or law firm and change is inevitable. Women running for Congress in the 1992 election repeatedly argued that, if elected, they would shake up the male-dominated House and Senate, producing unprecedented change, and in many ways they did. A three-year study by the Center for the American Woman and Politics at Rutgers University was summarized this way by Debra Dodson, senior research assistant with the Center: "Women members of the 103rd Congress had an impact in every area of legislation studied, whether or not the legislation dealt with 'women's issues.' But much of their impact is missed if we look simply at floor votes. Without the efforts of women members, some legislation might never have made it to a final vote, or it might have looked very different when it got to the floor" (in Goldston, 1995, p. 2A).

Openness and Boundaries The degree, rate, and desirability of change are three general factors that influence a group's ability or willingness to adapt successfully to change. The unhappy experience of a friend of mine illustrates all three. As the owner of a small business, he decided to go high-tech and computerize his office with the very latest, most sophisticated equipment. At the same time, he embarked on an office renovation project. To add to the disruption, he moved in a new partner. His office staff went berserk. They hadn't been trained to run the sophisticated computer programs and equipment. They resented the renovation, which displaced them from their normal work areas and created a huge mess that they had to work around. The new partner turned out to be a very demanding individual who thought little about expecting instant results from the beleaguered staff. The final change, however, that toppled this house of horrors was my friend's insistence that his staff work on weekends until the office was returned to a more normal state. Three of the four members of his staff quit, and they were spitting fire as they stomped out of the office never to return.

Too much change (degree) was required in too concentrated a period of time (rate) without a concerted effort to persuade the staff of the value (desirability) of the changes demanded. Groups can often adapt to significant change if given sufficient time to absorb the changes and if members are convinced the changes have merit.

Boundaries regulate the degree of openness and consequent exposure to change in a system. Boundaries determine the amount of freedom or constraint within a system (Barge, 1994). When groups establish boundaries they regulate the degree, rate, even the desirability of change. Boundaries control *input*— access to people, ideas, information, values, and events. Every group maintains **boundary control** to some extent.

Setting boundaries is a critical group function. Boundaries allow a group to perform, even to exist. So-called counterculture groups in the 1960s and 1970s sought a more tranquil life of self-sufficiency by closing themselves off to some of the disturbing outside influences of mass society. Rejecting the heart-thumping, vein-popping, stomach-churning lifestyle of urban dwellers, counterculturists limited group access to potentially disruptive outside information, people, ideas, values, and events in an effort to "return to nature."

Boundaries, however, are permeable (Conrad, 1990). They leak. No group can close off so completely to its environment that no change is possible. There is always some interchange with the environment that leaks through the boundaries.

Methods of Boundary Control <u>Groups establish boundaries by erecting physical, psychological, and linguistic barriers, and by establishing rules, roles, and networks.</u> Members may erect **physical barriers** to reduce or cut off interaction with outsiders. Locked doors, walls, inconvenient location in a building to discourage people from just "dropping by," partitions and cubicles in offices (sometimes derisively referred to as rabbit warrens), dividing space, and mapping out a defendable territory all set physical boundaries.

In some cases the physical boundaries are less obvious. Gangs may designate a few city blocks as their "turf." Certain streets act as lines of demarcation. In some instances, graffiti painted on signs or buildings serve as markers indicating a gang's turf. Conquergood (1994), in his long-term study of Chicago gangs, explains the importance of boundaries:

> Embedded within a larger system, the branch provides an encircling web of support, attachment, and solidarity against a hostile world. . . . Every branch is rooted in a clearly bounded territory called the hood. . . . Within this territory, particularly near the boundaries, graffiti announce self-consciously, "LK Camp," "This is King's World." The communicative task of the gang group is to transform marginal, somewhat forbidding urban space into a hood—to make a world of meaning, familiarity, adventure, and affective intensity. (p. 39)

Psychological barriers make an individual feel that they do not belong in the group. Kanter (1977) found that if members of management teams are mostly male (85 percent or more) in an organization, then women in the management group are viewed as "tokens." As tokens, women are defined as outsiders and excluded from group decision making, even though they are supposedly members of the team. Male managers, for example, were more likely to make sexual remarks in front of women than in front of men. At meetings they sometimes even apologized for a suggestive remark they were about to

Graffiti marks gang turf.

make and then made the remark anyway. This behavior has the effect of spot-lighting the presence of women in the group and underlining their token status. Women in this context are seen as not belonging and as not "real" members of the team, even as interfering with the day-to-day functioning of the group by diverting attention from the task to peripheral issues of sexual innuendo encouraged by their mere presence. Creating an unpleasant environment for women in management teams may also have the added effect of driving them out of the group entirely.

Linguistic barriers can also be used by a group to erect boundaries. Disaffected groups and groups that feel threatened by the larger society use argot as self-defense. An *argot* is a private vocabulary peculiar to a specific group. Prostitutes, because they engage in illegal behavior repudiated by much of society, conceal not only the sexual acts themselves but also "camouflage discussion of the acts to avoid arrest" (Samovar and Porter, 1995, p. 173). If you heard this statement: "I tried for a lobster, thought I had a roast beef, but had to settle for a steak," would you know what this meant if groceries were obviously not being discussed? In a pimp-prostitute conversation this argot, in some parts of the country, would translate into a client willing to pay one hundred and fifty dollars (lobster), a seventy-five dollar client (roast beef), and a fifty-dollar client (steak) (Samovar and Porter, 1995).

Members of ethnic groups and nationalities concoct new words to create distance between each other. Croats and Serbians, Slovakians and Czechs, and Indians and Pakistanis all emphasize relatively minor differences in the mostly shared language that they speak in order to create boundaries between groups (Greenway, 1993).

Rules also establish boundaries. Membership rules, for instance, determine who can be members of a group and who cannot. Monitoring group membership is one way groups control exposure to the "outside" and protect themselves from loss of group identity that results from granting membership to individuals who do not fully share common goals and commitment.

Rules define appropriate behaviors in specified social situations. Rules may specify who can talk to whom, thus controlling input from outside. Within organizations there is usually a chain-of-command rule. You do not normally leapfrog your immediate supervisor and communicate directly with the president of the company. In order to prevent information overload and inefficiency, the Big Cheese will want you to talk to the Cheez Whiz. In this way, *subsystems*—units that function as smaller systems within the larger system (e.g., departments within divisions, divisions within organizations)—are restricted from providing direct input.

Roles are another way groups set boundaries. A role is a pattern of behavior exhibited by a member of a group. All roles have expectations attached to them. These expectations specify appropriate behavior, thereby fostering predictability and controlling variability. Once the pattern of behavior is associated with a group member, a boundary is set.

The role of manager in an organization defines what behaviors are expected and appropriate and which are not. In the United States, managers are expected to respect the boundary between an employee's work life and private life.

Commenting on a female employee's lack of a husband and informing her that she will be attending a luncheon to meet an eligible male would be viewed as clearly overstepping the boundaries separating supervisor and employee.

The same reaction may not occur, however, in India where many Indians prefer a leadership style called "paternal authoritativeness." Indians expect that someone in a supervisory leadership role, typically a male, will act like a father who cares about a family member. Going to the trouble of arranging a luncheon for a female employee to meet an eligible male would likely be perceived as showing personal interest and concern for the employee's welfare (Brislin, 1993). The employee would likely appreciate the gesture (and attend the luncheon), whereas in the United States charges of sexual harassment might be filed. Role boundaries and culture are inseparably interconnected.

Finally, groups set boundaries by establishing networks. Networks control the access and flow of information within the group and they may also isolate the group from outside influences. A **network** is a structured pattern of information flow and personal contact. The more open the network, the more accessible information is to a broad range of individuals. <u>Open networks encourage change while closed networks emphasize stability and permanence</u>.

In some cases, becoming a link in the network is the hard part. One study of African Americans in the banking industry (Irons and Moore, 1985) found that not being included in the network was rated as the most serious problem to advancement in their jobs by 75 percent of the respondents. Other studies of Asian Americans found similar barriers to upward mobility (see Morrison and Von Glinow, 1990).

The "good old boy" network serves the purpose of thwarting change, particularly sharing power and resources with women. The Supreme Court has ruled that groups such as Kiwanis, Rotary, and traditionally all-male organizations cannot exclude women from joining if such organizations serve as networks for business opportunities. Having access to information from these groups can make the difference between becoming an active player in the business world and remaining a benchwarmer.

⊙⊙ CLOSER LOOK
Bound and Gagged: Cult Boundary Control

From the Manson Family and the Heaven's Gate Cybergroup to the Moonies and the Rajneesh, cults small and large have emerged in the United States. Some have disintegrated in violent clashes with law enforcement or in mass suicides, while others continue to troll the waters of the disenchanted and dispossessed for new converts. Depending on the definition, there are between 3,000 and 5,000 cults in the United States with between two million and five million members (Singer, 1995). These are rough estimates at best since there is no precise way to make a membership head count.

Singer (1995) defines a cult as "a group that forms around a person who claims he or she has a special mission or knowledge, which will be shared with those who turn over most of their decision making to that self-appointed leader" (p. xx). There are four important characteristics of cults which separate them from other religious, political, or social groups (Appel, 1983; Galanter, 1989; Singer, 1995). These four characteristics are:

1. Cults have strong, charismatic leaders who exercise control in an authoritarian power structure.
2. Cults have a shared belief system whose adherents accept that they alone are gifted with the revealed truth.
3. Cults insist on regimented behavior of followers, strict obedience to authority figures, and unquestioning acceptance of the group's norms and beliefs.
4. Cults create rigid boundary control.

It is this last cult characteristic that I wish to explore here.

Cults exercise boundary control in the same ways that other groups do, just with greater enthusiasm and extremity. First, they create physical isolation. The most obvious examples are the Jonestown complex in Guyana and the Branch Davidian fortress in Waco, Texas. Reverend Jim Jones, dubbed the "Messiah from Ukiah" by the media, awash in his paranoid delusions and threatened by a series of exposés in newspapers and magazines, moved the bulk of the membership in his People's Temple from San Francisco to the jungles of Guyana, South America. There, in "splendid isolation," Jones ruled his cult followers with an iron fist until it came to an end with the mass murder/suicide of 912 people, 276 of whom were children. David Koresh followed a similar pattern to Jones. Followers of this Branch Davidian leader built a 77-acre fortress of isolation in the middle of Texas. The Koresh cult also ended tragically in a 1993 fiery battle with federal authorities.

Physical isolation is also achieved through secrecy, in some instances. The manual of the Free Militia, a Midwest paramilitary cult, reads in part:

> The identities of cell members are known only within the cell and by their immediate superior. . . . All codes, passwords, and telephone networks are determined by and held in confidence within the cell. All fortified positions are determined, prepared and concealed by the cell. . . . The cell leader easily conveys clear orders to a small group of men. [Cell members] can communicate freely and openly while shrouding the particulars of their tactics, positions, and signals to everyone outside the group. (in Conway and Siegelman, 1995, p. 344)

These cells, or subterranean secret units, are "reserved for hard-core insurgent operations" (Conway and Siegelman, 1995, p. 354).

A second way cults maintain rigid boundaries is through information control. As Galanter (1989) explains, if a cult "is to maintain a system of shared beliefs markedly at variance with that of the surrounding culture, members must sometimes be rigidly isolated from consensual information from the

Isolated locations and fences clearly mark boundaries of Branch Davidian and Montana Freemen compounds. The boundaries, however, are permeable. Note the satellite dish, power, and phone wires connecting the compounds to the outside world.

general society that would unsettle this belief system" (p. 112). Working hand in hand with physical isolation, information control is exercised partly by creating closed networks that prevent outsiders such as parents, friends, and the media ("unbelievers") from entering the cult's premises. A member's support network (e.g., family) is severed. Access to outside information is cut off. Cult members are encouraged to read cult literature. Of course, the best means of information control is self-censorship (Pratkanis and Aronson, 1992). Information that is not "of the cult" is labeled "of the devil," "lies of the government," and so forth. Members are made to feel guilt and shame for showing interest in such information.

Cult followers are also fed a diet of misinformation (Singer, 1995). Sheltered from outside information, the only reality for members of Jonestown, for instance, was what Jim Jones and his band of cohorts created for the group. Jonestown members were told that Los Angeles had been abandoned due to severe drought, that the Ku Klux Klan was boldly marching through the streets of San Francisco, and that the U.S. government was preparing to destroy Jonestown and kill its inhabitants. So restricted was the information entering Jonestown that even misinformation served to control the membership and create a paranoid atmosphere.

A third method of cult boundary control is the use of a group argot incomprehensible to outsiders. How, for example, are outsiders to know that *the devil disguise, just flesh relationships,* and *pollution* are derogatory terms for parents (Singer, 1995)? *Being too horizontal* is being too sympathetic to peers. Moonies refer to all relationships between people as either a *Cain-Abel* (superior-subordinate) or a *chapter 2* (sexuality) problem (Hassan, 1988). The Divine Light Mission refers to their services as *satsang* and *darshan.* Scientologists talk about the *thetan* (soul) and *engrams* (aberrations). Deceptive fundraising practices are referred to by some cults as *transcendental trickery.* This **groupspeak,** as Singer terms it, shuts down members' critical thinking. "Eventually, speaking in cult jargon is second nature, and talking with outsiders becomes energy-consuming and awkward. Soon enough, members find it most comfortable to talk only among themselves in the new vocabulary. To reinforce this, all kinds of derogatory names are given to outsiders: wogs, systemites, reactionaries, unclean, of Satan" (Singer, 1995, p. 70).

A fourth method of cult boundary control involves erecting psychological barriers. This practice is most clearly evident in the "them versus us" in-group/out-group mentality that fosters either-or thinking within cults. You're *either* "with us" and right, redeemed, saved, *or* you're "against us" and therefore wrong, evil, unenlightened, doomed (Singer, 1995). To be an in-group member is to be a "chosen one." Those in the out-group are hated as enemies (Pratkanis and Aronson, 1992). The beast in David Koresh's worldview was the U.S. government—also the object of virulent hatred from various militia cults in the United States (Conway and Siegelman, 1995). The Children of God encourage members to hate their parents. "Fearfulness of outsiders, or xenophobia, a common characteristic of cults, is an important manifestation of boundary control. It holds groups together but it can reach the dimension of outright paranoia" (Galanter, 1989, p. 114).

Cults also erect psychological barriers against "bad thoughts." Questions that might arise in a member's mind that indicate less than total acceptance of the belief system of the cult are forcefully discouraged. These are "disagreeable thoughts," "evil," or "the work of Satan" (Pratkanis and Aronson, 1992). Members become their own mind police trying to clear their heads of Orwellian thought crimes.

Finally, <u>cult boundary control is created by rigid rules</u>. There are dress codes, dietary restrictions, and rules governing with whom a member may associate, marry, or talk. Some cults have rules stipulating whether members may raise their own children and where they may live (Singer, 1995). Gag rules that prohibit gossiping or "nattering" where members might express doubts or misgivings about the cult and the cult leaders are commonplace. Members are instructed to report any violations of the gag rule.

Although cults have extremely tight boundary control, no group can exist as a totally closed system. Boundaries are permeable even for cults. Seeking new converts requires some interaction with the outside world. The Branch Davidians, isolated in their fortress though they were, equipped their compound with a satellite dish, and some members, including Koresh, regularly jogged through Waco neighborhoods and shopped in local stores ("Cult compound," 1993). Members of the Heaven's Gate cult designed Internet web sites for San Diego businesses and used their own web sites to recruit members and proselytize their beliefs.

All groups exercise boundary control, but cults make boundary control a top priority, sometimes an obsession. This rigid boundary control is self-protective and has the effect of maintaining stability within the group and stifling change.

Questions for Thought

1. Can you have a cult without rigid boundary control?
2. Although cults are often religious or quasi-religious in nature, can cults be secular?
3. Can you have a cult without a charismatic cult leader?
4. How are cults different from the U.S. Marine Corps? The Catholic Church?

Openness and Group Effectiveness

Although all groups set boundaries, varying in degree from rigid to flexible, there is a strong bias in American culture that encourages openness and discourages closedness. We preach the value of fostering an "open society" and maintaining an "open mind." Having a "closed mind" is linked to an authoritarian personality and dogmatism. A closed society is likened to China or North Korea. As I've already noted, highly closed, isolated groups are often referred to as cults. The fact that cults are excessively closed, however, shouldn't prompt the opposite problem—excessive openness. According to Klapp (1978), <u>the belief that openness is always good and closedness is always bad is a faulty one</u>.

The degree of openness in a system is a critical factor in a group's ability to adapt to change successfully. The pervasive bias for overly abundant openness found in U.S. society, however, is simply misguided. No group can long endure unless it closes off to some outside influences and restricts access to some information (Galanter, 1989).

A group must close off when both the quantity and type of outside influences place undue stress on the group and/or prevent it from accomplishing its task. Members need time to reflect, to absorb information, to determine proper direction, to arouse enthusiasm for tasks, and to establish cohesion among themselves. These activities are not accomplished easily, maybe not at all, when input from outside the group competes for attention and complicates decision-making processes.

There are times, for instance, when a family seeks advice and counsel from friends and relatives and there are times when a family closes off to the intrusion of outsiders. In-laws who are overly free with advice and criticism impose stress on the family. Permitting even well-intentioned relatives and friends to hammer immediate family members with unsolicited counsel can easily lead to bickering, increased tension, and conflict.

The U.S. Supreme Court, although certainly not a closed group, does not permit open access by just anyone to the deliberative process. Only certain individuals and groups with a direct interest in an issue are allowed to provide input (Woodward and Armstrong, 1979). Open access to the justices would subject the Court to undue influence from special interests. Momentous decisions might become more political than judicial. In some groups, a good deal of closedness is essential for the work of groups to take place in an appropriate way.

Groups can also close off too much (Klapp, 1978). Boundary control can become overzealous, as is the case with cults. Galanter (1989) cites an example, however, of overzealous boundary control in a more ordinary group taken from his own experience in a Tavistock training institute in group behavior. Most participants were mental health professionals. At one point participants were asked to form small discussion groups, retire to separate rooms, and define a common position on a social issue.

Paul, a respected psychiatrist, was given the role of screening outsiders for his group. He took his role too seriously. When a slight, elderly woman entered the room where his group was deliberating, Paul insisted that she not infringe on the group's territory. The woman did not heed his directive but instead asked a few questions. Paul rushed over to the woman, tried to shove her out the door, and ended up angrily flinging her to the floor, wrenching her leg in the process. Decking a little elderly woman is not appropriate boundary control. Nevertheless, Paul exhibited no remorse for his bizarre behavior. He excused his action by blaming the woman for intruding on the group's deliberations.

The process of opening and closing in a group is not a mechanical one, operating like a pendulum swinging back and forth from rigid to flexible boundaries. Mechanical models of openness in human systems rely on static measures of change. Degrees of openness in a group system, however, are largely perceptual, not mathematical. What appears rigid to one group or individual may appear very flexible to another group or individual. Some groups are capable of coping with a great deal of change. Other groups fly apart when even minimal change occurs. It is the *perception* by group members of the degree, rate, and desirability of change coupled with the perceived permeability of the group's boundaries that determine adaptability, not some quantitative measure of change in the system.

When groups experience debilitating stress and tension, divisive conflicts, boredom and malaise, and poor productivity, members should take these as possible <u>signs of excessive openness or closedness</u>. Loosening or tightening boundary controls may be in order because groups must be able to adapt successfully to change.

 SECOND LOOK

Openness and Group Boundary Control

Types of Group Boundaries Regulating Change	Boundary Control and Group Effectiveness
• Physical barriers • Psychological barriers • Linguistic barriers • Rules • Roles • Networks	• Groups should close off when both quantity and type of information place undue stress on the group and/or prevent it from accomplishing its task • Groups can also close off too much • Debilitating stress/tension, divisive conflicts, boredom, malaise, and poor productivity are signs of excessive openness or closedness

<u>Communication is central to the adaptability of a group whatever the degree, desirability, and rate of change affecting it.</u> Through communication, group members indicate how much adaptation is permitted in the system. Here feedback is critical. A group cannot adequately adapt to change by adjusting boundaries if individuals within the group do not provide sufficient feedback to indicate problems they are having coping with the disruption precipitated by change.

INFLUENCE OF SIZE

Size is a central element in any human system. Fluctuations in the size of a group have enormous influence on the structure and function of the group. An increase in group size increases complexity and decreases member satisfaction.

Focus Questions

1. What is the most appropriate size for a decision-making group?
2. What distinguishes a small group from a large one?
3. How are groups and organizations different?

Group Size and Complexity

Change in a system creates greater complexity. One of the most significant changes affecting groups is an increase in size. As groups increase in numerical size, complexity increases. This increase in complexity has significant ramifications for how groups function. In this section, I will discuss the influence of size variations on groups from a quantitative and qualitative standpoint. I will also identify some of the primary differences between small groups and large organizations.

Quantitative Complexity Bostrom (1970) observes that as the size of the group increases arithmetically (linearly), the possible number of interactions between group members increases geometrically (exponentially). These are his calculations:

Number in Group	Interactions Possible
2	2
3	9
4	28
5	75
6	186
7	441
8	1056

Bostrom shows that in a dyad, only two relationships are possible, namely, person A to person B and vice versa. The relationship that A has to B may be quite different from the relationship B has to A. Person A may perceive the relationship with B as a close friendship whereas B sees the relationship with A as merely acquaintanceship. In a triad, or three-member group, there are nine possibilities:

1. A to B	4. C to A	7. A to B and C
2. B to A	5. B to C	8. B to A and C
3. A to C	6. C to B	9. C to A and B

In a special issue of *Newsweek* on the subject of the family, a practical example of the Bostrom calculations in real life is described:

> The original plot goes like this: first comes love. Then comes marriage. Then comes Mary with a baby carriage. But now there's a sequel: John and Mary break up. John moves in with Sally and her two boys. Mary takes the baby Paul. A year later Mary

meets Jack, who is divorced with three children. They get married. Paul, barely 2 years old, now has a mother, a father, a stepmother, a stepfather and five stepbrothers and stepsisters—as well as four sets of grandparents (biological and step) and countless aunts and uncles. And guess what? Mary's pregnant again. (Kantrowitz and Wingert, 1990, p. 24)

<u>Complexity increases rapidly as the size of the group grows</u>. Adding even a single member to a group enormously complicates the group dynamics. As newscaster Jane Pauley once remarked, "Somehow three children are many more than two."

I should note here, however, that although increasing the size of a group increases its complexity, <u>the loss of a group member, especially a key one, does not automatically reduce complexity even though the group size has diminished</u>. The reality of single parenting is not less but more complex. When two parents are raising children the workload can be shared (although women typically assume the greater burden). With single parenthood, the burdens remain but there is only one parent to perform the task and shoulder the responsibilities. So decrease in size does not reduce complexity in a group in all cases, although an increase in size inevitably increases the complexity of the group.

Complexity and Group Decision Making   As groups increase in size, complexity increases, but does this affect the decision-making process? The answer is yes. The most extensive research on this question of group size and decision making has been conducted on the jury system. If no important differences can be found between smaller-sized juries and larger ones, then the state could save a substantial amount of money by using juries with fewer members.

Important differences, however, have been discovered, although the research does not lead to any firm conclusions regarding the advisability of using smaller juries. <u>Participation rates are affected significantly by differences in the size of the group</u>. Kessler (1973) compared six-member and twelve-member juries and found a greater number of nonparticipants in the larger jury than in the smaller one.

Although participation is broader in smaller groups than in larger ones, the content of the communication is different in one important way. <u>Smaller groups inhibit overt disagreement and signs of dissatisfaction more than do larger groups</u>. Smaller groups can apply pressure to conform to majority opinion more directly and effectively on members than can be applied in larger groups (Bettinghaus and Cody, 1987). Splinter groups and factions are more likely to emerge in larger groups. In a six-person group there may be only a single deviant who must stand against the group. In a twelve-person group, however, two or more deviants may more easily emerge, forming a supportive faction. <u>Having an ally makes nonconformity easier to sustain</u>.

In the movie *Twelve Angry Men*, Henry Fonda's character votes "not guilty" when the other eleven jurors vote "guilty." Hailed by many as a dramatization of the importance of one person standing against the many in a fight for truth and justice, one scene is often overlooked. When Fonda's character stands alone, he debates with fellow jurors for a while but indicates that he is unwilling to continue if no other juror will support his position. He makes a deal with the jury. If no other juror votes not guilty on the next ballot, then he will join the majority and also vote for conviction, thereby sending the defendant to the electric chair. When he gains an ally, the fight is continued to its dramatic conclusion. Nonconformity is easier when you don't have to stand alone against the group.

The decision-making process is altered as the size of the group increases, but is the ultimate group decision affected? Although clear generalizations regarding the influence of size on group decisions cannot be made in regard to juries (Hastie et al., 1983), research on groups other than juries is more conclusive. The appropriate size for a group is the smallest size capable of performing the task effectively (Hackman, 1987; Sundstrom et al., 1990).

So what is the irreducible minimum size for small decision-making groups to be effective? The answer depends on the goals of the group. There is a trade-off between quality and speed when trying to determine ideal group size (Pavitt and Curtis, 1994). If the primary group goal is the quality of the decision, then a moderately sized group of seven to ten is advisable. (Groups larger than this, especially substantially larger, can easily become unwieldy and inefficient.) Moderate-sized groups are especially effective if there is little overlap of knowledge and skills among group members and the group task requires substantial diversity in knowledge and skills (Valacich et al., 1994). If the primary goal of the group is speed, however, then groups of four or fewer members are advisable. Since juries are faced with momentous choices that significantly affect people's lives, the twelve-member jury has been the norm. If your well-being depended on a jury verdict, you would certainly want the primary group goal to be the quality and not the speed of the decision. Nevertheless, as groups become larger, decision making becomes more complicated. Consensus (unanimous agreement) becomes difficult and majority vote is often used to make final decisions when groups are large. Some research (see Pavitt and Curtis, 1994) suggests five-member groups are a nice compromise when both quality *and* speed are important group goals. Ultimately, there is no magic number that constitutes the ideal-sized group. Even five-member groups can circumvent quality deliberations by a quick majority vote. Contextual factors (politics, legal requirements, institutional norms, availability of members, task complexity, etc.) may necessitate groups larger in size than five. Nevertheless, competent communicators can work effectively in larger than five-member groups although increased size magnifies the difficulties.

Group Size and Member Satisfaction

As groups increase in size and therefore complexity, satisfaction with the group experience diminishes (Pavitt and Curtis, 1994). Why should larger groups create greater dissatisfaction among members than smaller groups?

When groups grow larger and therefore more complex, there are fewer opportunities for each member to participate, generating dissatisfaction (Gentry, 1980). A few members, usually the talkative ones, tend to dominate the group (Pavitt and Curtis, 1994). Larger groups permit greater member anonymity, as any student can readily testify if exposed to a mass lecture class. In a small seminar, individual members have difficulty hiding. The relative anonymity provided by a larger group, while viewed as a plus by uninformed, reticent, or apathetic members, encourages isolates to form in the group. Isolates are individuals who occupy space but contribute nothing to the group. Their participation amounts to a physical presence (they make roll call) but nothing more. Isolates are unproductive and often unsociable. Although some individuals become isolates because of shyness, not indifference, their unproductive presence can easily frustrate other group members.

Isolates emerge in larger groups more than smaller groups because larger groups tend to be more intimidating. Unless an individual member is self-confident and assertive, he or she can be ignored easily by the group as a whole. Most members do not like being ignored or made to feel unimportant. If ignored, most individuals will withdraw from group participation. They remain members in name only.

Increasing group size produces diminished member satisfaction not only because of fewer opportunities for participation. In larger groups, access to information is not as readily available on the whole as in most smaller groups. Sheer size often prevents such ready access. As groups grow larger, the complexity of the group makes access to information more difficult to obtain. Complicated networks are established to regulate the flow of information. Tracking down the location of important data may become a trial. In the computer age, however, keeping information inaccessible is increasingly difficult. Member satisfaction with the group experience is directly related to perceived accessibility of information (Spiker and Daniels, 1981).

Groups versus Organizations

When groups grow, they reach a point where they may become organizations with bureaucracies. For instance, suppose you and two friends decide to open a small business together. Let's say you call it New Age Repair & Care (NARC for short). Your business specializes in "holistic healing" of automobiles in addition to conventional automotive services.

In its initial stages, the structure of your group is informal and the division of labor is most likely equal. Since the three of you work at the establishment, communication is not hampered by cumbersome chains of command, middle managers, and the paper chase of a large formal organization. Standards of operation and procedures for decision making are informally negotiated among the three of you as situations occur.

If your little enterprise booms, employees will have to be hired, thus expanding the business and increasing the complexity of the entire operation. Work schedules will have to be coordinated. Standardized codes of dress and conduct on the job may be required. Some training in New Age automotive techniques may be necessary. Formal grievance procedures may also be required to settle disputes. You may decide to open additional NARC outlets, even become a chain, selling franchises around the country. Now you must hire managers, accountants, and lawyers, establish a board of directors, sell stock in the company, and become business executives. What began as a small enterprise can grow into a large organization.

When small groups grow into larger groups, finally graduating into complex organizations, the structure and function of these human systems change. With increasing group size comes greater formality. Small groups are more personal than large organizations. Small groups usually can function well as a committee of the whole with relatively equal distribution of power. Large organizations become hierarchical, with clearly demarcated power structures and lines of authority, although recently there has been a trend toward *flattening the hierarchy* by moving away from tightly defined roles of superiors and subordinates and placing greater emphasis on teamwork (Skrzycki, 1989). The company becomes more important than any single individual. Employees in the organization can be replaced with relative ease whereas in a small intimate group, loss of a single member may bring about the demise of the group.

The flow of information is one of the most important differences between small groups and complex organizations. Normally, little negative information from below reaches the top of the corporate hierarchy, or if it does it is delayed (Conrad, 1990). In the spring of 1995, software producer Intuit, Inc., confessed that there were bugs in its tax-preparation software. Those using the software would likely file erroneous income tax returns with the IRS. Intuit's tax-preparation programs were the market leaders and the timing of the announcement that the programs were defective came just six weeks prior to the April 15 income tax deadline, too late for eager beavers who filed an early return. Intuit President Scott Cook admitted at a news conference that the firm's technical support team knew about the software bugs in December 1994 but didn't pass the information up the corporate ladder for many weeks. Cook sheepishly explained, "This one is particularly embarrassing because we didn't know we knew about it. I am very disappointed that we did not act more quickly on this. We really let our customers down" (in Gomes, 1995, p. 4C).

Although negative information and blunders can be hidden in small groups, it is far more difficult than in organizations. Bad decision making cannot be hidden easily when the group is small. Almost any blunder will become incandescent when the black hole of bureaucracy is not present to shroud it. If you have three people running a small business and one of the three does something boneheaded that affects the enterprise, your choices immediately narrow to two possibilities (unless, of course, you are guilty but playing dumb). One of your two partners has to be the culprit.

Information distortion usually is a bigger problem in organizations than in smaller groups. Managers act as gatekeepers, screening messages, selecting which ones will be brought to the attention of higher-ups. By the time a message from below reaches top executives in an organization, it can easily become unrecognizable nonsense. Similarly, information from the top can be distorted by the time it filters down to the bottom of the organization (Conboy, 1976).

In smaller groups, however, the communication is usually more direct with fewer opportunities for distortion from messages transmitted serially through several people. If the message is communicated to the entire group at the same time—a comparatively easy task if the gathering is small—then the problems of message distortion are reduced.

SECOND LOOK

Effects of Increasing Group Size

Increases	Decreases
• Complexity	• Participation in group discussion/ talkative members become dominant
• Factionalism/splinter groups	
• Formality—more hierarchical	• Pressure to conform—coalitions likely to form in opposition to group norms
• Information distortion	
• Quality decision making (unless group becomes too large and unwieldy)	• Member satisfaction with group experience
	• Access to information
• Difficulty achieving consensus— majority vote often substituted	• Flow of negative information to top of hierarchy
	• Speed of decision making

CLOSER LOOK

The Beatles as a System

In February 1966, John Lennon made the provocative and not-very-bright remark that the Beatles rock group was "more popular than Jesus Christ." Although this offhand bit of hyperbole by the most volatile member of Britain's famous rock quartet was not well received by many fans and foes alike of the Beatles, there was no doubt that this rock band was an international phenomenon of no small proportion. They sold over one *billion* recordings—which continues to be the current world record.

To this day, the Beatles have international name recognition even among the generation of young people born long after the disbanding of the "Fab Four." When the Beatles *Anthology, Vol. I,* a CD of previously unreleased tracks, was made available on November 21, 1995, to coincide with a six-hour ABC-TV documentary on the rock group, it sold 450,000 copies the first day it was released, the highest single-day sales ever for an album ("They're still on top," 1995, p. 4A). More than a quarter of a century after the Beatles disbanded, their popularity has risen to new heights. Thirteen million of their first two anthology albums were sold in 1996 and six million of their old albums were purchased, making 1996 the best year commercially that the Beatles ever had. Their third anthology album hit the top of the Billboard chart in November, 1996. Forty-one percent of the album-buyers were not even born when the Beatles split up in 1970 (''Who's the hot group,'' 1996, p. 2A).

Albert Goldman (1988) described the phenomenon of the Beatles as ''the most triumphant career in the history of show business'' (p. 326). Music critic Robert Christgau, writing in 1973, gave tribute to the Beatles by defining ''rock'' as ''all music deriving primarily from the energy and influence of the Beatles—and maybe Bob Dylan . . .'' (in Stokes, 1980, p. 151).

The Beatles are credited with revolutionizing the economics of the music industry by inventing the rock tour on a grand scale emulated to this day by subsequent rock bands (Stokes, 1980). The Beatles seized artistic control of their recordings from record companies, leading the way for future groups and musicians. They popularized the concept album (e.g., *Sgt. Pepper's Lonely Hearts Club Band*), convincing other rock musicians that an album didn't have to consist merely of a conglomeration of hit singles and filler recordings. ''The Beatles broke down the barriers between low art and high art, the visceral and the intellectual—rock became something to think about as well as feel about. And telling us how to think and feel about the music were rock critics, something else we have the Beatles to thank/curse for'' (Brumley et al., 1995, p. 8).

The Beatles serve as an interesting historical case study illustrating the groups-as-systems perspective. It is difficult to find well-researched accounts of the life cycle of any long-standing group. Since much has been written chronicling the Beatles' decade-long lifespan, however, all three primary elements of a system—interconnectedness of parts, adaptability to change, and influence of size—can be usefully illustrated by examining this famous rock group.

Originally called the Quarrymen and composed of John Lennon, Paul McCartney, George Harrison, Stuart Sutcliffe (who dropped out early on), and any drummer they could find, by 1960 they had become the Beatles with Pete Best at the drums. The cohesiveness of the group did not gel, however, until Best was replaced by Ringo Starr (Richard Starkey).

McCartney described the early Beatles, who played predominantly in pubs and strip joints in Hamburg, Germany, this way: ''We're all really the same person. We're just four parts of the one'' (in Stokes, 1980, p. 53). As the band developed and rocketed to superstardom following appearances on the Ed Sullivan show in February 1964, the interconnectedness of the four became increasingly obvious. Ward and his associates (1986) note that ''John needed Paul's melodic sense; Paul needed John's skepticism; George needed their sense of pop; and because he kept his feet unhesitatingly on the ground, they all needed Ringo, who cherished them like a fan'' (p. 348). Famed conductor Leonard Bernstein waxed rhapsodic when describing the synergistic effect of John and Paul's songwriting collaboration plus the meshing of all four band members: "These two [John and Paul] made a pair embodying a creativity mostly unmatched during that fateful decade [the Sixties]. . . . And yet, the two were merely something, the four were it. The interdependence was astonishing" (in Stokes, p. 3).

Faced with adulation from fans on an unprecedented scale, the Beatles were forced to erect boundaries for their own protection and sanity. These boundaries included hiding away in hotel rooms during tours, ducking out back entrances to avoid shrieking throngs of Beatles worshippers, and avoiding most public establishments. In order to record their albums and most of all protect the band's initial image of wholesomeness, the prying eyes of outsiders were steadfastly blocked from view. Boundary control was so stringent that a rumor began circulating that Paul had died in a bloody traffic accident in 1966. This rumor "explained" why the Beatles had stopped touring and had sequestered themselves in recording studios where Paul's demise could be camouflaged by electronic gimmickry.

Adaptability to change became essential to the Beatles' long survival as a rock band. Some of the changes they faced included wealth and notoriety, marriages and kids, serious drug use (especially by John), drug arrests (John and Paul), the death by drug overdose of their long-time manager Brian Epstein, who skillfully created the image of the Beatles, and a foray into Eastern mysticism (primarily by George). Yet by closing off to the public and placing the primacy of the Beatles above petty conflicts and artistic differences, the Beatles managed to stay together despite some rocky moments. The final straw of change that broke the band's back was the arrival of Yoko Ono (Lancashire, 1970). This was one change too many (degree) and an unwanted one, besides (desirability).

John became fascinated with Yoko in 1966 but did not begin an intimate relationship with her until two years later. Their celebration of newfound love together culminated in the *Two Virgins* album they recorded in a six-hour period one night. Consisting mostly of "random bird calls, screeches, and nose-blowings" (Stokes, 1980, p. 222), the most noteworthy feature of the album

Yoko Ono was the "fifth Beatle" and a disruptive influence.

was its cover displaying John and Yoko nude. The controversy surrounding this album strained the already turbulent relationships among the foursome, but when John tried to impose Yoko's musical suggestions onto the Beatles' compositions, she became an intolerable threat. When John married Yoko, the end was near. Paul, George, and Ringo had not contemplated a "fifth Beatle," yet Yoko's intrusive presence had the effect of increasing the group's size and thus magnifying complexity and conflict.

On April 10, 1970, Paul announced to the world that the Beatles were no more. Yet even in divorce, he recognized the continued interconnectedness of band members. "No matter how much we split, we're still very linked. We're the only four people who've seen the whole Beatlemania bit from the inside out, so we're tied forever, whatever happens" (in Lancashire, 1970, p. 1).

Questions for Thought

1. Could rock bands like the Beatles ever survive long without stringent boundary control? Why?
2. The intrusion of Yoko Ono demonstrates the significant impact a single individual can have on a group, especially when that individual is not regarded as a true group member. Can you think of similar instances where a single individual has had such a dramatic effect on a rock band?

DEFINITION OF A SMALL GROUP

Now that I have sketched the face of what a system looks like, let me provide a suitable definition of a group. A group is a system. As a system, a group is characterized by interconnectedness of its constituent parts, adaptability to change, and the influence of size. Consequently, I offer the following <u>definition of a **group**</u>: *a group is a human communication system composed of three or more individuals, interacting for the achievement of some common purpose(s), who influence and are influenced by one another.*

A group, then, is different from a mere collection of individuals called an aggregation (Goldhaber, 1990). Twenty-five people standing in line to buy tickets for a movie are not a group but simply a collection of people. Since they do not interact in order to achieve a common purpose (i.e., strangers standing in line are not there expressly to help each other secure tickets), they do not qualify as a group. The same holds for a crowd shopping in a mall or waiting for a plane departure delayed by fog. In both cases the presence of other people is irrelevant to the achievement of the specific purpose (i.e., buying clothes or traveling from point A to point B). A collection of individuals must succeed or fail as a *unit* in a quest to achieve a common purpose in order to be called a group. Crowds, of course, can become groups if they satisfy the definition provided above.

Which of the above qualifies as a group according to the definition of a group? Why?

👀 CLOSER LOOK

The Night Stalker

The capture of the infamous Night Stalker serial killer in Los Angeles on August 31, 1985, provides an interesting application of the definition of a group. Richard Ramirez, a twenty-five-year-old drifter, was guilty of thirteen vicious murders and thirty other felonies mostly committed at night during the summer months of 1985. Fleeing from police who had released a picture of their suspect to the newspapers, Ramirez ended up in an East Los Angeles neighborhood. He pulled a young woman from her car and tried to grab her keys. She recognized Ramirez from the newspaper photo and screamed, "It's the killer, the killer!" The woman's brother-in-law grabbed a metal stick and clubbed Ramirez on the head three times. The killer took off. Neighbors emerged from their homes, discovered what had happened, and joined in the pursuit, chasing the Night Stalker down the street. Before long the crowd had cornered Ramirez, gang-tackled him, and held him down until police arrived (Holguin, 1985).

This collection of determined neighbors constituted a group. They were a system. All pursuers were interconnected, since what the woman did directly affected the brother-in-law who in turn affected the actions of other neighbors. The neighbors had to adapt to change when the Night Stalker tried to steal a car then fled down the street. The size of the group was influential because there was strength in numbers. The neighbors interacted by communicating verbally and nonverbally (e.g., facial expressions, shouts, the woman's scream, the pursuit) in order to achieve a common purpose—surrounding the killer and gang-tackling him. Obviously the neighbors were influenced by one another's actions. The courage to chase after a mass murderer who had terrorized Los Angeles for months probably came from collective action. On all counts, the Night Stalker's captors qualify as a group.

Some theorists, however, may disagree with my analysis because the collection of individuals who captured Ramirez did not interact over a period of time longer than a few minutes and therefore cannot qualify as a system with a discernible structure. This was a group with no history and a fleeting life span. I could argue that there were identifiable roles and norms exhibited by these individuals working together in common purpose, but those who wish to discount my example as inapplicable are free to do so. I raise no protest. As Fisher and Ellis (1990) contend, "Arguing whether a particular collection of persons makes up a group is about as worthwhile as arguing about the number of angels who can dance on the head of a pin" (p. 13). If you understand the essential characteristics of a group identified in my definition and illustrated by the Night Stalker example, then I am satisfied.

Questions for Thought

1. Do you think the collection of individuals that captured the Night Stalker qualifies as a group? Explain.

2. Does it seem reasonable to you to designate a collection of individuals as a group when they have only a fleeting interaction with each other? Explain.

This text will focus on small groups with special emphasis in Chapters Six and Seven given to decision-making and problem-solving groups. Trying to draw a meaningful line between small and large groups, however, can prove to be fruitless. When does the addition of one more member transform a small group into a large one? Over the years, communication theorists typically have set the upper limit of small groups at between twelve and twenty members, with fifteen often cited. Brilhart and Galanes (1995), however, prefer to define "small" in terms of process, not number. A group must be composed of "a small enough number of persons for each to be aware of and have some reaction to each other" (p. 8) in order to qualify as small. I think this approach is preferable to setting an arbitrary upper limit on group size.

Although I will not concentrate on organizations in this book, I will include examples from organizational settings because many of you can relate meaningfully to such an environment. Virtually all of what I will discuss is immediately relevant to enhancing communication competence in organizations. After all, "an organization itself may be viewed as a group of groups" (Haslett et al., 1992, p. 103).

In summary, groups are systems. The three main elements of a system are interconnectedness of parts, adaptability to change, and the influence of size. A small group is defined in terms of function and the "ideal size" for most decision-making and problem-solving groups is the smallest group capable of performing the task effectively. Having now laid the theoretical foundation for analyzing small groups, I will discuss the process of group development in the next chapter.

QUESTIONS FOR CRITICAL THINKERS

1. How does the effect of a disruptive group member demonstrate the interconnectedness element of a system?
2. In groups that you belong to, what boundaries are erected?
3. Do organizations always require a hierarchical structure? Explain.
4. How far can you flatten an organizational hierarchy and still maintain effectiveness?

Group Development

Years ago when General Motors had the notion that the Chevy Vega would compete effectively against imports, an interesting situation developed at one of its plants. Unhappy with what workers perceived to be bad treatment from management and unfair negotiations during contract talks, some individuals broke into brand new Vegas parked in a lot awaiting transport. They tore out gear shifts and glove compartments, trashed upholstery, and generally vandalized the automobiles. The perception among workers that management exhibited a single-minded concern for task accomplishment (producing Vegas) with little regard for employee welfare helped create an environment ripe for sabotage. Although this incident occurred in an organizational setting, it demonstrates a relevant point concerning all group situations: there is a strong interconnectedness between the task and social dimensions of groups.

I have four principal <u>objectives</u> in this chapter. They are:

1. to explain the relationship between the task and social dimensions of a group,
2. to discuss periodic phases of group development,
3. to delineate the factors that affect a newcomer's acceptance into a group and what the newcomer can do to enhance that acceptance, and
4. to discuss the relationship between gender, ethnicity, and group development.

TASK AND SOCIAL DIMENSIONS

Focus Questions
1. How do the task and social dimensions of groups interconnect?
2. How are the task and social dimensions integral to both the formation and development of decision-making groups?

<u>All decision-making groups have both task and social dimensions</u>. The **task dimension** is the work performed by the group and its impact on the group. The **social dimension** is the relationships between members in the group and their impact on the group as a whole. These two dimensions of decision-making groups are not independent entities that stand in opposition to each other. As I have already emphasized, groups are systems and, as such, all aspects of a group are interconnected. Consistent with this perspective, the task and social dimensions of a group are interrelated. Degree of concern for a task affects the social or relationship aspects. Conversely, degree of concern for relationships in the group affects the accomplishment of the task.

Management at the Chevy Vega plant apparently failed to appreciate the dynamic interconnectedness of task and social dimensions in groups. Driving workers to finish a task while concurrently alienating them invites retaliation.

Unhappy employees do not make an efficient team. The Chevy Vega plant eventually closed because of poor productivity.

Although excessive focus on task may disrupt the interpersonal harmony of the group, excessive attention to social relationships may likewise thwart the task accomplishment of the group. I have observed numerous groups fall victim to the "enjoying each other's company" enticement.

CLOSER LOOK
The Case of "Hormones with Feet"

Anxious to make friends and not infrequently hopeful that romance is in the offing, students preparing group symposium presentations in my classes often become sidetracked. They devote disproportionate energy toward cultivating interpersonal relationships at the expense of the group's overall performance on the task. Sometimes this involves only certain members, and other times the total membership becomes involved in pursuing a good time at the expense of task accomplishment.

I would never wish to thwart burgeoning romance nor interfere with blossoming friendship, but there is a time and place for everything. I still remember with some amusement the couple in one group a few years back who aptly illustrated Mark Twain's definition of an adolescent as "hormones with feet." This couple's group was desperately attempting to put together a symposium presentation on some issue of national import. Meanwhile, these overheated lovers were fixated with each other. Their conversation gushed with honey-coated affection. Meaningful squeezes, tender hugs, starry-eyed gazes, the entire repertoire of longing for each other was amply demonstrated for all to observe.

I'm confident that you can predict the reaction of other group members to this overt display of adolescent behavior. At first, group members were uncomfortable, then mildly amused, irritated, exasperated, and finally just plain hostile. Two group members self-absorbed in promoting a social relationship while ignoring the task at hand seriously undermined the entire group's ability to function productively. In other circumstances, I am certain the entire group membership would have applauded this couple's newly discovered love for each other. In this particular context, however, members viewed the couple's behavior as disruptive. This couple did not exhibit communication competence because they showed insensitivity to the needs of the group, a pronounced Me-orientation, and no commitment to group goals. They put their agenda ahead of the group's.

When whole groups decide that it is better to socialize than to work, task accomplishment obviously suffers. It is not unusual for a group to waste valuable time socializing with one another only to realize too late that deadlines are fast approaching and sufficient work has not been finished.

Questions for Thought

1. If your group meets at a member's house to work on a project, is it a good idea to order pizza and drinks at the start of the meeting? Why?
2. Have you experienced a similar case of oversocializing to the detriment of task accomplishment?

In a system, the results of a group's interactions are called **outputs.** The output from a group's task dimension is **productivity** and the output from the social dimension is **cohesiveness.** Productivity is the result of the efficient and effective accomplishment of a group task. Cohesiveness, the degree of liking members have for each other and the group and the commitment to the group that this liking engenders, is the result primarily of attention to social relationships. Cohesive groups have a We-orientation. Neither the task nor the social dimensions can be ignored for a decision-making group to be successful. Both dimensions are interconnected. Too much attention to productivity can diminish cohesiveness by producing stress and conflict. Conversely, too much emphasis on cohesiveness can produce a group of social loafers who like each other a great deal but accomplish nothing in particular. This is a problem unless, of course, the purpose of the group is merely to have a good time and no task needs to be accomplished.

As Fisher and Ellis (1990) correctly observe, common sense indicates a close relationship between productivity and cohesiveness. Productive groups tend to be cohesive (group accomplishment creates positive feelings among members) and cohesive groups tend to be productive. This latter relationship, however, requires some qualification. In general, cohesiveness enhances group productivity unless overemphasized (Evans and Dion, 1991). This relationship, however, was stronger in small groups than larger ones, for ongoing natural groups than for artificially created groups, and for cooperative groups than for competitive groups (Klein, 1996). The nature of the task also affects the relationship between cohesiveness and productivity. The more interdependent group members must be in order to accomplish a task (e.g., flying a passenger jet, performing surgery, playing team basketball) the stronger is the cohesiveness-productivity relationship (Gully et al., 1995).

So how do groups build cohesiveness? There are several ways. The main strategies for instilling cohesiveness in a groups are:

1. *Encourage compatible membership.* When group members enjoy each other's company and share an attraction for one another, cohesiveness can build easily. When difficult, disruptive individuals join the group, cohesiveness can suffer. Of course, a group doesn't always have the luxury of choosing who can join. Sometimes membership is mandated from outside (e.g., by an institution or corporation).

2. *Develop shared goals.* One aspect of cohesiveness is sharing a common vision. When all group members are pulling together to achieve a goal valued by all, cohesiveness increases.
3. *Accomplish tasks.* Productive groups usually become more cohesive as a result of task accomplishment. If group members feel good about work accomplished, this often pulls the group together and promotes an *esprit de corps.* As a rule, successful teams exhibit little disharmony. Unsuccessful teams, however, frequently manifest frustration and disappointment by sniping, sniveling, and finger-pointing. Poor productivity can lead to group disintegration.
4. *Develop a positive history of cooperation.* If group members work together co-operatively rather than competitively, cohesiveness can flourish (Klein, 1996). I will elaborate on constructing cooperation in small groups in Chapter Four.
5. *Promote acceptance of group members.* If members make each other feel valued and err on the side of praise, not blame, then they will be encouraging each other to excel.

The task and social dimensions are integral to both the formation and development of decision-making groups. Just where these two dimensions fit into the life of a group can be ascertained by exploring the periodic phases of group development.

PERIODIC PHASES OF GROUP DEVELOPMENT

Many communication scholars have classified group development into specific stages. Tuckman (1965) describes the four phases of group development as forming, storming, norming, and performing. His nomenclature for the four phases is clever—one I plan to use here. His conceptualization of specific phases of group development occurring in sequence, however, is mechanistic. Groups do not pass through predictable phases of development in linear fashion like a person does when growing older (i.e., youth, middle age, old age). Groups do not necessarily travel from forming to storming, then to norming, and finally to performing in perfect sequence. Groups tend to be far messier than this, sometimes cycling back around to a previous phase seemingly completed (Hare, 1994). (Unhappily, such cycling back is not possible with aging.)

Admittedly, group development can be classified in terms of an initial phase where individuals join together for some reason (forming), a tension phase (storming), a standards and rules of conduct for members phase (norming), and a phase where effort is targeted toward goal achievement (performing). I prefer to add the modifier "periodic," however, when discussing phases of group development. Adding "periodic" indicates that the phases are apt to appear, disappear, and reappear, even overlap. A "periodic phase" reaffirms the inevitability of change in a system and the necessity of adaptability to that change. A periodic phase implies no changeless, step-by-step progression with no turning back, as does the term "phase" by itself.

Let me add one other note of clarification. Forming, storming, norming, and performing are global phases of group development relevant to groups in general, large or small. I will discuss *specific* phases relevant to the process of decision emergence in small groups in Chapter Seven.

Focus Questions

1. Does why we join a group make any difference to the group?
2. Is tension in a group undesirable?
3. Where do group norms come from? Why do we conform to group norms?
4. Do groups outperform individuals?

FORMING: Why We Join Groups

We join groups for many reasons. These reasons act as catalysts for group formation. We join groups to satisfy some need (Shaw, 1981). This need satisfaction divides into five principal categories:

1. interpersonal attraction (we are drawn to members of the group),
2. attraction to group activities,
3. attraction to group goals,
4. establishment of meaning and identity, and
5. attraction to the fulfillment of needs outside of the group.

Let me briefly elaborate on each category.

Interpersonal Attraction We join groups because we are drawn to its members. Human beings have a strong need to affiliate with others, particularly others who are similar to ourselves (Shaw, 1981). <u>We seem drawn to others when we perceive them to be similar to us in personality, attitudes and beliefs, ethnic origin, and economic status.</u>

We also seem attracted to those who experience similar feelings to our own in distressing situations (Schachter, 1959). Victims of natural disasters are attracted to each other because of shared misery. They are bonded by trauma. Misery may love company, but usually of a particular type. "Misery loves *miserable* company" (Firestone et al., 1973).

If you just flunked a big exam, chances are you will be more inclined to seek out others who likewise bellyflopped than those who aced the test. We seem drawn to those who are experiencing similar emotions to our own. Who wants to be around someone who glories in his or her good fortune while you sink into a blue mood over your misfortune? Blubbering in our beer is so much more satisfying when we are joined by fellow blubberers.

Membership in groups such as Alcoholics Anonymous, Smokenders, and Weight Watchers partly stems from this attraction to individuals who share common trials and tribulations or experience even more trying times than your own. You can expect similar emotional reactions from similarly tormented individuals.

There are exceptions, however, to the relationship between similarity and interpersonal attraction. We are hesitant to interact with people described as "emotionally disturbed" even if they have similar attitudes to our own (Novak and Lerner, 1968). This reaction is hardly surprising in light of the study by Tringo (1970), who found that the "mentally ill" were the least preferred of twenty-one disabled groups, even less attractive than actual lepers. Some perceived dissimilarities between ourselves and others cancel out other usually salient areas of similarity.

Other factors influence interpersonal attraction besides similarity between individuals. <u>Physical attractiveness is probably the most obvious source of attraction</u>. Women seem drawn to good-looking men. There is evidence to support the common observation, however, that physical attractiveness is more important to men than it is to women as a factor influencing attraction (Ritter, 1996), a fact surprising only to someone new to the planet. Although other factors of attractiveness may be more important determinants of group membership, physical attractiveness certainly matters to some people.

Attraction to Group Activities An attraction to the group's activities is a second reason we join groups. Hackers' groups have emerged all over the United States. One such group of twelve members ranging in age from teenagers to a man in his fifties was interviewed by Dawn Yoshitake (1996) in the Union Station train terminal in Los Angeles. Meetings are open to anyone, including security specialists, law enforcement agents, or the curious. These hackers meet to share information about equipment and new techniques for manipulating technologies. They may also bond in the process. One hacker, a sixteen-year old, put it this way, "I can't talk to a lot of my friends about computers and phone (hacking). But here, people understand. It's an acceptance thing" (p. A7).

Joining a group because you are attracted to the group's activities doesn't require a person to embrace the primary goals of the group. <u>We may in fact harbor disdain for the primary goals of the group yet still wish to join the group because of what the group does</u>. You may not approve of what the hackers do, which is essentially criminal invasions of privacy via computers and phones, but you may find their ability to manipulate technology fascinating and educational.

When I coached intercollegiate debate, it was not unusual to have students join the debate team for primarily social reasons rather than academic ones. Despite the fact that the debate team existed primarily to train students in argumentation, several students joined the team in order to travel around the country, cultivate friendships, fall in love, and engage in the inevitable social activities that are attached to debating. Doing well in the team competition was secondary for these group members.

Softball leagues are frequently rated "A," "B," and "C" for the same reasons. The hard-core athletes can be separated from the Budweiser crowd. The team competition is the primary focus of softball leagues. Nevertheless, some players are drawn to the social activity more than the sport itself.

Attraction to Group Goals   A third reason why we join groups and wish to remain as members is an attraction to the group's goals (Reckman and Goethals, 1973). <u>When you are drawn to a group because of its goals, commitment to it is likely to be strong</u>. Those of you who may have worked for a political candidate know full well that commitment to the cause, namely electing the person of your choice for political office, acts as an adhesive binding members of political groups together. When the goal is achieved such groups normally disband until the bid for reelection surfaces. Then again, campaign veterans and neophytes form to advance the goals of the group.

When you join a fund-raising group for a worthy cause, you don't have the luxury of interacting only with members that you'd enjoy inviting to dinner. You're stuck adapting to the various personalities and quirks of fellow fundraisers. Your commitment to the goal of the group, however, may be enough to keep you coming back. The competent communicator, of course, has a better chance of adapting effectively to difficult circumstances posed by groups whose membership has formed to advance a cause than does someone who is less skillful and aware.

Establishment of Meaning and Identity   We sometimes join groups to make sense of our world. As I indicated in Chapter One, the human imperative to make sense out of our world does not happen in social isolation. Take cults, for instance. This making sense of the world is the fundamental basis of cult conversions. Individuals who join cults are in the throes of an identity crisis. They are searching for meaning in their lives, and cults offer such meaning and identity. Social psychologist George Cvetkovich notes that studies of ex-cult members reveal that 75 percent are recruited during an identity crisis and 25 percent "had always been in an identity crisis" (in Valdez, 1983, p. 7).

Former Massachusetts Commissioner of Public Health Deborah Prothrow-Stith's (1991) study of youth violence in the United States draws this comparison between "anti-social groups" such as gangs and "pro-social groups" such as fraternities:

> Pro-social and anti-social, they satisfy the adolescent need to belong to a group, separate from one's family. Pro-social and anti-social, they provide young people with goals and objectives, a world view, and a place where they are valued. Group membership gives some purpose to life. The more adrift a young person feels, the more powerful the attraction of the peer group, but even well-adjusted young people need what groups offer. (p. 97)

<u>When situations are ambiguous, and we're looking for answers, we often join groups as a means of better understanding ourselves, our world, and others who cross our paths</u> (Goethals and Darley, 1987). Joining a group can give meaning and purpose to our lives. Working with the Red Cross and other relief groups, joining the local chapter of Amnesty International, becoming an active

member of a church group, or associating with a local protest group fighting for a cause all give us an identity and a purpose. In the process, our lives become more meaningful.

Fulfillment of Unrelated Needs   Finally, we join groups to satisfy needs that are unrelated to the group's task, goals, members, or even our desire to belong. Sometimes we join because it looks good to do so or may further our career. We may become group members to enhance our resume or establish business contacts. In some cases we are told by persons in authority to join a group and we think it wise to comply lest we suffer unhappy consequences. The instructor of your class may put you into a group of people who interest you very little. If you are pragmatic, you will make the best of a less-than-satisfactory situation since your grade may depend on it. As a competent communicator you remain committed to the group even when the group does not "trip your trigger," as one of my students phrased it.

Goldhaber (1990), in his own research at the University of New Mexico, found that the average tenured faculty member served on six to eight committees simultaneously, not counting departmental and university faculty meetings. Most faculty members reported that they were exasperated with all the committee work.

So why do professors join such groups? Perhaps we join one or two committees because of the reasons already discussed, maybe even three or four committees if we're strongly committed to the institution, but eight? Hardly! Committee work comes with the job. We frequently "do committees" because we're looking out for our best interests.

SECOND LOOK

Why We Join Groups

- Interpersonal attraction (we are drawn to members of the group)
- Attraction to the activities of the group
- Attraction to group goals
- Establishment of meaning and identity
- Attraction to the fulfillment of needs outside of the group

The reasons why individuals join groups have noticeable effects on the productivity and cohesiveness of those groups. If you join because you are attracted to the other members, the likelihood of cohesiveness in the group is certainly more probable than if you join to meet outside needs. If you join because you are attracted to the group's goals, productivity is likely to be enhanced. If you join groups for personal gain only, you'll likely end up as dead weight and drag the entire group down. The reasons why you join groups influence the outcomes of the group. Exhibiting a sensitivity to the needs of the group during the forming phase is therefore vital.

The competent communicator can show sensitivity to the needs of the group during the forming phase in the following ways (Andersen, 1988):

1. *Express positive attitudes and feelings.* Avoid disagreement and disagreeableness. This phase is the getting-acquainted stage of group development. This is not an appropriate time to be deviant (e.g., embarrassing lapses in social etiquette, abrasive remarks, provocative statements, outrageous dress). Refrain from zealous and indiscriminate self-disclosures. Because members are unfamiliar with you at this juncture, displays of deviance or disagreeableness will invite negative evaluations. Don't put your foot in your mouth. Put your best foot forward.
2. *Appear friendly, open, and interested.* Be approachable by establishing eye contact with group members, initiating conversation, responding warmly to interactions from others. Superficial conversation on frivolous topics (e.g., the weather, sports, fashion) is appropriate. You're not trying to "Free Tibet" or "Save the Whales" during the forming phase. Your purpose is to become acquainted with other group members and to work out how you will relate to other group members and how they in turn will relate to you.

Storming: Tension in Groups

The inevitability of change within a system ensures stresses and strains in any group. These stresses and strains usually surface in the form of conflict. All groups experience some social tension because change can be an ordeal. Tension among group members should be viewed as a positive force. We are usually at our best when we experience some tension. Athletes perform best when they find the proper balance between complete relaxation and crippling anxiety. Excessive tension, however, can produce damaging conflict that may split the group apart. The relative absence of tension in a group can result in lethargy, haphazard attention to the task, and nonproductivity. Finding the level of tension that solidifies the group and effectively managing group tension are important factors in successful group development.

Ernest Bormann (1990) identifies two types of social tension—primary and secondary. All groups experience both types.

Primary Tension When you first congregate in a group you normally feel some jitters and unease. This is **primary tension.** Instructors meeting classes for the first time usually experience some primary tension. When you initially meet roommates, classmates, or teammates, primary tension occurs.

Group interaction during periods of primary tension is usually of very low intensity. Social inhibitions make group members cautious and hesitant in their communication. Long periods of uncomfortable silence, discussion of frivolous subjects, and tentative statements are all indicators of primary tension. Group members are often overly polite and careful to avoid controversy. Interruptions normally invoke profuse apologies.

Primary tension overlaps the forming and storming periodic phases of group development. The reasons you are attracted to a group may have a great deal to do with the degree of primary tension you experience in the group. If you join a group primarily because you are attracted to the members of the group, then making a favorable first impression may be very important to you. Your primary tension will probably be quite high.

Competent communicators recognize that primary tension is a natural dynamic of group life, so don't avoid it. Understand it and deal with it; don't run from it. In most instances primary tension tends to be short-lived and cause for little concern. With time, you become comfortable with the group and your primary tension diminishes. <u>Joking, laughing, and chitchatting about your interests, experiences, and beliefs on noncontroversial subjects all serve to reduce primary tension</u>. As you get to know one another better, there is less perceived threat.

If a group is too anxious to get down to business and foregoes the small talk, however, primary tension is likely to create an atmosphere of formality, stiffness, and insecurity. Communication will be stilted and hesitant. The ability of the group to work on a task will be hindered by excessive and persistent primary tension.

Engaging in small talk to relieve primary tension has cultural variations. In the United States, we tend to view small talk as wasting time. Many Asian (e.g., Japan, China, and Korea), Middle Eastern (e.g., Saudi Arabia), and Latin American (e.g., Mexico, Brazil, and Chile) cultures, however, view small talk as a necessary ritual engaged in over many cups of coffee or tea for several hours or even several meetings during which the group's task may not even be mentioned (Samovar and Porter, 1995). Ethiopians attach prestige to tasks that require a great deal of time to complete, so lengthy small talk, viewed by most Americans as "doing nothing," is considered highly significant and purposeful.

Even groups that have a lengthy history should not assume that communication aimed at diminishing primary tension is no longer relevant. Long-standing groups experience primary tension at the outset of every meeting. This is especially true if groups such as the PTA and homeowners associations meet infrequently. Members test the water to reaffirm their standing in the group. A brief period of free and open communication on topics of no particular importance is a constructive way to deal with primary tension present at the beginning of any group meeting.

Secondary Tension The stress and strain that occurs within the group later in its development is called **secondary tension.** Having to make decisions produces secondary tension. Disagreements and conflicts—storming—inevitably emerge when group members struggle to define their status and roles in the group. Shortage of time to accomplish a task often increases secondary tension. Differences of opinion regarding how best to solve a problem or make a decision induces tension. A deviant member can rattle the tranquillity of a group. Whatever the causes, secondary tension should be expected. Low levels of secondary tension may mean that the group is highly harmonious. It may also mean that you've created a cult of dullness composed of unmotivated, apathetic, and bored idlers.

Signs of secondary tension are many and varied. Frequently, secondary tension is marked by an abrupt departure from the group's routine. A sharp outburst, a sarcastic barb, or hostile and antagonistic exchanges between members will stoke the fires of secondary tension. Rules of polite communication may be replaced by shouting matches. Extreme secondary tension is unpleasant for the group. If left uncontrolled, the group's existence may be threatened.

Secondary tension was palpable during the second Rodney King trial, a civil suit, in 1993. According to interviews with three of the jurors, tempers flared on the fifth day of deliberations. Jurors argued over taking time off. The foreman quarreled with another juror and refused to apologize claiming that if he tried he'd probably end up punching her in the face. Another juror questioned the masculinity of a thirty-year-old engineer on the jury who had insisted that deliberations terminate early because his brain couldn't absorb any more information. The young man responded to this insult by threatening to beat up his detractor. Half the jurors broke into tears as the emotional bloodletting continued. One juror demanded to see his doctor (Rohrlich, 1993). Similar tension was evident during jury deliberations in the trials of the Menendez brothers and of O.J. Simpson.

Let me emphasize that the goal is not to eliminate secondary tension. All decision-making groups will unavoidably experience secondary tension. <u>Within tolerable limits, such tension can be a positive force</u>. Tension can energize a group, challenge the members to think creatively, and bring the group together.

As we will see when I discuss the problems associated with groupthink, trying to avoid or camouflage secondary tension merely tricks us into believing the group is functioning well. Beneath the surface, the group may be disintegrating or the decisions coming from the group may be ill-conceived, even disastrous.

<u>The real challenge facing competent communicators is to manage secondary tension within tolerable limits</u>. But how do we know when tension passes the tolerable level and becomes intolerable? There is no mathematical formula for determining such limits. Every group operates as a unique system of interconnected parts. Some groups can tolerate a great deal of disagreement and conflict. Other groups are more vulnerable to disintegration because members are more thin-skinned or insecure and view disagreements as personal repudiations and attacks. Some families operate well in an atmosphere of considerable screeching and yelling. Other families function successfully only in an atmosphere of civility; raising a voice would be most unsettling for the group. Communication appropriateness, thus, is contextual.

Wilson and Hanna (1990) offer a <u>general rule of thumb for determining excessive tension in a group</u>. "Too much tension can be measured by a group's inability to function in the task area and to maintain a satisfying social climate" (p. 135). The Rodney King jury clearly experienced excessive tension based on this standard. Unlike most other decision-making groups, however, a jury doesn't have the freedom to disband, as many groups would when tension becomes intolerable, so the King jury recovered and finished its work.

In the trial of defendants accused of seriously beating trucker Reginald Denny during the Los Angeles upheaval precipitated by the Rodney King verdict, jurors also experienced excessive tension. One juror was dismissed by the judge at the request of the other eleven exasperated jurors for "failure to deliberate." One female on the sequestered Denny jury became so upset about not being able to see her boyfriend that she ran down a hallway of the courthouse yelling, "I can't take it anymore" (Kramer, 1993, p. 1A). The judge gave jurors the weekend off from their deliberations to recharge their batteries and reduce the tension. Part of being a competent communicator is showing sensitivity to the needs of your group—recognizing when limits have been reached and knowing how to manage effectively the tension in the group.

A competent communicator can exhibit sensitivity to the needs of the group during the storming periodic phase of group development by handling secondary tension as follows (Andersen, 1988):

1. *Tolerate, even encourage, disagreement and deviance.* Suppressing differences of opinion will likely increase tension and exacerbate conflict. The trick is to keep the disagreement and deviance within tolerable limits. One way to do this is to focus the disagreements and deviance on the task (unless, of course, the conflict is social in nature). Resist the temptation to drift into irrelevant side issues, especially contentious ones.
2. *Keep a civil tongue.* When disagreements become more social than task related (e.g., personal attacks and disparaging remarks) they easily degenerate into interpersonal combat. Disagree without being disagreeable, although there are contexts where civility may not make a point forcefully enough. You want to foster a cooperative, not a competitive, atmosphere for discussion. You can express points of view with conviction and exuberance without "going nuclear" on those who do not agree with you.
3. *Be an active listener.* Encourage all group members to express their opinions and feelings. Clarify significant points that are confusing. Resist the temptation to interrupt, especially if this produces defensive behavior from group members. Make an honest effort to understand the point of view that is in opposition to your own.

There are numerous sources of conflict within a group that raise the level of tension. Reasons for stormy transactions in groups and strategies for effectively managing them will be discussed in greater detail in later chapters. For now, recognize that conflict and tension are a normal part of the group experience. Dealing with tension may be smooth sailing for some groups and whitewater rafting for others.

Norming: Regulating the Group

A group will establish rules or standards. Rules define appropriate behaviors in specified social situations. *"They stipulate what a person must do (obligation), ought to do (preference), or must not do (prohibition) in order to achieve certain goals"* (Smith, 1982, p. 63). In other words, rules regulate behavior. In groups, these rules are called **norms.**

Types of Norms   There are two types of norms, explicit and implicit. Explicit norms are rules that expressly identify acceptable behavior. Such rules are codified as in constitutions and bylaws of fraternal organizations, religious orders, and the like. All laws in our society act as explicit norms.

Most norms, however, are implicit. These rules regarding what is and is not socially acceptable are usually covertly determined. You ascertain implicit norms by observing uniformities in the behavior and expressed attitudes of members and by noticing what fosters negative consequences and thus constitutes deviance for a particular group.

I can illustrate the difference between explicit and implicit norms by examining a college seminar class. If participating in a seminar qualifies as a new experience for you, group norms could be determined in several ways. Usually, the professor teaching the seminar will provide a syllabus explicitly specifying what students are expected to do during the term. Such norms as "refrain from tardiness and absenteeism," "all assignments must be turned in on time," "all papers must be typed—no exceptions," and "active participation in the discussions is imperative" are just some of the possible explicit rules of classroom behavior you might find specified in your seminar. One colleague of mine used to tell her students that she would lock the classroom door exactly at the start of the hour when class was supposed to begin. Any student who was late for any reason would be barred from entry. This worked well until the professor was sued by one of her students. The claim was made that the professor's strict, no-exceptions policy caused her student, who was running late, to drive unsafely one day in order to avoid being locked out when an important exam was scheduled. The student lost control of her car and suffered serious injuries when she crashed her automobile.

The implicit rules for the seminar class might be such things as "don't interrupt the professor when he or she is speaking," "sit in chairs stationed around the rectangular table," "be polite when disagreeing with classmates," and "don't hide the professor's notes, even in jest" (you had to be there). These norms are ascertained by observing the behavior of your classmates and the professor.

Purpose and Development of Norms   The main purpose of norms is to achieve group goals. Shimanoff (in Cathcart and Samovar, 1992) cites the example of Overeaters Anonymous to illustrate the goal-oriented nature of norms. Change (i.e., losing weight) in Overeaters Anonymous groups is regulated by rules, one of which is that members are permitted to talk about food only in generic terms (carbohydrates, protein, etc.) but not in terms of specific foods (Twinkies, burgers, cookies). The rule is based on the assumption that references to particular foods will stimulate a craving for those foods and make goal achievement more difficult, while references to foods in generic terms will produce no such cravings. Apparently you won't hear the refrigerator calling your name when merely talking about carbohydrates, but mention Häagen-Dazs and there better be a clear path to the Frigidaire or somebody's going to get trampled.

The norming process takes place almost immediately in groups. When a group is formed, members cast about trying to determine what behavior will be acceptable and what will be unacceptable. Part of the primary tension in a group may stem from this concern for proper group etiquette.

There are three principal sources of norms in small groups. First, <u>some norms are from systems outside the small group</u>. Standards of excellence and specific norms of performance for work teams within organizations can be and often are externally influenced by management outside of the team (Sundstrom et al., 1990). Charters and bylaws of local chapters of fraternal organizations, therapeutic groups, and others are usually set by parent organizations or agencies. In a clear case of interconnectedness of parts in a system, the small groups work within the normative framework set by the organization. These small groups have varying degrees of freedom to develop unique norms not stipulated externally.

<u>A second source of small group norms is the influence of a single member</u>. Research shows that a single person can influence the group to accept higher standards of behavior and performance than would exist without the influence of this member. Even when that influential member leaves the group, the norm typically remains (MacNeil and Sherif, 1976). Sometimes these influential individuals are designated group leaders and sometimes they are newcomers joining an established group.

<u>A third source of small group norms is the group itself</u>. Small group norms most often develop from transactions within the group. Sometimes this is explicitly negotiated (e.g., juries deciding what procedures will be used to arrive at a verdict), but most often it emerges implicitly from trial and error ("Oops, the group disapproves—guess I'll try something else.").

Conforming to Norms   The propensity toward **conformity,** the adherence to group norms, can be seen from a study of bulimia, a disorder characterized by binge eating followed by self-induced vomiting (Crandall, 1988). Bulimia is typically found in certain social groups such as cheerleader squads, sports teams (e.g., gymnastics), dance troupes, and sororities. Norms are established within these groups, which promote the binge-and-purge behavior. Instead of viewing this bizarre behavior as abnormal or unhealthy, sororities studied by Crandall promoted bulimia as a reasonable method of controlling members' weights. Group norms even established a preferred rate of binging and purging. Popularity in the group depended on sticking to this standard. Even those group members who initially felt no desire to binge or purge began to follow the crowd.

So why do we conform to norms in groups? In a society as individualistic as the United States, why do we adhere to the rules of acceptable behavior in groups? We conform for three reasons that flow from the purposes for norms.

First, <u>conforming to group norms reduces ambiguity and makes functioning in a group a smoother operation</u>. Maintaining order—controlling change—is the first purpose of norms. Conforming to norms in a group manifests a desire for order and a reduction of ambiguity. Most people are not comfortable with rapid, unregulated change. We conform because we like things orderly and predictable.

A second reason why we conform to norms is that <u>conformity results in social acceptance, support, companionship, and recognition</u>. We must "go along to get along." Loyalty to the group manifested in conformity to group norms is rewarded with approval from the members. Norms create solidarity with group members. Our natural desire to belong makes such solidarity attractive. Individual goals such as making friends or increasing social activities can be satisfied by conforming to group norms. Why shouldn't we want to conform?

Third, <u>groups have informational power</u>. Group norms "serve as frames of reference for assessing the reasonableness of one's own opinions and behaviors" (Smith, 1982, p. 171). We match our view of the world with that of the group. We thus learn whether we are in step or out of step with prevailing points of view. In addition, groups can act as a source of information for evaluating or perfecting our abilities and for accomplishing certain ends. A chess team, writers' group, bridge club, or work group may have its social function, but such groups also provide information on our level of skill and accomplishment and they assist us in improving our abilities. Failure to conform to the norms of the group will often mean the withholding of valuable information that can assist us in our quest for personal improvement.

Conditions for Conformity to Norms   There is greater conformity to group norms when certain conditions exist. First and foremost, <u>the stronger the cohesiveness in the group, the greater is the conformity to group norms</u> (Shaw, 1981). The relationship between cohesiveness and conformity is hardly surprising. Cohesiveness, by definition, is the degree of attraction we have to a group and our desire to be a member. If there is minimal attraction to the group and nebulous desire to be a member, then there is scant reason to adhere to the rules of behavior. A group has little leverage against apathetic or scornful members. How can the group command conformity when you don't care if you're unceremoniously booted out of the group? Conversely, individuals who are strongly attracted to the group and wish to remain members in good standing are much more likely to conform and bow to pressure for uniformity of opinion and behavior.

Second, <u>conformity is greater when individuals expect to be group members for a long time</u> (Smith, 1982). After all, you must live with this group. Why make your life unpleasant by not conforming, particularly in job situations where economic considerations may make job switching impractical.

Melanie Singer, a Los Angeles Highway Patrol officer called to testify on behalf of the accused officers in the second Rodney King trial in 1993, admitted on the witness stand that she didn't give medical assistance to the hogtied, bleeding King following his horrific beating because she didn't want her fellow officers to start heckling her ("Fearing heckling," 1993). When you have to live with the group in your life's profession you tend to conform to implicit norms of behavior even when your conscience may dictate otherwise.

Third, <u>conformity is greater when individuals perceive that they have somewhat lower status in the group</u> than other members or are not completely accepted by the group (Smith, 1982). Higher-status members have earned the right to dissent but lower-status members must still earn that right to occasional nonconformity. Lower-status members also feel a greater need to prove themselves to the group, to show fealty.

👀 CLOSER LOOK

Hazing Rituals

Recognizing the strong link between cohesiveness and conformity to norms, groups will sometimes go to great lengths to foster cohesiveness. Hazing rituals of college fraternities purposely subject prospective members to a series of activities, often ludicrous and sometimes dangerous, designed to test the limits of physical exertion, psychological strain, and social embarrassment. Cialdini (1993) lists numerous examples of silly, stupid, dangerous, and lethal activities actually required by some fraternities as part of Hell Week initiations. Examples include forcing pledges to swallow quarter-pound hunks of raw liver slathered with oil, abandoning pledges on mountain tops or in remote areas in bitter-cold conditions without suitable clothing, repeatedly punching the stomach and kidneys of pledges who forget parts of ritual incantations, and incarcerating pledges in a locked storage closet for two days with only salty foods, no liquids, and only a small plastic cup to catch urine. Dennis Jay, a fraternity pledge, was forced to drink huge quantities of alcohol from a beer bong—a funnel contraption. He was rushed to a hospital in a coma. His blood alcohol level was 0.48, six times the legal definition of drunk in most states and 0.02 below the normal fatal dose (Grogan, B. et al., 1993).

Between 1978 and 1985, twenty-nine college students died as a result of hazing ("The hazards," 1986). An NBC News report on November 10, 1989, updated this statistic to fifty-one deaths. By 1986, seventeen states had outlawed hazing. Stopping hazing, however, is not easy. When Richard Swanson, a University of Southern California student, gagged on an oil-soaked hunk of liver then choked to death before anyone could help him, the university applied stringent rules to initiation practices. Students rioted in protest. Outlawing hazing likely drives it underground rather than eliminates the practice.

Hazing or initiation rituals in groups is widespread. Clubs, gangs, even some businesses subject new members to hazing. Anthony Roberts lost his right eye and almost his life when, as part of an initiation ritual into a rafting and outdoor group called Mountain Men Anonymous, he stood with a fuel can on his head so a group member could shoot it with a bow and arrow. The arrow missed the can and passed through his eye into his brain. Miraculously he survived with no serious brain damage. He said he felt "really stupid" ("Man survives," 1993, p. 9A).

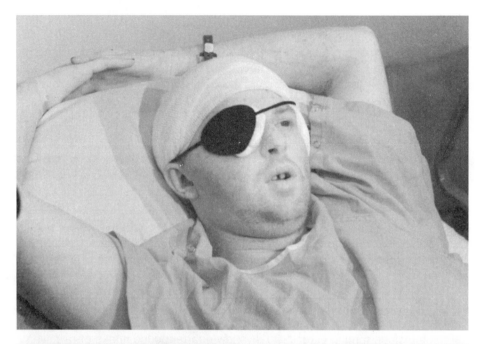

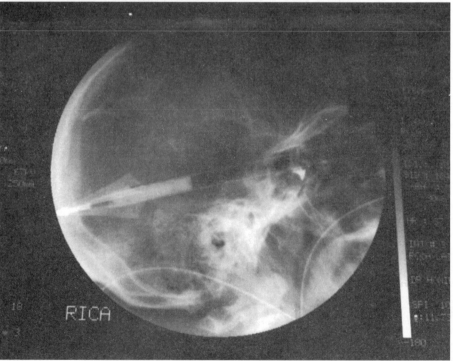

Anthony Roberts took an arrow through his eye and into his brain (see his X ray above) in a hazing ritual gone bad.

Five teenage girls had unprotected sex with an HIV-infected male gang member as part of an initiation rite to gain entrance into the gang. Jo Ann King-Sinnett, spokeswoman for Planned Parenthood of San Antonio, Texas, explains the teens' behavior this way: "If the test (for HIV) came up negative, then it was like they were brave enough to have unprotected sex and they were tough enough, and their body was tough enough to fight the disease" ("Unsafe sex," 1993, p. 4A).

Rohlen (1973) cites an elaborate initiation ritual required by a Japanese bank. Over a three-month period, new employees are forced to meditate and fast together at a Zen monastery, participate in rigorous basic training at an army base, perform community service, vacation at an isolated youth hostel, and complete a strenuous twenty-five-mile hike. All this so employees can cash checks for customers and turn down their loan applications.

West Point cadet John Edwards experienced an ironic twist to the hazing controversy. In 1988, he was expelled from the U.S. Military Academy because as an upperclassman he refused to subject first-year cadets to the ritual hazing. He felt it was absurd and dehumanizing behavior, not to mention dangerous. In 1996, just months after four women were admitted to the Citadel, a previously all-male military college, two of the women were sprayed with a flammable liquid and their clothes were set on fire. Fortunately, they were not injured ("I suspended," 1996, p. 9A).

Why do groups insist on such bizarre and risky membership rituals? Moreland and Levine (1989) cite several reasons. First, groups harshly initiate their newcomers because the harder it is to get into a group the greater will be the loyalty and commitment to the group once membership has been attained. We tend to value more that which is difficult to achieve than that which requires minimal effort. The more severe the hazing ritual, the more desirable a group appears to be. In one experiment, the more electric shock a woman received as part of the hazing ritual, the more she convinced herself that the group and its activities were valuable, interesting, and desirable despite the clear effort of the experimenters to make the group appear uninteresting and worthless (Gerard and Mathewson, 1966). A study by Young (1965) of fifty-four tribal groups found that those with the most severe and difficult initiation rituals had the greatest group solidarity.

If you had to swallow a slimy, oil-soaked slab of raw liver, freeze off the southside of your anatomy, or risk your life in order to gain membership, chances are quite good that you would slavishly conform to the norms of the group. Deviance is not likely to emerge from a tight-knit group bonded by ordeals.

Second, a harsh initiation provides the group with valuable information about the newcomers. If newcomers refuse to be initiated, fail the initiation tasks, or participate in the rites of passage grudgingly, then this informs the group that such newcomers are not likely to fit in with the group. They probably will not conform to group norms.

Third, a harsh initiation discourages newcomers who have a weak commitment to the group or have a half-hearted desire to join the group. The sooner such individuals leave before becoming members, the less trouble they are likely to pose for group members. Troublemakers can destroy the cohesiveness of the group.

Fourth, <u>a harsh initiation may convince newcomers how dependent they are on long-time members (old-timers)</u>. The old-timers make the decisions regarding who is granted membership and who is not. The old-timers must be convinced that the newcomers are worthy of that membership.

Questions for Thought

1. Have you ever participated in hazing either as the perpetrator or the recipient? Was it for the reasons stated above?
2. Should hazing rituals, especially the high-risk ones, be outlawed? Would outlawing such practices stop them?
3. Is it possible to have hazing rituals that are not dangerous and still serve the purpose of creating cohesiveness and subsequent conformity in the group?

SECOND LOOK

The Norming Process

Types of Norms
Explicit—preferences and prohibitions specifically stated in some form
Implicit—preferences and prohibitions determined from observation

Sources of Norms
Other larger systems outside the small group
Influence of a single member
Transactions within the group

Why Group Members Conform to Norms
Reduction of ambiguity
Social acceptance, support, companionship, and recognition
Information—assesses reasonableness of one's opinions/behaviors

Conditions for Conformity to Norms
Stronger cohesiveness, greater the conformity
Greater conformity when individuals expect to be group members for a long time
Greater conformity when individuals perceive they have lower status in group

---

Nonconformity   Since behavior in groups is governed by rules, a <u>violation of a norm can be quite disturbing for group members</u>. A colleague of mine once told me of a surprising incident that occurred in her beginning public speaking class. She asked all students to give a four-minute introductory speech to loosen everyone up. She instructed students to describe a significant event which they had experienced that had a profound impact on their lives. She expected to hear straightforward presentations on trips taken to foreign countries, geographic relocations, the college experience, and so forth. She did hear this—and more. After most of the students had given their presentations, a woman in her thirties gave her speech. She began by telling the class that she had never achieved sexual fulfillment in her life until the previous weekend when she and her lover experienced carnal bliss. She then proceeded to tell the astonished class what it was like experiencing her very first orgasm.

It is difficult to imagine what could possibly have possessed this woman to believe that such a revelation was appropriate for this environment. Communication competence is a real issue here. As Littlejohn and Jabusch (1987) observe, "One of the signs of communication competence is the ability to move in and out of a variety of communication situations with ease, adapting to the rule systems of others" (p. 38). This woman clearly exhibited scant awareness of which rule system was appropriate for this situation. Her revelation and description of sexual fulfillment might have fit the rules system in a professional counselor-client relationship, even perhaps in a conversation with a close friend, but in front of a group of relative strangers in a formal classroom situation? Her unpredictable behavior produced plenty of red faces and eyes cast downward from embarrassed classmates.

Groups usually do not appreciate nonconformity except within fairly limited boundaries. How groups deal with nonconformity, especially in its intentionally bold form as defiance, will be discussed at length in Chapter Nine.

The norming periodic phase of group development provides a structure for appropriate communication. Norms are rules that regulate change, promote group solidarity, and serve as a reference for assessing the reasonableness of our opinions and behavior. Norms of different groups vary greatly. Group norms are maintained until they no longer serve functional purposes for the group. If a norm tends to divide a group rather than solidify it, for instance, or thwarts achievement of group goals (i.e., establishes an overly open or excessively closed system), then it becomes dysfunctional and needs to be changed.

A competent communicator exhibits a sensitivity to the needs of the group during the norming periodic phase of development as follows:

1. *Adapt communication to the norms of the group.* As previously noted, communication becomes inappropriate when, without sacrificing goals, violation of norms could be averted by more prudent action.
2. *Encourage change when norms are excessively rigid.* Norms are not sacrosanct. Some norms can be suffocatingly rigid—too closed to permit adaptation to change in the system. The place to begin initiating such change is with the group whose norms are too rigid and exclusionary. Norm rigidity fosters nonconformity and disruption. Violating the norm is one avenue of change if rational argument proves unsuccessful, but expect backlash from the group. Leaving the group is certainly an option. Failure to loosen norms from within may require intervention from without as in court suits and protest.

3. *Encourage change when norms are too elastic.* Excessive openness in a system can be counterproductive. The same guidelines for changing overly rigid norms apply here as well.

Performing: Group Output

If I had a dollar for every time I have been told that a camel is a horse designed by a committee, I would be sipping Mai Tais on a white sand beach in the tropics enjoying a blissful state of very early retirement. Then there is the equally moth-eaten description of a committee as a group of people who can do nothing individually but, as a group, can gather and decide that nothing can be done. Along the same line is this anonymous offering: "Trying to solve a problem through group discussion is like trying to clear up a traffic jam by honking your horn." Winston Churchill, always armed with his sardonic wit, fired this salvo: "A committee is the organized result of a group of the incompetent who have been appointed by the uninformed to accomplish the unnecessary." On my own campus, committees metastasize like malignant cancer, eating up professors' and administrators' time and sucking the lifeblood from the institution. There was even a recent proposal to establish a "committee on committees," ostensibly to bring this blood-sucking monster under control, but nothing ever came of the proposal.

In terms of performance, groups as decision-making units are in need of better public relations. Too many people are inclined to believe that groups are assembled to stymie progress and to serve as roadblocks to decision making, not to produce better alternatives. Grouphate is real.

So, are groups as inept as the moldy jokes and acerbic assessments indicate? Berg's (1967) study of 124 discussion groups is not very encouraging. He found that groups pursued their discussion topics for an average of only 58 seconds at a time before diverting to an irrelevant topic. The range varied from a low of 28 seconds to a high of 118 seconds. One group leader in this study described his job as "chairman of the bored." Other studies support Berg's results. "Whether groups were composed of women in a Lebanese college, Japanese graduate students, university undergraduates, first-line managers at IBM, or educators in public-health nursing, the average attention span for all the groups was about one minute" (Bormann and Bormann, 1988, p. 120).

Although the tired jokes about groups and the research on group attention span suggest that groups hinder rather than help solve problems and make decisions, the evidence is far more mixed. One of the most researched areas of group communication is the comparison of individual to group performance. The key issue from this research is not whether individuals or groups are superior performers. <u>The central point is under what conditions do groups outperform individuals and vice versa</u>? Since grouphate is often a result of poor group productivity, group versus individual performance seems to be a significant issue to explore.

Individual versus Group Performance Groups outperform individuals in some circumstances but not others (Forsyth, 1990; Pavitt and Curtis, 1994). I will initially consider under what conditions groups are likely to outperform individuals. Then I will discuss under what conditions individuals are likely to outperform groups.

Groups will probably outperform individuals when certain conditions exist. First, <u>when the task requires a wide range and variety of information and skills, groups tend to be superior to any individual</u>. Group members *pool knowledge,* thus producing results superior to those produced by any individual. One study found that the group scored significantly higher than its highest scoring member (Stasson and Bradshaw, 1995). It did this by pooling knowledge. When the highest scoring member didn't know the answer to a question, another member typically knew the answer to that specific problem. Thus, the group as a whole benefited because members had nonoverlapping knowledge. As humorist Will Rogers once said, "Everybody is ignorant, just on different subjects." <u>A key to successful group performance is putting together a team composed of members who do not share ignorance, but instead pool nonoverlapping areas of knowledge</u> (Stasson and Bradshaw, 1995).

Dr. Don Wukasch spent nineteen years as part of a high-performance cardiac surgery team. He cites two instances (in Larson and LaFasto, 1989) of outstanding team performance that resulted from pooling nonoverlapping knowledge. In the first instance, emergency surgery on a woman with a ruptured spleen ran into immediate and potentially life-threatening complications. As Wukasch opened up the woman's abdomen, the lights went out from a power outage caused by the onset of a hurricane. The surgical team had about four seconds to clamp a gushing artery before the woman would bleed to death. Unknown to Wukasch, the nurses had flashlights hanging in the corners of the operating room. Within three seconds the surgical team was back in action and the woman's life was saved.

Wukasch cites a similar instance when he performed surgery at the Texas Heart Institute. Again a hurricane hit, the power was knocked out, and the heart-lung machine quit, leaving about a minute or two before the patient would start to die. Wukasch didn't know how to restore the heart-lung machine, but functioning as a cohesive, well-trained unit, team members began hand-cranking the machine and surgery continued within fifteen seconds.

Besides pooling knowledge, another reason groups outperform individuals when the task is comprehensive is the *group remembering* phenomenon or what some call collective recall of information. Quantitatively, the research on group remembering has consistently shown that groups are superior to individuals (even the best individual compared) in recall of information (Clark and Stephenson, 1989).

Why is group remembering significant? Juries more often than not arrive at verdicts on the basis of recall of the evidence and pertinent information reflecting guilt or innocence. In one study, individual jurors averaged only a 60 percent accuracy rate on recall of specific evidence and less than 30 percent on questions pertaining to the judge's instructions to the jury. As a group, however, the jury scored 90 percent accuracy on evidentiary material and 80 percent accuracy on the judge's instructions (Hastie et al., 1983). "The group memory advantage over the typical or even the exceptional individual is one of the major determinants of the superiority of the jury as a legal decision mechanism" (Hastie et al., 1983). I should also note that larger-sized (twelve-member) juries have superior recall of evidence compared to smaller-sized (six-member) juries (Hastie et al., 1983).

Another example of the relevance of group remembering is personnel-interviewing panels that often must sift through huge amounts of information and listen to hours of oral responses to questions from numerous candidates for a job. Having more than one person who can recall vital details can aid the group in making a final quality decision.

Second, groups generally outperform individuals <u>when both the group and any individual compared are without expertise on the task</u>. Here *synergy* is at work. As Johnson and Johnson (1987) remark in somewhat overstated fashion, "None of us is as smart as all of us" (p. 131). In a recent study, even though no individual group member knew the correct answer on a test question, the group as a whole selected the correct answer in 28 percent of the cases. Individual members working alone, however, selected the correct answer only 4 percent of the time (Stasson and Bradshaw, 1995).

Third, groups will usually outperform an individual <u>when both the group and the individual have expertise and the task is an especially complicated and complex one</u>. The ability of a group to divide labor, to *share the load,* will normally result in a better decision than any overburdened individual could manage. Legal cases such as the Pennzoil multi-bizillion dollar suit against Texaco in 1987 require armies of attorneys. O.J. Simpson hired a team of high-priced attorneys to defend him in his 1995 murder trial. In cases such as these, a single attorney would be easily overwhelmed by workload and information overload without extensive assistance from other attorneys.

A group of experts is especially effective when members are highly motivated and they are trained to work as a team. One study found that groups outperform their best expert member 97 percent of the time (Michaelson et al., 1989). *Teamwork* allows a group to coordinate efforts and work at optimum effectiveness.

Fourth, <u>even when comparing a group of reasonably bright and informed nonexperts to an individual with special expertise, group decisions are sometimes superior</u>. One of the reasons for this superiority is that when groups are functioning effectively, members perform an *error correction* function for the group (Hastie et al., 1983). Assumptions are challenged and alternatives are offered that an individual might overlook. In addition, the collective energy and chemistry of the group may produce a synergistic result.

Although groups frequently outperform individuals, this is not always the case. Under certain conditions, individuals outperform groups. There are five such conditions supported by research.

First, <u>groups composed of uninformed laypersons will not usually outperform someone with special expertise</u> such as a doctor or lawyer on issues of medicine and law. There is certainly no advantage to be gained from *pooling ignorance.* As already noted, however, even in uninformed groups synergy sometimes compensates for lack of knowledge. *Negative synergy,* nevertheless, is more likely when group members are uninformed.

A second condition in which groups usually perform no better and perhaps worse than individuals occurs <u>when groups establish norms of mediocrity,</u> or what radio commentator Paul Harvey once called "the best of the lousiest and the lousiest of the best." Some groups are composed of members who are satisfied with relatively low productivity. If norms of mediocrity prevail in a group, performance will be lackluster or worse (Stogdill, 1972). Even individual members who may wish to perform at a higher level will become discouraged because of *insufficient motivation to excel.* Since the group rewards middling performance, why bother trying harder than the rest?

A third condition in which groups usually perform no better than and perhaps worse than individuals occurs <u>when groups become too large.</u> Again, the rule of thumb is the smallest-sized group capable of performing the task effectively is the ideal-sized group. Quality performance is usually enhanced in moderately sized groups (i.e., seven to ten members). Much above this size, however, and *problems of coordination and efficiency* increase. Just assembling a dozen members can be daunting when schedules have to be coordinated. More important, however, is the problem of **social loafing**—the tendency of individual group members to reduce their work effort as groups increase in size (Gerow, 1995) as displayed by the inclination to "goof off" when performance is needed in a group, miss meetings, show up late, or fail to start or complete individual tasks. Please note here that reticence to participate in group discussion because of shyness does not constitute social loafing. Loafers put out little effort because of poor motivation, disinterest, or bad attitude.

⊙⊙ CLOSER LOOK

Social Loafing: Sapping a Group's Vitality

Social loafing can suck the energy from a group. A group cannot ignore a social loafer because the group is a system of interconnected parts. Social loafing is not an insignificant problem for groups. Some of the greatest frustration and exasperation expressed by my students occurs because someone in their group is a slacker.

Social loafing has been observed in groups working on a variety of tasks, among both males and females, people of all ages, and in many different cultures (Forsyth, 1990). Social loafing occurs more often in larger groups because sluggards can idle away their time less noticeably than in smaller gatherings (Zimbardo, 1992). Since other members presumably can pick up the slack resulting from loafers' listless participation, larger groups act as breeding grounds for loafers. When groups become populated predominantly with social loafers, nothing much gets accomplished.

Social loafing is more common in an individualist culture such as the United States than it is in a collectivist culture such as Taiwan, Japan, China, and other Asian countries (Early, 1989; Gabreyna et al., 1985). In a collectivist culture, social striving or the desire to produce for the group because group membership is highly valued is strong. Personal efforts and achievements are

Social loafers can diminish overall group performance and become a burden on the entire group.

less visible in a group and more likely to go unrecognized, however, so social loafing is more likely in an individualist culture.

So what can you do about social loafers? Ask them to get their thyroid checked or suggest that they down a few cans of Jolt cola? Here are several steps that can be taken to address the problem of social loafing (see also Lumsden and Lumsden, 1993):

1. *Establish a group responsibility norm.* Emphasize as a group individual responsibility to the team and the importance of every member contributing a fair share to the successful completion of a task.
2. *Note the critical importance of each member's effort.* Impress upon all members that their individual effort is special and essential to the group's success.
3. *Identify and evaluate individual contributions.* Provide each member with specific and easily identifiable tasks and set aside time for the group to evaluate each member's contribution to the overall project. Gerow (1995) claims that "social loafing can be virtually eliminated" (p. 711) by combining Step 2, making each member's effort seem valuable and essential, and letting members know that their individual tasks will be clearly identified and

evaluated by the group. Despite Gerow's optimism, however, I know from experience that more is sometimes required.

4. *Talk to the individual privately.* The first three steps attempt to prevent loafing. This step calls for either the leader of the group or a designated member to approach the loafer and ask why the lethargic attitude exists. Encourage stronger participation, reaffirm the importance of the loafer's contribution to the team effort, and solicit suggestions regarding how the group might help the person become a contributor.

5. *Confront the loafer as a group.* Identify and describe the problem behavior in specific detail. Ask the loafer directly how the problem can be solved. DO NOT name-call or personally attack the recalcitrant member.

6. *Consult a higher power* (not to be confused with divine intervention, although that would be impressive). When all of the above steps fail, consult a supervisor, teacher, or someone with greater authority than group members and ask for advice. The authority figure may need to discuss the problem with the loafer.

7. *Boot out the slacker.* This is a last resort. Do not begin with this step as many groups prefer. You may not have this option available, however.

8. *Sidestep the loafer.* Reconfigure individual responsibilities and tasks so even if the loafer contributes nothing to the group effort, the group can still maneuver around the loafer and produce a high-quality result.

Questions for Thought

1. Does the group task have any bearing on the frequency of social loafing? Explain your answer. Give examples from your own experience.
2. Do you agree that an individualist culture such as the United States has a bigger problem with social loafing than collectivist cultures do? Explain.

A fourth condition in which groups typically perform no better than individuals occurs <u>when the task is a simple one</u>. When faced with a remedial task there is no special advantage in having a group work on it. *Minimal resources* are required. If any individual can likely do the task, why involve a group?

Finally, <u>when time is a critical factor</u>, groups usually perform less effectively than individuals. In emergency situations or in circumstances where speed and efficiency are paramount, individuals can often perform better than groups, especially large groups. The reason is simple. Groups tend to be *abominably slow.* There are exceptions, however. A disaster team trained to perform under pressure and time constraints is one such exception. Most groups, though, are not trained to operate swiftly and efficiently under pressure. As previously noted, small groups are faster than larger groups, but even small groups can lag behind a single individual in the performance of a task.

Groups outperform individuals in a variety of conditions. There is no magic, however, in assembling groups to perform tasks. There are conditions in which groups perform abysmally.

SECOND LOOK

Individual versus Group Performance

Group Superior to Individual

Conditions	Reason(s)
• Broad-range task	• Pool knowledge, group remembering
• Neither have expertise	• Synergy
• Experts, complex task	• Share the load, teamwork
• Individual expert, informed group	• Error correction, synergy

Individual Superior to Group

Conditions	Reason(s)
• Individual expert, uninformed group	• Pooling ignorance, negative synergy
• Groups establish mediocrity norms	• Insufficient motivation to excel
• Group becomes too large	• Difficulty coordinating, social loafing
• Simple task	• Minimal resources required
• Time critical factor	• Groups too slow

Risk-taking and Polarization   Researchers of small group decision making used to believe that groups almost inevitably influence individuals to take greater risks than those same individuals might take alone. This was called the risky shift phenomenon. Teenagers in groups who goad each other to engage in goofy and dangerous actions is a common example. Terrorists concoct riskier, bolder, fanatical acts of violence when they discuss their schemes in a group (McCauley and Segal, 1987). After hundreds of studies, however, there is ample evidence that groups sometimes have a conservative shift rather than a risky shift (Levine and Moreland, 1990). Thus, group decisions tend to polarize.

    Group polarization is the group tendency to make a decision that is more extreme, either riskier or more cautious, after discussion has occurred than the initial preferences of group members. (Group polarization, however, does not mean that the attitudes of individual group members become more polarized with disagreement among members.)

    Groups tend to polarize decision making if there is a clear majority leaning one way (risk) or the other (caution). If most members of a group lean slightly toward risk-taking initially, they will become more prone to take risks, and if most members of a group lean slightly toward playing it safe, they will likely become even more cautious in their decisions than they were initially. When a group contains two unified subgroups holding strong opposing viewpoints (risk and caution), however, a typical result is *depolarization* and compromise, not polarization (Vinokur and Burnstein, 1978). Committees in the U.S. Congress composed of Democrats and Republicans often depolarize out of necessity. One subgroup proposes scrapping the progressive income tax and replacing it with a flat tax (risky) and another subgroup proposes tinkering with the tax code but making no substantial change. The committee might depolarize with the compromise of a flatter tax (less cautious) but with some progressivity (less risky).

The direction of the group polarization appears strongly influenced by culture. For instance, U.S. groups are more likely to polarize in the direction of risk while Chinese groups are more likely to polarize in the direction of caution (Hong, 1978).

The group polarization effect also occurs in decision making that doesn't involve issues of relative risk. When moderately prejudiced high school students discussed racial issues in groups they exhibited even greater prejudice after the discussion. Conversely, groups of high school students with only slight prejudice became even less prejudiced after discussion (Myers and Bishop, 1970).

Lefton (1991) identifies three explanations for the group polarization effect. The first is the social comparison theory (normative influence). The assumption here is that an individual uses the group norm regarding riskiness or caution as a point of reference. The individual is inclined to shift after group discussion in order to conform more closely to the perceived expectations of the group in this regard. The individual member compares his or her position on riskiness or caution to that of the group as a whole. If most group members initially tend toward riskiness, cautious members are inclined to move in the direction of the majority. If most members initially favor caution, all members feel pushed to be cautious.

A study by Kalvin and Zeisel (1966) supports the social comparison explanation. They found that of 215 juries that contained an initial majority, only six reached a verdict that went contrary to the majority support on the first ballot. Nemeth (1977), however, found that the legal rule "beyond a reasonable doubt" may be such a strong norm for a jury that when the initial majority favors acquittal, the final verdict is likely to be for acquittal. When the initial majority favors conviction, the probable results are far more mixed. This shows polarization toward risk-taking (i.e., possibly letting a criminal go free to repeat the crime).

A second explanation for the group polarization effect is the persuasive arguments hypothesis (informational influence). This perspective takes the position that individuals in a group will move toward either greater risk or caution when exposed to arguments and information that were not available to individuals when they made their initial choice.

In general, the greater the number of arguments advanced during discussion that support the initial majority group opinion, the more cogent, reasonable, and persuasive they seem to be, and the more original or nonredundant the arguments are, the greater will be the polarization (Smith, 1982). Naturally, if the majority is predisposed toward risk-taking (or caution), the number of arguments advanced will usually favor that predisposition.

One qualifier, however, should be added to the persuasive arguments explanation for the group polarization effect. Laughlin and Ellis (1986) found that polarization toward the majority point of view is not automatic. Minorities tend to move to the majority when there are no demonstrably correct answers. When the correct decision can be demonstrated, however, a "truth wins" process emerges. Applying truth wins to the polarization effect, then, you must allow for a minority to swing the majority over to its side if the minority's arguments are virtually irrefutable. In the movie *Twelve Angry Men*, the majority is swayed systematically by the minority when presented with demonstrably correct refutation of the prosecution's case. The arguments that an assailant would not stab downward with a switchblade; that a female witness could not have gotten up, put on her glasses, and moved to a window to identify an assailant through an El-train rushing by all in just a few seconds; and that the switchblade was not "the only one of its kind" persuaded the initial majority to vote for acquittal, not conviction.

The last explanation for group polarization is the <u>diffusion of responsibility hypothesis</u>. This point of view explains riskier decisions but not more cautious decisions. Because it is a group that is identified with a decision and not a single individual, responsibility for the decision is spread out. The responsibility for a decision is felt less by individuals in a group than by an individual acting alone. Groups become lawless mobs for the same reason. It is the perception that an abstract group made a decision. If you were a member and agreed with the group decision but later are challenged, you can blame the decision on the group and pretend to have disagreed but lost out. Groups can also make members anonymous. We may recognize the Committee for Safer Streets but not the individuals who sit on the committee.

Shaw (1981) argues that the research supports all three explanations for group polarization. In some cases it may be social comparisons that encourage the polarization. In other instances it may be persuasive arguments or diffusion of responsibility. It may be all three operating together. What is clear and unmistakable, however, is that <u>groups do tend to polarize decision making when there is a clear majority initially favoring either risk or caution, and that group discussion is the primary means of inducing the change of mind</u>.

The performance phase of group development is a complex process. I have merely laid the groundwork for more detailed discussion of group performance in later chapters. Nevertheless, I can give some general advice at this juncture regarding communication competence. <u>A competent communicator exhibits a sensitivity to the needs of the group during the performance periodic phase of group development as follows</u>:

1. *Focus on the task.* Since task and social dimensions of groups are interconnected, focusing on the task to the detriment of social relationships among members obviously makes little sense. Nevertheless, when there is work to be done, the primary focus of the competent communicator is on the accomplishment of the task. Opportunities to build cohesion occur most often in the norming phase.

2. *Encourage participation from group members.* The group needs to utilize its resources fully, which means that even social loafers may have much to contribute. A <u>note of caution</u> here: Encouraging member participation

should not be a blanket rule. Some group members should not be encouraged to participate because they disrupt the group's decision-making process (more on this in Chapter Seven).

Communication competence requires flexibility. What is appropriate communication in one phase of group development will prove to be inappropriate in other phases. As Andersen (1988) summarizes, "Competent communicators are skilled in all phases of group development, and they are adaptable enough to implement effective communication behavior at the appropriate phase of group development. You can improve your overall group competence by becoming sensitive to group phases and the appropriateness of your communication skills" (p. 456).

 SECOND LOOK

Competent Communication and Group Development

Forming Periodic Phase
- Express positive attitudes and feelings
- Appear friendly, open, and interested

Storming Periodic Phase
- Tolerate, even encourage, disagreement and deviance
- Keep a civil tongue
- Be an active listener

Norming Periodic Phase
- Adapt communication to the norms of the group
- Encourage change when norms are excessively rigid
- Encourage change when norms are too elastic

Performing Periodic Phase
- Focus on the task
- Encourage participation from group members (in most instances)

NEWCOMERS AND GROUP DEVELOPMENT

The interconnectedness of all components of a system makes the entry into a group of even a single new member a highly significant event. Moreland and Levine (1989) note that as groups develop, relationships among members stabilize and the roles and norms in the group become more complex. "The entry of a newcomer into the group can threaten this development by forcing members to alter their relationships with one another" (p. 156).

Nature of Group

Moreland and Levine (1989) cite several characteristics of a group that directly affect the acceptance of a newcomer. First, the level of group development has a direct bearing. Katz (1982) studied several research and development groups in a large corporation for four months. Members of those groups that had been in existence for a relatively short time communicated more with newcomers and were more open to their ideas than were members of older groups.

Younger groups have only recently formed and still may be establishing norms and working out differences. A newcomer is less disruptive since he or she enters early on in the group development process. Entering a long-standing group, however, where development has progressed far beyond the initial stages can be a far greater shock to the system and requires greater adaptation to the change by the members. The newcomer seems more like an outsider in older groups than in younger ones.

Second, the level of group performance affects the acceptance of newcomers. When the system is functioning well, group members may not want to take a chance on altering a successful formula. Accepting a newcomer may pose a big risk. When a group is performing poorly, however, there is a strong impetus for change. The arrival of a newcomer may be perceived as a welcome addition. The group's fortunes may take a turn for the better. The benefits seem to outweigh the risks by a considerable margin.

Third, the number of members is an important characteristic affecting acceptance of a newcomer into a group. Those groups that have too few members to perform necessary tasks well usually are eager to accept newcomers into their group. Newcomers mean less work for each member and potentially greater success for the group. Groups that have too many members to function efficiently, however, will probably view a newcomer as an additional burden.

Finally, the degree of "openness" in a group also affects acceptance of newcomers. Here Moreland and Levine define openness as frequent entry of new members and exit of old members. Open groups, then, are more comfortable with, and experienced in, member turnover. Therefore, newcomers have an easier time getting accepted in open groups than they do in closed groups that have little turnover and minimal experience adapting to changes in membership.

In Alan Alda's movie *The Four Seasons,* a long-time (older) group of close, successful, middle-aged friends whose group membership has not changed in years (closed) is thoroughly disrupted when one member marries a young woman after divorcing his wife. Initially, the young woman is given an icy reception. The friends quarrel as a result of the perceived intrusion of this outsider. Having experienced a long period of stability with no exits of old members and no entrances of new members before this, they are unskilled in adapting to such change. The period of adjustment to this newcomer is lengthy.

Sometimes newcomers have a tough entry into a long-standing group. Sometimes the system is disturbed significantly by the newcomer. The characteristics I have just discussed are all related to the nature of the group. Acceptance of newcomers into a group, however, is transactional. This means that the newcomer also contributes to the acceptance or rejection by the group. There are steps newcomers can take to improve their chances of group acceptance.

Newcomer Strategies

Moreland and Levine (1989) identify several strategies newcomers can employ to improve their chances of gaining acceptance from a group. The competent communicator will employ such strategies.

First, <u>newcomers can conduct a thorough reconnaissance of the group</u>. I've already discussed at length why individuals join groups, but reasons for joining don't guarantee wise choices. Most newcomers do a poor job of scouting out a group to determine whether they and the group are a good match (Wanous, 1980). Newcomers should exploit all available sources of information about the group in order to form a reasonably accurate assessment of the group they contemplate joining.

Second, <u>play the role of newcomer</u>. Seek the advice of old-timers (long-time members), avoid disagreements with old-timers, and talk less than old-timers. This obviously is not a permanent role. As you become more accepted by the group your communication can move away from the newcomer role pattern.

Third, <u>seek patrons within the group</u>. Patrons are old-timers who help newcomers become accepted by the group. The best patrons are called mentors. Mentors are old-timers who develop a close personal relationship with the newcomer and assist the newcomer's entry into the group.

Fourth, <u>collaborate with other newcomers</u>. When more than one newcomer enters a group, they stand to gain from banding together in common purpose. Newcomers can lend emotional support and encouragement to one another. They can provide useful information about the group. They can act as a friendly face, making the group climate more inviting.

 **SECOND LOOK**

Newcomer's Entry into Group

Characteristics Affecting Newcomer's Acceptance

- Level of group development
- Level of group performance
- Number of members (too many or too few members)
- Degree of openness (member turnover rate)

Newcomer's Strategies for Acceptance

- Conduct thorough reconnaissance of group
- Play the role of newcomer
- Seek patrons within the group
- Collaborate with other newcomers

FOCUS ON GENDER/CULTURE

Gender/Ethnicity and Group Development

Women and ethnic minorities have typically experienced unequal treatment in small groups (Forsyth, 1990). Women and African-Americans have reported dissatisfaction with their relatively low status in mixed-membership groups (Hembroff, 1982). The good news is that women and ethnic minorities, although required to put extra effort into their tasks just to remain on par with white male members, can increase status in small groups eventually through successful performance (Hembroff and Myers, 1984; Martin and Sell, 1985). The bad news is that overall group performance can suffer during the lag period when contributions of women and ethnic minorities are overlooked because they are accorded low status in the group (Kirchler and Davis, 1986).

There are significant differences between groups composed of diverse members (mixed company) and groups whose membership is uniform. Unfortunately, the focus of research in this area has mostly ignored ethnic minorities and concentrated on gender differences. Unquestionably, however, female ethnic minorities experience the greatest disadvantage because they face a double bias (Morrison and Von Glinow, 1990).

In mixed-sex groups, men are normatively assumed to be the task experts whereas women are assumed to be the relationship experts (Acker, 1990). This assumption puts women at a disadvantage in task groups. The norm emphasizes a lower status role for women (i.e., keeping the peace) while dictating a higher status role for men (i.e., making important decisions and solving problems).

Do women perform as well as men in small task groups? The answer depends on two primary factors—the <u>type of task</u> and <u>gender balance</u>. Studies reveal that men tend to excel at tasks requiring mathematical expertise or physical strength. Women tend to excel on verbal tasks (Wood, 1987). Perhaps more importantly, recent research shows that the performance of women in small groups is significantly affected by gender composition. If a woman is alone in an otherwise all-male group, her performance will be adversely affected. As Taps and Martin (1990) explain, "The opportunities for a solo woman to speak, or to show she is competent and has a contribution to make, are low in otherwise male groups; and the larger the size of the group, the lower these odds are" (p. 475). Taps and Martin recommend balanced gender groups to overcome the normative bias of mostly male task groups.

There is definitely a benefit to women and, by extrapolation of the research, ethnic minorities when group composition is more diverse. One study showed that gender diversity in small groups enhanced the team performance even on a "male-oriented task" (Rogelberg and Rumery, 1996). In situations where group composition can be considered during the formative phase (e.g., task force or ad hoc groups), a maximum effort should be made to have a diverse membership with women and ethnic minorities fairly represented. The **Twenty Percent Rule** is an important *minimum* standard to achieve in this regard. Researchers have observed that <u>discrimination against minorities, and</u>

presumably women, drops substantially when no less than 20 percent of a group, and not fewer than two members, are from a minority (Pettigrew and Martin, 1987).

Questions for Thought

1. Why does the Twenty Percent Rule work to diminish discrimination against minorities and women?
2. How important do you think it is to have a diverse group membership? Any connection to group synergy? Explain.

In summary, all groups have a task and social dimension. The output of the task dimension is productivity. The output of the social dimension is cohesiveness. Productivity can affect cohesiveness and vice versa.

Group development encompasses four periodic phases: forming, storming, norming, and performing. These periodic phases do not occur in rigid sequence. These phases frequently overlap and groups may jump around between phases depending upon the circumstances and situations they face. Some groups never progress beyond the forming and initial storming phases. These are groups that for many reasons dissolve because they do not work.

Finally, the entry of newcomers into a group can be a disturbing event. Competent communicators learn about the nature of the group to which they seek membership, and they learn the strategies that will assist their acceptance into the group. Women and ethnic minorities, who are often in the newcomer role, have had a difficult time gaining acceptance into groups.

QUESTIONS FOR CRITICAL THINKERS

1. When is it appropriate to be a nonconformist in a small group?
2. Are there ever times when the task is so important that concern for the social dimension of the group must be ignored?
3. Should group members make an effort to integrate newcomers into the group or is it primarily the task of the newcomer to adapt to the group?

Developing the Group Climate

IDEO, a design firm in California's Silicon Valley, produces ninety products on average each year and has gross revenues of about $25 million. IDEO has designed, among other things, AT&T's new line of answering machines and telephones, the insta-cholesterol test, virtual reality headgear, a long list of computer products, Levolor blinds, and the Crest toothpaste tube that stands perpendicular on the bathroom counter (O'Brien, 1995).

What IDEO has accomplished, however, is not nearly as impressive as how the firm accomplished it. David Kelley, the founder and driving force behind IDEO, is the most uncorporate corporate executive you're likely to find. Kelley has established a corporate climate that is the antithesis of what you're likely to see in most of the Fortune 500 companies and most small businesses as well. Kelley wanted three things when he established IDEO: to work with friends, to have no bosses in charge of employees' lives, and to not work with jerks.

IDEO has a flattened hierarchy characterized by few titles, no "bosses," and no time clocks or specified vacation schedules. Kelley organizes weekly company bike rides, hosts birthday celebrations for workers according to their zodiac signs, and often conducts Monday morning meetings seated on the floor of a purple-and-aqua room devoid of furniture. Kelley treats his employees the way he wishes he had been treated when he worked for Boeing Corporation and National Cash Register. At Boeing, Kelley says engineers were treated like scum. "We were like cattle. There were 200 of us in a room" (O'Brien, 1995, p. 13).

At IDEO, employees are treated as equals who set their own schedules (typically fifty- to sixty-hour workweeks) while meeting demanding standards and strict deadlines. Employees are free to transfer to overseas offices in London or Tokyo or to transcontinental offices in Chicago and New York as long as someone from those offices agrees to swap jobs. The open, free-wheeling climate at IDEO is a large part of its appeal (O'Brien, 1995). Client John Melin, CEO of Smith Sport Optics in Ketchum, Idaho, says, "His [Kelley's] people are easy to work with and willing to listen. . . . At other firms, they tell you this is the best way to do it" (p. 11). Bob Sutton, a Stanford professor of organizational behavior, spent fifteen months studying IDEO to understand the secret of its success. His conclusion: "The secret is simple but complex. It's about people who aren't focusing on office politics" (p. 25). IDEO has a positive group climate.

A communication climate permeates all groups. A positive climate exists when individuals perceive that they are valued by the group and treated well. A negative climate exists when group members do not value and respect one another, when trust is minimal, and when members perceive that they are not treated well. Every group creates an atmosphere that varies according to how members conduct transactions. Decision making, problem solving, and conflict management are all made more difficult, perhaps even impossible in a negative climate. Climate sets the stage for how groups will function. <u>The purpose of this chapter is to identify and explain those communication patterns that enhance the productivity and satisfaction of group members and those patterns that thwart such outcomes.</u>

Toward accomplishing this purpose, I have three <u>objectives</u>:

1. to explain the different results of a competitive versus a cooperative climate on group effectiveness,
2. to describe which communication patterns promote a counterproductive, defensive group climate and which produce a productive, supportive one, and
3. to provide a specific plan for dealing with difficult group members who disrupt the group climate.

<u>The underlying premise fundamental to this discussion is that prevention is preferable to cure</u>. Establishing a constructive group climate of trust, openness, directness, and accomplishment will prevent many problems from occurring, thus making cures for hostile conflict and disruptive dissension among members largely irrelevant. Those conflicts that do arise can be solved more easily and constructively in a cooperative, supportive climate than in a competitive, defensive one. Decision-making and problem-solving techniques will be more meaningful when operating in the context of a constructive climate.

COMPETITIVE VERSUS COOPERATIVE CLIMATES

Our culture pays lip service to the desirability of human cooperation, while our behavior shows a clear preference for competition. Apologists for competitiveness lament, "Wouldn't it be nice if we could get along with others and work together?" Then they quickly add, "But since that doesn't seem possible, let's make sure we learn to out-compete our adversaries." The message is clear. We live in a dog-eat-dog world. Mutts get devoured by Dobermans. It's better to be a Doberman.

This rather primitive, law-of-the-jungle, "them versus us," polarized thinking is the focus of this section. I will train a critical eye on the mindset that views competition as constructive or at least necessary and unavoidable, while cooperation is viewed as largely unattainable. I will make a special effort to compare the effects of competition versus cooperation on small group climate and goal attainment.

Focus Questions
1. What is the relationship between communication competence and competition/cooperation?
2. Do most people prefer competition to cooperation?
3. Does competition increase motivation to succeed? Group cohesiveness?
4. Does competition improve achievement and performance?
5. Does competition build self-esteem and character?

Definitions

Alfie Kohn (1992) in *No Contest: The Case against Competition* defines **competition** as "mutually *exclusive* goal attainment (MEGA)" (p. 3). When transactions in groups are competitive, your success is achieved at the expense of other group members. Competition by definition requires losers. Usually, winners are in the distinct minority and losers constitute the vast majority. Tim Montgomery, a sprinter on the 1996 U.S. 4 × 100-meter Olympic relay team, put it succinctly when faced with the prospect of earning a silver, not a gold medal: "Second place is first place for losers" (in Killion, 1996, p. 6A). The players on the Buffalo Bills football team have often been branded as "losers" because they lost four straight Super Bowl games. Coming in second in a competitive society doesn't usually win accolades, but it can draw ridicule.

Competition necessitates the failure of the many for the success of the few. There is only one World Series champion in baseball, one world chess champion, one female and one male world figure skating champion, and one woman crowned Miss America. Competition for a job produces a single happy candidate and, in some cases, hundreds, even thousands, of disappointed applicants. In the fall of 1996, the city of San Francisco solicited applications for fifty new firefighters. More than ten thousand individuals applied. Pick any contest and the disproportionate number of losers compared to winners is usually enormous.

Linda Putnam (1986) describes competitive climates in the group setting this way:

> In competitive climates, decision outcomes emerge from the suspicion and distrust of group members. . . . The tensions inherent in decision dilemmas are managed through power plays by dominant members who control decision rules, procedural directives, and topics of discussion. Ineffective decisions often emerge from the constrained patterns of communication that typify these competitive climates. (p. 179)

Cooperation can be defined as mutually *inclusive* goal attainment (MIGA). Your success is tied directly to the success of other group members. The spirit of cooperation was captured and its logic was communicated succinctly by Benjamin Franklin when he reputedly remarked upon signing the Declaration of Independence, "We must all hang together—or, most assuredly, we shall all hang separately."

Putnam (1986) describes a cooperative climate in the group setting this way: "In cooperative climates, decision outcomes emerge from coping effectively with differences of opinion, personality clashes, and rival alternatives for courses of action. Group supportiveness, commitment, and interdependence constitute the content themes of cooperative climates" (p. 179).

Independently attempting to attain a goal previously unrealized, such as performing more push-ups than ever before or earning a higher grade on a calculus exam than at any other time in your academic life, is neither competition nor cooperation. Often mistakenly referred to as "competing with one-self," the effort to improve on a previous performance is not competition unless the aim is to defeat another party to achieve such a goal. If being number one requires a number two, three, four, and so forth, then we are competing. If being better than before is attained at no one else's expense, then this is individual achievement not competition.

As Kohn (1992) explains, competition requires interaction. It is not a solitary undertaking. Claiming that we compete with ourselves is like saying we arm-wrestled with ourselves. Arm wrestling is an interactive phenomenon necessitating at least one other party. Competition is likewise interactive.

Kohn's definitions of competition and cooperation and Putnam's descriptions of competitive and cooperative group climates have a direct relationship to my previous explanation of competent communication. The mutually inclusive nature of cooperation reflects the We-orientation of competent communication whereas the mutually exclusive, win-lose nature of competition reflects the Me-orientation. Competent communication is predicated on effectiveness or the achievement of group goals. If cooperation proves to be superior to competition in producing group productivity and achievement (an issue for later discussion), then there is another link between cooperation and communication competence.

Prevalence of Competition

Fisher and Ury (1981) relate an amusing story that reflects the preoccupation of western cultures with competition.

> In 1964 an American father and his twelve-year-old son were enjoying a beautiful Saturday in Hyde Park, London, playing catch with a Frisbee. Few in England had seen a Frisbee at that time and a small group of strollers gathered to watch this strange sport. Finally, one Homburg-clad Britisher came over to the father: "Sorry to bother you. Been watching you a quarter of an hour. Who's *winning*?" (p. 154)

Our inclination to view most human interactions in a competitive light is real and pervasive. Kohn (1992) argues that life in America "has become an endless succession of contests. . . . It is the common denominator of American life" (p. 1). Nathan Miller (in Bolton, 1979) bitingly asserts that "conversation in the United States is a competitive exercise in which the first person to draw a breath is declared the listener" (p. 4). Paul Wachtel (1983), author of *The Poverty of Affluence,* declares, "Competition is almost our state religion" (p. 284). George Leonard refers to our "overblown, institutionalized, codified worship of winning" (p. 128).

Competition in the United States is everywhere. Our economic, judicial, and political systems are based on competition. U.S. universities are "intensely individualistic and highly competitive. Student is pitted against student through the grading system, and faculty member against faculty member for promotion and other academic favors" (Smith, 1990, p. 13). Even our leisure time activities are often dominated by sporting events, where we serve as either a spectator or a participant whose central purpose is to win—to beat others.

The toddler race and children's chess match show that emphasis on competition begins at an early age.

The competitive obsession in the United States is graphically illustrated by an incident that occurred in Lakewood, California. On March 19, 1993, police arrested eight members of a high-school boys' clique called the "Spur Posse" (named after the San Antonio Spurs professional basketball team). The boys were charged with seventeen counts of lewd conduct, unlawful intercourse with minors, and rape allegedly involving girls from ages ten to sixteen. The boys readily admitted that one of the main activities of this group was to "hook up" (have sex) with as many girls as possible (Seligman, 1993).

The boys, many of them top athletes at their high school, coolly admitted to investigators that they kept count of the young girls they had sex with, boasting as many as sixty conquests. Apparently, this was more of a contest about "scoring" than simply having sex. As sociologist Donna Eder of Indiana University explains, "They take the competitive sense and move it into the realm of sexuality" (in Gelman and Rogers, 1993). Contests in the United States can be about almost anything imaginable and even unimaginable.

Some parents defended their sons with a "boys will be boys" excuse. One father boasted to reporters about the virility of his son, a founder of the Spur Posse. Other members of the Lakewood (dubbed "Rapewood" by some upset by this incident) community rationalized that what these boys did was no different from behavior bragged about by professional sports icons such as Wilt Chamberlain, who claims to have slept with more than 20,000 women (commitment to a relationship apparently isn't one of his strong points).

Competition is everywhere in the United States, but is it predominantly a male fascination? After all, Tannen (1990) argues that men view conversations from a status (competitive) perspective but women view them from a connec-

Members of the Spur Posse argue with a female antagonist on a talk show.

tion (cooperative) perspective. According to Kohn (1992), women—although not as competitive as men overall—are becoming more competitive in order to succeed in a cutthroat society. A study of conflict management practices in the workplace found that women are no less competitive than men when conflicts arise (Gayle, 1991). In some instances, women who have advanced in their professions exhibit the "Queen Bee Syndrome" (Mathison, 1987). They climb up the competitive ladder of success and then, instead of assisting other women to do likewise, they protect their position as top woman in the company. They do this by making it tough for other talented women, possible rivals for the typically few positions open to women in organizations, to advance.

In business, sports, entertainment, medicine, law—virtually all facets of our society—women are increasingly emulating the previously male preoccupation with competition. Kohn (1992) laments this recent trend. He argues: "Choice in the fullest sense has been in scarce supply for both sexes as regards competition. It might be said that while women *couldn't* compete, men have *had* to compete. . . . The fact that men have had a virtual monopoly on competitiveness does not, in itself, make it desirable" (p. 179). What women should be saying, Kohn continues, is not "Me, too!" but "What a mess!" Imitation may be the highest form of flattery, but when has the predominantly male obsession with

Women have become increasingly fascinated with competition.

the competitive model and its pronounced Me-orientation shown that it de-serves imitation?

Let me clearly state my point of view here so there is no misunderstanding. It is the *pervasiveness of competition* to the virtual exclusion of cooperation in our culture that troubles me. I can't realistically envision the eradication of com-petition and the substitution of total cooperation in the United States. I prefer to keep my feet planted firmly on the ground and not get lost in the ether of utopian thinking. We do have to deal with the realities of our competitive society. I'm not convinced, however, that we have to eliminate competition. We don't have to replace one extreme (hypercompetitiveness) with another extreme (ultracooperativeness). There will be numerous times in groups where despite Herculean efforts, competition prevails. In such cases, the competent communicator has to have the flexibility of skills to adapt to an adversarial, competitive situation. As we will see when conflict management is discussed in the final chapter, sometimes a competitive communication style is required in order to manage the conflict effectively. Competition, however, should be drastically de-emphasized in small groups, and cooperative systems should be established in groups whenever the possibility arises.

But if cooperation and communication competence are linked, how can competitive patterns of interaction be anything but incompetent communica-tion? First, communication competence is a matter of degree. Drinking a small amount of alcohol does not make you an alcoholic and it may be beneficial in some instances if kept to a minimum. Likewise, a limited amount of competi-tiveness in groups does no harm and may be beneficial to the group. The prob-lem in the United States currently is that we are drunk on competition, stu-porous with the single-minded goal of beating others. Second, although competent communication requires a We-not-Me orientation, this does not ex-clude any consideration of individual needs. Likewise, cooperation is We-oriented but not to the complete exclusion of individual (me) needs. Orientation implies primary, not exclusive focus. The emphasis matters, not the mere pres-ence of occasional competitive communication patterns.

⚆⚆ CLOSER LOOK

Competing for No Good Reason

The mental set that predisposes us to compete easily pervades situations that do not demand a win-lose mentality. An interesting instance of this occurred in my group communication class. Students were assigned a symposium project. The assignment required a discussion of the full range of viewpoints on a topic of national or international import.

Three of the term groups working on this assignment were extremely reti-cent to indicate their topic choice when asked for this information by a repre-sentative of the fourth group. Despite the fact that I had not ruled out the pos-sibility of two groups presenting a symposium on an identical topic, such a restriction was assumed by all. When we discovered that two of the four term groups had chosen rain forests as their topic, the winds of competitiveness blew chill indeed. One of the groups doing rain forests immediately negotiated with me to present its symposium first, thereby hoping to steal the thunder of the other group. When members of the competitor group overheard the negotiations, they screamed foul. Bitter recriminations flew between the antagonists. I stepped in to calm tempers. I instituted a random drawing to designate the order of presentation. Despite my assurance that both groups could work on the same topic and that grades would not be determined on any comparison between groups, the competitors seemed unmollified.

Outside of class the antagonism continued. Members of the two competing groups verbally accosted each other during lunch in the cafeteria. When class resumed, both groups could be heard muttering unflattering comments about their adversaries. On her own initiative, one member asked to speak to the rival group, but her rivals curtly ordered her to leave.

A contest of sorts ensued. Members of one group swarmed the library, hoping to preempt efforts by members of the competing group to secure necessary informational resources. Library books were jealously guarded. Magazines were checked out and hoarded. Independent sources of information, such as interviews with professors, material garnered from environmental groups, and the like, were kept secret.

What is most interesting about this feud is that neither group needed to compete, yet cooperation never seemed to enter the consciousness of participants in this skirmish. Since their grades would be determined by a set of criteria applicable to all groups, and no comparison between groups would transpire, neither of the rivals had any good reason to compete. They both had excellent reasons, however, to collaborate and share information. If they were worried about the redundancy of two identical presentations, the antagonists could have worked together and organized their symposiums in such a way that redundancy could have been kept to a minimum. By pooling resources, they could have improved both of their final presentations. Instead, the two groups became instantly rigid and systemically hostile, each demanding that the other group choose a different topic. The result? Both groups gave mediocre symposium presentations.

The We-not-Me orientation of the competent communicator necessitates less emphasis on competitive win-lose and more emphasis on cooperative win-win approaches to these kinds of conflicts of interest. In my students' defense, they learned from their experience of competing when it wasn't necessary. Their second symposium was a more cooperative effort and a better overall performance.

Questions for Thought

1. Why do you think the two groups were unable to break their competitive mindset? Why didn't they see the wisdom of cooperation and act accordingly?

2. Can you think of experiences you've had in groups that closely parallel these two groups?

Effects of Competition versus Cooperation

The pervasiveness of competition in American society and the vehemence with which it is defended makes competition difficult to challenge. Bruce Ogilvie, a professor emeritus at San Jose State University and a pioneer in sports psychology, states, "We have to be careful in our country about ever attacking winning. It's a deeply embedded ethic in our culture" (in Kutner, 1994, p. D2). The instant anyone claims that competition can produce many serious adverse consequences, testimonials from true believers assume a kind of religious fervor. "Competition brings out the best in each of us;" "Winning is better than sex;" and, of course, "You hate competition because you're a loser"—these and similar statements are heard repeatedly. They sound like incantations to the guru of gamesmanship, Vince Lombardi, who claimed, "Winning isn't everything; it's the only thing."

Those who seem most convinced that competition is a constructive force in American life usually have had some success competing, typically in sports and business enterprises. Sports stars, not surprisingly, tout the virtues of competition. They have profited mightily from it. They are paid staggering sums of money to display their talents on the fields of athletic combat. In 1996, basketball superstar Michael Jordan signed a one-year contract with the Chicago Bulls for $25 million. He was paid an additional $20 million to advertise athletic shoes for Nike, an amount that exceeded the total combined annual pay of the thousands of Third World Nike shoe-factory workers (Derber, 1996). Shaquille O'Neal signed a seven-year contract for $121 million to play for the Los Angeles Lakers. Even lesser-known players such as Allan Houston ($56 million for seven years) and Chris Childs ($24 million for six years) earn enormous salaries ("Lakers ante up," 1996). In a study of the compensation paid to top executives in Silicon Valley, California, the ten highest-paid executives averaged almost $11 million annually ("Are salaries," 1996).

Asking the superstars of the sports and business world to defend competition is self-serving at best. If you were making similar sums of money for playing a sport or running a business, would you complain about the negative side of competition? But few can ever achieve such rewards in our hypercompetitive culture. Frank and Cook (1995) argue that the United States has become a "winner-take-all society." Rewards for competing have become enormous in size but fewer in number, encouraging economic waste, income inequality, and an impoverished cultural life. The increasing concentration of rewards deludes many into believing that they should try for the few gargantuan prizes even though almost none of them will succeed. Somehow translating the benefits of competition enjoyed by superstars to the weekend warriors of this country and to the workers who lose their jobs from "downsizing" and corporate takeovers seems like a stretch.

The joy of victory is exhibited by the victorious 1996 Women's Olympic gymnastics team.

The pain of defeat, even when it results in silver and bronze medals, is exhibited by the "losing" Russian and Romanian Women's Olympic gymnastics teams.

Achievement and Performance   In September 1989, President George Bush expressed his belief in the merits of competition. He called for "a new spirit of competition between students, between teachers and between schools" (in Jacobs, 1989, p. 5B) in order to improve student achievement and performance in the classroom. Republican presidential candidate Bob Dole echoed the Bush sentiment in his acceptance speech at the Republican national convention in the summer of 1996 when he called for "school choice and competition" to improve education in the United States (in Baxter, 1996). This belief in the merits of competition is cultural dogma accepted by most Americans without question.

Do we function more effectively in groups when the climate is competitive? Almost without exception, the resounding answer is NO! Johnson and Johnson (1981 and 1987) conducted the most extensive review of the research on the effects of competitive, cooperative, and individualistic learning experiences ever undertaken. They found 65 studies conducted by other researchers that showed the superiority of cooperation over competition on achievement and performance and 108 studies demonstrating the same clear advantage of cooperation over individual work. Only 14 studies contradicted these remarkably consistent results. An additional 21 studies conducted by Johnson and Johnson found that cooperation, not competition, clearly leads to higher achievement. As David Johnson (in Kohn, 1987) concludes, "There's almost nothing that American education has seen with this level of empirical support" (p. 54).

The essence of cooperative learning in the classroom is team learning. Students work together in small groups. Credit for a project is given to the entire group, not each individual separately. Thus, each small-group member must pull his or her own weight or the whole group suffers. Let me note here that it is not my purpose to explain in detail how to structure the classrooms of America for cooperative learning. Others (Johnson and Johnson, 1987) have already done that admirably. Nevertheless, later in this chapter I will discuss methods you can employ to structure cooperation into small groups, which will serve as a framework not only for cooperative learning but also for cooperative work teams for all manner of tasks.

The issue of student performance and cooperative versus competitive classroom environments is particularly significant when considering ethnic minority students. Based on their own research, Widaman and Kagan (1987) conclude:

> Traditional and competitive classroom structures are not optimal environments for stimulating achievement among cooperatively oriented students. Considered together with the strong evidence that minority students are generally more cooperative than majority students . . . and that minority students show dramatic gains in cooperatively structured classrooms . . . , the present findings support the conclusion that inherent in traditional classroom structures there is probably a general, systematic bias against the achievement of minority students. (p. 364)

The clear advantage of cooperation compared to competition is reflected in other arenas besides education. Robert L. Helmreich, a professor of psychology at the University of Texas, conducted seven studies with a wide variety of subjects (e.g., scientists, businesspeople, airline pilots, and airline reservation agents). All seven studies (see Kohn, 1992) showed clear advantages of cooperation over competition on achievement and performance. Helmreich's research shows that highly competitive individuals do not perform as well in work as those who are less competitive. Business school graduates who exhibited low levels of competitiveness earned about $6,000 a year more than those who showed high levels of competitiveness (in Sit, 1989).

A large group of studies by Dean Tjosvold (1986) of Simon Fraser University in British Columbia echoed Helmreich's results. "Cooperation makes a work force motivated," but "serious competition undermines coordination" (p. 29). More recently, another study (Van Oostrum and Rabbie, 1995) was added to the growing mountain of research showing the superiority of cooperation over competition. When competitive groups were compared to cooperative groups within an organization, the cooperative groups overall vastly outperformed the competitive groups. Even the *worst* cooperative groups that were relatively weak on task accomplishment, on average, outperformed the *best* competitive groups.

Why do the results of these studies run counter to the cultural dogma that encourages competitiveness in order to achieve and perform at optimum levels? Directly put, the cultural dogma is wrong. Kohn (1992) offers three primary reasons why cooperation promotes and competition dampens achievement and performance for most groups and individuals.

First, <u>attempting to achieve excellence and trying to beat others are different goals</u>. Academic debate illustrates the point. Careful reasoning, meticulous regard for the authenticity and credibility of evidence, and skillful communication of oral argumentation have been replaced mostly by such dubious practices as the canned recitation of prepackaged "argumentative briefs," an emphasis on quantity—not quality—of arguments, and the delivery of refutation at hyper-speed by bombastic, spittle-spraying debaters. These latter practices are part of an elaborate and complex game squarely targeted on winning, not rhetorical excellence.

None of these competitive communication practices would be encouraged much less taught in any basic speech course because these practices cannot be justified as competent communication. They are inappropriate for any communication arena other than perhaps competitive debate—a very specialized context. As William Southworth (in Freeley, 1986), a long-time debate coach at the University of Redlands, observes, "What passes now for oral persuasion in the typical debate has virtually no application at all in any other setting demanding persuasive skills" (p. 406). He decries "the seemingly constant reduction in the level of oral comprehensibility by our practicing . . . debaters" (p. 405). Victory over opponents becomes the goal, not development of competent communication skills and in-depth analysis of complex issues. Winning doesn't motivate someone to become a competent communicator if less desirable communication practices lead to "victory."

Kohn offers a second reason why a cooperation promotes higher achievement and productivity than does competition. <u>Resources are used more efficiently in a cooperative atmosphere than a competitive one.</u> A cooperative climate promotes the full utilization of information by a group, whereas a competitive climate typically promotes information hoarding (Johnson and Johnson, 1986). When group members work interdependently toward a common goal, not competitively to advance individual goals, there is likely to be less duplication of effort, better utilization of members' skills, and greater pooling of information and knowledge. The synergistic effect already explained is more likely to occur in a cooperative climate.

A third explanation by Kohn for the superiority of cooperation over competition as regards achievement and productivity is that <u>competition diminishes performance because of the antagonism associated with beating others</u>. The goal of competition is victory over opponents. Since your opponents stand in the way of your victory, they are the enemy. Any system that is structured in a zero-sum fashion—I win only if you lose—is bound to create hostility, even hatred and aggression toward those who block your path to victory (Kohn, 1992). A competitive small-group system is structured to frustrate the achievement of most group members. If only one member of a sales team can get the "Salesperson of the Year" bonus, then every other member will be disappointed by his or her failure to achieve a personal goal. Cooperating with other members of the sales team by sharing leads would be defeating your own purpose.

Group Cohesiveness Closely associated with group achievement and performance is group cohesiveness. Does competition enhance intragroup cohesiveness? As I already indicated, intragroup competition usually increases hostility and aggressiveness among group members. But what about intergroup competition? Doesn't wanting to defeat another group increase cohesiveness within your group? This is true to an extent. Van Oostrum and Rabbie (1995) found "weak indications" that intergroup competition generates internal group cohesion. This is primarily true, however, for winning teams. Losing teams typically fall apart and members look for someone to blame, such as the group leader (Van Oostrum and Robbie, 1995).

<u>Even if intergroup competition stimulates internal group cohesion, however, this method is a questionable way to achieve such a result</u>. The group will have to manufacture enemies to defeat in order to maintain cohesion within the group. Cohesion, then, is artificially induced. It doesn't flow naturally from group interaction. Once the foe has been bested, the reason for cohesion is removed (Filley, 1975). A cooperative group climate, on the other hand, enhances the social relationships within the group thereby increasing cohesiveness and group productivity as a by-product.

Self-esteem Jules Henry noted that "a competitive culture endures by tearing people down." Question the athletes who never play and ask them how they feel about competition. Better yet, ask those who aren't even good enough to make the team and earn the "privilege" of acquiring splinters in their backsides from warming the bench. Anywhere <u>from 50 to 80 percent of adolescents who participate in sports quit because they aren't having any fun</u> (Brue, 1989 and Orlick, 1978). A September 11, 1990, NBC special entitled "Sports and Kids" put the figure at 75 percent. A study of kids involved in Little League (a competitive enterprise Kohn [1992] describes as "institutionalized child abuse") revealed that the more winning is emphasized, the higher the dropout rate. Highly competitive coaches had a team dropout rate five times greater than teams coached by a more cooperative manager who emphasized skill development, not winning ("Put enjoyment ahead," 1994). As sports psychologist Terry Orlick (1978) observes, "For many children competitive sports operate as a failure factory which not only effectively eliminates the 'bad ones' but also turns off many of the 'good ones' " (p. 129).

While many adolescents quit sports because they fear failure and they can't handle the pressure of competition, many others never try out because they wish to avoid the embarrassment of not making the team. Remember those agonizing moments in childhood when you engaged in the ritual of choosing up sides for basketball, soccer, or some other competitive game? If you were considered a star by your schoolmates your inclusion on the team was assured. Your main concern was the prestige that accompanies being chosen first, second, or third. If you were viewed as inept at sports by schoolmates, however, then your main concern was whether you would be chosen at all to join the team, and if so, would you suffer the humiliation of being taken last in the playground draft.

In a competitive environment, only the most skillful are valued. The less skillful just make defeat more probable and thereby become a burden on the team. Olympic swimming sensation Amy Van Dyken, winner of four gold medals in the 1996 Games, took seven years to win her first race. While she was in high school, she overheard her relay teammates complaining that "with Van Dyken anchoring [the race], we're not even going to get second." Van Dyken recalls that "I found out later that some of them had gone to our coach several times and said they would refuse to be in the relay with me because I was so terrible" (in Meacham, 1996, p. 8DD). To her credit, Van Dyken plugged away for years, quitting at one point in college but coming back "because of how greasy my hair got when I wasn't in the pool two times a day" (p. 8DD). Hers is a story of incredible persistence against the forces that tried to beat her into submission. Most people quit rather than absorb the torment of being called a loser.

Roger Johnson (in Kohn, 1987) makes the point this way: "You know where self-esteem comes from? It comes from peers, from being liked, accepted, connected." Competition offers a very different message. "The minute you lose, your value ends. That's a terrible thing to tell a kid," says Johnson, "or an adult" (p. 54). Daniel Gould, professor of exercise and sports science at the University of North Carolina in Greensboro, makes this assessment: "We find that children believe that if you win, you're worthy, but if you lose, you're not worthy. They pick up the subtle message that outcome is the only thing that counts" (in Kutner, 1994).

Unquestionably, competition has an effect on an individual's self-esteem and this effect is mostly negative, while cooperation enhances self-esteem (Deutsch, 1985). An extensive review of the research on the effects of competition and cooperation on self-esteem revealed that of those studies that showed a significant difference between the two, eighty-one showed an advantage for cooperation and *only one* gave the advantage to competition (Johnson and Johnson, 1989). Cooperation bolsters individual self-esteem, but competition typically does not.

Character Building and Ethics You've heard the claim. Competition builds character. It teaches you, in the words of an editorial in the *San Jose Mercury News* lamenting the demise of spelling bees in the Gilroy, California, school district, "how to work hard, to sacrifice, to concentrate and to lose" ("It spells success," 1991, p. 5B). The editorial concludes, "We don't need less healthy competition in our schools, we need more. Kids need to learn how to lose if they are going to learn how to win" (p. 5B).

Such sweeping claims of character building are typically offered as self-evident truisms with not the slightest effort to support such generalizations with evidence. Hocker and Wilmot (1995) claim that losing "does not build character; it builds frustration, aggression, or apathy" (p. 85). Sports psychologist Susan Butt (1976) states that "the traditional assumption that competitive sport builds character is still with us today in spite of overwhelming contrary evidence" (p. 54). There is "no empirical support for the tradition that sport builds character" (Ogilvie and Tutko, 1971, p. 61).

On the contrary, the evidence shows that competition typically produces cheating. In business, insider trading scandals made headlines more than once. In education, cheating among students is epidemic (Derber, 1996). Two studies (in Yates, 1985)—one by John Baird of the psychology department at Bloomsburg State College in Pennsylvania and a second by Joseph Trimble of the psychology department at Western Washington University—found that about three-quarters of the students they surveyed admitted cheating. Baird's student sample gave competition for grades as the number one reason for cheating. One of the most popular books on college campuses is *Cheating 101* by Michael Moore. This primer on cribbing provides detailed strategies for surreptitiously passing answers from one student to another during an exam. Moore claims that everybody's cheating and that he's just making "an honest living" teaching students how to be dishonest (in Derber, 1996).

On the other side of the podium, professors fake research results published in scholarly and scientific journals far more frequently than we care to admit, and the dishonest practice of piggy-backing, attaching one's name to a publication for which little or no work was performed, is widespread (Sykes, 1988). When much is at stake and few can be winners, <u>cheating and dishonesty flourish in a competitive climate</u>. As Sissela Bok (1978), in her widely acclaimed book *Lying,* explains, "The very stress on individualism, on competition, on achieving material success which so marks our society also generates intense pressures to cut corners . . . such motives impel many to participate in forms of duplicity they might otherwise resist" (p. 258).

Surely you have to wonder how competition, which glorifies the victors and is indifferent, even contemptuous, toward the losers in a contest, teaches the ethical and moral lessons of sportsmanship, fair play, honesty, empathy, and compassion toward opponents—all key elements in character building. <u>If, in order to feel good about myself (winner) I have to make you feel bad about yourself (loser), how does this make me a better person?</u> How does this build character? As Alice Walker so eloquently observes, we live in a culture where "the only way I can bloom is if I step on your flower, the only way I can shine is if I put out your light" (in Lanka, 1989, p. 24). Does this strike you as even a remote incentive to improve one's character?

If any character building does occur, it seems to occur in spite of, not because of competition. It's not the competition that produces the fair play since being a good sport may diminish your chances of winning. What team, for instance, would keep a player simply because he or she is a really good sport, a nice person, and a graceful loser? Answer: a team that de-emphasizes winning. The more competitive the team and the bigger the stakes associated with winning, the more likely we are to cheat and be ugly to others. "Nice guys finish last" is a cultural cliché. Boasting, taunting, and other overt displays of bad taste and questionable character are typically ignored if a player has exceptional talent.

By contrast, in a cooperative system, where the focus is placed on working together to achieve a common purpose, not on beating an adversary to gain personal advantage, there is no incentive nor benefit derived from dishonesty and cheating. In a cooperative system, group pressure is aimed at discouraging individualism and a Me-orientation. Rewards come from working and achieving as a team.

Preference for Cooperation

Do we prefer competition to cooperation when given a choice? You would think that given the clear disadvantages of competition that most people would answer no. Since most Americans have known little else but a competitive environment, however, the answer is likely to be yes.

The question is largely meaningless, though, since in the hypercompetitive climate of American society we rarely have an opportunity to sample cooperation as an alternative to competition. If I were to ask you to list games you have played, how many of these games would be cooperative rather than competitive? Can you even think of any cooperative games you have ever played? (See Butler, 1986, and Rabow, 1988, if you're interested in pursuing the cooperative alternative.) Even in our schools, cooperation is often confused with conformity and obedience. Stating a preference when comparing two possibilities, only one of which has been learned and experienced to any substantial degree, reveals a choice made in a void.

Johnson and Johnson (1985) cite seven studies demonstrating that when given the rare opportunity to experience *both* cooperation and competition, most subjects prefer cooperation. Haines and McKeachie (1967) found that college students prefer a cooperative, not a competitive, group-discussion technique in a learning environment. Kohn (1992) could not find a single study showing a preference for competition over cooperation when subjects had an opportunity to experience both and then make a choice between the two. He concluded that "it is not unusual for people to say they prefer to compete but then to change their minds when they see at first hand what it is like to learn or work or play in an environment that does not require winners and losers" (p. 32).

FOCUS ON CULTURE

Culture and Competition

The pervasiveness of competition in the United States can easily delude us into believing that humans are competitive by nature. But where is the evidence that humans must compete because nature makes it inescapable? Even the depiction of life in the animal and plant world as "survival of the fittest" and "red in tooth and claw," to use Tennyson's metaphorical description, vastly overstates the competitive aspects of life on Earth. Anne Fausto-Sterling (1993) observes that "research in the past two decades shows that cooperation among species plays at least as big a role as violent struggle" (p. 24). Zoologist Frans de Waal notes, "Aiding others at a cost or risk to oneself is widespread in the animal world" (in Boyd, 1996). Cooperation, according to this new school of thought, has survival value. Animals that help each other find food and ward off predators do better than those that go it alone (Boyd, 1996).

Comparing cultures reveals that "it is the norms of the culture that determine its competiveness" (Kohn, 1992, p. 39), not human nature. Anthropologist Margaret Mead (1961) claimed that "it is the way the structure of the society is built up that determines whether individual members shall cooperate or shall compete with one another" (p. 481).

Consider the typical case of an elementary student who experiences difficulty discerning the correct answer to a math problem. The teacher urges the student to "think harder," applying further pressure to the intimidated youngster desperately hoping for a flash of brilliance. Meanwhile, fellow classmates are frantically waving their hands, certain in their own minds that they have deduced the right answer. Finally, giving up on the perplexed child, the teacher recognizes another student who excitedly shouts the correct answer. One child's misery is another child's triumph. Henry (1963) summarizes this commonplace competitive situation in U.S. classrooms this way: "So often somebody's success has been bought at the cost of our failure. To a Zuni, Hopi, or Dakota Indian, [besting another student] would seem cruel beyond belief, for competition, the wringing of success from somebody else's failure, is a form of torture" (p. 35).

Chuck Otterman's experience coaching football to students at Arizona's Hopi High School illustrates the normative nature of competitiveness. Football, with its emphasis on hitting opponents, psyching up for the game, and total commitment to victory, contradicts almost nine centuries of Hopi culture and religion.

Located on a reservation, Hopi High hardly embraced football. As Otterman (in Garrity, 1989) explains, "They aren't used to our win-at-all-costs, beat-the-other-man mentality. Their understanding of life, of what it means to be a good Hopi, goes against what it takes to be a good football player" (p. 11). Hopi football players did not initially understand the game. Hopi fans didn't know what to do at games, so Otterman had to be both coach and cheerleader, frequently urging the slim crowds to stand up and shout their support for the team.

In the second year of the program, the team went a respectable 6-4 thanks to an excellent quarterback and sure-handed wide receivers. Nevertheless, their quarterback, Jarrett Huma, was uncomfortable with his impressive record-setting personal statistics. Huma and his teammates felt more comfortable when his proficiency at quarterback fell off the next season. "Individual success makes them uneasy," Otterman observes.

After three seasons of bringing football to a community that was skeptical from the outset, Otterman resigned, citing lack of community support for the program. Otterman explains, "These people (were) just waiting to say, 'Football is bad, we don't want it.' And maybe they're right. I really don't know. I don't think the Hopis knew what they were getting into" (p. 16).

There is plentiful evidence demonstrating that American hypercompetitiveness does not have to be imitated. Kagen and Madsen (1971) showed that rural Mexican children were more cooperative than Mexican American children, who, in turn, were more cooperative than Anglo American and rural Mexican children. Nelson and Kagan (1972) state:

> Anglo-American children are not only irrationally competitive, they are almost sadistically rivalrous. Given a choice, Anglo-American children took toys away from their peers on 78 percent of the trials even when they could not keep the toys themselves. Observing the success of their actions, some of the children gloated, "Ha! Ha! Now you won't get a toy." Rural Mexican children in the same situation were rivalrous only half as often as the Anglo-American child. (p. 53)

Norwegians almost always reciprocated cooperative behavior in an experimental game, but American subjects responded to cooperative behavior with cooperation of their own only about half the time (Marwell and Schmidt, 1975). Israeli kibbutz children exhibited far more spontaneous cooperative behavior than did urban Israeli children (Shapiro and Madsen, 1974). Australian aborigines, the Inuit of Canada, the Tangu of New Guinea, and the Kikuyu of Kenya all exhibit much greater cooperation than is found among Americans (Kohn, 1992).

Questions for Thought

1. In your judgment, was it appropriate to introduce football to the Hopis? Explain.
2. Is it possible for a subcultural group to remain mostly cooperative when the predominate culture is largely competitive?
3. Have you had experience with other cultures where cooperation is emphasized?

Whether the arena is business, education, politics, medicine, or even religion, competition prevails and cooperation is a rarity. So how do we reverse this emphasis? How does the competent communicator establish greater cooperation in small groups? Not simply, but persistently!

 SECOND LOOK

Cooperation Compared to Competition

Cooperation	Competition
Improvement of achievement/ performance	Diminishment of achievement/ performance
• efficient utilization of resources	• hoarding of resources
• goal of achieving excellence	• goal of beating others
• promotion of harmonious relationships	• fostering of antagonism/ divisiveness
Increased cohesiveness	Diminished cohesiveness for ''losers''
Enhancement of self-esteem	Typical creation of ''failure factor''
Encouragement of openness/honesty	Encouragement of cheating/ dishonesty

Teamwork: Constructing Cooperation in Groups

Cooperation is often mistaken for fuzzy-headed, impractical altruism or misplaced idealism. Actually, cooperation is quite practical and pragmatic. If we sink or swim together, then it serves the interests of all parties to assist one another in treading water. Urgent pleas and pious pronouncements, however, will not produce teamwork in groups, even if our intentions are noble.

Group cooperation requires more than good intentions and altruistic attitudes. Cooperation must be transacted between parties, not pronounced from the pulpit. One study (Shure et al., 1965) found that aggressive subjects will exploit those using a pacifist strategy of complete cooperation. If one party perceives an advantage from dominating the cooperative party, then such exploitation is likely. Filley (1975) concludes that "while cooperation based upon moral values—pacifism, helping, or avoiding the exploitation of others—may occur, the more important ingredient for inducing cooperative behavior is rational self-interest" (p. 71).

Teamwork must become systemic. This is especially true since most of us are expert competitors but novice cooperators. As Wachtel (1983) explains, "People in a system with competitive values tend to become competitive, and in so doing they keep the system competitively oriented" (p. 144).

For teamwork to become systemic in a small group, cooperation has to be *structured into the framework of the group* for the benefit of all members. There are <u>five criteria that must be met in order to establish a cooperative team structure</u>: interdependence, equality, participation, individual accountability, and cooperative communication patterns. Leave out any one of these criteria and you diminish the teamwork potential of the group.

Interdependence   When we must all work together in order to achieve a desirable goal, we are interdependent. The goal is unattainable without the cooperation of group members, so we depend on each other for success. <u>Success is not defined individually but in terms of the group</u>. If three people set out in a sailboat to circumnavigate the globe, all three individuals have the same goal. Additionally, no single person can achieve the goal without the teamwork of the other two individuals. All three individuals depend on each other for a safe and successful mission. If they fail, it is a collective failure. If they achieve their goal, it is a collective achievement.

Sometimes groups choose a cooperative goal of simply doing the best they can for all members of the team. The first women's team to be invited to climb Mount Kongur in China didn't set as its target getting one team member on top of the mountain. Instead, the team chose a cooperative goal to get as many team members as high up the mountain as possible (Larson and LaFosto, 1989). Here success is determined by everyone pulling together to produce the best results for every member—no winners or losers.

Cooperative goals can be reinforced by an <u>interdependent division of labor and resources</u> within the group. Journalists working on a complex story often must work cooperatively in teams in order to complete the final product. Each member of the journalistic team must research a facet of the total story because no single journalist could complete the project by himself or herself and still make the deadline. Pooling labor and resources structures interdependence.

Equality   There are essentially three ways rewards can be distributed in a group: winner-take-all, equitable distribution (proportional), and equal distribution. Deutsch (1985) discovered that when success depends on group members working together, an equal distribution of rewards "gives the best results and the competitive winner-take-all system gives the poorest results" (p. 163).

A merit system of rewards (winners-take-all) is intrinsically competitive. Only the winners receive the rewards. This sets up a win-lose dichotomy and sets in motion all the negative consequences associated with competition already discussed. Merit systems may motivate the few who believe they have a reasonable chance of being "number one." Everyone else, however, is demoralized because the rewards are forever out of reach.

Profit-sharing programs based on equitable reward distribution (i.e., the more a group member contributes to the team success the higher the bonus paid) is preferable to winner-take-all schemes. The biggest drawback, however, to equitable reward distribution is identified by Brislin (1993) when he points out, "The goal is to reward the efforts of *individuals* in the group rather than to ensure that the group will survive into the future. The quest for individual rewards often leads to a great deal of tension when benefits are to be distributed. People disagree if they do not receive as much as expected" (p. 53).

Schuster (1984) studied twenty-eight firms engaged in some form of financial sharing plan. The majority showed productivity gains from the plans, but the productivity improvements occurred more frequently in firms with system-wide distribution of bonuses that were equally distributed.

The incentive of systemwide equal distribution plans is to share the rewards of a team effort to excel. Equal distribution of rewards provides potential motivation for all group members and, as Deutsch (1979) notes, enhances mutual self-esteem and respect, group loyalty, and congenial personal relationships within the group. The superiority of equal rewards distribution is supported by the results of hundreds of studies (Deutsch, 1985).

Both interdependence and equality as means of structuring cooperation in a group were experimentally tested in a school setting by psychologist Elliot Aronson (1975), using what he terms the "jigsaw classroom." Students were formed into small learning groups to prepare for an upcoming examination. Each student was given only a portion of the material, a piece of the overall puzzle, necessary to pass the test. Everyone needed each other, and test scores were determined on the basis of how well the group did, not on individual performance. Thus, group members had to teach each other and work together in order to do well. So the group goal, division of labor, and distribution of rewards were all structured for cooperation.

When the jigsaw method was used by Aronson in classrooms that had been recently desegregated, impressive results were obtained. Jigsaw learning produced significantly more friendships and less prejudice between ethnic groups than occurred at the same school using competitive learning techniques. Self-esteem, test scores, and liking for the school experience all improved for minority students. White students also experienced similar positive results.

Participation Group members must have a stake in the outcomes for cooperation to occur. Participative decision making is essential to the institution of cooperation in groups. Collaborative effort will disintegrate if group members feel that their cooperation merely rubber-stamps decisions already made by others with more power.

Participative decision making occurs at two levels. First, group members' participation in decision making is valued, encouraged, and respected. Members feel they are a part of a team making important decisions. Second, the decisions of the team (subsystem) are valued, encouraged, and respected by the system as a whole. Teams are given a great deal of autonomy to determine their own success. Team decisions are not vetoed by upper management. Cooperation occurs in a climate of trust. If the team is not trusted to make careful, deliberative decisions, and if the team's choices are not respected, then participative decision making will quickly be perceived as a deceptive game that creates only the illusion of choice.

A review of forty-seven studies revealed that meaningful participation in decision making increased worker productivity and job satisfaction (Miller and Monge, 1986). When participative decision-making programs fail, they typically fail because participation was minimal, only some individuals were allowed to participate, the program was too short-term, the decisions teams were allowed to make were relatively inconsequential, or the team's choices were essentially ignored by upper management (see Kohn, 1993). I will discuss participative decision making in greater detail in Chapter Seven. The important point here is that the meaningful participation is essential to the establishment of teamwork in groups.

Individual Accountability   Interdependence, equality, and participation all sound great, I picture you saying, but what about social loafers who could benefit from the toil of others? Group effort is not truly cooperative if some members are slackers who let others do all the work but expect to receive equal reward for lounging on their ample backsides. You must have a mechanism for individual accountability in order to discourage free rides on the group's gravy train (Johnson and Johnson, 1987).

Let me note at the outset that smaller groups naturally have greater individual accountability than larger groups. As I previously indicated, social loafing typically occurs in larger groups because slackers can diminish their effort without being easily noticed. Keeping groups small makes individual accountability less of an issue.

I have already discussed in Chapter Three a plan to deal with social loafing. Institute it. If loafing continues despite the group's best efforts, however, then deny the loafer some rewards as a last resort. Denial of rewards can be justified by the group based on the rationale that equal distribution of rewards among all group members should be based on a genuine effort to produce for the group (We-orientation), not based merely on equal rewards for all members who still register a pulse. Individual accountability establishes a *minimum standard of performance* in order to share the fruits of team labor. The standards should not be set so high that they assure failure. Opportunities for loafers to redeem themselves should be available. The focus should be on raising all team members above the minimum standards, way above if possible, not on looking for ways to designate failures. Minimum standards agreed to in advance by the group might include the following: no more than two missed meetings, no more than two tardies or early exits from meetings, work turned in to the group on time, and work determined by the group as satisfactory quality.

Individual accountability is not the same as rank ordering of group members' performances or distributing rewards based on merit. Individual accountability merely establishes a *minimum* standard of performance that all can reach (mutually inclusive). Rewards based on merit automatically disqualify the vast majority even when performance of group members is quite good, but simply not the best (mutually exclusive).

⊙⊙ CLOSER LOOK

Habitat for Humanity

In 1993, it became the seventeenth-largest homebuilder in the United States. By 1995, more than 40,000 homes occupied by a quarter of a million people had been built by this remarkable organization. More than 400,000 people in more than 1,200 U.S. cities and towns and in forty-eight other countries have donated their time and energy to the cause of building new homes for the world's poor (Gaillard, 1996). In 1997, Habitat for Humanity was building homes at a rate of 20,000 per year.

The success of Habitat for Humanity is a case study in cooperative team building. Habitat was begun in 1968 by Millard Fuller, a lawyer and business-man who became a self-made millionaire but gave away his riches and dedi-cated his life to helping poor people own decent housing. Habitat embodies the first four criteria for establishing teamwork and constructing cooperation in groups.

First, Habitat structures interdependence into every housing project. Build-ing houses for Habitat is a community project, not the work of unrelated individ-uals. As Fuller (1995) explains, "We are all connected. Who doesn't want their community to flourish? And as long as there are shacks in any community, the community is less than well. A Habitat home can be the first step to bringing those who've been left behind into the fullness of community life. The commu-nity is always the better for it" (p. 10).

The building of Habitat homes is based on interdependent teamwork. Work crews composed of volunteers divide the labor, with each small subgroup erecting portions of the total structure a section at a time. Work crews are syn-ergy in action. Most volunteers who build Habitat homes have no expertise in such tasks. In fact, one Habitat construction team in Bend, Oregon, calls itself "Chris's Bad Girls" and advertises on the Internet, encouraging women ages 16 to 100, "experienced or inexperienced, walking or in a wheelchair, sighted or unsighted" to volunteer their labor to build Habitat homes. On their first pro-ject, women from ages 16 to 84 volunteered to build a Habitat home con-

An all-woman construction team works cooperatively to build a Habitat home.

stucted entirely by women (at the time the third of its kind in the United States). With the exception of Chris, who was the leader of the group and a general contractor, none of the women were builders. The second-in-command was picked because she had once built a doghouse. Nevertheless, they successfully constructed a Habitat home by working together as a team of committed volunteers with a common goal.

Second, Habitat promotes the equality criterion. Qualifications to own a Habitat home are applied equally to all applicants. All Habitat homeowners are given no-interest home loans. Habitat does not make any profit on the homes so there is no winner-take-all or equity reward system. Mortgage payments are sunk back into new Habitat construction projects. All houses are basic structures with no frills; just solid, standardized houses varying in size only on the basis of number of family members who will occupy the homes.

Third, Habitat also encourages participation in several ways. The entire community is involved in fund-raising, land acquisition, donation of construction materials, and plans for building Habitat homes. Volunteers contribute their time and effort and for this they are valued, encouraged, and respected members of a team. Future homeowners participate along with volunteers, helping to build their own homes.

Fourth, individual accountability is an essential part of Habitat's success. Future homeowners are not accepting charity. As Fuller (1995) puts it, Habitat is "a hand up, not a handout. It's empowerment on the most basic level. Each homeowner family is expected to help build their own house and others" (p. 8). Fuller calls the minimum contribution the future owners must make to the home-building effort "sweat equity." Homeowners are expected and required to contribute 500 hours of labor on their own home and other Habitat projects. They also pay an average of $240 per month in mortgage payments. They are accountable for their loans like any other homeowner. An impressive 89 percent of Habitat homeowners make their mortgage payments on time and fewer than 1 percent of all Habitat loans end in foreclosure (Fuller, 1995, p. 125). Habitat, a Christian-based organization that practices what it preaches, helps people help themselves in an exemplary exhibition of cooperation in groups.

Habitat for Humanity takes shacks and replaces them with modest new homes by instituting essential elements of cooperation and teamwork.

Questions for Thought

1. What problems do you think Habitat runs into when developing plans to build low-income homes? How might it overcome these problems?
2. Do you see any limitations on Habitat's ability to achieve its stated goal to wipe out all substandard housing in the world?

Cooperative Communication Patterns All of the other criteria are largely irrelevant if the communication patterns in the group are competitive, not cooperative. <u>Learning cooperative communication patterns is vital if you hope to build teamwork</u>. Competent communicators show sensitivity to other team members by working to establish a noncompetitive climate. Consequently, I will devote the next section to a detailed discussion of defensive (competitive) versus supportive (cooperative) communication and how it influences group climate.

 SECOND LOOK

Structuring Teamwork

Interdependence
- Establish cooperative goal structure (interdependent individual/group goals)
- Develop interdependent division of labor and resources

Equality
- Avoid winner-take-all reward distribution
- Avoid equity reward distribution
- Share rewards equally among group members

Participation
- Establish participative decision making on important issues
- Give teams decision-making autonomy
- Value, encourage, and respect group members' participation

Individual Accountability
- Keep groups small—discourages loafing
- Employ plan to stop social loafing (see Chapter Three)
- Establish minimum standards of performance—denial of rewards

Cooperative Communication Patterns
- Avoid defensive communication patterns
- Encourage supportive communication patterns

DEFENSIVE VERSUS SUPPORTIVE CLIMATES

Certain communication patterns encourage a competitive, defensive atmosphere and other communication patterns promote a cooperative, supportive climate. Competent communicators look for ways to make groups work. As you'll see in this section, defensive communication patterns impede while supportive communication patterns enhance group effectiveness.

Focus Questions

1. In what ways do defensive communication patterns adversely affect groups?
2. In what ways do supportive communication patterns enhance groups?

Defensive versus Supportive Communication

Jack Gibb (1961), in an eight-year study of groups, identified specific communication patterns that both increase and lessen defensiveness. They are

Defensive	Supportive
1. Evaluation	1. Description
2. Control	2. Problem orientation
3. Strategy	3. Spontaneity
4. Neutrality	4. Empathy
5. Superiority	5. Equality
6. Certainty	6. Provisionalism

As I discuss each of these communication patterns, see if you recognize any of them in your own experience with groups.

Evaluation versus Description   I survived the 1989 Loma Prieta earthquake in Santa Cruz County, California. A 7.1 magnitude temblor can rearrange your house in unusual ways. Spaghetti sauce, Italian dressing, honey, olive oil, ground coffee, and generous quantities of shattered glass, china, and dishware make an odd and sticky amalgamation on your kitchen floor.

A friend of mine was in his townhouse when the earthquake hit. Objects flew across the rooms, kitchen cabinets emptied onto the counters and floor, and glass shattered throughout his home. When the fifteen seconds of rocking and rolling to Mother Nature's syncopation subsided, a momentary quiet ensued. Then from the back room came the timid, frightened little voice of his five-year-old daughter: "Daddy, it wasn't my fault."

We live in a society that manifests a propensity for evaluating others, and we are quick to defend ourselves even when no evaluation is offered. One study revealed that 97 percent of nurse managers and 96 percent of staff nurses reported experiencing verbal abuse, a potent form of evaluation. Although the sources of verbal abuse of nurses come from physicians, patients, patients' families, and peers, nurses are most affected by abuse from physicians. A quarter of the annual turnover rate for both nurse managers and staff nurses is attributable to verbal abuse from doctors (Cox, 1991). As Helen Cox (1987), associate dean of nursing education at Texas Tech University, observes, "Verbal abuse is so prevalent in nursing that it is surprising that any of us stay in nursing" (p. 50).

We tend to be more sensitive to negative feedback than positive feedback (Hamachek, 1982), although sometimes even positive evaluations in the form of praise can make us defensive when offered with an ulterior motive attached or presented in a condescending manner. Unsolicited criticism that denigrates another person invites retaliation, not change. It is inappropriate, insensitive communication. Imagine how you would respond if someone, especially a stranger, volunteered that you needed to lose weight. A friend of mine has a standard retort when someone offers comment on her weight: "I may be fat, but you're stupid and only one of us has any hope of changing." Most of us don't take criticism lightly.

Who criticizes us, stranger or loved one, for instance, does make a difference regarding whether we are likely to be defensive when evaluated. A study in West Germany (in "Ditch hubby," 1989) revealed that 86.5 percent of the women surveyed "willingly accept" criticisms from their best female friends. Another survey by Simmons Market Research Bureau/Bright Enterprises (in "Criticism that hurts," 1989) revealed that people most resent criticism from their spouse's parents, followed closely behind by criticism from their mates, then criticism from a subordinate at work. Men resent criticism from their children more than women do. What is criticized also influences our level of defensiveness. The Simmons survey revealed that respondents were most hurt by criticism questioning their integrity.

Evaluation clearly promotes a defensive climate in groups, especially when group members seem to be ganging up on an individual member. Description, however, acts as a kind of antidote to evaluation and promotes a supportive climate. So how do we become more descriptive in our communication with group members?

There are three primary steps necessary to become more descriptive. First, use what Narcisco and Burkett (1975) refer to as *"first person singular" language*. First person singular uses I-statements, not you- or we-statements at the beginning of the sentence. Typically, first person singular statements begin with an identification of the speaker's feeling, followed by a description of behavior linked to the feeling. "I feel excluded and isolated when my contributions receive no response from the group" is an example of a first person singular descriptive statement. Such an I-statement focuses the attention on the person speaking. A you-statement, however, places the focus on someone who is an object of attack. "You have excluded me from the group and you make me feel isolated" is a statement dipped in the acidic juices of accusation and blame. Finger-pointing invites defensive reactions and abusive conflict.

First person singular statements require each of us to take responsibility for our feelings and to *own* our assertions from the very start. You cannot reasonably contradict a first person singular statement unless you have an indication that the person is not being honest with you. "I feel overwhelmed" doesn't warrant a "No you don't" response. In fact, denying what someone else feels sounds ludicrous. Imagine how strange it would sound if you shared with your group, "I am unhappy with our group performance and worried that we will receive a low grade on our term project," and were then told, "You just think you're unhappy and worried, but trust us, you really aren't."

You-statements most often lead to heated denials. "You've upset the entire group by showing up late for all of our meetings" will likely produce a defensive denial, "No I haven't. No one seems to care whether I'm alive or dead."

Second, *make your descriptions specific, not vague.* "I feel weird when you act inappropriately around my boss," is an inexact description. "Weird" and "inappropriately" require specific elaboration. Get to the point. "I feel awkward and embarrassed when you tell my boss jokes that ridicule gays and women," is much more specific.

Third, *eliminate editorial comments* from descriptive statements. This is perhaps the most challenging step. Some I-statements are undisguised personal assaults. "I feel ashamed when you act like a social retard in front of my colleagues" uses the I-statement form without the supportive intent or phrasing. Even an I-statement that may appear to be a specific description devoid of judgment sometimes inadvertently travels into evaluative territory. "I get irritated when you waste the time of this committee by commenting on trivial side issues, and you change the topic before we have had a chance to discuss the issues," loads the statement with provocative phrasing. "Waste time" and "trivial" retain the evaluative and attack elements likely to induce defensive responses. Simply jettison the loaded language.

Need I do more than mention the obvious futility of viewing descriptive statements as some magic formula for building a supportive group climate? Textbook-perfect first person singular statements induce no supportive climate if the tone of voice used is sarcastic or condescending, eye contact is threatening, facial expressions and body language are intimidating, and gestures are abusive. We must be willing and able to place the focus on our own feelings and spotlight the specific behaviors we find objectionable without sending mixed messages composed of verbal descriptions and nonverbal evaluations.

Control versus Problem Orientation   In the fall of 1989, a remarkable event took place in full view of the international community of nations. That stark symbol of repression, the Berlin Wall, began to crumble with the acquiescence of the East German government. Faced with intractable economic problems and social upheaval the likes of which had never been seen since Germany was severed in two after World War II, the East German leadership loosened travel restrictions to the West (openness and change go hand in hand). Hundreds of thousands of East Germans danced on the wall and celebrated their newly acquired freedom to travel into West Germany. Sections of the wall were removed by construction workers. More than a million East Germans poured into the West during a single weekend. Most did not remain, but many would return for additional visits, heady with the experience of their newly acquired travel privileges. The jackboot of repression had finally been lifted off the throat of East Germans when the onslaught of human desire for freedom became unstoppable.

Samuel Butler once said, "He who agrees against his will, is of the same opinion still." The human need for individual freedom is so universal that Jack Brehm (1972) developed a theory of psychological reactance to explain our resistance to efforts aimed at controlling our behavior and limiting our personal freedom to choose for ourselves how to live our lives. Simply put, psychological reactance means the more someone tries to control us and restrict our choices, the more we are inclined to resist such efforts, especially if we feel entitled to our freedom to choose. If the pressure becomes intense, we may be strongly attracted to that which is prohibited. The following bit of wisdom captures this well: There are three ways to make sure something gets done—do it yourself; hire someone to do it; forbid your kids to do it (in Landers, 1995).

Tell someone they can't do something and, typically, it is what they want to do most. Levine (1984), in his fifteen-year study of "radical groups" involving more than a thousand subjects, concluded that the coercive practice of deprogramming individuals who join cults "can drive young people back into their group, or into a pattern of cult-hopping, for years" (p. 27). Conversely, tell group members that they must do something and they will resist. Worchel and Brehm (1971) found that 83 percent of the members of a group refused to go along with one of their members who said, "I think it's pretty obvious all of us are going to work on task A."

The competitive battle for control in groups is not a one-way process. In some cases the gauntlet is thrown down by the person who initiates the interaction. In other cases control is communicated by those who respond to the initial message. A tangential or interrupting response can be disconfirming and both may exhibit an effort to control conversations (Sieberg and Larson, 1971). A tangential response minimally acknowledges what the speaker had to say, then steers the conversation in another direction. An interruption steps into the middle of a speaker's statement and may maneuver the conversation in a different direction.

<u>We help prevent a defensive climate from emerging when we collaborate on a problem and seek solutions cooperatively</u>. The orientation is on the problem and how best to solve it, not on how best to control those who have less power. The problem needs to have a kind of separateness from the individuals involved. Personality conflicts and power struggles have to fade into the background while the spotlight illuminates the problem, and the solution is explored by all parties together in a collaborative effort.

When labor and management sit down at the bargaining table, both parties must lay aside their personal differences in order to tackle the issues that need to be resolved. If one side begins by demanding concessions from the other side, a competitive framework emerges and resistance to the power play will almost certainly result. If both sides decide to approach the negotiations as a collaborative problem-solving challenge, however, a cooperative framework can emerge. In this spirit the challenge becomes how best to satisfy the needs of both parties, not how to satisfy one party at the expense of the other.

Despite the recent encouraging trend away from emphasis on controlling employees in the workplace toward a more problem-solving approach manifested by greater participation by employees in the decision-making process, old patterns die hard. One study (Fairhurst et al., 1984) found that when supervisors are faced with poor employee performance, controlling, not problem-solving strategies predominate.

Wanting to be less controlling and more problem solving is not the complete answer. The competent communicator must know how to problem solve, have the requisite skills, and be committed to finding solutions. More will be said on problem solving and how to develop a problem orientation in later chapters.

Strategy versus Spontaneity   The experience of buying a new car is a trial for me. I loathe the initial fake friendliness from the salesperson. I recoil when the salesperson starts in with the transparent compliments (e.g., "You look like a smart guy" or "You strike me as the kind of guy who can spot a steal when you see one"). I retreat (usually out of the showroom entirely) when the auto hucksters try to double-team me, one on each side, with their transparent stereophonic sales pitch.

Most people resent and resist being manipulated. If you are like most people, simply knowing that someone is attempting to influence you for his or her own benefit is repellant. If you suspect that dishonesty is part of the stratagem, you are probably doubly put off.

Hidden agendas, those personal goals of group members that are not revealed openly, can create a defensive atmosphere when members suspect that there is a conflict between individual and group goals. I have seen several efforts by part-time instructors to denigrate other part-timers with greater seniority while at the same time trying to bolster their own image. These part-time instructors consistently camouflaged their competitive strategy to gain a more favorable position in the departmental pecking order as just their concern for the students' education and their desire to improve the department. All of these attempts have backfired. Members of the department, full-time and part-time, have uniformly resented the manipulative ploys. Their strategy was seen as disruptive to the department, creating conflict and intrigue where none needed to exist. In one instance, the offending instructor was terminated.

Inoculation theories on resistance to persuasion (Smith, 1982, and Trenholm, 1989) add another factor to the defensive equation. Not only do we recoil from deceitful, self-oriented efforts to influence us, but the mere knowledge that someone plans to try to influence us at all can put us on the defensive. When we anticipate that someone will try to change our attitudes and beliefs on a subject, especially if it is an important one to us, we resist. If forewarned, we will build our defenses in the form of counterarguments to fend off the attack.

Petty and Cacioppo's cognitive response theory claims that forewarning is a primary factor in the resistance to influence process. In two studies, Petty and Cacioppo (1977) gave students a three-minute and a five-and-a-quarter-minute forewarning of an impending influence attempt. The first attempt was on the issue of student housing and the second was on the issue of a comprehensive examination in a student's declared major. In both cases, students who were forewarned of the influence attempt and given a short time to mount an argumentative defense exhibited substantial resistance to the influence effort. A comparative group of students not forewarned, however, showed considerable acceptance of the persuasive message. Not only do coercive attempts to control us produce defensiveness, but even noncoercive influence attempts incline us toward resistance.

Gibb (1961) calls for spontaneity as the answer to strategic communication. I consider the term ill chosen for two reasons. First, how do you manufacture spontaneity, and if you do, is that not strategic? I can just imagine people concerned about developing supportive communication patterns muttering to themselves, "Be spontaneous." My point is simple. You can't be spontaneous on command. To argue that spontaneity is the antidote to strategic communication misleads us into the mistaken notion that we can will spontaneity into existence. Spontaneity just happens because it feels appropriate at the moment. Planned spontaneity is an oxymoron, a contradictory term.

My second objection to using the term spontaneity is that it can also mean off-the-top-of-your-head, ill-conceived, inappropriate remarks—the kind that a competent communicator would edit. Impulsive behavior doesn't seem like a useful model for competent communication.

What Gibb seems to be calling for is not so much spontaneity, but instead directness and honesty. If we are straightforward with others they will often be straightforward with us. In my own experience, I have noticed that people are sometimes taken aback by directness at first, but they soon adjust to it. Usually they will reciprocate in kind, if not sooner, often later. In any case, straightforwardness sends a clear message: DON'T PLAY GAMES WITH ME. I DON'T LIKE IT. In the long run, defensiveness is reduced by a consistent, straightforward pattern of communication. How to be straightforward without being hostile or sounding threatening will be discussed when I outline the essential elements of assertiveness in Chapter Nine.

Neutrality versus Empathy   We like being acknowledged when we are present in a group. We dislike being treated like a piece of the furniture, sitting alone in a corner. Indifference to group members, or what Gibb calls neutrality, makes us defensive. Making little or no effort to listen to what a member of your group has to say exhibits indifference and treats the communicator as a nonperson. Allowing a group member to become an isolate can easily result in the isolate's alienation from and rejection of the group. If no one in the group seems to care what the isolated person has to say, why should that person contribute to the group at all?

When parents ignore their child's requests, questions, or comments, the child feels unvalued. Such communication is called an **impervious response** (Sieberg and Larson, 1971). Failure to even acknowledge another person's communication effort either verbally or nonverbally treats that individual as a nonperson. Such indifference is disconfirming. Failure to return phone calls, write letters, or send cards and presents at Christmas or on birthdays all communicate an indifference.

An **irrelevant response** also communicates an indifference and is disconfirming (Sieberg and Larson, 1971). A committee member says, "I think I know what we should do to increase productivity," only to be met with the irrelevant question from the committee chair, "Did you pick up the applicant files from personnel?" A teenager asks her parents for advice on a personal matter and is irrelevantly queried about her choice of attire. Such responses communicate an insensitivity to the other person's needs—a Me-not-We orientation.

You counter indifference with empathy. Howell (1982) defines empathy as "thinking and feeling what you *perceive* another to be thinking and feeling (p. 108)." Empathy is built on sensitivity to others, a quality of the competent communicator. Empathy requires that we deal with what we perceive to be the needs, desires, and feelings of group members because that is what we would want others to do for us. "How would you like it if I treated you the way you treat me?" is a plea for empathy from others.

Rosenfeld (1983) determined that creating a supportive climate in the college classroom was a key determinant of whether classes would be liked or not by students. Liked classes are characterized by instructor behaviors that are predominantly empathic. These behaviors include showing interest in the problems students face, exhibiting a perception of subject matter as students see it, and making students feel that the instructor understands students. Showing that we understand and relate does make a difference.

Superiority versus Equality   A superior attitude is a turn-off for most people. Treating employees with contempt, for example, wins no friends but it certainly can induce defensiveness. Studs Terkel (1972), in his book *Working*, provides this description by a steelworker of a superior attitude in action:

> This one foreman I've got, he's a kid. He's a college graduate. He thinks he's better than everybody else. He was chewing me out and I was saying, "Yeah, yeah, yeah." He said, "What do you mean, yeah, yeah, yeah. Yes, *sir*." I told him, "Who the hell are you, Hitler? . . . I came here to work, I didn't come here to crawl. . . . " One word led to another and I lost. I got broke down to a lower grade and lost twenty-five cents an hour, which is a hell of a lot. It amounts to about ten dollars a week. He came over—after breaking me down. The guy comes over and smiles at me. I blew up. He didn't know, but he was about two seconds and two feet away from a hospital. (p. xxxii)

The Rosenfeld (1983) study on defensiveness in the college classroom underscores the experience of the steelworker and his antipathy for the superior attitude of his foreman. Behavior of instructors in disliked classes are characterized as predominantly superior. "My teacher makes me feel we are not intelligent" was one of the key factors attributed to disliked classes. One of the key factors characterizing liked classes was "My teacher treats us as equals with him/her."

Whatever the differences in our abilities, talents, intellect, and the like, treating people with respect and politeness, as equals on a human level, encourages harmony and productivity. Treating people like they are IRS agents at the awards ceremony for the state lottery winner will invite enmity and retaliation.

Equality does not mean we all have the same abilities. Equality from the standpoint of group climate means that we give everyone an equal opportunity to succeed. We accord all group members respect unless they earn our disrespect. We do not make people feel stupid. Despite variability in talent, ability, achievements, money, and so forth, we do not make issues of these differences in the group. We do not sabotage the efforts of one person in the group by demeaning that member as inferior. Task accomplishment is thwarted by diminishing the self-esteem of any member. The diminishment of even one member may send a systemwide message to all members—you could be the next target. *Be on guard.*

Certainty versus Provisionalism   There are very few things in this world that are certain—death, taxes, and that your clothes dryer will eat your socks. Communicating certainty to group members, however, is asking for trouble. I listened to students in my class argue with one of their group members who insisted that crystals really do have healing powers and that only pig-headedness kept the group from accepting the truth of what he was adamantly asserting. This individual would entertain no contrary point of view, so certain was he of the unalterable correctness of his belief, nor would he accede to requests from members for hard evidence of crystal healing power. He was certain he was right and anyone who couldn't accept this truth must be stupid. This was dogmatism in action.

Dogmatism is the belief in the self-evident truth of one's opinion. The dogma, or declaration of truth, warrants no debate in the mind of the dogmatist. A dogmatic individual exhibits closed-mindedness and rigid thinking. Alternative ideas are not seriously considered. Interestingly, the word dogma spelled backwards is *am-god*. Dogmatists act god-like in the certitude of their own point of view. These self-appointed deities can easily inflame the tempers of group members. Some people derive pleasure from trying to prove the dogmatist wrong. Competitive contests fought over assertions of truth by dogmatists and their antagonists can degenerate into adolescent bickering.

Leathers (1970) conducted a study where typical dogmatic statements were introduced into group discussions. The five statements used were:

1. That's a ridiculous statement. I disagree.
2. Are you serious in taking such an absurd position?
3. You are wrong. Dead wrong!
4. I don't understand why I ever agreed with you.
5. That's downright foolish.

Subjects responded to these statements of certitude (and evaluation) with increased tension (e.g., rubbing hands together nervously and squirming in their seats). These statements also elicited opinionated statements from group members. A climate of inflexibility was produced and trust among group members deteriorated.

A provisional or flexible attitude is an effective substitute for dogmatism. As previously noted, the competent communicator must remain flexible and adapt to changes in the system. You approach problems in groups as issues to be investigated. You remain open to possibilities and options that you may not have explored.

Provisionalism does not require you to be open to nonsense, however. I'm not suggesting that you should entertain flat-earth-type arguments and points of view. Some issues have been settled for all practical purposes and necessitate no further discussion unless startlingly new evidence surfaces challenging accepted beliefs. As I indicated earlier, a system can be too open and endanger your well-being. Let others speak their piece. Encourage contributions from all group members. Discuss issues thoroughly, but beware the absolute statement.

Reciprocal Patterns

Defensive communication from one group member can provoke like communication from other group members. The same is also true of supportive communication. Since communication is transactional, how one party communicates affects how other parties in the group communicate. Incompetent communication can produce similarly deficient communication from others. Competent communication can likewise encourage the same from group members.

If you disparage others, they will more than likely retaliate in kind. One such famous verbal parry and thrust occurred between Lady Astor, the first female member of the British Parliament, and Winston Churchill. Exasperated by Churchill's opposition to several of the causes she espoused, Lady Astor acerbically remarked, "Winston, if I were married to you, I'd put poison in your coffee." Churchill replied, "And if you were my wife, I'd drink it" (in Fadiman, 1985, p. 122). Verbal attack begets verbal attack.

The moment we begin to interact with another person we establish a communication climate. Once this climate develops, it can set in motion a reciprocal pattern—like begets like (Adler, Rosenfeld, and Towne, 1989). One study (Burggraf and Sillars, 1987) found that supportive/confirming communication patterns by one party during a conflict elicited similar responses from the other party. The same held true for defensive/disconfirming communication patterns. Sundell (1972) verified this in a study of junior high school teachers and students. Confirming teachers were confirmed by their students while disconfirming teachers were disconfirmed by their students.

The challenge in any group experience is to maintain the positive reciprocal pattern of support and confirmation and to break the cycle of the negative reciprocal pattern of defensiveness and disconfirmation. <u>The maintenance of the social relationships within your group is a vital process</u>. As I indicated in the previous chapter, the interconnection between the task and social dimensions of a group is inextricable. If members of your group fail to create a positive supportive climate, task accomplishment will be jeopardized and conflict will be aroused.

A positive reciprocal pattern of support and cooperation must emerge from the communication transactions among group members. Group leaders may play an important role in this process by setting the tone for the group. If the leader exhibits competitiveness, the group will likely compete. If the leader has the ability and authority to structure cooperation into the group process, then group members will more likely cooperate than compete. The responsibility, however, for establishing a positive group climate rests on all group members. Norms of cooperation emerge from patterns of group interaction. You must encourage cooperation, suggest ways to cooperate rather than compete, discourage competitive communication patterns, and model the appropriate communication behavior for a positive climate to develop. These behaviors are part of how the competent communicator demonstrates a commitment to the group.

⊙⊙ CLOSER LOOK

The Robbers Cave Experiment

Social psychologist Muzafer Sherif and his colleagues conducted studies in 1949, 1953, and 1954 on intergroup conflict and cooperation (Sherif, 1966). These studies are noteworthy because they took place in a natural environment (campsites in remote areas), not in a laboratory setting, and because the magnitude of the endeavor has never since been duplicated (Sherif et al., 1988). Many experiments have since confirmed the findings of these three studies (Brewer, 1979, and Brewer & Miller, 1984), but not one of these efforts by itself was nearly as ambitious in scope.

The 1954 study, commonly referred to as the Robbers Cave experiment in reference to the Oklahoma state park where it was conducted, is the most important of the three experiments. The subjects were twenty-two eleven-year-old boys from established middle-class Protestant families. Two groups of eleven boys apiece were formed by the experimenters and matched on the basis of observed skills and athletic ability. The reduction of intergroup tension and conflict was the primary focus of this study.

The experiment had three stages. Stage One brought the two groups of boys to the campsite on separate days. Neither group even saw each other until the end of the first week. Activities and problem situations with common appeal to the boys that necessitated interdependent action were created to induce cooperation within each group. Toward the end of the first week, each group adopted a team name. One called itself the *Rattlers* and the other designated itself the *Eagles*.

Stage Two was the friction phase. The two groups were brought together to participate in a tournament. Competitive events in the tournament included several tug-of-war contests, baseball games, a touch football game, tent pitching, cabin inspections judged by staff members, a skits and songs contest, and a treasure hunt. Prizes were awarded to the winning team based on accumulated points.

Stage Three was the friction-reducing phase. This stage had two parts. First, the Rattlers and the Eagles came in contact with each other in situations varying in duration from fifteen minutes to an hour. These situations were meant to test the effects of pleasant contacts on intergroup conflict. The second part introduced goals that were compelling for both groups, the attainment of which was beyond the efforts and resources of either group alone. Sherif referred to these as **superordinate goals.** The staff sabotaged the water supply to encourage the two groups to pitch in together and discover the source of the problem. A copy of *Treasure Island* was rented after both groups pooled their money to secure the film. The Eagles and Rattlers worked together to help start a stalled truck used to bring in food supplies. All of the boys had to pull on a rope attached to the truck. This tug-of-war with the truck was required on more than one occasion.

The results of this study were many and varied. First, when the Eagles and the Rattlers, physically separated from each other, worked interdependently on goals with common appeal value within their groups (e. g., learning to pitch a tent, make meals, and an unplanned group effort to kill a copperhead snake eight feet from the campfire), cooperation was promoted. This cooperation, however, did not transfer to intergroup relations. The realization that a second group was present at another part of the campsite immediately induced a "them versus us" mentality.

When the competitive interactions between the two groups commenced, conflict escalated. Boys on both teams took the tournament extremely seriously. Both sides prayed for victory.

The tournament produced reciprocal patterns of attack-counterattack. Competition produced aggression and hostility, even hatred. Name-calling and invective became standard practice. The Eagles and Rattlers hurled insults back and forth. They called each other "cowards," "yellow bellies," "stinkers," "braggarts," "sissies," "little babies," even "communists" and "nigger campers." Evaluation was met with counter-evaluation, insult with insult. Assertions of superiority ("Our pitcher's better than yours") were immediately countered ("Our catcher's better than yours").

The competitive phase of this experiment provoked territoriality. Both groups made frequent reference to "our diamond," "our swimming hole," "our Upper Camp," and the like. The Rattlers tried to lay claim to the ball field by placing "their flag" on the backstop. It was burned later by the Eagles. Fist-fights broke out and challenges to fight were frequent. Both groups raided each others' cabin, turning over beds, ripping screens off windows, and stealing personal possessions. One member of the Eagles, just prior to the tournament, expressed the opinion that "maybe we could make friends with those guys and then somebody would not get mad and have any grudges" (in Sherif et al., 1988, p. 98). During the tournament this same individual became one of the most enthusiastic name-callers. A competitive system produces competitive individuals.

During the final stage of the experiment, mere contact in pleasurable activities did not reduce the friction and antagonism between the two warring groups. In fact, these contact situations merely provided additional opportunities for both groups to wage war on each other. Putting the Eagles and Rattlers together in the mess hall produced several food fights. Whenever the Rattlers entered a building ahead of the Eagles, they were taunted with the remark, "Ladies first."

The establishment of superordinate goals succeeded where mere contact failed. At first, the boys returned to bickering and name-calling following their joint effort. Gradually, however, their hostility diminished as they worked together for the common good. Members of both groups began to intermingle. At a joint campfire, one of the Rattlers performed his Donald Duck imitation for the Eagles and was received with great enthusiasm. The Eagles responded with their own "spitball act." The evening ended with both groups singing their favorite songs. On the last day, the Rattlers took their $5 won earlier in one of the contests and bought everyone, Eagles and Rattlers alike, malts at a refreshment stand.

The Eagles and Rattlers pursue superordinate goals.

A comparison of friendship choices by members of both groups graphically shows how successful superordinate goals were in reducing friction and promoting cooperation. At the end of Stage Two (friction phase), only 6.4 percent of the Rattlers identified members of the Eagles as their friends. At the end of Stage Three (friction-reducing), this figure had increased to 36.4 percent. Among the Eagles, the figures were 7.5 percent after Stage Two and 23.3 percent at the end of Stage Three. Perhaps even more impressive were the unfavorability ratings of the former ''enemies.'' At the end of Stage Two, 53 percent of the Rattlers' ratings of the Eagles were unfavorable but only 4.5 percent were unfavorable after Stage Three. Similarly, 76.9 percent of the Eagles' ratings of the Rattlers were unfavorable after Stage Two. After Stage Three, however, only 22.6 percent were unfavorable (Sherif et al., 1988).

Clearly, when groups perceive advantages to cooperating, they will cooperate. Sherif (In Trotter, 1985) sums up the essence of this remarkable study: ''In short, hostility gives way when groups pull together to achieve overriding, superordinate goals which are real and compelling to all concerned'' (p. 59).

Questions for Thought

1. Do you think the results of the Robbers Cave experiment would have been similar if the subjects had been eleven- and twelve-year-old girls? Adults? Why?
2. Can superordinate goals be established to prevent or resolve any conflict?
3. Can you think of examples where intergroup rivalry such as occurred in this experiment produced similar results? Different results?
4. Do you think the results of this study would be the same if the experiment was replicated today?

DEALING WITH DIFFICULT GROUP MEMBERS

Unfortunately, it is not uncommon to have a member of a group who hasn't learned supportive communication patterns or who chooses competitive defensive patterns regardless. Such an individual can prevent a group from operating as a cohesive, fully functioning team. Gouran (1988) notes, "Disruptive behavior perhaps is the one occurrence with which the average participant in a decision-making or problem-solving group feels least equipped to cope" (p. 202). There are several fundamental steps that should be taken by the group when dealing with a difficult member.

First, <u>make certain your own house is in order</u>. Has the group made a genuine effort to create a supportive, noncompetitive climate? If not, then refrain from looking for scapegoats to blame for group disharmony and conflict. The problem is you. Get busy and clean up your environment. You can hardly expect others to be supportive and cooperative when you haven't made the effort either.

Second, <u>stop wishing that difficult individuals were different</u>. This is wasted energy. Chronic behaviors have been learned usually over long periods of time. If your disruptive member is a bigot, don't expect to change him or her into a generous, open-minded person. Change *your* communication in relation to that person's difficult behavior. Communication in groups is a transaction operating within a system. What one party does affects the other parties. You may change the troublemaker's behavior toward the group even though you will not likely change him or her from a difficult person into a likable one. So how do you act in relation to the difficult member so the problem person becomes less of a disruption? Consider the next step.

Third, <u>try not to encourage the disruption</u>. Groups unwittingly encourage the disrupter in several common ways. Avoid the following:

a. *Don't placate the troublemaker.* Laughing nervously when the disrupter cracks sexist or racist jokes or makes offensive remarks about group members merely encourages further moronic behavior. Staring at the disrupter in dead silence, however, can be intimidating. When the entire group does it, even the most obnoxious individual can be induced to reconsider the inappropriate behavior. Permitting frequent interruptions from the offending party, enduring this ploy for conversational control, is a strategy of appeasement with little potential for success. Allowing the disrupter to manipulate the group in order to "keep the peace" rewards the troublemaker for objectionable behavior.

b. *Refuse to be goaded into a reciprocal pattern.* Resist the very real temptation to meet firepower with firepower. Don't counter abusive remarks with abusive remarks of your own. <u>Be unconditionally constructive</u> (Ury, 1991). Disrupters thrive on provoking retaliation. Your insistence that the dogmatist is "completely wrong" will only brand you as sounding just as dogmatic and unyielding. Becoming aggressive with aggressors escalates into intractable power struggles. Meeting dominance with dominance invites a tug-of-war. So don't take the bait. Keep telling yourself that if you do, you're engaging them on their terms and on their familiar ground, to your disadvantage. Resisting the temptation to "fight fire with fire" requires self-control (and in some cases deserves a medal of commendation). Consciously resisting the natural desire to match the behavior of an obstreperous individual won't be easy. In some extreme cases it won't be possible.

c. *Have an out-of-body experience* (Lulofs, 1994). Remove yourself mentally from the conflict. Listen to the disrupter as if you were an uninvolved third party with no energy in the outcome. Picture yourself as a mediator whose job it is to resolve the problem.

d. *Don't provide a soapbox for the troublemaker.* On two occasions in my teaching career, I have had a disruptive student interrupt me in the middle of a lecture/discussion to complain about the class. On the first occasion, I handled the situation poorly. My difficult student blurted out in a loud voice, "Can we do something relevant for a change? I'm tired of discussing other people's problems." I mistakenly took the bait and tried to carry on a dialogue with this person in front of the entire class. I began justifying what I had been doing in the class. Not surprisingly, he was unmoved by my response and undeterred in his obnoxious behavior. He was more than happy to mount the soapbox and focus attention on his personal agenda. The rest of the class became restless and annoyed with this interruption. I felt angry and ineffectual.

On the second occasion, my disrupter demanded to know why I was "wasting so much time on the relationship between gender and communication patterns." In this instance, I immediately deferred to the entire class. I put it to the class directly, "Do the rest of you agree that this is a waste of time?" When they indicated that they did not, I then asked the class, "Do you want to take class time to discuss his complaint?" They again indicated that they did not. With the support of the group, I then deferred a confrontation with this student until after the class was over. He was ill-prepared to challenge the entire group. Notice, however, that I said *deferred* the confrontation. You can't ignore disruptive behavior especially when it becomes chronic.

Fourth, <u>attempt to convert disruption into a constructive contribution</u> (Gouran, 1988). Suppose in the middle of a group discussion your disrupter blurts out, "That's a completely stupid suggestion, but typical of a woman" (I didn't say this was going to be easy). You could reply in kind, thereby setting in motion a reciprocal pattern of derision. Instead, you could attempt to divert the disrupter away from abusive remarks and toward constructive contributions to the group by responding, "Perhaps you could provide a better suggestion." This response does not invite your obnoxious member to mount a soapbox and launch into an irrelevant monologue. You are requesting a pertinent contribution. Bell's (1974) research indicates that substantive comments in a group discussion encourage a focus on content not on relationship conflicts. Disrupters are less likely to continue their abuse when they are focused on the substance of the discussion. If the disrupter does not respond appropriately to your invitation to be constructive, then you can proceed to the next step.

Fifth, <u>confront the difficult person directly</u>. If the entire group is upset by the behavior of the difficult person, then the *group* should confront the disrupter. Even truly abrasive individuals whose behavior seems to indicate a complete lack of regard for the group will find it tough to ignore pressure from group members. Confrontations, of course, should be descriptive not evaluative.

Even when there is a power disparity, such as when your supervisor in your work group is the difficult person, confrontation is important. If you are suffering constant criticism and it demoralizes you, let your boss know that less criticism and more encouragement will likely result in higher productivity from you. There is, of course, one last step that you may have to take if none of the above steps proves to be fruitful.

Sixth, <u>separate yourself from the difficult person if all else fails</u>. Communication is not a panacea for every problem that comes up in groups. Some individuals leave no other option except ostracism (a competitive choice) by the group. Removing the troublesome individual is one way of ridding the group of the disruption. If the difficult person is powerful, however, ostracism may not be an option. In this case, try putting physical distance between you and the problem person. Stay out of each other's way whenever possible. Keep interactions to a minimum. In a few instances, you may have to leave the group in order to restore your sanity. Some jobs, for instance, are just not worth keeping when abuse is heaped on you daily by an individual with more power than you have.

 **SECOND LOOK**

Dealing with Difficult Group Members

Make certain your own house is in order
Stop wishing difficult individuals were different
Don't encourage the disruption
• Don't placate troublemakers
• Refuse to be goaded into a reciprocal pattern (tit-for-tat)
• Have an out-of-body experience—become a "third party observer"
• Don't provide a soapbox for troublemakers
Try to convert disruption into a constructive contribution
Confront the difficult group member directly
Separate yourself from the difficult group member if all else fails

Let me include an addendum to this plan for dealing with difficult group members. I have presented you with a rational model for handling troublemakers. I encourage you to try these methods. I am confident that they will work well for you. Nevertheless, we are not strictly rational beings. Difficult people can provoke intense anger and deep frustration from group members. In my own experience, I have found that even if I lost my temper and let my emotions get the better of me, this response is not as problematic as simply ignoring or enduring the disruptive behavior. Even if your anger translates into personal attacks, at the very least you have served notice on the troublesome group member that his or her pattern of behavior is unacceptable and will not be suffered in silence.

I do not counsel emotional explosions as a means to resolving conflicts with difficult individuals, yet I know that occasionally we give in to our impulses. Sometimes it just feels s-o-o-o-o-o g-o-o-o-o-d to tell off our tormentors. If you do lose your self-control, at least follow up at a later time with direct confrontation. You may find that your initial outburst got the attention of your troublemaker. A more rational, deliberate strategy may still work even after a shouting match.

In summary, there is perhaps no greater challenge nor more important task in a group than establishing a positive, cooperative climate. A negative, competitive climate will bode ill for your group. Defensive climates promote conflict and disharmony in groups. Supportive climates do not free groups entirely from conflict, but such an atmosphere enhances the likelihood of constructive solutions to conflict in groups.

QUESTIONS FOR CRITICAL THINKERS

1. Why do you think supervisors faced with poor employee performance use predominantly controlling, not problem-solving, strategies?
2. Are there instances when you should act as a model of cooperative behavior even though other group members will take advantage of you?

Roles and Leadership in Groups

In a study of a surgical team at St. Joseph's Hospital in Ann Arbor, Michigan, the distinction between the role of doctor and nurse was evident. During a coronary bypass operation, the two surgeons (both males) began swapping stories about the Detroit Tigers while loud rock music played in the background. Two nurses (both women) assisting with the operation began a quiet discussion of their own, only to be reprimanded by the head surgeon, who bellowed, "Come on people, let's keep it down in here" (Denison and Sutton, 1990, p. 301). Nurses did not have the same leeway to talk, laugh, and joke with each other as did surgeons. Surgeons, by necessity, were in charge of the operation. Surgeons were in the leader role and nurses were in the follower role, expected to do the bidding of the surgeons without question. Surgical teams have clearly defined roles. Nurses, nevertheless, complained bitterly that the doctors were unnecessarily oppressive in exercising their superior power (i.e., used defensive communication patterns of control and superiority). Nurses complained that they were "slaves" and often were expected to perform demeaning tasks when ordered by surgeons to do so.

In the drama of life we play many roles. Whatever our roles, communication competence occupies center stage. When individuals fill certain roles, they are expected to behave in certain ways explicitly or implicitly indicated by the group. The group's expectations regarding appropriate role behavior serve as criteria for judging the relative communication competence of members.

Thus, any definition of group roles must be in terms of expectations prevailing among members of a group. Fisher and Ellis (1990) provide such a definition. Their definition of a role is *"a set of communicative behaviors performed by an individual . . . that involves the behaviors performed by one member in light of the expectations that other members hold toward those behaviors"* (p. 203). These expectations serve as boundaries for behavior within the group system.

Individuals act out their roles in transactions with members of the group. Group members play their respective parts during the periodic phases of group development and in a climate that they create by the nature of their communication. Roles are not static entities. When the composition of your group changes, when phases of development change, when the group climate shifts either toward or away from a cooperative/supportive one, or when you move from one group to another, you have to adapt to these changes in the system. The required behaviors for your role may change as a consequence or the roles members play may have to change.

In this chapter I will discuss roles with special focus on the prime group role of leader. My principal objectives are:

1. to explain the significance of roles in groups,
2. to discuss the role emergence process,
3. to describe how members gain and retain group leadership, and
4. to discuss how to be an effective leader in groups.

GROUP ROLES

Rules (norms) and roles form the basic structure of a group. **Structure** is the systematic interrelation of all parts to the whole. Structure provides form and shape for a group. Rules (norms) and roles interconnect. Whenever a group member adopts a role, certain normative behaviors are expected from the member. What may have begun as a casual or unnoticed pattern of behavior may quickly develop into an expectation. What is becomes what ought to be. You tell a few jokes during the initial meeting of your group. You may have just assumed the role of tension reliever without even noticing. Other group members, however, may come to expect you to interject humor into tense situations. In this section I will discuss the effects of roles on behavior, types of roles, role emergence, and role fixation.

Focus Questions

1. Are there some group roles that the competent communicator should avoid?
2. When two roles conflict, which role is likely to prevail?

Effects of Roles

The expectations attached to roles can "exert a pervasive influence on the perceptions and evaluations of role occupants by others" (Shaw, 1981, 277). This process was demonstrated in a study in which pairs of students performed the roles of questioner and contestant in a college bowl–type quiz game (Ross et al., 1977). Questioners were instructed to think of ten difficult questions for which they knew the answers. They then were to ask contestants these questions. Both students and the audience knew that the roles of questioner and contestant were randomly assigned. Yet, both the audience and the contestants thought that those students playing the questioner role were smarter than those students playing the contestant role. Questioners, of course, looked more impressive asking difficult questions for which they already knew the answers, while contestants looked less impressive trying to answer the questions and sometimes making mistakes. Despite the obvious advantage given to the questioners and despite the fact that students playing both roles were equally intelligent, the predominant perception was markedly influenced by the role each student played.

I have seen the effects of acting out roles in my own classroom. I conduct a simple exercise where I randomly assign roles to individuals in groups. The roles, however, are known to the group but not known to the individuals assigned the roles. The group then works on a task together, adapting to the roles each person is expected to play. When an individual is assigned the role of leader, for example, the group looks to that person for direction. If a person is assigned the role of an isolate, the group ignores that person. Individuals quickly recognize what role they have been assigned.

I have had some very interesting results from this simple exercise. When groups laugh at the "clowns," the clowns usually become instant comics and enjoy the attention. I have seen individuals who have never made a humorous comment in class, become genuinely funny playing the clown role. When "isolates" are ignored they usually struggle to get recognized for a time, then give up in disgust and become an isolate sitting in silence. When "leaders" are looked to for direction, they usually end up leading the group.

On one occasion, I assigned the role of leader to a very shy woman who had never uttered a peep the entire term. An amazing transformation took place. The attention she received from the group initially intimidated her. After a short time, however, she began directing the group toward the accomplishment of its task. She revealed afterward that she had never led a group and it was a heady experience. The group indicated what was expected of her and she responded. Playing a role we are not accustomed to can affect our perceptions of ourselves and the group.

The effects of roles on perceptions can be seen in a dramatic way by doing a **role reversal,** which is stepping into a role distinctly different from or even opposite a role we usually play. In a study (Geis et al., 1984) of the impact of high-status versus low-status roles, the power of role reversal was evident. Viewers of television commercials depicting a man in the high-status important person role (his wishes, needs, and preferences were the central concern of the commercial) and a woman in the relatively low-status helpmate role (her wishes, needs, and preferences were never addressed or acknowledged) described the man as a "rational, independent, dominant, ambitious leader." The woman, by contrast, was described as an "emotional, dependent, submissive, contented follower." A markedly different result from these stereotypic depictions of male-female interactions occurred when the roles were exactly reversed. When the woman in the commercial performed the high-status role and the man acted out the low-status role, viewers described the woman as a "rational, independent, dominant, ambitious leader" and the man as an "emotional, dependent, submissive, contented follower."

Role status, the relative importance, prestige, or power accorded a particular role apparently nurtures stereotypic perceptions of males and females (Hoffman and Hurst, 1990). The implication of this finding is significant. <u>One way to shatter the stereotype that women are followers and not leaders is to reverse roles—place more women in the high-status leadership role and fewer women in the lower-status follower role</u>. Let women be seen more often in power positions and less often in subservient positions. This conclusion would seem to apply to ethnic minorities as well.

The effects of roles can be seen in another way. When we find ourselves playing roles in different groups that contradict each other, we experience **role conflict.** Usually we are forced to make a choice between the two. For instance, when a disastrous fire in the 1950s in Texas City, Texas, endangered the entire city, police officers were faced with a serious role conflict. Should they continue to protect the citizens of the city in their role as police officers, or should they consider their role of parent and spouse as more important. They couldn't do both. In every case except one they chose their family role over their professional role. The exception was a man who knew his family was safe in another city (Killian, 1952). Which role would you choose if faced with such a dilemma?

Similarly, students who have children are often faced with conflict between their student role and their parent role. Do you take the final exam or do you stay home with your sick child? Women with careers and families are concerned increasingly with this perceived role conflict. When a woman is in an important business meeting where colleagues depend on her input and she receives a phone call from her child's school, what does she do? Let me note that the same role conflict could exist for a man as well, but women are still typically cast as the primary caretaker except in single-parent situations. The perception that family demands will intrude upon a woman's work world more than on a man's acts as an impediment to women's advancement in organizations (Haslett et al., 1992).

An extensive review of forty-two studies on role conflict (Fisher and Gitelson, 1983) showed significant effects. When individuals felt role conflict within organizations, they exhibited an increased propensity to leave an organization. They also showed decreases in commitment to the organization, involvement in the job, satisfaction with the job, and participation in decision making.

Some roles have a greater impact on us than others. The role that has the greatest importance and most potent effect on us is usually the one we choose when we have to decide between conflicting roles.

◎◎ CLOSER LOOK

The Stanford Prison Study

It happened one Sunday morning. Police officers with sirens screeching swept through the college town and arrested ten male students. Charged with a felony, they were searched, handcuffed, and taken to police headquarters for booking. Then they were blindfolded and transported to the "Stanford County Prison" located in the basement of the Stanford University psychology building. Upon arrival they were stripped naked, issued a smock-type uniform with an ID number across the front and back, and made to wear a cap made out of nylon to simulate a shaved head. Each prisoner received towels, soap, a toothbrush, and bed linen. Jail cells were sparsely furnished—cots and bucket toilets. Personal belongings were prohibited.

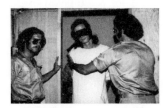

The ten inmates were guarded by eleven college students. These guards carried billy clubs, handcuffs, and whistles. They dressed in khaki uniforms and wore sunglasses to make eye contact impossible. They remained nameless.

Guards established a set of rules that the prisoners were to follow without hesitation or resistance. The rules were rigid: no talking during meals, rest periods, or after lights were out. Head counts were taken at 2:30 A.M. Troublemakers faced loss of "privileges." At first, these privileges included opportunities to read, write, or talk to other inmates. Later, "privileges" were defined as eating, sleeping, and washing.

The inmates revolted against the repressive conditions. Some barricaded the doors of their cells with cots. Some engaged in hunger strikes. Several tore off their ID numbers. The guards became increasingly abusive and authoritarian in response to the revolt. They used a fire extinguisher to quash the rebellion. Punishment for disobedience included cleaning toilets with bare hands, doing push-ups, and spending time in solitary confinement (a closet). Head counts were used as a means of harassment. Head counts took ten minutes or less on the first day. By the fifth day, the head counts lasted several hours as the guards vilified prisoners, who were standing at attention the entire time, for minor infractions of the rules.

Within a short time some of the prisoners began to act depressed, dependent, and disturbed by their incarceration. Several prisoners experienced severe stomach cramps. One prisoner wept uncontrollably. He flew into fits of rage and experienced disorganized thinking and bouts of severe depression. Three other inmates developed similar symptoms. Another inmate developed a psychosomatic rash over his entire body when his "parole" was denied.

The chief form of communication initiated by the guards to the prisoners consisted mostly of commands, insults, verbal and physical abuse, degrading references, and threats. The principal form of communication used by the prisoners when interacting with the guards consisted mostly of resistance and ridicule in the beginning, but became more compliant later (e.g., answering questions and giving information).

Stanford psychologist Phillip Zimbardo (1992), who conducted this mock prison study, terminated the experiment after only six days. The study was originally planned for a two-week period, but he decided that the roles had become real. As Zimbardo (1992) concluded: "In guard roles, college students who had been pacifists and 'nice guys' behaved aggressively—sometimes even sadistically. As prisoners, psychologically stable students soon behaved pathologically, passively resigning themselves to their unexpected fate of learned helplessness" (576).

Zimbardo had taken twenty-one healthy, well-adjusted male students who exhibited no signs of emotional instability or aberrant behavior when given extensive personality tests and clinical interviews prior to the experiment and had transformed them into pathological guards and compliant prisoners. The "guard" and "prisoner" roles were randomly assigned by the flip of a coin, so pathological behavior cannot be explained by looking for character flaws in the men acting as guards. Clearly, the young men in this controversial field study became the product of their designated roles.

Questions for Thought

1. Considering the effects this experiment had upon its subjects, do you have any ethical concerns about conducting similar studies?
2. Can you think of roles outside of a prison environment that exert similar influence and power over individuals' lives as exhibited in this experiment?
3. Would you have preferred to be a prisoner or a guard? Why?
4. As a guard, would you have treated the prisoners abusively? Are you uncertain how you would have behaved? Explain.
5. As a prisoner, would you have been docile or rebellious? Are you uncertain how you would behave in the prisoner role? Explain.

The expectations associated with group roles and the perception of the value, prestige, influence, status, or stigma attached to each role by both the group and the individual can strongly affect us. The types of roles we play, of course, can have a direct bearing on what effect playing roles can have on the person and the group.

Types of Roles

It is not possible to enumerate all the roles a person can play in groups. In its broadest sense, roles are categorized as formal and informal. **Formal roles** are assigned by an organization or group partly to establish order. This type of role identifies a position. Titles such as "president," "chair," and "secretary" usually accompany formal roles. Especially within larger organizations, a set of expected behaviors to fulfill the role is explicitly spelled out. A job description used to hire an individual to fill a specific position is an example. Formal roles exist within the structure of the group or organization. They are designated. They do not emerge naturally from communication transactions. Formal roles are often independent from any person filling the role.

In smaller groups, the roles are mostly informal. The roles emerge from the group transactions. **Informal roles** emphasize functions, not positions. A group member may fulfill leadership functions, that is, perform as a leader, without any formal designation. No single informal role is found in all or even most groups with the probable exception of leader (Fisher and Ellis, 1990).

Actual duties and specific behaviors expected from a group member playing an informal role are implicitly defined by communication transactions among members. The group does not tell an individual explicitly how to be a good leader, but members do indicate degrees of approval or disapproval when an individual assumes the role. Informal role playing is improvisational, not scripted.

Informal roles are typically classified into three types: task, maintenance, and self-centered (Benne and Sheats, 1948; Mudrack and Farrell, 1995). **Task roles** move the group toward the attainment of its goals. The central communicative function of task roles is to extract the maximum productivity from the group. **Maintenance roles** focus on the social dimension of the group. The central communicative function of maintenance roles is to gain and maintain the cohesiveness of the group. Self-centered or **disruptive roles** serve individual needs or goals (Me-oriented) while impeding attainment of group goals. Individuals who play these roles often warrant the tag "difficult group member." The central communicative function of self-centered, disruptive roles is to focus attention on the individual. This focus on the individual can diminish group productivity and cohesiveness. Competent communicators avoid these roles. Table 5-1 provides samples of task, maintenance, and disruptive roles with corresponding communication behaviors

Table 5-1 Sample of informal roles in groups

Task Roles

1. *Initiator-Contributor:* Offers lots of ideas and suggestions; proposes solutions and new directions.
2. *Information Seeker:* Requests clarification; solicits evidence; asks for suggestions and ideas from others.
3. *Opinion Seeker:* Requests viewpoints from others; looks for agreement and disagreement.
4. *Information Giver:* Acts as a resource person for group; provides relevant and significant information based on expertise or personal experience.
5. *Clarifier-Elaborator:* Explains, expands, extends the iOdeas of others; provides examples and alternatives.
6. *Coordinator:* Draws together ideas of others; shows relationships between facts and ideas; promotes teamwork and cooperation.
7. *Secretary-Recorder:* Serves group memory function; takes minutes of meetings; keeps group's records and history.
8. *Director:* Keeps group on track; guides discussion; reminds group of goal; regulates group activities.
9. *Devil's Advocate:* Challenges prevailing point of view for the sake of argument in order to test and evaluate critically the strength of ideas, solutions, or decisions.

Maintenance Roles

1. *Supporter-Encourager:* Bolsters the spirits and goodwill of the group; provides warmth, praise, and acceptance of others; includes reticent members in discussion.
2. *Harmonizer-Tension Reliever:* Maintains the peace; reduces tension through humor and by reconciling differences between members.
3. *Gatekeeper-Expediter:* Controls channels of communication and flow of information; encourages evenness of participation; promotes open discussion.
4. *Feeling Expresser:* Monitors feelings and moods of the group; suggests discussion breaks when mood turns ugly or energy levels flag.

Self-centered or Disruptive Roles

1. *Stagehog:* Seeks recognition and attention by monopolizing conversation; prevents others from expressing their opinions fully; wants the spotlight.

2. *Isolate:* Deserts the group; withdraws from participation; acts indifferent, aloof, uninvolved; resists efforts to be included in group decision making.
3. *Clown:* Engages in horseplay; thrives on practical jokes and comic routines; diverts members' attention away from serious discussion of ideas and issues; steps beyond the boundaries of mere tension reliever.
4. *Blocker:* Thwarts progress of group; does not cooperate; opposes much of what group attempts to accomplish; incessantly reintroduces dead issues; makes negative remarks to members.
5. *Fighter-Controller:* Tries to dominate group; competes with members; abuses those who disagree; picks quarrels with members; interrupts to interject own opinions into discussion.
6. *Zealot:* Tries to convert members to a pet cause or idea; delivers sermons to group on state of the world; exhibits fanaticism.
7. *Cynic:* Displays sour outlook (a person who ''smells flowers [and] looks around for a coffin''—H. L. Mencken); engages in fault-finding; focuses on negatives; predicts failure of group.

Playing roles is a fluid process. During a single committee meeting an individual may play several roles. A group member may even adopt a disruptive role following an unsuccessful attempt to play a maintenance role such as tension reliever or encourager. Individuals in a system are so interconnected that what one group member does can influence significantly the roles other group members play.

Role Emergence

In large groups and organizations roles are largely determined by their formal structure. Even within this formal structure, however, role emergence occurs. Functional roles operate in smaller group meetings within the organization or in factional subunits of large groups.

Role emergence, however, is a relevant concern primarily to small, informal leaderless groups without a history. These groups can be ad hoc project groups set up within formal organizations (e.g., self-managed work teams), classroom discussion groups formed for the purpose of completing a class project, or a jury in a criminal trial. The roles each member will play have not been designated in advance but emerge from the transactions conducted among group members. How roles emerge in zero-history groups has been studied extensively at the University of Minnesota (Bormann, 1990).

Individuals initially make a bid for those roles that they find most rewarding and enjoyable and that they have played successfully in other groups. **Group endorsement** of the bid to play a specific role, however, must occur before a person gets to play that role. This endorsement is determined primarily by a consideration of the relative performance skills of group members. The group will reinforce the bid of that member perceived to be most skilled in the relevant performance area by both verbal and nonverbal communication. The endorsement process proceeds by trial and error. A group member tries out a role, perhaps tension reliever, for example. If the group does not reinforce the effort (e.g., doesn't laugh at the jokes), then the member will try another role hoping to get endorsement. An individual who persists in an effort to play a specific role in the face of group resistance may be characterized as inflexible and uncooperative.

Once a role for a member has been endorsed by the group, **role specialization** occurs. An individual member settles into his or her primary role. If the group wants you to be an information giver, then that will be your principal function. This specialization doesn't preclude you from assuming other roles, however. Role specialization does not grant a monopoly to a single member. There may be more than one harmonizer in the group, although there is likely to be only one member with the primary responsibility. Too much effort to operate in what is perceived to be another member's primary role territory can invite negative feedback from the group.

Role Fixation

In the movie *The Great Santini,* Robert Duvall plays a Marine Corps pilot. He is a rather odd character because he interacts with members of his family as if they were military recruits at boot camp. He orders his children to stand at attention early every morning while he inspects them. The children are required to address their father as "Sir" in a snappy voice. Duvall expects absolute obedience from his kids as he would from his subordinates in the military. He is aggressive and savagely competitive with his son. Duvall's character is fixated in a single role. Despite the inappropriateness of this role acted out in a family context, despite the disruption it causes his wife and children, Duvall's character seems incapable of playing any role other than that of officer in the military.

Competent communication requires the ability and the willingness to adapt communication behavior to changing situations. Some individuals, however, get locked into the mindset that they must play a certain role and there are no good substitutes. Leader, information giver, feeling expresser, and tension reliever are among the most likely candidates for **role fixation**—the acting out of a specific role and that role alone no matter what the situation might require (Postman, 1976).

Professional comedians sometimes don't know when to be serious in social gatherings. They are always "on." Lawyers who cross-examine their spouses as they do hostile witnesses on the stand at a criminal trial may find their role fixation is a ticket to a court of a decidedly civil sort.

Role fixation in decision-making groups can occur when an individual moves from one group to another, or it can happen within a single group. If you were a gatekeeper in the last group, you may insist on performing the same role in your new group. There may be another member, however, who can play the role better. If you insist on competing for the role instead of adapting to the new group by assuming another role, you will be a source of conflict and disruption. If the other member is truly better in the role than you are, then the resources of the group will not be utilized to their fullest if you keep fighting for the role.

Sometimes the group insists on role fixation to its own detriment. The reluctance of men to accept women in a leadership role, for instance, can lead to role fixation against a woman's wishes. Expecting women to play feeling expresser in all or most groups erects overly restrictive boundaries within the system and uses group resources inefficiently. Women should have the opportunity to play roles that require more than nurturing (e.g., supporter-encourager) or low involvement (e.g., secretary-recorder).

So what suggestions do I offer regarding communication competence and group roles? The competent communicator exhibits a sensitivity to the needs of the group in relation to group roles as follows:

1. *Demonstrate flexibility.* Playing a variety of maintenance and task roles adapts to the needs of the group. Fighting for roles perceived to be more prestigious and desirable may leave vital group needs unattended.
2. *Avoid disruptive roles.* Show commitment to group effectiveness, not self-centeredness at the expense of group success.
3. *Be experimental.* Try different roles in different groups. Don't get locked into playing the same role in all groups. You'll become role fixated.

LEADERSHIP

Jack Gibb (1969) observes: "Almost every influential thinker from Confucius to Bertrand Russell has attempted some form of analysis of leadership" (p. 205). Scholars, philosophers, social scientists, even novelists have exhibited an intense interest in the subject. When Geier (1967) interviewed eighty students, males and females, who participated in sixteen discussion groups, all but two reported they would like to be the group leader. Bormann (1990) accumulated case studies outside of the academic setting indicating that the desire to provide leadership for a group is widespread.

Why do most people want to be leaders? There are numerous reasons, but the most obvious ones are *status* that comes from running the show, *respect* from group members for doing a good job of guiding the group, and *power* accorded leaders allowing them to influence others and produce change.

Wanting to be a leader in decision-making groups, however, is hardly sufficient. The competent communicator must acquire the knowledge and the skills necessary to be an effective leader. In this section I will define leadership, discuss how to gain and retain leadership, and explore several perspectives on what constitutes effective leadership in groups.

Focus Questions
1. How is the process for retaining the leader role different from the process for emerging as group leader?
2. Are women and ethnic minorities equally capable as white men to function as leaders in small groups? Does your experience parallel the research results on this question?

3. After considering all the perspectives on leadership, what is the central overriding point that can be made about leadership in small groups?

Definition of Leadership

There are numerous definitions of **leadership.** As far back as 1949, there were at least 130 different definitions of "leader" and "leadership" (Bass, 1960). Marak (1964), however, writes, "The most common definition of leadership . . . and the one closest to ordinary usage describes leadership in terms of interpersonal influence-compliance relationships" (p. 174). But what kind of influence-compliance relationship? Is leadership an influence-compliance process that "turns followers into children" as Eric Hoffer once remarked? Is it the "ability to inflict pain" on followers as one corporate head commented in a 1980 *Fortune* magazine article? Is leadership, as Fiedler (1970) viewed it, "power over other people, and power over others enables a man to do things, to get things, to accomplish feats that, by himself, are unattainable" (p. 1)? Sidestepping the objectionable sexism of Fiedler's statement, his viewpoint represents the sledgehammer school of leadership popular with those who view leadership narrowly as naked dominance of others.

Shaw (1981) claims: "Leadership is an influence process which is directed toward goal achievement" (p. 317). Since no particular goal achievement is specified, however, an individual goal achieved at the expense of group goals might qualify as leadership. Wilson and Hanna (1990) argue that Shaw's definition is satisfactory if it is slightly amended to read: "Leadership is an influence process which is directed toward *group* goal achievement."

Despite the differences among the various definitions of leadership, there does seem to be agreement that leadership is a social influence process (Husband, 1988). This consensus serves as a basis for indicating what I consider leadership to be and not to be.

First, leadership requires followership. The two roles either exist together or they exist not at all. A leader must have someone to lead and followers must have someone to follow. Behavior labeled as leadership in the absence of followership "is no more leadership than the behavior of small boys marching in front of a parade, who continue to strut along Main Street after the procession has turned down a side street toward the fairgrounds" (Burns, 1978, p. 427).

Second, leadership implies change. As Husband (1988) explains: "People expect leaders to bring change about, to get things done, to make things happen, to inspire, to motivate. To influence someone is to change them—their behavior, their attitude, their beliefs or their values" (p. 494). Standing still is losing ground in a world of constant flux. The world will pass you by.

Leadership, as noted historian James MacGregor Burns (1978) argues, can be transformational. The transaction between a leader and followers can elevate, mobilize, inspire, and uplift. Groups that are transformed—-changed—-seek higher goals, loftier purposes, and experience increased levels of motivation than are ordinarily found in groups.

Third, leadership is a transactional power relationship. Viewing leadership as a transaction signifies a two-way influence process. The social influence occurs with the consent of the governed. Leaders influence followers, but followers also influence leaders by making demands on them, requiring them to meet members' expectations, and evaluating their performance in light of these expectations. Managers who are democratically oriented in their transactions with subordinates become autocratic (directive and controlling) when subordinates expect and even prefer an autocratic leadership style. Conversely, autocratic managers behave more democratically when subordinates clearly expect and prefer a democratic style of leadership (Crowe et al., 1972).

Fourth, <u>leadership is a communication process</u>. Leadership is exercised through communication within the group (Barge and Hirokawa, 1989). Managers, for instance, spend a majority of their work time communicating with others (Luthans et al., 1988). The communication competence of the leader is therefore central to any discussion of leadership.

Fifth, <u>leadership should not be determined exclusively on the basis of outcomes</u>. There is a tendency to associate leadership with actual goal attainment. Although achieving group goals is a primary consideration, it should not be the only basis for determining leadership in groups. Leadership is a communication process, not an outcome. I am not arguing that outcomes are irrelevant to leadership. If the group never attains its goals, then members might contemplate a change in leadership. The group goal, however, may not always be attainable, or the goal may be unrealizable in the short term. Within organizations, leaders of work groups may be thwarted from achieving change by inflexible institutional policies or veto power by upper management.

Conceptualizing what constitutes leadership is a far cry from knowing how to exercise leadership in a group. How leaders emerge and the ways to retain leadership in groups will be discussed next.

Gaining and Retaining Leadership

Some zero-history groups never do settle on who will lead and who will follow. In Geier's (1967) study of sixteen such groups working for as long as twelve weeks, almost a third of the groups never had a leader emerge. These leaderless groups were uniformly unsuccessful at their tasks and were socially unsuccessful as well. Strife predominated. Time was wasted and members became frustrated. Cohesiveness suffered and members began skipping meetings rather than suffer more disharmony. In contrast, groups that had leaders emerge and that developed stable roles for their members were successful (De Souza and Kline, 1995). The emergence of leaders, therefore, is a significant event in the life of a group.

How Not to Become Leader It is often easier to determine what you shouldn't do if you wish to become leader than what you should. We know that corruption or sex scandals, for instance, can send the media into a feeding frenzy and can torpedo a promising political career, but the absence of such scandals won't capture any headlines. Having a spotless character may just brand you as dull in some people's minds. Lack of negatives do not necessarily equal positives.

Before I discuss how you should communicate in groups in order to improve your chances of emerging as the leader, I will indicate first what you should avoid. <u>The competent communicator who wishes to emerge as group leader should heed the following dictums</u> (Bormann, 1990; Fisher and Ellis, 1990; Geier, 1967):

1. *Thou shalt not show up late for or miss important meetings.* Groups choose individuals who are committed, not members who exhibit an insensitivity to the group. As an anonymous wit once observed, "Absence makes the heart grow fonder—of someone else."
2. *Thou shalt not be uninformed about a problem* commanding the group's attention. Knowledgeable members have a greater chance of emerging as leaders. The clueless need not apply.
3. *Thou shalt not manifest apathy and lack of interest* by sluggish participation in group discussions. Group members are not impressed by "vigor mortis." Indifference provokes defensiveness. Participation is a sign of commitment to the group, and commitment to the group and its goals is part of the leadership process (De Souza and Kline, 1995).
4. *Thou shalt not attempt to dominate conversation* during discussion. Learning when to shut up is a useful skill.
5. *Thou shalt not listen poorly* (Bechler and Johnson, 1995). Leadership is not a monologue; it's a dialogue. As someone once said, a monologue is "the egotist's version of a scintillating conversation." Dialogue means leaders and followers listen carefully to each other.
6. *Thou shalt not be rigid and inflexible when expressing viewpoints.* A hardened position is plaque on the cortex. It decays the mind and contracts the brain.
7. *Thou shalt not bully group members.* Browbeating members to do your bidding will gain few admirers. There may be no way to avoid issuing orders in some situations (e.g., in the military), but watch out for psychological reactance. Bullies get banished to the playground.
8. *Thou shalt not use offensive and abusive language.* Blue language produces red faces. This will surely alienate many, if not most, group members.

Geier (1967) found that some of these counterproductive communication patterns were more likely than others to prevent someone from becoming a group leader. The three he found most relevant, in order of importance, were being uninformed, not participating, and being rigid and inflexible.

General Pattern of Leader Emergence   The extensive research conducted at the University of Minnesota under the direction of Ernest Bormann (1990) discovered a pattern of leader emergence in small zero-history groups. <u>In general, a group selects a leader by a process of elimination where potential candidates are systematically removed from consideration until only one person remains to be leader.</u> We may be quite clear on what we don't want in a leader but not as sure about what we do want. Bormann (1990) notes that "there is difficulty in estimating who will emerge as leader, but little disagreement about who will *not* be the leader" (p. 205). This narrowing of the candidate field makes good sense. As we eliminate candidates, complexity is reduced. The breadth of possibilities is narrowed while the depth of understanding of each candidate's qualifications for the role is increased.

There are two phases to the process-of-elimination explanation of leader emergence. During the first phase, roughly half of the members are eliminated from consideration. The criteria for elimination are crude and impressionistic. Negative communication patterns—the "thou shalt nots" weigh heavily. Quiet members are among the first eliminated. Nonparticipation will leave the impression of indifference and noncommitment. There was not a single instance in the Minnesota studies of a quiet member who became a leader.

Conversely, talkativeness also influences the leadership emergence process. Those who talk the most are perceived initially as potential leader material (Pavitt and Curtis, 1994). Mere talkativeness, however, is not enough to emerge as a leader (Bormann, 1990). Group members who blather, who make pronouncements on subjects without making a great deal of sense, are quickly eliminated by the group from consideration as leader. Such individuals are reminiscent of William Gibbs McAddo's characterization of President Warren G. Harding as "an army of pompous phrases moving over the landscape in search of an idea." Windbags gain no favor.

The members who express strong, unqualified assertions are also eliminated. These individuals are perceived to be too extreme and too inflexible in their points of view to make effective leaders. The attitude of certitude will provoke defensiveness from group members.

The uninformed, unintelligent, or unskilled are next in line for elimination. Groups look for task-competent individuals who are committed to the group goals to emerge as leaders (De Souza and Klein, 1995). Inept members distract the group from goal attainment.

In the second phase, about half the group still actively contend for the leader role. This part of the process can become quite competitive. Frustrations and irritations can mount. As the field of contenders narrows, the choice may become more difficult since differences between candidates may be less obvious than in the first phase. Of the remaining contenders, those who are bossy or dictatorial and those whose communication style is irritating or disturbing to group members are eliminated.

So who emerges as leader if more than one member survives the elimination rounds? There are several possibilities. First, if the group feels threatened by some external or internal crisis (e.g., inability to choose a topic for a symposium presentation or members with expertise fall sick or leave the group), the group often turns to the member who provides a solution to the crisis and he or she becomes leader. Second, members who remain active contenders for the leader role often acquire lieutenants. A lieutenant is an advocate for one of the contenders. He or she boosts the chances of the contender becoming the group leader. If only one of the members gains the support of a lieutenant, then this person will likely become the leader. If two members each gain a lieutenant, then the process of leader emergence can be drawn out, or even end in stalemate.

The general tendency is for groups to accept as leader the person who provides the optimum blend of task efficiency and sensitivity to social considerations. This tendency, of course, does not translate into a tidy formula or precise recipe. Some groups prefer a leader who concentrates more on task accomplishment and less on the social dimension of the group. Other groups prefer the opposite.

In the final analysis, this explanation of leader emergence should not be viewed as a mechanistic process that progresses in unwavering, step-by-step fashion. Groups can divert from this general pattern and sometimes do, radically. Nevertheless, the Minnesota studies have identified an interesting pattern of leader emergence in groups.

Ultimately, if you want to become the leader of a group you should take the following steps (Bormann, 1990):

1. Manifest conformity to the group's norms, values, and goals.
2. Display proper motivation to lead.
3. Avoid the "thou shalt nots" previously identified.

Deviants, dissenters, and disrupters will be eliminated early as potential leaders. Groups prefer leaders who will assist them in the attainment of their goals, will defend the group vigorously against threats, and remain loyal to the group. Since most group members think of a leader as the single individual who does most of the work, anyone hoping to be leader must also demonstrate a willingness to work hard for the group (Hollander, 1978).

 FOCUS ON GENDER/CULTURE

Leadership and the Problem of Bias

The problem of gender and ethnic bias complicates the pattern of leader emergence just described. The research on gender bias is far more voluminous than it is on ethnic discrimination. The early studies (prior to 1969) of small groups at the University of Minnesota found that women were not generally regarded as appropriate for the leader role in mixed-sex groups. Men usually refused to follow directions issued by women in the presence of other men. Some men in the studies expressed the strong opinion that women should obey and men should lead.

I recently heard a "rebuttal" to this sexist point of view from a female student when she remarked, "Behind every successful male leader stands an amazed woman." Sexist stereotyping of both females and males in the role of group leader, of course, is a poor basis upon which to decide who should lead and who should follow, but some studies show that women are not exempt from discriminating against their own sex when considering who should play the leader role (Watson, 1988). A September 1993 Gallup Poll of 1,065 adults revealed that more women (44 percent) than men (33 percent) prefer a male boss. Although 49 percent of the men polled said a boss's gender doesn't matter, only 24 percent of the women surveyed felt likewise. As Gallup's David Moore concludes, "Women seem a little more sexist about the gender of their boss than men" ("Poll," 1993). Who should emerge as leader in a group should be a matter of who is the best *person,* not which is the preferred gender to fill the role.

Drawing any definitive conclusions in regard to gender differences and leader emergence is problematic because the relevant studies are both time- and culture-bound. Attitudes about women in the role of leader vary from decade to decade and from culture to culture. Nevertheless, gender stereotypes are gradually diminishing in the United States. Later studies (1969–1979) at Minnesota showed some erosion of negative male attitudes toward women in the role of group leader. A more recent survey of students at a leading business school ("Men more willing," 1988) revealed substantial acceptance of women in the role of leader. The acceptance of women as leaders has also increased dramatically in the ranks of male executives. In 1965, 41 percent of male executives opposed the idea of women as managers but by 1985, this number had dropped precipitously to a mere 5 percent (Sutton and Moore, 1985). The shift in attitudes regarding women as leaders, however, is perhaps best exemplified by reflecting on the incredulity that the question, "Are women executives people?" asked in a study by the *Harvard Business Review* (Bowman et al., 1965), would elicit today. Although subjects in this study indicated women executives were people, can you imagine asking such a question on any survey today?

Although gender bias is diminishing, this decrease does not necessarily translate into women becoming leaders in small groups. Generally, it is still more difficult for a woman to emerge as leader of a group than it is for a man to do so. The lone male in an all-female group will often become the leader, whereas the lone female in an all-male group will rarely become the leader (Crocker and McGraw, 1984). Even women who are interpersonally dominant have a difficult time emerging as leaders of small groups. Nyquist and Spence (1986) found that in same-sex groups the dominant member became the leader 73 percent of the time. When the dominant group member in a mixed-sex group was male, however, he became the leader 90 percent of the time, but when the dominant member was female, she became leader only 35 percent of the time.

Studies of gender bias in the workplace, where emerging leaders live their daily lives and engage in small group communication, provide reason to be both initially discouraged and ultimately encouraged. The issue of a **glass ceiling,** an invisible barrier of subtle discrimination that excludes women from top jobs in corporate and professional America, is apparent. Fewer than 10 percent of senior management positions in U.S. government service are filled by women. Only 5 percent of senior management positions at Fortune 1000 companies are filled by women (Jacobs, 1996). Fewer than one in eight positions on corporate boards of Fortune 500 companies are occupied by women (Ries and Stone, 1992). At colleges and universities nationwide little more than one senior position (dean or above) *per institution* is filled by a woman (Ries and Stone, 1992). Only 8 percent of tenured law school professors are women, and of the 178 law schools accredited by the American Bar Association, only fourteen have female deans ("Study's verdict," 1996). A mere 13 percent of law firm partners are women ("Equality still," 1996). A scant 12 percent of federal judges are women (Epstein, 1996).

A 1993 U.N. Human Development Report (in Wright, 1993) noted: "No country treats its women as well as it treats its men. . . . Women are the world's largest excluded group. Even though they make up half the adult population . . . they make up just over 10 percent of the world's parliamentary representatives and consistently less than 4 percent of Cabinet ministers or other positions of executive authority" (p. 10A). The report of the U.N. Conference on Women held in Beijing in September 1995 came to a similar conclusion. The report noted that there are fewer women in the parliaments of Europe and North America than there were a decade ago ("Study finds," 1995).

That's the bad news. The encouraging news is that women are making huge strides in several areas. Economic consultant Nuala Beck argues that women are well positioned to advance in the new knowledge-based economy driven by the microchip. She claims that the Fortune 500 companies, and women's place in their hierarchy, are largely irrelevant—a relic of the manufacturing economy that is dwarfed by the knowledge-based industries. The ratio of female-to-male knowledge workers (engineers, technicians, scientists, professionals, and senior managers) is almost one to one (Collingwood, 1997). The new economy is based primarily on the knowledge and skills of the workers instead of seniority, a decided advantage for women.

Twenty-five years ago fewer than 4 percent of MBA degrees went to women. Now, more than one-third of all MBAs are earned by women (Jacobs, 1996). At the turn of this century, women occupied only 4 percent of management positions in the United States. That number has increased more than *tenfold* as we approach the twenty-first century (Hackman and Johnson, 1996). Nearly half of all law students in the country are women (Epstein, 1996). In 1960, fewer than 3 percent of all law degrees conferred in the United States were earned by women. Now it is close to half (Jacobs, 1996). In 1971, only 3 percent of all lawyers in the United States were women. Now a quarter of all U.S. lawyers are women ("Equality still," 1996), and if law school enrollment of women continues at the present rate, 40 percent of the U.S. legal profession will be composed of women by the year 2010 ("Sexism prevails," 1996). Women earn almost half of all doctoral degrees ("Study shows," 1997). In the 1960s, only a handful of women were tenured college professors. Currently, almost a quarter of the nation's tenured faculty are women (Koury, 1996). In the medical profession, fewer than 6 percent of all M.D. degrees were earned by women in 1960. Now it is almost 40 percent (Jacobs, 1996).

Even the wage-salary disparity between men and women has narrowed substantially. On average, women earn 72 cents for every dollar men earn. As an hourly wage (men work more hours on average than women), however, it jumps to 82 cents (Jacobs, 1996). Post and Lynch (in Jacobs, 1996) conclude: "The gender pay gap virtually disappears when age, educational attainment, and continuous time spent in the workforce are factored in as wage determinants" (p. 7B).

Despite these historic gains in fields that prepare women for leadership roles, women still have difficulty becoming leaders despite convincing evidence that women and men are equally capable (Haslett et al., 1992; Morrison and Von Glinow, 1990). Sexism still exists, and equal treatment on the job is still an unrealized goal, prompting an ever-increasing number of women to shun the corporate and professional worlds and start up their own small businesses with themselves in charge. There are nearly eight million women-owned small businesses in the United States, employing sixteen million workers. That's about a third of all businesses in the United States. Women are creating businesses at twice the national average (Wasserman, 1996).

This is a good news-bad news record, but, overall, the outlook for the future is optimistic. Haslett and her associates (1992) conclude that "slowly, sporadically, and unevenly" women are being accepted as leaders in groups. "The winds of change may not be a gale, but at least they are breezes blowing in the right direction" (p. 14).

Although the research on gender bias is substantial, the issue of ethnic bias and leader emergence has been largely ignored (Morrison and Von Glinow, 1990). Nevertheless, if we extrapolate from the dismal statistics on ethnic minorities in management positions, the conclusion seems inescapable that ethnic bias is a modifying factor in leader emergence.

The U.S. Labor Department's Glass Ceiling Commission, in its final report, noted that African, Asian, and Hispanic Americans occupy only a scant 1 percent of the executive management jobs at Fortune 500 companies ("Glass ceiling intact," 1994). The report also noted that the glass ceiling is apparent in federal jobs as well. Minorities hold 28 percent of all federal jobs but fill only 8 percent of the top posts. Female ethnic minorities tend to have the toughest time emerging as leaders because they face a double bias (Morrison and Von Glinow, 1990).

How do we combat this gender-ethnicity bias in emergent leadership in groups? First, the Twenty Percent Rule again comes into play. When women and minorities find themselves flying solo in groups, the chances that they'll land in a leadership position is remote. As the number of women and minorities increase in a group, however, the likelihood that a woman or a minority will emerge as leader also increases (Shimanoff and Jenkins, 1996) because bias decreases.

Second, if group members are allowed to mingle, interact, and work on a project before determining a leader, the decision is more likely to be made on the basis of individual performance rather than gender (or ethnicity if we extrapolate the research findings). Small groups that met for six to fifteen weeks on a project were as likely to name a woman as their leader as they were a man (Goktepe and Schneier, 1989). Allowing women and minorities to display their strengths increases their chances of emerging as group leaders.

These first two suggestions are supported by research (Haslett et al., 1992). The more familiar both men and women become with leaders who are other than white males, the more women and ethnic minorities are judged as capable of leading groups. Even at the very traditional United States Air Force Academy, cadets rated female leaders less favorably than males before they experienced them in action (stereotypes), but once they had served with several women leaders over a period of time, cadets rated female leaders as equivalent to male leaders (Adams et al., 1984). When women and ethnic minorities are no longer perceived as tokens, but instead form a substantial portion of group membership and increasingly occupy top leadership positions, then competence will be judged less on gender and ethnic bias and more on actual performance.

Third, <u>engaging in task-relevant communication behavior is a key to emerging as leader of a small task-oriented group</u> (Hawkins, 1995). Task-relevant communication includes initiation and discussion of analysis of the group problem, establishment of decision criteria, generation of possible solutions to problems, evaluation of possible solutions, and establishment of group operating procedures. Task-oriented female group members are as likely to emerge as leaders of small task groups as are task-oriented male group members (Hawkins, 1995).

Fourth, <u>if women and minorities are among the first to speak in the group and they speak fairly frequently</u>, their chances of emerging as leaders increase (Shimanoff and Jenkins, 1996). Speaking early and often without dominating discussion is perceived as assertive. Speaking early is more important for women and minorities than it is for men.

Finally, women and minorities can advance their chances of becoming leaders in small groups by <u>honing their communication skills and abilities</u>. Developing competence in communication by using skills appropriately and effectively can go a long way toward combating gender and ethnic leadership bias (Hackman and Johnson, 1996).

Questions for Thought

1. Should group members encourage women and minorities to speak early and often by inviting their participation?
2. Do you feel that the glass ceiling will shatter soon as the number of women and minorities in the middle ranks of leadership swell? What might prevent this from happening?
3. What responsibilities do white males have regarding the issue of leadership bias?

 SECOND LOOK

Pattern of Leader Emergence

GENERAL PATTERN

(Process of Elimination)

Phase One

- Quiet members eliminated
- Members who express strong, unqualified assertions eliminated
- Uninformed, unintelligent, and/or unskilled eliminated

Phase Two, part one
- Bossy, dictatorial members eliminated
- Members with irritating or disturbing communication style eliminated

Phase Two, part two
- Member who provides solution in time of crisis
- Member who acquires a lieutenant
- If more than one member acquires lieutenant—possible stalemate

HOW TO BECOME LEADER
- Manifest conformity to group norms, values, and goals
- Display proper motivation to lead
- Avoid the "thou shalt nots"

MODIFYING FACTORS OF LEADER EMERGENCE
- Gender bias
- Ethnic bias

Retaining the Leader Role The process for retaining the leader role is not the same as the process for emerging as the group leader. An individual could conform to group norms, display a strong motivation to lead the group, and avoid the "thou shalt nots" and still not retain the role of leader, as many political leaders have learned. A leader is sometimes deposed if his or her performance is felt by members to be subpar. There are <u>three primary qualifications for retaining leadership</u> (Wood et al, 1986):

1. You must demonstrate your competence as leader.
2. You must accept accountability for your actions.
3. You must satisfy group members' expectations.

Retaining the role of leader can be a tricky business. Groups can be fickle. What seems to satisfy members one day may enrage them the next. Take, for instance, the case of Ann Reynolds. From 1982 to 1990 she was the chancellor of the California State University system. In December 1989, the *San Jose Mercury News* (Philp, 1990) reported several disturbing facts regarding the chancellor's behind-the-scenes maneuvering for executive perks and salary increases. Under her leadership, $99,999 ($1 under the legislative limit) was quietly spent on six cars for vice chancellors, $240,000 was spent on Reynolds' state-owned Bel-Air home, and members of the board of trustees for the CSU system were given a 43 percent raise. Members of the public and the state legislature were incensed, especially since all this had been done in secret.

Trustees for the CSU system expressed embarrassment publicly and turned on the chancellor for allegedly misleading them on the propriety of using the secret delegation method for increasing executive salaries. Her competence to retain the leadership position was in question. Members of the board of trustees felt Reynolds misled them. She failed to meet their expectations—specifically, to keep the board out of public controversy on sensitive issues. Ultimately, she was held accountable by the trustees and the public. Reynolds resigned just before a move was made to oust her as chancellor.

Retaining leadership in a group requires competent communication. The leader must adapt to ever-changing situations. Group expectations of the leader may shift as circumstances alter. Members' confidence in and loyalty to their leader may be as firm as a mattress in a fleabag motel. A leader must demonstrate competence and satisfy group expectations on a continuing basis or member loyalty may disappear quickly. Last year's success may not compensate adequately for this year's failure as many athletic coaches have learned to their dismay.

Retaining the role of leader in a small group may be more challenging for women than for men. Studies (see Haslett et al., 1992) have demonstrated that men's leadership is judged as superior in quality to identical leadership behavior exhibited by women. Men are typically rated as more competent than women even when the behavior of both is identical. In one study, both male and female group members nodded approval and agreement, smiled, and looked pleased more often in response to male leaders than to identical contributions from female leaders. Both male and female members also frowned, scowled, and looked displeased more often in response to female leaders than male leaders even though there was no difference in what was said or done (Butler and Geis, 1990).

Again, achieving a "critical density of women in the public sphere and in positions of authority" (Tavris, 1992, p. 300) is essential. The more experience groups have with women and minorities as leaders, the more this bias will erode. This is especially true as women and minority leaders demonstrate their communication competence, satisfy group expectations, and prove successful in their leadership role.

Perspectives on Effective Leadership

Scholarly perspectives on leadership have changed greatly over the three-quarters of a century since the first serious research was conducted on this central group role. In this section, I will examine the primary perspectives that have generated considerable interest.

Traits Perspective   This is the "leaders are born not made" perspective. The earliest studies on leadership set out to discover a universal set of traits applicable to all those who become leaders. A huge number of traits were studied. We know, for instance, that height, weight, and physical attractiveness have a bearing on social influence. Tall individuals usually have greater influence with others than shorter individuals (only Lincoln was a taller president than Bush or Clinton). Very heavy or skinny people have less influence than more "ideal weight" types (Hickson et al., 1989). Good-looking individuals can influence a group.

So why don't all tall, fit, physically attractive individuals become leaders instead of short, dumpy, plain-looking individuals? Why was physically unattractive Eleanor Roosevelt considered a world leader? How do we explain the popularity of Rush Limbaugh, a rotund, balding man with bad taste in ties? How did Michael Dukakis (short and registering zero on the charisma meter) become the Democratic candidate for president in 1988? How did diminutive Barbara Boxer become a U.S. senator? And what are we to make of Microsoft's CEO, Bill Gates, who is a walking advertisement for *Revenge of the Nerds*? NBC News anchor Tom Brokaw remarked after conducting a roving interview with Gates at a Comdex computer show in Las Vegas, "It's like walking the Vatican with the Pope" (in Levy, 1995, p. 54). Then, of course, there is the "billionaire Boy Scout" and legitimate presidential candidate H. Ross Perot, frequently described by political pundits as "jug-eared" and "squeaky-voiced." Fellow Texan Molly Ivins (1992), a newspaper columnist, described Perot as "a seriously short guy who sounds like a Chihuahua" (p. 38). I'm sure you can cite many examples of individuals in groups you belong to where no specific set of traits explains why this person is the leader.

Leader emergence and leadership effectiveness, however, are not identical. The characteristics necessary even to be considered for the leader role in a small group (e.g., talkative, confident, motivated, knowledgeable, punctual, adaptable, good listener) don't assure your emergence as leader. You may

The traits perspective on leadership isn't very enlightening. Which traits do Eleanor Roosevelt, Rush Limbaugh, Michael Dukakis, Barbara Boxer, Bill Clinton, Bill Gates, Colin Powell, and Ross Perot have in common that explain their leadership: Good looks? Height? Physical size? Charisma? Intelligence? Personality? Ethnicity? Gender?

possess other traits that the group finds annoying or obnoxious. More importantly, such traits don't assure success if you become a leader.

What traits make a leader effective? Fiedler and House (1988) claim that "effective leaders tend to have a high need to influence others, to achieve, and they tend to be bright, competent, and socially adept, rather than stupid, incompetent, and social disasters" (p. 87). Perhaps intelligence, social and verbal skills, integrity, sense of humor, extroversion, confidence, or some other list of characteristics accounts for effective leadership in groups. These and other traits seem appropriate, even essential for a leader to possess. These traits, however, may be *necessary yet not sufficient* to be an effective group leader. Certain basic traits move you into the leadership arena. They are the irreducible minimum qualifications to become a leader, but to retain the role of leader and ultimately to perform effectively in this role other factors play a more important part.

The principal problem with the trait approach to effective leadership is the assumption that leadership resides in the person, not in transactions conducted within the group context. As Hollander (1985) observes, "Leadership is a process and not a person" (p. 487). Why do individuals become leaders in some groups but not others if an individual possesses the requisite leadership traits? If you're leadership material in one group, shouldn't you be leadership material in all groups? If traits explain leadership, how could mass murderer Charles Manson inspire such fanatical obedience from his little "family" of compliant followers yet produce such revulsion from most of society? Some people saw Marshall Applewhite, Jim Jones, and David Koresh as messiahs; others saw only lunatics. If they had the requisite leadership traits for one group, why not all groups? Obviously, there is more to effective leadership than the trait approach can explain.

Effective leadership is not a single set of traits. As management expert Peter Drucker (1988) has concluded, effective leadership "has little to do with 'leadership qualities' and even less to do with 'charisma.' It [effective leadership] is mundane, unromantic and boring. Its essence is performance" (p. 1). To reinforce this point Drucker further notes that charismatic leaders (those who possess a constellation of personal attributes or traits that groups find appealing) such as Hitler, Stalin, and Mao were "the misleaders who inflicted as much evil and suffering on humanity as have ever been recorded. . . . Dwight Eisenhower, George Marshall, and Harry Truman were singularly effective leaders yet none possessed any more charisma than a dead mackerel" (p. 1).

Styles Perspective   Unsatisfied with the trait approach to leadership, Kurt Lewin and his associates developed a new approach based on three leadership styles: autocratic, democratic, and laissez-faire (Lewin et al., 1939). Autocratic style exerts control over group members. The autocratic leader is highly directive. This leadership style does not encourage member participation. Douglas McGregor (1960) describes autocratic leadership as a "my way or the highway" approach: Do what I say or hit the road. Autocratic leaders are not concerned about making friends or getting invited to parties. The autocratic style puts most of the emphasis on the task with little concern for the social dimension of the group (high task, low social).

How could these seriously weird individuals (Charles Manson, Jim Jones, David Koresh, and Marshall Applewhite) become leaders? The traits perspective doesn't explain much about their emergence or influence as leaders.

The democratic style is nondirective and participative. It encourages participation from and disseminates responsibility for important group functions among members. Democratic leaders work to improve the skills and abilities of group members (Gastil, 1994). Followers have a say in what the group decides. The democratic style puts a balanced emphasis on both the task and social dimensions of the group (high task, high social).

The laissez-faire style is not really leadership at all and was eventually dropped from serious consideration in most of the research. It is a do-nothing approach to the group. The laissez-faire style provides no direction and no regard is accorded the social transactions in the group (low task, low social).

An extensive leadership study of more than 12,000 managers in fifty different organizations both private and governmental showed a clear relationship between democratic-participative style and leadership success (Hall and Donnell, 1979). Successful managers usually sought the advice and opinions of subordinates. Average or unsuccessful managers did not seek the participation of subordinates in decision making (autocratic-directive style). Unsuccessful managers seemed more concerned about protecting themselves than advancing the goals of the organization (Me-not-We orientation).

The extensive research comparing autocratic-directive and democratic-participative leadership styles, however, presents mixed results (Gasil, 1994). Both directive and participative styles can be productive, and, although the participative style fosters more member satisfaction than does the directive style (Van Oostrum and Rabbie, 1995), the difference is neither large nor uniform (Gasil, 1994). Participative leadership seems to work best when it springs naturally from the group itself. Not all small groups, however, want nor expect their leaders to adopt the participative leadership style. Some cultures prefer the "paternal authoritative" (benevolently directive) style to the participative style (Brislin, 1993). In such cultures, the participative style may not work as well as the directive style.

Gender also plays a role in the leadership style-effectiveness equation. Male and female leaders are evaluated by group members as equally competent when the democratic-participative style is used (Eagly et al., 1992). When the autocratic-directive style is used, however, group members evaluate women as substantially less competent leaders than men. Apparently, group expectations influence judgments of leader competence. Female leaders are expected to adopt the participative leadership style, which complements the desire for connection, but groups are unaccustomed to seeing women use the directive style, which places more emphasis on independence and power than on connection (Tannen, 1990). Men clearly have more flexibility in choice of leadership style. With time, this stereotype that locks women into a single style of leadership should virtually vanish as women challenge the expectation.

One weakness of the participative-directive leadership style duality is that these styles are viewed as extreme opposites. Individuals operate *either* as participative *or* directive leaders, but not both. Realistically, though, a combination of participative and directive leadership styles is required in small groups. Intuitively, we know this is the case. When you're sitting white-knuckled in the jumbo jet that is experiencing engine trouble, do you want the captain to be democratic and take a vote on what should be done? Does it not make more sense to have someone in charge who takes action and tells the crew what to do immediately without pausing for conversation and debate? This is an emergency situation.

Or, consider the situation in which a person is new on the job. Should this person be consulted on how the job should be accomplished when he or she doesn't even have a good idea what the job entails? Should teachers consult their students before determining course content when the students know little or nothing about the subject? Should military commanders seek the advice of their troops before launching an offensive?

No one style of leadership will be suitable for all situations. This realization has led researchers to explore yet another approach to leadership—the situational or contingency perspective.

Situational (Contingency) Perspective   This is the "it depends" approach to leadership. Since no one style of leadership is appropriate for all situations, effective leadership is contingent upon adapting the right style to the specific situation. The situational perspective on leadership is well-suited to the systems approach to small groups. Adaptability to changing circumstances within the group system is the essence of situational leadership.

There are two principal situational models of leadership effectiveness. The first is Fred Fiedler's (1967) contingency model. Fiedler's model, however, does not offer guidance on how to become a more effective leader once you're in a group. In this sense it has rather limited application for our purposes, so I will spare you an explanation of his complicated model.

A more flexible and useful situational model of leadership effectiveness has been offered by Hersey and Blanchard (1988). Although their model is targeted at organizations, it applies well to groups large and small, especially ones with long life cycles. Their model is also well-suited to a systems perspective. Acknowledgment of the interconnectedness of leader and followers plus the recognition of the importance of leader adaptability to change within the system are noteworthy.

Hersey and Blanchard have combined three variables in their situational model:

1. The amount of guidance and direction (*task emphasis*) a leader provides.
2. The amount of relationship support (*socio-emotional emphasis*) a leader provides.
3. The *readiness level* in performing a specific task, function, or objective that followers demonstrate.

The interplay among these three variables will indicate the level of leadership effectiveness.

Effective leadership is dependent upon the transactions that take place between the leader and followers. For Hersey and Blanchard this is the vital, paramount contingency upon which leadership effectiveness rests. Let me add that central to this transaction is the communication competence of the leader. The leader must have the necessary knowledge of leadership styles, the skill to employ these styles, the sensitivity to adapt the styles to the changing circumstances of the leader-follower relationship, and the commitment to make the transaction work.

There are four leadership styles in the Hersey and Blanchard model. The **Telling style** (high task, low relationship emphasis) is directive. A leader using this style provides specific instructions regarding a task and closely supervises the performance of followers but places minimal focus on developing social relationships with followers. The **Selling style** (high task, high relationship) is also directive. A leader using this style explains and clarifies decisions but also tries to convince followers to accept directives. The **Participating style** (low task, high relationship) is nondirective. A leader using this style encourages shared decision making with special emphasis on developing relationships in the group. The **Delegating style** (low task, low relationship) is nondirective. A leader using this style allows the group to be self-directed. Responsibility for decision making and implementation of decisions rests with the group. The key to leadership effectiveness is matching the appropriate style to the group environment.

Fisher (1986) criticizes the situational approach to leadership by arguing that it is "intuitively reasonable" but "the number of variables which are potentially contingent on leadership and the possible combinations of those variables of situation, leader, and followers are virtually impossible to comprehend" (p. 203). Hersey and Blanchard agree with the thrust of Fisher's criticism. No leader could ever consider all possible situational variables before making a decision. Hersey and Blanchard contend, however, that there is no need to consider all or even most variables. The relationship between the leader and follower is the prime consideration because if the follower decides not to follow the leader, then all other situational variables (nature of the task, time involved, expectations, etc.) are irrelevant.

The primary situational variable that the leader must consider when adapting leadership styles to the specific group is the readiness level of the followers. Originally called "maturity," Hersey and Blanchard (1988) define readiness as "how ready a person is to perform a particular task" (p. 175). They identify two principal components of readiness: ability and willingness. "Ability is the knowledge, experience, and skill that an individual or group brings to a particular task or activity" (p. 175). They define willingness as "the extent to which an individual or group has the confidence, commitment, and motivation to accomplish a specific task" (p. 175). This all sounds remarkably like communication competence.

Decisions are leader directed at lower levels of readiness while decisions are follower directed at higher levels of readiness. As readiness levels increase, effective leadership requires reduced guidance and direction from the leader and less socio-emotional support for followers. These relationships are depicted in Figure 5-1.

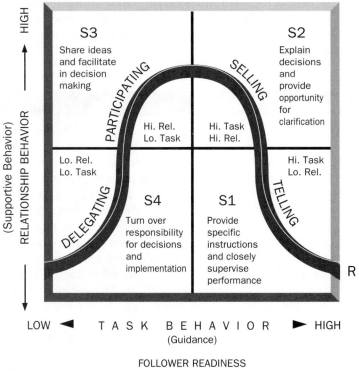

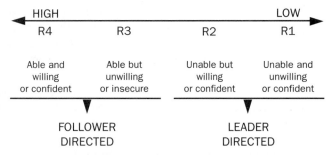

Figure 5-1 *The Telling (S1), Selling (S2), Participating (S3), and Delegating (S4) leadership styles related to follower readiness. Situational Leadership® is a registered trademark of the Center for Leadership Studies, Inc. Reprinted with permission. All rights reserved.*

Followers, for whatever reasons (e.g., divorce, midlife crisis, lack of challenges), may regress in their readiness levels, losing motivation or slipping in their skill performance. In such cases, the leader moves backward through the styles curve (i.e., from delegating to participating or even telling), adapting to the change in circumstances.

⊙⊙ CLOSER LOOK
Effective versus Ineffective Leadership

A friend of mine once worked in county government. She and another individual were hired to fill administrative positions in the personnel office. Her immediate supervisor employed the laissez-faire leadership style, which is to say no leadership at all was ever exercised. Upon my friend's arrival at her new job, she was delegated authority and responsibility for which she had no preparation. Office procedures were not explained. She was expected to perform by trial and error without direction or training. When she made mistakes, she was held accountable, while her supervisor literally sorted through his list of music records and tapes on a computer file in his office, disappeared on extended lunches, and attended numerous "meetings" (i.e., coffee breaks). The other employee hired along with my friend received similar treatment. Neither my friend nor her partner in frustration received any useful training from their supervisor during the first six months of their employment.

Here was a case of ineffective leadership. The supervisor employed an inappropriate style right from the beginning. When you start a job, you don't even know where the coffeemaker is located, much less the details of how you're expected to perform in your new position. An effective leader tells an employee at the start what that person needs to know in order to perform optimally. As the employee begins to learn the relevant tasks, encouragement and further clarification are provided (selling). The employee's input regarding decisions is solicited (participating) as he or she masters the relevant tasks, and *eventually* you delegate authority and responsibility to the employee because he or she can be trusted to perform well.

A second example illustrates effective leadership. Two friends of mine worked in the international finance division of a large computer software company as temporary employees. Their supervisor, a bright young woman, was a skillful leader. During the first week, the supervisor trained them, indicating what they needed to know in order to perform their job. Soon their supervisor solicited their opinions. Gradually, they both were delegated new responsibilities and tasks, but not at the same rate since one mastered her tasks more quickly than the other. The supervisor adapted to the readiness levels of her employees. What began as a temporary, expedient employment opportunity grew into an offer of permanent employment in a responsible position. Effective leadership is good for the leader and good for the followers.

Effective leadership requires adaptation of styles to individuals within the group. Some members will require a telling style for a longer period of time than will others. Some members may require a great deal of encouragement and support while others will require little. In the above cases, the ineffective leader had a "one style fits all" approach—the laissez-faire or sit-on-your-derriere style. He "managed" all of the employees in his department exactly the same way. Conversely, the effective leader adapted to the readiness levels of each individual employee within her department. She exhibited the flexibility of the competent communicator because she tailored her leadership style to the requirements of each follower.

Questions for Thought

1. Have you had a similar problem with a supervisor who exhibited poor leadership?
2. What should you do if faced with an ineffective leader in a group?

Is situational leadership effective? A study at Xerox Corporation (Gumpert and Hambleton, 1979) revealed that highly effective managers knew more about and used situational leadership more frequently than less-effective managers. When situational leadership was applied according to the Hersey and Blanchard model, subordinate job performance was higher than when it was not. Hersey and Blanchard (1988) cite additional studies in educational settings (e.g., classrooms, college boards of trustees) where situational leadership has proven to be highly effective.

Functional Perspective   Unlike the previous approaches to leadership that assume a leader has already been designated or emerged in the group, the functional perspective views leadership in terms of certain functions that must be performed for the group to be successful. Typically, those functions fall into two categories: task requirements and social or maintenance needs.

The functional perspective can be divided into two schools of thought. The first has been dubbed by William Schutz as the **"leader as completer"** viewpoint. Leaders are thought to perform those essential functions within a group that other members have failed to perform. Typically, the list of possible functions falls into the standard task requirements and social or maintenance needs categories. The list of task and maintenance roles previously identified indicates functions essential to a group (e.g., giving information, coordinating, directing, gatekeeping, and relieving tension). Leadership, then, is seen as an adaptive role. Leaders step in and assume whatever role in the group is required at a particular time but that has not been filled by any other member (e.g., researching background on group task, making list of group members' phone numbers).

A second school of thought, the **"vital functions"** viewpoint, sees leaders performing a list of vital group functions different in kind and/or degree from other members. Fisher and Ellis (1990) offer a list of such functions:

Group Procedures

1. *Plan an agenda.* Group meetings proceed more smoothly when the leader has constructed a list of topics for discussion and decision making. (See Appendix C.)
2. *Handle routine "housekeeping" details.* These include taking roll, calling the meeting to order, making important announcements, modifying the agenda before discussion proceeds, and so forth.
3. *Prepare for the next meeting.* Announce the time, place, and date of the next meeting. Plan ahead by making certain that the meeting room is appropriate in size and physical conditions.

Task Requirements

1. *Initiate a structure.* The leader identifies issues to be discussed, proposes procedures for such discussion, guides the discussion and focuses members on the agenda, and may suggest possible solutions to problems.
2. *Seek information.* More so than other members, the leader requests facts, asks for clarification of points that are unclear, and asks questions.
3. *Give information.* Leaders are the most prepared group members. They research the important issues in advance. They can inform other group members when there are gaps in their knowledge.
4. *Offer informed opinion.* Leaders give opinions based on evidence and sound reasoning. So as not to stifle discussion, these opinions will usually be offered after other group members have had their say.
5. *Clarify, summarize, and elaborate.* The leader provides closure for the group. Points agreed to and points still disputed are identified.

Social Needs

1. *Facilitate involvement and communication.* Leaders encourage participation from all members. Keeping meetings lively and fast-paced can prevent nonparticipation that results from boredom.
2. *Harmonize.* The leader is responsible for establishing a supportive climate. This may mean confronting members who are disrupting meetings or creating competitiveness. Humor helps relieve tension and improve group climate.
3. *Express feelings.* A leader expresses feelings when appropriate and promotes a supportive environment in which others can express their feelings.

Of the two functional viewpoints, <u>the leader as completer seems to have the greater merit</u>. A large-scale investigation of the question, "Which communicative functions do leaders perform more frequently or more characteristically than nonleaders?" revealed no unique functions associated with the leader role (Drecksel, 1984). <u>The set of leader behaviors listed are essential for the effective functioning of the group</u>, but Fisher (1986) also observes that "there is no particular reason to believe that leaders should or do contribute more of those functions than other members" (p. 212).

Reasonably, a leader has no preset list of functions to perform for the group, with the possible exception of certain procedural acts (e.g., constructing an agenda, arranging for an appropriate meeting room). A leader acting as a competent communicator, however, is responsive to the specific needs of the group. If tension needs to be relieved, the leader provides that function. If the group requires certain information, the leader can provide it. The leader as completer viewpoint does have merit.

From the functional perspective, leadership is a shared responsibility. If the group strays off task, any member can and should refocus the group. If a minority point of view has been ignored, any member can and should encourage the group to listen and give a fair hearing to a differing viewpoint. If conflict is smoldering beneath the surface of group discussion, any member can and should confront this. The group leader monitors the overall group process and progress, but the leader is not solely responsible for how the group performs.

Communication Competence Perspective   What do we really know about leadership in groups? With so many perspectives and viewpoints, what makes sense? Barge and Hirokawa (1989) offer a communication competence model of leadership as an integration of the traits, style, situational, and functional perspectives on leadership.

The communication competence model of leadership is grounded in three general assumptions about the nature of leadership:

1. Leadership is an active process of overcoming barriers to group goal achievement.
2. Leadership is exercised through the process of communication.
3. Communication skills (competencies) are the core of leadership in groups (Barge and Hirokawa, 1989).

The central, overriding point to make in regard to these assumptions about leadership is that leadership in groups is an adaptive process. This seems undeniable. As Ralph Stogdill (1975), a leadership researcher for more than four decades, puts it, "The most effective leaders appear to exhibit a degree of versatility and flexibility that enables them to adapt their behavior to the changing and contradictory demands made on them" (p. 7). In order to overcome barriers to goal achievement, leaders must be prepared and able to adapt to changing situations and circumstances. Being prepared and able requires knowledge, skill, sensitivity, and commitment. In other words, the best leaders are likely to be the most proficient communicators; or as Hackman and Johnson (1996) put it, "Extraordinary leadership is the product of extraordinary communication" (p. 81).

Leaders have to function within a system, and change is unavoidable in any system. As the most central role in a small group, the leader must be the most adaptive. Leaders should be able to analyze the needs of group members, analyze changing situations, inspire commitment from members, and exhibit behavioral flexibility (Wood et al., 1986).

Effective leaders do in fact adapt to changing situations in the group. Research shows that effective leaders change their behavior when the group experiences a crisis or is failing on a task (Wood, 1977). When leaders do not adapt in such situations, they lose status with group members.

Leaders should avoid the "thou shalt nots," work with members in structuring a cooperative group climate, and monitor group process, procedures, and progress. A competent leader will exhibit the knowledge of essential group functions, the flexibility to apply appropriate leadership styles depending on the circumstances, and the ability to respond to changes in the group. The "one leadership style fits all" approach is doomed to fail much of the time. Knowing what produces defective small group decision making and problem solving and what processes produce effective decision making and problem solving is part of the competent leader equation. These are the subjects of the next two chapters.

⊙⊙ CLOSER LOOK
Ethics and Leadership

Approximately $150 million is spent annually by U.S. businesses on controversial group-training programs for employees (Singer, 1995). These group-training programs include an amazing conglomeration of techniques to incite worker motivation, enhance cooperation, and improve productivity. According to the Equal Employment Opportunity Commission (EEOC), a federal oversight agency, training programs include mysticism, faith healing, aura readings, meditation, guided visualization, self-hypnosis, therapeutic touch, biofeedback, yoga, and fire walking (I've heard of lighting a fire under your employees but this takes a metaphor a bit literally). In one case, a woman who perceived herself to be very overweight was told to wear a bikini, go out on the street, and act like a Pied Piper singing and trying to get a band of men to follow her. In another instance, people cross-dressed and acted out caricatured versions of the opposite sex. Then there is the "rebirthing" exercise called "Cocktail Party" where group trainees writhe on the ground while exorcising their personal demons and shout at one another for up to two hours while trainers hand out vomit bags and exhort the trainees to purge their emotions (Singer, 1995).

These programs raise important ethical issues directly associated with leadership in groups. Employees are often told by management leaders that they must participate in these training programs even though the content and techniques of the programs may be offensive to employees or may violate employees' religious and moral beliefs. Do managers, supervisors, and leaders of small groups have a right to compel employees and group members to participate in a program they find offensive, immoral, or potentially harmful?

Ethical leadership is an important issue because the consequences of unethical leadership can be serious. Singer (1995) notes, "Besides making complaints to the EEOC, many employees have filed civil suits objecting to training program content or related pressures at the workplace. Some lost their jobs by objecting. Other employees have suffered psychological decompensation as a consequence of what occurred in the training programs" (p. 191).

Hackman and Johnson (1996) offer guiding principles for ethical leadership. I've condensed these principles into the following criteria:

1. *Honesty.* Ethical leaders avoid intentionally deceptive or harmful messages. Many of the training programs I referred to are deceptively packaged as seminars on job-related skills when they are actually confrontational, psychologically intense therapy groups (Singer, 1995).
2. *Concern for others.* A leader's concern for group members must supersede concern for his or her personal gain. Ethical leadership requires that you advance the goals of the group, not your own personal agenda at the expense of the group. Those who promote training programs that are self-serving ventures aimed primarily at fattening the wallets of those hustling such programs do not exhibit ethical leadership.
3. *Respect.* Ethical leaders treat all members with equal respect unless they earn disrespect (e.g., by exhibiting racist, homophobic, or sexist attitudes toward other group members). Treat others as you would want others to treat you. Trainers that abuse individuals in training programs show disrespect where none has been earned.
4. *Commitment.* Ethical leaders remain committed to the group and group members even in rough seas. Leaders don't jump ship and leave group members to sail into cannon fire. Groups sink or swim together and they accept the consequences of their actions as a unit. Many training programs have no follow-up. They are one-shot efforts. Trainers have no commitment to the group once the program is finished (often one or two days). If emotional damage is done to a trainee, there is usually no commitment to "right the wrong" done to the trainee.
5. *Even-handedness.* Ethical leaders apply and enforce policies and decisions without favoritism or cronyism. Racism, sexism, and homophobia have no place in decisions by leaders.

This list of ethical criteria should guide you in answering questions on ethical leadership. These criteria, however, are not absolutes. There are exceptions. In some cases criteria may conflict. Concern for others may conflict with honesty when telling the truth may severely harm a group member. Leaders frequently face ethical dilemmas where no clear answers emerge. If leaders are guided by these ethical criteria, however, then they are making a sincere effort to do what is right, and that is the essence of ethical leadership.

Questions for Thought

1. Should a group member have an absolute right to refuse to participate in a training program if he or she finds it offensive or objectionable? Should training programs ever be a requirement of employment?
2. Can you think of exceptions to each of the ethical criteria?

In summary, there are many roles to play in small groups. Competent communicators learn to play a variety of roles. Leaders emerge in a process of elimination. There are different requirements, however, for gaining the leader role and retaining it once the role has been secured. The key to effective leadership is communication competence, whose keystone is adaptability to changing situations and needs in the group.

I've discussed how groups develop and how to create a cooperative/supportive climate during that development, and I've explained the roles we play during the life of a group and how to function effectively in those roles. Now I will examine the principal work that most groups perform. In the next two chapters I will analyze first defective then effective decision making and problem solving in small groups.

QUESTIONS FOR CRITICAL THINKERS

1. Have you experienced role fixation? Have you observed it in others?
2. Do Adolph Hitler, Joseph Stalin, Jim Jones, David Koresh, Charles Manson, and Marshall Applewhite qualify as leaders? Explain your answer in terms of leadership perspectives.

Group Discussion: Defective Decision Making and Problem Solving

Irving Janis (1982) relates the story of a tragedy that occurred in the mining town of Pitcher, Oklahoma, years ago. The local mining engineer warned the inhabitants that due to an error, the town was in danger of imminent cave-in from undermining. Residents were advised to evacuate immediately. The warnings went unheeded. At a meeting of the local Lion's Club, leading citizens of the town joked about the doom-and-gloom forecast. One club member evoked raucous laughter from the membership when he entered the meeting wearing a parachute on his back in mock preparation for the predicted disaster. Within a few days, several of the club members and their families died when parts of the town caved in, swallowing some of those who spoofed the warnings.

Why would people ignore the threat? We read and hear stories every year of similar collective misjudgments and disasters. How do scandals such as Watergate, the Iran-Contra affair, and Whitewater ever occur in the first place? What gives rise to inept decision making in small groups? How can group fiascos be averted? These are some of the questions that will be addressed in this chapter.

Some theorists use the terms *decision making* and *problem solving* synonymously. Others draw distinctions between the two, using one or the other as the more general term. I see the terms as interconnected. A decision requires a choice between two or more alternatives. Groups make choices in the process of finding solutions to problems (e.g., where to meet, what process to use in making choices, what is the best solution to the problem, how to implement the solution). Problem solving necessitates decision making, and most decision making involves problem solving. Although I will use both terms together throughout the book, when I use either term alone I am indicating a primary emphasis on either decision making or problem solving, recognizing that the two are not neatly divided in actual practice.

In this chapter, I have four objectives:

1. to analyze the adverse effects of excessive or insufficient information quantity on group decision making/problem solving,
2. to explain the role of mindsets in defective decision making/problem solving,
3. to explore the contribution of collective inferential error to defective decision making/problem solving, and
4. to describe and analyze groupthink as an ineffective group decision-making process.

In other words, this chapter explores ways in which small groups manifest defective **critical thinking,** a major cause of bad decisions and poor solutions to problems. Critical thinking requires group members to analyze, criticize, and evaluate ideas and information in order to reach sound judgments and conclusions. Critical thinking, therefore, is central to any discussion of small group decision making and problem solving.

One note of caution, however. Russian author Fyodor Dostoyevsky once remarked that "everything seems stupid when it fails." Determining degrees of decision-making and problem-solving effectiveness simply on the basis of outcomes would be misleading and inaccurate. Although suggestive, bad outcomes do not automatically signal defective decision making and problem solving because bad luck, sabotage, poor implementation by those outside the group, or misinformation may have caused the undesirable result (Janis, 1982).

As I indicated earlier, groups often outperform individuals. Obviously, this will not be the case if the group is functioning like The Three Stooges. Groups generally outperform individuals in certain circumstances if they operate effectively rather than defectively.

INFORMATION: THE RAW MATERIAL OF CRITICAL THINKING

Information is critical to decision making and problem solving in groups. <u>Faulty information processing by a group will likely lead to low-quality decisions, but sound information processing will likely lead to high-quality decisions</u> (Hirokawa, 1987). Faulty information processing is partly the result of too much or too little information on which to base decisions.

Focus Questions
1. Which is the bigger contributor to defective decision making/problem solving in groups—information overload or underload?
2. Which method of coping with information overload is potentially the most effective?

Information Overload

Richard Wurman (1989) claims, "Information has become the driving force in our lives, and the ominous threat of this ever-increasing pile demanding to be understood has made most of us anxious" (p. 32). De Moor (1996) states, "Owing to the rapidly increasing number and connectivity of large databases, computer conferencing systems, World Wide Web sites, and so on, information chaos is arising" (p. 92). **Information overload** is a pervasive problem in virtually all decision-making/problem-solving groups. <u>Information load is based on the rate and complexity of information inputs into a system</u> (Farace et al., 1977). When the rate of information flow into a system and/or the complexity of that information exceeds the system's processing capacity, information overload (excessive input) has been reached. This section will focus on how pervasive the problem of information overload is and how to cope with it.

Extent of the Problem   Jeff Davidson (1996) puts the problem succinctly, "This generation is more besieged by information than any that preceded it, and perhaps more so than all previous generations combined" (p. 495). More information has been produced in the last 30 years than was produced in the previous 5,000 years. A single edition of *The New York Times* contains more information than the average person was likely to be exposed to in an entire lifetime in seventeenth-century England (Wurman, 1989). More information is generated worldwide in a 24-hour period than you could process and absorb in all your years on this planet. With the rise of the Internet, we are rapidly approaching a point in which more information will be generated in *one hour* than could be processed and absorbed in your lifetime (Davidson, 1996).

Pick any occupation, profession, vocation, or area of interest and the problem of information overload is epidemic. Academics in the sciences alone churn out articles for over 70,000 separate journals at a rate of two every minute or 2,880 every day (Sykes, 1988). This number does not include the blizzard of articles appearing in more than 3,000 social science journals plus academic publications in all other scholarly disciplines.

Chief executive officers in the business community spend, on average, more than four hours a day just reading in order to keep current with the accelerating production of information relevant to their business enterprises (Goldhaber, 1990). In a survey of 1,300 business managers from Great Britain, the United States, Australia, Singapore, and Japan by Reuters Business Information (in "Businesspeople suffering," 1996), 43 percent of senior managers claimed that information overload had made them ill. Nearly two-thirds of these same individuals said that their personal relationships had also suffered and that they had experienced diminished job satisfaction because of information overload. Psychologist Dr. Daniel Lewis, who analyzed the results of this study states, "Having too much information can be as dangerous as having too little. Among other problems, information overload can lead to paralysis of analysis, making it harder to find the right solutions or make the best decisions" (p. 10).

Students working on group projects recognize the problem of information overload and its disruptive quality. When surrounded by a Mount Everest of books and articles on a research subject, or a stack of printouts from the Internet, you lose sight of the larger picture. How does all this information fit together into a coherent package? The more you learn about the subject, the more confusing the larger picture may appear. You become lost in the trees while searching for the forest. In fact, Wurman (1989) argues that schools encourage **information bulimia,** a binge-and-purge cycle of information processing. Students cram facts into their heads, regurgitate them for a test or group presentation, then quickly purge them from their minds forever (sound vaguely familiar?). No meaningful decisions have been made in the process; no vital answers to problems have been discovered.

⊙⊙ CLOSER LOOK
The McMartin Preschool Case

All decision-making groups are adversely affected by information overload. Information is the lifeblood of decision making in groups, but if there is a hemorrhaging of information, then the capacity to make decisions is impaired. This can be seen by examining the McMartin Preschool child molestation court case (Goldston and Torriero, 1990; Schindehette et al., 1990), the longest and most expensive criminal trial in American history, lasting twenty-eight months and costing $15 million. (The O. J. Simpson criminal trial just *seemed* like the longest trial in human history.)

The case began when Judy Johnson, who claimed she had divine powers and whom the courts described as a psychotic alcoholic (Baker, 1996), charged that her two-and-a-half-year-old son had been sexually abused at a day-care center in Manhattan Beach, California. Ultimately, sixty-five sex abuse and conspiracy charges were filed against two defendants: Raymond Buckey, thirty-one, and his sixty-three-year-old mother, Peggy McMartin Buckey. Testimony in the trial was taken from 124 witnesses. One ten-year-old boy was on the witness stand for sixteen days.

Weeks of testimony were devoted to the meaning of turtle shells that children in the case claimed were part of threatening satanic rituals used to silence them. The jury was faced with the nearly impossible task of sifting through 63,000 pages of sometimes complicated testimony and 917 exhibits in order to determine the guilt or innocence of the defendants. Jury deliberations commenced a full year and a half after the last of nine children testified at the trial. The jury deliberated for *nine weeks* before acquitting the defendants on fifty-two counts but deadlocking on thirteen others. The jurors admitted afterward that they believed someone had committed child molestation at the daycare center but weren't sure who.

Critics argued afterward that the prosecution filed too many charges. They claimed that a case should have been built around a few strong charges and fewer children should have been involved (originally 400 children were interviewed and more than 200 charges filed, contributing to the overload right from the start). How can one feel confident that justice has been served when the sheer quantity of information overwhelms the jurors' ability to absorb it? As Michael Marien (in Didsbury, 1982) observes, "Paradoxically, as more information is made available to us, we become less well-informed and decisions become harder to make" (p. 63).

Raymond Buckey was retried on the thirteen charges that deadlocked the original jury. After yet another lengthy and expensive courtroom drama, the second trial ended in a hung jury. Charges against him were ultimately dismissed after he had served five years in a county jail awaiting trial and his entire family fortune of $3 million had been exhausted on lawyers' fees.

Questions for Thought

1. If you were on a jury such as the one in the McMartin case, how would you proceed to deal with the massive quantity of information?
2. Are there effective ways to present information so jury members aren't overwhelmed by the sheer volume of testimony and details?

178 CHAPTER 6 *Group Discussion: Defective Decision Making and Problem Solving*

An avalanche of information buries us in both relevant *and* irrelevant information. A glut of information makes it very difficult to distinguish useless from useful information. Effective decision making is consequently hampered because we have trouble finding the good stuff when we're up to our nostrils in the worthless stuff. Halpern (1984) cites a riddle illustrating this point. It goes as follows:

> Suppose you are a bus driver. On the first stop you pick up 6 men and 2 women. At the second stop 2 men leave and 1 woman boards the bus. At the third stop 1 man leaves and 2 women enter the bus. At the fourth stop 3 men get on and 3 women get off. At the fifth stop 2 men get off, 3 men get on, 1 woman gets off and 2 women get on. What is the bus driver's name? (p. 201)

Don't reread the riddle! Have you figured it out? The answer, of course, is your name since the riddle begins, "Suppose *you* are a bus driver." All the information about the passengers is irrelevant and merely diverts your attention from the obvious and correct answer. Information overload buries us with irrelevant as well as relevant information. Effective decision making is difficult when we have to sort through the heaps of useless information in order to find that which can assist us in making intelligent decisions.

Doing research for this textbook using the Internet proved to be a daunting experience for me. The amount of infotrash that surfaces when a search on the Internet is not well focused is amazing. On several searches, more than 10,000 items were accessed. One search accessed 406,632 separate items to peruse. More than 99 percent of my limited sampling of this information garbage dump revealed worthless, irrelevant junk. Occasionally, I found a nugget mixed in with the fool's gold. Ever-increasing quantities of information present a new challenge to small groups. How do you cope with information overload?

Coping with Information Overload   You can cope with information overload in several ways. **Screening information,** much as you do phone calls, by simply choosing to ignore much of the information, is one possibility. There are still a few faculty members at my campus who steadfastly refuse to use the computers that sit in their offices gathering dust. They want no part of e-mail, the Internet, or anything more technologically advanced than a portable typewriter. It is becoming extremely difficult to avoid the deluge of information cascading upon us, however, even if one desires to do so. Those faculty who refuse to use e-mail are left out of the information loop on campus. They are continually stunned to hear after-the-fact that certain decisions have been made when the rest of the campus was clued-in by e-mail weeks beforehand.

Screening can be useful, however. If you find a hundred e-mail messages waiting for your attention when you return from a vacation, how do you cope? One way is to purchase a software program called Bozo Filters that automatically screens e-mail messages from designated senders (Barnes, 1996). America Online announced in September 1996 that it would block messages from Internet sites that flood subscribers' e-mailboxes with unwanted bulk-mail advertisements (called *spams*). Spamming was the number one complaint from America Online members (Rae-Dupree, 1996). The move by America Online was immediately challenged in court by advertisers.

My solution is more low-tech than this. I regularly screen my e-mail messages by looking at their title. I delete most e-mail messages without reading them because I can determine from their titles that they are irrelevant to me (e.g., someone advertising their house for sale). This is the same way I screen my junk mail. About 80 percent of my daily mail is junk and gets tossed into the trash (or the recycling bin when possible) unopened.

Specialization is a second method for coping with information overload. In order to cope with the information deluge, individuals in government, business, education, and all occupational fields become increasingly more specialized, more narrowed in focus and expertise. Since the quantity of information is expanding exponentially in all fields of endeavor, there is no hope that individuals can keep pace with the changing informational environment unless they specialize. When you specialize you can manage to know a lot about a little. If you don't specialize, you may know very little about a lot.

Specialization in higher education, however, best illustrates the main drawback of this coping strategy. According to the report of the Study Group on the Conditions of Excellence in American Higher Education (in "Text of New Report," 1984), American two- and four-year colleges and universities offer more than 1,100 different majors and programs, nearly half of which are in occupational fields. The report goes on to observe that as undergraduates increasingly select very narrow majors "they become isolated from each other, and many students end up with fragmented and limited knowledge" (p. 36). <u>Students increasingly know more and more about less and less</u>.

Krimsky (1984) applies this analysis to the group decision-making arena. He notes in his examination of public policy decision making in groups: "The nonexperts may find it difficult to distinguish dogma from conjecture and scientific consensus. When individuals are recognized as experts, they may be inclined to wield that confidence beyond the issues of science or their particular area of expertise" (p. 168).

When our knowledge is limited in scope we become more dependent on experts, more vulnerable to their characterizations and perceptions of reality, and more prone to let them do our thinking for us. If we know little or nothing about the law, we may be forced to trust the advice of a lawyer counseling the group on some legal issue. The overuse of incomprehensible jargon by so many experts these days makes it doubly difficult for nonexperts to make intelligent decisions based on the advice of specialists. Although some specialization is undoubtedly necessary to cope with information overload, increasing specialization will probably not improve decision making in groups and may worsen it.

Selectivity is a third method of coping with information overload (Klapp, 1978). Since we can't attend to all information bombarding us, we must choose selectively on the basis of group priorities and goals. As George Mandler, director of the Center for Human Information Processing at the University of California at San Diego, explains:

> If I paid attention to all the things my senses are reporting at any moment and took them all into account, I'd have great difficulty acting. It would be very hard for me to decide what to do. . . . If you go to a restaurant and there are fifty entrees on the menu, you can't deal with it—you first have to narrow it down to, maybe, chicken dishes, or to veal dishes. (in Hunt, 1982, pp. 91–92)

Setting group priorities helps us select which information requires our urgent attention and which can be delayed or ignored entirely. Setting priorities distinguishes what we *need* to know from what there *is* to know. Learning how to *narrow the search* for information on the Internet, for instance, can overcome much of the problem of infotrash referred to previously. Selecting what information specifically is required avoids getting buried by the information dumptruck.

Dividing the labor can also assist in the selectivity process. Each group member can share the burden guided by a set of agreed-upon priorities and clear goals. Graduate students, as "slave labor," are often pressed into service at universities to search and select information relevant to a senior faculty member's scholarly endeavor. Reliance on others to search for relevant information, of course, requires trust in their skills; also, you run the risk of missing crucial information overlooked by someone with less commitment to the project and less concern about the outcome of any decision.

Limiting the search is a fourth way of coping with information overload. As Conrad (1990) observes, there is a curvilinear relationship between information seeking and the level of uncertainty and threat facing a group. When a group faces a simple, unimportant situation, the tendency is to seek out little information. Why make the effort? In more complex, confusing situations, however, more information is sought, but only to a point. When conditions of extremely high uncertainty and threat exist, gathering additional information may cause more confusion, increase anxiety, and possibly lead to decision-making paralysis because more information may produce an increased number of options to consider or may add too much complexity for quick decision making to take place. Thus, decision makers typically reduce the search for more information in highly ambiguous or threatening situations (Victor and Blackburn, 1987; Staw et al., 1981).

Even in situations that are not ambiguous or threatening, the information search must stop at some point for decisions to be made. As Alfred Korzybski liked to remind audiences, "You can never know everything about anything." There is a time for searching and a time for deciding.

Pattern recognition is a fifth means of coping with information overload and potentially the most effective. Discerning patterns is our best defense against information overload. As Klapp (1978) notes, "Once a pattern is perceived, 90 percent of information becomes irrelevant" (p. 13). Pattern recognition allows us to digest and process greater quantities of information if for no other reason than it assists our memory and helps us chunk information. *Chunking* is a process of recoding information into larger more meaningful patterns.

Consider the following example: 1776181218611917194119501964. Without chunking, these twenty-eight numbers would overwhelm the average person's memory and render the numbers useless. A closer examination, however, reveals that the above digits easily break into the generally accepted official starting dates for the United States' entry into major wars. These twenty-eight digits recode into seven more manageable chunks: 1776 1812 1861 1917 1941 1950 and 1964.

In order for chunking to help you cope with information overload, the units must be meaningful. You can't chunk units into just any pattern. For instance, look at the following set of letters: FEA TSO FST REN GTH AMA ZEF RIE NDS. This form of chunking offers no meaningful pattern. In the absence of a meaningful pattern, the sets of letters become clutter. Yet a recoding of the same letters results in the more meaningful and memorable message: FEATS OF STRENGTH AMAZE FRIENDS.

Chunking can be used by groups to cope with information overload. Football teams preparing for a game against an opponent could not possibly perform effectively if they had no specific game plan. A team's game plan acts as a chunking device. Only a small number of plays are chosen. The players are instructed by the coaches to concentrate on a few key strategies: "establish the running game," "contain the opponent's quarterback," "double-team the wide receivers." No player can concentrate on more than a few crucial strategies. The plan simplifies the team's approach to the game. It establishes recognizable patterns for players. The game plan makes sense out of what easily could become nonsense when the system, the team, becomes overwhelmed by too much information about an opponent or by too many plays.

Overall, groups can cope effectively with information overload by carefully defining the problem to be discussed (selectivity), setting a time frame for discussion of the problem and solutions and establishing deadlines for final decisions (limiting the search for information), and especially searching for meaningful patterns that suggest potential solutions to problems (pattern recognition).

 **SECOND LOOK**

Coping with Information Overload

- **Screening**—limit exposure to information
- **Specialization**—know a lot about a little
- **Selectivity**—attend to information that relates directly to group goals and priorities
- **Limiting the Search**—time for searching and time for deciding
- **Pattern Recognition**—chunk information into meaningful units

Information Underload

Although information overload is a far more prevalent and significant problem, information underload can also present problems for groups. **Information**

underload in groups refers to an insufficient amount of information (inadequate input) available to a group for decision-making purposes.

Kruglanski (1986) argues that the 1986 *Challenger* space shuttle disaster was partly a result of information underload. He claims that the compartmentalized deliberation and small-group discussion process at NASA prevented vital information concerning potential sources of an accident from being communicated to the responsible decision makers. This conclusion was supported by the Report of the President's Commission on the Space Shuttle *Challenger* Disaster (1986).

As tragic as the loss of the *Challenger* crew was, however, this flaw in group decision making could have been infinitely more serious if the faulty O-rings had failed on the very next shuttle flight scheduled, instead of during the *Challenger* flight. According to Berkeley professor Dr. John Gofman, co-discoverer of Uranium 233, if the O-rings had failed one flight later you could have "kissed Florida good-bye" (in Clanton, 1988). The next shuttle flight after the *Challenger* was scheduled to carry forty-seven pounds of Plutonium 238. According to Dr. Helen Caldicott in her book, *Nuclear Madness*, one ounce of Plutonium 238 could induce lung cancer in every person on earth. Effective group decision making is serious business.

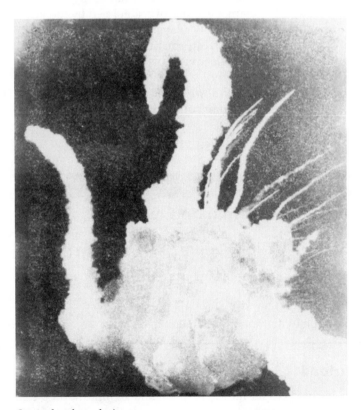

Space shuttle explosion

Information underload can pose a problem in a variety of arenas. Conrad (1990) notes that a consistent finding in studies of organizational communication is that "subordinates want their supervisors to 'keep them informed' and feel that they receive too little relevant and useful information from their supervisors, especially about events, policies, and changes directly involving them or their jobs" (p. 132). Supervisors do not usually provide enough job-related information to subordinates (Goldhaber, 1986).

The problem of unshared information in small groups is serious. Groups that pool information have an advantage over individual decision makers. This potential advantage of pooling information in groups, however, often goes unrealized because group members who have unique information fail to share that information with other members (Schittekatte and Van Hiel, 1996).

Not only is a potential advantage lost from unshared information, but disaster may occur because vital information was not shared with the group. A study (Foushee and Manos, 1981) of cockpit crews flying large commercial planes revealed a tendency of crews who shared little information not to perform as well as crews who shared a greater quantity of information. Seventy percent of all civil aviation accidents and near-misses during a five-year period reported by the NASA Safety Reporting System were caused by either improper transmission of information from one crew member to another or failure to transmit vital information at all (Burrows, 1982). Fewer errors related to mishandling of the engines, hydraulic systems, fuel systems, misreading and missetting instruments, and failing to use ice protection were found when sufficient information was communicated to all crew members.

Information underload is usually a problem of too much closing in a system. The general solution to this problem is greater openness in the lines of communication. All members of the group must have access to the relevant information in order to make quality decisions. Finding the balance between too little and too much information, however, requires critical thinking skills. The competent communicator must acquire sufficient knowledge to recognize within a specific context what information is directly relevant to the task and what is irrelevant or marginal. Increasing the quantity of irrelevant or minimally useful information will confuse the group, not assist it in making effective decisions and solving problems.

MINDSETS: CRITICAL THINKING FROZEN SOLID

Perceptual **mindsets,** psychological and cognitive predispositions to see the world in a particular way—such as biases, preconceptions, and assumptions—interfere with effective decision making and problem solving. Cognitively we are prepared to receive only certain messages and ignore others. We are conditioned to view the world narrowly.

Try this demonstration of mindset on your unsuspecting friends. Have them spell the word *shop* out loud. Now ask them to respond immediately to the question, "What do you do when you come to a green light?" The vast majority will unthinkingly reply, "stop." Why? Because spelling the word *shop* narrows our focus to rhyming words even though the correct answer does not rhyme. Our minds are set to view the world in a particular way even if this is inappropriate. You may be surprised by the power of mindsets. Follow the "shop-stop" demonstration with this version of the same illustration: Spell *joke* out loud. "What do you call the white of an egg?" Most people will be victimized a second time by answering "yolk."

Focus Questions

1. Why does confirmation bias lead to defective decision making/problem solving?
2. Why is dichotomous (either-or) thinking called false?

Confirmation Bias

Confirmation bias is a prime example of a mindset that can produce defective decision making and problem solving. **Confirmation bias** is a tendency among all of us to seek information that confirms our predispositions and to ignore or distort information that contradicts our currently held beliefs and attitudes (Hunt, 1982).

Consider this real example of confirmation bias. A man sued the phone company for several million dollars when he was seriously injured by an automobile that crashed into the phone booth he was occupying. The insurance industry has cited this as an obvious example of a frivolous lawsuit. Obviously, the injured man sued the "deep pocket," the party with the megabucks, not the party truly responsible for the injury, namely, the driver of the car. If you already hold a strong opinion that Americans suffer from lawsuit mania, then you probably would seek no additional or contradictory information regarding this case. Why look any further when your predisposition is confirmed? You give up the investigation before you have a chance to discover contradictory information that would challenge your predilections.

The facts, however, paint a more complex picture. The phone company had been notified on fifteen occasions that the particular phone booth in question had a defective door. The door stuck regularly and trapped occupants in the booth. Even in normal circumstances this could pose a danger and obviously a considerable inconvenience to occupants.

In the case in question, an automobile spun out of control and headed for the phone booth. The man tried desperately to escape from the phone booth but was unable to do so because the door jammed. The automobile crashed into the booth and permanently crippled the man. The victim won the suit because of negligence on the part of the phone company.

The predisposition many people have that Americans are lawsuit-happy acts as a filter for the facts in the case just described. Since our bias is to search for information that supports our points of view, once we think we've had a confirmation there is little motivation to search any further. The case is closed and so are our minds on the subject.

Confirmation bias is alive and well in small groups (Schittekatte and Van Hiel, 1996; Stasser and Titus, 1987). Janis (1982) summarizes research on small group decision making by noting the strong tendency among group members to "show interest in facts and opinions that support their initially preferred policy and take up time in their meetings to discuss them, but they tend to ignore facts and opinions that do not support their initially preferred policy" (p. 10). This confirmation bias is cited by Myers and Lamm (1977) as a contributing factor to the group polarization process previously discussed.

The consequences of confirmation bias to decision making and problem solving in groups are serious. Hirokawa (1985) found that assessing "the negative qualities or consequences associated with alternative choices" (p. 218) was an important determinant of high-quality group decision making. In other words, <u>looking for the potential weaknesses and disconfirming evidence regarding decisions and solutions is a significant element of effective group decision making and problem solving</u>. Assessing positive qualities or consequences was not determined by Hirokawa to be nearly as important. Thus, groups that resist confirmation bias and actively search for possible negative outcomes of decisions and solutions usually make better choices than groups that don't.

There is more to confirmation bias, however, than simply seeking confirmation of viewpoints and ignoring disconfirmation. Confirmation bias can also distort evidence that disconfirms our viewpoints and perceptions in a most interesting fashion. Neil Postman (1976) calls this **self-confirmation.** In this distortive process, all evidence and reasoning becomes confirming no matter how damaging it might first appear to be.

Let me first illustrate self-confirmation with a story (in Postman, 1976). This man goes to a psychiatrist with an unusual problem. He is firmly convinced that he is dead. The psychiatrist is a bit perplexed but she makes an effort to change her patient's mind. She asks the man, "Do dead men bleed?" He responds, "No, they don't." The psychiatrist then reaches into her desk drawer, pulls out a pin, grabs the man's hand and stabs it with the pin. The man looks at the blood spurting out of his wound and remarks, "Well, I'll be damned. Dead men do bleed." The man's mindset is unshakable. Seemingly disconfirming evidence indicating that the man is not dead is merely distorted to fit the predisposition and confirm the original conclusion.

Walter Anderson (1990) describes self-confirmation in a group setting this way:

> After events in the Oregon Rajneesh commune deteriorated into what would look to most people like complete and dangerous looniness—wiretappings, drug use, poisonings, importation of thousands of street people to vote in local elections, building of an arsenal of rifles and semi-automatic weapons, finally criminal charges against the leaders and virtual collapse of the whole setup—many followers remained convinced that Rajneesh had designed the whole thing as a part of his teaching. "I wouldn't have missed the experience for anything," one said. "Bhagwan showed us at firsthand how power corrupts. He showed us how Fascism comes into being. Where else could you learn something like that?" (p. 197)

Women often have to deal with self-confirming beliefs of supervisors in groups and organizations. Self-confirmation typically manifests itself in a kind of "damned if you do, damned if you don't" dilemma for women (Haslett et al., 1992). When women conform to stereotypes by acting in accommodating, unassertive ways, they have difficulty being taken seriously and thus garnering advancement and promotions. When they act more assertively, however, they also diminish their probabilities for promotion and advancement because they are viewed as uncooperative and too aggressive, even though similar behavior by males is usually viewed positively. Sexist stereotypes of women in business settings are thus perpetuated because "evidence" of women's inability to perform well as managers and executives is noted whenever unassertive, accommodating behavior is exhibited, but when women adopt a more assertive style this also is cited as "evidence" of their inadequacy because "no one can get along with them."

The perpetuation of unwarranted beliefs is the natural result of confirmation bias. How do we correct our false beliefs that pollute the decision-making/problem-solving process when we aren't open to refutation of such beliefs? How do we see the world more accurately so our group decisions have greater validity and our solutions to problems have more efficacy when we insulate ourselves from disconfirming information? The answer obviously is we don't.

So how does the competent communicator combat confirmation bias? The competent communicator combats the problem of confirmation bias as follows:

1. *Seek disconfirming information and evidence.* Since most group members will be predisposed to seek confirming evidence, someone will have to perform an error-correction function for the group. Consider it your personal responsibility to find the disconfirming information. If, after a concerted effort, you find little negative evidence of note, then your decision or solution has an excellent chance of turning out well.
2. *Vigorously present disconfirming evidence to the group.* Be persistent. Members will usually ignore negative news unless you assert yourself. Messengers with bad news aren't always killed. Sometimes they're received as heroes when they prevent the group from making a grave error.
3. *Play devil's advocate.* The term *devil's advocate* originated many centuries ago with the Roman Catholic Church (Forsyth, 1990). Investigations of claims of sainthood were viewed by the church as so important that a formal position called devil's advocate was instituted for the express purpose of challenging the qualifications of candidates. Develop the habit of asking yourself and others the question, "So what's another side of the issue?" Challenge the assumptions and claims of those defending a decision or solution in your group—play devil's advocate. Do it in the spirit of problem orientation (supportive), not as an effort to force your will on the group (defensive). Clearly indicate your intentions so there will be no misunderstanding of your motives or intent. Anyone may play devil's advocate in a group. If groups establish a norm of devil's advocacy, then the responsibility won't fall on one member's shoulders.

4. *Gather allies to help challenge confirmation bias.* Women and ethnic minorities especially profit from developing support with those members of a group who are respected and open-minded.

False Dichotomies

Dichotomous, either-or thinking is the tendency to view the world in terms of opposites and to describe this dichotomy in the language of extremes. Dichotomies are usually false because in most instances there are more than two opposing possibilities, thus, the term **false dichotomy.** Describing objects, events, and people in such extreme polarities as moral-immoral, good-bad, rich-poor, corrupt-honest, intelligent-stupid locks us into a mindset of narrow vision. Most objects, events, and people are more accurately described in gray shades, not black or white.

If a thousand people were chosen at random and plotted on a graph according to height, weight, intelligence, income, age, health, skin color, and other factors, most of these thousand people would bunch up in the middle (relatively average height, weight, income, etc.) and only a few individuals would appear at the extremes. This is called a bell-shaped curve or normal distribution. Dichotomous characterizations concentrate on the few extremes and ignore the far more numerous cases spread across the vast middle ground (DeVito, 1989). Thus, we describe people as short or tall, fat or thin, young or old, healthy or unhealthy, and so forth. Yet the lines of demarcation separating these polarized categories are anything but clear.

For instance, when does a man become bald? How many hairs does a man have to lose before we pronounce him bald? When does a molehill become a mountain? And once we have declared the molehill a mountain does it become a molehill once again by the removal of a single rock? When does a recession become a depression? When does success turn into failure? When does a small group become a large group and vice versa? Dichotomous descriptions of events and objects are usually false because most of reality consists of more-to-less, not either-or.

False dichotomies contribute to defective group decision making and problem solving. When group members are predisposed to see problems and solutions only in extremes, the vast middle ground goes largely unexplored. City councils, faced with reduced revenues during a recession, see only layoffs and reductions in public services when they think dichotomously (i.e., tax revenues up—fund services and jobs; tax revenues down—cut services and jobs). They may fail to explore other avenues for raising revenues besides taxes.

Dichotomous thinking can lead to a friends-enemies duality when controversy brews. Groups may then shrink from making hard decisions or they may be provoked into making decisions from less than pure motives. Even the decision to make a decision can be a product of dichotomous thinking. Groups locked into the mindset that a decision has to be made may never consider a third alternative besides voting for or against some proposal. Postponing the decision until adequate study of the problem can take place and potential solutions can emerge may be a more viable option.

In some few cases, however, it makes good sense to think dichotomously. It is very difficult to be sort of pregnant or almost a virgin. Some classes in college are graded on a pass-fail or credit–no-credit basis. The options are clearly either-or with no exceptions. All possibilities are included in these two choices. Most dichotomous thinking, however, inappropriately implies all possibilities are included within two extreme categories when clearly this is not the case.

The competent communicator combats the problem of false dichotomies in small groups as follows:

1. *Be suspicious of absolutes.* When group members argue only two extreme possibilities (e.g., a solution is either all good or all bad), look for a third or even fourth possibility.
2. *Employ the language of qualification.* When engaged in group discussion, speak in terms of degrees (i.e., to what extent an argument is true). You'll be using terms such as *sometimes, rarely, occasionally, mostly, usually,* and *moderately.* This is not the language of the wishy-washy fence-straddler. This is the language of precision in matters of human discourse.

◌◌ CLOSER LOOK

Blue Eyes versus Brown Eyes

In-group bias, a product of our tendency to dichotomize the world, is a source of racism, sexism, and discrimination. The in-group bias occurs when one group of individuals is differentiated from another group of individuals. The differentiations may be quite arbitrary and meaningless in any important sense (e.g., individuals wearing basic blue jeans versus individuals wearing designer clothes). Nevertheless, both groups will quickly develop a "them" versus "us" mentality. This we-they thinking between groups fosters a superior attitude toward your own group (the in-group) and a perception of inferiority toward the other group (the out-group). Once the superiority-inferiority dichotomy is established, hostility targeted at the out-group easily emerges. Perceived differences between the groups, even trivial ones, are magnified.

A remarkable demonstration of the arbitrariness of the in-group versus out-group phenomenon was devised by Jane Elliott (1977), a third-grade teacher in Riceville, Iowa. Elliott wanted her students from an all-white, rural community of about 900 people to experience prejudice and discrimination firsthand in order to appreciate its viciousness.

She divided her class into two groups according to eye color. Quite arbitrarily she designated the brown-eyed children as "superior" to the "inferior" blue-eyed children. "Brown-eyed people are better, cleaner, smarter, more civilized than blue-eyed people," she informed her wide-eyed pupils. Brown-eyed students were given special privileges, while blue-eyed children were told to obey certain demeaning rules that applied to them exclusively.

With their teacher constantly reminding the blue-eyed children of their inferiority and the brown-eyed children of their superiority, the we-they false dichotomy quickly affected the children's performance and self-esteem. The blue-eyed children immediately began to perform poorly in their schoolwork and became downcast, sullen, and angry. Brown-eyed children transformed from ''marvelously cooperative, thoughtful children'' into ''nasty, vicious, discriminating little third-graders.''

The following day, Elliott informed her class that she had been wrong the day before. The blue-eyed children were really the superior people and the brown-eyed children were inferior. Almost immediately the two groups switched behavior and self-perceptions. Now the brown-eyed children described themselves in derogatory terms such as stupid, dull, and bad while the blue-eyed children chose complimentary terms such as nice, good, and sweet. This was a complete turnaround for both groups from self-reports the day before. Academic performance suffered for the new ''inferior'' group and was enhanced for the new ''superior'' group.

The simplism and false perceptions fostered by dichotomous labeling of groups during this demonstration were apparent. The distinctions drawn by Elliott between the blue-eyed children and brown-eyed children were unequivocally either-or: superior or inferior designations with no in-between. The distinctions were obviously false since the two groups flip-flopped on the second day and suddenly became the opposite of what they were designated the previous day.

In addition to demonstrating the falseness of dichotomous, either-or thinking, Elliott's classroom experiment also clearly illustrates confirmation bias. Inappropriate or disruptive behavior by members of whichever group happened to be designated inferior was seized upon by Elliott as ''proof'' of their inferiority, and admirable behavior by members of the superior group was noted as ''proof'' of the group's superiority. In one instance, when brown-eyed children were labeled inferior, Elliott exclaimed, ''Everyone's ready except Lori—she's a brown eyes.''

When the blue-eyed children were designated as the inferior group, Elliott shook her head when a blue-eyed child had trouble reading, then allowed a brown-eyed child to read the passage correctly. Turning to one blue-eyed child she asked, ''Russell, where are your glasses?'' He had forgotten them. ''Susan has her glasses—she's a brown eyes,'' noted Elliott to the class. No matter what the children did, Elliott selectively spotlighted behavior that seemed to confirm the arbitrary designation of either superiority or inferiority. Throwing away a plastic cup was ''wasteful'' if done by a child in the inferior group, while keeping it might be labeled ''unsanitary'' (self-confirmation). Elliott, however, was not immune from confirmation bias. When she accidentally flipped up a screen while trying to pull it down, one of her pupils shouted, ''What do you expect, she's blue-eyed.''

Weiner and Wright (1973) found results similar to Elliott's when they conducted a controlled experiment with a third-grade class. In addition, however, they also found that a classroom experiment like the one Elliott created can significantly diminish racial prejudice among children.

Children are suggestible. Adults, however, are more sophisticated. Nevertheless, Elliott duplicated her results when she tried her experiment with adult groups, most notably with officials and employees at an Iowa state penitentiary. At first I didn't believe these results could be duplicated with adults. When I saw a movie on Jane Elliott and her experiments, however, I became a believer.

No matter how arbitrary and trivial the distinctions made between groups, human beings easily slip into a we-they frame of mind. Once the designation has been made regarding who the "we" are and who the "they" are, almost any behavior can be twisted to confirm a predisposition. In this way, prejudice is excused and nurtured.

Questions for Thought

1. Do you think Elliott's experiment should be conducted in public schools across the United States to combat racism fostered by confirmation bias and dichotomous thinking?
2. In your opinion is this experiment with third-graders ethical? Could children suffer serious psychological trauma from such an experiment?

COLLECTIVE INFERENTIAL ERRORS: UNCRITICAL THINKING

Two American women—a matronly grandmother and her attractive granddaughter—are seated in a railroad compartment with a Romanian officer and a Nazi officer during World War II. As the train passes through a dark tunnel, the sound of a loud kiss and an audible slap shatters the silence. As the train emerges from the tunnel no words are spoken but a noticeable welt forming on the face of the Nazi officer is observed by all. The grandmother muses to herself, "What a fine granddaughter I have raised. I have no need to worry. She can take care of herself." The granddaughter thinks to herself, "Grandmother packs a powerful wallop for a woman of her years. She sure has spunk." The Nazi officer, none too pleased by the course of events, ruminates to himself, "This Romanian is clever. He steals a kiss and gets me slapped in the process." The Romanian officer chuckles to himself, "Not a bad ploy. I kissed my hand and slapped a Nazi."

This story illustrates the problem of inferential error. **Inferences** are conclusions about the unknown based on the known. They are guesses varying by degrees from educated to uneducated (depending on the quantity and quality of information on which the inferences are based). We draw inferences from previous experiences, factual data, and predispositions. The facts of the story are that the sounds of a kiss followed by a slap are heard by all members of the group. Based on what is known, the three individuals who do not know for sure what happened all draw distinctly different and erroneous inferences.

Making inferences is not a problem in itself. The human thinking process is inferential. Our minds "go beyond the information given" (Nisbett and Ross, 1980). We could not function on a daily basis without making inferences. You can't know for certain that the grocery store is open. It may have burned down or closed due to a power outage. You draw the conclusion that it is open on the basis of what is known. If the store has always been open twenty-four hours, seven days a week, then you infer it will be open now, which is a relatively safe inference. <u>The principal problem with inferences is that we rarely question their accuracy</u>. We *assume* our inferences are true even when they rest on insufficient or faulty information, and, as the Felix Unger character in an episode of the old TV program *The Odd Couple* once explained, "To *assume* is to make an *ass* out of *u* and *me*." This can pose serious problems for group decision making. If we don't exercise our critical thinking abilities by closely examining important inferences central to decision making in groups, bad decisions are highly likely to result.

Focus Questions
1. What are the primary general sources of collective inferential errors?
2. Should we avoid making inferences?
3. Why are most correlations noncausal?

Prevalence of the Problem

The centrality of inferences to decision making and problem solving in groups is made apparent by Gouran (1982) when he explains:

> In virtually every phase of discussion, inferences come into play. Whether you are assessing facts, testing opinions, examining the merits of competing arguments, or exploring which of several alternatives best satisfies a set of decisional criteria, you will have occasion to draw inferences suggested by the information you are examining. How well you reason, therefore, can have as much to do with the effectiveness of a decision-making discussion as any other factor that enters the process. (pp. 96–97)

Individuals are inclined to make inferential errors (see Closer Look: The Uncritical Inference Test). The problem can be magnified in groups. Gouran calls this **collective inferential error.**

The research regarding group polarization suggests that when a group exhibits a predominant initial tendency, group discussion seems to amplify the initial position of group members. If the inference is a bad one, the group may engage in collective misjudgment. Studies by Gouran (1981, 1982, 1983) have established the prevalence of inferential errors in groups. As many as half of a group's discussion statements may be inferences. Groups often accept these inferences uncritically.

Gouran (1983) examined student group discussions in which eighty inferences were made regarding questions of policy. Only one inference was challenged. The rest were reinforced, extended, or new inferences were added. Why is this significant? Because Hirokawa and Pace (1983) and Martz (1984) found that <u>ineffective decision-making groups that arrived at faulty decisions dis-</u>

Look at the college basketball coach pictured above. How did you decide which individual was the coach? Did you assume that the male is the coach? If so, you made an inaccurate inference. Laura Mitchell coaches the University of California at Santa Cruz women's basketball team.

played more inferential deficiencies in their discussions than did effective groups.

👀 CLOSER LOOK

The Uncritical Inference Test

Individuals are prone to make inferential errors (Nisbett and Ross, 1980). See if you have such a tendency. Read the following story. For each statement about the story, circle "T" if it can be determined without a doubt from the information provided in the story that the statement is completely true, "F" if the statement directly contradicts information in the story, and "?" if you cannot determine from the information provided in the story whether the statement is either true of false. The story:

> Dr. Chris Cross, who works at St. Luke's Hospital, hurried into room #314 where Yoshi Yamamoto was lying in bed. Pat Sinclair, a registered nurse, was busy fluffing bed pillows when Dr. Cross entered. Dr. Cross said to the nurse in charge, "This bed should have been straightened out long ago." A look of anger came across Nurse Sinclair's face. Dr. Cross promptly turned around and hurried out the door.

1. Chris Cross is a medical doctor who works at St. Luke's Hospital. **T F ?**
2. Dr. Cross is a man in a hurry. **T F ?**
3. Yoshi Yamamoto, who is Japanese, was lying in bed. **T F ?**
4. Pat Sinclair was in room #314 when Dr. Cross entered and found her fluffing bed pillows. **T F ?**
5. Dr. Cross was irritated with Nurse Sinclair because the bed was not straightened out. **T F ?**
6. Yoshi Yamamoto is a patient at St. Luke's Hospital. **T F ?**
7. Nurse Sinclair's face reddened because Dr. Cross was stern with her. **T F ?**
8. When Dr. Cross entered he became the third person in room #314. **T F ?**
9. This story takes place at St. Luke's Hospital. **T F ?**
10. This story concerns a series of events in which only three persons are referred to: Dr. Cross, Nurse Sinclair, and Yoshi Yamamoto. **T F ?**

I created this version of what Haney (1967) originally devised and called *The Uncritical Inference Test.* I have given it to students for more than fifteen years. The huge majority *incorrectly* identify all or most of the statements as "T." If you circled "?" for all of the statements above, then you are not likely to make inferential errors unless you get sloppy. "?" is the correct answer for all of the statements. Without exception, these statements are based on assumptions—guesses regarding what is likely but not verifiably true from the information provided. All of the statements involve uncertainty—some more than others. The reasons these statements are uncertain are as follows:

1. Chris Cross is a doctor of some sort but not necessarily a medical doctor (Dr. Cross may be a Ph.D., chiropractor, dentist, etc.)
2. Dr. Cross is not necessarily a man.
3. Yoshi Yamamoto has a Japanese name, but isn't necessarily Japanese (married name, assumed name).
4. Pat Sinclair may be a *male* not a "her."
5. This requires an inference that Dr. Cross is irritated and that Nurse Sinclair and "the nurse in charge" are one and the same person, which cannot be ascertained from the information provided.
6. Yoshi Yamamoto may be an orderly taking a break or a visitor resting, not a patient.
7. This requires an inference that "a look of anger" automatically produces a "reddened face." Again, Nurse Sinclair may be male.
8. There may have been four people in room #314 if Nurse Sinclair and the nurse in charge are not the same person.
9. Dr. Cross works at St. Luke's. Nowhere does it say this story occurred there.
10. Again, four people may be in the story: Dr. Cross, Nurse Sinclair, the nurse in charge, and Yoshi Yamamoto.

Assuming that all doctors are male and all nurses are female unless designated otherwise (e.g., woman doctor; male nurse) are increasingly inaccurate inferences as traditional roles change. If we don't even recognize that we've made an inference, then we're not likely to notice when the inference is a bad one. If individually you do poorly on recognizing and critically evaluating inferences, imagine the quality of decision making in a group when most or all of the members are inclined to make inferential errors.

Questions for Thought

1. Is The Uncritical Inference Test merely splitting hairs over relatively minor assumptions or does the test sensitize us to an important and common deficiency in our critical thinking process?
2. Assuming some inferential errors are more serious than others, how do you determine the more serious from the less serious?

General Sources of Inferential Errors

Inferences that rely on a quality information base in plentiful supply are educated guesses—not always correct, but nevertheless probable. Inferences that are drawn from a limited, faulty information base, however, are "uneducated" guesses—likely to produce inferential errors (Gouran, 1989). The two general sources of inferential errors, then, are a faulty information base or misinformation, and a seriously limited information base.

Inferential errors from a faulty information base are common. Hirokawa (1987), in a study of ineffective decision making in small groups, provides an example of collective inferential error resulting from a faulty information base. The group task was to choose ten items from a list of thirty salvageable articles most crucial to surviving five days in a remote wilderness area of Canada in the middle of winter following a plane crash. In one group, the following discussion took place:

B: I think we should go with the wine next. . . . That would be helpful for survival, I would think.
C: How so?
B: Well, uh, first, it can help to keep us warm—we established that as one of our needs . . . plus, you know, like wine can be used for medicinal purposes.
A: I don't understand.
B: What? About keep us warm? Medicinal value?
A: Yeah.
B: Well, OK, wine . . . have you ever drunk wine, you have, haven't you? It warms you up, right? That's because of the alcohol in it, but also, that alcohol, that's how it can be used for medicinal purposes. Say if someone got cut, we could wash it with it, cleanse it, keep it from getting infected.
C: Plus, also, if we need to, I guess we could also use it to help us get a fire going. Like if the twigs and sticks were wet, and wouldn't burn, we could pour some wine over them and light it.
A: Like lighter, or what, yeah, charcoal-lighting fluid?

B: Yeah, right, same idea. So, see, the wine has several uses. . . .
C: Yeah, let's go with the wine. (pp. 17–18)

There are several bad inferences in this example of negative synergy because the information used to draw the inferences is faulty. The feeling of warmth from drinking alcohol does not mean the body is heated by drinking wine. Alcohol dilates the blood vessels in the skin, which in turn chills the blood when a person is exposed to very cold weather. An intoxicated person is more likely to get hypothermia. The low level of alcohol in wine also makes it ineffective as a disinfectant; and have you ever tried to ignite wine? There isn't a high enough level of alcohol in wine to act as a fire starter.

Inferential error resulting from severely limited information is equally problematic for a group. Foushee (1982) notes that there have been several documented near-collisions in the sky because pilots made faulty inferences. In addition, he cites an example where a critical alarm went off in the cockpit of a plane. Shortly thereafter, the alarm went silent, leading the captain to infer that it was probably a false warning. After landing, however, the pilot learned that the flight engineer had pulled the circuit breaker for the alarm system, that it was not a false warning, and that the alarm could have been potentially serious.

Upon questioning, the flight engineer revealed that he had asked the captain if he wanted the alarm turned off. When the captain made no reply, the flight engineer wrongly inferred that he was complying with the captain's wishes by switching off the alarm. The engineer based his inference on the extremely limited information that the captain did not specifically tell him to keep the alarm operational and check the source of the problem. The captain inferred that the alarm was a false one simply because it stopped. That's very limited information on which to draw such a significant inference.

The problem here is not that groups make inferences. Decision making requires inferences. Thinking is inferential. <u>The problem is that we are prone to make inferences based on extremely limited or faulty information without even realizing that we've made a guess, not identified a fact</u>. If no group member challenges the validity of inferences made during discussion, if members just assume as fact that alcohol makes you warm because you get a warm feeling from it, or that silence means consent, then groups may stack one faulty inference upon another. This makes a poor basis for quality decision making.

CLOSER LOOK
The Blandina Chiapponi Case

A dramatic example of inferential error made international headlines in 1989 (Brecher, 1989). A woman named Blandina Isabella Chiapponi said she had been raped by a man named Steven Lamar Lord, an unsavory character, in a Denny's parking lot in Fort Lauderdale, Florida, at 3:00 A.M. The case went to trial and the jury acquitted the defendant after two hours of deliberations. One of the jurors, Ray Diamond, gave the verdict worldwide attention when he explained after the trial, ''We all felt she was asking for it, the way she dressed'' (in Brecher, 1989, p. B1). Blandina Chiapponi was wearing a lace miniskirt, tank top, white high heels, and no underwear on the night in question.

Within days, the 22-year-old woman was an international celebrity. On both Oprah Winfrey's and Larry King's talk shows, she claimed, ''I was kidnapped, I was beaten, I was almost murdered before being raped three times. My life has been ruined, not only by the brute who raped me, but by a jury who decided I was to blame because of what I was wearing'' (p. B1). The media had a field day. The *London Daily Mail* described her as ''an innocent, convent-educated girl'' from a ''close-knit Catholic family who are standing by her'' (p. B1). Blandina Chiapponi, so went the story, had been victimized twice— once by her brutal rapist and again by the jury. A ''Take Back The Night'' march on the county courthouse made her case a central issue. On the basis of her version of the incident and the one inflammatory comment of the juror (who later ''explained'' that he simply meant that Chiapponi was a prostitute whose form of dress purposely advertised her desire to sell sex), most people seemed to think that the jury had performed a terrible injustice.

On closer inspection, the following inconsistencies and errors in Blandina Chiapponi's story created a reasonable doubt in the minds of jurors:

1. She said she was with friends the night of the incident, but she couldn't remember their names.
2. She asserted that she was going into Denny's for something to eat, yet she had no money nor any place to keep money on her person.
3. She changed her story on the witness stand regarding where the rape allegedly took place.
4. She told the investigating officer that she was wearing underpants, then admitted during the trial that she wasn't.
5. She claimed she worked at a modeling and talent agency, which was false; she actually worked at a massage parlor thought by police to be a front for prostitution.
6. After charging rape, she later refused to cooperate with the prosecution and was arrested for ignoring subpoenas—she resisted arrest.
7. She claimed she had inherited a substantial amount of money, which was never proven.
8. She asserted, ''I was hit over the head and cut up and left for dead,'' but although there was evidence of sexual intercourse, there was no evidence of physical violence except for a small finger wound that looked like a paper cut.
9. She claimed she had a close-knit family who staunchly stood behind her— this also proved to be untrue.

In fact, the jury did not decide its verdict on the basis of what this woman wore (Brecher, 1989). In their discussions, despite the later misleading remark by Ray Diamond, the jurors agreed that what she wore and how she lived her life were irrelevant to the verdict. The case ultimately was decided on whose story the jury believed—Chiapponi's or Lord's (he claimed she was a prostitute looking for money and cocaine). The fact that she was shown to be a liar of no small proportions left the jury with a reasonable doubt. Elinor Brecher (1990) summarizes:

> What mattered to the jury was this: Blandina Chiapponi had clearly misrepresented herself under oath, not once but several times. Although it pained them, in a case where the physical evidence was inconclusive, the jury had no choice but to look to the victim's credibility in order to remove that last shred of reasonable doubt, as the law demands. They looked but they still doubted. (p. B1)

Blandina Chiapponi may have been raped. It's not likely the truth will ever be ascertained. The inference that the jury had failed in its duty and had perpetrated an abomination, however, cannot be drawn validly from the facts. The jury in the Blandina Chiapponi case was an effective decision-making group since individuals in the group performed an error-correction function and overcame the serious temptation to make inferential errors. The fact that Steven Lamar Lord was an unsavory character, who even may have looked like a man capable of rape, and the attire of Blandina Chiapponi did not sway the jury to make faulty inferences. They drew conclusions from the facts available, not from assumptions concerning what could have happened or how they might have wanted the verdict to come out.

The public, in general, and the media, in particular, were guilty of collective inferential error, of jumping to a conclusion unsupported by the facts available. Based on the slimmest information—one inflammatory statement by Ray Diamond—the inference was drawn that this jury had perpetrated an outrageous injustice. Later, this faulty inference was bolstered by Blandina Chiapponi's one-sided and erroneous presentation of the "facts." It is understandable that Ray Diamond's comment would incite an angry response from the public. His was an example of communication incompetence. He made an insensitive, completely inappropriate remark. Yet, why assume he spoke for the entire jury of twelve members? Since faulty inferential leaps are more likely when the issues are emotionally charged, as was the case in the Chiapponi trial, scrutinizing inferences is all the more important when the issues are combustible.

Questions for Thought

1. Do you agree that the jury in this case was "an effective decision-making group"? Explain.
2. Can you think of instances when you have "jumped to conclusions" very much like the public reaction to Ray Diamond's incendiary statement?

Specific Sources of Inferential Errors

There are several specific sources of inferential errors that can adversely affect group decision making. I will discuss three of the most prevalent.

Vividness   The first specific source of inferential error is the vividness effect. Stanovich (1992) explains it this way:

> When faced with a problem-solving or decision-making situation, people retrieve from memory the information that seems relevant to the situation at hand. Thus, they are more likely to employ the facts that are more accessible to solve a problem or make a decision. One factor that strongly affects accessibility is the vividness of information. (p. 59)

The graphic, outrageous, shocking, controversial, dramatic event draws our attention and sticks in our minds. Producer Gary David Goldberg captured the essence of the vividness effect when he pointedly observed, "Left to their own devices, the networks would televise live executions. Except Fox—they'd televise live *naked* executions" ("TV or not TV," 1993).

We tend to overvalue vivid, concrete information and undervalue abstract, statistical information, which often depicts a more accurate picture of the way things are. When groups of college students and community residents were asked to estimate how often the insanity plea is used by defendants in their state they estimated 33 and 38 percent respectively. Yet the truth is fewer than 1 percent of defendants even attempt this defense. When asked to estimate how successful this plea is when tried, both groups estimated 45 percent of the time, yet the actual fact is, when tried, the insanity plea is successful only 4 percent of the time. Jeffrey and Pasewark (1983) argue that this misperception derives "from publicity accorded by the public media to criminal cases of notoriety" (p. 38). John Hinckley, who shot Ronald Reagan, made a successful insanity plea. Dan White, who killed San Francisco mayor George Moscone and city supervisor Harvey Milk, successfully used the "Twinkie Defense" to argue "diminished capacity" (junk food made him do it). These are vivid exceptions that can distort our perceptions regarding how often the insanity or diminished capacity defense is used and how successful it is likely to be.

Although the vividness effect does not always lead to poor decision making, Hamil and his associates (1979) demonstrated its potential for inferential error. They presented subjects with one of two videotaped interviews in which an individual identified as a guard at a state prison discussed his job. In the first videotape, the guard was a model of human decency, exhibiting compassion toward prisoners and concern for their rehabilitation. In the second videotape, the guard was a brutish individual who ridiculed the idea of rehabilitation and called the prisoners animals who had to be punished to maintain order and control. Some of the subjects were told that the guard depicted in the videotape was a typical example of guards at the prison, others were told that the guard was not typical, and still others were told nothing about whether the guard was typical or not.

What the subjects were told about the prison guard seemed to matter little. The videotape of the guard, however, apparently was too vivid to ignore. Subjects who saw the humane version of the interview reported that they believed prison guards in general were humane while, those subjects who saw the inhumane, brutish version reported that they believed prison guards in general were inhumane.

From students who give greater credibility to a friend's opinion of a professor than they do to statistical summaries of the ratings of all students who have taken a class from that professor (Borgida and Nisbett, 1977), to those individuals who give credence to the anecdotes and testimonials for all manner of inflated claims about diet plans and cancer cures, the power of the vivid example to shape and distort decision making is real. The potency of the vividness effect is so real that Stanovich (1992) concludes that it "threatens to undermine the usefulness of any knowledge generated by any of the behavioral sciences" (p. 141). Be immediately wary of any claim that rests on the veneer of the vivid example.

Unrepresentativeness   When we make a judgment, we assess the resemblance or accuracy of an object or event presumed to belong to a general category. Is a specific example representative of a general category? If the answer is yes, then the inference drawn from the representative example is on solid footing. If the example is unrepresentative, however, inferences drawn from it are likely to be erroneous. If the example is both unrepresentative and vivid, then the potential for inferential error is magnified.

Ray Diamond did not speak for the Chiapponi jury, yet the public and the mass media assumed that he represented all twelve members. If you said to yourself as I related the details of the Chiapponi case that you wished I hadn't chosen this example to illustrate collective inferential error because the issues are sensitive and some might erroneously assume that her conduct was typical of rape victims, then you have manifested an appreciation for the potential dangers of unrepresentativeness. Those who would assert from the Chiapponi case that rape victims frequently lie in such trials and therefore testimony from such victims is highly unreliable make a huge inference based on a single unusual instance. This inference has as much validity as asserting that because your second cousin is a pathological liar most of your family must be too. Blandina Chiapponi hardly qualifies as a representative complainant in a rape trial.

A study by Quattrone and Jones (1980) illustrates inferential error resulting from unrepresentativeness in a group context. College students indicated their belief that if one member of a group made a particular decision, then all members of the group would make the same decision. This was especially true if the students were observing the decisions of students from other colleges. In other words, we stereotype an entire group on the basis of a single individual who may or may not be representative of the group as a whole.

Correlation   A third specific source of inferential error is correlation. A consistent relationship between two or more variables is called a **correlation.** There are two kinds of correlations: positive and negative. A positive correlation occurs when X increases and Y also increases (e.g., as you grow older your ears grow larger—nature's practical joke on the elderly; as you increase in height your weight also increases). A negative correlation occurs when X increases and Y decreases (e.g., as adults increase in age their capacity to run long distances decreases; as cars increase in age they decrease in value).

Most correlations are not perfect; a perfect correlation has no exceptions. Not everyone who grows taller increases in weight, especially if a teenager aggressively diets to slim down as he or she grows. Not every automobile loses value as it ages, especially if it is an antique classic car.

The main problem with correlations is the strong inclination people have for inferring causation (x causes y) from a correlation (sometimes called a *post hoc ergo propter hoc* fallacy). A large research team collected data in Taiwan to determine which variables best predicted use of contraceptive methods for birth control (Li, 1975). Of all the variables, use of birth control was most strongly correlated with the number of electric appliances (i.e., toasters, ovens, blenders, etc.) found in the home. Birth control usage increased as the number of electric appliances increased (GE doesn't bring good things to life?). So does it make sense to you that a free microwave oven or electric blender for every teenager in high school would decrease teen pregnancy rates? I'm confident that you can see the absurdity of such a suggestion.

The birth control–electric appliances correlation is an obvious case where a correlation, even though a very strong one, is not a causation. The number of electric appliances more than likely is a reflection of socioeconomic status and education levels, which undoubtedly have more to do with rates of birth control usage than the number of electric irons and toasters found in the home.

Stephen Jay Gould (1981) explains that "the vast majority of correlations in our world are, without doubt, noncausal" (p. 242). The fact that most correlations are noncausal, however, does not prevent most people from making the inferential error of correlation mistaken for causation. As Gould states, "The invalid assumption that correlation implies cause is probably among the two or three most serious and common errors of human reasoning" (p. 242).

I have witnessed the correlation as causation inferential error in my own classes. Consider the following discussion that took place in a small group in one of my classes.

J: I think we should choose capital punishment for our topic. I just did a paper on it. We can show that capital punishment works. In a lot of states that have it, murder rates have decreased.

A: Yeah, did you ever see that video where they show executions? Really gross. You know most criminals would think twice about killing someone if they realize they'll fry in the electric chair.

B: Well, I heard that when they execute a guy, the murder rate goes up right after. I don't think capital punishment is a very effective solution to murder.

In this brief conversation, group members managed to allege the truth of an asserted causation based only on a correlation, affirm the validity of the inferential error with a little commonsense reasoning, then refute the effectiveness of capital punishment by introducing yet another correlation assumed to be a causation.

When capital punishment was instituted in some states, murder rates did decrease. Do we have a causation established? Not necessarily. Even if murders decreased after the institution of capital punishment, no causal connection can be assumed. Other factors, such as the economic outlook for the state or country and availability of support services for poor people, may be responsible for any decrease in murder rates. As social psychologist Dane Archer reports (in Wilkes, 1987), of the fifty-odd U.S. studies of the deterrence effect of the death penalty, only one asserted a causal connection and that lone study is suspect. None of the other numerous studies could establish causation. Archer concludes from this and his own research that "the overwhelming pattern in deterrence research shows that the death penalty has no effect on the homicide rate" (p. 31).

Conversely, if an assertion is made that murder rates increase after executions take place, this does not mean the two are causally connected. This may be coincidence. Executions *may* cause increases in homicide rates, but you certainly don't establish such a causal link by showing a mere correlation.

 SECOND LOOK

Sources of Inferential Errors

General Sources of Inferential Errors
- Seriously limited information base (insufficient quantity of information)
- Faulty information base (poor-quality information)

Specific Sources of Inferential Errors
- Vividness
- Unrepresentativeness
- Correlation (*post hoc ergo propter hoc* fallacy)

Error Correction: Practicing Critical Thinking

In order for the error-correction function of group discussion to kick in, competent communicators must recognize the sources of inferential errors just discussed. Assertively focusing the group's attention on sources of inferential error can help prevent faulty decision making from occurring. In other words, group members must put their critical thinking abilities into practice if effective decision making is to take place. As Hirokawa and Pace (1983) found, group discussion promotes higher-quality decision making when:

1. The validity of inferences are carefully examined.
2. Inferences are grounded in valid information.
3. At least one member of the group exerts influence to guide the group toward higher-quality decisions.

Notice the last point. <u>A single individual can prevent or minimize inferential error in group decision making</u> because one person can affect the entire system. Communication competence can be contagious. Collective inferential error, the manifestation of defective critical thinking by a group, is the product of the communicative efforts of individual members. Hirokawa and Scheerhorn (1989) note that "an individual can prevent the occurrence of errors by influencing the group to accept correct information and conclusions" (p. 78). If one person can create problems for a group, one person can also help a group perform effectively.

So what specifically does the competent communicator do to prevent bad inferences from occurring or identify them when they do occur? The competent communicator must ask a series of questions related to the general sources of inferential error. <u>The most important questions the competent communicator should ask are</u>:

1. Is the evidence sufficient to draw the inference?
2. Is the evidence the best available?
3. Is the evidence recent?
4. Is the evidence relevant to the inference? Does it really prove the claim?
5. Is the evidence one-sided (confirmation bias)? Is there contradictory information?
6. Can you verify the facts? How do you know what is said is actually true?
7. Are the sources of the information reliable? Any bias?
8. Are the sources of the information authorities? Are the authorities trustworthy?
9. Are the authorities quoted in their field of expertise?
10. Is the statistical sample representative of the whole? Is the sample size adequate?
11. Is the example typical or is it an exception?
12. Is the relationship only a correlation, not a causal relation?

Asking yourself these questions will help you sort out faulty inferences from valid ones. These questions will assist you in determining whether information used to draw inferences is too limited or faulty. (See Appendix B for further elaboration.)

GROUPTHINK: CRITICAL THINKING IN SUSPENDED ANIMATION

What are we to make of the monumental blunder at Pearl Harbor? How could this country have been caught so flat-footed that infamous morning of December 7, 1941? There were ample warnings that Japan was preparing for a massive military operation. On November 27, 1941, Admiral Stark in Washington, D.C., sent Pearl Harbor a "war warning" predicting an attack from the Japanese somewhere "within the next few days" (in Janis, 1982, p. 75). Since Pearl Harbor was not specifically cited as a likely target for the Japanese attack, however, the warning was discounted. No special reconnaissance was ordered to provide a sufficient alert that Japanese aircraft carriers were steaming toward Pearl Harbor. Two army privates spotted large unidentified aircraft on a radar screen heading toward Pearl Harbor an hour before the actual attack. They reported this to the Army's radar center. Again, the information was discounted. Patrols encountered hostile submarines in advance of the bombings. No action was taken.

As Vice Admiral William S. Pye testified after the disaster, with even ten minutes' warning, the Japanese airplanes could have been shot down before inflicting much damage on our vulnerable fleet. Incredibly, no alert was even sounded until the bombs were actually exploding. Eight battleships, three cruisers and four other ships were sunk or damaged. More than two thousand men were killed and at least as many were wounded or missing. Pearl Harbor was our worst military disaster. How could it have happened?

Focus Questions
1. What causes groupthink?
2. Do groups have to display all the symptoms of groupthink to exhibit poor quality decisions that accompany full-blown groupthink?

Definition

Sociologist Irving Janis (1982), who has extensively analyzed decision-making debacles, argues that Pearl Harbor, the Bay of Pigs fiasco, Watergate, the escalation of the Vietnam War, and other blunders of recent U.S. history sprang from a defective decision-making process he calls groupthink. Janis defines **groupthink** as "a mode of thinking that people engage in when they are deeply involved in a cohesive in-group, when the members' strivings for unanimity override their motivation to realistically appraise alternative courses of action" (p. 9).

Cohesiveness and its companion, concurrence-seeking, are the two central features of groupthink. Janis does not argue that all groups that are cohesive and seek agreement among its members exhibit groupthink. These are necessary but not sufficient conditions for groupthink to occur (Mullen et al., 1994). Obviously, a noncohesive group can spend most of its time and energy on social upheaval, diverted from task accomplishment, and cohesiveness in a group can be a very positive factor (Miranda, 1994).

Groupthink is rooted in *excessive* cohesiveness and a resulting pressure to present a united front to those outside of the group. The more cohesive a group is, the greater is the danger of groupthink. This is especially true as the size of the group increases (Mullen et al., 1994). Critical thinking and effective decision making are sacrificed when members are *overly concerned* with reaching agreement, avoiding conflict, and preserving friendly relations in the group. A study (in Cole, 1989) of 275 members of high-level management teams at twenty-six major U.S. companies by Robert Lefton and V. R. Buzzotta of Psychological Associates, Inc., found that 19 percent of the team members carried on business by "not making waves" and another 9 percent revealed that their teams preferred getting along instead of getting things done.

Wood and her associates (1986) point out that groupthink is "a result of system forces that arise out of the interaction among members" (p. 103). No group member has to squash dissent openly. The concurrence-seeking norm is so firmly established in the group system that critical faculties are often paralyzed seemingly without notice. Frequently, members fail to see issues that should be challenged, positions that should be questioned, and alternatives that should be explored. Even if they do recognize such problems, they choose to go along in order to get along.

Groupthink is not the cause of every decision-making fiasco. Information overload or underload, mindsets, collective inferential error, and sometimes plain stupidity of decision makers may be primarily responsible for blunders. As Janis (1982) argues, however, groupthink often is a contributing cause and sometimes is a primary cause. In this next section, I will summarize some of the evidence cited by Janis to support his thesis within the context of his symptoms of groupthink.

Identification of Groupthink

How do you recognize groupthink? Janis lists eight specific symptoms of groupthink, which he then divides into three types. I will discuss the eight symptoms within the context of these three types.

Overestimation of the Group's Power and Morality   Repeatedly, the main decision makers associated with the Pearl Harbor debacle communicated a sense of invulnerability. Pearl Harbor was thought to be impregnable, much as the French Maginot Line was thought to be an impenetrable defense until the Germans in World War II proved that to be a laughable notion. The U.S. command in Pearl Harbor ridiculed the idea of a Japanese attack. Torpedo planes were discounted because U.S. torpedoes required a water depth of at least sixty feet to function and Pearl Harbor had a thirty-foot depth. Little consideration was given to the possibility that the Japanese had developed a torpedo capable of striking a target in shallow water. The illusion of invulnerability exhibited by the fleet command at Pearl Harbor was exploded with nightmarish rapidity.

The U.S. sense of higher moral purpose contributed to the Bay of Pigs invasion. The purpose, after all, was to upend a communist dictator and free the Cubans. The Iran-Contra affair was partially the result of an excess of moral righteousness. The Reagan administration was trying to secure the release of the hostages. Sometimes you have to engage in unsavory dealings (so went the logic), such as trading arms for the hostages, when your purpose is righteous. This unquestioned belief in the inherent morality of the group is symptomatic of groupthink.

Closed-mindedness   Closed-mindedness is manifested by <u>rationalizations</u> that discount warnings or negative information that might cause the group to rethink its basic assumptions. David Stockman (1986), Ronald Reagan's budget director from 1981 to 1985, cites just such an instance of rationalization. In November 1981, as the country was sliding into a recession destined to be the most severe since the Great Depression, the president met with his advisors on the budget. Having been convinced that the "Reagan Revolution" was headed toward a balanced budget, you can imagine the consternation when the economy didn't cooperate as predicted. The Office of Management and Budget predicted huge budget deficits, reaching a high of $146 billion in 1984 alone. Even the "optimistic" budget forecasts of the Department of the Treasury showed a 1984 deficit of $111 billion.

When this gloomy news was communicated to President Reagan, according to Stockman, "the words he found most soothing were those of his Treasury Secretary" (p. 373). Reportedly, Donald Regan's soothing words were a rationalization encouraging the president to accept what was later dubbed the "rosy scenario"—a set of economic forecasts built on wishful thinking, not sound economic calculations and assumptions. Regan said, "Mr. President, your program has only been in effect thirty-three days. Let's not write it off yet. There's no reason for all the gloom and doom. We at Treasury think these figures are too pessimistic. They assume your tax cut isn't going to work" (p. 373). Little corrective action was taken. The federal government accumulated deficits even *larger* than what was predicted by the "pessimists."

Another aspect of closed-mindedness leading to groupthink is <u>negative stereotyped views</u> of "the enemy" as weak, stupid, puny, or evil. This characterization helps justify the recklessness of the group. The Japanese were characterized as a "midget nation" by the command at Pearl Harbor. Lyndon Johnson reputedly characterized the North Vietnamese during the war in this racist fashion: "Without air power, we'd be at the mercy of every yellow dwarf with a pocket knife" (in Lewallen, 1972, p. 37). President Kennedy's advisors considered Castro and his military force to be a joke. The real joke was the invasion plan that sent 1,400 Cuban exiles up against Castro's military force of 200,000. Simple arithmetic should have shot down that idea.

Pressures toward Uniformity   The last type of symptom of groupthink is the pressure to maintain uniformity of opinion and behavior among group members. Sometimes this pressure is indirect and in other cases it is very direct. An indirect form is manifested when group members engage in <u>self-censorship</u>, assuming an apparent consensus exists in the group. The importance of doubts and counterarguments are minimized as a result of the perceived uniformity of opinion. Silence is considered assent, which can lead to what some have called "pluralistic ignorance." Other group members have their doubts, but everyone assumes agreement exists, no one wants to rock the boat, so no one questions or raises an objection. Thus, an <u>illusion of unanimity</u> is fostered.

The film adaptation of Tom Wolfe's bestseller *The Bonfire of the Vanities* was a $50 million box-office bomb. Many people involved in making the movie, starring Tom Hanks and Melanie Griffith, had doubts about the casting choices and changes in the storyline, but they never voiced these doubts to the director, Brian De Palma (Stern, 1992). Apparently, De Palma also had some reservations, but because no dissent was voiced, he convinced himself that he had made the correct decisions. The illusion of unanimity led to a disastrous motion picture.

In order to maintain the uniformity of the group, <u>direct pressure</u> is applied to deviants. David Stockman became the center of a cyclone when he was quoted in an *Atlantic Monthly* article by Bill Greider characterizing the tax-cut portion of Reaganomics—the Reagan administration's policy of minimalist government—as a Trojan horse: a most unflattering metaphor. Here was President Reagan's budget director seeming to expose the fantasy of achieving a balanced budget, vigorous economic growth, and minimal inflation in part by lowering taxes. The winds of controversy swirled around the White House following the Stockman admission.

Reagan's group of advisors was furious with Stockman for his apparent treason. The president's chief of staff, Jim Baker, called Stockman into his office and coldly issued the following directive:

> "My friend," he started, "I want you to listen up good. Your ass is in a sling. All of the rest of them want you . . . canned right now. Immediately. This afternoon. If it weren't for me," he continued, "you'd be a goner already. But I got you one last chance to save yourself. So you're going to do it precisely and exactly like I tell you. Otherwise you're finished around here. . . . You're going to have lunch with the president. The menu is humble pie. . . . When you go through the Oval Office door, I want to see that sorry ass of yours dragging on the carpet." (In Stockman, 1986, p. 5)

Stockman was thrashed back into line with the group. Intellectually, he was convinced that a tax cut was economic folly. In order to remain a member of Reagan's inner circle, however, Stockman was coerced into an act of public humiliation—a confession of his supposed rhetorical excesses.

Finally, uniformity is maintained by information control. <u>Self-appointed mindguards</u> protect the group from adverse information that might contradict shared illusions. The system closes off to negative influences, protecting uniformity. Once John Kennedy had decided to proceed with the ill-fated Bay of Pigs invasion, his brother Robert dissuaded anyone from disturbing the president with any misgivings about the mission.

Dissent of group members is often suppressed or ignored. One study (Laughlin and Adamopoulos, 1980) found that in almost 75 percent of the cases, the one person in a six-member group who knew the correct answer to a problem was unable to convince the group because the group suppressed the divergent point of view.

<u>A group does not have to display all the symptoms to experience the poor quality decisions that accompany full-blown groupthink</u>. As Janis (1982) explains, "Even when some symptoms are absent, the others may be so pronounced that we can expect all the unfortunate consequences of groupthink"

(p. 175). He argues that "the more frequently a group displays the symptoms, the worse will be the quality of its decisions, on the average" (p. 175).

Preventing Groupthink: Promoting Vigilance

In order to prevent groupthink, groups must become vigilant decision makers. Vigilant decision making requires several steps be taken (Janis, 1982; Wood, Phillips, and Pedersen, 1986). First, and most obvious, members must recognize the problem of groupthink as it begins to manifest itself. Knowledge is required of the competent communicator. If even a single member recognizes groupthink developing and points this out energetically to the group, the problem can be avoided.

Second, the group must minimize status differences. High-status members exert a disproportionate influence on lower-status group members. The resulting communication pattern is one of deference to the more powerful person (Milgram, 1974). Such deference can produce ludicrous, even disastrous consequences.

Michael Cohen and Neil Davis (1981), Temple University pharmacy professors and authors of *Medication Errors: Causes and Prevention,* argue that the accuracy of a doctor's prescription is rarely questioned even when a prescribed treatment makes no sense. They cite one comical instance of blind deference to high-status authority. A physician ordered application of eardrops to a patient's right ear to treat an infection. The physician abbreviated the prescribed treatment to read, "Place in R ear." The duty nurse read the prescription and promptly administered the eardrops where they presumably would do the most good to "cure" the patient's "rectal earache." Neither the nurse nor the patient questioned the doctor's rather unconventional treatment.

On a more serious level, airline industry officials have become alarmed at what has been dubbed "Captainitis" (Foushee, 1984). The status and decision-making authority of the flight captain make it difficult for crew members to correct obvious errors that could lead to a plane crash. One study by a major airline showed that passengers have something extra to worry about besides wind shear, metal fatigue, and baggage being sent mistakenly to the Falkland Islands. In the experiment, crews were subjected to flight simulations under conditions of severe weather and poor visibility. Unknown to the crew members, the captains feigned incapacitation, making serious errors that would lead to certain disaster. Airline officials were stunned to learn that 25 percent of the flights would have crashed because no crew member took corrective action to override the captain's faulty judgment. Weick (1990) claims that this contributed to the Tenerife air disaster in 1977.

Thus, status differences in groups can encourage groupthink, especially when these status differences are magnified by an autocratic-directive style of leadership instead of a democratic-participative style (Leana, 1985; Mullen et al., 1994). John Kennedy, anxious not to commit another blunder like the Bay of Pigs, instituted several new procedures for top-level decision making. One of these procedures was leaderless group discussions. On occasion, especially during the initial stages of discussion where alternatives were being generated, Kennedy would absent himself from the proceedings. Robert Kennedy, the president's brother and close advisor, commented, "I felt there was less true give and take with the president in the room. There was the danger that by indicating his own view and leanings, he would cause others just to fall in line" (in Janis, 1982, p. 142).

The group leader, as high-status member, has the primary responsibility to minimize the influence of status differences. The leader could withhold his or her point of view from the group until everyone has had an opportunity to express an opinion. As management training consultant Michael Woodruff explains, "If I present an idea as something that I am excited about, then my staff has to go against me. But if I present it neutrally, they will be more likely to speak out if they think it is wrong. Staffers will seldom criticize what the boss has endorsed" (in Stern, 1992, p. 104). The high-status group member could also indicate ambivalence on an issue, thereby encouraging the open expression of a variety of viewpoints.

Seeking information that challenges an emerging concurrence is a third way to prevent groupthink. Assessing the negative consequences of choices is a mark of an effective decision-making group (Hirokawa, 1985). Closely related to this, developing a norm in the group that legitimizes disagreement during discussion sessions is a final way to prevent groupthink. This norm may have to be structured into the group process.

There are several ways to accomplish these last two ways of preventing groupthink. First, assign one or two group members or a subgroup to play **devil's advocate**. The primary group presents its proposals and arguments and the devil's advocates critique it. This process can proceed through several rounds of proposals and critiques until the group, including devil's advocates, is satisfied that the best decision has been made. This is a very effective method of overcoming the excessive concurrence-seeking characteristic of groupthink (Stasser and Titus, 1987).

Second, institute a **dialectical inquiry** (Sims, 1992). This procedure is very similar to devil's advocacy, except in dialectical inquiry a subgroup develops a counterproposal and defends it side-by-side with the group's initial proposal. Thus, a debate takes place on two differing proposals. One or the other may be chosen by the group, both may be rejected in favor of further exploration and inquiry before a final decision is made, or a compromise between the two proposals may be hammered out. Both devil's advocacy and dialectical inquiry are effective antidotes to groupthink, but dialectical inquiry may be slightly more effective (Pavitt and Curtis, 1994).

Third, assign a group member to play the **reminder role** (Schultz et al., 1995). This is a formally designated role. The reminder raises questions in a nonaggressive manner regarding collective inferential error, confirmation bias, false dichotomies, and any of the myriad symptoms of groupthink that arise. The reminder role is an effective method of combating groupthink tendencies (Shultz et al, 1995).

Groupthink can be a primary source of poor decision making in groups (Hensley and Griffin, 1986; Herek et al., 1987; Leana, 1985; Moorhead and Montanari, 1986). Recognizing the symptoms of groupthink and taking steps to prevent it from occurring play an important role in any effort to improve the quality of group decisions.

 SECOND LOOK

Groupthink

PRIMARY SYMPTOMS

Overestimation of Group's Power and Morality

- Illusion of invulnerability
- Unquestioned belief in the inherent morality of group

Closed-mindedness

- Rationalizations
- Negative stereotyped views of "the enemy"

Pressures toward Uniformity

- Self-censorship of contradictory opinion
- Illusion of unanimity
- Direct pressure applied to deviants
- Self-appointed mindguards

Preventing Groupthink

- Recognize groupthink when it first begins
- Minimize status differences
- Seek information that challenges emerging concurrence
- Develop norm that legitimizes disagreement

In summary, group members must exercise their critical thinking abilities. The quality of decision making and problem solving in groups is significantly affected by problems of information quantity, mindsets, inferential errors, and groupthink. If groups learn to cope with information overload and underload, recognize and counteract mindsets, avoid or correct collective inferential errors, and avoid groupthink, then decision making and problem solving probably will be of higher quality.

QUESTIONS FOR CRITICAL THINKERS

1. Why is information overload such a problem when we have "labor saving" technologies such as desktop computers to process huge quantities of data?
2. Why are collective inferential errors more likely when issues are emotionally charged?
3. If cohesiveness is a positive small group attribute, why can it lead to groupthink?

Group Discussion: Effective Decision Making and Problem Solving

An ancient Chinese proverb observes, "If you don't know where you are going, then any road will take you there." Most of us, however, are not satisfied arriving at no place in particular. Aimless deliberations in groups often result in restlessness and resentment because wasting time in discussion sessions is frustrating. Meeting for no significant reason and for no clear purpose contributes to grouphate. Having no specific destination, a group engaged in animated but pointless discussions resembles a caged hamster running feverishly on its exercise wheel, but getting nowhere.

In the previous chapter, I discussed *defective* decision making/problem solving. In this chapter, I will discuss the process of *effective* group decision making/problem solving. Toward this end I have three <u>objectives</u>:

1. to explain procedures for conducting productive group discussions that will result in effective decisions and solutions to problems,
2. to explore the pros and cons of participation in the decision-making/problem-solving process and how to encourage productive participation, and
3. to delineate several techniques of creative group problem solving.

Both creativity and reasoned discourse have an important place in group discussion. <u>Competent communicators manifest flexibility by exercising both their creativity and their reasoning skills when making decisions and discovering solutions to problems.</u>

DISCUSSION PROCEDURES

General Considerations

Effective decision making in groups doesn't just happen miraculously. Communication scholars have spent decades trying to determine which discussion procedures promote quality decision making and problem solving and which procedures retard it. In this section, I will discuss the general conclusions arrived at by researchers in this regard.

Focus Questions
1. How should group members proceed systematically to engage in productive discussion?
2. How does Standard Agenda relate to the functional perspective on effective group discussion procedures?
3. What constitutes a true consensus?

Periodic Phases of Decision Emergence   In Chapter Two, I argued that group development generally does not progress in an orderly, logical fashion from one phase to another. The term *phase* suggests a linear, step-by-step, unidirectional development as in "phases of the moon" (i.e., the moon never travels from its half-moon back to its quarter-moon phase without first becoming full) or "phases in child development" (i.e., children never return to the "terrible twos" phase—for this we can be thankful). I contended that sequential phasic models of overall group development are mechanistic and do not integrate well into a systems perspective. Phases are usually more periodic than perfectly sequential. The same is true of phasic models of group decision making.

Many scholars have attempted to discover phases of group decision making. Fisher (1970), for example, posits a four-phase sequence composed of orientation to the group, conflict over choices to be made, emergence of a proposed decision, and finally, reinforcement and commitment to a specific decision. Despite the popularity of Fisher's phasic model of group decision making, it has limited applicability. As Spiker and Daniels (1987) observe, Fisher's model may apply to some groups with limited life spans and no prior history (e.g., ad hoc project teams), but the model applies poorly to long-standing groups that must adapt to changes on a continuous basis. Linear models such as Fisher's implicitly assume decision-making groups follow an identical sequence of phases (Poole and Doelger, 1986).

More recently, Poole (1983) has introduced a *multiple sequence model* of decision emergence. The multiple sequence model pictures groups moving along three activity tracks—task, relational, and topic. Groups do not necessarily proceed along these three tracks at the same rate or according to the same pattern. Some groups may devote a significant amount of time to the relational (social) activities of groups before proceeding to a task discussion.

In recent studies, Poole and Roth (1989a; 1989b) discovered three principal paths that groups take in reaching decisions. The first path is called the *unitary sequence.* Groups on the unitary sequence path proceed in the same step-by-step fashion toward a decision. The second path is called *complex cyclic.* These groups engage in repeated cycles of focusing on the problem, then the solution, and back again to the problem, and so forth (periodic phases). Finally, the third principal path to decision making is *solution oriented.* Here the group launches into discussion of solutions with little focus on an analysis of the problem. Poole and Roth found that the complex cyclic path was chosen most frequently by groups they studied, followed by the solution-oriented path with the unitary sequence path used infrequently.

The value of Poole's multiple sequence model of decision development is that it shows that group discussion does not necessarily proceed along a single predictable path. There are several ways that decisions occur in groups. The limitation of the model is that it merely describes patterns of group discussion without indicating ways to improve communication competence during these discussions.

Functional Perspective   Discussions that follow some systematic procedure tend to be more productive and result in better decisions than do relatively unstructured discussions (Hirokawa, 1985; Schultz et al., 1995). In this regard, two generalizations are supported by research. First, effective group decision making requires an analysis and understanding of a problem *before* members search for solutions. Ineffective decision-making groups typically begin exploring solutions before thoroughly analyzing and understanding a problem (Hirokawa, 1983).

Second, effective decision-making groups normally engage in creative exploration of unusual, even deviant, ideas during initial discussions (Bormann and Bormann, 1988). At some point, the group ceases generating ideas and begins focusing on which ideas are best and should be implemented. This does not mean, however, that the group never considers a new idea once the winnowing process begins. Nevertheless, there is a time for freewheeling, open-ended, creative discussion and there is a time for more organized, systematic deliberation.

Let me add that following a set of steps stipulated in a systematic discussion procedure (e.g., The Standard Agenda) in sequential rigid fashion is probably too inflexible for natural discussion to take place. Steps in any systematic discussion procedure should be looked at as guidelines, not commandments. Some allowance should be made for cycling back to steps previously addressed as group members discuss problems and solutions.

Let me emphasize that there is no single systematic discussion procedure that guarantees effective decision making and problem solving. Gouran (1982) explains that you should not "assume that by simply going through a set of steps a group will automatically make a good decision. What happens at each stage and how well necessary functions are executed are the real determinants of success" (p. 30). Systematic discussion procedures work best when the group decision matters to group members and when members have received training and practice using such procedures (Pavitt and Curtis, 1994).

Hirokawa (1988) discovered that variations in the quality of decisions by groups can be accounted for by the relative ability of members to perform four critical decision-making functions. These four functions are the effective assessment of each of the following: the problem, the requirements for an acceptable choice, the positive qualities of alternative choices, and the negative qualities of alternative choices. This *functional perspective* is incorporated in The Standard Agenda discussion procedures explained in the next section.

The Standard Agenda

John Dewey (1910) described a process of rational problem solving and decision making that he called *reflective thinking*. There have been several adaptations of Dewey's reflective-thinking process for group discussion and decision making. All of these, however, begin with a focus on the problem, then move systematically to a consideration of possible solutions (Bormann, 1990).

The Standard Agenda is a direct outgrowth of Dewey's reflective-thinking process. The Standard Agenda is the most complete, flexible, and time-tested group problem-solving method (Wood et al., 1986).

Systematic Procedures   The Standard Agenda places the emphasis initially on the problem in order to counteract premature consideration of solutions. Let me briefly walk you through the six steps of The Standard Agenda.

1. *Problem Identification:* Let's suppose the problem area is smoking in the college cafeteria—a problem faced on my campus. The problem should be formulated into a question identifying what type of problem the group must consider. Questions may be phrased as fact, value, or policy. The choice will identify the nature of the problem. A **question of fact** asks whether something is true and to what extent. "Is smoking hazardous to your health?" is a question of fact. A **question of value** asks for a judgment—to what extent is something good or bad, right or wrong, moral or immoral, and so forth. "Is jeopardizing the health of nonsmokers with passive smoke morally justifiable?" is a question of value. A **question of policy** asks whether a specific course of action should be undertaken in order to solve a problem. "What changes should be made regarding smoking in the college cafeteria?" is a policy question. This is the question I will discuss here.

2. *Problem Analysis:* The group gathers facts, tries to determine how serious the problem is, what the harm associated with the problem is, if the harm is serious and widespread, and what causes the problem. For example, the college cafeteria is a place for students across the campus to congregate. The facility is small, not well ventilated, and has primary access through the main door that opens onto the smoking section, forcing nonsmokers to travel through a carcinogenic cloud before reaching fresh air. Smoking and non-smoking sections exist, but smoke drifts into the nonsmoking section. Nonsmoking students complained repeatedly to their student senators about this situation. In an open hearing instituted by the Student Senate on the question, tempers flared. One student, defending the "rights of smokers," told nonsmokers to "quit school if you don't like our smoking." A student defending "nonsmokers' rights" vehemently retorted, "Polluters have no rights." Another nonsmoker facetiously suggested, "public floggings as a penalty for smoking in the cafeteria." Licking a dirty ashtray and spraying foul-smelling perfume on smokers' clothing were also suggested as penalties. One note of caution here: Although analyzing the problem is important and should be undertaken before exploring potential solutions, bogging down by analyzing the problem too much can also thwart effective decision making. **Analysis paralysis** prevents a group from ever getting on with business and making a decision.

3. *Solution Criteria:* The group should establish criteria for evaluating solutions *before* solutions are addressed. Wood and her associates (1986) observe that "establishing criteria prior to discussing solutions enhances the probability that a group will avoid divisiveness and agree on a final solution that all members find acceptable" (p. 56). Not all criteria, however, are created equal. The group must consider the relevance and appropriateness of each criterion. For example, Jose da Silva, a civilian who oversees the police in Sao Paulo, Brazil, ran into an unexpected roadblock when he attempted to stop police killings of civilians, which had reached a hundred per month. Many civilians considered the body count to be a criterion of police competence in solving crime and they approved of eliminating rather than arresting suspects ("Sao Paulo," 1996). (A training program was introduced to dissuade police from killing suspects.) Some relevant and appropriate criteria on the

smoking question might be protect the health of nonsmokers, maintain a comfortable and attractive environment in the cafeteria for all students, cost less than $5,000, and avoid alienating either group (smokers or nonsmokers). The criteria should be ranked in order of priority. Health of students is unquestionably the most important criterion.

4. *Solution Suggestions:* The group brainstorms possible solutions without evaluating any suggestions until the best alternatives are likely to have been discovered. Some possibilities on the smoking issue include ban smoking from the cafeteria, switch smoking and nonsmoking sections, build a partition between the two sections, improve the ventilation of the smoking section, and move smokers to an adjacent lounge area away from the main entrance, closed off from nonsmokers.

5. *Solution Evaluation and Selection:* The story of a military briefing officer asked to devise a method for raising enemy submarines off the ocean floor illustrates the importance of this step. The briefing officer's solution? Heat the ocean to the boiling point. When bewildered Pentagon officials asked him how this could be done he replied, "I don't know. I decided on the solution; you work out the details." The devil is in the details. Explore *both* the merits and demerits (avoid confirmation bias) of suggested solutions. **Devil's advocacy** and **dialectical inquiry** (see Chapter Six) are useful techniques for accomplishing this aspect of the Standard Agenda. Consider each solution in terms of the criteria established earlier. For instance, banning smoking satisfies the criterion "protect the health of nonsmokers" but clearly "alienates smokers." Switching smoking and nonsmoking sections may help reduce nonsmokers' contact with polluted air but wouldn't eliminate drifting smoke, and the smoking section is a much smaller area than the nonsmoking section. Thus, the criterion on comfortable environment will likely remain unmet. Building a partition between sections would protect students' health, maintain a comfortable environment, and probably wouldn't alienate either group. The cost, however, might be prohibitive and it probably would not look attractive. Moving smokers to an adjacent lounge seems, on the surface, to satisfy all the criteria, but segregating smokers from nonsmokers doesn't entirely protect the nonsmoker from secondhand smoke since nonsmokers may need to interact with smokers in the lounge for a variety of reasons. Improving the ventilation in the smoking section seems like a Band-Aid solution. None of the criteria are satisfied fully. This is a partial solution at best. Since no solution satisfied all criteria completely, how the criteria were prioritized then becomes significant. Since health of students is the top priority, my campus decided to ban smoking from the cafeteria (and eventually banned smoking from the campus).

6. *Solution Implementation:* A common failing of decision-making groups is that once they arrive at a decision there is, like the backhand of an inept tennis player, no follow-through. Making the decision is one thing; implementing it is another.

Problems of Implementation The problems associated with implementation of small group decisions spring from the natural resistance of human beings to change. Social philosopher Eric Hoffer titled one of his books *The Ordeal of Change*. Change does not come easily to most of us. Zander (1961) cites a classic instance of such resistance. A farmer in the Tennessee Valley Authority area "assured us that he knew all about contour plowing, the rotation of crops, and the use of what he called 'phosaphate' for improving the soil. He allowed as how these were good ideas. 'But,' he said, 'I don't do it that way'" (p. 543).

Sometimes we're just suspicious of change especially when the need for change seems nebulous or nonexistent. The NBC morning show *Today* was humming along with first-place ratings when at the tail end of 1989, thirty-one-year-old Deborah Norville was brought onto the show to boost ratings among females aged eighteen to forty-nine. The move led to the departure of highly popular Jane Pauley, showing once again that the addition or subtraction of one member to a group can have systemwide implications. *Today*'s ratings took an immediate drop (some were calling it a "ratings meltdown"). ABC's *Good Morning America* zoomed into first place. One former network executive, unidentified in a *Newsweek* article (Waters, 1990), summed up the situation succinctly: "What they've (NBC) done is pioneer a new philosophy: 'If it ain't broke, break it (p. 58).'" The consensus in the industry was that NBC had shot itself in the foot, an act of self-inflicted sabotage reminiscent of Coke changing its formula.

Change poses risks. With change comes unfamiliarity and uncertainty. Implementing change may lead to unforeseen disasters. Playing it safe may seem like the wisest choice for a group, yet no system can stand still. Change is ubiquitous and inevitable. Every system must learn to adapt to change, which requires overcoming resistance to change.

Four primary factors influence our resistance to change in a group (Tubbs, 1984). First, as noted in the last chapter, <u>people are more likely to accept change when they have had a part in the planning and decision making</u>. Imposing change produces psychological reaction and therefore increases resistance to change.

Second, <u>changes are more likely to be accepted if they do not threaten the security of group members</u>. When management at colleges and universities start talking about "program review," faculty often become alarmed. In the past, this process has frequently served as a mechanism for eliminating faculty positions. In a context of threat, changes suggested by a program review committee will likely be stubbornly resisted.

Third, <u>changes are more likely to be accepted when the need for change affects individuals directly</u>. Discovering for yourself that change is required is more convincing than having someone else tell you it is so. Our personal experience can convince us more readily than all the statistics and public service announcements on TV combined. Candy Lightner started MADD (Mothers Against Drunk Driving) after her daughter was killed by a drunk driver. MADD chapters have sprung up all over the country, usually composed of individuals who have suffered the loss of a loved one from an accident caused by a drunk driver.

Finally, <u>there will be less resistance to change when the change is open to revision and modification</u>. Since there is no room for revision or modification in the complete abstinence school of alcoholic treatment, alcoholics usually have to hit bottom before they will join Alcoholics Anonymous because treatment calls for total lifelong sobriety.

Let me note here that the three factors (degree, rate, and desirability) affecting a group's ability to adapt to change in a system also affect resistance to change. For instance, individuals often resist changing their eating habits because dieting seems like such a huge alteration in lifestyle and most diets relegate their victims to lifetime rations of rabbit food. Facing a diet of foods that are as enjoyable to eat as chewing cardboard or munching weeds is discouraging. The first three letters of the word diet are, after all, D-I-E. Some people would rather die than diet because the change is too great, it requires a sudden alteration in lifestyle, and it is perceived as wholly unpleasant. This is why Weight Watchers groups emphasize that members can eat well and enjoy great food while losing weight gradually.

When the four conditions above are not met, resistance to change and difficulty implementing a group's decisions increase. Overcoming resistance to change may be the most serious problem groups face once decisions have been made.

 SECOND LOOK

The Standard Agenda

Six Steps

- Problem identification
- Problem analysis
- Solution criteria
- Solution suggestions
- Solution evaluation and selection
- Solution implementation

Overcoming Resistance to Change (Solution Implementation)

- Participation in group planning and decision making reduces resistance
- Change is more easily accepted if it does not threaten security of group members
- Change is more easily accepted when need for change affects group members directly
- There is less resistance to change when change is open to revision and modification

A decision-making method that stipulates systematically how to implement small group decisions is called **PERT** (Program Evaluation Review Technique). Once the group has settled on a solution, details of its implementation must be discussed. PERT provides a systematic method for reviewing all the steps required to carry out a solution to a problem. The basic steps are:

1. Determine what the final step should look like (e.g., a No Smoking policy for the cafeteria will be instituted).
2. Specify any events that must occur before the final goal is realized (e.g., the Board of Trustees must endorse the Student Senate decision on banning smoking in the cafeteria).
3. Put the events in chronological order (e.g., secure the support of the college president before going to the board for endorsement).
4. If necessary, construct a diagram of the process in order to trace the progress of implementation (useful only if there are numerous steps).
5. Generate a list of activities, resources, and materials that are required between events (e.g., hold a strategy session before student senators meet with the president to gain endorsement).
6. Develop a time line for implementation. Estimate how long each step will take.
7. Match the total time estimate for implementation of the solution with any deadlines (e.g., end of school year approaching). Modify your plan of action as needed (e.g., take any appointment time available with president that will move along the process).
8. Specify which group members will have which responsibilities.

Group Decision-making Rules

Decision making is guided by rules. As I stated earlier, rules help groups achieve their goals. They foster stability and reduce variability in a system. With rules there is greater predictability and less likelihood of chaotic decision making. The three principal decision-making rules are majority, minority, and unanimity rules. Any of these decision-making rules can be applied to the Standard Agenda format.

Majority Rule   The U.S. democratic political system is predicated on majority rule. No one should be surprised that this is a popular method of decision making in the United States. Majority rule in groups, however, is not exactly the same as majority rule in our political system. Minorities are protected by the Bill of Rights. Congress is guided by the realization that legislation must not violate constitutional guarantees.

In most groups, however, majority rule provides no protection for minorities. Here lies the principal drawback of this decision-making rule. Groups may be tempted to vote too quickly once a majority favors a particular decision. Full discussion of controversial issues may be short-circuited. The decision-making process can become adversarial (Hastie et al., 1983). Minorities may be bullied and run over by the more powerful majority. Discussions tend to be dominated by the majority faction of the group (Hans, 1978). When majority rule is invoked, there are winners and losers. All of the negative attributes associated with competition apply to majority rule. Commitment to implement the group decision can suffer, especially when a vocal minority feels cheated because their voices were not heard. Minority alienation may even lead to sabotage of the majority's decision.

Studies comparing juries using the unanimous decision rule and majority rule (Oregon requires a 10–2 majority and Louisiana a 9–3 split for felony convictions) found several deficiencies in majority rule (Abramson, 1994; Hastie et al., 1983). First, deliberations are significantly shorter and less conscientious. Deliberations typically end once a requisite majority is reached. Consequently, less error correction takes place, sometimes resulting in faulty verdicts. Second, minority factions participate less frequently and are less influential, thereby underutilizing the group's resources. Third, jurors' overall satisfaction with the group is lower. Minorities feel that their point of view is ignored and the style of deliberation in majority rule juries is typically more combative, forceful, and bullying.

The quality of the group's decision is a particularly troublesome problem with majority rule. Majorities can sometimes take ludicrous, even dangerous positions. The "tyranny of the majority" is no casual slogan. In 1970, the National Guard was ordered onto the campus of Ohio's Kent State University in the midst of student protests against the Cambodian invasion during the Vietnam War. At one point, the Ohio National Guard inexplicably opened fire on students. Nine students were wounded and four were killed (none of whom were involved in the protest). A public opinion poll was conducted in Kent, Ohio, following the shootings. The majority of subjects polled felt that the National Guard should have shot more students (Michener, 1971). Mob rule is a manifestation of the tyranny of the majority.

Despite the disadvantages of majority rule, there are some advantages. When issues are not very important, decisions must be made relatively quickly, and when commitment of all members to the final decision is unimportant, then majority rule can be useful. Majority rule is efficient and provides quick closure on relatively unimportant issues. In large groups, majority rule may be necessary in order for democratic decision making to take place since consensus becomes increasingly difficult the larger the group becomes.

Minority Rule Majorities don't always make the decisions. South Africa is a prime example. There are approximately five million whites and twenty-eight million blacks and ethnic minorities in the country, yet whites were in control of the government until Nelson Mandela rose to power.

Minority rule as a group decision-making method occurs in several forms. First, the *group designates an expert* to make the decision. This method relieves group members from devoting time and energy on problems to be solved. Decision by designated expert, however, is mostly ineffective. Trying to determine who is the clear expert in the group is often difficult, even impossible. Lack of group input also fails to capitalize on synergy.

Second, a *designated authority* (usually from outside the immediate group) makes the decision for the group, either after hearing discussion from group members or without their consultation. Decision by designated authority is popular in business organizations because it reinforces hierarchical power

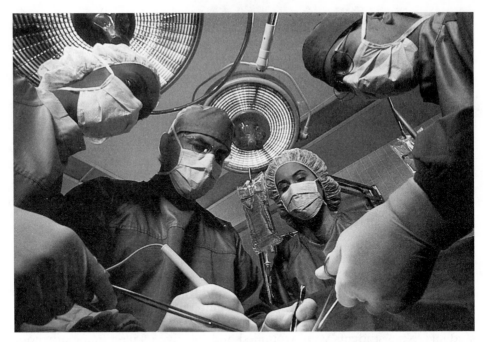

Some group decisions should not be made by majority rule. Surgical decisions are usually made by minority rule, that is, by the chief surgeon who is the designated authority.

structures and it is efficient especially when applied to simple, routine, or administrative details. Sometimes the group acts in an advisory capacity and sometimes not. Since the group has no ultimate authority, however, this method of decision making has drawbacks.

The quality of the designated leader's decision will depend a great deal on how good a listener he or she is. If the group discussion is merely a formality, which the leader views as an annoyance more than a way to sort through relevant alternatives, then none of the benefits of group discussion will accrue. Competent communication requires sensitivity to the needs of the group—which includes having a meaningful voice in decision making. If the leader takes the group's discussion seriously, however, then this is normally a vastly better system of decision making than one in which the designated leader makes decisions about important issues without the benefit of group discussion.

Since power is unevenly distributed in a designated leader method of decision making, group members are likely to vie competitively for attention and seek to impress the leader (Johnson and Johnson, 1988). Members will be tempted to tell the leader what he or she wants to hear, not what should be said. Groups in such an atmosphere become fawning, obsequious, ratifying committees—spineless jellyfish doing the bidding of the authority figure. An effective leader, of course, must set the climate for the group. If the leader encourages genuine disagreement and in no way penalizes members for their honesty, then the leader can benefit enormously from the dialectical clash of ideas that will likely occur in such a cooperative atmosphere.

Third, in some instances, *executive committees* must be delegated responsibility for making certain decisions because the workload for the group as a whole threatens to overwhelm or the time constraints are prohibitive. The challenge here is to persuade the group to get behind the decision.

Finally, minority rule can take the form of a *forceful faction* making a decision for the group by dominating less forceful members. On rare occasions this may be advisable when the minority faction consists of the most informed, committed members. Too often, however, dominant group members who flex their muscles focus on personal gain more than on what's good for the group (Murnighan, 1985).

Unanimity Rule (Consensus)   The unanimity rule governs some groups. Juries are the most obvious example. Persuading all members of a group to agree on anything can be daunting. The most prevalent form of the unanimity rule is group **consensus.** Not all unanimous decisions can be considered a consensus (Fisher and Ellis, 1990). On occasion, groups will agree on a decision, not because they think the alternative chosen is an acceptable one, but because they fear the consequences of dissent or grow weary deliberating. This would be a unanimous decision—all members choose the same alternative—but not a true consensus.

DeStephen and Hirokawa (1988) experimentally validated five criteria intrinsic to a conceptual definition of consensus. They are:

1. *Members agree with the group decision.* Consensus does not require adoption of every member's personal preference. Consensus usually requires some give-and-take. If all members can agree on an acceptable alternative, even if this alternative is not everyone's first choice, then you have come close to achieving a consensus.
2. *Members exhibit a commitment to the group decision.* There is more to consensus than mere agreement. As Fisher and Ellis (1990) contend, "Consensus implies not just agreement with the decision reached, but commitment to it" (p. 142). When candidates for president of the United States lose to their party's eventual choice, consensus is determined not by mere statements of support for the party's candidate but by manifestations of commitment to the choice. When losing candidates campaign vigorously for the party's selection, consensus is exhibited, even though, presumably, the losers feel the party made a less-than-perfect pick.
3. *Members are satisfied with the group decision.* The group decision cannot contradict deeply held values of group members and still produce member satisfaction. Obviously, not all decision making in groups can be by consensus, but consensus is worth attempting even when it seems remote.
4. *Members are satisfied with their participation in the decision making.* Members must feel that their voices have been heard by the group. A fair hearing is

required for consensus. A fair hearing, however, is not the same as agreement. Members will often disagree, sometimes vociferously, on the way to consensus. But as DeStephen and Hirokawa (1988) note, the "perceived freedom to participate in decision making does indeed lead to higher involvement and stronger support for the group decision" (p. 236). We rarely exhibit commitment to a decision when we had little part in formulating it. Consensus requires the opportunity to influence group discussion and choice.

5. *Members are satisfied with the group decision-making process.* This may involve a range of issues including the group climate, degree of openness in the system, and groupthink. Overall, group members must feel that there was commitment to effective decision making and a sensitivity to the needs of group members.

<u>True consensus, thus, requires agreement, commitment, and satisfaction.</u> Achieving consensus in groups is not easy. Consensus seeking is time-consuming and tension-producing, which most people tend to view as negatives, although they may actually be positives. When consensus seeking is conducted correctly, groups do not jump to solutions. They avoid confirmation bias, dichotomous thinking, and groupthink. Tension can encourage reconsideration of options.

<u>Arriving at a consensus necessitates strong motivation and communication</u> <u>competence among members.</u> Consensus will not likely be reached by the unskilled, the uninformed, the insensitive, and the uncommitted. Even if groups exhibit strong motivation and communication competence, some groups cannot achieve a consensus because they lack cohesiveness and members' values are in conflict. Groups, however, that use a consensus approach tend to produce better decisions; members feel more confident about the correctness of their decisions and are more satisfied with the decisions and with the group as a whole (Abramson, 1994; Miller, 1989).

Hall and Watson (1970) identify the specific rules for discussion when groups seek a consensus:

1. *Avoid stubbornly arguing for your own position.* Present your position clearly and logically, but listen openly to the positions of other group members (don't adopt the role of blocker).
2. *Avoid win-lose stalemates.* When impasses occur, look for the next most acceptable alternative (avoid false dichotomies).
3. *Avoid switching positions simply to sidestep conflict.* Withstand pressure to yield unless another position seems logically sound (resist groupthink).
4. *Avoid conflict-suppressing techniques* such as voting, averaging, coin flipping, and the like. Provisional straw votes may be taken to determine sources of differing opinion, but they should not be used as a pressure for conformity strategy (resist groupthink).
5. *Seek differences of opinion.* The clash of viewpoints tests ideas. Encourage participation by all members (combat confirmation bias).
6. *Be suspicious of initial agreement,* especially when it has occurred with little struggle. Explore the reasons members agree. Make sure they have agreed for either the same or complementary reasons (combat groupthink).

⊙⊙ CLOSER LOOK

The People vs. Juan Corona

On May 20, 1971, sheriff's deputies uncovered a body in an orchard near Yuba City, California. In the next two weeks, twenty-five victims were unearthed. All had been savagely mutilated by a knife or meat cleaver-type weapon. On May 26, 1971, before all the bodies were discovered, Juan Corona, a labor contractor, was arrested. He was eventually charged with all twenty-five murders.

Victor Villasenor (1977), in a remarkable book *Jury: The People vs. Juan Corona,* reconstructed the jury deliberations by painstakingly interviewing all twelve jurors. Since jury deliberations are conducted behind closed doors, how juries arrive at a consensus verdict is difficult to know. Villasenor provides the most thorough account ever attempted of a jury engaged in the often-contentious process of arriving at a unanimous determination of guilt or innocence. His re-creation of the jury in action was meticulous and thoroughly credible. The jury's deliberations were an admirable example of effective decision making in groups. How the jury conducted business and arrived at its verdict is instructive. Several aspects of effective group decision making are illustrated by the jury in the Juan Corona trial.

A juror named Ernie Phillips, highly talkative and the first to speak, was nominated and appointed foreman almost immediately. Ernie proved to be a capable leader. Information overload was the initial problem facing the jury. The task of sorting through testimony on twenty-five separate murders from 117 witnesses and thousands of pieces of evidence presented over a five-month period was daunting. To compound the problem, all jurors agreed that the prosecution's case was mistake-ridden, confusing, complex, and totally circumstantial. There were no eyewitnesses and no one had reported any of the murdered persons as missing.

Ernie immediately established rules of discussion so no one would monopolize and dominate conversation. Then the jury brainstormed possible procedures for tackling the voluminous evidence. After a lengthy period of discussion, jurors agreed to organize their deliberations victim by victim.

Criteria for weighing the evidence were established by specific instructions read to the jury by the judge. Early on in the jury's deliberations, they asked the judge to reread the instructions. The criteria for a verdict of guilty were innocent unless proven guilty, beyond a reasonable doubt, and to a moral certainty. The Corona jury continually returned to these criteria throughout their deliberations as Standard Agenda requires. For instance, in the latter stages of the process, a juror named Rick argued forcefully for a guilty verdict on the basis of the reasonable doubt criterion. Here is some of what he said: "What I'm trying to say, simply, is that we have no more doubts that are reasonable. We only have doubts that are possible, or imaginary, or in the realm of speculation, and we're not supposed to go that far . . . because we're supposed to follow the law, the Judge's instructions, and be reasonable" (p. 234).

The jury discussed procedures and criteria for decision making before discussing outcomes (a verdict)—essentials of effective group decision making.

In fact, the jury resisted taking a vote the first day of deliberations before reviewing the evidence. The judge had warned against premature commitment to a verdict before a fair discussion had taken place. On the second day, the jury took its first vote by secret ballot. There were seven for innocent and five for guilty.

Repeatedly, jurors resisted the temptation to fall victim to collective inferential error. Every time assumptions and speculation occurred, at least one juror would call attention to the unwarranted inferences and the potential for faulty decision making. For instance, Naomi, destined to be a lone holdout, at one point drifted into dangerous inferential territory when she said: "I got one thing to say. If Corona is so guilty, then why didn't the sheriff himself ever testify? Ah, why didn't the sheriff come and tell us that he knows Corona is guilty?" Donald Rogers, another juror, shot back the answer: "Because that's not evidence! That would be hearsay! Dammit, why don't you ask why God doesn't come down here and tell us everything about everybody, then we don't even need the jury system and we can all go home!" (p. 149).

When individual jurors wondered aloud why Corona never took the witness stand (his attorney worried he might have a heart attack, which he actually did have during the trial), why there was no case presented for the defense (just refutation of the prosecution's case), and why Corona looked startled when a witness named Pervis came to testify, at least one juror reminded everyone that this did not constitute evidence in a murder trial. Drawing any conclusions regarding Corona's guilt from these observations would require questionable inferences. The group performed an error-correction function admirably.

Not surprisingly, obtaining a consensus was the most difficult part of the eight days of deliberations. When the decision is important and the emotions run strong, achieving a consensus can be torturous. Tempers flared. Conversations were not always polite. Sometimes jurors screamed at each other. Rick, toward the end, shouted at Naomi, the lone vote for innocent, "Dammit! It's so simple if you just follow the Judge's definition and don't go daydreaming all over the place" (p. 230). He suddenly realized he had been shaking his fist in Naomi's face. The jurors complained about little things such as someone "always smiling." When Naomi needled Donald for speculating (making questionable inferences), he angrily retorted, "I only speculated after you started speculating" (p. 182).

Naomi became a source of some concern late in the deliberations. The second oldest member at sixty-one, she began to imagine sensational "facts" about the case that plainly never happened. She gobbled "nerve pills" throughout the jury's deliberations. Several jurors expressed concern to Ernie that Naomi was cracking under the strain.

Despite the dissension, the weariness, and the contentiousness, the jury refused to accept a verdict unless all members were committed to the decision. <u>A true consensus is one in which, not only is there unanimous agreement, but also satisfaction with and commitment to that decision.</u> Naomi seemed adamant in her resolve to acquit Corona. Apart from an occasional outburst by a juror, she was treated well despite her deviance from the group. When she asked a juror named George, "Should I tell them I'll vote their way and do it just to get it over with?" George replied, "No, you can't do that. You got to vote the way you think'' (p. 254). When Naomi finally did make the guilty verdict unanimous, two other jurors named Faye and Jim insisted that Naomi's vote not be accepted unless she honestly believed that Corona was guilty. When she stated that her decision was not made because of exhaustion or for the sake of convenience, the deliberations ended.

POSTSCRIPT: On August 1, 1990, Juan Corona was refused parole by the California Board of Prison Terms. When asked if he killed twenty-five people, Corona responded, ''I don't remember'' (''Corona is silent,'' 1990). He is serving twenty-five concurrent life terms in Soledad State Prison in Monterey County, California.

Questions for Thought

1. True consensus requires members' satisfaction with the group process. Do you think the Corona jury was satisfied with the group process? Explain.
2. If the legal requirement mandating a unanimous verdict hadn't existed, do you think the Corona jury would have achieved a consensus? Explain.

Some individuals complain that the Standard Agenda and the consensus method are rational approaches to decision making. Unfortunately, they argue, groups do not act in strictly rational ways (Conrad, 1990; Fisher and Ellis, 1990). This is true. Nevertheless, as Hirokawa (1988) has verified, the degree to which groups satisfy the four critical functions of effective decision making in a systematic manner is of central concern. These four functions (problem assessment, criteria, merits and demerits of decisions) can be satisfied without insisting that group members become Spock-like automatons—touting pure logic while shunning emotion. Clearly, groups can be affected by nonrational influences and still reap the benefits of a systematic, rational approach to decision making, as the jury in the Juan Corona trial demonstrated. Neither the Standard Agenda nor consensus decision making guarantee quality group choices. Both do improve the likelihood of effective decisions, however, compared to groups that exhibit more haphazard, nonrational approaches.

SECOND LOOK

Group Decision-Making Rules

RULES	PROS	CONS
Majority Rule		
	Quick	Minorities vulnerable to tyranny of majority
	Efficient	Quality of decision suspect
		Usually alienates minority
	Expedient in large groups	Underutilization of resources

(continued)

RULES	PROS	CONS
Minority Rule		
Designated Expert	Saves time	Expertise hard to determine
		No group input
Designated Authority	Clear	Members vie for attention
	Efficient	Members try to impress authority
Executive Committee	Divides labor	Weak commitment to decision
Forceful Faction	Faction may be most informed/committed	Likely Me-not-We oriented
Unanimity Rule (Consensus)		
	Quality decisions	Time consuming
	Commitment	Difficult
	Satisfaction	Tension producing

CRITICAL THINKING AND EFFECTIVE DECISION MAKING

The gathering and evaluation of information play a significant role in small group decision making. Group members must exercise their critical reasoning abilities at every stage of the Standard Agenda in order to maximize the probabilities of effective decisions (Hirokawa, 1992). Consequently, how you go about gathering information and the critical eye you focus on information gathered should be primary concerns.

Gathering Information

A cliché of the computer age is "garbage in, garbage out." Applied to decision-making groups, this little piece of wisdom means that the output of the group is likely to be no better than the input available to its members. Faulty or insufficient information easily produces collective inferential error.

Information gathering impinges on all six steps of the Standard Agenda, but it most directly affects the problem analysis step. Pooling ignorance about a problem, its causes and effects, can produce fiascoes (negative synergy).

Gathering information should be a focused effort by all group members. As Wood and her associates (1986) explain, "Only if your search for information is focused will you be able to manage the flood of information available to you. There is little hope for those who wander about in libraries hoping for some inspiration to come their way" (p. 158).

A group can focus its information gathering by asking certain standard questions (Wood et al., 1986). Use the following questions to guide your information search, especially if the group is considering a policy question:

1. *Is the problem significant?* This can be established quantitatively (e.g., a compilation of stats and facts showing tangible harm) and/or qualitatively (e.g., are important values jeopardized such as right to privacy or presumption of innocence?).
2. *What has caused the problem?* This may require testimony of experts and results from scientific studies. In some cases causes may be unknown.
3. *Can the problem be resolved without substantial change in present policy?* Sometimes the present policy requires sufficient time to be implemented and other times the policy is seriously flawed from the start with no hope of success.
4. *Has the problem occurred elsewhere, and if so, how was it handled?* Groups can learn from the previous experience of others.
5. *What solutions have been suggested for this problem?* Often several proposals have been offered to solve a specific problem.
6. *What are the advantages and disadvantages of each proposed solution?* Change is warranted if there is likelihood for improvement, but not if worse problems may result from the change.

With these questions in mind, <u>the group should divide the labor</u>. Some members may concentrate on certain questions while other members research different questions. The library is usually the place to start the information search. There are numerous standard references that can be enormously helpful on most topics. Let me list just a few.

The Readers' Guide to Periodical Literature is the research bible for many students. As a reference work, however, it is rather limited. Better sources of statistical information on a wide range of topics include the *Statistical Abstract of the United States, Facts on File, Information Please Almanac, Vital Statistics of the U.S., World Almanac, Monthly Labor Review, Report of the President's Council of Economic Advisors, Survey of Current Business,* and the *FBI Uniform Crime Report.* Excellent guides to professional and scholarly articles include *Psychological Abstracts, Sociological Abstracts,* and *International Index: Guide to Periodical Literature in the Social Sciences and Humanities.* The standard card catalog, of course, indicates books available in a specific library, but don't stop there. Check out *Books in Print* for a list of all books currently in print indexed by authors, topics, and titles. *Book Review Digest* may also be helpful. For government-related information, consult the *Monthly Catalog of United States Government Publications, The Congressional Index, Congressional Quarterly Weekly Report,* and *The Congressional Record.* For information of general interest, consult encyclopedias such as *Encyclopedia Britannica, World Book Encyclopedia,* and *Collier's Encyclopedia* as well as newspaper indexes such as *New York Times Index* and an index to your local newspaper.

For the most up-to-date information, use the Internet. Learning to use the proper search engines and focusing your search take time to master. Consult your librarian for assistance if you have no experience using the Internet. Some useful research sites on the Internet are:

http://www.apa.org (psychology)
http://www.census.gov/ (U.S. Census Bureau STATS)

http://www.ed.gov/NCES/ (National Center for Education Statistics)

http://www.census.gov/ftp/pub/ipc/www/idbprint.html (International Database)

http://www.ciesin.org/ (International Earth Science Information Network)

http://www.census.gov/main/www/stat-fed.html (U.S. Federal Statistical Agencies)

http://sosig.ac.uk/ (Social Science Information)

http://law.house.gov/ (Law Library of U.S. House of Representatives)

http://www.public.asu.edu/corman/infosys (International Communication Association)

Searching for information can be a tedious process. Remaining focused by following the suggestions I've offered will reduce the tedium and increase group efficiency.

Evaluating Information

Knowing where to find appropriate information is helpful, but group members must also know how to evaluate information. All information is not created equal. As a critical thinker, you must decide which information is most credible, current, relevant, and representative, and when the information gathered is sufficient to support adequately claims made by the group.

1. **Credibility.** Is the information believable and reliable? <u>When the source of your information is biased (gains something by taking certain positions), credibility is low</u>. A few years ago, sugar manufacturers in print advertisements labeled "Note to Mothers" claimed that white sugar was better than artificial sweeteners because: "Exhaustion may be dangerous—especially to children who haven't learned to avoid it by pacing themselves. Exhaustion opens the door a little wider to the bugs and ailments that are always lying in wait. Sugar puts back energy fast—offsets exhaustion. Synthetic sweeteners put back nothing. Energy is the first requirement of life. Play safe with your young ones—make sure they get sugar every day." Does this require a comment? Then there are the psychic hotline wars on TV. Individuals with dubious credentials battle over whose psychics are legitimate and whose are fakes, begging the credibility question: Are *any* phone psychics legitimate? Cash-conscious, self-proclaimed seers who make vague predictions about people's lives after fleeting interactions over the phone hardly seem credible. And do you ever hear how often these phone psychics make incorrect predictions (re-emphasizing the need to combat confirmation bias)? Credible evidence for the existence of legitimate phone psychics is still lacking—and I predict that this will not change in the foreseeable future.

   <u>Authorities quoted outside of their field of expertise are also not credible</u>. Iben Browning predicted a major earthquake for December 3 and 4, 1990, along the New Madrid Fault located in the Midwest. Schools in several states were dismissed during these two days as a result of his prediction. Was Browning a credible expert on earthquakes? He had a doctorate in physi-

ology and a bachelor's degree in physics and math. He was the chief scientist for Summa Medical Corp. He studied climatology in his spare time. Earthquake experts around the country repudiated Browning's predictions. He was not a credible source since his earthquake predictions were not in his field of expertise. (As you undoubtedly know, his predictions were wrong.)

Let me also note here that the Internet itself is not a credible source. The Internet is merely a search vehicle for finding information. There is garbage galore on the Internet. As a critical thinker, you must separate the gems from the garbage. Quoting "the Internet" as your source is tantamount to quoting "the radio."

2. **Currency.** Information should be as up-to-date as possible. What used to be taken as fact may be called into question with new information. Only a few years ago cholesterol levels below 300 were thought to pose no significant risk of heart disease. Now, the current advice calls for cholesterol levels below 200, and a 150 level is preferred in order to keep heart disease risk low. Currency is especially important when an event or situation is volatile and likely to change rapidly. Quoting last month's or even last week's stock prices could leave you a pauper if you act on such dated information. Interest rates on home mortgages change daily. You must have current rates before you decide to lock in a fixed-rate mortgage on a house you're purchasing.

3. **Relevance.** Information should relate directly to the claims made. A popular ad on television, which played for what seemed like the life span of a sequoia redwood tree, alleged that one analgesic worked better than all the rest because it had "800 milligrams of pain reliever" while the others had only 650 milligrams. More doesn't always mean better, however. For the vast majority of people, no additional pain relief is accrued beyond 650 milligrams (Willis, 1986). The information (800 milligrams) is therefore irrelevant to the claim of "more pain relief."

4. **Representativeness.** A single example or statistic may or may not accurately reflect what is true in a particular instance. If a vivid example (e.g., testimonial from a victim of black lung disease on the health risks of mining coal) illustrates the truth of a claim already supported by solid scientific evidence, then it is representative and provides dramatic impact to the claim. If, however, a claim rests merely on a few or even many examples, then a real question of representativeness exists. Examples to support a claim may be selectively chosen (confirmation bias), so they may not reflect what is true generally.

There are two principal guidelines for determining whether statistics are representative. First, the sample size (in polls, surveys, and studies) must be adequate. This can be determined most easily by the *margin of error*, which is the degree of sampling error accounted for by imperfections in selecting a sample. As the margin of error increases, the representativeness of the statistic decreases. If the margin of error reaches more than plus or minus 3 percent, the representativeness of the statistic becomes questionable. A study ("Pre-employment," 1990) of 103 California companies testing job applicants for drug use revealed that 17.8 percent of the applicants tested positive. The margin of error, however, was 7.8 percent. Thus, the results are questionable since the true level of drug use among the job applicants may have been 10 percent (17.8 percent minus 7.8 percent margin of error) or 25.6 percent (17.8 percent plus 7.8 percent margin of error) and still fall within the sampling error rate. The drug use problem may be substantially overstated or under-stated by the 17.8 percent statistic.

A second guideline for assuring representative statistics is that <u>the sample must be randomly selected, not self-selected</u>. A *random sample* is a part of the population drawn in such a manner that every member of the entire population has an equal chance of being selected. A *self-selected sample* is one in which the most committed, aroused, or otherwise atypical parts of the population studied are more likely to participate in the study. Shere Hite (1987) published a study entitled *Women and Love*. She based her conclusions on 4,500 surveys, composed of 127 essay questions, returned to her from a total mailing of 100,000 surveys. One startling conclusion from the study was that *98 percent* of women are dissatisfied with their relationships with men, a finding completely contradicted by national surveys using randomly selected samples, but nevertheless so sensational that it fueled the "men are jerks" argument for some time on the talk show circuit.

Hite's sample was adequately sized, but it was a self-selected sample. Women angry or disenchanted with their men are more likely to return the survey than those who are satisfied with their relationships with their men, because anger powerfully motivates action but contentedness will not likely rouse you from the couch.

Similarly, the tabloid television show *Hard Copy* conducted a call-in poll of potential voters on the day of the 1992 presidential election. The eventual sample was slightly more than 70,000, more than adequate if the sample had been random. This self-selected sample, however, produced a wildly inac-curate result. Bush received 41 percent of the call-in votes, Clinton only 31 percent, and Perot 28 percent. As you may recall, the actual election didn't give Bush a near-landslide victory as indicated by the self-selected sample of callers. A self-selected sample such as the ones in the Hite Report and on *Hard Copy* will not produce representative statistics that can be generalized beyond a very selective, narrow, highly motivated population.

5. **Sufficiency.** When do you have enough information to support your claims? Is there sufficient information to conclude that smoking cigarettes is hazard-ous to your health? After more than 40,000 studies, all showing the connec-tion between smoking and heart disease, lung cancer, and other deadly ill-nesses ("Advertising is hazardous," 1986), the answer is unquestionably yes, despite the Tobacco Institute's (biased source) fervent denial. Most other claims, however, do not have such overwhelming support. There is no magic formula for sufficiency. Determinations of sufficiency are judgment calls. Nevertheless, there are some guidelines for making such a determination.

First, <u>what type of claim are you making</u>? Causal relations require more evidence than a single study. In December 1990, a long-term study of nurses showed a significant correlation between levels of red meat consumption and colon cancer. Should we give up red meat? One study is insufficient to establish a causal relationship, so the answer is no. Claiming that violence depicted on television "may contribute to antisocial behavior," however, requires less stringent criteria for sufficiency since only a weak connection is claimed.

Second, <u>extraordinary claims require extraordinary proof</u> (Abell, 1981). When a claim contradicts a considerable body of research and knowledge, extraordinary proof must accompany such a claim. A claim that Earth has been visited by extraterrestrials requires much more evidence than a few alleged sitings. Likewise, accusing former *Entertainment Tonight* star and New Age musician John Tesh of being an "interplanetary mole" for an invading space-alien army, as the National Anti-Tesh Action Society did in June 1996 ("Wacky life forms," 1996), requires out-of-this-world evidence. On a less ethereal plane, claims of cancer cures must be rigorously tested. The claims are extraordinary, so they require more than ordinary, commonplace evidence. Ordinary claims, however, such as "flu viruses pose a serious health hazard to the elderly" can be demonstrated sufficiently with one authoritative statistic from the Center for Disease Control.

Third, <u>consider the context for the claim</u>. In a criminal trial, sufficiency means "beyond a reasonable doubt." In political debate and most arenas of public discourse, a "preponderance of evidence" (favors one side over the other) is sufficient. (See Appendix B for additional relevant material on critically examining information and claims.)

PARTICIPATION

Tom Peters (1989), coauthor of the bestseller *In Search of Excellence,* offers an illustration of the importance of participation in the decision-making process. When Keith Dunn, head of McGuffey's Restaurants in Asheville, North Carolina, attempted to follow Peters' advice and become more "people oriented," the results were discouraging. He instituted several morale-boosting schemes—contests with big prizes, benefits for workers, sweatshirts with catchy slogans, and so forth. Morale and performance dropped with each new gimmick. Why?

The missing ingredient in this management-by-decree minestrone he had cooked up was participation from those on the receiving end of his recipe for success. The managers and employees had no say in his decisions. He imposed them on his workers without consulting them. Top-down decision making without participation from those below easily produces antagonism and resentment. When Dunn opened up communication with employees and instituted some of *their* suggestions for change, productivity and profits turned around.

Is participation the panacea for competing successfully in the international marketplace? Does involvement by all members of the group inevitably lead to quality decision making and problem solving? In the next section, I will discuss the pros and cons of participation in the decision-making/problem-solving process.

Focus Questions

1. In what ways is communication competence central to the issue of how much participation in group decision making/problem solving is useful?
2. Which group members should be encouraged to participate and which should not?

Pros and Cons of Participation

During World War II, an experiment (Lewin, 1953) was conducted for the purpose of convincing "housewives" to serve less desirable types of meat such as kidneys, beef hearts, pork brains, and sweetbreads (a euphemism for calf innards). The federal government hoped to alleviate some of the problem of meat shortages by altering the choices of consumers. The subjects were Red Cross volunteers. One set of subjects listened to a persuasive lecture arguing that these types of meats were nutritious, tasty, and would help in the war effort, while another set of volunteers engaged in a guided discussion of how to overcome difficulties in serving these meats. Only 3 percent of the women in the lecture group actually served these meats to their families. An impressive 32 percent of the discussion group, however, served these meats to their families. Participating in a discussion dramatically influenced the behavior of group members. Other studies have supported these results (Tubbs and Carter, 1977).

Involving people in the decision-making process, especially when the decisions affect their lives directly, can be very beneficial. Self-managed or autonomous work teams are structured on the participatory decision-making model. Companies that establish self-managed teams in which workers are given a great deal of latitude in making decisions affecting production and sales, even hiring and firing of team members, typically show improvements in worker productivity, quality of products, and worker satisfaction and retention (Freeman, 1996).

Johnson and Johnson (1991) claim three advantages associated with participating in decision making. First, participation increases members' allegiance to the group because they feel they are active and valued contributors. Second, participation improves the quality of the decisions because the full resources of the group are utilized. Third, participation increases the commitment of group members to implementing decisions once they have been made because members all had a say in the decision and the result was not imposed on them from the outside.

 FOCUS ON CULTURE

Cultural Diversity and Participation in Small Groups

One of the significant challenges facing teachers in an increasingly multicultural educational environment is how to increase the participation level in class of some ethnic minority students. Japanese students, for example, initiate and maintain fewer conversations and are less apt to talk in class discussions than are American students (Ishii et al., 1984). This reticence to participate verbally in class carries over to small-group situations. Contributions to group decision making by ethnic minorities are consistently lower than nonminorities (Kirchmeyer, 1993). In 76 percent of the small groups in one study (Kirchmeyer and Cohen, 1992), the member who contributed the least was Asian.

Why is there this difference in verbal participation in small-group decision making? First, the value of verbal participation in decision making is perceived differently from culture to culture. As already noted, silent individuals are not seriously considered for the role of leader in American culture. Speaking is highly valued in the United States. Silence is not prized. Americans usually interpret silence in mostly negative ways: as indicating sorrow, critique, obligation, regret, or embarrassment (Wayne, 1974). Talking in an individualist culture is a way of showing one's uniqueness (Samovar and Porter, 1995).

In collectivist cultures and subcultures, by contrast, speaking is not highly prized. Students from collectivist cultural traditions typically see speaking too much in class as a sign of conceit and superficiality (Samovar and Porter, 1995). Among the Japanese, Vietnamese, Cambodians, and Chinese, emphasis is given to minimal vocal participation. Inagaki (1985) surveyed 3600 Japanese regarding their attitude toward speaking. He found that 82 percent agreed with the saying, "Out of the mouth comes all evil" (p. 6). For the Japanese "silence is considered a virtue as well as a sign of respectability and trustworthiness" (McDaniel, 1993, p. 19). In business negotiations, Japanese, Chinese, and Koreans are more at ease with long pauses and silences than are Americans. As Andersen (in Samovar and Porter, 1995) explains, "Cultures reflecting Buddhist tradition hold that knowledge, truth, and wisdom come to those whose quiet silence allows the spirit to enter" (p. 246). Many Native Americans equate silence with a great person (Samovar and Porter, 1995). Johannesen (1974) claims that the Native American "derives from silence the cornerstone of character, the virtues of self-control, courage, patience and dignity" (p. 27).

Second, a relative disadvantage in ability to communicate effectively in groups limits verbal participation of ethnic minorities. Minorities report considerably less facility for communicating with others in a college setting (Kirchmeyer, 1993). Not only are ethnic minorities at a distinct disadvantage if English is their second language, but minorities are at a disadvantage "in groups dominated by others who communicate more effectively and appropriately, [are] more assertive, and express less concern for others" (Kirchmeyer, 1993, p. 142).

Third, lackluster participation from ethnic minorities in decision making may result from weak commitment to the group. Weak commitment may result from group members' failure to indicate that participation from minorities is valued, or cultural differences with members of the dominant culture may make minorities feel less attachment to the group and less like they belong (Kirchmeyer and Cohen, 1992).

If tapping the resources of cultural diversity is an important group goal, and this would seem to be significant given the synergistic potential inherent in diversity, then finding ways to boost the verbal participation rates of ethnic minorities in an American culture that values speech is a worthy undertaking. The methods outlined in this chapter for encouraging constructive participation from low-contributors in general apply well to ethnic minorities.

Questions for Thought

1. Should nonminority Americans value silence as much as some ethnic minorities do?
2. Should Americans de-emphasize speaking ability?
3. Should you expect ethnic minority group members to become more assertive and outspoken participators in small groups even though this is not highly valued in their culture? Explain.

Participation, as important as it is to produce group synergy, is not the ultimate remedy for bad decision making. Those members who have weak oral communication skills may find participation intimidating. Individuals with high communication anxiety will likely find participation threatening and reason for refilling the Valium prescription. Enthusiastic participation by those who have demonstrated their lack of knowledge regarding the task will not improve the quality of decisions. Those who do not possess the requisite knowledge may bog down the group in worthless discussion about pointless issues.

Communication competence is central to the issue of participation levels in group decision making. Generally speaking, you should determine whether members have the necessary knowledge, skills, sensitivity, and commitment to the group to be a positive contributor. Pooling ignorance can generate negative synergy. High participation levels among the uninformed, unenlightened, unmotivated, or the insufferable will not result in quality decisions. Participation generally should be encouraged. Nevertheless, participation of all group members is not necessarily wise nor appropriate.

Increasing Constructive Participation

Assuming that participation of group members is worth increasing because low-participators are merely reticent, loafing from boredom, or feeling unappreciated, there are several steps that can be taken. (Steps for increasing constructive participation from group members in general vary somewhat from steps that a group must take to address the special problem of social loafers discussed in Chapter Three.)

First, overtly encourage contributions from low-participators. This is especially important for involving those ethnic minorities whose cultural values discourage assertiveness (Tang and Kirkbride, 1986). Solicit input from reticent members by asking open-ended questions (e.g., ''What do you think?''). When low-participators do offer contributions, indicate that this is valued by actively listening to what that person has to say.

Second, make issues and problems for discussion relevant to the interests of low-participators. When groups work on interesting, involving, or challenging tasks, member contributions increase (Forsyth, 1990).

Third, <u>give low-participators responsibility for certain tasks</u>. When individuals are designated as responsible for certain important tasks, they are less likely to sit back, waiting for someone else to assume the responsibility. If low-participators believe that their efforts have an impact on the group's final decision or product, they are less likely to remain uninvolved (Kerr and Bruun, 1983).

Fourth, <u>establish a cooperative group climate</u>. This is particularly important for ethnic minorities from collectivist cultures who are likely to feel more comfortable and committed in such an atmosphere.

Fifth, <u>encourage devil's advocacy and dialectical inquiry</u>. These two methods of combating groupthink also encourage constructive participation from all group members. With their emphasis on stimulating a variety of ideas and opinions, fully sharing information, openly confronting differences of opinion (using supportive, not defensive, communication patterns), and carefully evaluating alternatives, devil's advocacy and dialectical inquiry, sometimes referred to as constructive conflict, substantially increase the participation of ethnic minorities (Kirchmeyer and Cohen, 1992).

⊙⊙ CLOSER LOOK

Electronic Meetings: Mediated Participation

Humorist Dave Barry (1991), comparing meetings to funerals, seems to prefer funerals. He claims, "The major difference is that most funerals have a definite purpose. Also, nothing is ever really buried in a meeting" (p. 311). Milo Frank, author of *How to Run a Successful Meeting in Half the Time,* relates the story of an experiment at one of the major contractors for the Defense Department. Someone called a large meeting for no reason. People gathered, talked, began to argue, became animated, and wasted three hours without ever learning why the meeting was called in the first place.

Business consultant Mitchell Nash (in Dressler, 1995) lists six common complaints associated with group meetings. These six complaints are as follows: there is an unclear purpose for the meeting, participants are unprepared, key individuals are absent or late, discussion drifts into irrelevant conversation on unrelated topics, some participants dominate the conversation and stifle discussion, and decisions made at meetings are not implemented.

John Kenneth Galbraith viewed meetings as "indispensable when you don't want to do anything." Meetings, however, don't have to be time wasters or sedatives. Whoever chairs a meeting has specific responsibilities. As the chair, there are several ways that you can structure meetings to make them efficient and effective decision-making arenas. First, don't call a meeting unless there is no other good alternative. If an immediate response is required, group participation is essential, participants are prepared to discuss relevant issues, and key players can be present, then hold a meeting. Disseminating information, meeting because you are scheduled to do so every Tuesday afternoon, using the meeting as an opportunity to recruit help in researching a topic, or hoping to try out new ideas on colleagues are not solid reasons to hold meetings. If these objectives can be accomplished without meeting in a group, then don't meet. One of life's little pleasures is the surprise notification, "Meeting has been cancelled."

Second, contact every participant. Indicate in a memo or e-mail what the specific purpose of the meeting is, where, when, and how long it will be held, and what materials, if any, each participant should bring to the meeting.

Third, prepare a clear agenda and distribute it to all participants three days or more in advance of the meeting. The agenda should list the topics of discussion (see Appendix C for sample agendas). If reading materials must accompany the agenda, make certain that they are concise and essential to the discussion. Avoid information overload.

Fourth, provide accurate information on issues discussed, clarify complex issues, correct misconceptions, and especially keep the discussion on track and on point. Aimless discussions suck the life out of meetings and cause participants to do face-plants into tabletops from mind-numbing boredom. Do not allow any participant to be a stagehog and dominate the discussion.

Fifth, designate a specific time allotment for every discussion item. A time keeper should be assigned at the start of each meeting. When the time on a discussion item has elapsed, the group may decide to extend the time allotment or move to the next item. Time limits establish a crisp pace for the meeting. Keep meetings as short as possible.

Sixth, reserve a few minutes at the end of the meeting to determine whether the objectives of the meeting were accomplished. If further work and discussion is deemed necessary, schedule discussion for unfinished business for the next meeting. If decisions have been made by the group, implementation of these decisions must be monitored. This is usually the chair's responsibility, but all participants have some responsibility for this.

Seventh, distribute the minutes of the meeting as soon as possible. The minutes should indicate what was discussed, who said what, what action was taken, and what remains to be deliberated and decided.

In-person meetings are what most of us are accustomed to, but there are several electronic alternatives to the standard format. The teleconference, commonly referred to as the conference call, is a meeting conducted over the telephone. When face-to-face meetings are expensive to convene because participants are separated by geography, the conference call is a useful option. Teleconferences are easy to set up. Most business and many residential phone services provide conference call capability. Most of the guidelines for conducting efficient and effective meetings already discussed apply to teleconferences. The conference call should be necessary, focused, organized (have an agenda), and short.

Videoconferences are more technologically sophisticated. Meetings are conducted via closed-circuit or satellite-linked television. The videoconference, similar to the teleconference, is a useful option when participants cannot meet easily in person. Videoconferences also provide nonverbal cues such as facial expressions, posture, and eye contact unavailable in teleconferencing. Body language cues help participants to assess messages more accurately and they are instrumental in defining relationships between participants. Videoconferences should also be necessary, focused, organized, and short.

Electronic mail, or e-mail, meetings are a third technological alternative to the in-person meeting. E-mail discussions take place in written form only. Messages appear on computer screens. This encourages low-status members to participate in discussions and to stand their ground more firmly on controversial or contentious issues (Sproull and Kiesler, 1991). In-person discussions can be intimidating, especially if some participants are dominating and aggressive when expressing their points of view. Typing responses on a computer keyboard can embolden reticent participants to say exactly what they are thinking.

There are also electronic aids for in-person meetings. Group Decision Support Systems (GDSS) are hardware and software options that facilitate in-person meetings. The simplest version permits participants to register votes electronically on issues discussed during meetings. This allows for anonymity. Another version of GDSS is for brainstorming ideas. Other systems can provide structure for group discussions.

Despite the advantages of electronic alternatives to standard meetings, there are some drawbacks. First, electronic alternatives may be cost prohibitive. Computers, satellite hookups, videocameras, hardware, and software can be expensive. There are additional costs associated with using and maintaining these electronic alternatives once they are available.

Second, one can be seduced easily into believing that technology is a quick fix for fruitless meetings. Sophisticated technologies are just complicated toys if they are not matched properly with the purposes and objectives of the group. If participants are unfamiliar with or intimidated by computer alternatives, then expensive hardware will gather dust. The surest way to discourage reticent group members from participating is to conduct meetings electronically when members feel intimidated by the hardware and unskilled in the use of software alternatives. Proper training, which can be time-consuming and expensive, is necessary for optimum utilization of electronic meetings.

Third, electronic meetings may produce information overload. E-mail meetings can degenerate easily into message fatigue. Participants can be bombarded with facts, figures, opinions, and the ever-popular "attachments." The easier it is to send large amounts of information, the more information overload becomes a serious roadblock to effective decision making.

Fourth, electronic meetings usually require more planning and organization than simpler in-person meetings. Setting up equipment, having an expert standing by in case of equipment failure or glitches, and making sure that all participants are familiar with the systems they are using can produce a four-aspirin headache.

Fifth, e-mail meetings may encourage indiscriminate or overzealous expressions of anger or disagreement. Participants may not edit their written communication as carefully as they edit their oral communication during in-person confrontations. They may experience rage regret (e.g., "Why did I call my boss a pig-headed moron with a brain the size of a quark?"). It is also more difficult for participants to claim that they were misunderstood when a hard copy of their intemperate statement can be printed and disseminated.

Sixth, viewpoints and opinions may become more polarized and extreme, making consensus more difficult. The more removed participants feel from personal contact, the more this is likely to be true.

Electronically mediated meetings have their place. When issues are complex or ambiguous and emotions are running high, however, in-person meetings are preferred. Both in-person and electronically mediated meetings benefit from following the guidelines for efficient and effective meetings.

Questions for Thought

1. Can you think of additional advantages and disadvantages of electronically mediated meetings?
2. Do you think that we'll ever get to a time when in-person meetings will be replaced entirely with electronic alternatives? Explain.

CREATIVE PROBLEM SOLVING

Years ago, a prisoner escaped from a penitentiary in the western United States. He was recaptured after a few weeks. On his return, prison officials grilled him. "How did you cut through the bars?" they demanded. Finally, he confessed. He said he had taken bits of twine from the machine shop, dipped them in glue, then in emery. He smuggled these makeshift "hacksaws" back to his cell. For three months he laboriously "sawed" through the one-inch-thick steel bars. Prison officials accepted his story, locked him up, and kept him far away from the machine shop. End of the story? Not quite. Three-and-a-half years later, he escaped again by cutting through the cell bars. He was never recaptured, but how he escaped became a legend in the underworld. It seems that his original story was a phony. He hadn't fashioned a hacksaw from any materials in the machine shop. Instead, he had used woolen strings from his socks, moistened them with spit, and rubbed them in abrasive dirt from the floor of his cell, then painstakingly sawed through the cell bars (Rossman, 1931). The prisoner had fashioned a creative solution to a challenging problem. Creative problem solving is the focus of this section.

Focus Questions
1. How do imagination and knowledge relate to creative problem solving?
2. How do rational and creative problem solving relate to each other?

General Overview

The story of the prisoner's resourceful escape highlights several important points about creativity and problem solving. First, to borrow Thomas Edison's comment on genius, <u>creativity is more perspiration than inspiration</u>. We have to work at it. Imaginative solutions to problems don't usually spring from thin air. Even when they do seem to materialize from nowhere by some serendipitous, unexpected occurrence, you have to be prepared to see the usefulness of the discovery or it will go unnoticed.

Second, <u>creativity is spurred by challenges</u>. According to the adage, "Necessity is the mother of invention." We are creative in response to some felt need, to some problem that requires a solution. The bigger the challenge, the more complex the problem, the greater is the need for creativity.

Third, <u>creativity requires more than just imaginative ideas</u>. As Vincent Ruggiero (1988) puts it, creative ideas must be more than uncommon; they "must be *uncommonly good*" (p. 77). Or, as former prime minister of Great Britain, Harold Macmillan, once sarcastically remarked: "As usual the Liberals offer a mixture of sound and original ideas. Unfortunately, none of the sound ideas is original and none of the original ideas is sound" (in Metcalf, 1986, p. 148). Creative solutions are original, but they also must solve problems; they must satisfy goals or meet needs. They must work.

I once heard a radio commentator read recipes submitted by young kids for preparing a Thanksgiving turkey. One child wrote: "Put ten pounds of butter on the turkey and five pounds of salt. Cook it for twenty minutes." M-m-m-m-m good! Some culinary concoctions just don't work. The recipes are imaginative, but repulsive, like spaghetti and liver sauce or a tofu and oyster milkshake. Alfred North Whitehead makes my point succinctly: "Fools act on imagination without knowledge; pedants act on knowledge without imagination." Creative problem solving and decision making require imagination *and* knowledge. Children create foolish things because they don't know any better. Competent communicators have the knowledge and the skills to complement their imagination. They create solutions that are workable and effective.

Fourth, <u>creativity requires fluency and flexibility</u> (Bormann, 1990). Fluency is the ability to generate a great quantity of ideas quickly. Although sheer quantity doesn't guarantee solutions, the fewer the ideas, the less probable is the discovery of at least one good idea—that flower among all the thistles. Flexibility is the ability to break away from ordinary, usual ways of looking at problems and to adopt different ways of approaching problems.

Specific Creative Techniques

As I have emphasized already, group decision making and problem solving are usually more effective when systematic procedures are followed. Systematic procedures apply to group creativity as well (Firestien, 1990). <u>Haphazard, unfocused efforts to induce creativity are often not as productive as more focused efforts</u>.

Brainstorming and Nominal Group Techniques   "Encourage Wild Ideas" appears in large print on the walls of each brainstorming room, sanctuaries of creativity where product design teams composed of engineers, industrial designers, and behavioral psychologists at IDEO Product Development in Silicon Valley, California, fling ideas back and forth in a frenzy of mental activity

(O'Brien, 1995). IDEO brainstormed the design of Apple Computer's original point-and-click mouse, the Macintosh Duo docking system for laptops, and a host of diverse products. Faced with the problem of an electric car that is so quiet that it would likely cause accidents, the brainstormers attack the problem with relish. "How about tire treads that play music?" one team member offers. "How about a little Eric Clapton?" another chimes in, and the ideas begin to fly.

The **brainstorming** technique was introduced in 1939 by Alex Osborn. Brainstorming is designed to open up the problem-solving process. Rational approaches to decision making and problem solving run the danger of becoming methodical, stale, and unimaginative. Brainstorming can regenerate a group by opening up a stuffy, plodding, and inhibited group process.

There are several guidelines for using this technique:

1. *Don't evaluate ideas while brainstorming.* Critiques will inhibit contributions from group members. Evaluation stifles creativity (Amabile, 1983). Thus, a group needs to be self-monitoring. Idea slayers, such as "You can't be serious," "That will never work," and "It's completely impractical," should be squelched by members. Even positive evaluations, such as "Great idea," "I think you're on to something," and so forth, are out of order for the brainstorming process to work. Once positive evaluations are introduced into the process, group members will be looking for the negative reactions to surface, or they might assume that the absence of positive reactions equals a negative judgment of their idea.

2. *Don't clarify or seek clarification of an idea.* This will slow down the process. Clarification can come later after a list of ideas has been generated.

3. *Encourage zany ideas.* What appears to be a dumb idea initially can provoke a really good solution to a problem. Bolton (1979) cites the example of a brainstorming session by managers of a major airport who were generating ideas regarding ways to remove snow from the runways. One participant offered the idea that snow could be removed by putting a giant frog on the control tower. The frog could push the snow aside with its enormous tongue. This idea obviously was not selected, but it provoked an idea that eventually was adopted—a revolving cannon that shoots a jet airstream. Even if zany ideas never trigger effective solutions to problems, they at least loosen up the group. Goofy, crazy, off-the-wall ideas encourage a freewheeling climate conducive to creativity.

4. *Expand on the ideas of other group members.* Halpern (1984) cites the example of a food manufacturer seeking better ways to bag potato chips. Corporate executives were asked to identify the best packaging solution they had ever seen. One brainstormer said that bagging leaves wet was the best method. Dry leaves crumble and use up more air space. Wet leaves pack more easily and require fewer bags. Expanding on this idea, the manufacturer tried packing potato chips wet. When the potato chips dried they became tasteless crumbs. Nevertheless, from this initial failure sprang the popular potato chips in a can, in which a potato mixture is cooked in chip-shaped molds and then stacked in the can. From a bad idea came a good one.

5. *Record all ideas without reference to who contributed the idea.* Do not censor any ideas, no matter how silly they may seem.
6. *Encourage participation from all group members.* The maximum number of ideas requires the maximum effort from every group member.

Brainstorming complements the rational approach to decision making. Brainstorming normally is instituted during the solutions suggestion step of the Standard Agenda. Determining the quality of the ideas generated from brainstorming comes during the solution evaluation and selection step. Ideas are evaluated in terms of solution criteria established earlier in the Standard Agenda process.

Despite the popularity of the brainstorming technique, research has cast doubt on the superiority of brainstorming compared to individuals working alone (Paulus et al., 1993). Researchers (Valacich et al., 1994) offer three reasons for the inferior performance of group compared to individual brainstorming: evaluation apprehension (fear of negative critiques of ideas even though none may be verbalized), free riding (social loafing, which increases as groups grow larger), and production blocking (forgotten or suppressed ideas while group members wait their turn to speak).

Research suggesting that brainstorming may not be superior to individuals working alone has led to the **nominal group technique** (Delbecq et al., 1975). This technique utilizes key elements of brainstorming without group interaction. Individuals work by themselves generating lists of ideas on a problem, then convene in a group where they merely record the ideas generated (usually on a chart or blackboard for all to see). Interaction occurs only to clarify ideas, not to discuss their merits and demerits. Individuals then select their five favorite ideas, write them on a card, and rank them from most favorite to least favorite. The rankings are averaged and the ideas with the highest averages are the ones selected by the group.

There is some question regarding the research that shows nominal group technique superior to brainstorming. Mongeau (1993) argues that "although considerable research has been performed on brainstorming, little of this research is a valid test of Osborn's ideas" (p. 22). He explains that "brainstorming groups in the literature tend to be zero-history (and zero-future as well) groups where members are strangers. Members are not chosen with any concern for their problem-solving ability or experience with the topic under discussion" (p. 19). Several studies have had students "generate ideas about the practical benefits and difficulties that would arise if everyone had an extra thumb on each hand" (Paulus et al., 1993, p. 79; see also Paulus et al., 1996). Unlike ideas generated at IDEO, there is no way to test the practicality and effectiveness of any ideas generated on this task (or most tasks used in brainstorming studies).

Whenever I peruse the literature on group brainstorming, I am perplexed by the results. My own experience contradicts the findings of these studies. On numerous occasions I have worked with my colleagues in the speech communication department, and together we have brainstormed creative solutions to problems that had previously vexed me. The activities included in the

Instructor's Manual that accompanies this textbook are almost wholly the product of a group brainstorming effort. In one case, my colleagues and I spent two weekends together devising an effective exercise that I had tried by myself for ten years to create, every time giving up in frustration.

I agree with Mongeau (1993) that the research on group brainstorming is not an adequate test of the technique. Results derived from student groups that have no history together and no future, have no training and experience using the brainstorming technique (aside from a perfunctory explanation of the rules), are provided no opportunity to research the task prior to brainstorming, are given little time to think about the task, and are given tasks that are often unrelated to students' interests are dubious at best. Brainstorming, *if done properly,* should produce, if not more ideas, certainly better ideas on average than the nominal group technique, and quality, not quantity, of ideas is the real test. Your interest is in creating one great idea, not fifty lousy ones. The voluminous research on group synergy suggests that group brainstorming should be superior to individual brainstorming in generating great ideas.

Osborn actually suggested that the proper brainstorming format should involve first an individual, then a group, followed by an individual brainstorming session. Members should be provided with the topic a few days in advance of the brainstorming session to research it and to think of ideas to contribute. Then members meet as a group to brainstorm. After the group session, individuals are given a few days to contemplate further ideas on their own. In addition, members should not be strangers and they should belong to a long-standing (not a zero-history) group. They should also receive training and experience in how to use the brainstorming technique. Research shows that training and experience in brainstorming vastly improves idea generation (Firestien, 1990).

Electronic brainstorming offers an additional method for improving idea generation and creativity. Group members sit at computer terminals and brainstorm ideas using a computer-based file-sharing procedure (Group Decision Support System). Group members type their contributions, then send the file to a shared pool. Comments are made, ideas are added and shared with group members. This can even be done anonymously. Electronic brainstorming diminishes production blocking and evaluation apprehension that retard idea generation. Consequently, electronic brainstorming has even outperformed nominal groups in idea generation (Valacich et al., 1994).

Despite the advantages of electronic brainstorming, it has many of the drawbacks of electronic meetings previously discussed. First, the appropriate technology must be available. This is not always feasible or affordable. Second, electronic brainstorming requires greater, more meticulous planning and organization than does ordinary face-to-face, unmediated brainstorming. Third, some may feel electronic brainstorming is impersonal, lacking the more personal face-to-face interaction of unmediated brainstorming. Finally, electronic brainstorming may intimidate those who view technology with suspicion or even revulsion. Nevertheless, electronic brainstorming certainly offers an interesting, potentially promising method for generating creative ideas and solutions to problems.

Framing/Reframing   Consider the following problem offered by psychologists Kahneman and Tversky (1981):

> Imagine that the government is preparing for an outbreak of a rare disease that is expected to kill six hundred people. Two programs are available. If Program A is adopted, then two hundred people will be saved. If Program B is adopted, then there is a one-third chance that six hundred people will be saved, and a two-thirds chance that nobody will be saved. Which program should be adopted?

When the problem is framed in this way, the vast majority of subjects prefer Program A over Program B. People want to avoid the risk that nobody will be saved. Now consider this statement of the problem:

> Imagine that the government is preparing for an outbreak of a rare disease that is expected to kill six hundred people. Two programs are available. If Program X is adopted, then four hundred people will die. If Program Y is adopted, then there is a one-third chance that nobody will die, and a two-thirds chance that six hundred people will die.

When the problem is framed in this way, the vast majority of subjects choose Program Y over X. Subjects want to avoid the certainty that four hundred people will die. Yet, Programs A and X have identical outcomes, as do B and Y. So why did one group predominantly choose Program A while the other group predominantly chose Program Y? The wording of the problem is identical and the outcomes are identical, yet the choices are opposite. The reason for the difference lies in how the problem is framed—the way in which it is presented.

When MBA students and managers were informed that a particular corporate strategy had a 70 percent chance of success, most favored it. When it was framed as a 30 percent chance of failure, however, the majority opposed the strategy (in Wolkomir and Wolkomir, 1990). When people were presented with two options for treating lung cancer, 84 percent chose the surgery option when it was framed in terms of living, while 56 percent chose the surgery option when it was presented in terms of dying (McNeil et al., 1982).

Our frame of reference can lock us into a mindset, making solutions to problems difficult if not impossible to discover. Someone once said that an optimist sees the silver lining in every cloud, but the pessimist sees the cloud around every silver lining. Our frame of reference predisposes us to see the world in certain ways. This mental gridlock can block the free flow of creative ideas. Postman (1976) provides an example.

> You have the number VI. By the addition of a single line, make it into a **7**. The answer is simple: VII. Now consider this problem: You have the number IX. By the addition of a single line, make it into a **6**.

The answer is not so obvious because of your frame of reference, which identifies the number as a Roman numeral and all lines as straight. Not until you break away from this frame of reference by <u>reframing the problem</u>—by no longer assuming that the answer must be in terms of a Roman numeral and that all lines are straight—will you solve the problem. Have you found the answer? How about SIX?

Reframing <u>is the creative process of breaking a mindset by placing the problem in a different frame of reference</u> (Watzlawick et al., 1974). In a photograph, the way you frame the shot determines which part of the subject will be your focus and which part will be excluded. If you cut off people's heads or have the main focus of interest off to the side, then the picture will be poor in quality. So it is with framing problems. If you cut off possibilities by framing a problem in only one way, then potentially effective solutions will be excluded from view. Frames determine whether people notice problems, how they understand and remember problems, and how they evaluate and act on them (Fairhurst and Sarr, 1996). You must consider the problem from a different frame of reference, or reframed, in order to see new solutions.

Learning to reframe problems can be a highly useful skill for the competent communicator and it is an essential part of effective leadership in groups (Fairhurst and Sarr, 1996). Reframing a dispute from a competitive exercise to a cooperative one can assist groups in finding mutually satisfactory solutions for both sides (Brett et al., 1990). Breaking through mindsets can generate creative solutions to seemingly intractable problems.

When groups become stumped by narrow or rigid frames of reference, <u>interjecting certain open-ended questions can help reframe the problem and the search for solutions</u>. My personal favorite is "What if . . . ?" The group asks, "What if we don't accept this cutback in resources as inevitable?" "What if management isn't playing games with the budget?" "What if employees really want to produce quality work but find the work environment unmotivating?" "What if we tried working together instead of against each other?"

Napier and Gershenfeld (1989) suggest these additional reframing questions:

This situation or problem is just like . . . ?
A different way to describe this is . . . ?
The only time anything like this happened before was . . . ?
This feels like a . . . ?
This situation reminds me of . . . ? (p. 342)

CLOSER LOOK

Reframing Problems

A service station proprietor put an out-of-order sign on a soda machine. Customers paid no attention to the sign, lost their money, then complained to the station owner. Frustrated and annoyed, the owner changed the sign to read "$2.00" for a soda. No one made the mistake of putting money in the faulty soda pop dispenser. The problem was reframed. Instead of wondering how to get customers to realize that the machine was on the fritz, the owner changed the frame of reference to one that would make customers not want to put money in the dispenser.

When a 7-Eleven store in British Columbia faced a problem of teenagers loitering in front of the store, instead of framing the problem as an issue of coercion (i.e., how to force the teenagers to stop congregating), the problem was reframed into a question—what would motivate the teenagers to leave of their own volition? Answer: The store piped Muzak into the parking lot. Loitering stopped. Was this cause and effect? It's difficult to know for sure, but as one teen put it when faced with listening to loud Mantovani recordings, "I'm out of here, dude. They want to listen to that stuff, they can have it" ("As they see it," 1990, p. 2C).

If your group is faced with a cut in resources, group members can frame this as a dispiriting event bound to affect adversely the product of members' endeavors. This situation could be reframed, however, by posing the question, "What if we accept this as a challenge to be embraced?"

I once observed an academic department faced with a substantial loss of resources reframe just as suggested. Two members of the speech department retired and were not replaced. This was a small department to begin with, and the loss of almost one-third of its faculty was discouraging. Nevertheless, faced with the reality, the faculty pulled together and devised new and effective ways to teach the 300 speech majors. The faculty team taught larger classes, started a tutorial internship program where advanced speech majors earned academic credit for tutoring beginning speech students in the basic courses, streamlined a curriculum heavy with courses no longer central to the discipline, concentrated on highly visible programs that enhanced the image of the department (e.g., debate team, readers' theatre program, student speakers' bureau, and a department-sponsored outside speakers' forum), and worked energetically for restoration of faculty positions based on productivity increases. Within five years, two faculty positions were restored and the department was at its most vigorous.

In all three of these cases, reframing the problem was the key to finding an effective solution. Breaking our mindsets is an important step in the process of creative problem solving.

Questions for Thought

1. Can all problems be reframed or are there problems that have just one frame of reference?
2. Can you think of examples where you have reframed a problem and a solution has emerged?

One of the nice advantages of reframing is that <u>once a different frame of reference is presented, the mindset often is broken permanently</u>. For instance, what is the correct answer to the following problem?

Radar is to level as pup is to:
a. Mitten
b. Madam
c. Bird
d. Pope

Stuck? If so, then the likely reason is your frame of reference. When faced with questions framed as analogies, we are inclined to look for strictly logical connections. Try looking for a nonlogical relationship. What if you reframed the problem as a search for a common construction of the words? Does this help? Well, you've probably already checked for the solution before you've even read this sentence, so I'll give you the answer. The correct response is "b." All four words are palindromes—words that read the same forward and backward. Now that you know the frame of reference, you're not likely to be stumped in the future by such an analogy on a standardized test. Likewise, once your group has met a challenge in the past by reframing the problem, it has the experience and know-how to meet similar challenges when they present themselves.

Integrative Problem Solving Decision making often involves conflicts of interest. Groups, or factions within groups, perceive each other as desiring mutually exclusive goals. Thus, they compete, entering into a power struggle hoping that the other side will capitulate. Integrative problem solving is a creative approach to conflicts of interest built on cooperation.

An integrative approach to conflict searches for solutions to problems that benefit everyone. Pruitt and Rubin (1986) identify five types of integrative solutions. Two of these types—expanding the pie and bridging—are particularly appropriate for this discussion of creative decision making.

Expanding the pie refers to increasing the resources as a solution to a problem. When faced with scarce resources, groups often become competitive and experience serious strife, warring over who gets the biggest or "best" piece of the limited pie. Groups, however, sometimes accept the inevitability of scarce resources—what Bazerman and Neale (1983) call the "bias of the fixed pie"—without fully exploring options that might expand the resource pie.

Bridging is the second type of integrative solution to conflicts. **Bridging** offers a new option devised to satisfy all parties on important issues. Bridging was used to solve a conflict of interest over where to eat dinner involving a couple, a friend of the couple's, and her two teenage children. All three adults wished to eat dinner at a moderately priced restaurant specializing in fresh fish entrees served with wine. The teenagers wanted burgers, fries, and colas. After a fair amount of wrangling, the pouting and whining began—from the teenagers, not the adults. Frustrated, the mother of the teenagers declared, "I think we'll just take off and eat at home. This isn't working out." A suggestion was made by one of the other adults: "Why don't we send the kids over to that burger joint up the street, have them bring back their meal, ask the restaurant if they mind having food brought in by the kids, and if not, the adults will order fish dinners with all the trimmings topped off with a bottle of wine." Not surprisingly, this solution proved satisfactory to all. The restaurant cooperated, the adults ate a satisfying meal, and the teenagers enjoyed America's finest cholesterol.

◉◉ CLOSER LOOK
Finding Integrative Solutions

Because integrative problem solving is often challenging for a group, let me provide more extensive illustration of this creative technique in order to demonstrate its potential and diverse application. School districts in California, faced with ever-present lean budgets, could issue a collective sigh and proceed to cut programs and teachers. Instead, many districts have found creative ways to increase resources beyond what the state legislature provides. Some districts have established private foundations, raising as much as $435,000 each year in community donations. Some foundations throw $125-a-plate dinners, organize black-tie auctions, stage celebrity tennis and golf tournaments, do car washes, and one district foundation purchased a ten-acre vacant school site, developed it, and sold it for a $4 million profit for the schools (Le, 1995). These efforts to expand the resource pie save teachers' jobs and maintain important educational programs.

A more whimsical yet ultimately serious effort to expand the resource pie, rather than simply try to make do with what resources are offered, occurred at Western Washington University in early June 1985. Students in my persuasion class were required to demonstrate their grasp of persuasion concepts and strategies in a real-life situation. The Washington state legislature was about to pass an education budget shortchanging Western some $3.2 million compared to other comparable regional universities in the state. Students chided legislators by holding a bake sale to raise money for the university. Hoping to garner wide publicity and thereby influence the legislature to expand Western's resource pie, students set $3.2 *million* as the goal for their bake sale. The project mushroomed. The local and regional mass media covered the event. One television station in Seattle featured the bake sale as the opening story on its five o'clock news. Even the Associated Press gave the bake sale national coverage, putting a lengthy story and a photo on the AP wire.

Although the sale raised only $320 ($3.2 hundred as my class referred to it), the publicity may have helped. The legislature increased Western's budget substantially. This example illustrates that integrative solutions do not always expand the pie as much as desired, but resource expansion improves the situation even if the problem is not totally eliminated.

ABC News, on December 12, 1989, reported one successful effort to bridge the concerns of power companies, consumers, and environmentalists. Five New England states entered into an imaginative conservation program. Power company employees took the conservation program door-to-door throughout the five states. They replaced regular 100-watt lightbulbs with 16-watt flourescent bulbs of equivalent brightness but longer life span. They also checked for air leaks, caulking those they found. There was a slight increase in the rate per kilowatt hour of power usage to pay for this program. Boston alone saved enough energy to heat and light 38,000 homes.

This solution was ingenious. All primary concerns of the three parties were satisfied. Power companies and their investors saved money because no new expensive power plants had to be built to meet energy needs. The slight increase in rates provided additional revenue. Environmentalists were happy because replacement of a single 100-watt regular bulb with a 16-watt fluorescent bulb helps the environment by eliminating 1,000 pounds of carbon dioxide pumped from power plants into the atmosphere over a year's period. Carbon dioxide is the chief culprit in the greenhouse effect. Likewise, caulking leaks further reduced carbon dioxide. In addition, no new power plants mean less consumption of precious energy resources. Consumers were happy even though their energy rates increased slightly because the lower utilization of electricity reduced their monthly energy bills. This is an elegant integrative solution, bridging the important concerns of all parties in conflict.

Questions for Thought

1. Choose a difficult problem (e.g., budget crisis at your school, proposal to close libraries in the county in order to balance the budget, inadequate and out-of-date computer technology at your place of employment). What would be a potential integrative solution to the problem?
2. If integrative problem solving is such an effective technique, why isn't it used more often? What would be some of its limitations?

Competent communicators vigorously explore possible integrative solutions to problems. In order to do this successfully, there are several steps involved in finding an integrative solution to conflicts of interest (Pruitt and Rubin, 1986). They are:

1. *Integrating requires a clear statement of issues and goals from the conflicting parties.* If all are to benefit from the integrative solution, what the parties want to accomplish must be apparent. Rausch and his colleagues (1974) discovered that 66 percent of the conflicts they examined were successfully resolved when the issues were clearly stated; only 18 percent of the conflicts were effectively resolved where the issues remained vague or unstipulated.
2. *Parties in conflict must determine whether a real conflict of interest exists.* Family members argue over whether to get a dog or not. The two kids say they want a dog very much, the father and mother say they do not. On the surface this looks like a standard conflict of interest. Yet when the issue is discussed, what becomes clear is that the mother doesn't want to take care of the dog and the father dislikes barking. When asked whether a cat would serve as an adequate substitute, the kids enthusiastically agree since they really just want a pet. No conflict really exists since the parents actually like cats, which are low maintenance and mostly quiet, and the kids get their pet.

3. *The parties in disagreement should stick to their goals but remain flexible regarding the means of attaining them.* Some friends of mine—a married couple and a man recently divorced—decided to buy a house together. They decided to pool their resources because the cost of real estate where they lived was astronomical; far beyond either party's ability to afford the mortgage payments for a decent home. Both parties saw this as an investment opportunity as well as a means of acquiring a comfortable domicile.

A conflict developed, however, regarding the bachelor's lifestyle. The couple was not interested in having his girlfriends, all of them strangers, paraded through their home, possibly staying overnight or settling in for a long stay. The bachelor hated to be alone, especially during a time when his personal life was in turmoil. Both sides stuck firmly to their goals, budging not a centimeter. The couple, however, did offer a proposal that seemed to fulfill the goals of both parties. Rather than buy a very large house for a substantial price, they suggested purchasing a somewhat more modest house and with the money saved from the price difference, they could jointly purchase a nice trailer and set it up on the property for the bachelor's guests. The house would be jointly occupied at all other times except when the bachelor had strangers stay. The bachelor could maintain his lifestyle without interfering with the couple's privacy needs.

This was obviously an unconventional arrangement, but it worked for this group. Both sides stuck firmly to their goals, but demonstrated the flexibility of competent and creative communicators when it came to the means of attaining their goals.

4. *If stalemated, concede on low-priority issues or discard low-priority interests.* The prime goals remain intact. The focus continues to be a solution that satisfies the goals of both parties. You give on subissues that are relatively unimportant to you but are perhaps important to the other party.

 SECOND LOOK

The Effective Problem-Solving Process

Standard Agenda	Techniques
Problem identification	Framing/reframing
	Formulate question of fact, value, or policy
Problem analysis	Gather/evaluate information
Solution criteria	Consensus
Solution suggestions	Integrative problem solving
	Brainstorming/nominal group
Solution evaluation/selection	Consensus
	Devil's advocacy
	Dialectical inquiry
Solution implementation	PERT

NOTE: Although the consensus technique is used most directly during the solution criteria and solution evaluation/selection steps of Standard Agenda, consensus rules may operate throughout the problem-solving process. Majority or minority rule may also be inserted at various steps if appropriate conditions exist.

In summary, there is no dichotomy between rational and creative decision making and problem solving. The two can be complementary paths to effective decisions in groups. The discussion process, however, should be systematic, not haphazard. Consideration of the problem should come before deliberations on solutions. Standard Agenda is the most common and useful set of procedures for rational decision making. Consensus, when applicable, is an effective process for guiding members toward rational decisions. Brainstorming and nominal group technique, framing/reframing, and integrative problem solving all provide systematic techniques for the discovery of creative solutions to problems.

In the final three chapters, I will discuss the interconnected concepts of power and conflict. These concepts have already been addressed superficially in earlier chapters. Those brief references, however, were merely the preliminaries. Power and conflict are integral parts of the small group process—inescapable in any human system.

QUESTIONS FOR CRITICAL THINKERS

1. Why is majority rule so popular since consensus decision making, by comparison, is more advantageous?
2. Since a true consensus requires agreement, commitment, and satisfaction of group members, do you think groups are likely to achieve a true consensus or is this mostly an ideal?
3. What are some drawbacks to the Standard Agenda approach to decision making? Explain your answer.

Power in Groups:
A Central Dynamic

"Power tends to corrupt, and absolute power corrupts absolutely," Lord Acton reputedly observed. This is a popular view. We are used to thinking of power in illegitimate or unpleasant terms. The terms *power politics, seizure of power, power struggles, power brokers, power hungry, power mad, power play, high powered,* and *overpowered* reflect just some of the negative ways we associate this central element of human interaction.

Most people are simply uncomfortable with power. For many people "explicit references to power are considered in bad taste" (Kipnis, 1976, p. 2). When asked about relative amounts of power exercised by individuals in relationships with others, most people are awkwardly silent, obviously embarrassed, reluctant to answer, or halting in their replies (Hocker and Wilmot, 1995). Naomi Wolf (1994) claims that women in particular harbor "great ambivalence about claiming power" (p. 235), a position supported by others (Haslett et al., 1992). Some individuals find the very thought of power so unsavory that they innocently assert that it plays no part in their relationships. Rollo May (1972) terms this denial of one's own power "pseudoinnocence," where we "make a virtue of powerlessness, weakness, and helplessness" (p. 49). Edgar Friedenberg (1965) answers those who shun the very thought of power: "All weakness tends to corrupt, and impotence corrupts absolutely" (p. 47). There is no virtue in weakness, but there is temptation. Weakness can entice us into seeking power by illegitimate means in order to escape the grip of those strangling our spirit and stifling our motivation to improve our lot in life.

In this chapter, I have four objectives:

1. to explain the significance of power in the small-group arena,
2. to define what power is and is not,
3. to delineate the most common sources of power, and
4. to examine the primary indicators of power in small groups.

How we specifically transact power in groups will be discussed in the next chapter. The fact that virtually all group communication textbooks treat power as a peripheral phenomenon is an oversight that will be corrected here.

POWER: AN OVERVIEW

Focus Questions

1. In what ways is power central to small groups?
2. Where does power come from? Do group members possess power or is it conferred on them by the group?

Significance of Power

Power is unavoidable in human transactions. "It permeates human relationships. It exists whether or not it is quested for. It is the glory and the burden of most of humanity" (Burns, 1978, p. 15). Whenever you communicate with another person, power is present. As noted previously, every message has two basic dimensions: content and relationship. The content of a message communicates information regarding events and objects. The relationship dimension communicates information regarding the power distribution between group members. Every time you communicate with a person in a group, the relationship dimension is present.

Even marginal members exert influence on a group. I have had numerous groups approach me after class and request permission to dump one of their members for poor attendance and anemic participation at meetings. This is never a casual event. Frustration and anger are evident. As long as a person remains a member of a group, even marginally, he or she influences group decision making. If a marginal member misses several meetings, do you assume he or she no longer wishes to remain a group member? Do you count on this individual to play a part in a group presentation? Intermittent appearances foster ambiguity and can disrupt the group.

Abuses have given power a bad reputation. Illegitimate assertions and usurpations of power by scoundrels color our vision. None of you, however, can achieve your individual goals, none of you can communicate competently, nor can any group achieve its goals without exercising some power. I am not suggesting that you use power in groups as a Machiavellian manipulation for the achievement of self-centered, dubious goals. Hocker and Wilmot (1995) explain that "one does not have the option of not using power. We only have options about whether our use of power will be destructive or productive for ourselves and our relationships" (p. 74).

Power is central to decision making and problem solving in small groups. "It is not possible to discuss group functioning without discussing power" (Johnson and Johnson, 1975, p. 203). Your options lie not in whether to be influential, but in how best to exercise the influence you do have in a group.

Definition of Power

Power *is the ability to influence the attainment of goals sought by yourself or others.* This is a general definition. Let me explain more specifically what power is and conversely what it is not.

The Nature of Power   First and foremost, power is group-centered. The power that you wield is dependent on the relationships you have with group members. The interconnectedness of components in a system means that all group members have some influence. What one member does or does not do influences other members. The degree of power exercised by a single member at any moment will depend on transactions between members.

The degree of power exerted by a whining child in a supermarket, for instance, rests on the response of the parents. If the parents persistently instruct an ill-behaved child to "Stop it," or ask the child one of the world's silliest questions, "Do you want to get a spanking?" without taking additional steps to quell the obnoxious din, then the child has the upper hand. This is especially true if the parents, out of sheer frustration and a desire to get the kid to cork his or her inflated bellows, give in to some demand by the child (e.g., candy).

Power, however, is distributed differently if the parents are unwilling to assuage the child's whining. Parental resistance may take the form of strategic inattention to the child's boisterous display or firm disciplinary action. In any case, power resides in the transactions between group members.

The static view of power regards power as a property that resides in an individual. This is the perspective that views leaders as all-powerful and followers as powerless. A powerful person (e.g., leader) does not operate in a vacuum, but instead is a product of ever-changing transactions within a group. If power were indigenous to a person irrespective of the social environment, then no matter what the circumstances, that person would remain powerful. The absurdity of this position is readily seen the moment we consider a once-powerful political leader—Richard Nixon.

As president of the United States, Nixon wielded immense power. When Watergate dethroned our imperial president, he became an easy target for savage ridicule and scorn. Nixon was chastened by his public humiliation brought about by revelations of palpable wrongdoing. Power did not reside in the persona of Richard Nixon. Power came from the relationship Nixon shared with the public. When that relationship turned sour, our thirty-seventh president fell from power.

Similarly, while power is not a static property of any individual, it is also not a dichotomous concept. We often speak of powerful *or* powerless individuals. This is more the result of our penchant for false dichotomies than it is an accurate assessment of power distribution. If all group members have some degree of power, as I have already explained, then a more accurate description of power distribution in a group would be phrased in terms of *degrees* of power. The relevant question then becomes, "How much power does Person A exert relative to other members in that group?" rather than, "Is Person A powerful or powerless?"

Forms of Power   There are three forms of power (Hollander and Offermann, 1990). The most widely understood form of power is **dominance** or *power over* others. Dominance flows from a hierarchical structure or from structured differences in status among group members. Dominance is a product of dichotomous, either-or thinking (e.g., leader versus followers). My gain in power is your loss. Your way precludes my way. Thus, a power struggle must ensue to sort out who gets to be the top dog and who plays the junkyard dog—who is dominant and who is submissive.

A second form of power is called **prevention** or *power from* the influence efforts of others (e.g., followers resist leader dominance). When someone tries to dominate us, psychological reactance occurs. We try to prevent the dominance. Successful efforts to thwart the power plays of others exhibit a different kind of power—the power to prevent.

A third form of power is called **empowerment** or *power to* accomplish your own goals or help others achieve theirs (Bate, 1988). Empowerment is cooperative, not competitive. From this vantage point, the group as a whole profits most from all of its members gaining the ability to succeed together. One of the positive aspects of the model of effective leadership offered by Hersey and

Blanchard (1988), as discussed in Chapter Five, is the emphasis on empowerment rather than dominance. In their view, the leader role is not geared toward ordering underlings around and keeping followers in their place. Instead, effective leaders actively seek to increase the readiness levels of followers, thereby empowering them to accomplish tasks without the leader watching their every move.

These three forms of power are substantially different from one another. Those who try to dominate see power as finite, as an *active* effort to advance personal goals at the expense of others. The power pie is only so large and cannot be expanded. The few, not the many, can exercise power. Power, then, is seen as a struggle between the haves and have-nots. Thus, power must be seized actively by controlling access to power resources.

Those who try to prevent domination by others see power as *reactive*. Power is seen in competitive win-lose terms by those who try to dominate and those who try to prevent the domination. Those who try to prevent domination, however, react to the power initiatives of other group members by fighting back. They don't seek power for personal gain or to advance their own goals.

Those group members who try to empower see the power pie as expandable. As the range of resources and abilities shared by group members grows, so does the group power. Since the power pie can be expanded, all members may exercise power. Therefore, power can be inclusive rather than exclusive, shared rather than fought over. Group members can assist one another in gaining access to power resources rather than hoarding resources. Empowerment is *proactive,* meaning group members take positive action to assist self and others attain goals cooperatively.

SECOND LOOK

Forms of Power

Type	Definition	Description
• Dominance	• Power Over	• Active
• Prevention	• Power From	• Reactive
• Empowerment	• Power To	• Proactive

Those who harbor a negative concept of power are more than likely responding to the dominance form of power and its companion form—prevention. I would be naive to argue, however, that we can replace dominance with empowerment in all cases. Dominance will assuredly remain as the primary form of power in a competitive society. What can be hoped for is that empowerment will gain a wider audience and become more broadly applied.

Additionally, the dominance form of power is the most relevant in some instances. When resources are scarce, the power pie is not always expandable. Sometimes dwindling resources require layoffs and terminations. In four of the five speech departments where I have worked, severe budget reductions forced loss of some faculty members despite the best efforts of department members to find integrative solutions. Initially, cuts can be absorbed or additional funds can be found by creative problem-solving efforts. Eventually, if the cuts accumulate over several years, the "last hired, first fired" rule is difficult to avoid. Learning to cope with a climate of dominance is the task of a competent communicator and a subject for specific analysis in the next chapter.

CLOSER LOOK

Empowerment and Self-help Groups

Self-help groups have become a national movement. More than six million Americans are in self-help groups and the growth rate is accelerating (Jacobs and Goodman, 1989). The diversity of such groups is astonishing (see Leerhsen et al., 1990). Imitating the granddaddy of them all, Alcoholics Anonymous, are groups such as Depressives Anonymous, Gamblers Anonymous, Cocaine Anonymous, Batterers Anonymous, Impotents Anonymous, Prostitutes Anonymous, and Overeaters Anonymous. There is a self-help group for almost every medical disorder identified by the World Health Organization (Balgopal et al., 1992).

But this is merely the beginning. Consider just a handful of the more offbeat varieties—Hot Flashes (for menopausal women), Trichotillomania Support Network (for people who pull out their hair), Good Tidings (for women who continually fall in love with priests), Crossroads (for male transvestites), The International Intractable Hiccups Organization, Compulsive Shoppers, and an unnamed self-help group organized in 1993 by a hypnotherapist to assist poor unfortunates who have been abducted by extraterrestrials (the ultimate illegal aliens) and lived to tell about it. There are even self-help groups to provide comfort for distraught fans of recently departed rock stars, such as the group that formed after The Grateful Dead's Jerry Garcia died in 1995.

Most self-help groups, except for a few such as AA, are small and local. They usually emerge spontaneously from a condition of relative powerlessness. Self-help groups generally fall into four helping categories (Leerhsen et al., 1990): (1) addictive behavior, (2) physical and/or mental illness, (3) transitions (e.g., Recently Divorced Catholics), and (4) friends and relatives of those with a problem (e.g., Adult Children of Alcoholics).

The self-help movement got its biggest boost from the women's consciousness-raising groups in the 1960s (Leerhsen et al., 1990). The principal activity of self-help groups is information sharing (Fawcett, 1988), but with a purpose. What self-help groups do best is empower their members. Self-help groups are vehicles for change. Their attraction is not only the sharing of a common bond (similar problems), but the desire to learn how to solve vexing problems and cope with tribulations of life by receiving the support, comfort, and advice of fellow sufferers.

Self-help groups usually are leaderless. They operate democratically and encourage high participation. New members are usually warmly accepted into the group. Open communication is the norm. The climate is cooperative, and negative advice (e.g., "Tell your boss to take a flying leap") is normally discouraged.

How effective are self-help groups in producing change through empowerment? The research is inconclusive on this question (Jacobs and Goodman, 1989). Although several studies reveal positive outcomes, methodological problems with the designs of these studies prevent any firm conclusions. Regardless, self-help groups illustrate that viewing power as simply dominance (power over) ignores the vast arena of empowerment (power to).

Questions for Thought

1. Have you ever belonged to a self-help group? If yes, did you feel empowered by it?
2. Can a person become dependent on a self-help group even though the central purpose is to empower individuals?
3. Is the self-help movement really another manifestation of the "nation of victims" problem Sykes (1992) identifies, as in we're all victims and must seek out fellow sufferers for comfort and support?

POWER RESOURCES

As I stated previously, power is the ability to influence the attainment of goals sought by yourself or others. This ability to influence is derived from resources. A power resource is "anything that enables individuals to move toward their own goals or interfere with another's actions" (Folger at al., 1993, p. 100). The range of power resources is broad. I will discuss the primary resources from which power is most extensively derived in group situations.

Focus Questions
1. Information is power, but is all information power?
2. For expertise to serve as a power resource, must the expert always avoid errors?
3. What are the primary drawbacks of punishment as a power resource?
4. Where does an individual acquire charisma?
5. How does authority become legitimate?

Primary Power Resources

There are five primary power resources relevant to group situations. These five resources are information, expertise, rewards and punishments, personal qualities, and legitimate authority. These resources closely parallel French and Raven's (1959) classic types of power in groups.

Information Unquestionably, information is power. In an age of information, how could it be otherwise? Information has become a vital resource for the nations of the world. The U.S. economy has become information-dependent. About half the jobs in this country are in the "information sector" (Dizard, 1989).

Not all information, however, serves as a source of power. I have already explained that if the quantity of information becomes overwhelming, it is difficult to separate useless from useful information. Information must be valuable or useful to the group for it to have power potential.

Information assumes value or usefulness when it is perceived to be unavailable. If information is readily available to everyone, it has no power potential. Consultants can charge thousands of dollars to groups and organizations because they have information not readily available to members of the group. Who would bother to hire a consultant if that individual merely reiterated what everyone in the group already knew? Information becomes unavailable primarily from restrictions and scarcity (Brock, 1968). Let's discuss *restrictions* first.

Studies of censorship conclusively demonstrate that restricting information increases both its perceived value and the credibility of the information (Cialdini, 1993). A large-scale research study by the University of Chicago Law School (Broeder, 1959) dramatically demonstrates these effects on juries. Individuals actually serving their jury duty were formed into thirty separate juries, presented with tape recordings from previous trials, and asked to decide the outcome of the trial as if they were actually deciding the case. The results were fascinating.

The case involved a woman who had been injured by a careless male driver. When the driver said he was not insured, the woman was awarded an average of $33,000. When the driver said that he was insured, the woman was awarded an average of $37,000. The most interesting result, however, occurred when the driver indicated he was insured but the judge instructed the jury to disregard this information. In this circumstance, the jury awarded an average of $46,000. When the judge restricted the use of the information the jury actually gave the information more credence in deciding the award than if the judge had said nothing.

How many times have you seen courtroom dramas on TV or in movies where a jury is instructed to "disregard the testimony" of some witness? Erase damning testimony from your brain like it never happened? The Chicago Law School jury study shows that this amnesia-on-command is unrealistic, and any such attempt to restrict the information increases its perceived importance.

Scarcity also makes information seem more valuable and useful (Cialdini, 1993; Pratkanis and Aronson, 1992). In this era of information overload, scarcity of information is the exception, not the rule. Thus, when information is scarce, whatever is available seems terribly important. When there is only one witness to a serious crime, that witness becomes a far more important source of information than if five individuals witnessed the crime and were available to testify. Insider trading tips on the stock market are also prized for their scarcity.

In the 1980s, a controversial woman named J. Z. Knight, who portrayed herself as a celestial "channeler" in contact with a 35,000-year-old Cro-Magnon prophet named Ramtha, ran her School of Enlightenment in rural Washington state (Conway and Siegelman, 1995). The main attraction for small groups of Ramtha devotees was to hear the "wisdom" of this prophet as he spoke to seminar-like gatherings of fascinated followers. Ramtha spoke to these groups through Knight, who appeared to be in a trance, in a seemingly transmogrified guttural voice. Ramtha didn't speak to just anybody. He spoke to those who joined Knight's enlightenment school (and presumably paid the fee to join). It's not every day that you bump into a 35,000-year-old guru from another spirit dimension. The scarcity of such elder prophets makes what Ramtha had to say more enticing. If a 35-year-old guy named Fred said that every orgasm brings you nearer to death, and that when you die, you do not want to seek the light but instead go to the void, the darkness, because there are "light beings" waiting who will suck the experience from your spirit and leave you to reincarnate with no memory of your last life, do you think many people would find this insightful? Well, many did when it was viewed as scarce information from Ramtha (Conway and Siegelman, 1995).

Clearly, <u>information that is perceived by the group to be valuable and useful has power potential</u>. In order for information to be perceived as valuable and useful it must be restricted and scarce. Information that is readily available to group members is not a power resource. <u>The competent communicator can capitalize on information as a power resource as follows</u>:

1. *Provide useful but scarce or restricted information to the group.* Careful, diligent research often produces valuable information relevant to the group task. If this information is not known to other group members, it then assumes a power potential by increasing your prestige and influence in group decision making. I am not suggesting, however, that you act coy about giving the information to your group. There may be an appropriate moment when revealing the scarce information may have more dramatic impact on group members than some other moment, but trying to manipulate the group could easily invite animosity and reprisals. Competent communicators are We-not-Me oriented so withholding information for personal gain is counterproductive.
2. *Be certain information is accurate.* Sharing misinformation could earn you the enmity of group members. Misinformation could easily lead to collective inferential error, a prime cause of faulty decision making.

Expertise   We have a real love-hate relationship with experts. We often require their skills and advice, but seem to resent them for simply occupying positions of power or for making a buck off their expertise. Lawyers are a good example of this. Jokes deriding lawyers have become commonplace (e.g., How can you tell the difference between a dead lawyer and a dead snake in the road? Answer: There are skid marks in front of the snake).

With the twin problems of information overload and the explosion of change in our global village, no individual nor group could ever hope to function effectively without at some time requiring the services of experts. What academic department is not dependent on the expert who repairs the computers and Xerox machines? What board of directors has never needed the advice of

The power of information and expertise is depicted in this doctor-patient conversation.

an attorney? Families require plumbers, hair stylists, financial advisors, roofers, exterminators, counselors, mechanics, and those who repair our appliances, phones, televisions, and broken hearts.

In order for expertise to function as a power resource, at minimum, two conditions must be met. First, <u>the group must be convinced that the person has the requisite skills, abilities, knowledge, and background to function as a real expert</u>. Normally, the constituents of real expertise include appropriate education and training, intelligence, experience, and demonstrated mastery of relevant information. Ronald Reagan, revered by many, diminished his claim of expertise that usually is accorded sitting presidents when he continued his bad habit of inventing facts during speeches and press conferences. Reagan signaled what was in store for the nation during the 1980 presidential campaign when he asserted that trees and other vegetation cause more air pollution than automobiles. This prompted an anonymous wag in California to post a sign on a tree the next day that read: "Chop me down before I kill again." Reagan's apparent fascination with misinformation became so total that Mark Green and Gail MacColl chronicled more than 300 of "The Gipper's" most egregious errors in a book entitled *There He Goes Again: Ronald Reagan's Reign of Error*. This was followed by an update entitled *To Err Is Reagan*.

Expertise, however, is not a property of the person, but a judgment by others. Bradley (1980) found that individuals were more influential in small discussion groups when they appeared to have background experience relevant to the discussion topic than when they did not have such minimal expertise. In some cases it doesn't take much to be designated an expert in a group. This is more valid for male group members, however, than it is for female members. As Propp (1995) states, "The expertise brought to the decision-making process by women is at a disadvantage. Even if they hold critical information, it is evaluated more stringently than if the information is held by men" (p. 471). Men more than women are encouraged by groups to contribute their expertise, partly because group members, both males and females, don't initially think of women as experts (Propp, 1995). They need to be confronted directly and assertively with the expertise of female group members. Once the group accepts as an expert an individual of either sex, however, members are strongly influenced by the expert even to accept recommendations contradictory to members' initial points of view (Foschi et al., 1985).

Second, the person who has been accorded status as an expert must <u>demonstrate trustworthiness</u>. Power is not derived from expertise if the group suspects that the expert will lie for personal gain or self-protection. People the world over are more influenced by experts who stand to gain nothing personally than by those who would gain substantially by lying or distorting information (McGuinnies and Ward, 1980).

In the summer of 1992, the *National Law Journal* and LEXIS, a database service, conducted the most comprehensive national poll of jurors ever undertaken. Of the nearly 800 individuals who had recently sat on a jury, 95 percent said that they were impressed by expert testimony during a trial and 70 percent felt that expert testimony influences the outcome of a trial. Nevertheless, 51 percent of the jurors said that they didn't necessarily trust the testimony of police officers and 70 percent of African American jurors felt police testimony was suspect ("Jurors' views," 1993). The power potential of expertise is substantially reduced when trustworthiness is questionable.

Expertise has power potential, but the group determines who is an expert and who is a pretender to the title. There are some interesting intercultural differences related to power and expertise. Although expertise is an important consideration for Americans in choosing individuals for negotiating teams, status is more important to French, British, Chinese, Japanese, and Saudi Arabians (Hellweg et al., 1994). How expertise is perceived also varies from culture to culture. In the United States, an individual with exceptional expertise in one field might be perceived as irrelevant when the group discusses issues unrelated to that person's specialization. In Africa, however, opinion leaders are respected and valued over a broader range of topics for which they have no special technical knowledge (Dodd, 1994). Expertise is in the eye of the beholder.

Assuming a group member has special knowledge, skills, or abilities useful to the group, <u>he or she functions as a competent communicator while capitalizing on the power potential of expertise as follows</u>:

1. *Maintain skills, abilities, and knowledge currency.* You're only an expert for as long as the group perceives you as such. Let your knowledge grow out-of-date or your skills and abilities diminish and the group will quickly see you as yesteryear's expert—a relic.

2. *Demonstrate trustworthiness and credibility.* You should exhibit a We-not-Me orientation. Your expertise should be used to benefit the group, not merely bring personal advantages to yourself. Even when a group hires an expert from outside, the group expects that the lawyer, accountant, consultant, or whoever will show commitment to helping the group gain its goals, not simply make a buck for himself or herself.

3. *Be certain of your facts before advising the group.* Bad advice is like misinformation. The results can be disastrous for the group. Advice should be based on the best available information. An occasional error may not tarnish your credibility as an expert. Relatively frequent or serious error will.

4. *Don't assume an air of superiority.* Putting on an air of superiority will trigger defensiveness among group members.

Rewards and Punishments   Parceling out rewards or meting out punishment can be an important source of power. Salaries, bonuses, work schedules, perks, hirings, and firings are typical job-related rewards and punishments. Money, freedom, privacy, and car keys are a few of the rewards and punishments found in family situations. Grades, letters of recommendation, and social approval or disapproval are a few of the rewards and punishments available to teachers when dealing with students.

Rewards and punishment go hand in hand. Denial of rewards can be punishment. Cessation of punishment can be a reward. Not receiving abusive derision in front of your group when there is an expectation of public reprimand can be taken as a reward.

The greater the certainty that punishments will be administered, the greater is the power potential of punishment. Idle threats have little influence on group behavior. Parents who threaten spankings or denial of privileges but never follow through soon realize that children easily learn to ignore such impotent bluster. If employees are protected from termination by civil service regulations or tenure, then threatening to fire them is laughable.

Consider the relationship between crime and punishment in the United States. According to the U.S. Justice Department (Butterfield, 1996), more than forty million serious crimes are committed annually in the United States. Approximately 90 percent of all serious crimes in the United States are unreported or unsolved, meaning no punishment was ever administered (Vasconcellos, 1994). Economist Morgan O. Reynolds (in Methvin, 1991) of Texas A&M University conducted an extensive study of the relationship between serious crime and probability of punishment. His statistics are unsettling. Fewer than 2 *percent* of all criminal arrests result in a prison sentence. For every 100 murders, only 17 result in any prison sentence. For rape, the imprisonment rate is only 5.1 percent, for assault a mere 1.5 percent, and for auto theft a minuscule .3 percent. White-collar crime or what Ralph Nader calls "crimes in the suites" typically receives even less attention from our system of justice than do "crimes in the streets," so the rate of punishment for insider trading, fraud, graft, deceptive trade practices, and the like are close to nonexistent.

In this country, odds are very good that crime will go unpunished. Threats of punishment, however, seem to be more effective when the public perceives that the chances of punishment for a crime become more probable (Wooton, 1993). As the certainty of punishment for drunken driving increases, for instance, the incidence of drunken driving decreases (Ross, 1984). Punishment is a source of power if it can be and likely will be exercised.

Punishment as a source of power is a tricky business. As Shaw (1981) indicates, reward power tends to induce rewarding behavior from those on the receiving end whereas punishment power can have the opposite effect. If you disseminate rewards, you become more attractive in the eyes of those rewarded. Equal distribution of rewards systemwide, of course, creates a more supportive climate than rewards distributed on a merit system. Negative feelings, however, are aroused toward the person administering punishment. We normally don't like our tormentors.

Consequently, if you threaten group members with punishment, you may produce a **boomerang effect** (Hamachek, 1982). Threats of punishment may backfire. The more the group tries to bludgeon a deviant member into line, the more this person is likely to resist and do exactly what the group finds unacceptable. Psychological reactance takes over. Most of us don't like being pushed around or told by others what to do. If the punishment doesn't achieve the desired effect, this could have systemwide implications. Other members may be encouraged to engage in similar deviance. Issues of fairness and just cause may surface and escalate into ugly conflicts.

The ultimate punishment in a work setting, namely firing, can produce a disastrous boomerang effect. The chemical leak at a Union Carbide plant in Bhopal, India, in 1985, which killed and injured thousands, was partly the result of a disgruntled employee angry because he had been fired for breaking what he perceived to be illegitimate rules (Conrad, 1990). And, of course, disgruntled workers wreaking vengeance for loss of their jobs by pumping bullets into innocent fellow workers (referred to as "going postal" in the popular slang) seems sadly commonplace because of its frequency.

Punishment also has an additional drawback—it indicates what *not to do* but not what *to do* (Hersey and Blanchard, 1988). A case study by Huberman (1967) demonstrates this. A Douglas fir plywood mill experienced sloppy workmanship and discipline problems from some of the members of its work crew. Management relied heavily on punishment as a means of correcting the problems. The results from the punitive approach were negative. As Huberman noted, "not a single desirable result could be detected" (p. 64). He continued, "The people who had been disciplined were generally still among the poorest workers; their attitude was sulky, if not openly hostile. And they seemed to be spreading this feeling among the rest of the crew" (p. 65).

Please understand that I am not arguing that punishment should never be used. There are guidelines, however, that should chart your course when using punishment and rewards. Competent communicators use rewards and punishments as power resources as follows (Yukl, 1981):

1. *Rewards are a first resort; punishments are a last resort.* Punishment as a power resource must be exercised with caution and discretion. Punishment is coercive. It can easily backfire. Punishment can be a powerful means of

influencing behavior of group members, but punishment should be used sparingly in concert with heavy reliance on rewards.

2. *Rewards and punishments must be appropriate to the deed.* Rewards for mediocre or mundane performance will usually be seen as phony and manipulative. Anemic punishment for seriously flawed performance or severe punishment for relatively inconsequential error is out of proportion to the deed. In the former instance, group members will likely ridicule the ineffectual action, and in the latter instance, group members will likely rebel against the severity of the sanction. Rewards and punishments must be appropriate to the deed to maintain their power base.

3. *Group rules and penalties should be clear.* Ambiguity can lead to charges of injustice and unfairness.

4. *Verify the facts before acting.* This is especially important when using punishment. Don't punish based on a bad inference (e.g., conclude from rumor or hearsay that wrongdoing was committed).

5. *Make good on promises.* Expectation of reward must be fulfilled or backlash will result.

6. *Be generous with praise that is warranted.* Praise recognizes accomplishment and nurtures a positive group climate.

7. *No idle threats; use threats rarely.* Idle threats will be seen as weakness, not strength. Don't threaten if you don't intend to follow through on the threat or you can't make it stick. You'll lose face in the group.

8. *Be consistent and prompt in application of rewards and punishments.* Inconsistency in conferring rewards will invite charges of favoritism, promoting dissension within the group. Inconsistency in meting out punishment will foster inconsistent compliance from group members. "Justice delayed is justice denied," so be prompt in applying both rewards and punishments.

Personal Qualities   We all know individuals who exert some influence over us, not because of any of the previous power resources already discussed, but because of personal qualities they seem to possess in abundance that we find attractive. The research on interpersonal attraction presented in Chapter Three applies to this power resource. We are more likely to be influenced by those individuals whom we find attractive than by those we don't.

Physically attractive individuals especially have an advantage in the power arena. Although theoretically justice is blind, there is substantial evidence to indicate that the blindfold slips a bit when juries decide the fate of an attractive defendant. Sigall and Ostrove (1975) found that a pretty woman received special treatment by a mock jury compared to an unattractive defendant when the defendant's beauty had nothing to do with the commission of a felony. (The attractive woman, however, was dealt with more severely when the jury perceived that the defendant had used her beauty to commit a felony.)

Handsome men apparently gain a similar advantage. Stewart (1980) found that attractive male defendants received significantly lighter sentences and were twice as likely to avoid jail altogether than less-attractive defendants. The same pattern emerges in negligence trials. When the defendant was better-looking than the victim, the average jury award was $5,623. When the victim was better-looking than the defendant, however, the average award was $10,051 (Kukla and Kesler, 1978). Both male and female jurors exhibited the bias favoring the attractive individual. Group decisions are influenced by the attractiveness of an individual.

The influence accorded individuals who are perceived to be physically attractive goes beyond the judicial arena. Those students who have drawn from a more advantageous attractiveness gene pool receive higher grades for identical academic work than do those whose facial appearance tends toward the less attractive end of the looks continuum (Landy and Sigall, 1974). Frieze and Olson (in "Face it," 1989) also found that good-looking people make more money in business organizations than less attractive individuals. In their study, the two researchers had four judges rate the attractiveness of 737 MBA graduates on a scale from 1 to 5. Salaries increased about $2000 for every 1-point increase in men's and women's attractiveness ratings. In addition, the more attractive men (but not the more attractive women) were given higher starting salaries than their less fortunate counterparts.

Physically attractive people enjoy enormous social advantages in our culture. Mark Knapp (1980) summarizes these advantages when he notes that "it is not at all unusual to find physically attractive persons outstripping unattractive ones on a wide range of socially desirable evaluations, such as success, personality, popularity, sociability, sexuality, persuasiveness, and often happiness" (p. 98).

Although good looks do not always translate into social advantages and therefore power (e.g., attractive individuals may be the targets of unwanted, unrelenting, even threatening attention from "admirers"), you don't hear many attractive people wishing they had ordinary looks. One's overall degree of attractiveness, however, is not solely dependent on physical good looks, a point made obvious when actress Julia Roberts married country singer Lyle Lovett, although their subsequent split-up might suggest otherwise.

Some people are attractive to a group because they have charisma. The term **charisma** loosely refers to a constellation of personal attributes that people find highly attractive about an individual. Communication researchers have known for some time that expertise and mastery of certain persuasive skills, dynamism, trustworthiness, reliability, similarity of values and outlook, and identification with the group all contribute to an individual's ability to influence others.

Some people have a great deal of charisma and others have the charisma of the two principal contenders for the presidency in 1988 (George Bush and Michael Dukakis for those of you suffering a memory lapse due to these candidates' charisma deficit). Charisma, however, is not determined objectively. Groups decide what is attractive and what is not. When John and Jacqueline Kennedy visited Paris in 1962 as president and first lady, they made a lasting impression, Jacqueline more than John. Jacqueline, with her combination of beauty, poise, grace, and ability to speak French, charmed President Charles de Gaulle and the people of France. She stole the spotlight away from her normally charismatic husband who, as president, characteristically commanded center stage. Jacqueline's impact on the French was so complete that when the couple departed, John Kennedy held a press conference (a rare moment when he became the center of attention). In typical witty fashion and with a recognition of the irony of his wife's upstaging of the president of the United States, he began, "I do not think it is altogether inappropriate to introduce myself to this audience. I am the man who accompanied Jacqueline Kennedy to Paris, and I have enjoyed it" (in Fadiman, 1985, p. 328). Jacqueline Kennedy exercised little tangible power, but she displayed a powerful presence.

Charisma and leadership are often connected, especially in the public mind during political elections. Charismatic or **transformational leaders** communicate a vision to followers. Change is the central mission of the charismatic leader—change in followers' values, goals, needs, and behavior (Fiedler and House, 1988). Charismatic leaders induce fierce loyalty, commitment, and devotion from followers. There is a strong identification with the leader, and the followers' goals, self-esteem, and values become entangled with the charismatic leader-follower relationship. The leader's beliefs are thought to be correct, often absolutely correct.

One study (Smith, 1982) found that followers of charismatic leaders were more self-assured, worked longer hours, and had higher performance than followers of noncharismatic but effective leaders. Another study (Howell, 1985) found that only charismatic leaders had success overcoming the negative effects of a low performance norm in groups. In other words, they motivated workers to produce even when the group norm originally encouraged loafing. Other types of leaders (e.g., directive and considerate) were not successful in this regard.

As I indicated in Chapter Five, the trait perspective on leadership does not adequately explain how or why leaders emerge, nor their degree of effectiveness. Charisma is a power resource and charismatic leaders are often capable of generating intense reactions, even collective hysteria. There is no one constellation of traits, however, that makes a person charismatic. What makes a person attractive to a group is contingent on members' preferences. Charismatic leaders such as Charles Manson, Marshall Applewhite, Jim and Tammy Bakker, Jimmy Swaggart, and David Koresh obviously were attractive to their followers but unattractive to most outsiders. Charismatic movie producer Louis B. Mayer, of Metro-Goldwyn-Mayer (MGM) fame, helped shape the future of the movie industry in the 1930s, yet he was perceived by many to be a tyrant. Samuel Goldwyn reputedly claimed that the reason so many people attended Mayer's funeral was to make certain that he was really dead. The Mario Cuomos, Elizabeth Doles, Anita Hills, Jesse Jacksons, Jacqueline Kennedys, Rush Limbaughs, Ronald Reagans, and Ann Richardses of this world are charismatic because groups find them personally attractive, not because there is some precise formula that can create charisma.

So how does a competent communicator capitalize on personal qualities as a power resource in small groups? Get a personality transplant? Pay the big bucks for plastic surgery to improve physical attractiveness? Dress to impress those whose idea of appropriate attire never stretches beyond the power suit? Hardly! There are ways of enhancing personal attractiveness to a group even though such attempts offer no guarantee of success. <u>To be a competent communicator and increase power through personal qualities, try the following:</u>

1. *Enhance attractiveness.* Dress for context. Dress appropriately for the context, don't assume one style fits all occasions and situations. Sometimes dressing casually is more powerful than donning a power suit, which may look ridiculous at a sorority meeting to plan a charitable event. The same guideline applies to all other steps taken to improve physical appearance (e.g., cosmetics, hair length, and so forth).
2. *Learn effective presentational skills.* Charismatic individuals are often effective public speakers (e.g., Mario Cuomo, Jesse Jackson, Barbara Jordan, Martin Luther King, Ann Richards, Ronald Reagan, Bill Clinton, Malcolm X). In a Michigan poll of 500 adults (in Ross, 1989), speaking ability was ranked second on a list of factors deemed most influential in choosing a political candidate, behind party affiliation and ahead of appearance or good looks.

Legitimate Authority   We all play roles, but some of us exercise greater influence in groups because of our acknowledged position or title. <u>Power is derived from the shared belief that some individuals have a legitimate right to influence us and direct our behavior by virtue of the roles that they occupy.</u> Parents occupy a position of legitimate authority. In addition to other power resources they have at their disposal, parents are supposed to be accorded respect and deference simply because they are parents. We believe parents have the right to discipline their children and to expect obedience. Similarly, teachers and supervisors at work occupy an authority position considered legitimate by most groups.

Obedience to legitimate authority is deeply absorbed into the fabric of our society. We learn about the virtues of obedience to authority figures in school, at work, in church, in courtrooms, and in military barracks. The result is a mental set lasered into our brains: OBEY LEGITIMATE AUTHORITY.

Just how strong is our mental set that programs us to blindly obey legitimate authority? Kelman and Lawrence (1972) report the results of an unsettling nationwide study concerning perhaps the most notorious event of the Vietnam War. Lieutenant William Calley ordered soldiers under his command to slaughter all inhabitants (men, women, children, and babies) of a village called My Lai. Of those responding to the Kelman and Lawrence survey, 67 percent believed most people would follow orders and shoot villagers as soldiers did at My Lai, and 58 percent said they personally would shoot and kill women and children, even babies, if ordered to do so by someone in authority. Kelman and Lawrence conclude that "many Americans feel they have no right to resist authoritative demands. They regard Calley's actions at My Lai as normal, even desirable, because he performed them (they think) in obedience to legitimate authority" (p. 45).

◉◉ | CLOSER LOOK

The Milgram Studies

An amazing series of studies conducted by Stanley Milgram (1974) in the 1960s lends substantial support to the fear that as a society we have absorbed the lesson of obedience to legitimate authority so completely that <u>we are inclined to blindly and automatically obey authority figures</u>. We may obey even when it is dangerous or morally questionable to do so.

The basic experimental design of the obedience to authority studies by Milgram consisted of a naive subject who acted as "teacher" and a confederate who acted as "student." The naive subjects were told that the purpose of the experiment was to determine the effects of punishment on memory. Punishment consisted of electric shocks. The electric shocks were administered to the student for every wrong answer on a word-association test. Shocks began at fifteen volts and increased by fifteen-volt increments up to a maximum of 450 volts for each wrong answer from the victim. The experimenter directed the subjects to administer the increasingly intense shocks for every wrong answer even when the subjects objected. The experimenter served as legitimate authority in each of Milgram's experiments.

Milgram shock generator

A group of thirty-nine psychiatrists, thirty-one college students, and forty middle-class adults were asked to predict the maximum shock levels subjects would administer to the victim. No one predicted 450 volts. The vast majority predicted that subjects would stop at 150 volts or less. Nevertheless, <u>almost two-thirds of the subjects progressed to 450 volts</u> and delivered the maximum shock until they were instructed to stop by the experimenter. Subjects continued to administer the shocks even when they could hear the victim's screams of pain and agony. (The victim's anguish was cleverly faked: no electric shocks were actually delivered, but all except an insignificant few of the subjects perceived the punishment to be real.)

In one of the experiments, the victim complained of a heart condition exacerbated by the shocks. Nevertheless, twenty-six of the forty subjects administered the maximum shocks at the direction of the experimenter. In another version, Milgram had subjects administer the test but someone else deliver the shocks. Thirty-seven of the forty subjects served as accessories, taking no steps to halt the punishment of the innocent victim (this is "Milgram's 37" referred to by rock star Peter Gabriel in the lyrics of his song, "We Do What We're Told").

In all, Milgram conducted eighteen variations of the obedience to authority study. More than 1,000 subjects from all ages and walks of life participated.

Strapping the victim into the chair "connected" to the shock generator

Others replicated his experiments in America and abroad sometimes gaining as high as 85 percent compliance (in Milgram, 1974).

One of the more dramatic replications was conducted by Sheridan and King (1972). In this experiment, the victim was a cute fluffy puppy dog, not a human confederate. Although the victim in Milgram's studies appeared to be, but was never actually, shocked, Sheridan and King had the subjects actually shock the helpless puppy. The puppy, however, received a lower shock level than subjects believed. Regardless, the shocks were intense enough to cause yelping and highly animated protest from the dog.

Despite the disbelief commonly manifested by my students that anyone would continue to shock an adorable puppy held captive in a box whose floor was an electrified grid from which there was no escape, the results of the experiment contradict conventional wisdom. <u>Three-quarters of the subjects, all college students, were obedient to the end</u> (54 percent of the men and 100 percent of the women). At the behest of the experimenter, they delivered the maximum intensity shock (450 volts so they thought) to the cute puppy dog whose pain they could witness directly.

The Milgram studies and replications that followed reveal the awesome power of legitimate authority. Milgram (1974) argues that <u>the ''most fundamen-</u>

Would you administer 450-volt shocks to this helpless dog? In one experiment 100 percent of the women and 54 percent of the men did just that to a puppy.

tal lesson'' of his studies is that "even when the destructive effects of their work become patently clear, and they are asked to carry out actions incompatible with fundamental standards of morality, relatively few people have the resources to resist authority" (p. 6).

A case in point is the September 1, 1987, incident involving Brian Willson (in Cialdini, 1993). Protesting U.S. shipments of military equipment to Nicaragua, Willson and two other men laid their bodies across railroad tracks leading out of the Naval Weapons Station in Concord, California. Having notified the navy and railroad officials of their intended protest three days in advance, the three men were confident that they could stop the train at least for a day or two. The civilian train crew, however, had been ordered by their superiors not to stop despite the protest. Even though the crew could clearly see the men on the tracks 600 feet ahead, they never slowed the train. Two of the men successfully scrambled out of the way of the oncoming train, but Brian Willson was not fast enough. Both of his legs were severed below the knee. Willson, a Vietnam veteran, didn't blame the crew for his injuries. "They were just doing what I did in 'Nam. They were following orders that are part of an insane policy. They're the fall guys" (p. 177). In a mind-staggering instance of blaming the victim, the train crew filed a lawsuit against Willson asking for punitive damages for the "humiliation, mental anguish, and physical stress" they claim to have suffered because Willson prevented them from obeying their orders without having to cut off his legs.

Whether it is a defenseless puppy, a man with a heart condition, or perhaps even a protester sitting on train tracks who serves as the victim, most of you will follow the dictates of authority figures because you have learned the obedience lesson well (Kelman and Hamilton, 1989). The subjects in the Milgram experiments are like you and I. Milgram argues that they *are* you and I. Those subjects who obeyed showed no psychosis on psychological tests. They trembled, stammered, shook, wept, pleaded to be let out of the experiment, bit their lips until they bled, dug their fingernails into their own flesh, hung their heads and covered their faces with their hands; some even broke into uncontrollable fits of nervous laughter. These are not the signs of sadistic, twisted individuals who enjoy inflicting pain and suffering on helpless people and puppies. Milgram's subjects were normal people who preferred not to hurt the victims of the experiments. When Milgram offered subjects the option of choosing the shock level administered to the victim, thirty-eight of forty subjects chose to go no higher than 150 volts, and twenty-eight of these chose no higher level than 75 volts.

More convincing still that it is the power of legitimate authority that causes blind obedience and not sadism of subjects is a study by Martin and his associates (1976). When subjects were ordered to inflict a high-pitched sound on themselves that they were told might result in a 50 percent permanent hearing loss, the results of the Milgram studies were replicated. The subjects followed orders even when the punishment was self-inflicted and might cause them serious injury.

Perhaps you still think that these are merely laboratory results unrelated to real life. No such luck. In one field study (Hofling et al., 1966), twenty-one out of twenty-two nurses followed orders from an individual posing as a physician over the phone and headed for a patient's room to administer a potentially lethal dose of a drug. They were intercepted by an observer. The September 28, 1986, issue of the *Los Angeles Times* reported an incident in which an AIDS patient was killed when a nurse administered a lethal injection on the orders delivered over the phone of someone posing as a physician.

As my nursing students are quick to point out, however, we should not conclude from these examples that nurses should be feared. The image of zombie-like nurses marching down hospital corridors with lethal hypodermics in their hands mindlessly obeying orders from strangers posing as physicians is melodramatic. Perhaps as a result of obedience to authority studies, procedures have been instituted in hospitals to prevent these types of occurrences. Nevertheless, the power of legitimate authority is real and requires vigilance if tragedies are to be averted.

Questions for Thought

1. Are the Milgram studies ethical research? Should you have serious concerns about the psychological effects on subjects of such experiments who involuntarily discover their potential for evil, or do the benefits outweigh the drawbacks? (Some of the volunteer experimenters who assisted Milgram were asked by university authorities why they continued the experiment when they could plainly see that the subjects were deeply distressed. They replied, "Milgram told us to!")
2. Do you believe that blind obedience to authority is as widespread as the Milgram studies indicate?
3. Do you think you would have refused to obey the experimenter in these studies? If yes, explain what makes you different from the majority who inflicted the maximum intensity shock to the innocent victim.
4. Would the results of the Milgram studies have been the same if he had used a woman as the authority figure? A woman as the victim? A child as the victim? Explain.
5. In Sheridan and King's (puppy dog as victim) replication of the Milgram studies, 100 percent of the female subjects but 54 percent of the male subjects blindly obeyed. Why the difference in results? Do you think women are more inclined to blindly obey legitimate authority? This study was conducted in 1972. Would similar findings result from replication of this study now? Explain.

An important point to note here is the power potential of *legitimate* authority. <u>We are not inclined to comply with directives from those individuals acting authoritatively but who are not deemed legitimate.</u> Group members must grant legitimacy before authority will have any weight. Those individuals perceived to be authorities without legitimacy will exercise substantially less influence in a group than those perceived to be authorities with legitimacy. A study of groups (Read, 1974) revealed that how the leader becomes an authority figure can be a decisive issue. Leaders who usurp authority are not granted legitimacy by the group. These pretenders to the throne of power have less influence than appointed or elected group leaders. Groups whose leaders have a weak basis of legitimacy (e.g., randomly appointed leaders) exhibit inferior performance compared to groups whose leaders have a strong basis of legitimacy (e.g., leaders appointed for their competence or elected by the membership) (Hollander, 1986).

The sad, sorry lot of inexperienced substitute teachers illustrates the problem of authority without legitimacy. Students frequently subject them to a kind of ritual hazing. I'm reminded of the old westerns on TV where the timid stranger in town is forced to dance to the beat of a six-shooter firing lead at the newcomer's vulnerable tootsies. Students can make an exasperated substitute teacher perform a little dance of sorts by hurling verbal shots of disrespect and insult at the stranger in the schoolroom. Teachers are authority figures in a school environment, but substitute teachers must struggle to establish legitimacy in students' eyes. They must combat the strong impression that as a substitute, they are not "real teachers." This is a perceptual challenge. No individual possesses legitimate authority. This power resource is conferred by the group.

Although the results from the Milgram studies (see Closer Look) and subsequent replications by other researchers are disturbing, defiance of all authority is as empty-headed as blind compliance. Both are manifestations of communication incompetence. What kind of society would you live in if few people obeyed police, teachers, parents, judges, bosses, or physicians? There are solid reasons why you should obey legitimate authorities in most circumstances. The answer to the excessive influence of legitimate authority rests with your ability to discriminate between appropriate and inappropriate use of authority, the task of a competent communicator, not the exercise of indiscriminate rebellion against all authority.

Those who aspire to be competent communicators while capitalizing on legitimate authority as a power resource should:

1. *Become an authority figure.* There are two principal sources of authority: appointed (designated) leader and emergent leader (Forsyth, 1990). Becoming either grants you authority. Emergent leader has already been discussed in Chapter Five. Appointed leader occurs because you gain favor of a powerful person, earn the right to be appointed (e.g., seniority), or are the only group member willing to accept the appointment.
2. *Gain legitimacy.* Legitimacy comes from conforming to accepted principles, rules, and standards of the group. Authority that is imposed on the group (leader appointed from outside the group) usually has problems of legitimacy because the group resents nonparticipation in making the

appointment. Authority that springs from the group (e.g., voted by membership to represent the group in bargaining talks or earned by demonstrating competence) has a solid base of legitimacy.

3. *Encourage participative decision making.* Keeping in mind the qualifiers attached to participative decision making discussed in the preceding chapter, if you are in a position of authority, encouraging participative decision making can help maintain the legitimacy of that authority by retaining the goodwill of group members.

 SECOND LOOK

Competent Communicator's Guide to Power Resource Use

Power Resource	Communication Guidelines
Information Power	• Provide group scarce but useful information • Be certain information is accurate
Expertise	• Maintain knowledge currency • Demonstrate trustworthiness and credibility • Be certain of your facts before advising • Don't assume air of superiority
Rewards and Punishments	• Rewards first resort; punishments last resort • Rewards/punishments appropriate to deed • Group rules and penalties should be clear • Verify your facts before acting • Make good on promises • Be generous with praise that is warranted • No idle threats; use threats rarely • Be consistent and prompt in application
Personal Qualities	• Enhance attractiveness • Learn effective presentational skills
Legitimate Authority	• Become an authority figure • Gain legitimacy • Encourage participative decision making

Group Endorsement

No resource is an inherent source of power. Power resources are not properties of individuals. A person does not possess power, but is granted power by the group. Power occurs within a system. As such, the group must endorse the resource for it to be influential (Folger et al., 1993). There are a number of factors that contribute to group endorsement. Not all of these factors need be present for any single resource to serve as a basis of power.

Significance of Resource   <u>Group endorsement usually depends on whether the resource meets a need of the group</u>. Will the group find this resource valuable and significant? Will it assist the group in attaining an important goal?

Rewards, for instance, have little power potential unless important group needs are met by the reward. When teachers fear for their lives because the school environment resembles a combat zone, the prospect of increased salaries may seem much less important than the establishment of a safer teaching environment. A rewarding job, one that is perceived to be fulfilling, interesting, and challenging will often be more desired than high salaries or generous fringe benefits. Rewards are transactions between those who control the resources and those who desire the resources. What is rewarding to one person may be unrewarding to another. Some students are powerfully motivated by grades and others could not care less. There is no power potential in a resource that group members do not value, for whatever reasons.

Similarly, a person who exhibits charisma has an ability to influence a group. This would not be the case, however, if the group did not value charisma. A colleague of mine once had a situation that soured him on charisma. The chair of his academic department exuded charisma. He was a dynamic personality, a powerful voice outside the department. Unfortunately, charisma does not always substitute for hard work. The chair was a loafer who was careless about details. He was uninformed about essential matters pertaining to intradepartmental welfare. He delegated much of his own work to freshly minted faculty members who did not have the security of tenure, and he made arbitrary and capricious decisions without consulting members of the department.

When the chair retired, charisma was not an important consideration for the hiring committee. The department had experienced flash without follow-through, inspiration without perspiration. The committee was far more interested in efficiency, hard work, and expertise. They had become wary of charisma. They selected a rather dull but diligent, competent but unspectacular individual to chair the department.

Control of Resource   <u>Group endorsement depends on whether you can deliver the goods</u>. Can you help the group gain access to the resource (empowerment) or can you restrict the availability of the resource for others (dominance)?

One of the groups working on its symposium presentation in my group communication class had a member (I will call her Darlene) who assured everyone that she had access to "all the information we need on offshore oil drilling." The group was so convinced that she could deliver the essential information that it adopted offshore oil drilling as the topic for its symposium. No one in the group knew anything useful on this topic. Group members imagined that they could forego tedious research in the library because Darlene would save them the effort. Darlene seemed heaven-sent. Information was power, but only if Darlene could make good on her promise.

The group met on several occasions. Darlene missed the first meeting and failed to deliver on her promise of an information bonanza when she appeared at a second meeting. Nevertheless, she insisted that the group trust her. Hesitantly, group members reaffirmed their faith in her and waited. No one in the group made a move toward the library. Meanwhile, Darlene assumed a leadership role since she was the resident expert on the topic and seemingly controlled vital resources.

One week prior to the designated date for the symposium presentation, Darlene informed her stunned group that she would not be able to provide the promised information. She sheepishly suggested that the group change its topic. If looks could kill, Darlene would be embalmed. Her group was enraged. Naturally, the group felt betrayed. Darlene was ostracized. She dropped the class. Her group muddled through a rather lame symposium presentation, still smarting from the shortcut that led the group down the primrose path.

In like manner, if you threaten punishment but cannot deliver on the threat, you actually lose power. Such failure to administer the punishment reveals to the group members that they have little to fear from you. This may embolden group members to defy your dictates even more than before. Parents are well acquainted with this turn of events when dealing with reluctant children.

The same holds for rewards. If you promise rewards (a salary increase, promotion, special privileges, etc.) but you fail to deliver on the promise, then you lose power. Future promises from you are likely to be met with a collective yawn, catcalls, or even less flattering gestures of derision.

Availability of Resource   Group endorsement depends on the availability of the resource from other sources. Restricted access increases the power potential of the resource. Darlene would have been in a less powerful position had other members of her group had access to essential information on the topic chosen for investigation. Group members could have empowered themselves by conducting research on the chosen topic. The group would not have been so dependent on Darlene's input, and Darlene in turn would not have wielded such influence over the group had other group members become informed on the subject. When she didn't produce the information as promised, other group members could have taken up the slack.

What should be clear by now is that groups determine the power any individual member wields. If the resources that we bring to the group are endorsed by the group, then we will exercise some degree of power with the membership. Power is not a static entity. Power is a transaction among the members of a group.

INDICATORS OF POWER

Hocker and Wilmot (1995) observe, "Since power is a dynamic product of shifting relationships, precise measurement of the amount of power parties have at any one time cannot be accomplished" (p. 79). Assessing the resources valued by the group is a starting place in ascertaining the power dynamics in a group. Determining the relative degree of power each member wields, however, is more complicated than a resource inventory.

Focus Questions

1. Those who define, control. What does this mean?
2. In what ways do male and female communication patterns differ in regards to verbal dominance?
3. What are the effects of "powerless" verbal and nonverbal communication patterns?

Problems of Power Assessment

Tabulating the resources of each member, even when these resources have been endorsed by the group, will not provide an accurate indication of where the power is predominantly located. If one member has legitimate authority, and another member has valued information, while a third group member has expertise, and a fourth member is charismatic and has rewards to distribute, which member is most powerful? This type of resource inventory merely tells you that all four group members have some degree of power. You wouldn't be able to assess the relative degree of power wielded by each individual by simply noting who has what resource.

Ascertaining relative degrees of power for each group member is further complicated by the complex ways in which human beings exercise power. Power is not always overtly displayed. If you are the designated leader of the group (e.g., appointed chair of a committee), but you are eager to garner the approval of one particular committee member, do you really have the most power in the group as the recognized leader? You are enormously influenced by this individual and may even alter your behavior significantly to curry favor with this important person. Meanwhile, this person may remain largely indifferent to your efforts. So who influences whom?

Despite these difficulties in accurately assessing the relative degree of power exercised by individual group members, there are many indicators of power present in all group transactions. Without complete precision, you can ascertain in a general way the distribution of power in a group. Determining such a distribution requires an ability to recognize indicators of power.

There are three main categories of power indicators: general, verbal, and nonverbal. Indicators are simply the ways in which relative degrees of power are communicated in groups.

General Indicators

There are several general indicators of power in groups. First, who defines whom and makes the definition stick? Those who define, control. The group, of course, must endorse the definition. Ordinarily we define people by attaching a label to them. Teachers define students (e.g., smart), physicians define patients (hypochondriac), psychiatrists define clients (schizophrenic), parents define children (incorrigible), and bosses define employees (good worker).

The relationship between definition and power can be seen clearly by considering just a few of the more embarrassing and controversial mental illness designations of the past from the field of psychiatry. There was the form of "insanity" called *drapetomania,* the mental disease afflicting slaves who contin-ually tried to escape from bondage. Then there was *masturbatory insanity.* An editorial on this "mental illness" appearing in a mid-nineteenth century issue of the *New Orleans Medical and Surgical Journal* (in Szasz, 1980) asserted: "Nei-ther plague, nor war, nor smallpox, nor a crowd of similar evils, have resulted more disastrously for humanity than the habit of masturbation: it is the destroy-ing element of civilized society" (p. 18). *Protest psychosis* branded as crazy pri-marily black militants who reject white culture. Finally, there was *homosexuality,* which the American Psychiatric Association designated a mental illness until 1973. Then APA members in 1974 had a change of heart and instantly trans-formed a so-called mental illness into an "alternative lifestyle."

The power of definition can be highly consequential. When the APA in May 1993 proposed labeling women who experience severe premenstrual syn-drome as having *premenstrual mood disorder,* a firestorm of opposition erupted. The National Organization of Women denounced the idea. Fearful that in child custody, rape, and sexual harassment cases women with severe PMS (broadly defined by the APA) would be branded as mentally ill and thus discredited, NOW organized a street protest outside the APA conference in San Francisco. Deborah Glenn, the vice president of NOW's San Francisco office said, "When women become aware of this, they become outraged" (in Alvarado, 1993, p. 1A).

The fact that such labeling is taken seriously indicates that psychiatrists, physicians, teachers, parents, bosses, and the like do have influence even if they're pinheads or bigots. If the individual or group, however, discounts the definition, then this indicates relative powerlessness in this situation. If a teacher labels a student a troublemaker but the entire class does not, then the teacher exercises little influence in this regard. In fact, any effort to punish this student may be viewed as unfair and encourage a backlash against the teacher's authority in class.

Whose decisions are followed is a second general indicator of power in a group. In a family, do the kids obey the father but ignore the mother or vice versa? Does it depend on the type of decision being made? Who is accommo-dated in the group? An alcoholic father may command obedience from his kids only by coercion. He may lose the respect of his children due to his obnoxious drinking and acts of physical violence. If the father loses respect, he erodes his legitimate authority. In this case, the mother may actually exercise greater power because she has the respect and trust of the children. Whenever the hammer of repression is not directly swung, the children will likely follow the mother's directives and ignore the father's whenever possible.

Who opposes significant change is a third general indicator of power. Those who have been accorded power by the group are usually uncomfortable with change that goes much beyond a little fine-tuning. Substantial change may alter the power relationships. The disaffected and relatively powerless individuals and groups clamor for substantial change as a general rule. Adapting to change in any social system is critically important, yet significant change is normally the product of the disgruntled, not those ensconced in positions of authority.

Verbal Indicators

Power is reflected in the way we speak. Many communication researchers have argued that the language choices and sentence construction of the relatively powerful tend to be distinctly different from the language choices and sentence structure of the less powerful.

The speech of a subordinate is often flooded with self-doubt, hesitancy, approval seeking, overqualification, and self-disparagement (Henley, 1977). Examples of "powerless" speech patterns include the following:

HEDGES: *"Perhaps* the best way to proceed is . . ." "I'm a *little* concerned that this *might* cause problems."

HESITATIONS: *"Well, uhm,* the important thing to remember is . . ." "Gosh, ah, shouldn't we, *ah,* delay the decision?"

TAG QUESTIONS: "The meeting will be at noon, *okay?"* "This point seems irrelevant, *doesn't it?"*

DISCLAIMERS: *"You may disagree with me,* but . . ." *"This is probably a silly idea,* but . . ."

EXCESSIVE POLITENESS: "I'm extremely sorry to barge in like this, but . . ." "Yes, *sir/ma'am* . . ."

Powerless speech suggests uncertainty, indecisiveness, lack of confidence, vacillation, and deference to authority. As Henley (1977) argues, these verbal indicators of submissiveness "advertise the powerlessness of those who must constantly acknowledge their subordinate status and must approach initiative gingerly, lest they be reminded it's not their prerogative" (p. 69). "Powerful" speech is generally direct, fluent, declarative, commanding, and prone to interrupt or overlap other group members' speech (Pearson et al., 1991).

The consequences of using powerless speech are revealed in a study set in a courtroom arena (Erickson et al., 1978). The researchers constructed two distinctly different versions of a witness's key testimony in a trial. The powerless version included many hedges, hesitations, tag questions, and other variants of verbal submissiveness, while the powerful version included none of these. A male and female were trained to read each version of the testimony to subjects. Both male and female speakers were rated as more credible, competent, likable, strong, and active when they read the powerful version. Power is perceptual. Choosing language that may connote weakness to the group will often produce the perception that you are also weak (Hackman and Johnson, 1996).

Dominance is on the other end of the power spectrum from submissiveness. Power is sometimes indicated by verbal bullying. Interrupting, contradicting, berating, and sheer quantity of speech are examples of **verbal dominance.** Monopolizing a conversation, for example, has obvious power implications. Those who dominate conversations are able to get their point presented to an audience. Those who can't sandwich a word into the conversation are unable to articulate their point of view. More importantly, as previously discussed, those who talk the most are more likely to be perceived as leaders in groups than are quiet members.

Interruptions to seize conversational control clearly reflect the status of individuals in a group. Relatively powerful individuals may interrupt the less powerful, but not vice versa. The peons are expected to defer to the pooh-bahs when interrupted.

Henley (1977) speculates that "a hierarchy of power in a group could be plotted by ordering people according to the number of successful interruptions they achieve (and maybe subtracting the number of times they're successfully interrupted)" (p. 69). Eakins and Eakins (1976) found just such a relationship. They analyzed faculty meetings of a university communication department for one year. Interruption patterns were strongly related to the relative position in the hierarchy of each faculty member. The department chair, for example, was interrupted least while the lone faculty member without a Ph.D was interrupted the most.

Presumptuousness—self-promoting overconfidence, arrogance—is closely akin to verbal dominance as an indicator of power. Presumptuous group members make verbal comments that suggest their superior knowledge, wider experience, and better judgment than other "lesser" group members (Godfrey et al., 1986). Presumptuousness is also revealed when verbal statements contain substantial quantities of *advisement* (e.g., "You should present the information this way"), *interpretation* (e.g., "You're obviously disappointed with the group's performance and you think we're loafing"), *confirmation* or *disconfirmation* of others' viewpoints (e.g., "That's the correct answer;" "You've made a huge mistake"), and *reflection* (e.g., "You're contradicting what you said yesterday"). The relatively powerful are more prone to presumptuousness than the relatively powerless (Godfrey et al., 1986; Stiles et al., 1979). Maybe that's why the statement "It's lonely at the top" is often repeated.

 FOCUS ON GENDER/CULTURE

Powerful Language Differences

Verbal indicators of power in our culture follow a gender pattern in several instances. Men are typically more verbose, more given to long-winded verbal presentations, and more talkative in mixed-sex groups than are women (James and Drakich, 1993). Talkativeness is associated with leader emergence. Men are more verbally aggressive than women (Nicotera and Rancer, 1994; Stewart et al., 1996), meaning men are more inclined to verbally attack the self-concepts of others. Men are also more argumentative than women (Stewart et al., 1996), meaning men are more likely to advocate controversial positions or to challenge the positions on issues taken by others. Women are inclined to view verbal aggressiveness and argumentativeness as strategies of dominance and control; a hostile, combative act (Nicotera and Rancer, 1994). Since men are more likely to seek status and women are more likely to seek connection in conversations (Tannen, 1990), these gender differences in verbal indicators of power are not surprising.

Tavris (1992) argues, however, that the use of relatively powerless speech by women—the use of hedges, tag questions, disclaimers, qualifiers, and hesitations—can be used to influence men. A study by Carli (1990) supports this interpretation. Carli found that women are more inclined to use powerless speech patterns when conversing with men, but not with other women. Tag questions, hesitations, and the like seem to reassure men that women are not attempting to enhance their status. Thus, women pose no threat to male status in groups, so men are more likely to listen to nonthreatening women. Does the strategy work? Apparently it does, because women are more influential with men when using powerless speech. Other women, however, view powerless speech as annoying when it is used to influence them.

The issue of powerless versus powerful speech takes on added complexity when culture is added to the mix. What is viewed as powerful speech is culture-specific. The Japanese, for example, and most Asian cultures would view our version of powerful speech as immature because it indicates insensitivity to others and is likely to make agreement more difficult (Wetzel (1988). In Malagasy society (Madagascar) ''women have lower status than men but they use our stereotypical 'powerful' language; they do the confronting and reprimanding and in so doing . . . their constant violation of societal norms is seen as confirmation of their inferiority'' (Smith-Hefner, 1988, p. 536). In Western societies, verbal obscenity and swearing is perceived as powerful language. Neither Japanese men nor women, however, use such language except in rare instances (De Klerk, 1991). In Malagasy and the Bhojpuri community in northeast India, ''women are more abusive than men, and this . . . increases as we go down in the caste hierarchy'' (Misra, 1980, p. 177).

When cultures clash over issues of significance, these different views of powerful and powerless speech can pose serious problems. When negotiating teams from Japan and the United States meet, misunderstandings easily arise (Hellweg et al., 1994). The language of Japanese negotiators is rife with indirect language viewed as powerless to American negotiators unfamiliar with cultural differences in perception. Japanese negotiators use such expressions as *I think, perhaps, probably,* and *maybe* with great frequency. They will also expect no interruptions while they speak. Americans negotiate in blunt terms, will interrupt, and view indirect and qualifying language as signs of weakness and lack of resolve. Misunderstandings of this nature make negotiations difficult and decision making troublesome.

Questions for Thought

1. If the powerless speech used by some women influences men, doesn't that make the language powerful, not powerless?
2. Do you think there is a relationship between powerful-powerless speech patterns in a culture and the individualism-collectivism focus of the culture?

Powerful speech is not always appropriate. Abusive and obscene language may be perceived in our culture as powerful speech, but it will offend group members and can destroy the cohesiveness of the group. Sometimes deferential language is a sign of respect and not merely powerless speech. Even tag questions can sometimes be used powerfully. If the leader of a small group says, "You'll see that this is done, won't you?" this may be issued more as a directive than a request. Then the tag question is authoritative, not weak.

Nonverbal Indicators

There are many nonverbal indicators of power. Let me provide just a sample of the more important ones.

Space is the prerogative of the powerful. Parents get the "master bedroom" while children may have to share a bedroom. The best offices with the most space are occupied by those individuals with the greatest power (Durand, 1977). The prime parking spaces are reserved for the higher-status individuals, as students experience on college campuses across the nation. Allocation usually follows a pecking order. Privacy of space is the prerogative of the powerful. Those individuals who are regarded as powerful may violate the space of those less powerful, but not vice versa. Peons must ask for permission to enter the domains of the influential. You must be granted access to the chambers of the privileged.

Posture and gestural communication are also markedly different for superordinates and subordinates. Generally, the powerful exhibit more relaxed, casual posture (Pavitt and Curtis, 1994). They feel free to slouch in chairs, place feet on tables, spread their arms and legs wide. The less powerful must be more concerned about posture, lest they offend. Their posture tends toward the stiff, tense, erect, and inhibited. Arms are kept close to the body or folded across the chest, and when sitting, knees may appear welded together. Subordinates can be directed to "sit up straight" or told to "stop slouching" by superordinates. Parents can tell children how to stand, sit, and move their bodies, but children do not have the same prerogative.

Touch clearly indicates power relationships in groups. Superordinates touch subordinates far more frequently than vice versa (Henley, 1977). The less-powerful often feel required to yield to the touch of their superiors even when the touching is unwanted and offensive. Laws prohibiting sexual harassment have been established in the United States to protect the less powerful from the tactile abuse (among other inappropriate acts) of the more powerful. These statutes recognize that uneven power distribution plays a primary role in most cases of sexual harassment. Harassers take advantage of their power position and the vulnerability of those who are their targets.

Eye contact is yet another nonverbal indicator of relative degrees of power. Staring is done more freely by the powerful. The less-powerful must monitor their eye contact more carefully. If a superordinate is speaking to a subordinate, eye contact connotes active listening and deference to authority. Superordinates, however, may feel no obligation to exhibit interest or attentiveness to subordinates by maintaining eye contact. Submissiveness is also manifested by lowering your eyes and looking down.

Finally, nonverbal symbols of power include a wide variety of <u>objects and tangible materials</u>. Large desks, plush carpets, office windows, master keys, company cars, computers, the list could go on and on.

The consequences of using powerful versus powerless nonverbal communication can be seen from a study by Lee and Ofshe (1981). Subjects in this study read a summary of a personal-injury lawsuit. They then estimated how much money should be awarded to the injured party. Initially, all subjects favored no less than $10,000. A videotape was shown to the subjects showing a man arguing that the plaintiff should receive only $2,000. Although the man's arguments remained exactly the same, there were three separate nonverbal conditions. As Forsyth (1990) labels them, there was the "deference-demanding condition" (exhibited powerful nonverbal behaviors), the "deferential condition" (exhibited powerless nonverbal behaviors), and the "neutral condition" (moderate mixture of powerful and powerless nonverbal behaviors). The deference-demanding (powerful) speaker on the videotape influenced subjects to reduce the award by an average of $4,273. The neutral speaker influenced the subjects to reduce the award substantially less—an average of $2,426. The deferential (powerless) speaker, however, did not fare so well. Subjects *increased* the award an average of $2,843.

In a similar study (Tuzlac, 1989), males argued for a specific financial award. Black males and white males exhibiting a powerful nonverbal style were influential to an equivalent degree. Those males who exhibited a powerless nonverbal style, however, were not influential.

Much more could be added here regarding nonverbal indicators of power, but my point has been made. You can discern the relative distribution of power in a group by observing both verbal and nonverbal indicators and noticing a few general communication patterns.

 **SECOND LOOK**

Indicators of Power

General Indicators	**Nonverbal Indicators**
• Who defines whom	• Space
• Whose decisions are followed	• Posture and gestural communication
• Who opposes significant change	• Touch
	• Eye contact
Verbal Indicators	• Objects and tangible materials
• Verbal dominance	
• Presumptuousness	

In summary, power is a central dynamic in all groups. I have defined power as the ability to influence the attainment of goals sought by yourself and others. Power is not a property of any individual. Power is the product of transactions between group members. Information, expertise, rewards and punishments, personal qualities, and legitimate authority are primary resources of power. Groups must endorse these resources before they have power potential. The influence that you wield cannot be determined precisely. Nevertheless, you can approximate the distribution of power in groups by observing certain general patterns of communication, plus verbal and nonverbal indicators.

QUESTIONS FOR CRITICAL THINKERS

1. Information is power. Can misinformation also serve as a power resource? Explain your answer.
2. Can a person learn to be charismatic?
3. If punishment has significant drawbacks, why is it typically used more frequently than rewards by those in power positions?

Power:
An Architect of Conflict

Henry Kissinger once said, "Power is the ultimate aphrodisiac." Unquestionably, power does have sex appeal. It can be a titillating experience. Who among you has not fantasized what life would be like if you were in charge? "If only I were running things." Tacitus observed long ago, "Lust of power is the most flagrant of all the passions." For some, lust for power can degenerate into an obsessive need to influence and dominate others. Powermongers easily embrace the self-satisfying and ego-inflating notion that they are the prime movers of group members' productive behavior. When groups function effectively, powermongers often believe it is because of their influence, but when groups function ineffectively, powermongers believe the cause is poor member motivation (Kipnis, 1974).

The primary focus of this chapter will be on how we transact conflict in groups, especially when power is unequally distributed. My <u>objectives</u> are:

1. to discuss the relationship between the imbalance of power in groups and conflict,
2. to explain the five general responses to power differences in groups, and
3. to describe ways that the competent communicator can transact power in small groups.

IMBALANCE OF POWER

Focus Questions

1. How are power imbalances and violence related?
2. "Dominance is an architect of conflict." What does this mean?

When power is inequitably distributed in a group and dominance becomes the focus, systemwide power struggles often ensue (Hocker and Wilmot, 1995). In an atmosphere of dominance and submissiveness, those who exercise the greatest influence are stimulated by their ability to manipulate and control events and people. They usually jealously guard their power. Those who exercise relatively little power, however, will often feel angered, frustrated, or disheartened by their impotence (Baumeister et al., 1996). This emotional disparity between the relatively powerful and the relatively powerless can serve as a catalyst for conflict. Ugly instances of violence may result.

Deng Xiaoping and the fossilized decision makers of China's gerontocracy were willing to slaughter students and citizens protesting nonviolently for democratic reforms in Beijing's Tiananmen Square in 1989 rather than relinquish power. Deng and the hard-liners supporting him displayed a savagery against the Chinese dissidents that was daunting. As repression goes, however, this butchery of unarmed demonstrators was unremarkable. History has recorded worse incidents of carnage. In another sense, though, the Beijing massacre was remarkable. It demonstrated the extremities that some will travel in a desperate journey to maintain dominance even when the whole world is watching, horrified and repulsed.

On a less global level, significant power disparities, especially when the more powerful individual acts on his or her advantage, often fosters violent confrontations. Two studies (Allen & Straus, 1980, and Coleman & Straus, 1986) found that violence is much more prevalent in relationships where either the husband or the wife has far more power than in relationships where the distribution is more equivalent. Gelles and Straus (1988) in their extensive study of family violence conclude:

> The greater the inequality, the more one person makes all the decisions and has all the power, the greater the risk of violence. Power, power confrontations, and perceived threats to domination, in fact, are underlying issues in almost all acts of family violence. (p. 82)

Violence easily spills beyond the husband-wife relationship and becomes a systemwide problem. The anger and frustration a victim of violence feels often becomes displaced when the victim attacks innocent, even less powerful targets, such as children. A cycle of violence may infiltrate the entire family system.

This chain reaction of violence can extend beyond the permeable boundaries of the immediate family to extended family members (e.g., grandparents or in-laws) and friends. Worse still, children learn patterns of dominance and violence from watching parents who physically and emotionally abuse one another. A large national study (Kalmuss, 1984) found that teenagers who witness physical abuse between parents are likely to beat their spouses when they are married. Violence resulting from power imbalance can become self-perpetuating.

This connection between a dominance-submissive power imbalance and expressions of aggression is demonstrable in teacher-student relationships. In one study (Wilmot, 1976), students were asked to indicate what options they considered employing to resolve conflicts between themselves and more powerful teachers. Their answers on paper included "Use a .357 magnum," "Blow up his mailbox," "Sabotage him," and "Beat him up." Although students may have been engaging in cathartic overstatement, recent reports in the news media of increased violence against teachers by students make one pause.

There are two instances of violence against teachers reported in the national media that are unsettling to any educator. A professor at a California university was literally hammered to death because he rejected a graduate student's dissertation, preventing him from acquiring his doctorate. In the second incident, a graduate engineering student at San Diego State University killed his entire thesis committee as he was about to defend his master's thesis.

Although violence is a frequent companion of the relatively powerless, nonviolent sabotage of the group is also encouraged by a dominance-submissiveness perspective. The common refrain, "Desperate people do desperate things," has a real ring of truth. When a pet project is ignored or repudiated by the membership, an individual who feels powerless to influence the group may try to threaten the group's existence. Going to the news media and alleging corruption, misappropriation of funds, questionable ethical practices, and the like all challenge the integrity and credibility of the group. The charges do not have to be true in order to cause substantial, even irreparable damage.

When people exercise power over us, aggression often results. <u>Dominance is an architect of conflict</u>.

 FOCUS ON CULTURE

Power Distance and Cultural Differences

In the United States, power imbalances are often the catalyst for aggressive behavior. The responses to power imbalances in some cultures, however, are strikingly different from the United States. <u>Cultures vary in their attitudes concerning the appropriateness of power imbalances</u>. Hofstede (1980) terms these variations the **power distance dimension** (herein referred to simply as PD).

Countries that are culturally classified as low-PD (relatively weak emphasis on maintaining power differences), such as the United States, Sweden, Denmark, Israel, and Austria, are guided by norms and institutional regulations that minimize power distinctions among group members and between groups. Challenging authority (not easy in any culture, as the Milgram studies demonstrate), flattening organizational hierarchies, and using power legitimately are subscribed to by low-PD cultures. Low-PD cultures do not advocate eliminating power disparities entirely, and in a country such as the United States, power differences obviously exist. The emphasis on maintaining hierarchical boundaries between the relatively powerful and powerless, however, are de-emphasized in low-PD cultures. Workers in low-PD cultures may disagree with their supervisors, in fact, disagreement may be encouraged by bosses. Even socializing outside of the work environment and communication on a first-name basis between workers and bosses is not unusual (Brislin, 1993).

Countries culturally classified as high-PD (relatively strong emphasis on maintaining power differences), such as the Philippines, Mexico, India, Singapore, and Hong Kong, are guided by norms and institutional regulations that accept, even cultivate, power distinctions. The actions of authorities are rarely challenged, the powerful are thought to have a legitimate right to use their power, and organizational and social hierarchies are encouraged (Lustig and Koester, 1993). Workers normally do not feel comfortable disagreeing with their bosses, and friendships and socializing between the two groups are rare.

The reactions by members to power imbalances in small groups are likely to reflect where a culture falls on the power distance dimension. One study (Bond et al., 1985) compared people's reactions to insults in a high-PD (Hong Kong) and a low-PD (United States) culture. Subjects from Hong Kong were less upset than those from the United States when they were insulted, as long as the initiator of the insult was a high-status person. As Brislin (1993) explains, ''When people accept status distinctions as normal, they accept the fact that the powerful are different than the less powerful. The powerful can engage in behaviors that the less powerful cannot, in this case insult people and have the insult accepted as part of their rights'' (p. 255).

Differences in power distance do not mean that high-PD cultures never experience conflict and aggression in small groups emanating from power imbalances. <u>Members of low-PD cultures, however, are more likely to respond with frustration, outrage, and hostility to power imbalances than members of high-PD cultures</u> because low-PD cultures value power balance even though the experience of everyday life in such cultures may reflect a somewhat different reality. In a low-PD culture, the struggle to achieve the ideal of balanced power in small groups is more compelling and the denial of power is likely to be perceived as more unjust, even intolerable, than in a high-PD culture where power balance is not viewed from the same vantage point.

Questions for Thought

1. Is it merely ethnocentric bias (''My culture is better than your culture'') that Americans typically regard power balance as preferable to power imbalance?
2. Which leadership style would likely be preferred in high-PD cultures, directive or participative? How about low-PD cultures? Explain.
3. If you were an exchange student in a high-PD culture, would you have difficulty adjusting to the ''don't challenge your teachers'' norm in the high-PD culture?

TRANSACTING POWER

Power is transacted in groups in far more complicated ways than by merely going ballistic when there's a power struggle. Transacting power in groups can involve any of five general responses. These responses are Compliance, Alliance, Resistance, Defiance, and Significance **(C-A-R-D-S)**. <u>The last four alternatives are the ways members attempt to balance the power in groups.</u>

Compliance: Social Influence

Compliance is the process of consenting to the dictates and desires of others. Compliance involves both obedience to authority and conformity to group norms.

Focus Questions
1. How are obedience and conformity similar to and different from each other?
2. ''Expedient conformity can lead to private acceptance.'' How?
3. How does deindividuation and pressure toward uniformity encourage conformity?
4. Is altruism a strong compliance-gaining strategy?

Conformity versus Obedience When compliance is the result of group influence on the individual, it is usually referred to as conformity, since we are expected to comply with norms established by the group. When compliance is the result of a high-power group member (e.g., leader) influencing lower-power members, it is normally referred to as obedience. Both conformity and obedience are powerful forms of compliance. "Obedience and conformity both refer to the abdication of initiative to an external source" (Milgram, 1974, p. 114).

An interesting variation of the standard Milgram obedience-to-authority studies pitted conformity against obedience. In this modification (Milgram, 1974), there were two confederates and one naive subject. The two confederates administered the test and the naive subject administered the punishment (increasing levels of electric shock) for incorrect answers. At the 150-volt shock level, one of the confederates refused to continue taking part in the experiment despite the experimenter's insistence. At 210 volts, the second confederate bailed out of the experiment.

With two defectors for support, 90 percent of the naive subjects refused to comply with the experimenter's command to increase the shocks all the way to 450 volts. Most of the forty naive subjects, 60 percent, stopped at 210 volts or less. Yet in a comparison study where the naive subject faced the experimenter alone, only 35 percent refused to comply with the experimenter's command and *refusal never occurred before 300 volts.*

Conformity to group norms can sometimes prove to be a more powerful tendency than obeying authority. In this study just described, the defectors created a group norm that opposed shocking a victim against his will. Most subjects complied with the norm instead of following the authority figure's insistent directives (Shaw, 1981).

Compliance in either form (conformity or obedience) seems to be the rule, not the exception. The ease with which individuals can be directed to behave compliantly has been demonstrated countless times by Allen Funt's *Candid Camera*. Consider just a small sample of vintage routines from this television show. Recall the person who stopped eating a hamburger whenever the "Don't Eat" sign flashed; the man who turned right, then left, then faced the rear of an elevator whenever a group of fellow travelers led the way; the people who stopped at a red light hanging over a sidewalk; and the drivers who, when presented with a roadblock and a sign reading, "Delaware Is Closed Today," turned around and drove away. One woman asked meekly if New Jersey was open. As a rule, most people are compliant in most situations.

The ease with which individuals will conform to group norms can be used for socially constructive purposes. A sign hung in a men's shower room at the University of California in Santa Cruz urged students to conserve water by shutting off the shower while soaping up. Only 6 percent of the men complied. The power of a group to instill conformity, however, was demonstrated by Aronson (1988) when he had several male students serve as models of appropriate behavior by turning off the shower while soaping their bodies. In this case, conformity shot up to 67 percent among those observing the appropriate behavior from others.

Two Types of Conformity   There are two types of conformity relevant to group communication: expedient conformity and private acceptance (Smith, 1982). **Expedient conformity** occurs when an individual expresses attitudes and exhibits behaviors acceptable to the group, yet harbors private beliefs at odds with the group. Expedient conformity happens primarily because the conformist wishes to avoid specific punishment for noncompliance or hopes to gain a specific reward for publicly parroting the party line. Expedient conformists remain true to the group only when they are under surveillance.

The aftermath of the Beijing massacre is a stark illustration of expedient conformity. Mandatory "study sessions," indoctrination meetings aimed at intimidating the population into submissiveness and proselytizing the big lie that no one was killed in Tiananmen Square in June 1989, were scheduled at workplaces throughout China after the popular uprising was squashed. Some actually came to believe the Orwellian version of events, but as journalist Lewis Simons (1989) reported, many citizens simply engaged in expedient conformity. As one young Chinese man explained, "No one makes any comments. If it's absolutely unavoidable, we give a very short answer and try to make it seem that our thinking is very close to the mainstream. Not exactly the same, because that looks suspicious, but similar" (p. 2A).

Closer to home, you are often faced with circumstances requiring expedient conformity. The consequences are likely to be far less severe than what the Chinese people experienced. Nevertheless, there will be times when being a team player is expected of you even though you may privately disagree with the group's decision. Your job, even friendships, may depend on following group orthodoxy.

In contrast, **private acceptance** occurs when an individual's public *and* private attitudes and beliefs are compatible with the group's norms and viewpoint. The individual accepts the norms of the group as his or her own. The individual and the group are congruent in their values and outlook. Close surveillance is unnecessary because the individual has internalized the norms of the group and the values and attitudes that act as the underpinnings of these norms.

⊙⊙ | CLOSER LOOK

The Bizarre Case of Patty Hearst

<u>Expedient conformity can lead to private acceptance</u>. One of the most dramatic and publicized instances of such conversion began on February 3, 1974. Patricia Campbell Hearst, granddaughter of the late newspaper tycoon William Randolph Hearst, was kidnapped from her Berkeley, California, apartment by a small group of self-proclaimed revolutionaries who called themselves the Symbionese Liberation Army. The SLA demanded that the wealthy Hearst family purchase several million dollars' worth of food and distribute it to the poor of California. The SLA threatened to execute Patty Hearst unless this ransom was disseminated to the "people oppressed by capitalism." The demand was met.

The nation watched transfixed by this prisoner-of-war melodrama. After two months of captivity, two weeks of which Patty Hearst spent blindfolded and incarcerated in a closet, the melodrama took a startling twist. The captive became an SLA convert.

Patty Hearst, nineteen-year-old politically naive college student and kidnap victim, announced that she had joined the SLA. She renounced her family and proclaimed herself Tania, "an urban guerrilla." A disbelieving public was further shaken when, on April 15, she participated with the SLA in a bank robbery recorded on camera for all to see. Just in case anyone doubted Patty Hearst's conversion, on May 16, she assisted the escape from arrest of two of her captors, William and Emily Harris, by covering their retreat with a fusillade of bullets from her automatic rifle. The next day, all members of the SLA except the Harrises and Tania were killed in a shootout with police in Los Angeles. Patty Hearst eluded an intensive twenty-month search spearheaded by the FBI before she and the Harrises were captured.

So the facts are these: The SLA kidnapped Patty Hearst, brutally beat her boyfriend during the commando-like capture, blindfolded her and threw her in a closet for two weeks, abused her, and threatened to execute her if the ransom wasn't paid. Sure sounds like a group I'd want to join. How about you? So why did this heir to the Hearst newspaper empire choose to become an SLA member? How could such a radical transformation have happened to Patty Hearst? How could she have moved from expedient conformity (e.g., doing everything the SLA told her to say and do in order to stay alive) to actual private acceptance, from average college student to defiant revolutionary?

Patty Hearst before her kidnapping by the SLA and after her conversion when she becomes Tania, "urban guerrilla."

There are several explanations for Patty Hearst's bizarre conversion. First, she fell victim to the **Stockholm Syndrome,** named for a hostage situation that developed during a bank robbery in Sweden's capital city. The Stockholm Syndrome is a psychological process whereby the victims come to identify with their aggressors. Galanter (1989) explains why this occurs: "The agent inflicting distress on the dependent person is also perceived as the party who can provide relief. Thus, pressure is exerted on those experiencing distress to accommodate to the party who comes to be seen as the only one able to offer relief" (p. 105).

Patty Hearst feared for her life during the initial stages of her confinement. When the SLA eventually released her from the closet, then treated her well, she was understandably relieved, even grateful to her captors. As Galanter (1989) further explains, "Victims implicitly hope that by means of fidelity and compliance, they may elicit the aggressor's protection" (p. 106). Members of the SLA were the only ones who could allay Patty Hearst's fears for her well-being and the only ones who could release her because help from the outside did not appear to be coming anytime soon, if ever. She became dependent on her captors for her safety and eventual release from captivity. The SLA was transformed in the mind of Patty Hearst from aggressor to protector.

Second, the SLA used **boundary control** as a means of inducing internalization of their political views. The only information Patty Hearst was exposed to during her captivity was news that supported the SLA mindset. Politically naive and indifferent at the outset, Patty Hearst had no reservoir of knowledge, no means of independently assessing the validity of SLA propaganda, and no ability to solicit informative counterarguments from experts. She was also isolated from her usual sources of social support. She was unable to receive feedback from others who could bolster any attempts she might make to resist the SLA persuasion effort.

Third, Patty Hearst gradually came to believe that she had the freedom to walk undeterred out the door and return to her family and friends. She was strongly encouraged, however, to join the SLA. This was an important final step in the conversion of Patty Hearst. The internalization of an attitude or belief as one's own emanates from a **perception of free choice,** not coercion. Expedient conformity is induced by threats of punishment or extrinsic rewards (e.g., payoffs in money or gifts). Private acceptance flows from the perception of unimpeded choice. Patty Hearst came to believe that she had arrived at her new worldview through thoughtful discussion and debate with her captors. She voluntarily internalized the viewpoint that "U.S. imperialism is the enemy of all oppressed people."

Patty Hearst ultimately survived her harrowing group experience, but not without consequences. She reverted to her more conventional worldview following arrest. A "brainwashing" defense put on by internationally renowned lawyer F. Lee Bailey, however, failed to sway the jury in her trial on bank robbery charges. The jury accepted the less melodramatic explanation for her behavior, namely, that conversion from expedient conformity to private acceptance of the SLA came through some coercion but mostly through standard persuasive techniques and was therefore of her own volition. She served almost two years in prison before her sentence was commuted by President Jimmy Carter. After her release, she married her former bodyguard, had two daughters, and in 1996 she published her first novel.

Questions for Thought

1. Can you think of experiences in your own life where expedient conformity to a group has led eventually to private acceptance?
2. Would you have found Patty Hearst guilty if you had been on the jury? Explain.

Group Influence and Conformity On a warm April night in 1989, a pack of teenagers went "wilding"—a variety of gang rampage—into New York City's Central Park. Originally a band of about thirty youths, a smaller group of seven split off from the main crowd. Spotting a slightly built twenty-eight-year-old Wall Street investment banker out jogging by herself, the predators leaped on their relatively helpless prey.

After brutally beating and raping their victim, they left her to bleed to death. She didn't. She did suffer some permanent brain damage, but remarkably she returned to her Wall Street job eight months after the attack. Yusef Salaam, age fourteen, after his arrest, explained why he had bludgeoned the woman with a lead pipe. "It was fun," he said. "Something to do."

This instance of group viciousness certainly lends credence to Nietzsche's opinion that "Madness is the exception in individuals but the rule in groups." Why would a group of teenagers commit such a barbaric act? The answer seems to lie more in the nature of group influence than in any focus on individual pathology. These youths were hardly casebook sociopaths. They were described by friends, teachers, and relatives as industrious, churchgoing, even shy (Gelman and McKillop, 1989). The power of the group to incite aberrant behavior is a more credible explanation.

There is a psychological process called **deindividuation** that liberates group members' inhibitions to behave antisocially. Deindividuation occurs when individuals shed their personal identities and replace them with a group persona (Jessup et al., 1990).

Why does deindividuation occur in groups? *Anonymity* is the principal reason (Wade and Tavris, 1990). As a group increases in size, an individual can meld into the group more easily. An antisocial act becomes a group act, not an individual one. Anonymity provided by the mask of groupness can embolden even normally hesitant individuals. Once the individual assumes a group identity, responsibility becomes diffused among the many. Individual acts appear relatively inconsequential even though the collective result may be horrific. When a band of rowdies at a soccer match attacks a referee and supporters of the opposing team, no individual will likely feel any more than marginally responsible for the ensuing loss of life and serious injuries inflicted on innocent spectators. After all, screaming at an official or throwing a few punches at

Deindividuated sports fanatics riot during a soccer match.

members of the opposition may seem relatively harmless. Collectively, however, it may precipitate an ugly riot.

The term "fan" is short for "fanatic," and deindividuated sports fanatics worldwide have produced ugly riots with increasing frequency. Fans enraged by England's loss to Germany in a soccer match in 1990 rioted throughout Great Britain, resulting in three deaths, dozens of injuries, and 600 arrests. Championship victories led to riots by celebrating fans in Montreal, Dallas, and Chicago in 1993. Celebration of the Chicago Bulls' third straight NBA championship erupted into a riot that left two dead, 700 arrested, and caused massive property damage.

Returning to the "wilding" example, we can see deindividuation resulting from anonymity. Individually, none of the assailants fit the profile of a sociopath. Feeling anonymous in a group, however, diffused accountability for a criminal atrocity. As Robert Panzarella, a professor of political science at New York's John Jay College of Criminal Justice, explains in reference to the wilding attack, "Basically, it's a loss of the individual's personality. Things he (each individual attacker) would never think of doing by himself he does in the group" (in Gelman and McGillop, 1989, p. 65). Caught up in the frenzy of the moment, the anonymity of the group conferred a perceived freedom from accountability, a diffusion of responsibility, and a release from restraint.

In addition to the process of deindividuation, group influence manifests itself in **pressure toward uniformity** among members. As I indicated previously when discussing groupthink, this pressure toward uniformity is sometimes an explicit process. Members may specifically indicate that uniformity is expected. In the 1994 trial of a Pennsylvania woman accused of attempted murder, one juror held out for three days in favor of a not guilty by reason of insanity verdict. She finally caved in to the group pressure from her fellow jurors and voted to convict. She explained that she was "tired of being badgered, and she agreed to vote for a guilty verdict even though she had not changed her mind" (Farley, 1994, p. A1). More typically, however, the pressure toward uniformity is implicit (Turner, 1981). There is an understanding from experience and observation that to go along is to get along. There are rewards for compliance and there are sanctions for noncompliance.

Many studies document the pressure toward uniformity process of group influence (see Johnson, 1986). One of my favorites (Tuddenham & McBride, 1959), however, found that group pressure toward uniformity can convince a subject to go along with silly group conclusions, such as that an average person eats six meals a day and that the United States is populated mostly with old people. Group influence is a significant factor inducing compliance in individuals.

Compliance-Gaining Communication Strategies   The research on compliance-gaining has identified numerous ways to induce people to accede to our requests. Trenholm (1989) has condensed the abundant lists of verbal strategies for gaining compliance into four general categories.

The first general strategy is the use of *threats and promises*. Punishments and rewards are actualized as power resources by the communication of threats and promises. We demonstrate and test our power in groups by threatening to punish noncompliance and by offering rewards for compliance.

The skillful use of threats and promises to induce compliance from group members depends on five main factors (Folger et al., 1993). When trying to induce compliance, threats and promises need to be specific (e.g., "Join me or I'll fire you"; "Join me and I'll promote you to office manager"). They should be credible (i.e., presented by someone who can demonstrate a willingness and ability to actually punish noncompliance or reward compliance). They must be immediate (e.g., "Turn off the TV or go to your room now"). They should be presented as equitable (i.e., threats that seem fair and just; rewards that appear deserved). They should be adjusted for climate (i.e., a promise is more believable in a cooperative group climate than in a competitive one; a threat in a cooperative climate may be viewed as "for my own good" but in a competitive climate it may be seen as outright coercion to be resisted).

The threats and promises strategy typically degenerates into a polarizing "You're either for me or against me" false dichotomy for group members. Allies garner rewards; enemies earn enmity and retribution.

A second compliance-gaining strategy is *exchange and reciprocity*. When someone does us a favor, we feel an implied contract to return the favor either in kind or in excess of what was done for us. Suppose your work team covers for you while you're ill by taking on your responsibilities and tasks during your absence. When group members ask you to cover for them in some future circumstance, you will be hard pressed to ignore this felt obligation, even if the effort required of you exceeds the original favor performed by the group. Every society subscribes to this principle of reciprocation (Gouldner, 1960). Those individuals who violate the principle are called "moochers," "ingrates," or names too indelicate for me to repeat here.

The limitation of reciprocation as a constructive compliance strategy is that it rests on paybacks, not the merits or demerits of the issue in question. This can easily lead to poor decisions based on irrelevant past concerns.

The third compliance-gaining strategy is *value and identity appeals*. Here compliance is sought by references to shared values and a common identity among group members. "Catherine, surely you see the importance of fighting the politicians that advocate the transformation of a pristine forest into an asphalt jungle." Here the appeal is to perceived shared values. "It's an issue of public trust, George. We can't just turn our backs and walk away. As a friend I implore you; as a colleague I beseech you to become a team player." Here the appeal is a combination of value and identity appeals. The implication is that the two parties share certain values, and appealing to them will encourage compliance. In addition, an appeal to a common identity as friends, colleagues, and members of the same team seeks to unite individuals under one banner.

Altruism is the last compliance-gaining strategy. Altruism is a demonstrated concern for the welfare of others. This is an appeal to selflessness. We comply in order to help someone else without reaping any tangible reward for ourselves. In a supposedly cold, callous, violent society like the United States, this strategy may seem anemic by comparison to the three already discussed. The infamous case of Kitty Genovese certainly calls into question the strength of altruism as a compliance-gaining strategy. In 1964, Genovese was repeatedly stabbed while thirty-eight neighbors heard her cries. No one came to her aid nor called the police until more than half an hour had passed.

The Genovese case became a symbol of the absence of altruism in American society. In August 1995, a malicious act of violence in Detroit seemed reminiscent of the Genovese case. Deletha Word, a thirty-three-year-old woman, was involved in a minor traffic accident. She hit the car driven by nineteen-year-old Martell Welch. She drove off. Welch, accompanied by friends, took off after Word, caught her on a bridge, dragged her out of her car and proceeded to beat her up and smash her car with a tire jack in full view of dozens of onlookers. Fearing for her life, Word jumped off the bridge into the Detroit River thirty-two feet below. She drowned.

Initial media reports called it another case of the Kitty Genovese syndrome or bystander inaction. This incident, however, is more complicated than that. Two men, Lawrence Walker and Orlando Brown, did come to Word's aid, diving into the river to save her. Unfortunately, she apparently mistook them for her attackers and swam away from them. Several motorists also called 911 during the attack. Onlookers could reasonably do little more, however, since they could not be sure that an enraged Welch, assisted in the attack by his friends, didn't have a gun.

Another event challenges the absence of altruism assumption made in these previous cases. Lenny Skutnik, a Washington, D.C., office worker, heroically rescued a drowning woman, a victim of the crash of a Boeing 737 that plunged into the frozen Potomac River on January 13, 1982. When asked in an interview why he leaped into the river at the risk of his own life to rescue the woman, he stated, "It was in my heart. I just felt sorry for the girl."

Field studies show that altruism is a powerful motivator of behavior. In four separate studies (Clark and Word, 1972, 1974) staged in Florida, a "maintenance man" acted out an accident scene for bystanders. When the man seemed clearly hurt and required aid, bystanders came to his assistance 100 percent of the time in two of the experiments. In the other two experiments, helping the injured man involved contact with potentially lethal electrical wires. The victim, nevertheless, received assistance 90 percent of the time.

When the emergency is clear, not ambiguous (e.g., Is that a homeless person sleeping on the sidewalk or a diabetic in a coma from insulin shock?), most people will lend assistance even when it threatens their personal safety. If the situation is ambiguous, we may not want to look foolish helping out when personal safety may be an issue or when no assistance is required.

Whether a particular situation is interpreted as requiring altruism also influences the likely responses. Culture again plays a part. In the United States and Northern European cultures, societal norms dictate that husband-wife arguments are strictly private. In one field study, when bystanders observed a staged argument between a woman and a man, two-thirds came to the assistance of the woman when she yelled, "Get away from me; I don't know you!" but only 19 percent tried to help her when she yelled, "Get away from me; I don't know why I ever married you!" (Shotland and Straw, 1976). In Mediterranean and Latin cultures, however, intervention by passers-by into a conflict between two people is the norm (Wade and Tavris, 1990).

There is also strong evidence to indicate that people will help those in need due to uncontrollable or unintentional circumstances (Fiske and Taylor, 1984). They are far less likely to be altruistic, however, if they perceive that the person in need has brought on the problem themselves through stupidity, cupidity, duplicity—well, you get the idea. This is why heroic efforts are made on behalf of a toddler trapped in a well, but mostly disapproving glares are offered to a drug-dazed panhandler on the street.

Finally, the size of the group present influences altruistic bystander intervention (Zimbardo, 1992). As the group size increases, the likelihood of intervention decreases. The most probable reason is that each person assumes others will help. This is a credible explanation for the Kitty Genovese incident (remember there were thirty-eight witnesses to the event). In larger groups the assumption that others will help may be based on a belief that others could be more effective than you could be given the situation (e.g., a small female bystander witnessing a victim attacked by a man the size of a refrigerator would defer to male bystanders to take effective action). In the Deletha Word incident, the fact that her attacker was a huge young man probably persuaded many onlookers to defer to other bystanders who could possibly restrain an out-of-control Martell Welch.

The compliance-gaining strategies outlined by Trenholm (1989) in no way exhaust all possibilities. There are numerous additional strategies available to induce compliance from group members. Nevertheless, those discussed illustrate a broad range of strategies available for compliance-gaining.

SECOND LOOK

Compliance

Types of Conformity
• Expedient conformity: public attitudes and behaviors at odds with private
      beliefs
• Private acceptance: public and private attitudes/beliefs are compatible

Group Influence and Conformity
• Deindividuation: personal identity replaced with group persona
• Pressure toward uniformity

Compliance-Gaining Communication Strategies
• Threats and promises
• Exchange and reciprocity
• Value and identity appeals
• Altruism

Alliance: Coalition Formation

Subgroups inevitably form in a human system of any size larger than two. These subgroups often develop around some issue or idea that triggers a conflict within the system. **Alliances** are associations in the form of subgroups entered into for mutual benefit or a common objective. Groups normally splinter into subgroups especially when there is a disagreement concerning how best to achieve a group goal. In most circumstances, alliances in groups are temporary. They are expedient unions between two or more group members primarily to <u>increase the influence of specific individuals in matters of mutual importance</u>. These temporary alliances are called **coalitions.**

Power is central to coalition formation (Grusky et al., 1995). Disputes within the group trigger coalition formation. Group members form coalitions to increase their power and thus control decisions made in the group when group members don't agree on issues of significance to the group.

Focus Questions
1. Which theory of coalition formation is stronger: minimum power or minimum resources?
2. From your experience and observations, do coalitions form primarily from attitude similarity, identification with group members, or determinations of power distribution and potential rewards?

Minimum Power versus Minimum Resources Weaker members of groups increase their power primarily by forming coalitions (Folger et al., 1993). Weaker members acting alone pose no threat to stronger members unless weaker members organize and form coalitions. The less powerful seek coalitions to balance power in groups more evenly.

Because coalitions can change the distribution of power in a group, coalition formation is adversarial, competitive, and contentious. Coalitions are formed not simply to advance the goals of the allied members, but also to thwart the attainment of noncoalition members' goals. Consequently, powerful members often move to stymie formation of coalitions among weaker members. This can be accomplished by forming their own coalitions with weaker parties or by confusing issues and arousing discontent in the ranks of the weak, thus splintering potential allies.

There are two classic theories of coalition formation. The first is Caplow's (1968) **minimum power theory** or the "weakness is strength" perspective. In a triad (group of three), the weakest member will be the only one who will always be included in a coalition. Coalitions form on the basis of the minimum power necessary to overcome an opponent. Group members are guided by a desire to maximize their control over others and to minimize the control others exercise over them.

Gamson's (1961) **minimum resources theory** rests on a "strength is weakness" point of view. Group members with the most power are included in coalitions less often than are weaker members (Murnighan, 1978). This is true because more powerful members are entitled to a larger share of the rewards than weaker members, leaving less for other members. Also, sometimes powerful members are unaware of the necessity to protect their power position by forming alliances (Komorita and Ellis, 1988).

Practical application of these two theories can be ascertained by considering three simple situations. First, there are three business partners—Tom, Dick, and Harry—all with equal power. There are three coalitions possible: Tom-Harry, Tom-Dick, and Dick-Harry. Both theories predict that all three coalitions are equally likely. No single member gains more power nor any larger share of the rewards by joining with one member as opposed to the other. If Tom, for instance, allies himself with Harry, he gains no greater advantage than if he allies himself with Dick since all parties share equal power.

Consider a second situation. There is a family named Harmony consisting of parents, Rose and Fred, and a daughter named Crystal. Both Rose and Fred exercise an equal amount of power, but Crystal has less power than either parent. Again, both theories predict the same coalition formation. Crystal will enhance her power by allying herself with either parent and she will gain no advantage in rewards by choosing one parent instead of the other. Rose and Fred, however, will not likely form a coalition with each other because they already exercise more power than Crystal does. There is no advantage in power or rewards to be gained by such an alliance. An alliance between either parent and Crystal, however, does provide an advantage over the other parent. Thus, the most likely combination is Crystal and either parent.

A third situation reveals a difference in predictions made by the two theories. Suppose that the Harmony family had a different power ratio. Let's say that Rose had a power ratio of five, Fred a four, and Crystal a three. The key distinction now is that the parents do not share equal power. The minimum power theory predicts that Rose-Crystal and Fred-Crystal are equally likely coalitions. Rose allies with Crystal in order to prevent a Fred-Crystal coalition of greater power than Rose alone. Fred and Crystal may ally with each other to accomplish this very thing.

Minimum resources theory, however, predicts that Fred-Crystal is a far more probable alliance than is Rose-Crystal. Both Rose and Fred will seek to ally with Crystal, but Crystal will prefer Fred. Why? Because Crystal will expect a larger share of the rewards from such a coalition than she could expect from an alliance with Rose. Her contributed resources are proportionately greater with Fred (three-sevenths of their combined resources) than they are with Rose (three-eighths of their combined resources).

So whose theory is correct? Research shows that <u>minimum power theory is most accurate when the group members are highly sophisticated strategic players. Minimum resource theory is most accurate when group members are inexperienced and naive about coalition formation</u> (Komorita and Kravitz, 1983). Neither theory offers a complete explanation for how coalitions form in groups.

In addition, neither the minimum power nor the minimum resources theory deals well with the difficulty of assessing levels of power, discussed in the previous chapter. It's convenient to assign power ratios of five, four, and three, or fifty, forty, and thirty, or whatever to individuals in groups. This makes application of each theory clear and tidy. In reality, however, no such precise measure of power distribution can be designated

<u>Power is more a perceptual than quantitative entity</u>. On a scale of 1 to 100, what numerical ratio should be assigned to an individual who possesses scarce information highly prized by the group compared to a member with charisma? This evaluation assigns a precise numerical weight to a subjective perceptual choice. That's like saying God is a thousand times more powerful than all human beings collectively. Why not a million, a billion, a trillion? Ten to the quadgillionth power? God is more powerful in what sense? Total firepower? Transcendent love? Awesome authority? We have no way of precisely measuring such things. The best we can do is estimate power distribution on the basis of indicators, but this results in imprecise general approximations (e.g., God definitely has the advantage).

Additional Perspectives   Some coalitions obviously form not on the basis of minimum power or resources, but on the basis of <u>identification with another member</u> (personal qualities as a power resource). Adcock and Yang (1984) argue that in a family, children are more likely to ally with the same-sex parent because they can identify more closely with that parent. Thus, the likelihood of coalition formation with *either* parent would not be equal as predicted in the minimum power or minimum resources theories.

Personal observation also reveals that despite the predictions, coalition formation doesn't always follow probabilities. Parents do form alliances in order to present a united front against their children, especially on matters of potential disagreement, such as discipline, curfews, drug use, or dating. A recent study (Grusky et al., 1995) found that 41 percent of the coalitions that formed in four-person families were parental coalitions that reinforce the status differences between parents and their children. Coalitions that split parents risk eroding family solidarity and may threaten the survival of the family system. This study is an interesting addition to coalition research because it involved four-member families, complicating the possible coalition combinations. Coalitions involving the father were the strongest whereas coalitions involving the younger child were the weakest.

As useful as these explanations of coalition formation are, there is one crucial element missing from all of the theories discussed. <u>Coalitions do not form in the absence of communication.</u> Coalition formation is not like computer dating, where a machine makes the selection on the basis of objective data. Coalitions form on the basis of communication transactions between potential allies. Human beings don't always choose what is in their best self-interest. Sometimes we make choices based more on interpersonal attraction or revulsion than we do on more objective determinations of rewards, attitudinal similarity, or power potential.

It's plausible that you might form a coalition with another group member in order to command a larger share of the rewards or because of similarity of worldviews and goals. But as sure as mildew finds a home in Seattle, incompetent communication can dampen enthusiasm for the development of such an alliance. Skillful, competent communication, however, can enhance the probabilities that a coalition will form even in unlikely circumstances. Sometimes a potential ally must be convinced (by compliance-gaining strategies) of the advisability of a coalition.

 SECOND LOOK

Theories of Coalition Formation

Theory	Explanation
• Minimum Power	• Weakness is strength
• Minimum Resources	• Strength is weakness
• Identification	• Affiliation with/attraction to group members
• Attitude Similarity	• Commonality of goals—expedience

Resistance: Covert Noncompliance

In comparison to compliance-gaining strategies, little research has been conducted on compliance-resisting strategies (Pearson, 1989). The skimpy research that has been conducted makes no distinction between resistance and defiance (see Burroughs, Kearney, and Plax, 1989). I see a distinct difference between the two.

Resistance is a covert form of communicating noncompliance, and it is often duplicitous, and manipulative. Resisters are subtle saboteurs. Resistance is the prevention form of power (power from). Done craftily, resistance can be difficult to identify unequivocally for those who are its targets because the sabotage is ambiguous, often communicating a seemingly sincere effort to comply. The target is often left mostly convinced that resistance is taking place, but is unable to make this apparent to the group due to the mixed messages being sent. <u>Resistance strategies are normally the choice of the less powerful</u>. When faced with a dominant individual (supervisor, parent, or group leader) it is often safer to employ indirect means of noncompliance than direct confrontation or open defiance. Nevertheless, even high-power individuals on occasion will use resistance strategies. If undercurrents of dissatisfaction are apparent, openly defying the wishes of group members may provoke outright rebellion.

Defiance is an overt form of communicating noncompliance. It is unmitigated, audacious rebellion against attempts to induce compliance. Defiance is also a prevention form of power, but there is no ambiguity in defiance. There is no subtlety. No one is left guessing whether an individual supports a specific norm or goal of the group. <u>Those who are defiant dig in their heels, while those who merely resist drag their feet</u>.

In this section I will discuss specific strategies of resistance, or what Bach and Goldberg (1972) term "passive aggression." I have combined their list of strategies with my own.

Focus Questions
1. Since resistance strategies rely on deceit and mixed messages, should competent communicators always avoid them?
2. How should a competent communicator deal with resistance strategies?

Strategic Stupidity Your group is working on an important class presentation. Each member has been assigned a topic area to research. At one of your meetings, an inventory is taken regarding information collected up to this point on relevant topic areas. When asked for a status report, one of the members of your group whines, "I couldn't find anything on world hunger." Are you faced with a drooling dolt or is this person covertly resisting active involvement in the group project? Bet your money on the latter.

When you do not want to expend energy on a project, especially if the project was not of your choosing, you may feel hesitant directly complaining to the group about your dissension. If you have been outvoted in the group when the proposal for the project was decided, you may resent having little influence on the group decision. You may feign stupidity in order to penalize the group and to exercise influence, at least in a negative way. When the success of the group presentation depends on all members pulling a load, one resistant member can create systemwide problems.

Strategic stupidity can be a time-honored tradition in some families. Consider just a few examples, all of them aimed at resisting unpleasant duties or tasks forced on recalcitrant individuals: A family member whines, "But I don't know how to use the vacuum" (it takes a big active brain to figure out such a complicated machine); Teenage computer whizzes pretend stupefaction when asked to interrupt their computer game to load and start the dishwasher—"But Mom, you never taught me how to stack the dishwasher and I don't understand how to work it"; A spouse who doesn't want to deal with family finances even in limited ways claims an inability to understand even simple arithmetic necessary to balance a checkbook.

These are just a few illustrations of a maddeningly effective power strategy. Why is it effective? Strategic stupidity can effectively thwart compliance attempts by more-powerful group members because in most instances the strategy is part of a recurring pattern. If used only once, it becomes an isolated incident. If used time-and-again as is often the case, strategic stupidity can frustrate the dominant party to the point of capitulation. If group members must spoon-feed their strategically stupid member on where to look in the library for information on world hunger, they may decide that this takes too much effort, surrender in exasperation, and do the research themselves.

Strategic stupidity works exceedingly well when the low-power person claims stupidity, is forced to attempt the task anyway, then performs the task ineptly. In a study of 555 married adults conducted by Special Report Network ("Home chores," 1993), 14 percent of the men admitted that they've purposely botched chores around the house in order to get out of doing them again. Doing a half-baked job of a simple task can exasperate even the most patient person. If criticized for doing a poor job, the low-power person can always retort, "How was I supposed to know," or "I told you I didn't know how to do it." The pathetic performance becomes proof that the stupidity was "real." To expect any better performance in the absence of careful and persistent tutelage would be an injustice.

Loss of Motor Function This resistance strategy is an effective companion to strategic stupidity. Here the low-power person doesn't pretend to be stupid. The resister just acts incredibly clumsy, often resulting in costly damage. There is a mixed message here. The nonverbal behavior displays resistance but the verbal statement that often accompanies it feigns a genuine attempt to comply.

I still remember an incident that happened to me years ago when as a college student I worked summers at a can factory. I was a worker in quality control. In a less-than-admirable effort to avoid the horrid press department, I kept ducking out of sight at the start of the morning shift in order to avoid the supervisor, who had a habit of selecting some poor college student employee to replace a worker who had quit the press department. The press department was where can lids were stamped out and sent through a machine, coated, and packed in boxes or paper sleeves stacked onto wood pallets.

One day the supervisor spotted me and sent me to the press department to replace someone who had quit. I went reluctantly. The job I was given pitted me against a machine that pumped out can lids in rapid fashion. I had to stack the lids without spilling them onto the floor. I purposely adopted the loss of motor function strategy in order to get out of the job. By the end of my shift, I had spilled thousands of lids onto the factory floor, shut the machine down four times, incensed the machinist who had to spend time starting up the machine each time it was shut down, and forced my supervisor to call in two workers to clean up my mess. I was making the system adapt to my act of sabotage. All the while I insisted in bellicose tones to my upset supervisor that I was trying hard but that the job was impossible to do. The next day I returned to my previous job (half-expecting to be fired), hid out, watched my supervisor pick another college student to take my press job, and I spent the rest of the summer free from press department duties. I even received a promotion. Ironically, I ended up in the press department the next summer and managed to master the job with little difficulty.

<u>It is the apparent effort exerted that makes this strategy so effective.</u> In my can factory incident I had sweat rolling down my face. I seemed to be making every effort possible to keep up with the diabolical machine. I just couldn't quite stay with it. If the high-power person alleges deliberate sabotage, the low-power person can always become incensed, even incredulous that anyone would even suggest such a thing. It's an awkward position for a high-power person. How does one conclusively prove willfulness? You don't want to look like you're beating up on a less-powerful group member. If you make an accusation of willfulness but fail to convince the group, then you may lose power by diminishing your credibility (personal qualities as a power base).

The Misunderstanding Mirage   This is the "I thought you meant" or the "I could have sworn you said" strategy. The resistance is "expressed behind a cloak of great sincerity" (Bach and Goldberg, 1972, p. 110).

I have observed numerous instances of this strategy in my group communication classes. Typically, a student will deliberately miss an important meeting with his or her group then claim, "Oh, I thought we were going to meet on *Thursday*. Sorry. I just got confused." I can't count the number of times students have used this strategy to excuse their late assignments. "You said it was due Friday, not today, didn't you?" they'll say hopefully. If I were to respond, "No, your paper is due today," my resistant student often replies, "Well, I thought you said Friday so can I turn my assignment in then without a penalty?" The implied message attached to this ploy is clear: "Since this is a simple misunderstanding, penalizing me for a late assignment would be unfair."

Again, the high-power person is placed in a seemingly awkward position. The teacher may lose some power (legitimate authority) if the class sees his or her behavior as capricious and unfair.

<u>High-power persons sometimes use this strategy of misunderstanding in order to avoid felt obligations.</u> Teachers may purposely miss appointments with students or committee meetings on campus because they'd prefer to leave

town before the rush-hour traffic. Pretending to have misunderstood when the meeting was scheduled relieves them of having to confront directly their own irresponsibility.

Selective Amnesia Have you ever noticed that some people are very forgetful? This seems especially true regarding those things that these same individuals find distasteful. This temporary amnesia is highly selective when used as a resistance strategy. We rarely forget what is important to us and what we like doing.

The message is again mixed. You manifest no outright signs of noncompliance. You outwardly agree to perform the distasteful task. Appointments, promises, and agreements just "slip your mind." If your group insists that you assume a larger share of unpleasant tasks, you can always agree, then forget to do them.

A more sophisticated version of this strategy, however, is truly selective. Take an errand such as purchasing office supplies for your department. Remember to buy all the items except one or two important ones. Hey, you did pretty well, didn't you? So you forgot the disks for the computers and now the entire office staff is affected. No one's perfect. If your selective amnesia proves to be a recurring problem, that errand gig may shift to someone else.

Tactical Tardiness When you really don't want to go to a meeting, a class, a lecture, or whatever, you can show your contempt by arriving late. If you don't arrive too late, you can still claim that you attended the event, so you're protected from punishment for being absent. Showing up late irritates, frustrates, and even humiliates those who take the meeting seriously. Tactical tardiness is intended to produce these very feelings in those requiring attendance.

Tactical tardiness asserts power in disguised form. The group is faced with a dilemma. The group may wait for your arrival, but this holds the entire group hostage until you arrive. Members' plans for the day may be trashed by the delay. The other alternative is to commence without you. This also may prove to be problematic, however. Once you saunter in you'll naturally expect an update on the meeting. If you offer reasonable-sounding excuses for your late arrival, the group will feel bound to clue you in on what has already transpired, thereby halting progress until you have been informed.

Tactical tardiness is a recurring strategy of resistance used by some students who dislike having to take certain classes, especially ones that are required. Normally, I hear excuses such as, "I couldn't find a parking place," "My math teacher kept us late," and "I had to walk way across campus after my last class." These are all legitimate-sounding excuses. One excuse that did not strike me as legitimate but was certainly creative occurred a few years back. A female student arrived late for class. Her excuse? "I had to give mouth-to-mouth resuscitation to my epileptic pet rat." You'll be pleased to know that the rat survived, so I was informed.

All instances of tardiness are not necessarily tactical. Occasionally, getting to meetings on time is not possible through no fault of our own. Tactical tardiness is a recurrent pattern of resistance, not a rare occurrence.

Tactical tardiness is not the sole province of the less powerful. High-power persons may also use this strategy to reinforce their dominance. Self-important celebrities with egos swelled like puffer fish often arrive late to functions. They hope to underscore their perceived superiority over the peons who admire them by making them wait.

Purposeful Procrastination   Most people put off doing that which they dislike. There is nothing purposeful about this. There is no strategy involved. Procrastinators just tend to be hedonistic: they pursue pleasure and avoid pain. Procrastination, or what someone once called "the hardening of the oughteries," can become a resistance strategy when it is purposefully aimed at a target.

Purposeful procrastinators play their deceitful game by pretending that they will pursue a task "soon." While promising imminent results, they deliberately refuse to commit to a specific time or date for task accomplishment. Trying to pin down a purposeful procrastinator is like taking a knife and stabbing Jell-O to a wall—it won't stick. They'll make vague promises. When you become exasperated by the ambiguity and noncommittal attitude, the purposeful procrastinator will try to make you the problem. "Relax! You'll stroke out if you're not careful. I said I'd get to it, didn't I?" The implication is clear. You're impatient and unreasonable. The job will get done—not without delay after delay, however. If the task doesn't get accomplished, it is because "something came up unexpectedly." If you express irritation at the delays, you're a nag.

Here is how one student in a group communication class confessed his use of procrastination as a resistance strategy:

> I hated the topic the members of my group chose for their symposium. Since I was absent the day they decided and several members had already started researching their part of the group presentation, I didn't see how I could insist on choosing a different topic. This didn't stop me from despising the choice. I also really resented being told what my area of responsibility was. I decided that there was no way I would do any work on this project. If my group wanted a good grade, they'd have to do the work for me. I delayed on purpose. I told my group, "Oh yeah! I'm going to prepare. I'll be at the practice sessions." Then I did nothing and I didn't show. Of course, they were really bent by this. I simply made up excuses like "I had to work unexpectedly" or "I had a big exam to study for." They tried to tell me what to do from the start and I decided, "Forget you." I got what I wanted. They flipped out, panicked, and concluded that they couldn't count on me so they researched and wrote my speech for me. VICTORY. Naturally, I expressed surprise and mild indignation when they handed me my speech—like they didn't trust me or something.

There is not much to admire in this student's conduct, especially since the initial problem was of his own making, namely absenteeism. Nevertheless, aside from any heavy-handed moral judgments we might like to make, the reality is that his strategy worked. His group told him what to do (dominance) and he responded with purposeful procrastination. Power shifted to him because the group could not ignore his resistance.

SECOND LOOK

Resistance Strategies

Strategic Stupidity—smart people acting dumb on purpose; feigned stupidity
Loss of Motor Function—sudden attack of the clumsies
The Misunderstanding Mirage—illusory mistakes
Selective Amnesia—no fear of Alzheimer's; forgetting only the distasteful
Tactical Tardiness—late for reasons within your control
Purposeful Procrastination—promising to do that which you have no intention
　　of doing anytime soon, if ever

All six resistance strategies I have discussed result from a dominance form of power. When power is imbalanced, low-power group members will often fight a covert battle of resistance to domination.

Resistance strategies are generally viewed as negative and unproductive (Bach and Goldberg, 1972). This is true in an ideal sense. Resistance strategies are underhanded, deceitful, and rest on mixed messages. This doesn't make for terribly competent communication, nor do such strategies make conflict resolution easy. Resistance strategies are not the type of skills a competent communicator needs to learn. Nevertheless, I am not willing to rule them out unequivocally. Low-power members may have no better tools to resist dominant group members. The essence of the problem doesn't lie in the resistance strategies. The dominance form of power creates a group atmosphere where resistance strategies are nurtured and encouraged.

I have already described how to use resistance strategies should you ever need to do so. From the standpoint of competent communication, however, my emphasis must be on how to deal effectively with resistance, since the resistance may not always be noble. There are two principal ways for the competent communicator to deal with resistance strategies in groups:

1. *Confront the strategy directly.* Identify the communication pattern and ferret out the hidden hostility. Once this has been accomplished, efforts must be made to discover alternatives to dominance-submissiveness power patterns. Care should be taken to use the descriptive pattern of communication discussed in Chapter Four on group climate.
2. *Thwart the enabling process.* We become enablers when we allow ourselves to become ensnared in the resister's net of duplicity. The more we continue to explain the proper way to wash the windows, the more we are entangled in the strategic stupidity of the resister. When we continue to wait for the chronically late, we generate tactical tardiness. If we perform the tasks for those who use loss of motor function to resist, we reward their behavior and guarantee that the behavior will persist.

　　Group members thwart the enabling process by their own acts of noncooperation. You have to refuse to be a party to the resistance. If a staff member "forgets" an item at the supplies store, guess who gets to make a return visit? If you hear the old refrain, "I can't be expected to remember everything," tell him or her to make a list. If someone is continually late for appointments, inform them that you will leave after ten minutes if it happens in the future, then follow through with your threat if tardiness actually recurs. If the person is repeatedly late for committee meetings, refuse to fill them in on what they missed and encourage them to come on time. Continued tardiness may necessitate expulsion from the group.

Again, I must emphasize that <u>the appropriate focus should not be on how to combat resistance, but instead on why the resistance occurs in the first place.</u> If the main cause of resistance resides in the dominance form of power, then the focus of attention should be on how to reduce the power disparity, or at least its perception.

Defiance: Bold Noncompliance

When I previously explained the difference between resistance and defiance, I noted that defiance is overt, audacious noncompliance. Defiance presents no mixed messages. Defiant communication is unambiguous. When individuals exhibit behaviors that do not conform to group norms, they are called deviants. <u>When this deviance is a purposeful, conscious, overtly rebellious act, it is called</u> **defiance.** Group members typically turn to defiance when they perceive little or no chance of enhancing their power position through formation of an alliance, resistance strategies seem either inappropriate or ineffective, or they feel like exhibiting independence from group conformity. Defiance is often the final "I can't take it anymore" response to incompetent communication from the group and the reliance of more powerful members on dominance as an approach to group decision making.

Cookson and Persell (1986) cite one example of defiance in the "I can't take it anymore" mode. At one of the private prep schools that they studied, students engage in "treeing." This is a form of defiance in which the entire student body climbs into trees and screams, refusing to cease the protest until the administration of the school agrees to negotiate small matters of individual freedom.

Focus Questions
1. Why are defiant members a threat to the group?
2. What is the best strategy for a defiant member to take when trying to convert the rest of the group to his or her viewpoint?
3. What strategies are typically used by a group to command compliance from a defiant member?

Threat of Contagion   Someone who refuses to conform to group norms— who defies conventions—can be a threat to the group. If a group tolerates even a single deviant, the degree of uniformity in decision making and behavior will be significantly affected. A single act of defiance can have systemwide implications.

When a group composed of confederates of the experimenter *unanimously* judged the length of a line incorrectly, 35 percent of the naive subjects unaware of the set-up consistently conformed with the obviously erroneous group judgment (Asch, 1952). When one of the confederates deviated from the group judgment, however, naive subject conformity dropped precipitously to 8 percent. A single deviant encourages independent decision making, even outright rebellion. Even when the deviant was wearing glasses with "Coke bottle" lenses and the task required visual discrimination, the influence of the deviant was so strong on the group that even the support of a visually impaired person was sufficient to induce naive subjects to defy the collective misperception of the group (Allen and Levine, 1971).

One rather interesting field study (Lefkowitz, Blake, and Mouton, 1955) demonstrates the power of a single defiant act in a natural setting. Observations were made on a street corner in Austin, Texas, on three afternoons during mid-day. Violations of the traffic signal were recorded. In the control condition where no interference occurred, the signal was violated in 8 of 742 instances. When a well-dressed (a nonverbal indicator of high status) confederate waited for the signal to change, violations occurred only 4 times in 771 instances. Yet, when the well-dressed confederate violated the signal, there were 52 violations by pedestrians in 526 instances. Of those 52 violations, 40 followed on the heels of the confederate's small rebellion. Defiance is contagious, especially if a powerful-looking person encourages the deliberate nonconformity.

A defiant individual threatens the power of a group to command compliance from its members. A defiant individual is a rebel. It may not matter whether a defiant member is a "rebel without a cause" or a "rebel without a clue." The fact that one group member refuses to comply for whatever reason may be enough to fortify other members to defy group pressure toward uniformity. The entire group must either try to crush the rebel or adapt to the change precipitated by the defiant member.

Variable Group Reaction All defiance is not created equal. There are several factors that determine group reaction to noncompliance. Some instances of deviance will produce nary a ripple of concern in the group. Other instances will be perceived as intolerable. Whether a group takes steps to squash noncompliance, adopts a calculated indifference to the defiance, or explores ways to adapt to the challenge posed by the deviant depends in large part on four factors.

First, some norms are not as important to a group as others, so the reaction to defiance will vary. For a basketball team, curfews and eating meals together before a game may be considered terribly important, but socializing with team members outside of the basketball environment may be perceived as relatively unimportant. In the military, the liberal use of scatological and profane language is the norm and so is the proper form of address when an enlisted soldier speaks to an officer. The sanctions that result from defiance on the first norm are likely to be far less severe than the sanctions that result from defiance on the second norm. Really interesting results can be observed, of course, if compliance with the first norm contradicts the second norm as when an enlisted person addresses an officer in obscene or profane language.

A second factor influencing whether a group will make an effort to deter defiance is that some norms are accepted by the entire group whereas other norms are accepted by some and rejected by other members. I have been in several groups where the norm stipulating that racist references will not be tolerated is never questioned by any group member. These same members, however, have been divided on the norm prohibiting sexist references and language. No group member needed to be reminded that referring to an African American male as "boy" smacks of racism and would not be condoned. Some of the same members, however, became quite testy when reproached for consistently referring to adult females as "girls." The group as a whole seemed to think the trivialization of women was significantly less of an issue than the diminution of African American males, thus requiring different responses to deviance.

Third, the degree of deviation from the norm also affects whether a group discourages nonconformity and, if so, to what extent. A group may have a norm requiring punctuality. If a member is a few minutes late to a meeting, this deviance is usually ignored. If a member arrives two-thirds of the way through a meeting, however, group members may not look so kindly on this degree of noncompliance.

Fourth, the deviation from the norm has to be a matter of obvious defiance, not inadvertent noncompliance. Showing up for a new job dressed inappropriately is rarely an act of defiance. Normally, this show of deviance will be interpreted as a clueless blunder, not an act of rebellion. *Not all deviance is defiance*. Deviance must be overt, conscious, and clearly intended to flout group norms before it becomes defiance. The group reaction to inadvertent deviance will likely be mild compared to unmistakable defiance. We smile indulgently when a small child bangs on the bathroom door and inquires, "Whatdya doin' in there?"

Extinguishing Defiance As I previously pointed out, defiance is the exception, compliance is the rule. Small wonder. When a group decides noncompliance is intolerable, the group often applies intense pressure on defiant members to get them back in line. Leavitt (1964) identifies four general strategies of pressure by a group to command compliance from recalcitrant members. These general strategies tend to follow a sequential order, although there may be variation in some circumstances.

First, group members attempt to *reason* with the deviant. Schachter (1951) found that the quantity of talk aimed at the deviant increases substantially when nonconformity is first recognized. Groups show an intense interest in convincing deviants of their folly. Clearly, groups expect deviants to change their point of view and behavior. Groups, however, will not usually show any inclination to change in the direction of the deviant.

If reason fails to sway a deviant into compliance, a group will often try *seduction*. This is usually a psychological ploy to make the deviant feel guilty or uncomfortable because the group is made to look bad in the eyes of outside observers. Telling the deviant that his or her efforts are wasted and will accomplish nothing is another form of the seduction strategy.

Then there is the classic seduction referred to as **co-optation.** Here you offer the rebellious individual a piece of the power pie, thus, effectively buying their support instead of their defiance. Offers of promotions, perquisites, monetary incentives, and the like in exchange for compliance are examples of attempts to co-opt deviants. Seduction strategies are virtually limitless.

Whistleblowers are often hit with the seduction strategy in one form or another. Whistleblowers are individuals who expose to the light of public scrutiny such abuses as waste, fraud, corruption, and dangerous practices in corporations and organizations. The standard seduction goes like this: "Think of how this will tarnish the reputation of (fill in the blank) if you go public and air our dirty laundry." "You won't get anywhere anyway so why cause such turmoil?" "We've been considering you for a promotion. Naturally, we'd expect you to be a team player."

The third line of defense against deviants is *coercion*. This is where groups begin to get rough. Communication turns abusive and threatening. Groups attempt to force compliance by using nasty and unpleasant tactics; what Zimbardo (1988) refers to as the "three deadly R's: ridicule, repression, and rejection" (p. 631).

As the disparity in power between conflicting parties increases, the temptation to use coercive tactics also increases. As Shaw (1981) concludes on the basis of several studies, "In general, the more power a person has, the greater the probability that he or she will use it" (p. 301). If someone challenges your authority defiantly and you have the power to crush them like a cockroach, you will be sorely tempted to squish them underfoot even though this may be an unwarranted overreaction. Not employing the full range of power resources at your disposal is sometimes a better response to noncompliance than unleashing your entire arsenal. Unfortunately, we too often kill an insect with hand grenades. A measured response often proves to be more effective for all parties involved, as I will discuss later.

Glazer and Glazer (1986) studied fifty-five whistleblowers over a period of several years. Coercive tactics against these whistleblowers included threats of firing and sometimes actual terminations (amputating the offending member will restore the group's cohesiveness swiftly, although not without consequences). In addition, some were transferred to undesirable jobs and locations, demoted, harassed, and intimidated by supervisors and peers. On December 10, 1993, CNN, reporting on a study of whistleblowers, noted that 88 percent of whistleblowers had suffered personal reprisals for their defiance. Oregon congressman Ron Wyden accused authorities at four military nuclear plants of harassing four whistleblowers by requiring them to see a psychiatrist as a means of intimidation and repudiation. As Wyden put it, "This is an old strategy that goes on in totalitarian countries. It's incredibly grotesque that it's being pursued here" (in "Whistle-blowers claim," 1989, p. 11A).

The final stage of group pressure to induce compliance from a deviant is *isolation.* There are situations (e.g., tenure or civil service protections) where the group cannot eliminate the deviant from the group, at least not immediately. In such an instance, the group can physically and psychologically isolate the deviant. Here the offending member remains part of the group only artificially. If the isolation is prolonged, the deviant may eventually submit to the pressure and become compliant. If not, the deviant is at least contained.

Shannon Faulkner's effort to become the first female cadet at the Citadel, a military academy in Charleston, South Carolina, was met with open hostility. She became the campus leper. Forced by the courts to accept her first as a student, then later as a cadet, the students hit Faulkner with derision, isolation, and ostracism. She was "booed, mooed, hissed at and scorned as 'Shrew Shannon' and 'Mrs. Doubtgender' " (Goldstein, 1994, p. 13A). Bumper stickers advocating "Save the Males" and "Shave Shannon's Head" appeared. One teacher observed that Faulkner was wise to sit in the front of her class so she couldn't see the looks from boys sitting behind her.

Those who defended Faulkner's attempt to crack the all-male brotherhood at the Citadel received similar treatment. Faulkner's mother, Sandra, a social studies teacher, was ostracized by some of her colleagues. Faulkner's father, Ed, saw his fence company business suffer. A black student, Von Mickle, defended Faulkner because it reminded him that blacks were not welcome at the Citadel until 1966. He was "spoken to" by other students and was ridiculed in the student newspaper.

Are these strategies to extinguish noncompliance successful? Faulkner caved in to the pressure of the ostracism and the media attention her defiance provoked. She left the Citadel in her first week as a cadet.

Even if these strategies fail to induce compliance, however, they certainly have their nasty consequences. Coworkers often disassociate themselves from whistleblowers to protect their own jobs. Friends and family become impatient with the battle and may come to view the effort as a tedious, even destructive, waste of time. Donald Soeken, formerly a psychiatric social worker for the U.S. Public Health Service and a one-time whistleblower, turned a farm in West Virginia into a haven for whistleblowers he calls The Whistlestop. Soeken says, "Most whistleblowers get a feeling of hopelessness that it probably seems to take a lifetime of therapy to get over. Blowing the whistle is not easy. And it's almost insurmountably lonely" (in Anderson, 1991, p. 17).

On March 6, 1989, CBS News reported a study of whistleblowers. As a result, at least partially, of pressures to induce their compliance, 17 percent of the whistleblowers studied lost their home, 15 percent divorced, and 10 percent attempted suicide.

Given the tremendous pressure to conform exerted on those who defy, how do we explain the individual who converts the group to his or her way of thinking, as Henry Fonda dramatized in *Twelve Angry Men*? Admittedly not a frequent occurrence, minorities (defiant members) do influence groups.

If the immediate group cannot reject you (e.g., jury or elected official), then the deviant's best chance of converting the group is to remain unalterably and confidently defiant throughout discussions—in other words, defy without cracking (Gebhardt and Meyers, 1995). If, however, the group has the power to exclude the deviant from the group or the deliberations, then the deviant stands a better chance if he or she remains uncompromisingly defiant until the group seems about fed up. At this point the deviant should indicate a willingness to compromise some (Wolf, 1979). The group is more likely to modify its position if it sees the deviant as coming around and being more reasonable. Remaining intransigent when the group can reject you is a losing battle. Your consistent defiance will be taken as legitimate justification for your ostracism.

I should note that remaining unalterably defiant will win you no friends. As Moscovici and Mugny (1983) indicate, unwavering deviants are seen as less reasonable, fair, warm, cooperative, liked, admired, and perceptive than other group members. This is not surprising since the deviant creates secondary tension in the group. Although the consistent deviant is not viewed as competent by the group, deviants are perceived to be confident and self-assured, independent, active, even original.

Consistency may increase the influence of minorities in groups, especially when there is some ambiguity and indecision among majority members, but it does not necessarily improve group decision making (Gebhardt and Meyers, 1995). Flexibility is a key to communication competence in groups. Intransigence aimed at winning over the group will likely produce counter-rigidity from the majority group members. When both minority and majority members remain rigidly consistent, majorities prevail (Gebhardt and Meyers, 1995).

 **SECOND LOOK**

Defiance by Group Member

Factors Affecting Group Reaction
- Significance of norm to group
- Level of group acceptance of norm
- Degree of deviation from the norm
- Obvious defiance or inadvertent noncompliance

Extinguishing Defiance
- Reason—convincing with logic
- Seduction—make deviant feel ineffectual or co-opt him or her
- Coercion—ridicule, repression, and rejection
- Isolation—psychological/physical ostracism; group member in name only

Minority (Defiant Members) Influence Strategies
- Group cannot ostracize—deviant remains consistent throughout discussion
- Group can exclude—remain consistent until group is about fed up, then indicate willingness to compromise

Significance: Self-empowerment

When group members grow tired of being dominated by more powerful individuals, they can do more than merely resist or defy demands for compliance.

Less powerful members can enhance their relative influence, they can balance the power in the group more evenly, by increasing their value to the group. Becoming more significant to the group can occur in two primary ways: by developing communication assertiveness and by increasing personal power resources.

Focus Questions
1. In what ways do aggressiveness and assertiveness differ?
2. Why should group members learn to be assertive?
3. How do mentoring and networking enhance personal power resources?

Assertiveness   Sue Townsend (in Metcalf, 1986) relates a story that depicts a common misconception regarding assertiveness:

> My mother has gone to a woman's workshop on assertiveness training. Men aren't allowed. I asked my father what "assertiveness training" is. He said, "God knows, but whatever it is, it's bad news for me." . . . then my mother came home and started bossing us around. She said, "The worm has turned," and "Things are going to be different around here," and things like that. Then she went into the kitchen and started making a chart dividing all the housework into three . . . she put the chart on the wall and said, "We start tomorrow." (p. 22)

The image many people have of an assertive person is that of an obnoxious, overbearing, argumentative, self-centered individual bent on intimidating others. This hardly qualifies as a description of a competent communicator, and yet assertiveness is an important skill for the competent communicator to acquire.

I continue to hear the terms assertive and aggressive used synonymously. Infante and his associates (1993) define assertiveness as a tendency to be "dominant, ascendant, and forceful" (p. 162) and they claim that it is a "generally constructive aggressive trait" (p. 163). Defining assertiveness as dominance and constructive aggression, however, produces conceptual confusion. It defines assertiveness in terms of power over others (dominance), but calls this constructive. Considering the voluminous research already discussed on the negative aspects of competition, defining assertiveness as dominance (win-lose) hardly fits well in a communication competence model. How does one make the "constructive aggression" that forces submissive behavior from others a positive force for the losers in this dominance game? How do you dominate without denying others their rights?

Simply calling aggression "constructive" doesn't make it so. In fact, Infante and his colleagues (1989) define "verbal aggressiveness" as "attempts to inflict psychological pain, thereby resulting in the receiver's feeling less favorable about self, i.e., suffering self-concept damage" (p. 164). This definition makes "constructive verbal aggression" difficult to conceptualize. Distinguishing assertiveness and aggressiveness conceptually does seem appropriate. This is especially true in light of research on family violence and abusive relationships that shows a clear connection between verbal aggression and physical attacks (Coleman, 1980).

I prefer Adler's (1977) definition of assertiveness as *"the ability to communicate the full range of your thoughts and emotions with confidence and skill"* (p. 6). Assertiveness falls in between the extremes of passivity and aggressiveness and is distinctly different from either. Aggressiveness puts one's own needs first, while passivity underemphasizes one's needs (Lulofs, 1994). Assertiveness takes into account both your needs and the needs of others.

Adler is very careful to emphasize the "ability" and "skill" aspects of his definition, thus emphasizing communication competence. Assertiveness is perceived by many people to be merely communicating the full range of thoughts and emotions—period. The ability and skill part of the equation is blithely overlooked. So they sound like arrogant little Nazis in the process of telling others what they think or feel. They come off sounding like self-absorbed, Me-oriented twits. William Howell (1982) cautions us to "balance assertiveness with empathy" (p. 3). Assertiveness is not a "looking out for number one" competitive communication strategy. <u>To be assertive is to be sensitive to others while also looking out and standing up for yourself</u>. You can stand up for yourself without trampling others in the process. Power doesn't have to be viewed as a zero-sum game where your acquisition of power must result in the loss of power for others. Defining assertiveness in terms of empowerment makes this point obvious.

<u>Assertiveness is not a strategy of resistance</u>. As I already explained, resistance tactics are acts of passive aggression. Assertive communication can be employed to defy a group. I have not included assertiveness in the section on defiance, however, because I view it as *a primarily empowering form of communication.* We most often use assertive communication not to defy the group, but instead to assure that our individual needs, rights, and responsibilities are not submerged or ignored by the group. Assertiveness is a positive self-enhancing form of communication. Assertive members seek to enhance their significance in the group, not diminish their role. When a formerly passive member is assertive, the group may view this as a highly constructive change, wholly consistent with the norms of the group, and worthy of encouragement, not ostracism.

⊙⊙ CLOSER LOOK
Conspicuously Unassertive

Are we generally an assertive bunch? Not really. <u>Assertiveness is conspicuous by its absence</u>. Zimbardo (1977) questioned 5,000 men and women regarding shyness, a common form of nonassertion. He found that 80 percent reported feeling shy at some time in their lives and 40 percent considered themselves shy at the time of the study.

Several studies by Moriarty (1975) demonstrate how difficult it is for most people to assert themselves. In the first experiment, he had male college students, two at a time, take a difficult twenty-minute test. One of the two test-takers was a confederate. Shortly after the test commenced, the confederate turned on a boom box at high volume. Unless their fellow test-taker complained, a seventeen-minute rock music concert ensued. Some subjects exhibited nonverbal signs of displeasure, but 80 percent made no verbal objection. Fifteen percent made mild requests of the confederate, who was instructed to continue the rock concert until subjects asked the accomplice three times to turn off the music. One subject acted aggressively by leaping up and demanding that the confederate snap off the music. This so startled and intimidated the confederate that he complied.

Moriarty followed this experiment with several interesting field studies on the same question of nonassertiveness. He subjected forty people reading in a library to loud seven-minute conversations. Only one of the forty subjects asked the noisy conversationalists to quiet down, while nine left. The remaining thirty subjects endured the disruption. In a similar study in a movie theater, only 35 percent of the subjects verbally complained when confederates conversed loudly during the movie.

Moriarty had his confederates act even more outrageously in yet another experiment conducted in Grand Central Station in New York City. This time the subjects were twenty men dressed in business suits using the pay phone. As each man finished his call, he was approached by the experimenter who asked the subject if he had seen a ring left in the booth. All subjects answered "No" since no ring was actually left. Then the experimenter said, "Are you sure you didn't see it? Sometimes people pick up things without thinking about it." Another denial followed, whereupon the experimenter asked each subject to empty his pockets as if to verify the subject's truthfulness. Remember, this is New York City, a place renowned for its aggressive citizens. Did the subjects tell the experimenter to take a hike? Did they verbally assault the experimenter for having the audacity to imply that subjects were being less than honest? You might expect such a response, but actually only four of the twenty subjects refused to comply. The rest, sixteen subjects (80 percent), emptied their pockets.

Considering previous evidence on compliance rates already cited, these results are not that surprising. We find it difficult to stand up for ourselves, so much so that some individuals have advertised their willingness to act as paid surrogate asserters. That's right! In Chicago, a woman named Marti Hough started her "Speak Up Service" from her home. For a small fee, she delivered messages for her reticent clients because they feared doing it themselves.

Questions for Thought

1. Does the pervasiveness of passivity derive mostly from shyness or does the fact that we live in a violent society, where volatile strangers may do harm to us if we are assertive, play a part?
2. How would you rate your own level of assertiveness? Are there some situations where you are assertive and others where you are either aggressive or passive? If so, which conditions produce aggressiveness and which passivity?

There are distinct <u>advantages to learning assertiveness</u>. The most obvious advantage is that you won't have to pay someone like Marti Hough to do your asserting for you. More importantly, self-assertion makes you a more significant person in a group. Your potential influence in group decision making will be enhanced. Passive members become isolates and are easily ignored by the group. Assertive members make their presence felt and express their ideas and feelings to the group for consideration. This increases the group's resources and helps promote group synergy.

Assertiveness is empowering. Dipboyle and Wiley (1977) found that job recruiters deemed assertive candidates to be more suited to supervisory positions than nonassertive candidates. In addition, assertive candidates were more frequently invited for a second interview and their qualifications were perceived more positively than nonassertive candidates even though there was no actual difference.

Assertiveness may also prove to be life-saving. Following an airline crash in 1978, the National Transportation and Safety Board recommended that training for cockpit crews include assertiveness, implying that the lack of assertiveness was a causal factor in the crash (Foushee, 1984). In another incident, a jet slid off the runway because of excessive speed. Although the captain was apparently unaware of the excessive speed, the first officer knew but could only manage a sheepish comment about a possible tailwind.

<u>The competent communicator, however, cannot assume that assertiveness is always appropriate</u>. Mathison (1987) discovered that while male managers reported positive perceptions of assertive communication from female managers, other female professionals reported negative perceptions of assertive female managers.

Part of the explanation for the negative reaction among female professionals may be the "Queen Bee Syndrome" previously discussed. Assertive women may be viewed as strong competitors. The Queen Bee may also find it difficult to identify with her female competitors since she had to adopt an aggressive male communication style in order to succeed in a male-dominated hierarchy.

Schmidt and Kipnis (1987) also discovered that you can be overly persistent in asserting yourself. They found that excessive assertiveness can result in less favorable evaluations from supervisors, lower salaries, greater job tension, and greater personal stress than a less-vigorous assertion of one's needs and desires.

Cultural differences must also be taken into account. Assertiveness is not valued in Japan and many Asian cultures (Samovar and Porter, 1995). Standing up for yourself and speaking your mind are seen as disruptive and provocative acts likely to create disharmony. North American Native Indians "have developed a distaste for Western assertiveness and tend to avoid those who interact in assertive ways" (Moghaddam et al., 1993, p. 124).

<u>These results underline how important it is that you not assume that assertiveness is always preferable to passivity or aggressiveness in every circumstance</u>. The advantages and disadvantages must be weighed within each context. This is, of course, standard operating procedure for any competent communicator. As a general rule, however, assertiveness is empowering, es-

pecially in American culture, and more advantageous with far fewer and less severe disadvantages than aggressiveness or passivity.

So how do you become more assertive? Bower and Bower (1980) provide a useful framework for learning assertiveness. They call it **DESC** Scripting. The **D** is for *describe;* **E** is for *express;* **S** is for *specify;* and **C** is for *consequences.*

D*escribe:* When there is a conflict between you and group members, you initiate resolution of the conflict by first <u>describing the behavior that is trouble-some</u>. My previous discussion of descriptiveness as a supportive alternative to evaluation that produces defensiveness applies here. To recapitulate, descriptiveness requires first person singular language, specificity, and elimination of editorial comments. Thus, description does not in-volve denouncement of the offending party. For example, instead of attacking the offender (e.g., "That does it! You're not going to get away with stealing any more of my ideas."), you describe as precisely as pos-sible what behavior irks you (e.g., "Last week I suggested we reorganize the program. Now I see my idea attributed to you. I think I deserve an explanation.").

E*xpress:* Here you <u>express how you think and feel</u> about the offending behavior. Again, this is not a verbal assault on the offender. All an attack will do is precipitate defensiveness and counterattack. Instead, you formulate a state-ment from your perspective (e.g., "I believe," "I feel," "I disagree"). The express step is not an opportunity for finger pointing and accu-sation (e.g., "You made me feel . . ."). This step requires a statement of per-sonal reaction from you to the offensive behavior from another group member.

S*pecify:* This step <u>identifies the behavior you would like to see substituted for the bothersome behavior</u>. Once more, the request needs to be concrete and spelled out, not vague or merely suggestive. "I think it is only fair that I receive sole credit for this proposal, and in the future I expect to receive credit for my ideas" is better than "I want you to stop plagiarizing my ideas immediately."

C*onsequences:* The <u>consequences of changing behavior or continuing the same behavior patterns should be articulated to the offending party</u>. The em-phasis, if possible, should be on rewards, not punishments. "I like working here and expect to continue as long as I'm treated fairly" is better than "If you continue to steal my ideas I'll be forced to quit."

The **DESC** guidelines for assertiveness will prove to be nothing more than an idealized fantasy cooked up by academic types unless "powerless" language and anemic nonverbal behavior are eliminated from the process. Description should not include requests for permission to speak, think, or disagree. Scrap the "Do you mind if I" or the "If it's okay with you, may I please speak with you" forms of passivity. Replace permission requests with direct declarative statements, such as, "I'd like to discuss this matter with you," or "I need to schedule a meeting with you."

Expressing your thoughts and feelings must be accomplished with confidence and skill. This requires direct eye contact, not looks cast downward or side-to-side. Posture should be erect, not slouched in a cowering "whipped puppy" stance. Tone of voice should be modulated so aggression doesn't spill out or passivity creep in. Tag questions, hedges, hesitations, disclaimers, and overly polite references should be minimized or eliminated if possible. If you are interrupted, calmly indicate, "I'm not finished with my thought."

Everything I've suggested regarding how to be assertive requires practice. To become a competent communicator you must be willing to expend some energy honing your skills. In some circumstances, you will find that assertiveness is far easier than in others. In a few instances, assertiveness may be unwise. Some individuals become physically threatening when crossed in any way. Some powerful individuals feel threatened by a direct, no-nonsense style of resolving disagreements.

Nevertheless, I strongly advocate a direct, assertive communication style in all but a few exceptional situations. Passivity is "powerless" communication—a ticket to nowhere. Aggressiveness is contagious. Combative communication can easily escalate into nasty scenes and unfortunate outcomes.

Increasing Personal Power Resources   Since the group confers power on the individual, a person can enhance his or her power by increasing personal resources valued by the group. There are a number of avenues available for personal power enhancement.

First, women who have been homemakers may increase their value in the family by returning to college, earning a degree, and finding employment. The additional income obviously has systemwide implications. The entire family benefits from extra money. In turn, the wife and mother becomes a "professional" with all the prestige that is accorded such a title. Her self-esteem may be bolstered by her sense of independence resulting from a college education and employment in her field of study.

Husbands who assume a greater portion of the domestic chores may increase their value in the family. Children whose parents are unemployed or underemployed can exercise greater power if they find a part-time job to supplement family income.

Second, learning certain skills valued by the group can enhance your power position. If you master the skills required to use computers and no one in your group is computer-literate, then your power increases when the group requires such technical expertise.

Third, developing a close friendship or intimate relationship with a powerful member of a group can enhance your power position. This is often a premise of numerous cheap and sleazy novels that occupy our summer vacations. If an adult marries into a family and becomes a stepparent, legitimate authority is enhanced. If the children do not accept the new parent, however, conflict can easily arise in the family.

Finally, the *mentoring* and *networking* processes can enhance personal power resources. **Mentors** are knowledgeable individuals who have achieved some success in their profession or jobs and who assist individuals trying to get started in a line of work. Mentors can provide information to the newcomer that prevents mistakes by trial and error. Mentoring seems to have been especially useful for women in their rise to upper echelons of organizations (Noe, 1988). One study showed that women who have mentors move up the corporate ladder much faster than women without mentors. Women also receive more promotions faster when they are helped by mentors (in Kleiman, 1991). Mentors are essential for women trying to advance to the highest levels of corporate leadership (Hackman and Johnson, 1996).

Networking is a form of group empowerment. Individuals with similar backgrounds, skills, and goals come together on a fairly regular basis and share information that will assist members in pursuing goals. Networks also provide emotional support for members, especially in women's networks (Stewart et al., 1990).

 SECOND LOOK

Significance (Empowerment)

Assertiveness
- **D**escribe the behavior that is troublesome
- **E**xpress how you think and feel about the offending behavior
- **S**pecify behavior preferred as a substitute for bothersome behavior
- **C**onsequences of changing behavior or continuing without change should be articulated

Increasing Personal Power Resources
- Personal improvement
- Learn valued skills
- Develop close relationship with powerful group member
- Mentoring and networking

In summary, an imbalance of power in groups promotes conflict and power struggles, and in some instances can lead to violence. The five ways we transact power in groups, especially when power is unequally distributed, are compliance, alliance, resistance, defiance, and significance. Compliance primarily aims to bring the less powerful in line with the dictates of the more powerful and to discourage deviance, which can be contagious. Alliance, resistance, defiance, and significance are all means used by members to balance the power more equitably in small groups.

QUESTIONS FOR CRITICAL THINKERS

1. Field research supports altruism as a very powerful compliance-gaining strategy. Do your own experiences and observations agree with this assessment?
2. Have you ever used resistance strategies? Did they work? Were they used against dominant individuals?
3. Can you think of instances in your own experience where assertiveness was inappropriate?

Conflict Management in Groups

John Dewey observed many years ago that conflict "stirs us to observation and memory. It instigates invention. It shocks us out of sheep-like passivity, and sets us at noting and contriving." Brent Rubin (1978) provides a similar kind of statement when he argues that "conflict is not only essential to the growth, change, and evolution of living systems, but it is, as well, a system's primary defense against stagnation, detachment, entropy, and even extinction" (p. 202). So, what do you think? Would you rather have conflict in your group or not? My guess is that most of you would opt for conflict-free group experiences if you were given a choice.

I also believe that conflict can be a constructive force in small groups, but I appreciate the widespread wish to avoid conflict if possible. Entering into a struggle with another party or parties can be quite disconcerting. There's tension, unpleasantness, vulnerability, and uncertainty in most conflict transactions. I'm convinced, however, that it is the uncertainty inherent in conflict that produces the greatest unease. What will happen if I do X? Our imaginations can easily shift us into disaster mode. Most people feel ill-prepared and ill-equipped to deal effectively with life's disputes. Disaster can seem to be ever-lurking in the dark shadows when our alternatives are unclear and our confidence in our own abilities to handle conflict constructively is shaky.

Nevertheless, conflict is a fact of group life. About a quarter of a manager's time is spent dealing directly with conflicts in groups (Thomas and Schmidt, 1976). A group composed of members living in perfect harmony is a fiction. Even striving for such an illusory goal can easily degenerate into groupthink. The absence of conflict in small groups may indicate sluggishness, apathy, and disinterest, all of which normally result in low productivity and may lead to the eventual disintegration of the group.

My purpose here is to show you ways to manage conflict constructively in groups, not to teach you ways of avoiding conflict and becoming boringly harmonious. Unquestionably, if conflict is handled ineffectually, group productivity, cohesiveness, and satisfaction will be threatened. Conflict, managed poorly, can tear a group asunder. Incapacitation and serious disruption of the group can be prevented, however, if you learn to manage conflict adroitly.

In previous chapters, I have already discussed at length several sources of conflict and their corresponding antidotes. Briefly, these are:

Sources	Solutions
Competitive group climate	Structure cooperative group climate
Defensive communication patterns	Structure supportive communication
Self-centered disruptive roles	Adopt strategies for dealing with difficult group members
Imbalance of power	Balance power among group members
Conflicts of interest	Integrative problem solving

I wish to build on this foundation of previous discussion by accomplishing these three <u>objectives</u>:

1. define conflict specifically,
2. explain the communication styles available for dealing with conflict, and
3. discuss how to effectively transact conflict in small groups.

DEFINITIONS OF TERMS

Consider the following events (based on a real situation) as a case study illustrating conflict:

Village Haven Townhomes

Once upon a time there was a quiet little condominium complex composed of eighteen units beside a meandering creek in a forest setting. The residents enjoyed seeing the deer wander down in the evening from their habitat above the complex. Wildlife was abundant. A climate of tranquillity enveloped this special place.

Then one day, bulldozers and earth movers of every variety rumbled in unannounced. Peace and quiet were abruptly replaced by ear-splitting noise, incessant vibration from the heavy equipment thundering back and forth across the once-emerald terrain. Families residing in Village Haven were understandably shaken by the realization that thirty-two additional units were about to be squeezed onto every speck of available space a mere thirty feet across from the original eighteen residences.

The situation, however, did not improve once construction of the condos began. Residents were awakened regularly at 6:30 a.m. on weekdays and sometimes on weekends to the sounds of hammering, sawing, and shouting from workers. Cars previously parked along the curb of the one-way road into and out of the complex had to be moved to a small paved area in the center of the development where bulldozers and forklifts whizzed by, showering the autos with dirt and debris. Tires were regularly punctured by nails strewn across the road by careless workers. Huge trucks and construction equipment frequently blocked the single-lane road into and out of the complex, stranding residents in their cars, sometimes for ten to fifteen minutes. Residents occasionally found pathways to their homes dangerous to traverse.

At one point, a signed message from the developer and contractor was taped to the doors of the condos. Residents were instructed to remove their cars from the street so "demolition and reconstruction" could take place. Residents were now ordered to park their cars on a street overlooking the complex about two blocks up a very steep, poorly lighted hill. During the demolition, two residents had stereos stolen out of their cars while parked on this street. The homeowners as a group were not happy!

The inhabitants of Village Haven, working under the auspices of the complex's Homeowners Association, considered legal action, but ran into numerous technical and political roadblocks. The developer and the contractor were asked to begin construction at 8 a.m. instead of 6:30 a.m. Residents were informed that early starts were "the nature of construction" and couldn't be changed. When representatives of the association raised objections to the edict requiring removal of all cars to the street above, they were told that this was an unavoidable inconvenience. Several residents got into shouting matches with the developer and the contractor.

Vandalism started to crop up here and there. The professionally painted sign at the entrance to the complex that read, "Village Haven Forest Townhomes," was painted over to read, "Village of the Damned." Another sign that read, "Welcome to Village Haven" was changed to read, "Welcome to Hell." Windows freshly installed in new units were sporadically smashed. Security patrols were increased to thwart the vandals, with little apparent success.

A few days after the message ordering the removal of all cars from paved areas was attached to residents' doors, a tongue-in-cheek message appeared on everyone's doorstep. Attributed to the contractor and developer (real author unknown), but obviously intended as an underground satirical jibe at these two individuals, the message was addressed to Village Haven Residents and purported to answer complaints from homeowners. The bogus message was signed under the names of the contractor and developer, with the appellation "The Village Idiots" added.

Frustrated and weary, residents began listing their units for sale. The project was finally completed, some of the original residents left, but the animosities lingered.

Definition of Conflict

The Village Haven Townhomes battle provides us with a means of explaining the definition of conflict in a group context, which is as follows: **Conflict** is the interaction of interconnected parties who perceive incompatible goals and interference from each other in attaining those goals. This definition is a slightly modified version of that offered by Hocker and Wilmot (1995) and Folger and his associates (1993). Let me explain each element of my definition in terms of the Village Haven fracas.

First, conflict in groups requires <u>interaction</u> between parties. Conflict is not a solitary endeavor. If the homeowners of Village Haven had merely sat and stewed over perceived outrages, then no conflict would have existed because the developer and contractor wouldn't have known there was a problem. Parties in conflict act and react to one another, sometimes over long periods. Often this interaction is manifested in shouting matches, such as occurred between the residents of Village Haven and the developer and contractor. Sometimes interaction is more indirect, such as the exchange of written messages placed on residents' doorsteps. Occasionally, the interaction is of a nonverbal nature. Vandalism and the reaction to it (beefed-up security) are examples from the Village Haven conflict.

Second, conflict occurs between <u>interconnected parties</u> in a group system. (Some experts prefer the term *interdependent,* but *dependence* denotes submission, thus suggesting that interdependence is mutual submission. I prefer *interconnected* because it strikes me as a more neutral term.) *Interconnected parties* means that for a conflict to exist, the behavior of one or more parties must produce consequences for the other party or parties. The invasion of the bulldozers significantly affected the residents of Village Haven. Likewise, the developer and contractor could not completely ignore residents' reactions. People shouting at them, needling them in a bogus message, and vandalizing property (although it is unclear whether residents were actually the vandals) are acts difficult to ignore.

Third, conflict involves <u>perceived incompatible goals</u>. Sometimes we perceive incompatible goals where none exist. This perception, however, is reality until both parties are convinced that they are not working toward mutually exclusive goals. In other cases, the goals are incompatible. The residents of Village Haven would have preferred an eighteen-unit complex to a fifty-unit complex. The developer and contractor couldn't make any money that way. The goal of the builders to erect thirty-two additional units collided squarely with the desire of the residents for peace and quiet. Construction is obtrusive and disruptive. Other goals were perceived at least by one party to be incompatible, but probably didn't need to be. A plan to begin construction later than 6:30 in the morning and reduce some of the frustrating side effects of living in the middle of a construction zone (e.g., nails in the road, or equipment blocking access to residents' units) should have been achievable.

Finally, conflict involves <u>interference from each other</u> in attaining desired goals. Unless one party attempts to block the attainment of another party's goal, there is no conflict. You and I may interact and be interconnected parties, and we may even perceive our goals to be incompatible, yet conflict may not exist even then. You may, in an act of pure selflessness, assist me in the attainment of my goal at the expense of attaining your own goal. Interference must be present for conflict to exist.

In Village Haven, interference abounded. Builders interfered with residents' tranquillity and convenience and transformed the environment from a low-density to a high-density development. None of the original occupants wanted this change. Residents' reaction to this interference was interference of their own in the form of verbal abuse and vandalism (again assuming the culprits were residents).

Conflict Resolution versus Management

The two terms used most frequently to describe the process for dealing with conflict are *resolution* and *management*. I have chosen the term management because it is more appropriate for a systems perspective of small-group communication. Resolution suggests settling conflict or terminating the struggle, as if ending conflict by any means is always desirable. Since conflict can be an essential catalyst for growth in a system, resolving conflict is not necessarily desirable. In some instances, increasing conflict may be required to evoke change. Civil rights demonstrators purposely provoked conflict to challenge racist laws in the South. Women who file sexual harassment lawsuits provoke conflict in order to end an evil.

Managing conflict implies no end to the struggle. Although some conflict episodes do end within a group and are therefore resolved, conflict overall in a system is a continuous phenomenon varying only in intensity. Management of conflict also implies no judgment on the goodness or badness of struggles in general.

Effectively managing conflict means keeping the struggle constructive, not allowing it to become destructive (Lulofs, 1994). *Constructive conflict* is characterized by flexibility. You adapt to changing circumstances and situations without getting locked into a one-style-fits-all approach. *Destructive conflict* is characterized by a tendency to escalate the conflict while losing sight of primary goals and issues. Attention gets diverted to inflicting punishment on an antagonist, seeking revenge, or dominating others.

STYLES OF CONFLICT MANAGEMENT

Communication is central to conflict in groups. Our communication can signal that conflict exists, it can create conflict, and it can be the means for managing conflict constructively or destructively (Hocker and Wilmot, 1995). Consequently, communication styles have been the center of much research and discussion. A communication style is an orientation toward conflict (Folger et al., 1993). Styles exhibit predispositions or tendencies regarding the way conflict is managed in groups.

Blake and Mouton (1964) initiated the styles approach to conflict management. Kilmann and Thomas (1977) elaborated and modified the styles approach. There are five communication styles of conflict management articulated by these theorists. I will explain each of the five styles adding some modifications of my own.

Focus Questions

1. How do communication styles of conflict management differ on task and social dimensions of small groups?
2. Should group members always use the collaborating style and avoid the competing (forcing) style?

Collaborating (Problem Solving)

The most complex and potentially productive conflict style is collaborating, or what some refer to as problem solving. Someone employing this style has a high concern for both task and social relationships in groups. The **collaborating** style recognizes the interconnection between the task and social components of groups and deals directly with both requirements. This is a win-win approach to conflict. The collaborating style attempts to satisfy all parties. This style is cooperative.

A collaborating style has two key components. The first is *confrontation*. When you confront, you bring conflict out into the open for examination. There is a recognition that conflict exists and must be faced directly or the clash will become dysfunctional for the group. Problems between parties in a dispute cannot be solved and the dispute resolved unless grievances and differences are discussed openly.

Although the news media are fond of using the term confrontation in a negative sense, as in "There was a violent confrontation between protesters and police," this is not the meaning relevant to this discussion. Confrontation as a conflict style incorporates all the elements already discussed at length regarding assertiveness (describe, express, specify, and consequences), supportive communication patterns (description, problem orientation, etc.), and consensus decision making. The purpose of confrontation is to manage conflict in a productive way for all parties involved.

Not all issues are worth confronting. Members who confront even trivial differences of opinion or can't let a momentary flash of pique go unattended can be quite tiresome. Groups have to decide which issues and concerns are priorities and which are tangential. You can overuse confrontation and make yourself a nuisance.

The second component of collaboration is *integration*. Since I have already discussed how to find integrative solutions to problems in Chapter Seven, I will not belabor the point. Integration as a collaborative technique, however, has not been given the attention that it deserves. Brett and her associates (1990) argue that negotiators in organizations are better at maximizing their own gains (competitive) than they are at maximizing joint gains (integrative). Pruitt (1981) also notes that negotiators tend to reach agreement on the first satisfactory proposal that comes along rather than looking for a better solution. Training through lecture, reading, and exercises, however, has excellent success in improving integrative skills of group members (Neale et al., 1988).

Since confrontation and integration are such effective communication techniques for solving conflicts of interest, why aren't they always used in these situations? There are several reasons. Using confrontation and integration usually requires a significant investment of time and effort along with greater-than-ordinary communication skills. Even if you are willing and able to employ these techniques, collaboration requires mutually agreeable parties. I have witnessed several instances where an integrative solution was constructed, yet the group rejected it because the members disliked the person who originated the proposal. Collaboration is built on trust. If parties are suspicious of each other and worry that one will betray the other by not honoring agreements, then even an integrative solution may be rejected. Also, parties in a conflict sometimes do not share the same psychological investment in finding an agreeable solution for all involved.

Accommodating (Smoothing)

A second communication style of conflict management is **accommodating** or what some refer to as smoothing. This style yields to the concerns and desires of others. Someone using this style shows a high concern for social relationships but low concern for task accomplishment. This style may camouflage deep divisions among group members in order to maintain the appearance of harmony. If the task can be accomplished without social disruption, fine. If accomplishing the task threatens to jeopardize the harmonious relationships within the group, however, a person using this style will opt for appeasing members, even though this may sacrifice productivity. Generally, group members with less power are expected to accommodate more often and to a greater degree than more powerful members (Lulofs, 1994).

Although we tend to view accommodating in a negative light, as appeasement with all its negative connotations, <u>this style can be quite positive</u>. A group that has experienced protracted strife may rejoice when one side accommodates even on an issue of only minor importance. Yielding on issues of incidental concern to you but of major concern to other parties can serve as a cooperative gesture. Group members who feel slighted or picked on during conflict interactions may need to have their ruffled feathers smoothed out. Tending to the concerns and needs of others, rather than merely looking out for number one, can be a constructive way of dealing with conflict and an indication of communication competence. Supportive, confirming remarks bolstering the image of group members who disagree with you can rejuvenate their interest in finding a viable solution to a problem. The remarks, of course, must seem genuine or they will exacerbate the tension and strife.

Compromising

When we compromise, we lower our expectations and goals. We give up something in order to get something. Some have referred to this as a lose-lose style of conflict management because neither party is ever fully satisfied with the solution. **Compromise** is a middle ground. Someone using <u>this style shows a moderate concern for both task and social relationships in groups</u>. The emphasis is on workable but not necessarily optimal solutions. Someone using this style shows moderate concern for group harmony but takes the attitude that a solution the group can live with should be satisfactory, if not exactly cause for celebration.

Compromise evokes ambivalence—both negative and positive reactions. We speak disparagingly of those who would "compromise their integrity." On some issues, usually moral or ethical conflicts such as abortion or capital punishment, compromise is thought to be intolerable. Pruitt and Rubin (1986) argue that compromise arises "from one of two sources—either lazy problem-solving involving a half-hearted attempt to satisfy the two parties' interests, or simply yielding by both parties" (p. 29). Yet despite this negative view of compromise, negotiations of labor-management contracts and political agreements are expected, even encouraged, to end in compromise. Members of task forces, ad hoc groups, and committees of many shapes and sizes often seek a compromise as an admirable goal.

Half a loaf is better than starvation—not in all circumstances, but certainly in some. When an integrative solution cannot be achieved, when a temporary settlement is the only feasible alternative, or when the issues involved are not considered critical to the group, compromise can be a useful conflict style.

◉◉ CLOSER LOOK

The Case of the Effective Compromise

<u>Compromise can be effective when used as a fallback approach after other styles have proved to be relatively unproductive</u>. I was once a member of an

academic search and selection task force composed of fifteen members and charged with writing specific procedures for hiring new faculty. One of the contentious issues that incited the most divisiveness concerned the presence of deans on hiring committees. This issue was debated at length with little progress. Virtually all faculty representatives on the task force wanted deans off the hiring committees. The faculty felt that having deans on such committees made candidate interviews and meetings for final selection difficult to schedule. In addition, choosing a colleague was thought to be outside the responsibilities of a dean, who usually had little or no knowledge of the relevant discipline. Also, their presence was thought to be intimidating because their power position could influence deliberations and even the final selection.

Management was adamant that deans remain because some overview of the process was essential if for no other reason than to protect the college from potential lawsuits on issues of Affirmative Action or committee bias. Management also felt an overall responsibility for ensuring that the college select the highest-quality candidates.

At one point in the deliberations, a proposal that deans remain on committees but have no voting power nor say in the final selection was offered. Initially, the proposal was virtually ignored. When it became apparent that stalemate was looming on the horizon, the same proposal was introduced a second time. Faculty were mostly opposed to it. Management seemed marginally satisfied with the compromise since they still had oversight of the committee process. In private, hesitant faculty members were encouraged to accept the compromise as a step toward the eventual elimination of deans from selection committees. The argument that the faculty could expect no better agreement at the moment was advanced vigorously by several committee members. Under this agreement, the deans may prove themselves irrelevant, making their elimination easier to argue in the future, so went the reasoning. The faculty accepted the proposal with resignation if not enthusiasm. Stalemate would have accomplished nothing after many hours of negotiations.

Questions for Thought

1. If none of the parties in conflict are actually happy with a compromise, how can it be viewed as effective?
2. How would you determine whether a compromise is acceptable or not?

Avoiding (Withdrawing)

Avoiding is a strategy of withdrawing from potentially contentious and unpleasant struggles. Gouran and Baird (1972) found that groups typically change the subject under discussion soon after a period of disagreement among members. *Flights from fights* may seem constructive at the time because they circumvent unpleasantness. In the long run, however, facing problems proves to be more effective than running from them. Someone using the avoiding conflict style shows little concern for both task and social relationships in groups. Avoiders shrink from conflict, even fear it. By avoiding conflict they hope it will disappear. Group tasks are sacrificed to a preoccupation with avoiding trouble. Social relationships within the group have scant possibility of improving when the conflict distorts the behavior of those doing the avoiding.

Avoiding, nevertheless, is sometimes appropriate. If you are a low-power person in a group and the consequences of confrontation are potentially hazardous to you, <u>avoiding might be a reasonable strategy until other alternatives present themselves</u>. Standing up to a bully at school may work out well in movies, but confronting antisocial types who look like they eat raw meat for breakfast and might eat you for lunch may not be a very bright choice. Staying out of a bully's way, although not ego-boosting, may be the best *temporary option in a bad situation.*

The study of family violence by Gelles and Straus (1988), based on interviews of more than 6,000 individuals, found avoiding to be <u>a sometimes effective strategy for dealing with spousal violence</u>. Avoiding was the most common method women used for dealing with physical abuse. Sixty-eight percent of women whose husbands had pushed, slapped, shoved, or thrown things at them said that simply keeping out of their husband's way and trying to anticipate what they should avoid saying or doing that might anger their husbands proved to be an effective strategy for preventing further physical abuse. *Fewer than a third* of those women, however, whose husbands had choked, beaten, punched, or kicked them found that avoiding was an effective approach to prevention of further violence against them.

By inference, children in a family dominated by an abuser would also find avoiding a sometimes necessary strategy for dealing with an ugly situation. Children learn avoiding as a strategy of survival when one or both parents are abusers.

Preventing violence in this manner, of course, can take its toll on the victims' self-esteem and sense of personal power. This style of conflict management is hard to recommend except in the most dire situations where <u>avoiding may be a temporary expedient necessary for self-protection</u>. Avoiding to prevent being pulverized promotes a dominance power perspective. Living in fear of triggering a spouse's or parent's violent rages through even the most innocent comment or innocuous behavior puts the abuser in charge of the lives of the less powerful family members.

<u>If the advantages of confrontation do not outweigh the disadvantages, avoiding the conflict might be a desirable course of action</u>. In some cases, tempers need to cool. Avoiding contentious issues for a time may prove to be constructive. When passions run high, reason usually trails far behind. We often make foolish, irrational choices when we are stressed out.

<u>In most cases, however, avoiding rather than confronting is highly counterproductive</u>. From their research, Gelles and Straus (1988) conclude: "Delaying until the violence escalates to a frequency or severity that would generally be considered abusive is too late. A firm, emphatic, and rational approach appears to be the most effective personal strategy a woman can use to prevent future violence" (p. 159). They suggest *confronting the very first incident of even minor violence*, not waiting to see if it happens again before firmly communicating to the perpetrator of the violence that such behavior is unacceptable and must stop.

Competing (Forcing)

The **competing** or forcing style flows from the dominance perspective on power. Competing and forcing your will on others is a win-lose style. Someone using a competing or forcing style shows high concern for task but low concern for relationships in groups. Task comes first. If accomplishing the group task requires a few wounded egos, that is the price of productivity. Someone using the competing/forcing style sees task accomplishment as a means of furthering personal more than group goals (Me-not-We orientation). Making friends and developing a positive social climate is secondary and expendable.

Since I have already discussed at length the consequences of competitiveness, communication patterns that aim to control others, and power imbalances, I will not belabor the problems associated with a competing/forcing style. As with all other styles, however, this style also has its constructive side. If a troublemaker in the group shows no signs of ending disruptions and the seriousness of the situation is clear, then forcing out this difficult member may be the correct choice. As I have noted, one person can affect the entire group because in a system all components are interconnected. Eliminating a troublemaker can revitalize the remaining members and allow progress on the task to proceed unimpeded.

Competing/forcing is a style of last resort, except in times of emergencies in which quick, decisive action must be taken and discussion has no place. If all other approaches to conflict produce little result, then competing/forcing may be a necessary means of managing the dispute.

 **SECOND LOOK**

Communication Styles of Conflict Management

Style	Task-Social Dimension
Collaborating (Problem Solving)	High task, high social
Accommodating (Smoothing)	Low task, high social
Compromising	Moderate task, moderate social
Avoiding (Withdrawing)	Low task, low social
Competing (Forcing)	High task, low social

All five styles of conflict management exhibit predispositions or tendencies. These predispositions, however, are not 100 percent predictable. Someone using the competing/forcing style may, in some circumstances, manifest genuine concern for social climate. Low concern doesn't mean no concern. An accommodator on occasion may regard the task accomplishment as vital. All of these styles represent standard operating procedures, not unalterably fixed ways of managing conflict.

As a general rule, <u>research clearly favors some conflict styles over others</u>. Burke (1970) reported several studies comparing the five principal conflict styles. Confrontation (collaborating) and smoothing (accommodating) were more successful methods for managing conflict than were forcing (competing) and withdrawal (avoidance). Phillips and Cheston (1979) compared problem solving and forcing styles in fifty-two conflict cases. Forcing was used twice as often as problem solving, yet in about half the situations where forcing was used the outcomes were bad, whereas in all instances where problem solving was used the outcomes were good. More recently, a scant 5 percent of first-line supervisors, middle managers, and top managers and administrators admitted to actually using the collaborating style in specific conflict situations while 41 percent selected competing and 26 percent chose avoiding styles (Gayle, 1991). Both male and female supervisors and managers, according to this study, typically select the least effective styles of conflict management.

<u>The competent communicator tends to use the collaborating/problem-solving conflict style, whereas the less-competent communicator opts most often for competing/forcing</u> (Conrad, 1983). Overall, the collaborating style in a variety of contexts produces better decisions and greater satisfaction from parties in conflict (Gayle-Hackett, 1989; Tutzauer and Roloff, 1988).

The results of research comparing the effectiveness of conflict styles are not surprising. I've already discussed at length the negative aspects of competing. Psychological reactance is the likely response to forcing. The collaborative/problem solving style is a win-win cooperative approach to conflict. Since the goal is to satisfy all parties, collaboration by its very nature should prove to be a more effective style in a greater number and variety of instances than competing/forcing.

<u>Overall, the probabilities of successfully managing conflict are higher with collaborating/problem solving than with competing/forcing</u>. As Fisher (1980) states, "When in doubt, confront" (p. 252). He further states, "Avoiding any type of conflict is the most ineffective method of management" (p. 252). Fisher overstates his case, but not by much.

Probabilities, however, do not mean certainties. Thus, the danger of over-emphasizing the superior probabilities of one style over another can produce rigidity, making adaptation to change in the system difficult. Flexibility is a key ingredient of communication competence. Individuals can become locked into a ritualistic, inflexible pattern of conflict management where every time a conflict arises, the same conflict styles are employed, regardless of the circumstances. Some people with tripwire tempers escalate conflicts into pyrotechnic events with annoying regularity no matter how minor the provocation. Others avoid conflicts or accommodate antagonists, never attempting to confront or find an integrative solution.

<u>Within systems, inflexible patterns of managing conflict can lead to interlocking behavior whose rigidity stymies effective management of disputes</u>. Parents may use competing/forcing styles to deal with all clashes with their children. "Do what I say and don't ask questions." The children reluctantly may, in turn, accommodate the parents because they fear the consequences, but resentment and hostility build with each act of yielding, and the family unit

experiences recurrent tensions and strife. Group leaders may try to confront every difference of opinion among members, producing frustration and annoyance because the leader seems incapable of discriminating between important and trivial differences. Effective conflict management is adaptive, not rigid.

TRANSACTING CONFLICT

Conflict is a transactional process. To understand how to transact conflict effectively in a small-group context, I will discuss three areas: primary situational variables, the problem of escalating spirals of conflict, and negotiating strategies.

Focus Questions
1. How do group members short-circuit conflict spirals?
2. Why is principled negotiation superior to other negotiating strategies?

Primary Situational Variables

Conflict styles function within a system, so they must be adapted to the changing dynamics of the group. Although some conflict styles have a higher probability of effectiveness than do others, the choice of styles always operates within a context. Effective conflict management is not a matter of deciding out of context what styles will be employed. "I think I'll use mostly collaborating/problem solving today and maybe round that out with a bit of accommodating/smoothing, but tomorrow I'm all competing/forcing, so look out" would be the strategy of the lame communicator.

Nature of the Conflict   The first situational variable that should be considered when deciding how to transact conflict in groups is the nature of the conflict. For instance, is the struggle primarily a *content or relationship issue*? At a college where I was employed, the faculty union and management engaged in bitter negotiations for two years. Resources were tight. The union's opening position called for a salary increase of 4 percent one year and 5 percent the next. Management countered with opening offers of 1 percent and 0 percent salary increase respectively. Management apparently hoped to send a message to the union that tough bargaining was ahead. The message received was quite different. Faculty members felt unvalued and were incensed by what they perceived to be an insulting and contemptible initial offer.

Management miscalculated. A tense, combative climate permeated the bargaining. Even though management eventually accepted the initial salary increase the union proposed, which should have been viewed as an achievement by the union, a residue of hard feelings remained. The nature of the conflict was relational rather than content-based. The dollars and cents proved to be less important than the attitude management communicated to the faculty. If you damage the relationship between disputing parties, even concessions or an integrative solution may not wash away the stains of ill feelings. The conflict may take on a different dimension of a more personal nature.

The following year, management shifted to a collaborative style of bargaining, made a reasonable opening offer, and negotiations were completed in record time without the bitter recriminations. If you focus on content issues when the conflict is primarily relational, you're headed for disaster.

A second aspect of the nature of the conflict is *how deeply held are the beliefs and values* that are at the source of the dispute among members (Borisoff and Victor, 1989). <u>The most difficult disputes to manage are value conflicts.</u> We may clash over ideas and still walk away friends, especially if the ideas do not touch on deeply held values. Beliefs such as, "Republicans favor big business," or "Alcoholism is not a disease" may provoke animated dissent among group members, but civility is usually maintained. When disputes over ideas and beliefs spill over into value clashes, however, especially when the values are held passionately, then you have a conflict of a different ilk. Battles over abortion, pornography, creationism versus evolution, flag-burning, hate speech, and the like leave little if any room for compromise. When dichotomous battle lines are drawn—friends versus enemies, saviors versus sinners—forcing is often the style required for conflict management. The courts have had to settle these issues by declaring what is permissible, even essential, and what is prohibited.

Values conflicts are especially difficult to manage when members of different cultures clash over divergent worldviews. Rubenstein (1975) presented a hypothetical situation to Arabs and Americans. Suppose that a small boat is occupied by a man and his wife, mother, and child when it capsizes. The man is the only one of the occupants who can swim. The man can save only one of the three nonswimmers. Which person should he save? All of the Arabs asked by Rubenstein would save the mother because a wife and child can be replaced, but not a mother. Sixty of 100 American college freshmen, however, would save the wife and forty would save the child. Saving the mother while sacrificing the wife and child was thought to be laughable. Intercultural value conflicts are probably the most difficult to manage.

When the nature of the conflict is *a power struggle,* the choice of styles will depend on the relative power relationships between the parties involved. A conflict between relative equals sets the stage for a collaborative effort or, at the very least, compromise. Conflicts between relative unequals, however, may require more accommodating and avoiding on the part of the low-power parties in the group than would be necessary if the power was more balanced.

Conflict is transactional. You choose your styles of conflict management within the context of communication choices made by all parties in the conflict. What one person does affects other group members. Low-power group members may want to collaborate. Dominating high-power group members, however, may see little need to collaborate since they can impose their will on you. Granted, competing/forcing may be an unwise choice for the powerful parties in the long run, but it may be an unavoidable reality you have to face. Until you can balance the power more equitably by employing strategies of alliance, resistance, defiance, or significance, collaborating with unwilling, dominating group members is wishful thinking.

Years ago a friend of mine worked as a temporary employee in the company headquarters for a large retail firm. The firm had a system of rules that seemed to have little purpose except to control employees. Office workers were required to punch in and out for their fifteen-minute breaks. Managers, without consulting anyone, assigned specific times for subordinates to take their breaks. No personal possessions were permitted on subordinates' desks (managers had no such restriction). This meant employees were not allowed to display family photos, keepsakes, or any items that might reflect an individual's personality. Subordinates were "written up" by managers for every three instances of tardiness (even if one minute late). Two write-ups in one year meant termination. One woman, a ten-year employee and revered by all the nonmanagement workers, was written up twice. This occurred even though she called the office to report each time she was delayed by personal problems such as a sick child and a car wreck. She was terminated despite an exemplary record of service.

The workers erupted. Formerly docile employees became activists. Workers began demanding that the union show some teeth. Long-standing grievances were formally filed. Management was confronted about its heavy-handed forcing style. The response? "If you don't like the way we run things—leave." Many employees followed the advice. The result was predictable. The company began to fail, in no small part because of the incompetent communication patterns of management. The parent corporation stepped in. There was a major shakeup in management and the company was renamed. If the relatively powerful refuse to collaborate, then different conflict styles and strategies are required.

Nature of the Relationships The nature of the relationships among group members is a second situational factor that should be considered when transacting conflict. In actual practice, we do make style choices in terms of our relationships with the other parties. Forcing is the most common style managers use in handling differences with subordinates (Phillips and Cheston, 1979). Managers typically handle conflict with superiors and peers differently (Rahim, 1985). They are primarily accommodating with superiors and compromising with peers.

These style choices revealed in the research do not represent ideal choices. As previously indicated, the Phillips and Cheston (1979) study found forcing to be an ineffective style about half the time. Nevertheless, we **style shift,** flexibly adapting our communication to the changes in the system, depending on the nature of relationships between ourselves and others.

If our relationship is one of trust and cooperation, regardless of the power disparities, then collaborating has real potential. As Tjosvold (1985) discovered, high-power supervisors in cooperative environments actually used their power to *assist* subordinates in solving problems. This was not so true in environments characterized by a competitive or individualistic climate. If our relationship is one of mistrust and suspicion, then collaborating will be difficult. Riccillo and Trenholm (1983) found that coercion (forcing) is the style of choice among supervisors dealing with subordinates they do not trust.

In relationships poisoned by mistrust, a collaborative attempt by one party may be seen as a ploy to gain some unforeseen advantage. Accommodating by one party, even as a gesture to change the negative dynamics of the parties in conflict, may be viewed as weakness and a sign that capitulation is likely to occur after a period of waiting.

Timing A third situational factor that should be considered by group members when transacting conflict is timing. Confrontation can be a highly effective style but not when used as a hit-and-run tactic (Johnson and Johnson, 1987). Confronting contentious issues five minutes before the group is due to adjourn or just before you leave for a luncheon date provides no time for the other person to respond constructively. <u>**Hit-and-run confrontations** look like guerrilla tactics, not attempts to communicate competently and work out disputes.</u>

I have a friend who is fond of the hit-and-run confrontation. As the other person starts to respond to his revelation, he abruptly excuses himself, pleading an "urgent" appointment that can't be missed or a "Sorry, I'm late for work" apology. This timing is strategic. If you hit, then run, you don't take the risk of getting hit back, at least not right away. The target of the hit-and-run gets to stew over your revelation and fume over your perceived insensitivity. The perpetrator, however, likely feels relieved that a great weight has been lifted by his or her self-disclosure. If you're going to confront, make time for it.

<u>At what point you are in the conflict is another timing issue that should influence your choice of styles</u>. Forcing may be required at some point in the conflict, but as a first choice during the initial struggle, forcing is almost always an unwise decision. Forcing typically produces psychological reactance. If you try to force, are met with resistance, then attempt to collaborate or accommodate, you may find that this sequence of styles suffers from poor timing. Trying to collaborate after unsuccessfully forcing will be seen as the disingenuous act of a person whose bluff and bluster were challenged. On the other hand, temporarily withdrawing after a protracted feud has stalemated might allow heads to clear and passions to cool. Sometimes we just need a break from the struggle, a chance to think calmly and dispassionately.

Conflict Spirals

Minor conflicts can easily escalate into major conflicts spiraling out of control when groups are faced with failure, poor working conditions, intense competition, stress, or a defensive climate. Managing conflict in challenging circumstances can be difficult. French (1941), in an early study of escalating aggression as an outgrowth of conflict in groups, documented how quickly conflict can spiral out of control. Offensive remarks flew back and forth among group members so rapidly that observers could only estimate the total number. In a forty-five minute period while group members worked on an insoluble and frustrating task, observers estimated that more than 600 offensive remarks were made.

As already noted, the principle of reciprocation operates universally in all societies. When someone assists us we feel obligated to return the favor. The principle of reciprocation can be exploited as a powerful compliance-gaining strategy or inducement for cooperation in small groups. There is another side to the strategy, however, called **negative reciprocation.** Here those who do harm to us or threaten our well-being are thought to deserve harm or threats in return, and as Carroll (1987) found, <u>negative reciprocation tends to be stronger than its positive form</u>.

Group members often overreact to perceived threats or offenses especially from more-powerful members, setting in motion a destructive conflict spiral (Youngs, 1986). This overreaction has a chain reaction or ripple effect on the whole system. Disputing group members often do more than merely reciprocate each other's negative behavior in exact proportion. They usually ratchet up the level of negativity. A mildly abusive remark from one member may invite a more aggressive remark from a second member that may in turn incite a highly abusive and threatening remark from a third member, and so forth.

⊙⊙ CLOSER LOOK

KILL Radio Conflict Case Study

The Situation (based on a real event): Open warfare has been raging for almost a year at public radio station K-I-L-L (slogan: "Live radio that'll knock you dead"). The station operates from facilities on the campus of Bayview Community College in Tsunami, California. KILL radio has 1,000 watts of power, enough to reach into the local Tsunami community (population 42,000).

The program director quit after a feud with the general manager (GM). The GM resigned soon after. His reasons for leaving, stated in his letter of resignation, were as follows:

1. The volunteer staff (community members who were not students) inappropriately editorialized while reading news on the air and presented only one side on controversial issues, both violations of Federal Communications Commission (FCC) regulations for public radio stations;
2. The volunteers were "insubordinate" when they refused to obey his directives concerning substitution of other programs for previously scheduled regular shows; and
3. They threatened him with bodily injury when he ordered the volunteers either to implement his directives or terminate their association with the station.

The volunteer staff countered these allegations with its own accusations: the GM showed them little respect and treated them abusively; they were overworked and underappreciated; and the GM never sought their input on programming and scheduling concerns.

The volunteers issued the following demands:

1. Programming should not be determined by one person, but by a consensus of the staff;

2. Program substitution should be made only when prior notice (at least two weeks in advance) has been given so staff members will not prepare material destined to be preempted at the last minute; and

3. Volunteers should run the station since they do the lion's share of the work and are the only ones with the necessary technical expertise.

The college supports the station with $85,000 annually, but is seriously considering a drastic cut in the station's budget due to the persistent conflict and because students are not actively involved in the station. The administration wants the station to be a learning laboratory for students interested in pursuing careers in broadcasting.

The volunteer staff has threatened to quit en masse unless their demands are met. The school's board of trustees is getting twitchy because of all the commotion; the faculty in the Department of Mass Communication are in a dither about the conflict because it is disruptive. The local community highly values the station and is upset by the dispute. The college administration named the chair of the mass communication department at Bayview College as the new general manager and temporary program director of the station. *Before reading further, analyze this dispute.* How would you manage this conflict if you were the new GM? Which conflict styles would you employ? When? How?

The Analysis: The KILL radio dispute is a power struggle. Competing/ forcing has become the primary style of managing the conflict. The previous GM threatened the staff with termination and the staff threatened the GM with bodily injury. So far, the forcing style has produced two resignations, the threat of a mass exodus by the staff, several demands from the staff, and a reservoir of ill feeling and disruption. If you, as the new GM, were to continue in this vein by terminating the volunteer staff, you might ignite a conflict spiral. Disgruntled volunteers might vandalize the station in retaliation, and relations between the college and the community would be strained further. The station would have to shut down until qualified staff could be found to replace those individuals terminated. In such an atmosphere, the board and administration just might decide to close the station permanently and cut their losses.

Since the staff has not been actively consulted in the past regarding programming (at least that's the allegation, and perception is the "reality" you must confront), the climate is one of control, not problem orientation. The staff feels disconfirmed and defensive. The perception exists among them that the previous GM treated them as expendable technicians, not talented employees worthy of respect.

This situation cries out for collaboration. The first step is confrontation. The new GM should immediately meet with the volunteers, probably individually first, to gather information from their perspective. This is a relational issue as well as a content issue. Staff members feel unappreciated and undervalued. Supportive, confirming statements concerning the essential role volunteers play in the functioning of the station should be made to all involved. Smoothing statements (e.g., "We're starting fresh. I want us to work together") should be delivered to the staff. You're seeking a cooperative working relationship with the volunteers.

In keeping with the desire for cooperation, an appeal to the superordinate goal of keeping the station on the air should be delivered. The new GM must impress on the staff that violations of FCC regulations could result in the revocation of the station's operating license. This is not a matter of personal preference but of law. The GM could further state, "Unless we handle our differences constructively, the college out of exasperation may shut the station down. None of us wants this to happen." There should be no threats about firing anyone. The tone and climate should be positive and focused on the central goal all can agree to, namely, maintaining the station.

Although final say on the programming issue is the GM's responsibility, input from the staff should be sought actively and given serious consideration. After all, the staff has to make the programming work on the air. That's difficult to accomplish if you'd like to play rhythm-and-blues but are ordered to play country-western. The staff could conduct a survey of the community (this is a public radio station) to determine programming preferences of the station's audience. The GM could then make programming decisions based on data from the survey and not on personal tastes of a single individual or the (possibly narrow) preferences of the staff. One or two experimental programs could be tried as a compromise if community preferences do not match staff preferences in programming. Some compromise may be possible on program substitution (perhaps one week prior notice, not two as demanded).

Integrating the radio station into the college curriculum should be a fairly simple process. Involving students in the actual operation of the station, perhaps as supervised interns earning class credit, would satisfy a primary concern of the administration and board. This would also expand the resources of the station by training additional individuals to help staff members who already feel overworked.

Finally, the demand that the volunteers run the station would have to be denied. More than likely, however, this demand was made without any expectation that it would be accepted. Avoid this issue unless a staff member raises it. Forcing would be required if this issue came to a showdown. Handling other issues effectively may reduce this issue to irrelevance. If disruptions or violations of FCC regulations recur, then those responsible should be terminated.

The key to the management of this conflict by a competent communicator is the flexible use of several conflict styles. No single style alone could effectively manage this complex dispute. The overriding conflict style, however, is collaboration. You begin by confronting central concerns of disputing parties, not competing/forcing. You find integrative solutions where possible. Termination is a last resort, not a first choice. You compromise only when a better solution cannot be found. You smooth hurt feelings because a supportive environment is essential to the management of conflict. You avoid emotional issues that seem tangential to the real sources of the conflict and are likely to provoke a power struggle.

None of these styles of conflict management, of course, will work unless you think through each step before you take it *(act, don't just react)*. The competent communicator must have knowledge of different conflict styles, the skill to use all the styles, a sensitivity for the requirements of the specific situation and the likely outcomes of each choice made, and a commitment to resolving the dispute as equitably as possible. Complex conflicts require sufficient time to be resolved. This means patience.

Questions for Thought

1. Before you read the analysis of this case study, what action would you have proposed to resolve the conflict? In what ways were your proposals different from the ones suggested in the analysis?
2. Do you disagree with any suggestions provided in the analysis? Explain.

How do groups short-circuit conflict spirals? The basic role of the competent communicator is to avoid negative reciprocation. <u>You must not match the abusive, insulting, or threatening behavior of other group members</u>. This can be best explained by examining negotiating strategies, a final aspect of transacting conflict in small groups.

Negotiating Strategies

Fisher and Ury (1981), in their excellent book on negotiation, *Getting to Yes*, state: "More and more occasions require negotiation; conflict is a growth industry. . . . Whether in business, government, or the family, people reach most decisions through negotiation" (p. xi). **Negotiation** is defined as "a process by which a joint decision is made by two or more parties" (Pruitt, 1981, p. 1). In this section, I will discuss commonly used strategies of negotiating conflict.

Tit for Tat A first strategy of negotiating is called tit for tat. This is an "eye for an eye, smooch for a smooch" approach to negotiating. Tit for tat reciprocates or matches the behavior of the other party or parties after an initial effort is made to cooperate. You do to them what they did to you in the previous move. You begin by cooperating, but if they compete, then you compete. <u>Since negative reciprocation is more likely than positive reciprocation, a spiral of competitive tit for tat is the usual pattern among group members</u>.

Fisher and Brown (1988) question the advisability of using the tit for tat strategy. They conclude that "as a strategy for building a working relationship—for improving the way we deal with differences—tit for tat would be a mistake" (p. 200). They argue that "the best guideline for building and maintaining a good working relationship is to act in various ways that are unconditional—ways that do not reciprocate what another does . . ." (p. 197).

Those who tout tit for tat (Axelrod, 1984) can make a case for the utility of the strategy when cooperation does occur. Tit for tat will maintain cooperation once it has been initiated because you reciprocate an act of cooperation, thereby encouraging further cooperation from the other party. <u>Tit for tat, however, is an incompetent strategy when you look at its negative sequences of potential moves and countermoves</u>. For example, if someone threatens you in a conflict, should you automatically threaten them back? If your antagonist demands outrageous concessions from you, should you mindlessly match the demands? If someone tries to cheat, blackmail, or exploit you in a dispute, should you reciprocate in kind? If another party has a snit fit, should you likewise throw a temper tantrum? Does any of this sound to you like competent communication? As Fisher and Brown (1988) explain, "If you are acting in ways that injure your own competence, there is no reason for me to do the same. Two heads are better than one, but one is better than none" (p. 202). Tit for tat predisposes us to stoop to whatever level the other party is willing to sink.

The most serious objection to tit for tat, identified by Fisher and Brown, is the likelihood of an endless "malignant spiral" of escalating competitive behavior. In a group, if even one member competes, tit for tat requires that all members compete. Thus, one competitive individual can make the entire group competitive. Since negative reciprocation is more likely than positive reciprocation, a cooperative gesture by one member is less likely to transform competitive members into cooperative ones than vice versa.

Tit for tat offers no way to break the competitive spiral once it has been set in motion, except maybe through outright exhaustion of the combatants or by taking disputants to the brink of catastrophe. Let's assume that every member of your group adopts a tit for tat strategy and sticks to it unswervingly. How do you ever short-circuit a destructive cycle of antagonism when everyone is waiting for someone else to make the first cooperative move? Tit for tat as a negotiating strategy seems extremely limited and mostly counterproductive.

Reformed Sinner A second strategy of negotiating is called reformed sinner (Pruitt and Kimmel, 1977). Someone using this strategy initially competes or acts tough, then cooperates and relaxes demands. The inducement to cooperate is the demonstrated willingness to compete if necessary. Unlike tit for tat, you try to break a conflict spiral by making the first move toward cooperation.

A rather interesting version of the reformed sinner strategy is Osgood's (1959 and 1966) GRIT proposal. GRIT stands for **G**raduated and **R**eciprocated **I**nitiatives in **T**ension reduction. Originally offered as a means to de-escalate the international arms race, the strategy has been employed in less-global conflicts. Lindskild (1978) summarizes game theory research supporting the effectiveness of the principal steps in the proposal.

GRIT tries to break the malignant spiral of escalating competitive conflict by initiating a cycle of de-escalation using the following sequence of steps (see Folger et al., 1993, for greater detail):

1. Issue a sincere public statement expressing a desire to de-escalate the conflict.
2. Specify the concession to be made, clarifying what, when, and how the action will be undertaken.
3. Follow through and complete the concession, but do not make this contingent on reciprocation by the other parties.
4. Encourage, but do not demand, reciprocation from the other parties.
5. Make no high-risk concessions that leave you vulnerable or in an indefensible position. Don't give away the store.

Someone using this method of promoting cooperation in a competitive conflict situation should consider following the first concession with another concession if no progress is made after a time. Don't pile concession on concession, however, with nothing offered in return. This strategy may take patience and persistence. Offering a minor concession and then withdrawing it when no immediate reciprocation is forthcoming from the other party is not a true GRIT.

Positional Bargaining   In positional bargaining, parties take positions on contested issues, then haggle back and forth until concessions are made and an agreement is reached. There are two styles of positional bargaining—hard and soft. *Hard bargainers* (sometimes called tough bargainers) see negotiation as a contest of wills. Hard bargaining is the "negotiate from strength" approach to conflicts of interest heard so often in foreign affairs deliberations. The focus is on conveying strength and resilience so the other party or parties will yield.

Hard bargaining is a competing/forcing strategy. Hard bargainers can be abusive or sarcastic in an attempt to gain an advantage over the other party. When both sides adopt a hard bargaining style, the battle is joined. Both sides attempt to cut the best deal for themselves (Me-not-We-orientation), not find the most equitable and constructive solution to the conflicts of interest. Opening positions typically are extreme and unreasonable. The more hard bargainers publicly defend these positions, the more hardened the positions tend to become. Egos become identified with positions. Concessions easily take on the appearance of "selling out." Walking out on the negotiations in a huff, refusing to budge even on trivial issues, and issuing ultimatums are commonplace tactics in hard positional bargaining.

Consider this example of hard positional bargaining among housemates:

GROUP MEMBER A: I want to have a party here at the house on Saturday.

GROUP MEMBER B: Hey, that's a great idea.

GROUP MEMBER C: Sorry, no can do. I have to study for my law exam and I sure can't do that with a couple of dozen Neanderthals belching, retching, and cranking the music beyond 125 decibels. I'd have to lug a truckload of books and notes to the library or anywhere else I might choose to study.

GROUP MEMBER A: Who appointed you king? This is our house too. Since when do you dictate what can and can't happen around here?

GROUP MEMBER C: Since I pay a third of the rent and am not about to sacrifice my standing in law school so you twits can get drunk with your brain-dead friends and act like imbeciles. I'm vetoing your little beer bash.

GROUP MEMBER B: I don't even know why we're bothering to ask for your permission to hold this party. There's no way you can stop us anyway. I say we just go ahead and do it. If you don't like it, sue us, Perry Mason.

GROUP MEMBER A: Yeah! Get used to the idea because we're going to have this party and there isn't anything you can do about it.

GROUP MEMBER C: On the contrary, there is a great deal I can do about it. Suing you is actually an option that appeals to me. I could sue you for damages especially if I do poorly on the exam. I could also argue in small claims court that you violated a verbal contract not to have parties without the consent of all housemates—I have witnesses affirming that you both agreed to such an arrangement. So don't start issuing ultimatums unless you want this party to cost a lot more than the price of beer.

And on and on it goes, a contest of wills complete with recriminations, threats, name-calling, and anger.

Hard bargaining doesn't have to mean ruthless bargaining and obstinacy. Chertkoff and Esser (1976) found that a party can achieve positive results by acting tough. Bartos (1970) revealed that hard bargaining achieved excellent results when both parties were tough. Eventually, though, there has to be some give and take in order for a stalemate to be avoided if all parties assume a hard bargaining strategy.

The main difficulty with this strategy is how tough should you be without seeming pig-headed? As with any competitive strategy, when hard bargainers face off against one another, their moves and countermoves can easily produce an impasse. Hard bargainers lower the odds of reaching an agreement (Pavitt and Curtis, 1994). If other parties perceive your opening position as unreasonable, even outrageous, negotiations get off to a rocky start. Hard bargaining that produces yielding by the other parties is also likely to foster bitterness and anger. The key to making this a constructive conflict strategy is to appear tough but fair. When I hear an opening position that is clearly extreme, I have doubts about that party's commitment to a fair settlement. Hard bargainers can slip easily into tough battlers, and that usually spells W-A-R-F-A-R-E.

Warfare is what resulted from hard bargaining that led to the baseball strike of 1994–95. Owners and players both ended up losers. Owners lost $800 million in revenue during the strike and additional millions from lower attendance resulting from fan disgruntlement once the eight-month strike ended a few days into the 1995 season. Players lost $350 million in salaries (Blum, 1995). This doesn't include the vendors who generated no revenue from ballgames canceled and the fans who felt betrayed. This strike can be summarized easily: greed times greed equals greed squared. Hard bargaining can produce nothing but losers. *Soft bargainers,* recognizing the high costs of hard bargaining on relationships with people you may have to interact with once the negotiations are concluded, yield to pressure. To soft bargainers, making an agreement and remaining friends is more important than winning a victory. The major drawback to soft bargaining is that you may give away too much in order to maintain harmonious relationships during negotiations. Soft bargainers are reticent to offend housemates by refusing to allow a party. Hard bargainers eat soft bargainers for hors d'oeuvres.

Principled Negotiation Fisher and Ury (1981) offer a third choice besides hard and soft positional bargaining—**principled negotiation** or interest-based bargaining. Principled negotiation embodies the essential elements of competent communication. All negotiations are conducted according to rules.

Principled negotiation changes the rules from competitive (hard bargaining) to cooperative. The four basic elements to this approach with corresponding principles for each element are:

PEOPLE: Separate the people from the problem.
INTERESTS: Focus on interests, not positions.
OPTIONS: Generate a variety of possibilities before deciding what to do.
CRITERIA: Insist that the result be based on some objective standard. (Fisher and Ury, 1981, p. 11)

Separating the people from the problem reaffirms the importance of supportive climates (e.g., description, problem orientation, equality, or provisionalism) and the inappropriateness of defensive communication patterns (e.g., evaluation, control, superiority, or certainty) during negotiations. Principled negotiation also focuses on content conflicts and strives to reduce relationship conflicts during negotiations.

When Frank Lorenzo became president of Eastern Airlines in 1986, relations between management and labor immediately became tense and personal, and after a year of fruitless negotiations, Eastern's machinists and pilots went on strike. The machinist union targeted Lorenzo as the issue in negotiations, painting him as an unscrupulous takeover artist. The Airline Pilots Association characterized Lorenzo as a Machiavellian sleazeball whose middle name was Greed. Lorenzo fired back, calling the pilots' role in the strike "suicidal" and akin to the Jonestown tragedy. Eastern filed for bankruptcy, and thousands lost their jobs because the parties in conflict could not separate the people from the problem.

Negotiating interests first, not arguing positions, is critical. Positions differ from interests. For instance, a group in my class working on a symposium presentation got into a dispute over topic choice. Two members wanted the group to choose "The Greenhouse Effect." Two other members pushed for "Capital Punishment." The three remaining group members advocated "Animal Rights." Bickering broke out as each faction chose a hard bargaining approach. Nobody was willing to budge. The focus of the bargaining became the weaknesses of each topic advocated by one faction or the other. Putdowns, snide comments, and abusive remarks were flung back and forth.

When instructed to explore their interests, not the positions of each faction, the group found a mutually satisfactory solution. The capital punishment faction had already done a great deal of research on the topic for other classes. Their primary interest was time management since they had families who wanted them home. They wanted to "double dip" by using research for two classes not just one. The greenhouse effect faction turned out to have a similar interest. They had done some research on environmental issues. The animal rights faction simply wanted to do a presentation that dealt with an issue of values, not some "dry, scientific report of facts and figures on the environment."

Once the interests of each faction were identified and discussed, the greenhouse effect faction realized that the capital punishment faction had already done most of the necessary research for the entire group presentation. This was far more extensive than the research already completed by those urging the environmental topic. The animal rights group agreed that capital punishment was an issue of values as well as "facts and figures" so they settled on capital punishment as the group topic.

Positions are the concrete things one party wants. Interests are the intangible motivations—needs, desires, concerns, fears, aspirations—that lead a party in the conflict to take a position (Ury, 1993). The struggle over which topic best fulfills the assignment is a position, but time management is the interest behind the position. Interest answers the question *why* a party takes a position. Focusing on interests instead of positions underlines the importance of structuring cooperation into the deliberations. Positional bargaining structures negotiations as a win-lose game. Negotiating interests structures cooperation into the deliberations because the focus is on the problem and a mutually satisfactory solution, not on the position or the people advocating the position. Focusing on interests, not on positions, is the basis of integrative conflict management.

Generating a <u>variety of options</u> is another aspect of principled negotiation. This involves brainstorming, as already explained in my discussion of problem solving. Integration by expanding the pie or bridging may be discovered in a brainstorming session. The nominal group technique may also prove to be useful here.

Finally, principled negotiation rests on <u>objective standards</u> for weighing the merits and demerits of any proposal. In the conflict over topic choice just discussed, one primary objective standard that was agreed to was "the least number of hours doing research in the library." An objective standard for "fairness" might be that both parties share equally all risks and financial costs.

<u>A specific comparison between hard and soft positional bargaining and principled negotiation is presented in the table constructed by Fisher and Ury</u> (1981).

Positional bargaining and principled negotiation compared

PROBLEM		SOLUTION
Positional Bargaining: Which Game Should You Play?		Change the Game— Negotiate on the Merits
SOFT	**HARD**	**PRINCIPLED**
Participants are friends.	Participants are adversaries.	Participants are problem-solvers.
The goal is agreement.	The goal is victory.	The goal is a wise outcome reached efficiently and amicably.
Make concessions to cultivate the relationship.	Demand concessions as a condition of the relationship.	**Separate the people from the problem.**

SOFT	HARD	PRINCIPLED
Be soft on the people and the problem.	Be hard on the problem and the people.	Be soft on the people, hard on the problem.
Trust others.	Distrust others.	Proceed independent of trust.
Change your position easily.	Dig in to your position.	**Focus on interests, not positions.**
Make offers.	Make threats.	Explore interests.
Disclose your bottom line.	Mislead as to your bottom line.	Avoid having a bottom line.
Accept one-sided losses to reach agreement.	Demand one-sided gains as the price of agreement.	**Invent options for mutual gain.**
Search for the single answer: the one *they* will accept.	Search for the single answer: the one *you* will accept.	Develop multiple options to choose from; decide later.
Insist on agreement.	Insist on your position.	**Insist on using objective criteria.**
Try to avoid a contest of will.	Try to win a contest of will.	Try to reach a result based on standards independent of will.
Yield to pressure.	Apply pressure.	Reason and be open to reason; yield to principle, not pressure.

From Getting to Yes *by Roger Fisher and William Ury. Copyright © 1981 by Roger Fisher and William Ury. Reprinted by permission of Houghton Mifflin Co.*

The principled negotiation approach to conflicts of interest must include two additional elements. You must <u>be *unconditionally constructive*</u> (Fisher and Brown, 1988) and you must <u>develop a **BATNA**</u> (**B**est **A**lternative **T**o a Negotiated **A**greement).

Being unconditionally constructive means you make choices and take only those actions that benefit both you and the other parties in the dispute regardless of whether the other parties reciprocate. <u>Remaining unconditionally constructive during negotiations short-circuits conflict spirals</u>. If they become abusive, you remain civil. If they purposely misunderstand or confuse issues, you clarify. If they try to bully, you neither yield nor bully back. You try to persuade them on the merits of your proposal. If they try to deceive you, neither trust nor deceive them. You remain trustworthy throughout the negotiations. If they do not listen carefully, you nevertheless listen to them carefully and empathically. This is not a guide to earning your way into heaven. This is a realistic, eyes-wide-open guide to *effective* negotiations. You remain unconditionally constructive because it serves your own best interests to do so.

A story told (in Fadiman, 1985) about Gautama Buddha, an Indian prince who lived in the sixth century BC and whose teachings formed the basis of

Buddhism, exemplifies the unconditionally constructive attitude necessary for principled negotiations. A man interrupted Buddha's preaching with a torrent of abuse. Buddha waited for the man to finish. He then asked his detractor, "If a man offered a gift to another but the gift was declined, to whom would the gift belong?" The man responded, "To the one who offered it." "Then," said Buddha, "I decline to accept your abuse and request you to keep it for yourself" (p. 84). Reciprocating abuse with abuse only sidetracks negotiations onto unproductive avenues of mutual disparagement. Abuse needs to be short-circuited, not encouraged.

You also need to develop a BATNA as a standard against which any proposal can be measured. Your BATNA tells you what's the best you can do if negotiations fail to produce an agreement. Most importantly, your BATNA keeps you from accepting an agreement worse than what you could have done without negotiations.

For instance, if you have ever visited towns on the Mexican side of the border with the United States, you have undoubtedly engaged in street negotiations with local merchants on items such as hand-crafted rugs, sunglasses, pottery, and other items. Not having a BATNA before entering into negotiations with merchants can lead you to overpay for merchandise. If you have no idea how much comparable items would cost in the United States, then you are likely to make a charitable contribution to the Mexican economy when negotiating with a savvy merchant on what you think is a hot deal. Your BATNA in this instance is a comparable item that sells at a slightly higher price in the United States, a similar item of better quality for more money, or a similar item of lesser quality for less money. You know when you've negotiated a real value if you have such a BATNA. Information is power. A BATNA can save you from making a serious mistake (Fisher and Ury, 1981).

What do you do if the other parties insist on hard bargaining, not principled negotiations? You remain unconditionally constructive. If one of your interests is fairness, ask the other parties to explain how their position is fair. Don't assert that the other side offers an unfair proposal. Asking the hard bargainers to justify their position translates positions (e.g., no parties on weekends) into interests (e.g., peace and quiet in order to study). Personal attacks, threats, and bullying tactics can be handled by confronting them openly and immediately. For example, "Threats are not constructive. I negotiate only on merit. Can we return to the substantive issues?" Openly confront any dirty tactics. If necessary, short-circuit the hard bargainers' game plan by forthrightly asking for the rules of the game. For instance, "Before we go any further, I need to know what rules we are following during this bargaining. Does everyone here want to achieve a fair settlement in the quickest amount of time, or are we going to play the hard bargaining game where blind stubbornness wins out?" Make them convince you that their intentions are honorable. In the process they may convince themselves that hard bargaining isn't appropriate. You want to bring hard bargainers to their senses, not to their knees (Ury, 1993).

In summary, conflict is a reality of group life. Although most people would prefer that conflict didn't exist, there are both positive and negative aspects to conflict. Constructive management of conflict can turn conflict into a positive experience for the group. The five primary communication styles of conflict management—collaborating, accommodating, compromising, avoiding, and competing—all have pros and cons depending on the situation. Nevertheless, collaborating has a higher probability of producing constructive outcomes than does competing. Negotiation is a universal process used to manage conflicts of interests. Principled negotiation is the most productive means of resolving conflicts of interests.

This concludes my discussion of communication competence in small groups. One of the central points that I hope has come through loudly and clearly is that one person can make an enormous difference in the quality of the group experience. What you individually do or don't do may be the difference between a successful and a less-than-successful group. Competent communication begins with you. The We-orientation is the core of group effectiveness. Don't look to others to make groups work. Take the knowledge you've garnered from this textbook and the skills that you will develop as you put this knowledge into practice and focus them on improving the group experience.

QUESTIONS FOR CRITICAL THINKERS

1. If competition has so many disadvantages, why would the competing/forcing style ever be appropriate for a competent communicator?
2. If principled negotiating is so effective, why isn't it used more often?

Public Speaking in Group Situations

Groups sometimes have public-speaking responsibilities. In some cases the group has been formed in order to present information orally before an audience of interested people. Examples of this are symposium presentations, where a panel of usually between five and seven individuals will express divergent points of view on a subject of controversy. An open forum also requires public-speaking knowledge and skill. Here a panel of experts comments on a subject of interest and audience members are given an opportunity to ask questions or comment on the speakers' presentations. In your small group class, your group may be required to give oral presentations. In order to assist those with little or no training and experience in public speaking, I am including this brief appendix, which will cover some of the basics of oral presentation. This will not be a comprehensive nor in-depth treatment of public speaking, but knowing a bit more about this typically fear-inducing activity can be some solace to the novice. I will discuss speech anxiety, attention strategies, organization, and use of visual aids.

SPEECH ANXIETY

Virtually everyone experiences some anxiety from having to make a public presentation. In one survey, 85 percent of the respondents reported that speech anxiety (also referred to by some as stage fright or performance anxiety) was a major and serious fear in their lives (Motley, 1988). My own surveys of college students in speech classes indicate that the vast majority of students experience at least some nervousness about presenting a speech in front of a class. A few students are terrified by the very thought of public speaking. Take any four individuals and odds are that two of the four will feel at least an occasional butterfly in the stomach before giving a speech. The third person will suffer nervousness that can be bothersome, but not incapacitating. The fourth person will be so anxiety-ridden that he or she will avoid classes that require oral presentations, skip meetings, refuse job promotions, or even change jobs or occupations in order to escape public speaking.

Even college instructors experience speech anxiety. In one study, 87 percent of psychology instructors confessed that they had experienced speech anxiety associated with some aspect of teaching (Leak and Gardner, 1992). Sixty-five percent of these same subjects rated their most extreme case of speech anxiety between "definitely unpleasant" and "severe or extreme." You're not alone if you are anxious about having to make an oral presentation in your class.

If I could offer you a cure for speech anxiety, would you take it? Your answer is probably yes. Actually, there is a cure, of sorts, for speech anxiety. Sedation induced by heavy doses of Valium, Librium, or Xanax will do the trick for even the most terror-stricken speaker. Aside from the physiological dangers associated with these tranquilizers (they're habit-forming and can kill you if used incautiously), these drugs, and others like them, will make you appear witless in front of an audience because they deaden mental acuity. So unless you don't mind appearing lobotomized in front of groups, avoid such a "cure."

Curing speech anxiety, however, is not necessarily a very desirable goal. *Managing* speech anxiety is the appropriate goal. If you are one of those individuals who considers a bad case of the flu on the day of your assigned speech to be a stroke of unparalleled good fortune, you may find it difficult to accept that speech anxiety isn't always an evil to be eradicated. The degree of anxiety, not the anxiety itself, requires attention. A moderate amount of anxiety can enhance performance. When kept under control, speech anxiety can be facilitative. Moderate anxiety can energize a speaker. You can present a more dynamic, forceful presentation when energized than when you feel so comfortable that you become almost listless and unchallenged by the speaking experience.

When the intensity of your fear about speaking in front of people gets out of control, however, it then becomes debilitative and detracts from your performance. Intense anxiety can be cause for real concern if ignored. It will congest your thought pathways, thereby clogging your free flow of ideas. In such a condition, every speaker's nightmare—going blank—will likely occur. Also, a terror-stricken speaker feels an urge to escape. Consequently, a seven-minute speech is compressed into three minutes by a staccato, hyperspeed delivery. The quicker the speech, the quicker the escape.

The causes of speech anxiety are complex and varied. Space does not permit a thorough discussion of these causes. Generally speaking, the causes of speech anxiety are self-defeating thoughts and situational factors.

Negative thoughts about your speaking performance are self-defeating. The tendency of many beginning speakers is to predict disaster. Those who think irrationally about their public-speaking performance wildly exaggerate potential problems and thus stoke the furnace of their fears. They predict not just momentary lapses of memory, but a complete meltdown of mental functions ("I know I'll forget my entire speech and I'll just stand there like a nitwit"). Minor problems of organization are magnified into graphic episodes of total incoherence and nonstop babbling. Perfectionists also anguish over every flaw in their speech and overgeneralize the significance of even minor defects. Flawless public-speaking performance is a desirable goal but why beat up on yourself when it doesn't happen? Perfectionists make self-defeating statements to themselves such as "I feel like an idiot. I mispronounced the name of one of the experts I quoted"; "I must have said 'Uhm' at least a dozen times. I sound like a moron"; and "My knees were shaking. The audience must have thought I was out of control." Ironically, the imperfections so glaringly noticeable to perfectionists usually go unnoticed by most people in the audience. Even the most talented and experienced public speakers make occasional errors in otherwise riveting performances.

Another self-defeating thought that triggers speech anxiety is the desire for complete approval from your audience, especially from those whose opinion we value (such as the teacher). It is irrational thinking, however, to accept nothing less than complete approval from an audience. You cannot please everyone, especially if you take a stand on a controversial issue. If you fear failure, then making complete approval from your audience a vital concern merely sets you up for inevitable failure. When you set standards for success at unreachable heights, you are bound to take a tumble.

The fact that you are evaluated by an audience every time you give a speech, even if no one is formally grading your performance, will usually trigger your anxiety. Human beings are social creatures who dislike, even fear, disapproval from each other. Even if you aren't seeking complete approval or adulation from your listeners, you would be a rare individual if you were completely immune to the judgments of others hearing you speak. Public speaking becomes doubly intense when formal grades are given for each speech performance.

There are many situational causes of speech anxiety. Novel situations—ones that are new to you—create uncertainty, and uncertainty can easily make you tense. For most students, public speaking is a novel situation. Few students have given many speeches in their lifetime, and some have never given a formal public address. Fortunately, as you gain experience speaking in front of audiences, the novelty wears off and your anxiety will diminish.

I have polled more than a thousand students in public-speaking classes over the years. When asked what causes their speech anxiety, many students will include "being on stage" or "being in the spotlight." The conspicuousness of the public-speaking situation increases most people's anxiety. Most students tell me that speaking to one or two persons is usually not very difficult, but speaking in front of an entire class or an auditorium filled with a thousand people really gives them the shakes. Here the interaction of conspicuousness and approval can be easily seen. Standing alone before a few people and possibly failing is not nearly as big a deal as possibly failing in front of a huge crowd. In the former situation, your potential failure would likely remain an isolated event, but in the latter situation the entire school might be in on your humiliation—so goes the logic. Substantially reducing the possibility of a poor performance by adequate preparation will certainly help counteract stage fright stimulated by conspicuousness.

So how do you manage your speech anxiety, given the variety of causes that induce it? Weatherman Willard Scott of the *Today* show has tried sticking a pin in his rump hoping to startle himself out of his stage fright. He has also tried screaming off camera (not a very practical solution for a classroom setting). Famous actor Laurence Olivier sometimes swore at his audience backstage hoping to replace anxiety with anger (also not subject to wide application). Numerous individuals have suggested to me that picturing your audience nude, or clothed only in underwear or in diapers, can be helpful (assuming you can stifle your laughter when the image pops into your mind). Breathing deeply is also a favorite tidbit of wisdom offered by many as a quick-fix coping strategy for stage fright, although if done too vigorously, this remedy can cause you to hyperventilate and fall flat on your face from light-headedness.

All of these remedies have some merit, especially if they work for you. None of them, however, offers a reliable solution to speech anxiety. There are many more effective methods for dealing with speech anxiety.

First, there is no substitute for *adequate preparation*. Conducting proper research on your speech topic, organizing your speech clearly and carefully, and practicing it several times are all essential if you hope to manage your anxiety effectively. Adequate preparation must include physiological preparation as well. This means proper nutrition just prior to the speech event. Ignoring your physiological preparation for a speech may cancel out the benefits of other methods used to manage your speech anxiety. Consequently, do not deliver a speech on an empty stomach, but do not fill your stomach with empty calories. You need quality fuel such as complex carbohydrates to sustain you while you're speaking. Simple sugars (donuts, Twinkies), caffeine (coffee, colas, chocolate), and nicotine (cigarettes) should be avoided or ingested in very small quantities. Adequate preparation of your speech and yourself will reduce uncertainty and the fear of failure. When you practice, practice, and practice your speech some more you reduce the novelty of the situation.

Second, use *positive imaging*. Counter negative, self-defeating thoughts with positive thoughts of success. Visualize in what ways your speech will be successful and occupy your mind with those thoughts, screening out thoughts of failure. Make affirmation statements to yourself when negative thoughts creep into your mind. "My speech will be a success" and "I know I can do this speech well" are examples of affirmations to use when self-doubt emerges.

Third, *gather perspective* on your speech situation. Consider the difference between rational and irrational speech anxiety. A colleague of mine, Darrell Beck, worked out a simple formula for determining the difference between the two. The <u>severity of the feared occurrence times the probability of the feared occurrence</u> provides a rough approximation of how much anxiety is rational and when you have crossed the line into irrational anxiety. Severity is approximated by imagining what would happen to you if your worst fears came true—you bombed the speech. Would you leave the state? Would you drop out of school? Probably not, since even dreadful speaking performances do not warrant such drastic steps. You might consider dropping the class, but even this is unlikely since fellow students are very understanding when a classmate delivers a poor speech. So even a poor speech does not rationally warrant significant life changes. The probability that your worst nightmare will come true and you will give a horrible speech, however, is extremely unlikely if you have adequately prepared. Thus, working yourself into a lather over an impending speech lacks proper perspective if you follow the advice given here.

Fourth, *refocus your attention* on your message and your audience and away from yourself. You cannot concentrate on two things at the same time. If you dwell on your nervousness, you will be distracted from presenting your message effectively. Focus on presenting your message clearly and enthusiastically. View the speaking experience as a challenge to keep your audience interested, maybe even an opportunity to change their minds on an issue.

Fifth, *make coping statements* to yourself as you give your speech, especially when you momentarily stumble. When inexperienced speakers make mistakes during a speech, they tend to make negative statements to themselves. You forget a point, momentarily lose your train of thought, or stammer. Immediately, the tendency is for you to say to yourself "I knew I would mess up this speech" or "I told everybody I couldn't give a decent speech." Instead, try making coping statements while you're delivering the speech. When problems arise say "I can do better" or "I'm getting to the good part of my speech." Talk to yourself during your speech in positive ways to counteract self-talk that defeats you. When parts of your speech go well, compliment yourself on a job well done. This sustains and energizes you as you proceed through the speech.

GAINING AND MAINTAINING ATTENTION

Renowned author G. K. Chesterton once remarked, "There is no such thing as an uninteresting subject, there are only uninteresting people." We've all suffered through conversations with the dreadfully dull individual whose idea of sparkling dialogue would make cartoon character Homer Simpson sound like Einstein by comparison. You may, however, find Chesterton's view on subject matter difficult to accept. Nevertheless, his viewpoint that no topic is inherently uninteresting has a strong ring of truth to it.

Topics may be poorly chosen for a specific audience, but dull speeches are usually a problem of how the information contained in the speech is presented. Audience interest doesn't just happen magically. Interest is garnered by carefully planning and utilizing strategies of attention.

Although gaining and maintaining attention throughout your speech is an important goal for any speaker, attention strategies should enhance a speech, not detract from it. A disorganized speech gains attention but in a negative way. Frequent verbal and vocal fillers such as "you know," "uhm," and "ah" draw attention to inarticulateness.

Some attributes of stimuli, by their very nature, attract attention. Consider just a few of these attributes and how they can become attention strategies.

First, *intensity* is concentrated stimuli that draw attention. Intensity is an extreme degree of emotion, thought, or activity. Relating a story of a woman fleeing for her life from a stalker can be intense, especially for those who fear such an occurrence. Don't be too graphic when describing emotionally charged events, however, or you may offend and alienate your audience.

Intensity, however, is created in ways other than by using fear- or anxiety-producing stories. There are several basic stylistic techniques that promote intensity and rivet an audience's attention. Direct, penetrating eye contact is a useful technique for producing intensity. Focusing your eye contact on an individual for a prolonged period of time during your speech can snap that person out of his or her daydreaming. How does an inattentive person continue to ignore you when you are zeroing in on the daydreamer with eye contact? The lack of eye contact so typical of manuscript speeches, where every word of your speech is written on the paper in front of you, underlines the importance of not reading a speech to an audience because you break connection with your listeners. Direct eye contact is an attention builder, but lack of eye contact is an attention destroyer.

Variation in vocal volume is a second technique for provoking intensity. A raised voice can be quite intense. It punctuates portions of your speech much as an exclamation point punctuates a written sentence. The use of a raised voice, however, can be a rather shattering experience for an audience. Incessant, unrelenting, bombastic delivery of a message irritates and alienates an audience. Punctuate with raised voice only those points that are especially significant and deserve closer attention.

Silence can also be intense. Silence as a technique for provoking attention can be used to punctuate important points in your speech in the same way that raising your voice can. A pregnant pause—silence held a bit longer than would be usual if you were merely taking a breath—interjects drama into your speech and spotlights significant points.

A second stimuli attribute that induces attention is called *the startling*. You try to stun, surprise, and shake up your audience. You want to blast them out of their complacency. A startling statement, fact, or statistic can do this quite effectively. Startling statements such as, "AIDS clearly has the potential to decimate the human population"; "Calories can kill you"; and "Did you know that all those fillings in your teeth may give you mercury poisoning?" can make an audience sit up and take notice. You, of course, do not want to make startling statements that can't be supported with evidence.

That it costs more to feed and house a criminal in prison than it does to send him or her to the most expensive university in the country is a startling fact. There are more homicides in the United States each month than in some war zones is another startling fact. According to the A. C. Nielsen Co., American television sets are turned on an average of more than seven hours each day, and that is a startling statistic.

Every startling stimulus, however, does not produce constructive attention from an audience. Speakers can startle and offend at the same time. A few examples from my own experience and those of my colleagues make this point. One student (during a speech on food poisoning) gained attention by vomiting scrambled eggs into his handkerchief, raising serious doubts about the speaker's good taste. Another student punched himself so hard in the face that he momentarily staggered himself (the speech was on violence in America). Yet another student fired a pistol at his audience (blanks only). After classmates dusted themselves off and reduced their heart rates, they showed no inclination to listen to the rest of his speech on gun control.

All of these examples have one thing in common. The speakers startled their audience but lost credibility in the process. Tasteless jokes, ethnic slurs, and offensive language will also startle an audience and gain attention, but at a substantial cost to the speaker. The general rule applies—attention strategies should enhance the effectiveness of your speech, not detract from it.

Making a problem or issue appear *vital* to an audience is a third attention strategy. There are two principal ways to make your topic seem vital to an audience. First, the problem must be made vital not in some abstract or general sense, but in a specific, immediate, and meaningful sense. An audience's primary question when told that a problem exists is "How does if affect me?" The problem becomes vital and therefore meaningful when the audience can see how the consequences of inaction directly affect its interests and well-being. "One out of every ten women in this audience will contract breast cancer and a similar number of men listening to me will contract prostate cancer. Those of you who escape the disease will likely know one or more friends or relatives who will die from these forms of cancer" is an example of how to personalize a problem and make it seem vital to an audience.

A second way that you can make your topic seem vital is to dramatize it. In April 1983, the National Commission on Excellence in Education issued its report called "A Nation at Risk." Not content to describe the problem of a failing educational system in the usual bland, technical language of most other reports on the subject, the authors of the Commission's report exhibited a flair for the dramatic. On the opening page, they woke up the nation to a crisis with these rhetorical flourishes:

> Our nation is at risk. . . . The educational foundations of our society are presently eroded by a rising tide of mediocrity that threatens our very future as a Nation and a people . . . If an unfriendly foreign power had attempted to impose on America the mediocre educational performance that exists today, we might well have viewed it as an act of war. . . . We have, in effect, been committing an act of unthinking, unilateral educational disarmament. ("National Commission," 1983, p. 5)

The nation and the media took notice. The report secured attention from a complacent public and it set an agenda for discussion.

Although characterizing problems and solutions as vital draws attention to urgent concerns, you must be careful not to overstate your case. Depicting even relatively trivial concerns as vital may brand you as simply overwrought or melodramatic. For an issue to be accepted as vital, it must have the ring of truth. Credible evidence must substantiate your claim that the problem is vital and so is its solution.

Using *novelty* is a fourth attention strategy. Audiences are naturally drawn to the new and different. Unusual examples, clever quotations, uncommon stories all attract attention because they are new and different.

Beginning your speech with a novel introduction is especially important.

<u>Do not begin by telling the audience what your topic is</u>. That is very unoriginal and boring. Create interest in your topic with a novel opening—an unusual news event, story, or human interest example related to your subject. For instance, notice how the following introduction grabs attention by using novelty:

> Acting as his own attorney, an Oklahoma City robbery suspect became agitated when a witness identified him in court as the guilty party. "I should have blown your head off," he screamed, adding on quick reflection, "if I'd been the one that was there." The verdict? Guilty. Lesson to be learned? Acting as your own attorney is a foolish idea.

Listing several novel examples related directly to your topic is another effective way to open your speech. For example:

> "The check is in the mail" used to be the standard ploy to ward off bill collectors. Not so anymore. Delinquent customers have adopted more original stalling tactics. Collection agencies have received excuses from the bizarre to the ridiculous. One woman claimed that she had run over her husband with a car, breaking both of his arms thereby making it impossible for him to write checks. Another woman living in Fargo, North Dakota, claimed that she slipped on her way to the post office, lost her checks in the snow and was forced to wait until the spring thaw before retrieving them. Then there was the businessman who placed his own obituary in the local newspaper and promptly sent the clippings to his creditors.

Novelty can be a very effective attention strategy, especially for the introduction to your speech, but also throughout your presentation.

Everyone seems to enjoy a good laugh. Using *humor* is a superior attention strategy if used adroitly. You should be able to incorporate humorous anecdotes, quotations, and personal stories throughout your speech.

<u>There are several important guidelines, however, for using humor effectively as an attention strategy</u>. First, don't force humor. If you aren't a particularly funny person and have never told a joke without omitting crucial details or flubbing the punchline, then don't try to be a comedian in front of your audience. Humorous quotations, funny stories, and amusing occurrences can be used without setting them up as jokes. Simply offer them as illustrations of key points and if the audience is amused then they will laugh.

Second, use only relevant humor. Unrelated stories and jokes may be suitable for a comic whose principal purpose is to make an audience laugh, but a formal speech requires you to make important points. Your use of humor needs to make a relevant contribution to the advancement of the speech's purpose.

Third, use good taste. Coarse vulgarities, obscenities, and sick jokes invite anger and hostility. Humor that rests on stereotypes and putdowns may alienate vast sections of your audience. Sexist, racist, and homophobic "jokes" that denigrate groups exhibit bad taste and poor judgment.

Fourth, don't overuse humor. Don't become enamored with your own wittiness. Telling joke after joke or telling one amusing story after another will likely produce laughter, but the audience will also be dissatisfied if you substitute humor for substance.

Humor can be risky but very satisfying when it works. Using humor is probably the most effective attention strategy when used appropriately and skillfully.

ORGANIZATION AND OUTLINING

Presenting a well-organized speech is critical to your success as a speaker. This section, by necessity, will be a cursory treatment of organization and outlining.

Perhaps the easiest way of developing the organization of your speech is to think of your speech as an inverted pyramid. The base of your upside-down pyramid represents the most general part of your speech, namely, the topic. Moving down toward the tip of the pyramid, you fill in the purpose statement, then the main points that flow from the purpose statement, then each main point is elaborated with subpoints, and subpoints are divided into sub-subpoints and so forth. You begin with the abstract and work toward the concrete and specific.

Let's say that your group has chosen for its symposium topic the problem of violence in America. First, your group must divide this general topic into manageable subtopics so each group member will have about a five- to seven-minute speech. Subtopics might include violence on television, violence in the movies, guns and violence, gang violence, social and economic causes of violence, and potential solutions to violence (which could be divided even further into specific proposals such as "three strikes and you're out," outlawing handguns, prison reform, social programs). Each group member would then be given his or her subtopic.

Once you have your subtopic for the symposium, each group member must construct a specific purpose statement. A purpose statement is a concise, precise declarative statement phrased in simple, clear language that provides both the general purpose (to inform or to persuade) and the specific purpose (exactly what you want the audience to understand, believe, feel, or do).

TOPIC: Violence on television
PURPOSE STATEMENT: To inform you that excessive violence on television can lead to acts of violence in society.
TOPIC: Guns and violence
PURPOSE STATEMENT: To inform you that handgun violence is a serious problem in America.

Your purpose statement becomes the blueprint for your entire speech. You determine your main points from your purpose statement.

PURPOSE STATEMENT: To inform you that handgun violence is a serious problem in America.
MAIN POINT I: Death from handguns is a serious problem.
MAIN POINT II: Serious injury from handguns also poses a serious problem for America.

Each main point is then divided into subpoints, sub-subpoints, and so on.

MAIN POINT **I**: Death from handguns is a serious problem.
SUBPOINT **A**: There are more than 16,000 murders from handguns every year in America; Japan has fewer than 100.
SUBPOINT **B**: More than 1,400 American youths between the ages of ten and nineteen commit suicide with a handgun each year.

Each subpoint is then broken down further with more detail, examples, and supporting evidence.

SUBPOINT **A**: There are more than 16,000 murders from handguns every year in America; Japan has fewer than 100.

SUB-SUBPOINT **1**: Teenage homicide from handguns has almost doubled in the last decade to more than 5,000 annually.

SUB-SUBPOINT **2**: The teenage handgun death rate now exceeds the mortality rate for young people from all natural causes combined.

SUB-SUBPOINT **3**: Three times more American young men are killed by handguns every 100 hours than were killed during the 100-hour Persian Gulf War.

SUB-SUBPOINT **4**: Provide examples of teenagers gunned down in street violence.

SUBPOINT **B**: More than 1,400 American youths between the ages of ten and nineteen commit suicide with a handgun each year.

SUB-SUBPOINT **1**: Most suicides are from handguns.

SUB-SUBPOINT **2**: Handguns put at risk large numbers of young people who consider suicide.

SUB-SUB-SUBPOINT **a**: More than one in four high school students seriously contemplate suicide.

SUB-SUB-SUBPOINT **b**: Sixteen percent of high schoolers make a specific plan to commit suicide, and half of these actually try to kill themselves.

SUB-SUB-SUBPOINT **c**: Ready availability of handguns makes teen suicide more likely.

SUB-SUB-SUBPOINT **d**: Tell the story of fourteen-year-old Paul Hoffman.

The resulting outline for your first main point would look as follows:

PURPOSE STATEMENT: To inform you that handgun violence is a serious problem in America.

I. **Death from handguns is a serious problem.**

   A. **There are more than 16,000 murders from handguns every year in America; Japan has fewer than 100.**
1. Teenage homicide from handguns has almost doubled in the last decade to more than 5,000 annually.
2. The teenage handgun death rate now exceeds the mortality rate for young people from all natural causes combined.
3. Three times more American young men are killed by handguns in 100 hours than were killed during the 100-hour Persian Gulf War.
4. Provide examples of specific teenagers gunned down in street violence.

   B. **More than 1,400 American youths between the ages of ten and nineteen commit suicide with a handgun each year.**
1. Nearly two-thirds of suicides are from handguns.
2. Handguns put at risk large numbers of young people who consider suicide.
   a. More than one in four high school students seriously contemplate suicide.
   b. Sixteen percent of high schoolers make a specific plan to commit suicide, and half of these actually try to kill themselves.
   c. Ready availability of handguns makes teen suicide more likely.
   d. Tell the story of fourteen-year-old Paul Hoffman.

You follow the same procedure for outlining your second main point. Note that every subpoint must relate specifically to the main point and likewise every sub-subpoint must relate specifically to the subpoint above it.

The form used in the sample outline (and in the outlines preceding each chapter in this text) follows a standard set of symbols composed of Roman numerals, capital letters, and Arabic numbers. Indent all subdivisions of a more general point. This will help you follow the development of your points as you speak. Every point that is subdivided has at least two subpoints.

Preparing the body of your speech is your most difficult and primary organizational task. The introduction, however, creates the all-important first impression with an audience. <u>Your introduction should satisfy the following objectives, usually in this order</u>:

1. Gain the attention of the audience.
2. Provide your purpose statement.
3. Relate the topic and purpose statement to the needs and interests of the audience (answering the question "Why should the audience care about your topic and purpose?")
4. Preview the main points of your speech (state them exactly as they appear in your outline.

The conclusion of your speech should strive to accomplish two objectives:

1. Wrap up the speech with a brief summary of your main points.
2. End the speech with an effective attention strategy that brings closure to the speech.

Once you have prepared your speech outline composed of your introduction, body, and conclusion, practice your speech several times. Speaking from an outline instead of a written manuscript is called the *extemporaneous style* of speaking (extemp for short). When you have prepared your full-sentence outline as already explained, you may want to condense full sentences into terse words or phrases for your actual speaking outline. Under pressure of performing before an audience, it is usually easier to speak extemporaneously when you do not have to read whole sentences. Glancing at a few words or a phrase to remind you of the point you wish to explain to your audience allows you to maintain strong eye contact with your listeners without losing your train of thought.

Finally, as you present your speech, *signpost* your primary points. Signposts indicate exactly where you are in your speech so the audience can follow along easily. Restating your main points as you get to each one is an example of signposting. If you had "three causes of gun violence in America" you would signpost each one as you addressed them in turn, such as "the first cause of gun violence is poverty"; "the second cause of gun violence is the ready availability of guns"; and "the third cause of gun violence is the breakdown of the criminal justice system." In this way, signposting underscores your important points as you present your speech.

USING VISUAL AIDS

Visual aids can add interest, clarify complex material, make points memorable, and enhance the credibility of the speaker. There are many types of visual aids and with the advent of computer graphics, laser disks, and technologies still being developed, the possibilities are almost limitless. For inexperienced speakers, however, it is best to keep visual aids simple. Photographs, diagrams, charts, graphs, physical models, video clips, and slides are the standard types of visual aids.

Poorly designed and clumsily used visual aids will detract from your speech. The following guidelines will assist you in preparing and displaying visual aids effectively:

1. Keep visual aids simple. Visual aids that work well in books, magazines, or newspapers rarely work well in a speech. In printed material a visual aid can be studied carefully. A complicated visual aid used in a speech will distract audience members from listening to the speaker while they try to figure out the complex graph, chart, or diagram.

2. <u>Visual aids should be large enough to be seen easily</u>. The general rule of thumb here is whether a person in the back of the room can see the visual aid easily.
3. <u>Visual aids should be neat and attractive</u>. Sloppy, hastily constructed visual aids are worse than no visual aids at all.
4. <u>Display the visual aid where it can be seen easily by all members of the audience</u>. Audience members should not have to stand up or elongate their necks to see the visual aid.
5. <u>Practice with the visual aids</u>. Remember Murphy's Law: Whatever can go wrong likely will go wrong. Slide projector bulbs burn out and poster boards can fall over even if placed on an easel. Check any equipment used before beginning your presentation. You look like an amateur when slides are up-side down, VCRs aren't tracking properly, or charts won't stand up in the easel or chalk tray.
6. <u>Talk to the audience, not the visual aid</u>. Don't turn your back on your audience while explaining your visual aid. Stand facing your audience, point the toes of your feet straight ahead, and imagine that your feet have been nailed to the floor. You can't turn your body toward the visual aid and screen out your audience when your feet are pointing straight ahead. Stand beside the visual aid when referring to it and use your finger or a pointer to guide the audience.
7. <u>Keep the visual aid covered when it is not in use</u>. Audience members may be distracted by the visual aid when you are talking about a point unrelated to the chart or graph.
8. <u>Do not circulate a visual aid among the audience members</u>. Passing around pictures or other visual aids while you're still speaking will distract listeners.

Critical Thinking Revisited: Fallacies

Chapters Six and Seven have already delved substantially into the process of critical thinking in small group decision making and problem solving. A critically thinking group member must be able to recognize and deal effectively with problems of information overload and underload, confirmation bias, false dichotomies, collective inferential error, and groupthink. In addition, critical thinking is involved in every step of the Standard Agenda, especially when information is gathered and evaluated, criteria for decision making are developed and applied, and final decisions are made by the group.

This bonus appendix is included because in classrooms in some parts of the country, heavier emphasis is placed on reasoning and use of evidence in the small group context than is true of other parts of the country. The list of fallacies below is not exhaustive. I have chosen only those specific fallacies that seem to occur frequently and that students are likely to encounter almost daily.

In order to understand fallacies clearly, let me first discuss the <u>structure of arguments</u> (Toulmin et al., 1979). An argument or "train of reasoning" is composed of several constituent parts. These parts are:

1. **Claim**—that which is asserted and remains to be proven.
2. **Data**—the grounds (support/evidence) for the claim. Statistical evidence; expert, authoritative testimony; documents; objects; exhibits; conclusions from test results; verifiable facts; and conclusions previously established constitute data.
3. **Warrant**—the reasoning used to link the data to the claim; usually assumed (implied), not stated directly. There are several types of warrants. For example:
   a. *Authority warrants*—data and claim are linked by the credibility of the authority used to support the claim.
      CLAIM: Infants can think conceptually.
      DATA: Professor Johnson claims that this is so.
      WARRANT: Professor Johnson is a highly acclaimed expert on this subject.

b. *Generalization warrants*—data and claim are linked by the asserted generalizability of one or more specific examples or sets of examples.
CLAIM: America supports the Republican agenda.
DATA: Polls in most major cities show strong support for the agenda.
WARRANT: Examples of support in large cities are representative of the entire country.

c. *Analogical warrants* (comparisons)—data and claim are linked by the literal similarity of two things compared.
CLAIM: The decline of moral values in the United States will destroy our country.
DATA: The Roman Empire crumbled from within because of moral decay.
WARRANT: The United States and the Roman Empire are very similar.

4. **Backing**—additional evidence and reasoning used to support the inference made in the warrant.
CLAIM: Poverty is the primary cause of America's social ills.
DATA: Studies show that poverty causes crime, drug abuse, divorce, and spousal abuse.
WARRANT: These are highly reliable studies conducted by experts.
BACKING: These studies were conducted by the New School for Social Science Research, the Camden Foundation, and the American Federation of Social Sciences, all highly respected, nonprofit think tanks.

5. **Reservations**—exceptions or rebuttals that diminish the force of the claim.
CLAIM: Jim Davis should be given antibiotics.
DATA: Davis suffered severe cuts and injuries on his arms and legs in an auto accident.
WARRANT: There is a risk of infection in such injuries.
BACKING: Hospital reports and studies indicate that risk of infection is serious and that antibiotics can prevent infection from occurring.
RESERVATION: Overuse of antibiotics can produce "super bugs." Antibiotics should be used only when absolutely necessary or they will eventually prove to be useless to fight disease.

6. **Qualifier**—degree of truth of the claim (i.e., highly probable, plausible, possible, etc.); depends on the degree to which you are confident that the claim is proven. The stronger the truth claim, the greater is the burden of proof.

Understanding fallacies will help you determine how valid is your claim, how strong is your data, and how solid is your warrant and backing. The arguments I used above to illustrate the elements of an argument are not necessarily good trains of reasoning. Study the fallacies listed below, then review these arguments and determine if they have any weaknesses.

I am dividing this list of fallacies into three types:

I. **Material Fallacies: errors in the process of using supporting materials as proof.**

II. **Logical Fallacies: errors in the process of reasoning.**

III. **Psychological Fallacies: claims that rest on emotional appeal rather than logic and evidence.**

I. **Material Fallacies**

A. <u>**Misuse of Statistics**</u>
1. **Manufactured or Questionable Statistics**—statistics that have been fabricated, or statistics whose validity is highly questionable because there is no reasonable method for compiling such statistics, or that which is quantified is too trivial to warrant the time, effort, and resources necessary to compile accurate statistics.
   a. Raymond Brown, in his *A Book of Superstitions,* claims that "about $275 million in business is lost on Friday the 13th because people are afraid of the danger so they stay home."
   b. "Researchers say anywhere from 1 in 10 and 1 in 100 Americans have genital herpes." (Difference between 1 percent and 10 percent of American population is enormous—statistics are imprecise, untrustworthy estimates.)
2. **Irrelevant Statistics**—statistics that do not directly prove the implied or stated claim yet they are offered as evidence supporting the claim.
   a. "Hot dogs are a nutritionally worthless food. They're 60 percent water." (So what? Fruit is 90 percent water. Statistic isn't relevant to claim.)
   b. "Handguns pose no serious threat to human life in this country. Only 34/10,000th of 1 percent of all handguns in America are involved in homicides." (Irrelevant whether small percentage of all handguns is used to kill people. If a person has thirty handguns but uses only one to kill you, who cares if the other twenty-nine handguns weren't involved in the homicide? Relevant statistic is what percentage of homicides involved a handgun.)
3. **Sample Size Inadequate or Unspecified**—sample size is very small, resulting in a margin of error in excess of plus or minus 3 percent, or you are left guessing what the sample size might have been.
   a. "Eighty percent of those surveyed support the cable TV legislation." (How many surveyed? Ten people, eight of whom favored the legislation?)
   b. "Four out of five doctors recommend aspirin for aches associated with flu."
   NOTE: <u>What makes an adequate sample size?</u>
   a. Sample of 1,000 is usually sufficient whether survey is national, state, or local.
   b. Sample must be randomly selected (typically from a table of random numbers).

    c. Margin of error should be no more than plus or minus 3 percent to be very representative.

4. **Self-selected Sample**—you choose to participate in a survey; you are not selected as part of a random, representative sample.

    a. Local TV station conducts a "call-in" poll on some controversial issue. Viewers choose to participate usually if they have a strong motivation, such as anger or a vested interest in the results turning out favorably for their point of view.

    b. Surveys or questionnaires printed in magazines asking readers to respond and mail in their answers.

5. **Dated Statistics**—statistics that are not current. Statistics should be as up-to-date as possible, especially if the event, phenomenon, or situation is volatile and likely to change quickly (e.g., number of unemployed, long-term interest rates on mortgages, murder rates in various cities, international monetary exchange rates).

NOTE: Some phenomena change very slowly, if at all, over time (e.g., rates of blind obedience to authority figures, deterrent effects of punishment on crime, percentage of U.S. population who call themselves Catholics, Protestants, etc.) requiring less attention to recency of statistics.

    a. "According to a 1985 United Nations Report, the number of AIDS cases is doubling every three years." (Too old to be valuable data. Substantial efforts have been made since 1985 to combat the spread of AIDS.)

    b. "According to the Department of Housing and Urban Development in a 1987 report to Congress, housing starts are at an all-time high in the United States." (Big recession occurred after 1987, significantly affecting housing starts, so statistics are dated and in this case useless except for historical comparison.)

B. <u>Misuse of Authority</u>

NOTE: Testimony of experts and authorities is useful as supporting material for claims because experts draw on a larger data and knowledge base than do nonexperts. Experts are not always correct (economists being a notable example), but they are more reliable than someone who is uninformed or only marginally knowledgeable about a subject, especially about a highly technical subject.

1. **Incomplete Citation**—reference to the authority is neither specific nor complete. <u>Minimum requirements for a complete citation include</u> qualification of authority if not obvious, place of publication, and date of reference.

    a. COMPLETE CITATION SAMPLE #1: The President's Commission on Mental Health, in its January 1994 report entitled

"Mental Health, Mental Illness," concludes, "The biggest stigma in America is the mental illness label."

b. COMPLETE CITATION SAMPLE #2: The latest report from the U.S. Census Bureau, last July, notes that 21 percent of children in the United States live in poverty.

c. "Research indicates" (unless offered by an expert interpreting the latest results in his or her field), "studies show," and the like are <u>incomplete</u> citations.

2. **Biased Source**—special interest groups or individuals who stand to gain money, prestige, power, or influence simply by taking a certain position on an issue or "crusaders for a cause" are all biased even though they may have expertise.

a. Quoting AT&T on the advantages of its phone company compared to MCI or Sprint.

b. Quoting the National Rifle Association on gun control.

c. Quoting R. J. Reynolds Tobacco Company on the safety of cigarette smoking.

3. **Authority Quoted Out of His/Her Field**—expertise is not generic. Quote experts in their area of specialization.

a. Professor of Biology, Dr. Ernhard Bousterhaus, claims, "Electric cars are impractical and will remain so for at least the next fifty years." (What expertise does a biologist have in regard to electric cars?)

b. Dr. Julia Esterhand, Professor of Anthropology at Moreland State University, claims that vitamin supplements are dangerous to your health.

II. Logical Fallacies

A. **Hasty Generalization** (overgeneralizing)—drawing conclusions (generalizations) from too few or atypical examples.

1. "German shepherds are mean, vicious dogs. I saw three different German shepherds on three separate occasions attack small children without provocation." (The vividness effect can lead to overgeneralization from a few isolated examples.)

2. Testimonials exalting cancer cures, faith healings, and so on are generalizations based on too few and probably atypical experiences of individuals.

3. The Talk Show Syndrome—audience members stand up and generalize on the basis of their individual experiences.

B. **False Analogy**—two items, events, or phenomena with similarities are viewed as identical. What is true of one is or should be true for the other, so goes the claim, even when a significant point or points of difference exist between the two things compared.

1. "Thousands of people are killed annually in automobile accidents but few if any have been killed in the United States by

an accident at a nuclear power plant. Yet, we ban nuclear power plants in many parts of the United States, while licensing drivers and automobiles. This makes little sense." (Banning cars would devastate the U.S. economy and create transportation havoc. Banning nuclear power plants has no such significant effects. Also, one major auto accident can kill dozens of people. One major nuclear power plant accident can wipe out an entire state and have international environmental effects for decades.).

2. "In Turkey, farmers grow poppies (source of heroin) as a cash crop. In the United States, farmers grow corn and soybeans for cash crops. Why outlaw poppies when we don't outlaw corn and soybeans?" (Poppy crop is not a critical food crop capable of feeding the hungry of the world. Corn and soybeans are critical food crops.)

C. **False Dichotomies** (either–or thinking)—false choice between only two opposites when other choices that fall between the extremes exist.
   1. "You either support the National Health Care proposal of the Administration or America will go broke from spiraling health-care costs. So make your choice." (Other proposals besides this one exist that may be better options to the health-care problems in America.)
   2. Responding to an Ann Landers column, 72 percent of 64,800 women said they would forego sexual intercourse with their partner if they could be held closely by their partner instead. (Only two choices provided when clearly a third exists, namely, the preference to be held closely *and* to have sexual intercourse.)

D. **Mistakes in Causation**
   1. **Correlation Mistaken for Causation** (post hoc ergo propter hoc)—when two phenomena vary simultaneously or one follows the other, a causal linkage is asserted based solely on the covariation of the two phenomena.
      a. "Since minority groups have been given more educational opportunities, we have had an increase in the crime rate in the United States. Educating minorities will simply increase crime."
      b. "I ate a lot of chocolate this week and now my face has acne. I guess I'll have to stop eating chocolate so I can get rid of these blasted pimples."
   2. **Single Cause**—attributing only one cause to a complex phenomenon with many causes.
      a. "Increasing interest rates is the cause of high inflation." (A cause but not necessarily the most important nor the only cause.)

      b. "Poor communication is the reason for the alarming increase in the divorce rate." (A cause but not necessarily the most important nor the only cause.)

E. Criterion Fallacies

1. **Missing Criterion**—claim requires definition of key term establishing standard for evaluating validity of claim, but no definition is offered.
   a. "*Hustler* magazine is an obscene magazine." (Term "obscene" must be defined before claim can be evaluated.)
   b. "The trouble with America is the failure to promote family values." (Must define "family values.")
2. **Questionable Criterion**—unreasonably broad or narrow definition of key term on which claim is based.
   a. "Those paintings are pornographic. They show naked men and women." (Overly broad definition of "pornographic.")
   b. "Intelligence is whatever the IQ tests measure." (Overly narrow view of intelligence.)

III. Psychological Fallacies

A. Personal Attack (ad hominem)—attacking the messenger in order to divert attention away from the message.

NOTE: Not all attacks on a person's credibility, character, qualifications, and so on are fallacious. If character or credibility is the real issue, then it is relevant argumentation (e.g., attacking Richard Nixon's integrity during Watergate was not a fallacious personal attack).

1. "Why are you always on my back for not studying? Last semester your GPA fell nearly a full point."
2. "Why should we listen to his charges of corruption in city government? He's nothing but a rabble-rousing troublemaker."

B. Popular Opinion (ad populum)—claim based on popular opinion rather than reasoning and evidence.

1. "Go ahead and smoke marijuana. More than a third of all college students do."
2. "Eighty-five percent of those polled believe fluoride in the water causes cancer. We should therefore ban fluoride from our water system."

C. Loaded Language—claim based on the emotional connotations of words rather than evidence and reasoning. The connotations may be negative or positive.

1. "This fanciful and ludicrous proposal for the establishment of a free campus bus system should be rejected."
2. "We engage in peaceful propaganda for the advancement of democratic ideals."

D. **Appeal to Tradition**—claim is made that what has always been done should continue to be done just because it has always been done that way.
   1. "We've never used cooperative learning in the classroom so we don't plan to start now."
   2. "I've always used a typewriter so I don't expect I'll be using a computer anytime soon."

Sample Agendas for Group Meetings

Agenda for a Business Meeting

Meeting of the Student Senate
October 1, 1997
Boardroom
2:00–3:30 P.M.

Purpose: Biweekly meeting

   I. Call meeting to order

  II. Approval of the minutes of last meeting (5 minutes)

 III. Additions to the agenda (2 minutes)

 IV. Committee reports
    A. Student fee committee (5 minutes)
    B. Student activity committee (5 minutes)
    C. Student union committee (5 minutes)

  V. Officers' reports
    A. Treasurer's report (5 minutes)
    B. President's report (10 minutes)

 VI. Old business
    A. Textbook prices (10 minutes)
    B. Campus parking problems (10 minutes)
    C. Pub on campus (5 minutes)

 VII. New business
    A. Computer access on campus (5 minutes)
    B. Safety on campus (20 minutes)

VIII. Building agenda for next meeting (5 minutes)

 IX. Adjournment

Agenda for a Discussion Meeting

Curriculum Task Force
March 17, 1997
Boardroom
3:00–5:00 P.M.

Purpose: To improve the curriculum change and approval process

    I. How does the current curriculum process work?

    II. What are the primary problems with the present curriculum process?

    III. What causes the problems?

    IV. What criteria determine an ideal curriculum process?

    V. What are some possible improvements in the curriculum process?

    VI. Which suggested improvements are the most promising? Why?

    VII. Are their any drawbacks to these suggested improvements?

    VIII. What needs to occur to implement the most promising suggested improvements?

In this text, I have attempted to keep jargon to a minimum. I am not fascinated with jargon, but it does facilitate communication by providing a verbal short-hand for complex concepts and ideas. Nevertheless, a glossary of terms does not substitute for clear understanding of the concepts represented. You can memorize a definition without knowing what it means. Clear understanding requires a context for the jargon. By reading the following terms in the context of this book, you will see the interconnections between and among the terms. All terms included in the glossary appear in **boldfaced** type in the body of the text.

Accommodating   Style of conflict management characterized by yielding to the concerns and desires of others.

Adaptability to change   The modification of the structure and/or function of the group in response to changing conditions.

Alliance   An association, in the form of subgroups, entered into for mutual benefit or the achievement of a common objective.

Analysis paralysis   Process whereby a group overanalyzes a problem, preventing itself from making a decision.

Assertiveness   The ability to communicate the full range of your thoughts and emotions with confidence and skill (Adler).

Avoiding   Style of conflict management characterized by withdrawing from potentially contentious and unpleasant struggles.

Boundary control   A system's regulation of the degree, rate, and desirability of change; controlling access to people, ideas, information, values, and events.

Brainstorming   A creative problem-solving technique characterized by non-evaluation of ideas, encouragement of zany ideas, and energetic participation of all group members in generating new ideas.

Bridging   A method of integrative problem solving whereby a new option is offered that satisfies the interests of all parties in a conflict.

Chunking   Process of re-coding information into larger, more meaningful units.

Cohesiveness   The degree of liking members have for each other and the group, and the commitment to the group that this liking engenders.

Collaborating   Cooperative style of conflict management characterized by confrontation and integration techniques.

Collective inferential error   Assuming as a group that certain inferences are facts without critically analyzing them, then based on these faulty inferences, making further inferences usually resulting in bad decision making.

Communication   A transactional process of sharing meaning with others.

Communication climate   The group atmosphere that varies according to how group members conduct transactions.

Communication competence   The ability to communicate in a personally effective and socially appropriate manner (Trenholm).

Communication skill   The successful performance of a communication behavior and the ability to repeat such a behavior (Spitzberg and Hecht).

Competing   A win-lose style of conflict management whereby one party in a conflict tries to force compliance from another party.

Competition   Mutually exclusive goal attainment (MEGA).

Compliance   The process of acquiescing to the dictates and desires of others.

Compromising   Style of conflict management characterized by giving up something in order to get something in return.

Confirmation bias   Tendency to seek information that confirms predispositions and to ignore or distort information that contradicts currently held beliefs and attitudes.

Conflict   The interaction of interconnected parties who perceive incompatible goals and interference from each other in attaining those goals.

Conformity   Adherence to group norms.

Consensus   Group decision-making process characterized by unanimous agreement, commitment to the decision, and satisfaction with the process and decision.

Cooperation   Mutually inclusive goal attainment (MIGA).

Co-optation   Seduction strategy that tries to buy off a defiant group member with promises of promotions, perquisites, money, and the like.

Correlation   A consistent relationship between two or more variables.

Credibility   Criterion used to evaluate information on the basis of its believability and reliability.

Critical thinking   The process of analyzing, criticizing, and evaluating ideas and information in order to reach sound judgments and conclusions.

Currency   Criterion used to evaluate information on the basis of how up to date it is.

Defensive communication   Competitive patterns of communication behavior that provoke the perception that one's self-esteem and identity as a person are being threatened.

Defiance   Purposeful, conscious, overtly rebellious form of communicating noncompliance.

Deindividuation   Psychological process that occurs when individuals shed their personal identities and replace them with a group persona.

Delegating style   Style of leadership that allows the group to be self-directed.

Denotative meaning   Relatively stable, neutral, shared meanings of a group.

Devil's advocacy   A role played by one or more group members to prevent groupthink, in which the devil's advocate critiques the group's proposal and arguments supporting the proposal.

Dialectical inquiry   A procedure for preventing groupthink, in which a subgroup develops a counterproposal and defends it side-by-side with the group's initial proposal.

Disruptive roles Informal roles that serve individual needs or goals while impeding attainment of group goals.

Dogmatism A belief in the self-evident truth of one's opinion, warranting no debate nor disagreement from others.

Dominance A form of power that emphasizes who is on top of the power hierarchy and in control and who is on the bottom and thus subservient.

Empathy Thinking and feeling what you perceive another to be thinking and feeling (Howell).

Empowerment The power to accomplish one's own goals or help others achieve theirs.

Equifinality Groups with a similar or identical final goal may reach that end in highly diverse ways; there's more than one way to achieve a goal.

Expanding the pie An method of integrative problem solving whereby resources are increased as a solution to a problem.

Expedient conformity Acquiescing in the dictates or desires of a group by expressing attitudes and exhibiting behaviors acceptable to the group while harboring private beliefs at odds with the group.

False dichotomies (pronounced DIE-COT-OH-MEES) Either–or thinking; the propensity to view the world in terms of only two opposing possibilities when other possibilities are available and to describe this dichotomy in the language of extremes.

Formal roles Designated roles that exist within the structure of a group or organization.

Group A human communication system composed of three or more individuals, interacting for the achievement of some common purpose(s), who influence and are influenced by one another.

Group endorsement Approval by group members of an individual's bid to play a particular informal role.

Grouphate The hostility people harbor from having to work in groups.

Group polarization The group tendency to make a decision that is more extreme, either riskier or more cautious, after discussion has occurred than the initial preferences of group members.

Groupthink A mode of thinking that people engage in when they are deeply involved in a cohesive in-group, when the members' strivings for unanimity override their motivation to appraise realistically alternative courses of action (Janis).

Hidden agendas Personal goals of group members that are not revealed openly to the group and that often directly conflict with group goals.

Hit-and-run confrontations Confronting another group member with a conflict of interest without giving that individual an adequate opportunity to respond.

Impervious response   A defensive communication pattern that is characterized by a failure to acknowledge another person's communication effort either verbally or nonverbally.

Individualism–collectivism continuum   Cultural variation in the degree to which people explore their uniqueness and independence versus their conformity and interdependence.

Inferences   Conclusions about the unknown based on the known.

Influence of size   The effect variation that size has on systems.

Informal roles   Roles that emerge from communication transactions within a group.

Information bulimia   A binge-and-purge process whereby information is crammed into one's head then quickly regurgitated without serious consideration of the impact of that information on decision making and problem solving.

Information overload   Condition where informational input into a system exceeds a system's capacity to process input effectively.

Information underload   Insufficient informational input available to a group for decision-making purposes.

Interconnectedness of parts   All parts of a system work together and affect each other and the system as a whole.

Irrelevant response   A defensive communication pattern manifested by questions or statements having nothing to do with the sender's message that indicates an indifference to the sender's needs.

Leader as completer   Functional leadership perspective that holds that leaders perform those essential functions within a group that other members have failed to perform.

Leadership   A two-way influence process that is directed toward group goal achievement.

Limiting the search   A method for coping with information overload whereby the search for information is stopped after a certain point in order for decision making to take place.

Linguistic barriers   Language restrictions, such as jargon, erected by a group to create an in-group/out-group division.

Maintenance roles   Informal roles that focus on the social dimension of the group, especially the nurturance of group cohesiveness.

Mentor   Knowledgeable individuals who have achieved some success in their profession or jobs and who assist other individuals trying to get started in a line of work.

Mindset   Psychological or cognitive predisposition to see the world in a particular way.

Minimum power theory   States that the weakest member of a triad will be the only member always included in a coalition.

Minimum resources theory   States that group members with the most power are included in a coalition less often than are weaker members because more-powerful members are entitled to a larger share of the rewards than weaker members.

Mixed messages   When verbal messages seem to contradict nonverbal messages and vice versa.

Negative reciprocation   Desire to do harm to another because he or she has done harm to you.

Negative synergy   When the joint action of group members produces a worse result than expected based on perceived individual abilities and skills of members; the whole is worse than the sum of its parts.

Negotiation   A process by which a joint decision is made by two or more parties (Pruitt).

Networking   Individuals with similar backgrounds, skills, and goals come together on a fairly regular basis and share information that will assist members in pursuing goals.

Networks   A structured pattern of information flow and personal contact.

Nominal group technique   A creative problem-solving procedure characterized by group members working alone to generate lists of ideas on a problem, convening the group and recording ideas generated, selecting the five favorite ideas, and ranking these five ideas on the basis of the group average.

Norms   Rules in a group that stipulate what a person must do, ought to do, or must not do in order to achieve certain goals (Smith).

Openness   Continuous interaction with the environment outside of the immediate system; degree of exchange of information, energy, and matter.

Output   The results of a group's interactions such as productivity (task dimension) and cohesiveness (social dimension).

Participating style   Nondirective style of leadership that encourages shared decision making with special emphasis on developing relationships in the group.

Pattern recognition   Potentially the most effective method for coping with information overload, whereby patterns are discerned from information in order to utilize information effectively.

Perception of free choice   Private acceptance of a belief or attitude flowing from the perception of unimpeded choice.

PERT (Program Evaluation Review Technique)   A decision-making procedure for implementing group decisions.

Physical barriers   Walls, partitions, or other material means of dividing space and segmenting territory.

Power   The ability to influence the attainment of goals sought by yourself and others.

Power distance dimension   Cultural variations in attitudes concerning the appropriateness of power imbalances.

Pressure toward uniformity   Influence applied to group members to comply with the prevailing attitude or viewpoint of the group as a whole, sometimes leading to groupthink.

Presumptuousness   Self-promoting overconfidence; arrogance as an indicator of power.

Prevention   A form of power that tries to thwart domination.

Primary tension   The normal jitters and feelings of unease group members experience when first congregating in a group.

Principled negotiation   A collaborative process of negotiating conflicts of interests on the merits, not on hard bargaining strategies.

Private acceptance   A type of compliance that occurs when an individual's public and private attitudes and beliefs are compatible with the group's norms and viewpoint.

Process   Events and relationships are dynamic, continuous, and ever-changing.

Productivity   The output from a group's task dimension.

Provisionalism   A flexible attitude; individuals remain open to possibilities and options that may not have been explored.

Pseudo-member   A group member in name only; pursuing individual goals unrelated to and sometimes at the expense of group goals.

Psychological barriers   Feelings that an individual experiences of not belonging in the group.

Psychological reactance   Theory that claims that the more someone tries to control an individual, the more that individual is inclined to resist such efforts.

Question of fact   Problem for group discussion formulated as a question that asks whether something is true and to what extent.

Question of policy   Problem for group discussion formulated as a question that asks whether a specific course of action should be undertaken in order to solve a problem.

Question of value   Problem for group discussion formulated as a question that asks for a judgment—to what extent is something good or bad, right or wrong, and so forth.

Reciprocal patterns   A tit-for-tat, spiraling pattern of mutuality; giving what you get and vice versa.

Reframing   The creative process of breaking a mindset by placing a problem in a different frame of reference.

Relevance   Criterion used to evaluate information on the basis of whether or not the information relates directly to claims made.

Representativeness   Criterion used to evaluate information on the basis of whether or not the specific example, statistic, or instance accurately reflects what is generally true.

Resistance   The prevention form of power; covert form of communicating noncompliance.

Ripple effect   Chain reaction of one system part on whole system.

Role conflict   Playing two roles that contradict each other.

Role fixation   Acting out a specific informal role, and that role alone, no matter what the situation might require.

Role reversal   Assuming a role considered "opposite" from a role an individual usually plays, such as student instead of teacher, employee instead of boss.

Roles   Patterns of behavior exhibited by members of a group in light of expectations that members hold toward those behaviors.

Role specialization   The primary informal role played by a group member.

Role status   The relative importance, prestige, or power accorded a particular role by group members or society.

Rules   Regulations that define appropriate behaviors in specified social situations.

Secondary tension   The stress and strain that occurs within a group (later in its development) manifested by disagreements and conflict.

Selectivity   A method for coping with information overload whereby an individual chooses on the basis of group priorities and goals what information to pay attention to and what to ignore.

Self-confirmation   Extreme form of confirmation bias whereby all evidence and reasoning, no matter how apparently contradictory, is distorted to confirm a belief or point of view.

Selling style   A directive style of leadership characterized by high emphasis on task accomplishment and high interest in social relationships among group members.

Social dimension   The relationships of members in groups and their impact on the group as a whole.

Social loafing   The tendency of individual group members to reduce their work effort as groups increase in size; the inclination to "goof off" in groups.

Social tension   Anxiety felt when interacting with other group members.

Specialization   A method for coping with information overload whereby an individual will know a lot about a little.

Stockholm Syndrome   Psychological process whereby victims come to identify with their aggressors.

Structure   The systematic interrelation of all parts to the whole.

Style shift   Using several styles of conflict management flexibly depending on the circumstances.

Sufficiency   Criterion used to evaluate information on the basis of whether or not there is enough information to support claims made.

Superordinate goals   Goals that are compelling for all parties in a conflict, the attainment of which are beyond reach without the cooperation of all parties.

Supportive communication   Cooperative patterns of communication behavior that bolster a person's self-image and self-esteem.

Synectics   An approach to group creativity in the business environment, characterized by cooperative participation, active listening, and reduction of role status.

Synergy   When the joint action of group members produces performance that exceeds expectations based on perceived abilities and skills of individual members; the whole becomes greater than the sum of its individual parts.

System   A set of interconnected parts working together to form a whole in the context of a changing environment.

Tangential response   A defensive communication pattern that minimally acknowledges what a speaker had to say, then steers the conversation in another direction.

Task dimension   The work performed by the group and its impact on the group.

Task roles   Informal roles that move the group toward the attainment of its goals.

Telling style   Directive style of leadership characterized by high emphasis on task accomplishment and low interest in social relationships among group members.

Transactional communication   Group members are both senders and receivers simultaneously and each influences the definition of the other and the relationship continuously.

Transformational leader   Charismatic leader who communicates a vision of change to followers.

Verbal dominance   Verbal bullying characterized by such communication behaviors as interrupting, contradicting, berating, and monopolizing the conversation.

Vital functions   Functional leadership perspective that sees leaders performing a number of vital group functions different in kind and degree from other members.

Work teams   Small groups of interdependent individuals who share responsibility for outcomes for their organization.

REFERENCES

Abell, G. Astrology. In G. Abell and B. Singer (Eds.), *Science and the paranormal.* New York: Charles Scribner's Sons, 1981.

Abramson, J. *We, the jury.* New York: Basic Books, 1994.

Acker, J. Hierarchies and jobs: Notes for a theory of gendered organizations. *Gender and Society,* 1990, 4, 139–58.

Adcock, A., and Yang, W. Parental power and adolescents' parental identification. *Journal of Marriage and the Family,* 1984, 46, 487–94.

Adams, J. et al. Follower attitudes toward women and judgment concerning performance by female and male leaders. *Academy of Management Journal,* 1984, 27, 636–43.

Adler, R. *Communication at work: Principles and practices for business and the professions.* New York: Random House, 1989.

Adler, R. *Confidence in communication: A guide to assertive and social skills.* New York: Holt, Rinehart, and Winston, 1977.

Adler, R., and Towne, N. *Looking out, looking in.* New York: Holt, Rinehart, and Winston, 1996.

Advertising is hazardous to your health. *University of California, Berkeley Wellness Letter,* July 1986, 1–2.

Alexander, N. How to stop wasting time at meetings. *San Jose Mercury News,* September 17, 1989, 1PC.

Allen, C., and Straus, M. Resources, power, and husband-wife violence. In M. Straus and G. Hotaling (Eds.), *The social causes of husband-wife violence.* Minneapolis: University of Minnesota Press, 1980, 188–208.

Allen, V., and Levine, J. Social support and conformity: The role of independent assessment of reality. *Journal of Experimental Social Psychology,* 1971, 7, 48–58.

Allen, V., and Wilder, D. Social comparison, self-evaluation, and conformity to the group. In J. Suls and R. Miller (Eds.), *Social comparison processes: Theoretical and empirical perspectives.* Washington, DC: Hemisphere Publishing, 1977, 196–201.

Alvarado, D. Furor over new diagnosis for PMS. *San Jose Mercury News,* May 22, 1993, 1A.

Amabile, T. *The social psychology of creativity.* New York: Springer-Verlag, 1983.

Andersen, J. Communication competency in the small group. In R. Cathcart and L. Samovar (Eds.), *Small group communication: A reader.* Dubuque, IA: Wm. Brown and Company, 1988.

Anderson, J. A haven for whistleblowers. *Parade,* August 18, 1991, 16–17.

Anderson, W. *Reality isn't what it used to be.* San Francisco: Harper and Row, 1990.

Appel, W. *Cults in America: Programmed for paradise*. New York: Holt, Rinehart and Winston, 1983.

Are salaries over the top or right on the money? *San Jose Mercury News*, June 23, 1996, 7A.

Aronson, E. The jigsaw route to learning and liking. *Psychology Today*, February 1975.

Aronson, E. *The social animal*. New York: Freeman Publishing, 1988.

Asch, S. *Social Psychology*. New York: Prentice-Hall, 1952.

As they see it. *San Jose Mercury News*, August 26, 1990, 2C.

A whole new way to communicate. *San Jose Mercury News*, May 6, 1988, 10F.

Axelrod, R. *The evolution of cooperation*. New York: Basic Books, 1984.

Bach, G., and Goldberg, H. *Creative aggression*. New York: Avon, 1974.

Baker, R. The silencing of the persecuting prosecutors. *Skeptical Inquirer*, May/June 1996, 42–45.

Balgopal, P. et al. Self-help groups and professional helpers. In R. Cathcart and L. Samovar (Eds.), *Small group communication: A reader*. Dubuque, IA: Wm. C. Brown, 1992.

Barge, J. *Leadership: Communication skills for organizations and groups*. New York: St. Martin's Press, 1994.

Barge, J., and Hirokawa, R. Toward a communication competency model of group leadership. *Small Group Behavior*, 1989, 20, 167–89.

Barnes, R. The new millennium workplace. *The Futurist*, March/April 1996, 30, 14–18.

Barry, D. *Claw your way to the top*. Emmaus, PA: Rodale Press, 1986.

Barry, D. *Dave Barry's guide to life*. New York: Wings Books, 1991.

Bartos, O. Determinants and consequences of toughness. In P. Swingle (Ed.), *The structure of conflict*. New York: Academic Press, 1970.

Bass, M., *Leadership, psychology and organizational behavior*. West Port, CT: Greenwood Press, 1960.

Bate, B. *Communication and the sexes*. New York: Harper and Row, 1988.

Baumeister, R. et al. Relation of threatened egotism to violence and aggression: The dark side of high self-esteem. *Psychological Review*, 1996, 103, 5–33.

Bavelas, A. et al. Experiments on the alteration of group structure. *Journal of Experimental Social Psychology*, 1965, 1, 55–70.

Baxter, T. Dole's attack is puzzling. *San Jose Mercury News*, September 13, 1996, 11B.

Bazerman, M., and Neale, M. Heuristics in negotiation: Limitations to dispute resolution effectiveness. In M. Bazerman and R. Lewicki (Eds.), *Negotiating in organizations*. Beverly Hills, CA: Sage, 1983, 51–67.

Bechler, C., and Johnson, S. Leadership and listening: A study of member perceptions. *Small Group Research*, 1995, 26, 77–85.

Beekeepers get set for "killer bees." *San Jose Mercury News*, March 18, 1990, 16A.

Bell, M. The effects of substantive and affective conflict in problem-solving discussions. *Speech Monographs*, 1974, 41, 19–23.

Benne, K., and Sheats, P. Functional roles of group members. *Journal of Social Issues*, 1948, 4, 41–49.

Benson, G. On the campus: How well do business schools prepare graduates for the business world? *Personnel*, 1983, 60, 63–5.

Benson, P. et al. Pretty pleases: The effects of physical attractiveness on race, sex, and receiving help. *Journal of Experimental Social Psychology*, 1976, 12, 409–15.

Berg, D. A descriptive analysis of the distribution and duration of themes discussed by task-oriented small groups. *Speech Monographs*, 1967, 34, 172–75.

Berge, Z. Electronic discussion groups. *Communication Education*, 1994, 43, 102–11.

Berlo, D. *The process of Communication*. New York: Holt, Rinehart, and Winston, 1960.

Bettinghaus, E., and Cody, M. *Persuasive communication*. New York: Holt, Rinehart, and Winston, 1987.

Biz grads focus too narrow. *USA Today*, May 20, 1985, 1C.

Blake, R., and Mouton, J. *The managerial grid*. Houston: Gulf Publishing, 1964.

Blum, R. Lawyers only winners. *Santa Cruz Sentinel*, March 3, 1995, B3.

Bok, S. *Lying: Moral choice in public and private life*. New York: Vintage, 1979.

Bolton, R. *People skills: How to assert yourself, listen to others and resolve conflicts*. New York: Simon and Schuster, 1979.

Bond, M. et al. How are responses to verbal insults related to cultural collectivism and power distances? *Journal of Cross-cultural Psychology*, 1985, 16, 111–27.

Bordevich, F. The country that works perfectly. *Reader's Digest*, February 1995, 101–106.

Borgida, E., and Nisbett, R. The differential impact of abstract vs. concrete information on decisions. *Journal of Applied Social Psychology*, 1977, 7, 258–71.

Borisoff, D., and Merrill, L. *The power to communicate: Gender differences as barriers*. Prospect Heights, IL: Waveland Press, 1992.

Borisoff, D., and Victor, D. *Conflict management: A communication skills approach*. Englewood Cliffs, NJ: Prentice-Hall, 1989.

Bormann, E. *Small group communication: Theory and practice*. New York: Harper and Row, 1990.

Bormann, E., and Bormann, N. *Effective small group communication*. Edina, MN: Burgess Publishing, 1988.

Bostrom, R. Patterns of communicative interaction in small groups. *Speech Monographs*, 1970, 37, 257–63.

Bower, S., and Bower, G. *Asserting yourself*. Reading, MA: Addison-Wesley, 1976.

Bowman, G. et al. Are women executives people? *Harvard Business Review*, 1965, 43, 14–28.

Boyd, R. Survival of the most cooperative? New insights into Darwin's theory. *San Jose Mercury News*, June 9, 1996, 1C.

Bradley, P. Sex, competence and opinion deviation: An expectation states approach. *Communication Monographs*, 1980, 47, 101–10.

Brecher, E. Furor over Florida rape case clouds disturbing facts. *The Seattle Times*, December 15, 1989, B1.

Brehm, J. *Responses to loss of freedom: A theory of psychological resistance*. Morristown, NJ: General Learning Press, 1972.

Brembeck, W., and Howell, W. *Persuasion: A means of social influence*. Englewood Cliffs, NJ: Prentice-Hall, 1976.

Brett, J. et al. Designing systems for resolving disputes in organizations. *American Psychologist*, February 1990, 162–70.

Brewer, M. In-group bias in the minimal intergroup situation: A cognitive-motivational analysis. *Psychological Bulletin*, 1979, 86, 307–24.

Brewer, M., and Miller, N. Beyond the contact hypothesis: Theoretical perspectives on desegregation. In N. Miller and M. Brewer (Eds.), *Groups in contact*. Orlando, FL: Academic Press, 1984.

Brilhart, J., and Galanes, G. *Effective group discussion*. Dubuque, IA: Wm. C. Brown, 1989.

Brislin, R. *Understanding culture's influence on behavior*. Fort Worth, TX: Harcourt Brace Jovanovich, 1993.

Broad, W. Flood of journals deluges scientists. *San Jose Mercury News*, March 8, 1988, 1C.

Brock, T. Implications of commodity theory for value change. In A. Greenwald, T. Brock, and T. Ostrom (Eds.), *Psychological foundations of attitudes*. New York: Academic Press, 1968, 243–75.

Broeder, D. The University of Chicago jury project. *Nebraska Law Review*, 1959, 38, 760–74.

Broome, B., and Fulbright, L. A multistage influence model of barriers to group problem solving: A participant-generated agenda for small group research. *Small Group Research*, 1995, 26, 25–35.

Brue, M. Youths deciding to quit sports. *San Jose Mercury News*, June 29, 1989, 7G.

Brumley, A. et al. You say you want a revolution. *San Jose Mercury News*, November 19, 1995, 3A.

Bryson, B. *The mother tongue*. New York: Avon Books, 1990.

Burggraf, C., and Sillars, A. A critical examination of sex differences in marital communication. *Communication Monographs*, 1987, 54, 276–94.

Burke, R. Methods of resolving superior-subordinate conflict: The constructive use of subordinate differences and disagreements. *Organizational Behavior and Human Performance*, 1970, 5, 393–411.

Burns, J. *Leadership*. New York: Harper and Row, 1978.

Burroughs, N., Kearney, P., and Plax, T. Compliance-resistance in the college classroom. *Communication Education*, 1989, 38, 214–29.

Burrows, W. *Psychology Today*, November, 1982, 43.

Businesspeople suffering information indigestion. *San Jose Mercury News*, October 25, 1996, IC.

Butler, D., and Geis, F. Nonverbal affect responses to male and female leaders: Implications for leadership evaluation. *Journal of Personality and Social Psychology*, 1990, 58, 48–59.

Butler, S. *Non-competitive games for people of all ages*. Minneapolis: Bethany House Publishers, 1986.

Butt, D. *Psychology of sport: The behavior motivation, personality, and performance of athletes*. New York: Van Nostrand Reinhold, 1976.

Butterfield, F. Justice survey shows big crime drop. *San Jose Mercury News,* September 18, 1996, 7A.

Caplow, T. *Two against one: Coalitions in triads.* Englewood Cliffs, NJ: Prentice-Hall, 1968.

Carli, L. Gender, language, and influence. *Journal of Personality and Social Psychology,* 1990, 59, 941–51.

Carroll, J. Indefinite terminating points and the iterated Prisoner's Dilemma. *Theory and Decision,* 1987, 22, 247–56.

The case for charm. *Self,* November 1989, 118.

Cathcart, R. , and Samovar, L. *Small group communication: A reader.* Dubuque, IA: Wm. C. Brown, 1992.

Census shows radical changes in family. *San Jose Mercury News,* September 5, 1989, 8A.

Chertkoff, J., and Esser, J. A review of experiments in explicit bargaining. *Journal of Experimental Social Psychology,* 1976, 12, 464–86.

Christensen, D. et al. Sensitivity to nonverbal cues as a function of social competence. *Journal of Nonverbal Behavior,* 1980, 4, 145–56.

Cialdini, R. *Influence: The new psychology of modern persuasion.* Glenview, IL: Scott, Foresman, 1993.

Cissna, K., and Keating, S. Speech communication antecedents of perceived confirmation. *Western Journal of Speech Communication,* 1979, 43, 48–60.

Clanton, J. The Challenger disaster that didn't happen. In Winning Orations 1988 by the Interstate Oratorical Association.

Clark, N., and Stephenson, G. Group remembering. In P. Paulus (Ed.), *Psychology of group influence.* Hillsdale, NJ: Lawrence Erlbaum, 1989.

Clark, R., and Word, L. Where is the apathetic bystander? Situational characteristics of the emergency. *Journal of Personality and Social Psychology,* 1974, 29, 279–87.

Clark, R., and Word, L. Why don't bystanders help? Because of ambiguity? *Journal of Personality and Social Psychology,* 1972, 24, 392–400.

Cleveland, H. People lead their leaders in an information society. In H. Didsbury (Ed.), *Communication and the future.* Bethesda, MD: World Future Society, 1982, 167–73.

Cody, M., and McLaughlin, M. Perceptions of compliance-gaining situations: A dimensional analysis. *Communication Monographs,* 1980, 46, 132–48.

Cohen, M., and Davis, N. *Medication errors: Causes and prevention.* Philadelphia: G. F. Stickley, 1981.

Cohen, P. *The gospel according to the Harvard business school.* Garden City, NY: Doubleday & Company, 1973.'

Cole, D. Meetings that make sense. *Psychology Today,* May 1989, 14–15.

Coleman, D., and Straus, M. Marital power, conflict, and violence in a nationally representative sample of American couples. *Violence and Victims,* 1986, 1, 141–57.

Coleman, K. Conjugal violence: What 33 men report. *Journal of Marital and Family Therapy,* 1980, 6, 207–13.

Collingwood, H. Forget the Fortune 500: For big bucks, think smaller and smarter. *Working Woman*, January 1997, 24–25.

Conant, J., and Wingert, P. You'd better sit down, kid. *Newsweek*, August 24, 1987, 58.

Conboy, W. *Working together: Communication in a healthy organization.* Columbus, OH: Charles Merrill, 1976.

Conquergood, D. Homeboys and hoods: Gang communication and cultural space. In L. Frey (Ed.), *Group communication in context: Studies of natural groups.* Hillsdale, NJ: Lawrence Erlbaum Associates, 1994.

Conrad, C. *Strategic organizational communication: An integrated perspective.* New York: Holt, Rinehart and Winston, 1990.

Conrad, C. Supervisors' choice of models of managing conflict. *Western Journal of Speech Communication*, 1983, 47, 218–28.

Conway, F., and Siegelman, J. *Snapping: America's epidemic of sudden personality change.* New York: Stillpoint Press, 1995.

Cookson, P., and Persell, C. The price of privilege. *Psychology Today*, March 1983, 31–35.

Cordell, A. *The socio-economics of technological progress.* Paper presented to the Faculty of Science Lecture Series on Human Environment: Problems and Prospects, Carleton University, February 23, 1973, mimeographed.

Cox, H. Verbal abuse in nursing: Report of a study. *Nursing Management*, 1987, 18, 47–50.

Cox, H. Verbal abuse nationwide, part I: Impact and modifications. *Nursing Management*, 1991, 22, 66–69.

Cox, J. Corona is silent. *The Sacramento Bee*, August 2, 1990, B1.

Crandall, C. Social contagion of binge eating. *Journal of Personality and Social Psychology*, 1988, 55, 588–98.

The criticism that hurts. *Psychology Today*, March 1989, 16.

Crocker, J., and McGraw, K. What's good for the goose is not good for the gander: Solo status as an obstacle to occupational achievement for males and females. *American Behavioral Scientist*, 1984, 27, 357–69.

Crowe, B. et al., The effects of subordinates' behavior on managerial style. *Human Relations*, 1972, 25, 215–37.

Cult compound grew on rules, isolation. *San Jose Mercury News*, March 3, 1993, 8A.

Daniels, T., and Spiker, B. *Perspectives on organizational communication.* Dubuque, IA: Wm. C. Brown, 1987.

Davidson, J. The shortcomings of the information age. *Vital Speeches*, 1996, 62, 495–503.

Davis, W. *The seventh year: Industrial civilization in transition.* New York: W. W. Norton, 1979.

De Klerk, V. Expletives: Men only? *Communication Monographs*, 1991, 58, 156–69.

Delbecq, A. et al. *Group techniques for program planning.* Glenview, IL: Scott, Foresman, 1975.

De Moor, A. Toward a more structured use of information technology in the research community. *American Sociologist*, 1996, 27, 91–102.

Denison, D., and Sutton, R. Operating room nurses. In J. Hackman (Ed.), *Groups that work (and those that don't)*. San Francisco: Jossey-Bass, 1990.

De Souza, G., and Kline, H. Emergent leadership in the group goal-setting process. *Small Group Research*, 1995, 26, 475–96.

DeStephen, R., and Hirokawa, R. Small group consensus: Stability of group support of the decision, task process, and group relationships. *Small Group Behavior*, 1988, 19, 227–39.

Deutsch, M. *Distributive justice: A social-psychological perspective*. New Haven: Yale University Press, 1985.

Deutsch, M. Education and distributive justice: Some reflections on grading systems. *American Psychologist*, 1979, 34, 391–401.

DeVito, J. Messages: Building interpersonal communication skills. New York: Harper and Row, 1990.

DeVito, J. *The interpersonal communication book*. New York: Harper and Row, 1989.

Dewey, J. *How we think*. Lexington, MA: D. C. Heath, 1910.

Didsbury, H. (Ed.). *Communications and the future*. Bethesda, MD: World Future Society, 1982.

Diehl, M., and Stroebe, W. Productivity loss in brainstorming groups: Toward the solution of a riddle. *Journal of Personality and Social Psychology*, 1987, 53, 497–509.

Diener, E. Deindividuation, self-awareness, and disinhibition. *Journal of Personality and Social Psychology*, 1979, 37, 1160–71.

Dillard, J., and Burgoon, M. Situational influences on the selection of compliance-gaining messages: Two tests of the predictive utility of the Cody-McLaughlin typology. *Communication Monographs*, 1985, 52, 289–304.

Dipboye, R., and Wiley, J. Reactions of college recruiters to interviewee sex and self-presentation style. *Journal of Vocational Behavior*, 1977, 10, 1–12.

Ditch hubby, keep pal, 2610 in Germany say. *San Jose Mercury News*, February 25, 1988, 6F.

Dizard, W. *The coming information age*. New York: Longman, 1989.

Dodd, C. *Dynamics of intercultural communication*. Dubuque, IA: Wm. C. Brown, 1995.

Downs, C., and Conrad, C. A critical incident study of effective subordinacy. *Journal of Business Communication*, 1982, 19, 27–38.

Downs, C. et al. *The organizational communicator*. New York: Harper and Row, 1977.

Drecksel, G. Interaction characteristics of emergent leadership. Ph.D. dissertation, University of Utah, 1984.

Dressler, C. Please! End this meeting madness! *Santa Cruz Sentinel*, December 31, 1995, 1D.

Driscoll, R., Davis, K., and Lipetz, M. Parental interference and romantic love: The Romeo and Juliet effect. *Journal of Personality and Social Psychology*, 1972, 24, 1–10.

Drucker, P. Leadership: More doing than dash. *The Wall Street Journal*, July 6, 1988, 1.

Du Bois, C. Portrait of the ideal MBA. *The Penn Stater*, September/October 1992, p. 31.

Durand, D. Power as a function of office space and physiognomy: Two studies of influence. *Psychological Reports*, 1977, 40, 755–60.

Dworetzky, J. *Psychology*. New York: West Publishing Company, 1991.

Eagly, A. et al. Gender and the evaluation of leaders: A meta-analysis. *Psychological Bulletin*, 1992, 111, 3–22.

Eakins, B., and Eakins, G. *Verbal turn-taking and exchanges in faculty dialogue.* Paper presented at the Conference on the Sociology of the Languages of American Women, 1976.

Early, C. Social loafing and collectivism: A comparison of the United States and the People's Republic of China. *Administrative Science Quarterly*, 1989, 34, 555–81.

Edelsky, C. Who's got the floor? *Language in Society*, 1981, 10, 383–421.

Egan, G. *The skilled helper*. Belmont, CA: Wadsworth, 1975.

Ekman, P., Friesen, W., and Bear, J. The international language of gestures. *Psychology Today*, May 1984, 64–69.

Elliott, J. The power and pathology of prejudice. In P. Zimbardo and F. Ruch, *Psychology and life*. Glenview, IL: Scott, Foresman, 1977.

Endicott, F. *The Endicott report: Trends in the employment of college and university graduates in business and industry*. Evanston, IL: Placement Center, Northwestern University, 1979.

Engleberg, I., and Wynn, D. DACUM: A national database justifying the study of speech communication. *Journal of the Association for Communication Administration*, 1995, 1, 28–38.

Epstein, A. Legal profession still makes it tough for aspiring women. *San Jose Mercury News*, January 8, 1996, 10A.

Equality still eludes female lawyers, experts say. *San Jose Mercury News*, August 18, 1996, 7A.

Erickson, B. et al. Speech style and impression formation in a court setting: The effects of 'powerful' and 'powerless' speech. *Journal of Experimental Social Psychology*, 1978, 14, 266–79.

Etzioni, A. *The spirit of community: Rights, responsibilities, and the communitarian agenda*. New York: Crown Publishers, 1993.

Evans, C., and Dion, K. Group cohesion and performance: A meta-analysis. *Small Group Research*, 1991, 22, 175–86.

Face it: Looks pay. *San Jose Mercury News*, August 13, 1989, 2PC.

Fadiman, C. (Ed.). *The Little, Brown book of anecdotes*. Boston: Little, Brown and Company, 1985.

Fairhurst, G., and Sarr, R. *The art of framing: Managing the language of leadership*. San Francisco: Jossey-Bass, 1996.

Fairhurst, G., Green, S., and Snavely, B. Face support in controlling poor performance. *Human Communication Research*, 1984, 11, 272–95.

Fandt, P. The relationship of accountability and interdependent behavior to enhancing team consequences. *Group and Organization Studies*, 1991, 16, 300–312.

Farace, R. *Communicating and organizing*. Reading, MA: Addison-Wesley, 1977.

Farley, R. Holdout juror said pressure was on. *Philadelphia Inquirer*, January 13, 1994, A1.

Fausto-Sterling, A. Is nature really red in tooth and claw? *Discover*, April 1993, 24–27.

Fearing heckling, CHP officer let King bleed. *San Jose Mercury News*, March 30, 1993, 3B.

Feathur, F., and Mayur, R. Communications for global development: Closing the information gap. In H. Didsbury (Ed.), *Communication and the future*. Bethesda, MD: World Future Society, 1982, 198–210.

Fernald, L. Of windmills and rope dancing: The instructional value of narrative structures. *Teaching Psychology*, 1987, 14, 214–16.

Fiedler, F. *A theory of leadership effectiveness*. New York: McGraw-Hill, 1967.

Fiedler, F. *Leadership*. Morristown, NJ: General Learning Press, 1970.

Fiedler, F., and House, R. Leadership theory and research: A report of progress. In C. Cooper and I. Robertson (Eds.), *International review of industrial and organizational psychology*. New York: John Wiley & Sons, 1988, 73–92.

Filley, A. *Interpersonal conflict resolution*. Glenview, IL: Scott, Foresman, and Company, 1975.

Firestein, R. Effects of creative problem solving training on communication behaviors in small groups. *Small Group Research*, 1990, 21, 507–21.

Firestone, I. et al. Anxiety, fear and affiliation with similar-state versus dissimilar-state others: Misery loves miserable company. *Journal of Personality and Social Psychology*, 1973, 26, 409–14.

Fisher, B. Decision emergence: Phases in group decision making. *Speech Monographs*, 1970, 37, 53–66.

Fisher, B. *Small group decision making: Communication and the group process*. New York: McGraw-Hill, 1980.

Fisher, B., and Ellis, D. *Small group decision making: Communication and the group process*. New York: McGraw-Hill, 1990.

Fisher, C., and Gitelson, R. A meta-analysis of the correlates of role conflict and ambiguity. *Journal of Applied Psychology*, 1983, 68, 320–33.

Fisher, R., and Brown, S. *Getting together: Building a relationship that gets to yes*. Boston: Houghton Mifflin, 1988.

Fisher, R., and Ury, W. *Getting to yes: Negotiating agreement without giving in*. New York: Penguin Books, 1981.

Fiske, S., and Taylor, S. *Social cognition*. Reading, MA: Addison-Wesley, 1984.

Folger, J. et al. *Working through conflict: A communication perspective*. Glenview, IL: Scott, Foresman, 1993.

Forsyth, D. *Group dynamics*. Pacific Grove, CA: Brooks/Cole Publishing Co., 1990.

Foschi, M. et al. Standards, expectations, and interpersonal influence. *Social Psychology Quarterly*, 1985, 48, 108–17.

Foushee, H., and Manos, K. Information transfer within the cockpit: Problems in intracockpit communications. In C. Billings and E. Cheaney (Eds.), *Information transfer problems in the aviation system* (NASA Report No. TP-1875). Moffett Field, CA: NASA-Ames Research Center, 1981.

Foushee, M. Dyads and triads at 35,000 feet: Factors affecting group process and aircraft performance. *American Psychologist*, 1984, 39, 885–93.

Frank, R., and Cook, P. *The winner-take-all society*. New York: The Free Press, 1995.

Freeman, K. Attitudes toward work in project groups as predictors of academic performance. *Small Group Research*, 1996, 27, 265–82.

French, J., and Raven, B. The bases of social power. In D. Cartwright (Ed.), *Studies in social power*. Ann Arbor, MI: Institute for Social Research, 1959, 150–67.

French, J. The disruption and cohesion of groups. *Journal of Abnormal and Social Psychology*, 1941, 36, 361–77.

Frey, L. *Group communication in context: Studies of natural groups*. Hillsdale, NJ: Lawrence Erlbaum Associates, 1994.

Friedenberg, E. *Coming of age in America*. New York: Random House, 1965.

Friedrich, O. Five ways to wisdom. *Time*, September 27, 1982, 66–72.

Fuller, M. *A simple, decent place to live*. Dallas, TX: Word Publishing, 1995.

Gabrenya, W. et al. Social loafing on an optimizing task: Cross-cultural differences among Chinese and Americans. *Journal of Cross-cultural Psychology*, 1985, 16, 223–42.

Gaillard, F. *If I were a carpenter: Twenty years of Habitat for Humanity*. Winston-Salem, NC: John F. Blair Publisher, 1996.

Galanter, M. *Cults: Faith, healing, and coercion*. New York: Oxford University Press, 1989.

Gallup, G. Public holds broad bias against cults. *San Jose Mercury News*, March 5, 1989, 22A.

Galvin, K., and Brommel, B. *Family communication: Cohesion and change*. Glenview, IL: Scott, Foresman, 1986.

Gamson, W. An experimental test of a theory of coalition formation. *American Sociological Review*, 1961, 26, 565–73.

Gardner, M. *Science good, bad and bogus*. New York: Avon Books, 1981.

Garrett, L. *The coming plague: Newly emerging diseases in a world out of balance*. New York: Penguin Books, 1994.

Garrity, J. A clash of cultures on the Hopi reservation. *Sports Illustrated*, November 20, 1989, 10–16.

Gartner, A., and Reissman, F. *Self-help in the human services*. San Francisco: Jossey-Bass, 1977.

Gastil, J. A meta-analytic review of the productivity and satisfaction of democratic and autocratic leadership. *Small Group Research*, 1994, 25, 384–410.

Gayle, B. Sex equity in workplace conflict management. *Journal of Applied Communication Research*, 1991, 19, 152–69.

Gayle-Hackett, B. Do females and males differ in the selection of conflict management strategies: A meta-analytic review. Presented at the Western Speech Communication Convention, Spokane, WA, February 17–21, 1989.

Gebhardt, L., and Meyers, R. Subgroup influence in decision-making groups: Examining consistency from a communication perspective. *Small Group Research*, 1995, 26, 147–68.

Geier, J. A trait approach in the study of leadership in small groups. *Journal of Communication*, 1967, 17, 316–23.

Geis, F. et al. Sex vs. status in sex-associated stereotypes. *Sex Roles*, 1984, 11, 771–86.

Gelles, R., and Straus, M. *Intimate violence: The causes and consequences of abuse in the American family*. New York: Simon and Schuster, 1988.

Gelman, D., and McKillop, P. Going "wilding" in the city. *Newsweek*, May 8, 1989, 65.

Gelman, D., and Rogers, P. Mixed messages. *Newsweek*, March 12, 1993, 28.

Gentry, G. Group size and attitudes toward the simulation experience. *Simulation and Games*, 1980, 11, 451–60.

Gerow, J. *Psychology: An introduction*. New York: HarperCollins, 1995.

Getter, H., and Nowinski, J. A free response test of interpersonal effectiveness. *Journal of Personality Assessment*, 1981, 45, 301–8.

Gibb, C. Leadership. In G. Lindzey and E. Aronson (Eds.), *The handbook of social psychology* (Vol. 4). Reading, MA: Addison-Wesley, 1969, 205–82.

Gibb, J. Defensive communication. *The Journal of Communication*, 1961, 11, 141–48.

Glass ceiling intact, statistics show at hearing. *San Jose Mercury News*, September 27, 1994, 1E.

Glazer, M., and Glazer, P. Whistleblowing. *Psychology Today*, August 1986, 37–43.

Godfrey, D. et al. Self-promotion is not ingratiating. *Journal of Personality and Social Psychology*, 1986, 50, 106–15.

Goethals, G., and Darley, J. Social comparison theory: Self-evaluation and group life. In B. Mullen and G. Goethals (Eds.), *Theories of group behavior*. New York: Springer-Verlag, 1987, 21–47.

Goffman, E. *The presentation of self in everyday life*. New York: Anchor, 1959.

Goktepe, J., and Schneier, C. Role of sex and gender roles, and attraction in predicting emergent leaders. *Journal of Applied Psychology*, 1989, 74, 165–67.

Goldhaber, G. *Organizational communication*. Dubuque, IA: Wm. C. Brown, 1990.

Goldhaber, G. et al. *Information strategies: New pathways to corporate power*. Englewood Cliffs, NJ: 1979.

Goldman, A. *The lives of John Lennon*. New York: William Morrow & Co., 1988.

Goldstein, S. Citadel's lone woman ostracized. *San Jose Mercury News*, April 11, 1994, 13A.

Goldston, L. Women make a big impact. *San Jose Mercury News*, November 19, 1995, 2A.

Goldston, L., and Torriero, E. McMartin sex case hinges on health of 12 weary jurors. *San Jose Mercury News*, January 8, 1990, 1A.

Gomes, L. Intuit fesses up again. *San Jose Mercury News*, March 3, 1995, 1C.

Gould, S. *The mismeasure of man*. New York: W.W. Norton, 1981

Gouldner, A. The norm of reciprocity: A preliminary statement. *American Sociological Review*, 1960, 25, 161–78.

Gouran, D. A theoretical foundation for the study of inferential error in decision-making groups. Presented at the Conference on Small Group Research, Pennsylvania State University, April 1982.

Gouran, D. Cognitive sources of inferential error and the contributing influence of interaction characteristics in decision-making groups. In G. Ziegelmueller and J. Rhodes (Eds.)., *Dimensions of argument: Proceedings of the Second Annual Summer Conference on Argumentation.* Annandale, VA: Speech Communication Association, 1981, 728–48.

Gouran, D. Communicative influences on inferential judgments in decision-making groups: A descriptive analysis. In D. Zarefsky et al. (Eds.), *Argument in transition: Proceedings of the Third Summer Conference on Argumentation.* Annandale, VA: Speech Communication Association, 1983, 667–84.

Gouran, D. Inferential errors, interaction, and group decision-making. In R. Hirokawa and M. Poole (Eds.), *Communication and group decision-making.* Beverly Hills, CA: Sage, 1986, 93–112.

Gouran, D. *Making decisions in groups: Choices and consequences.* Glenview, IL: Scott, Foresman, 1982.

Gouran, D. Principles of counteractive influence in decision-making and problem-solving groups. In R. Cathcart and L. Samovar (Eds.), *Small group communication: A reader.* Dubuque, IA: Wm. C. Brown, 1988, 192–208.

Gouran, D., and Baird, J. An analysis of distributional and sequential structure in problem-solving and informal group discussions, *Speech Monographs,* 1972, 39, 16–22.

Greenway, H. Making a demon of the enemy. *San Jose Mercury News,* January 3, 1993, 1A.

Grogan, B. et al. Their brothers' keepers? *People,* May 1993, 45.

Gross, M. *The psychological society.* New York: Random House, 1978.

Group therapy may help cancer patients. *San Jose Mercury News,* May 11, 1989, 5C.

Gruscky, O. The coalition structure of the four-person family. *Current Research in Social Psychology,* 2, 1995, 16–28.

Gudykunst, W. *Bridging differences: Effective intergroup communication.* Newbury Park, CA: Sage, 1991.

Gully, S. et al. A meta-analysis of cohesion and performance: Effects of level of analysis and task interdependence. *Small Group Research,* 1995, 26, 497–520.

Gumpert, R., and Hambleton, R. Situational leadership: How Xerox managers fine-tune managerial styles to employee maturity and tasks needs. *Management Review,* December 1979, 9.

Hackman, J. The design of work teams. In J. Lorsch (Ed.), *Handbook of organizational behavior.* Englewood Cliffs, NJ: Prentice-Hall, 1987, 315–42.

Hackman, M., and Johnson, C. *Leadership: A communication perspective.* Prospect Heights, IL: Waveland Press, 1996.

Haines, D., and McKeachie, W. Cooperative versus competitive discussion methods in teaching introductory psychology. *Journal of Educational Psychology,* 1967, 58, 386–90.

Hall, J., and Donnell, S. Managerial achievement: The personal side of behavioral theory. *Human Relations,* 1979, 32, 77–101.

Hall, J., and Watson, W. The effects of a normative intervention on group decision-making. *Human Relations*, 1970, 23, 299–317.

Halpern, D. *Thought and knowledge: An introduction to critical thinking.* Hillsdale, NJ: Lawrence Erlbaum, 1984.

Hamachek, D. *Encounters with others.* New York: Holt, Rinehart and Winston, 1982.

Hamill, R. et al. Ignoring sample bias: Inferences about collectivities from atypical cases. Unpublished manuscript, University of Michigan, 1979.

Haney, W. *Communication and organizational behavior.* Homewood, IL: Richard D. Irwin, 1967.

Hans, V. The effects of the unanimity requirement on group decision processes in simulated juries. Unpublished doctoral dissertation, University of Toronto, 1978.

Hare, A. Types of roles in small groups: A bit of history and a current perspective. *Small Group Research*, 1995, 25, 433–48.

Harper, C. et al. Study of simulated airplane pilot incapacitation: Phase II, subtle or partial loss of function. *Aerospace Medicine*, 1971, 42, 946–48.

Harwood, R. *The pursuit of the presidency 1980.* New York: Berkley Books, 1982.

Haslett, B. et al. *The organizational woman: Power and paradox.* Norwood, NJ: Ablex Publishing, 1992.

Hassan, S. *Combatting cult mind control.* Rochester, VT: Part Street Press, 1988.

Hastie, R. et al. *Inside the jury.* Cambridge, MA: Harvard University Press, 1983.

Hatfield, E., and Sprecher, S. *Mirror, mirror . . . The importance of looks in everyday life.* New York: State University of New York Press, 1986.

Hawkins, K. Effects of gender and communication content on leadership emergence in small task-oriented groups. *Small Group Research*, 1995, 26, 234–49.

Hellweg, S. et al. Cultural variations in negotiation styles. In L. Samovar and R. Porter (Eds.), *Intercultural communication: A reader.* Belmont, CA: Wadsworth, 1994.

Hembroff, L. Resolving status inconsistency: An expectation states theory and test. *Social Forces*, 1982, 61, 183–205.

Hembroff, L., and Myers, D. Status characteristics: Degree of task relevance and decision process. *Social Psychology Quarterly*, 1984, 47, 337–46.

Hendra, T. (Ed.). *Meet Mr. bomb.* New London, NH: High Meadow Publishing, 1982.

Henley, N. *Body politics: Power, sex, and nonverbal communication.* Englewood Cliffs, NJ: Prentice-Hall, 1977.

Henry, J. *Culture against man.* New York: Random House, 1963.

Hensley, T., and Griffin, G. Victims of groupthink: The Kent State University Board of Trustees and the 1977 gymnasium controversy. *Journal of Conflict Resolution*, 1986, 30, 497–531.

Herek, G. et al. Decision making during international crises: Is quality of process related to outcome? *Journal of Conflict Resolution*, 1987, 31, 203–26.

Hersey, P., and Blanchard, K. *Management organizational behavior: Utilizing human resources.* Englewood Cliffs, NJ: Prentice-Hall, 1988.

Hickson, M. *Nonverbal communication: Studies and applications*. Dubuque, IA: Wm. C. Brown, 1989.

Hillary: It will happen again. *Life*, August, 1996, 41.

Hirokawa, R. Communication and group decision-making efficacy. In R. Cathcart and L. Samovar (Eds.), *Small group communication: A reader*. Dubuque, IA: Wm. C. Brown, 1992.

Hirokawa, R. Discussion procedures and decision-making performance: A test of a functional perspective. *Human Communication Research*, 1985, 12, 203–24.

Hirokawa, R. Group communication and problem-solving effectiveness: An investigation of group phases. *Human Communication Research*, 1983, 9, 291–305.

Hirokawa, R. Why informed groups make faulty decisions: An investigation of possible interaction-based explanations. *Small Group Behavior*, 1987, 18, 3–29.

Hirokawa, R., and Pace, R. A descriptive investigation of the possible communication-based reasons for effective and ineffective group decision-making. *Communication Monographs*, 1983, 50, 363–79.

Hirokawa, R., and Scheerhorn, D. Communication in faulty group decision-making. In R. Hirokawa and M. Poole (Eds.), *Communication and group decision-making*. Beverly Hills, CA: Sage, 1986, 63–80.

Hite, S. *Women and love: A cultural revolution in progress*. New York: Alfred A. Knopf, 1987.

Hocker, J., and Wilmot, W. *Interpersonal conflict*. Dubuque, IA: Wm. C. Brown, 1991.

Hoffman, C., and Hurst, N. Gender stereotypes: Perception or rationalization? *Journal of Personality and Social Psychology*, 1990, 58, 197–208.

Hofling, C. et al. An experimental study in nurse-physician relationships. *Journal of Nervous and Mental Disease*, 1966, 143, 171–80.

Hofstede, G. *Culture's consequences: International differences in work-related values*. Beverly Hills, CA: Sage, 1980.

Holguin, R. Stalker suspect caught. *Santa Cruz Sentinel*, September 1, 1985, A1.

Hollander, E. Leadership and power. In G. Lindzey and E. Aronson (Eds.), *Handbook of Social Psychology*. New York: Random House, 1985, 485–537.

Hollander, E. *Leadership dynamics*. New York: Free Press, 1978.

Hollander, E., and Offerman, L. Power and leadership in organizations. *American Psychologist*, February 1990, 179–89.

Home chores still a battle of the sexes. *San Jose Mercury News*, February 16, 1993, 5A.

Hong, L. Risky shift and cautious shift: Same direct evidence on the cultural-value theory. *Social Psychology*, 1978, 41, 342–46.

Howell, J. A laboratory study of charismatic leadership. Working paper, the University of Western Ontario, 1985.

Huberman, J. Discipline without punishment. *Harvard Business Review*, May 1967, 62–68.

Hui, C. H., and Triandis, H. C. Individualism-collectivism: A study of cross-cultural research. *Journal of Cross-cultural Psychology*, 1986, 17, 225–48.

Hunt, M. *The universe within: A new science explores the human mind.* New York: Simon and Schuster, 1982.

Hurley, D. Getting help from helping. *Psychology Today,* January, 1988, 63–67.

Husband, R. *Leading in organizational groups.* In R. Cathcart and L. Samovar (Eds.), Small group communication, Dubuque, IA: Wm. C. Brown, 1992, 464–76.

Inagaki, Y. *Jiko hyogen no gijutsu* ("Skills in self-expression"). Tokyo: PHP Institute, 1985.

Infante, D. Test of an argumentative skill deficiency model of interspousal violence. *Communication Monographs,* 1989, 56, 163–77.

Irons, E., and Moore, G. *Black managers: The case of the banking industry.* New York: Praeger, 1985.

Ishii, S. et al. The typical Japanese student as an oral communicator: A preliminary profile. *Otsuma Review,* 1984, 17, 39–63.

Ivins, M. The billionaire boy scout. *Time,* August 1992, 38–39.

Jacobs, J. Designs for better education elude summiteers. *San Jose Mercury News,* October 2, 1989, 5B.

Jacobs, J. Who will raise the children? *San Jose Mercury News,* January 4, 1996, 7B.

Jacobs, M., and Goodman, G. Psychology and self-help groups. *American Psychologist,* March 1989, 536–45.

James, D., and Clarke, S. Women, men, and interruptions: A critical review. In D. Tannen (Ed.), *Gender and conversational interaction.* New York: Oxford University Press, 1993, 231–80.

James, D., and Drakich, J. Understanding gender differences in amount of talk: A critical review of research. In D. Tannen (Ed.), *Gender and conversational interaction.* New York: Oxford University Press, 1993, 281–301.

Janis, I. *Groupthink: Psychological studies of policy decisions and fiascoes.* Boston: Houghton Mifflin, 1983.

Jeffrey, R., and Pasework, R. Altering opinions about the insanity plea. *Journal of Psychiatry and Law,* 1983, 29–44.

Jessup, L. et al. Toward a theory of automated group work. *Small Group Research,* 1990, 21, 333–48.

Johannesen, R. The functions of silence: A plea for communication research. *Western Speech,* 1974, 38, 20–35.

Johnson, A. *Human arrangements: An introduction to sociology.* New York: Harcourt Brace Jovanovich, 1986.

Johnson, D., and Johnson, F. *Joining together: Group theory and group skills.* Englewood Cliffs, NJ: Prentice-Hall, 1975, 1991.

Johnson, D., and Johnson, R. *Cooperation and competition.* Hillsdale, NJ: Lawrence Erlbaum, 1987.

Johnson, D., and Johnson, R. *Cooperation and competition: Theory and research.* Edina, MN: Interaction Book Co., 1989.

Johnson, D., and Johnson, R. *Learning together and alone: Cooperative, competitive, and individualistic learning.* Englewood Cliffs, NJ: Prentice-Hall, 1987.

Johnson, D., and Johnson, R. Motivational processes in cooperative, competitive, and individualistic learning situations. In C. Ames and R. Ames (Eds.), *Research on motivation in education*, vol. 2. Orlando, FL: Academic Press, 1985.

Johnson, D., and Johnson, R. The socialization and achievement crisis: Are cooperative learning experiences the solution? In L. Bickman (Ed.), *Applied Social Psychology Annual 4*. Beverly Hills, CA: Sage, 1983.

Johnson, D. et al. *Circles of Learning: Cooperation in the classroom*. Edina, MN: Interaction Book Company, 1986.

Johnson, D. et al. Effects of cooperative, competitive, and individualistic goal structures on achievement: A meta-analysis. *Psychological Bulletin*, 1981, 89, 47–62.

Jurors' views differ on King beating trial. *San Jose Mercury News*, February 15, 1993, 3B.

Kagan, S. and Madsen, M. Cooperation and competition of Mexican, Mexican-American, and Anglo-American children of two ages under four instructional sets. *Developmental Psychology*, 1971, 8, 32–39.

Kalmuss, D. The intergenerational transmission of marital aggression. *Journal of Marriage and the Family*, 1984, 46, 11–19.

Kalven, H., and Zeisel, H. *The American jury*. Boston, MA: Little, Brown, 1966.

Kaminer, W. *I'm dysfunctional, you're dysfunctional*. New York: Vintage, 1993.

Kanter, D., and Mirvis, P. *The cynical Americans*. San Francisco: Jossey-Bass, 1989.

Kanter, R. *Men and women of the corporation*. New York: Basic Books, 1977.

Kantrowitz, B., and Wingert, P. Step by step. *Newsweek Special Issue*, Winter/Spring 1990, 24–34.

Katz, D. The effects of group longevity on project communication. *Administrative Science*, 1982, 27, 81–104.

Kelly, H., and Stahelski, A. Social interaction basis of cooperators' and competitors' beliefs about others. *Journal of Personality and Social Psychology*, 1970, 66–91.

Kelman, H., and Lawrence, L. American response to the trial of Lt. William L. Calley. *Psychology Today*, 1972, 41–45.

Kerr, N., and Bruun, S. Dispensability of member effort and group motivation losses: Free-rider effects. *Journal of Personality and Social Psychology*, 1983, 44, 78–94.

Kessler, J. An empirical study of six- and twelve-member jury decision-making processes. *University of Michigan Journal of Law Reform*, 1973, 6, 712–34.

Killian, A. VanDerveer ordeal proves worth it for well-drilled team. *San Jose Mercury News*, August 5, 1996, 1D.

Killian, L. The significance of multiple-group membership in disaster. *American Journal of Sociology*, 1952, 57, 309–14.

Kilmann, R., and Thomas, K. Developing a force-choice measure of conflict-handling behavior: The "MODE" instrument. *Educational and Psychological Measurement*, 1977, 37, 309–25.

King, A. *Power and communication*. Prospect Heights, IL: Waveland Press, 1987.

Kipnis, D. *The powerholders*. Chicago: University of Chicago Press, 1976.

Kirchler, E., and Davis, J. The influence of member status differences and task type on group consensus and member position change. *Journal of Personality and Social Psychology*, 1986, 51, 83–91.

Kirchmeyer, C. Multicultural task groups: An account of the low contribution level of minorities. *Small Group Research*, 1993, 24, 127–48.

Kirchmeyer, C. and Cohen, A. Multicultural groups: Their performance and reactions with constructive conflict. *Group and Organization Management*, 1992, 17, 153–70.

Klapp, O. Meaning lag in the information society. *Journal of Communication*, 1982, 32, 56–66.

Klapp, O. *Opening and closing: Strategies of information adaptation in society*. New York: Cambridge University Press, 1978.

Kleiman, C. A boost up the corporate ladder. *San Jose Mercury News*, July 28, 1991, 1PC.

Klein, S. Work pressure as a determinant of work group behavior. *Small Group Research*, 1996, 27, 299–315.

Kohn, A. It's hard to get left out of a pair. *Psychology Today*, October 1987, 53–57.

Kohn, A. *No contest: The case against competition*. Boston: Houghton Mifflin, 1992.

Kohn, A. *Punished by rewards*. New York: Houghton Mifflin, 1993.

Komorita, S., and Ellis, A. Level of aspiration in coalition bargaining. *Journal of Personality and Social Psychology*, 1988, 54, 421–31.

Komorita, S., and Kravitz, D. Coalition formation: A social psychological approach. In P. Paulus (Ed.), *Basic group processes*. New York: Springer-Verlag, 1983, 179–203.

Koury, Renee. UC spends millions on sex-bias cases. *San Jose Mercury News*, July 7, 1996, 1A.

Krimsky, S. Social risk assessment and group process. In W. C. Swap (Ed.), *Group decision-making*. Beverly Hills, CA: Sage, 1984, 151–80.

Kruglanski, A. Freeze-think and the *Challenger*. *Psychology Today*, August 1986, 48–49.

Kukla, R., and Kessler, J. Is justice really blind? The effect of litigant physical attractiveness on judicial judgment. *Journal of Applied Social Psychology*, 1978, 4, 336–81.

Kurtzman, L. New poverty class: Kids in single-parent homes. *San Jose Mercury News*, March 18, 1992, 1A.

Kutner, L. Winning isn't only thing that counts. *Santa Cruz Sentinel*, February 20, 1994, D2.

Labor force prediction foresees more women, minorities at work. *San Jose Mercury News*, March 13, 1988, 2PC.

Lakers ante up. *San Jose Mercury News*, July 19, 1996, 5D.

Lancashire, D. When Yoko walked in, McCartney said 'O No!' *New York Post*, April 13, 1970, 1.

Landers, A. Low income families need fire protection too. *Santa Cruz Sentinel*, February 25, 1995, D5.

Landy, D., and Sigall, H. Beauty is talent: Task evaluation as a function of the performer's physical attractiveness. *Journal of Personality and Social Psychology*, 1974, 29, 299–304.

Lanka, B. *I dream a world: Portraits of black women who changed America.* New York: Stewart, Tabori, and Chang, 1989.

Larson, C., and LaFasto, M. *Teamwork: What must go right, what can go wrong.* Newbury Park, CA: Sage, 1989.

Laughlin, P., and Adamopoulos, J. Social combination processes and individual learning for six-person cooperative groups on an intellectual task. *Journal of Personality and Social Psychology*, 1980, 38, 941–47.

Laughlin, P., and Ellis, A. Demonstrability and social combination processes on mathematical intellective tasks. *Journal of Experimental Social Psychology*, 1986, 22, 177–89.

Lawler, E., and Youngs, G. Coalition formation: An integrative model. *Sociometry*, 1975, 38, 1–17.

Leana, C. A partial test of Janis' groupthink model: Effects of group cohesiveness and leader behavior on defective decision making. *Journal of Management*, 1985, 11, 5–17.

Leary, M. *Understanding social anxiety.* Newbury Park, CA: Sage, 1983.

Leary, M. et al. Aspects of identity and behavioral preferences: Studies of occupational and recreational choice. *Social Psychology Quarterly*, 1986, 49, 11–18.

Leathers, D. *Successful nonverbal communication: Principles and applications.* New York: Macmillan, 1986.

Leathers, D. The impact of multichannel message inconsistency on verbal and nonverbal decoding behaviors. *Communication Monographs*, 1979, 46, 88–100.

Leathers, D. The process effects of trust-destroying behaviors in the small group. *Speech Monographs*, 1970, 37, 180–87.

Leavitt, H. *Managerial psychology.* Chicago: University of Chicago Press, 1964.

Leavitt, H. Some effects of certain communication patterns on group performance. *Journal of Abnormal and Social Psychology*, 1951, 46, 38–50.

Leerhsen, C. et al. Unite and conquer. *Newsweek*, February 5, 1990, 50–55.

Lefkowitz, M., Blake, R., and Mouton, J. Status factors in pedestrian violation of traffic signals. *Journal of Abnormal and Social Psychology*, 1955, 51, 704–6.

Lefton, L. *Psychology.* Boston: Allyn and Bacon, 1991.

Leonard, G. *The ultimate athlete.* New York: Viking, 1975.

Le, P. Foundations give schools a growing shot in the arm. *San Jose Mercury News*, October 23, 1995, 1A.

Levander, M. Report attacks "glass ceiling." *San Jose Mercury News*, August 9, 1991, 1A.

Levine, J., and Moreland, R. Progress in small group research. *Annual Review of Psychology*, 1990, 41, 585–634.

Levine, S. Radical departures. *Psychology Today*, August 1984, 20–27.

Levy, S. Bill's new vision. *Newsweek*, November 27, 1995, 54–57.

Lewallen, J. Ecocide: Clawmarks on the yellow face. *Earth*, April, 1972, 36–43.

Lewin, K. Studies in group decision. In D. Cartwright and A. Zander (Eds.), *Group dynamics.* Evanston, IL: Row, Peterson, 1953.

Lewin, K. et al. Patterns of aggressive behavior in experimentally created "social climates." *Journal of Social Psychology*, 1939, 10, 271–99.

Li, C. *Path analysis: A primer*. Pacific Grove, CA: Boxwood Press, 1975.

Likert, R. *The human organization*. New York: McGraw-Hill, 1967.

Lindskold, S. Trust development, the GRIT proposal, and the effects of conciliatory acts on conflict and cooperation. *Psychological Bulletin*, 1978, 85, 772–93.

Littlejohn, S. *Theories of human communication*. Belmont, CA: Wadsworth, 1989.

Littlejohn, S., and Jabusch, D. Communication competence: Model and application. *Journal of Applied Communication Research*, 1982, 10, 29–37.

Lubman, S. Volunteers bring schools more than they bargained for. *San Jose Mercury News*, September 15, 1996, 1A.

Lulofs, R. *Conflict: From theory to action*. Scottsdale, AR: Gorsuch Scarisbrick, 1994.

Lumsden, G., and Lumsden, D. *Communicating in groups and teams: Sharing leadership*. Belmont, CA: Wadsworth, 1993.

Lustig, M., and Koester, J. *Intercultural competence: Interpersonal communication across cultures*. New York: HarperCollins, 1993.

Luthans, L. et al. *Real managers*. Cambridge, MA: Ballinger Press, 1988.

Mabry, E. Some theoretical implications of female and male interaction in unstructured small groups. *Small Group Research*, 1989, 20, 536–50.

MacNeil, M., and Sherif, M. Norm change over subject generations as a function of arbitrariness of prescribed norm. *Journal of Personality and Social Psychology*, 1976, 34, 762–73.

Maier, N. *Problem-solving discussions and conferences: Leadership methods and skills*. New York: McGraw-Hill, 1963.

Man survives "stupid" arrow stunt. *San Jose Mercury News*, May 6, 1993, 9A.

Marak, S. The evolution of leadership structure. *Sociometry*, 1964, 27, 174–82.

Marks, M. The question of quality circles, *Psychology Today*, March 1986, 36–46.

Marks, M. et al. Employee participation in a quality circle program: Impact on quality of work life, productivity and absenteeism. *Journal of Applied Psychology*, 1985, 71, 61–69.

Martin, M., and Sell, J. The effect of equating status characteristics on the generalization process. *Social Psychology Quarterly*, 1985, 48, 178–82.

Mathison, D. Sex differences in the perception of assertiveness among female managers. *Journal of Social Psychology*, 1987, 126, 599–606.

Matlin, M. *Psychology*. Fort Worth, TX: Harcourt Brace, 1992.

May, R. *Power and innocence: A search for the sources of violence*. New York: W. W. Norton, 1972.

McCauley, C., and Segal, M. Social psychology of terrorist groups. In C. Hendrick (Ed.), *Review of personality and social psychology: Group process and intergroup relations*. Beverly Hills, CA: Sage, 1987, 9, 231–56.

McCrum, R., Cran, W., and MacNeil, R. *The story of language*. New York: Penguin Books, 1986.

McDaniel, E. *Japanese nonverbal communication: A review and critique of literature*. Paper presented at the Annual Convention of the Speech Communication Association, Miami Beach, FL, November 1993.

McGregor, D. *The human side of enterprise*. New York: McGraw-Hill, 1960.

McGuinnies, E., and Ward, C. Better liked than right: Trustworthiness and expertise as factors in credibility. *Personality and Social Psychology Bulletin*, 1980, 6, 467–72.

McLeod, H., and Cooper, J. Politically unplugged. *San Jose Mercury News*, July 31, 1996, 7B.

McNeil, B. et al. On the elicitation of preferences for alternative therapies. *New England Journal of Medicine*, 1982, 306, 1259–62.

Meacham, J. Revenge of the nerd. *San Jose Mercury News*, July 27, 1996, IDD.

Mead, M. *Cooperation and competition among primitive peoples*. Boston: Beacon, 1961.

Men more willingly accept women leaders. *The Wall Street Journal*, March 4, 1988, 31.

Metcalf, F. *The Penguin dictionary of modern humorous quotations*. New York: Penguin Books, 1987.

Michaelson, L. et al. A realistic test of individual versus group consensus decision making. *Journal of Applied Psychology*, 1989, 74, 834–39.

Michener, J. *Kent State: What happened and why*. New York: Random House, 1971.

Milgram, S. Group pressure and action against a person. *Journal of Abnormal and Social Psychology*, 1964, 69, 137–43.

Milgram, S. *Obedience to authority*. New York: Harper and Row, 1974.

Miller, C. The social psychological effects of group decision rules. In P. Paulus (Ed.), *Psychology of group influence*. Hillsdale, NJ: Lawrence Erlbaum, 1989.

Miller, K., and Monge, P. Participation, satisfaction, and productivity: A meta-analytic review. *Academy of Management Journal*, 1986, 29, 727–53.

Miranda, S. Avoidance of groupthink: Meeting management using Group Support Systems. *Small Groups Research*, 1994, 25, 105–36.

Misra, R. *The social stratification and linguistic diversity of the Bhojpuri speech community*. Unpublished doctoral dissertation. University of Poona, 1980.

Moghaddam, F. et al. *Social psychology in cross-cultural perspective*. New York: W. H. Freeman, 1993.

Mohrman, S., and Novelli, L. Beyond testimonials: Learning from a quality circles programme. *Journal of Occupational Behaviour*, 1985, 6, 93–110.

Mongeau, P. The brainstorming myth. Paper presented at the Western States Communication Association Conference, Albuquerque, NM, February 15, 1993.

Moorhead, G., and Montanari, J. An empirical investigation of the groupthink phenomenon. *Human Relations*, 1986, 39, 399–410.

Moreland, R., and Levine, J. Group dynamics over time: Development and socialization in small groups. In J. McGrath (Ed.), *The social psychology of time*. Beverly Hills, CA: Sage, 1987.

More women on boards. *Santa Cruz Sentinel*, December 12, 1996, B5.

Moriarty, T. A nation of willing victims. *Psychology Today*, April 1975, 43–50.

Morrison, A., and Von Glinow, M. Women and minorities in management. *American Psychologist*, February 1990, 200–208.

Moscovici, S., and Mugny, G. Minority influence. In P. Paulus (Ed.), *Basic group processes*. New York: Springer-Verlag, 1983.

Mudrack, P., and Farrell, G. An examination of functional role behavior and its consequences for individuals in group settings. *Small Group Research*, 1995, 26, 542–71.

Mulac, A. et al. Male/female language differences and effects in same-sex and mixed-sex dyads: The gender-linked language effect. *Communication Monographs*, 1988, 55, 315–35.

Mullen, B. Atrocity as a function of lynch mob composition: A self-attention perspective. *Personality and Social Psychology Bulletin*, 1986, 12, 187–97.

Mullen, B. Group cohesiveness and quality of decision making. *Small Group Research*, 1994, 25, 189–204.

Murnighan, J. Models of coalition formation: Game theoretic, social psychological, and political perspectives. *Psychological Bulletin*, 1978, 85, 1130–53.

Myers, D., and Bishop, G. Discussion effects on racial attitudes. *Science*, 1970, 169, 778–79.

Myers, D., and Lamm, H. The polarizing effect of group discussion. In I. Janis (Ed.), *Current trends in psychology: Readings from the American Scientist*. Los Altos, CA: Kaufmann, 1977.

Napier, R., and Gershenfeld, M. *Groups: Theory and experiences*. Boston: Houghton Mifflin, 1989.

Neale, M. et al. Joint effects of goal setting and expertise on negotiator behavior. Unpublished manuscript, Northwestern University, Evanston, IL, 1988.

Nelson, L., and Kagan, S. Competition: The star-spangled scramble. *Psychology Today*, September 1972, 53–56.

Nemeth, C. Interactions between jurors as a function of majority vs. unanimity decision rules. *Journal of Applied Social Psychology*, 1977, 7, 38–56.

Never married moms on rise in U. S. *The Sacramento Bee*, August 2, 1990, A4.

New Pentagon manual focuses on cooperation. *San Jose Mercury News*, December 19, 1991, 2A.

New rulers aren't sure what's next. *San Jose Mercury News*, December 12, 1989, 1A.

Nicotera, A., and Rancer, A. the influence of sex on self-perception and social stereotyping of aggressive communication predispositions. *Western Journal of Communication*, 1994, 58, 283–307.

Nieva, V. et al. *Team dimensions: Their identity, their measurement, and their relationships* (Technical report, Contract No. DAHC19–78–C-0001). Washington, DC: Advanced Research Resources Organizations, 1978.

Nisbett, R., and Ross, L. *Human inference: Strategies and shortcomings of social judgment*. Englewood Cliffs, NJ: Prentice-Hall, 1980.

Noe, R. Women and mentoring. *Academy of Management Review*, 1988, 13, 65–78.

Norman, J. So many meetings, so little time. *San Jose Mercury News*, March 6, 1996, 8G.

Novak, D., and Lerner, M. Rejection as a consequence of perceived similarity. *Journal of Personality and Social Psychology*, 1968, 9, 147–52.

O'Brien, T. No jerks allowed. *West*, November 5, 1995, 8–26.

Ogilvie, B., and Tutko, T. Sport: If you want to build character, try something else. *Psychology Today*, October 1971, 61–63.

One suspended in alleged Citadel hazing. *San Jose Mercury News*, December 15, 1996, 9A.

Orlick, T. *Winning through cooperation: Competitive insanity, cooperative alternatives*. Washington, DC: Acropolis Books, 1978.

Ornstein, R., and Ehrlich, P. *New world new mind: Moving toward conscious evolution*. New York: Doubleday, 1989.

Osgood, C. *An alternative to war or surrender*. Urbana, IL: University of Illinois Press, 1962.

Osgood, C. *Perspective in foreign policy*. Palo Alto, CA: Pacific Books, 1966.

Osgood, C. Suggestions for winning the real war with communism. *Journal of Conflict Resolution*, 1959, 3, 295–325.

Paulus, P. et al. Perceptions of performance in group brainstorming: The illusion of group productivity. *Personality and Social Psychology Bulletin*, 1993, 19, 78–89.

Paulus, P. et al. Social influences processes in computer brainstorming. *Basic and Applied Social Psychology*, 1996, 18, 3–14.

Pavitt, C., and Curtis, E. *Small group discussion*. Scottsdale, AZ: Gorsuch Scarisbrick, 1994.

Pearson, J. *Communication in the family*. New York: Harper and Row, 1989.

Pearson, J. et al. *Gender and communication*. Dubuque, IA: Wm. C. Brown, 1991.

Peters, T. Put this on your list: Listen with your heart. *San Jose Mercury News*, June 19, 1989, 2D.

Pettigrew, T., and Martin, J. Shaping the organizational context for black American inclusion. *Journal of Social Issues*, 1987, 43, 41–78.

Petty, R., and Cacioppo, J. Forewarning, cognitive responding and resistance to persuasion. *Journal of Personality and Social Psychology*, 1977, 35, 645–55.

Phillips, E., and Cheston, R. Conflict resolution: What works? *California Management Review*, 1979, 21, 76–83.

Philp, T. CSU leader resigns amid public furor. *San Jose Mercury News*, April 21, 1990, 1A.

Playing havoc with hormones. *San Jose Mercury News*, June 7, 1996, 14A.

Poll: More women than men say wives should stay home. *San Jose Mercury News*, September 20, 1993, 3A.

Poole, M. Decision development in small groups III: A multiple sequence model of group decision making. *Communication Monographs*, 1983, 50, 321–41.

Poole, M., and Doelger, J. Developmental processes in group decision-making. In R. Hirokawa and M. Poole (Eds.), *Communication and group decision-making*, Beverly Hills, CA: Sage, 1986, 35–62.

Poole, M., and Roth, J. Decision development in small groups IV: A typology of group decision paths. *Human Communication Research*, 1989a, 15, 323–56.

Poole, M., and Roth, J. Decision development in small groups V: Test of a contingency model. *Human Communication Research*, 1989b, 15, 549–89.

Porter, N., and Geis, F. Women and nonverbal leadership cues: When seeing is not believing. In C. Mayo and N. Henley (Eds.), *Gender and nonverbal behavior*. New York: Springer-Verlag, 1981.

Porter, R., and Samovar, L. Communication in the multicultural group. In R. Cathcart and L. Samovar (Eds.), *Small group communication: A reader.* Dubuque, IA: Wm. C. Brown, 1992.

Postman, N. *Crazy talk, stupid talk.* New York: Dell, 1976.

Pratkanis, A., and Aronson, E. *The age of propaganda.* New York: W. H. Freeman and Company, 1992.

Pre-employment drug tests ground almost 20% in state. *San Jose Mercury News,* May 24, 1990, 1A.

Propp, K. An experimental examination of biological sex as a status cue in decision-making groups and its influence on information use. *Small Group Research,* 1995, 26, 451–74.

Prothrow-Stith, D. *Deadly consequences.* New York: HarperCollins, 1991.

Pruitt, D. *Negotiation behavior.* New York: Academic Press, 1981.

Pruitt, D., and Kimmel, M. Twenty years of experimental gaming: Critique, synthesis, and suggestions for the future. *Annual Review of Psychology,* 1977, 28, 363–92.

Pruitt, D., and Rubin, J. *Social conflict: Escalation, stalemate, and settlement.* New York: Random House, 1986.

Purdy, M. Don't bow to King Carl. *San Jose Mercury News,* August 1, 1996, 1D.

Put enjoyment ahead of achievement. *Santa Cruz Sentinel,* February 20, 1994, D2.

Putnam, L. Conflict in group decision-making. In R. Hirokawa, and M. Poole (Eds.), *Communication and group decision-making,* Beverly Hills, CA: Sage, 1986, 175–96.

Quattrone, G., and Jones, E. The perception of variability within in-groups and out-groups: Implications for the law of small numbers. *Journal of Personality and Social Psychology,* 1980, 38, 141–52.

Rabow, G. The cooperative edge. *Psychology Today,* January 1988, 54–7.

Rae-Dupree, J. AOL fed up with "spam." *San Jose Mercury News,* September 5, 1996, 1C.

Rahim, M. Referent role and styles of handling interpersonal conflict. *The Journal of Social Psychology,* 1985.

Rathus, S. *Psychology.* Fort Worth, TX: Holt, Rinehart, and Winston, 1990.

Raush, H. et al. *Communication, conflict, and marriage.* San Francisco: Jossey-Bass, 1974.

Read, P. Source of authority and the legitimation of leadership in small groups. *Sociometry,* 1974, 37, 189–204.

Reckman, R., and Goethals, G. Deviancy and group orientation as determinants of group composition preferences. *Sociometry,* 1973, 36, 419–23.

Report of the Commission on the space shuttle Challenger *disaster.* Washington, DC: Government Printing Office, 1986.

Riccillo, S., and Trenholm, S. Predicting managers' choice of influence mode: The effects of interpersonal trust and worker attributions on managerial tactics in a simulated organizational setting. *Western Journal of Speech,* 1983, 47, 323–39.

Ridgeway, C. Status in groups: The importance of motivation. *American Socio-logical Review*, 1982, 47, 76–88.

Ries, P., and Stone, A. (Eds.). *The American woman 1992–93: A status report*. New York: W. W. Norton, 1992.

Ritter, M. Sometimes nice guys really do get the girl. *San Jose Mercury News*, August 12, 1996, 1A.

Rogelberg, S., and Rumery, S. Gender diversity, team decision quality, time on task, and interpersonal cohesion. *Small Group Research*, 1996, 27, 79–90.

Rohlen, T. "Spiritual education" in a Japanese bank. *American Anthropologist*, 1973, 75, 1542–62.

Rohrlich, T. On King jury: Bickering, tears and catharsis. *Seattle Times*, April 23, 1993, A1.

Rosenfeld, L. Communication climate and coping mechanisms in the college classroom. *Communication Education*, 1983, 32, 169–74.

Ross, H. Social control through deterrence: Drinking-and-driving laws. *Annual Review of Sociology*, 1984, 10, 21–35.

Ross, L. et al. Social roles, social control and biases in the social perception process. *Journal of Personality and Social Psychology*, 1977, 37, 485–94.

Ross, R. *Speech communication: The speechmaking system*. Englewood Cliffs, NJ: Prentice-Hall, 1989.

Rossman, J. *The psychology of the inventor*. Washington, DC: Inventors' Publishing Company, 1931.

Roszak, T. *The cult of information*. New York: Pantheon Books, 1986.

Rothstein, R. Give them a break. *The New Republic*, February 1, 1988, 20–24.

Rothwell, J. *Telling it like it isn't: Language misuse and malpractice*. Englewood Cliffs, NJ: Prentice-Hall, 1982.

Ruben, B. Communication and conflict: A system theoretic perspective. *The Quarterly Journal Speech*, 1978, 64, 202–10.

Ruben, B. *Communication and human behavior*. New York: Macmillan, 1984.

Rubenstein, M. *Patterns of problem solving*. Englewood Cliffs, NJ: Prentice-Hall, 1975.

Rubenstein, R. Changes in self-esteem and anxiety in competitive and noncompetitive camps. *Journal of Social Psychology*, 1977, 102, 55–57.

Russell, P. *The global brain*. Boston: Houghton Mifflin, 1983.

Sadker, M., and Sadker, D. Sexism in the schoolroom of the '80s. *Psychology Today*, March 1985, 54–7.

Salazar, A. Understanding the synergistic effects of communication in small groups. *Small Group Research*, 1995, 26, 169–99.

Samovar, L., and Porter, R. *Communication between cultures*. Belmont, CA: Wadsworth, 1995.

Sao Paulo tries to stop police from killing suspects, civilians. *Santa Cruz Sentinel*, August 1, 1996, A10.

Schachter, S. Deviation, rejection, and communication. *Journal of Abnormal and Social Psychology*, 1951, 46, 190–207.

Schachter, S. *The psychology of affiliation*. Stanford, CA: Stanford University Press, 1959.

Scheer, R. *With enough shovels: Reagan, Bush and nuclear war*. New York: Vintage Books, 1983.

Schindehette, S. et al. After the verdict, solace for none. *People*, February 5, 1990, 70–80.

Schittekatte, M., and Van Hiel, A. Effects of partially shared information and awareness of unshared information on information sampling. *Small Group Research*, 1996, 27, 431–49.

Schmidt, S., and Kipnis, D. The perils of persistence. *Psychology Today*, November 1987, 32–34.

Schultz, B. et al. Improving decision quality in the small group: The reminder role. *Small Group Research*, 1995, 26, 521–41.

Schuster, M. The scanlon plan: A longitudinal analysis. *Journal of Applied Behavioral Science*, 1984, 20, 23–28.

Schwartz, S. Individualism-collectivism: Critique and proposed refinements. *Journal of Cross-cultural Psychology*, 1990, 21, 139–57.

Scully, M. Bell condemns 'careerism' in colleges. *The Chronicle of Higher Education*, October 19, 1983, 1.

Secretary's Commission on Achieving Necessary Skills. *What work requires of schools: A SCANS report for America 2000*. Washington, DC: U.S. Department of Labor, June 1991.

Seligman, J. et al. A town's divided loyalties. *Newsweek*, March 12, 1993, 29.

Sexism prevails in law schools, bar study finds. *Santa Cruz Sentinel*, February 4, 1996, A7.

Shane, H. The silicon age and education. *Phi Delta Kappan*, January 1982, 303–8.

Shapiro, A., and Madsen, M. Between- and within-group cooperation and competition among kibbutz and nonkibbutz children. *Developmental Psychology*, 1974, 10, 140–45.

Shaw, M. *Group dynamics: The psychology of small group behavior*. New York: McGraw-Hill, 1981.

Shaw, M., Rothschild, G., and Strickland, J. Decision processes in communication nets. *Journal of Abnormal and Social Psychology*, 1957, 54, 323–30.

Sheridan, C., and King, R. Obedience to authority with an authentic victim. *Proceedings of the 80th Annual Convention, American Psychological Association*, 1972, 7, 165–66.

Sherif, M. *In common predicament*. New York: Houghton Mifflin, 1966.

Sherif, M. et al. *The Robbers Cave experiment*. Middletown, CT: Wesleyan University Press, 1988.

Shimanoff, S. Group interaction via communication rules. In R. Cathcart and L. Samovar (Eds.), *Small group communication: A reader*. Dubuque, IA: Wm. C. Brown, 1992.

Shimanoff, S., and Jenkins, M. Leadership and gender: Challenging assumptions and recognizing resources. In R. Cathcart, L. Samovar, and L. Henman (Eds.), *Small group communication: Theory and practice*. Dubuque, IA: Brown and Benchmark, 1996.

Shockley-Zalabak, P. *Fundamentals of organizational communication*. New York: Longman, 1988.

Shotland, R., and Straw, M. Bystander response to an assault: When a man attacks a woman. *Journal of Personality and Social Psychology*, 1976, 34, 990–99.

Shure, G., Meeker, R., and Hansford, E. The effectiveness of pacifist strategies in bargaining games. *The Journal of Conflict Resolution*, 1965, 9, 107–17.

Sieburg, E., and Larson, C. Dimensions of interpersonal response. Paper presented to the International Communication Association, Phoenix, AZ, 1971.

Sigall, H., and Ostrove, N. Beautiful but dangerous: Effects of offender attractiveness and the nature of the crime on juridical judgment. *Journal of Personality and Social Psychology*, 1975, 31, 410–14.

Simons, L. China's effort to control minds. *San Jose Mercury News*, June 19, 1989, 1A.

Simons, L., and Zielenziger, M. Culture clash dims U.S. future in Asia. *San Jose Mercury News*, March 3, 1996, 1A.

Sims, R. Linking groupthink to unethical behavior in organizations. *Journal of Business Ethics*, 1992, 11, 651–62.

Singer, M. *Cults in our midst: The hidden menace in our everyday lives.* San Francisco: Jossey-Bass, 1995.

Sit, M. Cultivating a corporate culture of cooperation. *San Jose Mercury News*, August 13, 1989, 1PC.

Skrzycki, C. Companies learn to listen. *San Jose Mercury News*, June 18, 1989, 1PC.

Skrzycki, C. Training is all the rage at U.S. firms. *San Jose Mercury News*, March 5, 1989, 1PC.

Smircich, L., and Morgan, G. Leadership: The management of meaning. *The Journal of Applied Behavioral Science*, 1982, 18, 257–73.

Smith, B. An initial test to a theory of charismatic leadership based on the responses of subordinates. 1982.

Smith, M. *Persuasion and human interaction: A review and critique of social influence theories.* Belmont, CA: Wadsworth, 1982.

Smith, P. *Killing the spirit: Higher education in America.* New York: Viking, 1990.

Smith-Hefner, N. Women and politeness: the Javenese example. *Language in Society*, 1988, 17, 535–54.

Snyder, M. Seek, and ye shall find: Testing hypotheses about other people. In E. Higgins, C. Herman, and M. Zanna (Eds.), *Social cognition: The Ontario symposium*, vol. 1. Hillsdale, NJ: Erlbaum, 1981.

Solid Glass. *San Jose Mercury News*, October 18, 1996, 1C.

Spiker, B., and Daniels, T. Information adequacy and communication relationships: An empirical examination of 18 organizations. *Western Journal of Speech Communication*, 1981, 45, 342–54.

Spitzberg, B., and Cupach, W. *Handbook of interpersonal competence research.* New York: Springer-Verlag, 1989.

Spitzberg, B., and Hecht, M. A component model of relational competence. *Human Communication Research*, 1984, 10, 575–99.

Sproull, L., and Kiesler, S. Connections: New ways of working in the networked organization. Cambridge, MA: MIT Press, 1991.

Stanovich, K. *How to think straight about psychology.* New York: HarperCollins, 1992.

Stasser, G., and Titus, W. Effects of information load and percentage of shared information during group discussion. *Journal of Personality and Social Psychology*, 1987, 53, 81–93.

Stasson, M., and Bradshaw, S. Explanations of individual-group performance differences: What sort of "bonus" can be gained through group interaction? *Small Group Research*, 1995, 26, 296–308.

Statham, A. The gender model revisited: Differences in the management styles of men and women. *Sex Roles*, 1981, 16, 409–49.

Staw, B. et al. Threat-rigidity effects in organizational behavior. *Administrative Science Quarterly*, 1981, 26, 501–24.

Stephan, W. School desegregation: An evaluation of prediction made in *Brown v. the Board of Education. Psychological Bulletin*, 1978, 85, 217–38.

Stern, A. Why good managers approve bad ideas. *Working Women*, May 1992, 104.

Stewart, J. Defendant's attractiveness as a factor in the outcome of trials. *Journal of Applied Social Psychology*, 1980, 10, 348–61.

Stewart, J. (Ed.). *Bridges not walls.* New York: Random House, 1986.

Stewart, L. et al. *Communication between the sexes: Sex differences and sex-role stereotypes.* Scottsdale, AR: Gorsuch Scarisbrick, Publishers, 1996.

Stiles, W. et al. Professional presumptuousness in verbal interactions with university students. *Journal of Experimental and Social Psychology*, 15, 1979, 158–69.

Stockman, D. *The triumph of politics: The inside story of the Reagan revolution.* New York: Avon, 1986.

Stogdill, R. Group productivity, drive, and cohesiveness. *Organizational Behavior and Human Performance*, 1972, 8, 26–43.

Strodtbeck, F., and Hook, L. The social dimensions of a twelve-man jury table. *Sociometry*, 1961, 24, 397–415.

Strodtbeck, F. et al. Social status in jury deliberations. *American Sociological Review*, 1957, 22, 713–19.

Stogdill, R. Historical trends in leadership theory and research. *Journal of Contemporary Business*, Autumn 1974, 7.

Stogdill, R. Personal factors associated with leadership: A survey of the literature. *Journal of Psychology*, 1948, 25, 64.

Study finds fewer female lawmakers. *San Jose Mercury News*, February 12, 1995, 10A.

Study shows women are gaining parity with men at work. *The Maui News*, January 3, 1997, B8.

Study's verdict: Law schools still sexist. *San Jose Mercury News*, February 3, 1996, 9A.

Sundell, W. The operation of confirming and disconfirming verbal behavior in selected teacher-student interactions. Doctoral dissertation, University of Denver, 1972.

Sundstrom, E. et al. Work teams: Applications and effectiveness. *American Psychologist*, February 1990, 120–133.

Sutton, C., and Moore, K. Executive women—20 years later. *Harvard Business Review*, 1985, 63, 43–66.

Swacker, M. Women's verbal behavior at learned and professional conferences. In B. Dubois and I. Crouch (Eds.), *The sociology of the languages of American women*. San Antonio, TX: Trinity University, 1976.

Sykes, C. *A nation of victims: The decay of the American character*. New York: St. Martin's Press, 1992.

Sykes, C. *Profscam: Professors and the demise of higher education*. Washington, DC: Regnery, 1988.

Szasz, T. *Sex by prescription*. New York: Penguin Books, 1980.

Tang, S., and Kirkbride, P. Developing conflict management skills in Hong Kong: An analysis of some cross-cultural implications. *Management Education and Development*, 1986, 17, 287–301.

Tannen, D. *You just don't understand: Women and men in conversation*. New York: Ballantine Books, 1990.

Taps, J., and Martin, P. Gender composition, attributional accounts, and women's influence and likability in task groups. *Small Group Research*, 1990, 21, 471–91.

Tavris, C. *Anger: The misunderstood emotion*. New York: Simon and Schuster, 1982.

Tavris, C. *The mismeasure of woman*. New York: Simon and Schuster, 1992.

Text of new report on excellence in undergraduate education. *The Chronicle of Higher Education*, October 24, 1984, 35–49.

They're still on top. *San Jose Mercury News*, November 25, 1995, 4A.

Thomas, K., and Schmidt, W. A survey of managerial interests with respect to conflict. *Academy of Management Journal*, 1976, 19, 315–18.

Thorne, B. *Public speech at Michigan State University*. East Lansing: Michigan State University Press, 1981.

Tjosvold, D. Power and social context in superior-subordinate interaction. *Organizational Behavior and Human Decision Processes*, 1985, 35, 281–93.

Tjosvold, D. *Working together to get things done*. Lexington, MA: Lexington Books, 1986.

To bee or not to bee. *Newsweek*, July 8, 1996, 60.

Toulmin, S. et al. *An introduction to reasoning*. New York: Macmillan, 1979.

Tracy, K. et al. The discourse of requests: Assessment of a compliance-gaining approach. *Human Communication Research*, 1984, 10, 513–38.

Trenholm, S. *Human communication theory*. Englewood Cliffs, NJ: Prentice-Hall, 1986.

Trenholm, S. *Persuasion and social influence*. Englewood Cliffs, NJ: Prentice-Hall, 1989.

Trenholm, S., and Jensen, A. *Interpersonal communication*. Belmont, CA: Wadsworth, 1988.

Triandis, H. Cross-cultural studies of individualism and collectivism. In J. Berman (Ed.), *Cross-cultural perspectives*. Lincoln, NE: University of Nebraska Press, 1990, 41–133.

Tropman, J. *Meetings: How to make them work for you*. New York: Van Nostrand Reinhold, 1988.

Tubbs, S. *A systems approach to small group interaction*. Reading, MA: Addison-Wesley, 1984.

Tubbs, S., and Carter, R. *Shared experiences in human communication*. Rochelle Park, NJ: Hayden, 1977.

Tuckman, B. Developmental sequences in small groups. *Psychological Bulletin*, 1965, 63, 384–99.

Tuddenham, R., and McBride, P. The yielding experiment from the subject's point of view. *Journal of Personality*, 1959, 27, 259–71.

Turner, J. *Sociology: Studying the human system*. Santa Monica, CA: Goodyear Publishing Co., 1981.

Tutzauer, F., and M. Roloff. Communication processes leading to integrative agreements: Three paths to joint benefits. *Communication Research*, 1988, 5, 360–80.

Tuzlak, A. Joint effects of race and confidence on perceptions and influence. *Canadian Ethnic Studies*, 1989, 21, 103–19.

Tversky, A., and Kahneman, D. Judgment under uncertainty: Heuristics and biases. *Science*, 1974, 185, 1124–31.

Tversky, A., and Kahneman, D. The framing of decisions and the psychology of choice. *Science*, June 30, 1981, 453–58.

TV or not TV. *San Jose Mercury News*, April 19, 1993, 5E.

Tziner, A., and Eden, D. Effects of crew composition on crew performance: Does the whole equal the sum of the parts? *Journal of Applied Psychology*, 1985, 70, 85–93.

Unsafe sex in gang rites alleged. *San Jose Mercury News*, April 27, 1993, 4A.

Ury, W. *Getting past no: Negotiating your way from confrontation to cooperation*. New York: Bantam Books, 1993.

Valdez, C. Cults focus on identity search. *Western Front*, November 1, 1983, 7.

Valacich, J. et al. Idea generation in computer-based groups: A new ending to an old story. *Small Group Research*, 1994, 57, 448–67.

Valenti, A., and Downing, L. Differential effects of jury size on verdicts following deliberation as a function of the apparent guilt of the defendant. *Journal of Personality and Social Psychology*, 1975, 32, 655–64.

Van Oostrum, J., and Rabbie, J. Intergroup competition and cooperation within autocratic and democratic management regimes. *Small Group Research*, 1995, 26, 269–95.

Vasconcellos, J. California strikes out. *San Jose Mercury News*, March 8, 1994, 7B.

Victim of power inequalities. *Hartford Courant*, November 15, 1984, F6.

Victor, B., and Blackburn, R. Determinants and consequences of task uncertainty. *Journal of Management Studies*, 1987, 18, 108–32.

Villasenor, V. *Jury: The people vs. Juan Corona*. Boston: Little, Brown and Company, 1977.

Vinokur, A., and Burnstein, E. Depolarization of attitudes in groups. *Journal of Personality and Social Psychology*, 1978, 36, 872–85.

Wachtel, P. *The poverty of affluence: A psychological portrait of the American way of life*. New York: Free Press, 1983.

Wackman, D., Miller, S., and Nunnally, E. *Student workbook: Increasing awareness and communication skills*. Minneapolis: Interpersonal Communication Programs, 1976.

Wacky life forms are pursuing "E.T." exile. *San Jose Mercury News*, June 21, 1996, 4A.

Wade, C., and Tavris, C. *Psychology*. New York: HarperCollins, 1990.

Wanous, J. *Organizational entry: Recruitment, selection, and socialization of newcomers*. Reading, MA: Addison-Wesley, 1980.

Ward, E. et al. *Rock of ages: The Rolling Stone history of rock and roll*. New York: Rolling Stone Press, 1986.

Warnemunde, D. The status of the introductory small group communication course. *Communication Education*, 1986, 10, 389–96.

Wasserman, E. Out from under the glass ceiling. *San Jose Mercury News*, July 28, 1996, 1A.

Waters, H. If it ain't broke, break it. *Newsweek*, March 26, 1990, 58–59.

Watson, A. Report criticizes colleges. *San Jose Mercury News*, November 2, 1986, 1A.

Watson, C. When a woman is the boss: Dilemmas in taking charge. *Group and Organizational Studies*, 1988, 13, 163–81.

Watzlawick, P. et al. *Change: Principles of problem formation and problem resolution*. New York: W. W. Norton, 1974.

Watzlawick, P. et al. *Pragmatics of human communication*. New York: W. W. Norton, 1967.

Weick, K. The vulnerable system: An analysis of the Tenerife air disaster. *Journal of Management*, 1990, 16, 571–93.

Weiner, E., and Arnold, B. Human factors: The gap between humans and machines. *The Futurist*, May-June 1989, 9–11.

Weiner, M., and Wright, F. Effects of undergoing arbitrary discrimination upon subsequent attitudes towards a minority group. *Journal of Applied Social Psychology*, 1973, 3, 94–102.

West, S. Behind a smoke screen. *Science 84*, June 1984, 12.

Westley, W. Secrecy and the police. *Social Forces*, 1965, 254–57.

Wetzel, P. Are "powerless" communication strategies the Japanese norm? *Language in Society*, 1988, 17, 555–64.

Whistle-blowers claim humiliating retaliation. *San Jose Mercury News*, August 6, 1989, 11A.

Whitkin, R. FAA says Delta had poor policies on crew training. *New York Times*, September 19, 1987, 1.

Who's the hot group in '96? The Beatles. *San Jose Mercury News*, October 23, 1996, 4A.

Widaman, K., and Kagan, S. Cooperativeness and achievement: Interaction of student cooperativeness with cooperative versus competitive classroom organization. *Journal of School Psychology*, 1987, 25, 355–65.

Wiemann, J., and Backlund, P. Current theory and research in communicative competence. *Review of Educational Research*, 1980, 50, 185–99.

Wiio, O. Organizational communication: Interfacing systems. *Finnish Journal of Business Economics*, 1977, 2, 259–85.

Wilkes, J. Murder in mind. *Psychology Today*, June 1987, 27–32.

Willis, L. More may not always be better. *The Seattle Times*, January 17, 1986, D5.

Wills, T. Downward comparison principles in social psychology. *Psychological Bulletin*, 1981, 90, 245–71.

Wilmot, W. *The influence of personal conflict styles of teachers on student attitudes toward conflict*. Paper presented to Instructional Communication Division, International Communication Association Convention, Portland, OR, April 15, 1976.

Wilson, G., and Hanna, M. *Groups in context*. New York: Random House, 1990.

Wolf, N. *Fire with fire: The new female power and how to use it*. New York: Fawcett Columbine, 1994.

Wolf, S. Behavioral style and group cohesiveness as sources of minority influence. *European Journal of Social Psychology*, 1979, 9, 381–95.

Wolfe, T. *The bonfire of the vanities*. New York: Bantam Books, 1987.

Wolkomir, R., and Wolkomir, J. How to make smart choices. *Reader's Digest*, February 1990. 27–32.

Women on welfare bear fewer children than norm, study finds. *San Jose Mercury News*, June 1, 1989, 2A.

Wood, J. Leading in purposive discussions: A study of adaptive behavior. *Communication Monographs*, 1977, 44, 152–65.

Wood, J. et al. *Group discussion: A practical guide to participation and leadership*. New York: Harper and Row, 1986.

Wood, W. A meta-analytic review of sex differences in group performance. *Psychological Bulletin*, 1987, 102, 53–71.

Woodward, B., and Armstrong, S. *The brethren: Inside the Supreme Court*. New York: Simon and Schuster, 1979.

Wooley, S. et al. BSCS cooperative learning and science program. *Cooperative Learning*, April 1990, 32–33.

Wooton, J. Lessons of Pop Jordan's death. *Newsweek*, September 13, 1993, 12.

Worchel, S., and Brehm, J. Direct and implied social restoration of freedom. *Journal of Personality and Social Psychology*, 1971, 18, 294–304.

Wright, R. Women are taking center stage in the worldwide political arena. *San Jose Mercury News*, July 1, 1993, 10A.

Wurman, R. *Information anxiety*. New York: Doubleday, 1989.

Yalom, I. *Theory and practice of group psychotherapy*. New York: Basic Books, 1985.

Yates, Don. Many students admit cheating. *Western Front*, May 9, 1985.

Yoshitake, D. Even hackers try support groups. *San Jose Mercury News*, August 5, 1996, A7.

Young, F. *Initiation ceremonies*. New York: Bobbs-Merrill, 1965.

Youngs, G. Patterns of threat and punishment reciprocity in a conflict setting. *Journal of Personality and Social Psychology*, 1986, 51, 541–46.

Yukl, G. *Leadership in organizations*. Englewood Cliffs, NJ: Prentice-Hall, 1981.

Zander, A. Resistance to change: Its analysis and prevention. In W. Bennis et al. (Eds.), *The planning of change*. New York: Holt, Rinehart, and Winston, 1961, 543–48.

Zander, A. The psychology of removing group members and recruiting new ones. *Human Relations*, 1982, 29, 1–8.

Zimbardo, P. *Psychology and life*. Glenview, IL: Scott, Foresman, 1988, 1992.

Zimbardo, P. *Shyness: What it is and what you can do about it*. Reading, MA: Addison-Wesley, 1977.

Zimbardo, P., Ebbesen, E., and Maslach, C. *Influencing attitudes and changing behavior*. Reading, MA: Addison-Wesley, 1977.

Acknowledgments

Brecher, Elinor. "Furor Over Florida Rape Case Clouds Disturbing Facts," *Seattle Times*, December 15, 1989, pp. B1–B2. Copyright © 1989 by Elinor Brecher. Reprinted with permission of the Miami Herald.

Fisher, B. and Ellis, D. *Small Group Decision Making*, 3rd edition by B. Fisher and D. Ellis. Copyright © 1990. Reprinted by permission of The McGraw-Hill Companies.

Fisher, R., Ury, W., and Patton, B. Excerpts from *Getting to Yes*, 2nd edition by Roger Fisher, William Ury and Bruce Patton. Copyright © 1981, 1991 by Roger Fisher and William Ury. Reprinted by permission of Houghton Mifflin Company. All rights reserved.

Gibb, Jack. "Defensive Communication," *Journal of Communication*, vol. 11, 141–148, 1961. Copyright © 1961 by *Journal of Communication*. Reprinted by permission of Oxford University Press.

Hershey, Paul and Blanchard, Kenneth H. *Management of Organizational Behavior*, 5th edition, © 1988, pp. 287 & 175. Reprinted by permission of Center for Leadership Studies, Inc., Escondido, CA. Situational Leadership® is a registered trademark for the Center for Leadership Studies, Inc. All rights reserved.

Hirokawa, R. "Why Informed Groups Make Faulty Decisions," *Small Group Behavior*, February 1987, vol. 18, No. 1, pp. 17–18, 22. Copyright © 1987 by R. Hirokawa. Reprinted by permission of Sage Publications, Inc.

Janis, Irving L. *Groupthink*, pp. 9, 142, 175, © 1982 by Houghton Mifflin Company.

Villasenor, Victor. From *Jury: The People vs. Juan Corona* by Victor Villasenor. Copyright 1977 by Victor Edmundo Villasenor. By permission of Little, Brown and Company.

Photo Credits

Chapter 1: p. 15, ©AP/Wide World Photos; p. 16, ©Susan Ragan/AP Wide World Photos

Chapter 2: p. 31, ©Kent Reno/Jeroboam, Inc.; p. 38 both, Dwight Conquergood/Northwestern University; p. 42 top, John Berry/The Gamma Liaison Network; p. 42 bottom, Woodcock/Gamma Liaison; p. 54 both, ©AP/Wide World Photos, p. 56 top left, ©Jane Scherr/Jeroboam, Inc.; p. 56 center left, ©Ron Heflin/AP Wide World Photos; p. 56 bottom left, ©Jane Scherr/Jeroboam, Inc.; p. 56 top right, ©Evan Johnson/Jeroboam, Inc.; p. 56 bottom right, ©Evan Johnson/Jeroboam, Inc.

Chapter 3: p. 76 both, ©AP/Wide World Photos; p. 84, ©Richard Hutchings/PhotoEdit

Chapter 4: p. 99 top, ©Steve Takatsuijo/Jeroboam, Inc.; p. 99 bottom, ©Bob Clay/Jeroboam, Inc.; p. 100, ©Robert Maass/Sipa Press; p. 101, ©Steve Malone/Jeroboam, Inc.; p. 105 top, ©Reuters/Mike Blake/Archive Photos; p. 105 bottom left and right, ©Amy Sancetta/AP Photo; p. 118, ©Julie Lopez/Habitat for Humanity International; p. 119 both, ©Ray Scioscia/Habitat for Humanity International; p. 132 both, ©Murafer Sherif/Wesleyan University Press

Chapter 5: p. 141 all, ©Philip G. Zimbardo; p. 159 top left, Leo Rosenthal/F.D.R. Library; p. 159 top center, ©John Mantel/Sipa Press; p. 159 top right, ©Peter Southwick/Gamma Liaison; p. 159 bottom left, Brad Markel/The Gamma Liaison Network; p. 159 bottom center left, ©Robert Sorbo-AP/Wide World Photos; p. 159 bottom center right, ©Corbis-Bettmann; p. 159 bottom right, ©Reuters/Corbis-Bettmann; p. 161 top left, ©UPI/Corbis-Bettmann; p. 161 top right, ©AP/Wide World Photos; p. 161 bottom left, ©Channel 9 Australia/Liaison; p. 161 bottom right, ©AP Photo/APTV

Chapter 6: p. 182, ©AP/Wide World Photos; p. 192, ©Dan Coyro/ Santa Cruz Sentinel

Chapter 7: p. 220, ©ATC Productions/Stock Market

Chapter 8: p. 260, ©Joseph Schuyler/Stock Boston; p. 268 and 269, ©1974 Stanley Milgram. Reprinted by permission of HarperCollins Publishers; p. 270, ©Kay Lawson/Jeroboam, Inc.

Chapter 9: p. 292 both, ©AP/Wide World Photos; p. 295, ©Allsport

AUTHOR INDEX

SUBJECT INDEX